Emerging Economic Models for Global Sustainability and Social Development

Bryan Christiansen
Global Research Society, LLC, USA

Irina Sysoeva
Independent Researcher, Russia

Alexandra Udovikina
Independent Researcher, Russia

Anna Ketova
Khabarovsk State Academy of Economics and Law, Russia

A volume in the Advances in Finance, Accounting, and Economics (AFAE) Book Series

IGI Global
DISSEMINATOR OF KNOWLEDGE

Published in the United States of America by
IGI Global
Business Science Reference (an imprint of IGI Global)
701 E. Chocolate Avenue
Hershey PA, USA 17033
Tel: 717-533-8845
Fax: 717-533-8661
E-mail: cust@igi-global.com
Web site: http://www.igi-global.com

Library of Congress Cataloging-in-Publication Data

Names: Christiansen, Bryan, 1960- editor. | Sysoeva, Irina, 1991- editor. | Udovikina, Alexandra, 1989- editor.
Title: Emerging economic models for global sustainability and social development / Bryan Christiansen, Irina Sysoeva, Alexandra Udovikina, and Anna Ketova, editors.
Description: Hershey : Business Science Reference, [2018]
Identifiers: LCCN 2017054601| ISBN 9781522557876 (hardcover) | ISBN 9781522557883 (ebook)
Subjects: LCSH: Sustainable development.
Classification: LCC HC79.E5 E475 2018 | DDC 338.9/27011--dc23 LC record available at https://lccn.loc.gov/2017054601

This book is published in the IGI Global book series Advances in Finance, Accounting, and Economics (AFAE) (ISSN: 2327-5677; eISSN: 2327-5685)

British Cataloguing in Publication Data
A Cataloguing in Publication record for this book is available from the British Library.

For electronic access to this publication, please contact: eresources@igi-global.com.

Advances in Finance, Accounting, and Economics (AFAE) Book Series

Ahmed Driouchi
Al Akhawayn University, Morocco

ISSN:2327-5677
EISSN:2327-5685

Mission

In our changing economic and business environment, it is important to consider the financial changes occurring internationally as well as within individual organizations and business environments. Understanding these changes as well as the factors that influence them is crucial in preparing for our financial future and ensuring economic sustainability and growth.

The **Advances in Finance, Accounting, and Economics (AFAE)** book series aims to publish comprehensive and informative titles in all areas of economics and economic theory, finance, and accounting to assist in advancing the available knowledge and providing for further research development in these dynamic fields.

Coverage

- Wages and Employment
- Banking
- Bankruptcy
- Fiscal Policy
- Behavioral Economics
- Accounting Standards
- Microfinance
- Theoretical Issues in Economics, Finance, and Accounting
- Applied Finance
- E-finance

IGI Global is currently accepting manuscripts for publication within this series. To submit a proposal for a volume in this series, please contact our Acquisition Editors at Acquisitions@igi-global.com or visit: http://www.igi-global.com/publish/.

The Advances in Finance, Accounting, and Economics (AFAE) Book Series (ISSN 2327-5677) is published by IGI Global, 701 E. Chocolate Avenue, Hershey, PA 17033-1240, USA, www.igi-global.com. This series is composed of titles available for purchase individually; each title is edited to be contextually exclusive from any other title within the series. For pricing and ordering information please visit http://www.igi-global.com/book-series/advances-finance-accounting-economics/73685. Postmaster: Send all address changes to above address.

Titles in this Series

For a list of additional titles in this series, please visit: www.igi-global.com/book-series

Agricultural Finance and Opportunities for Investment and Expansion
Augustine Odinakachukwu Ejiogu (Imo State University, Nigeria)
Business Science Reference • copyright 2018 • 236pp • H/C (ISBN: 9781522530596) • US $195.00 (our price)

Regaining Global Stability After the Financial Crisis
Bruno Sergi (Harvard University, USA) Filip Fidanoski (University of New South Wales, Australia) Magdalena Ziolo (University of Szczecin, Poland) and Vladimir Naumovski (University American College Skopje, Macedonia)
Business Science Reference • copyright 2018 • 383pp • H/C (ISBN: 9781522540267) • US $215.00 (our price)

Employment Protection Legislation in Emerging Economies
Samir Amine (Universite du Quebec en Outaouais, Canada)
Business Science Reference • copyright 2018 • 301pp • H/C (ISBN: 9781522541349) • US $195.00 (our price)

Fractal Approaches for Modeling Financial Assets and Predicting Crises
Inna Nekrasova (Southern Federal University, Russia) Oxana Karnaukhova (Southern Federal University, Russia) and Bryan Christiansen (PryMarke, LLC, USA)
Business Science Reference • copyright 2018 • 306pp • H/C (ISBN: 9781522537670) • US $215.00 (our price)

Regulation and Structure in Economic Virtualization Emerging Research and Opportunities
Denis Ushakov (Suan Sunandha Rajabhat University, Thailand)
Business Science Reference • copyright 2018 • 238pp • H/C (ISBN: 9781522549666) • US $145.00 (our price)

Accountancy and the Changing Landscape of Integrated Reporting
Ioana Dragu (Babes-Bolyai University, Romania)
Business Science Reference • copyright 2018 • 303pp • H/C (ISBN: 9781522536222) • US $195.00 (our price)

Foreign Direct Investments (FDIs) and Opportunities for Developing Economies in the World Market
Venkataramanaiah Malepati (University of Gondar, Ethiopia) and C. Mangala Gowri (University of Gondar, Ethiopia)
Business Science Reference • copyright 2018 • 315pp • H/C (ISBN: 9781522530268) • US $215.00 (our price)

Economic Growth in Latin America and the Impact of the Global Financial Crisis
Mauricio Garita (Universidad del Valle de Guatemala, Guatemala) and Celso Fernando Cerezo Bregni (Universidad del Valle de Guatemala, Guatemala)
Business Science Reference • copyright 2018 • 240pp • H/C (ISBN: 9781522549819) • US $180.00 (our price)

IGI Global
DISSEMINATOR OF KNOWLEDGE

701 East Chocolate Avenue, Hershey, PA 17033, USA
Tel: 717-533-8845 x100 • Fax: 717-533-8661
E-Mail: cust@igi-global.com • www.igi-global.com

To all of our wonderful colleagues, family, friends, and other loved ones around the world.

Editorial Advisory Board

Table of Contents

Foreword xvii

Preface xix

Acknowledgment xxiv

Chapter 1
The Effect of Globalization on Economic Growth: Evidence From Emerging Economies 1
Recep Ulucak, Erciyes University, Turkey

Chapter 2
The Relationship Between Globalization and Income Distribution: An Empirical Analysis in the Context of South Korea 20
Buhari Doğan, Süleyman Demirel University, Turkey
Muhlis Can, Hakkari University, Turkey

Chapter 3
Is Sustaniable Tourism a Leverage FOR Economic Development? A Critical Review 46
Hakan Sezerel, Anadolu University, Turkey
Cihan Kaymaz, Gumushane University, Turkey

Chapter 4
Selection of Renewable Energy Sources for Sustainable Development and an Economic Model Proposal for Countries 65
Alptekin Ulutaş, Cumhuriyet University, Turkey
Coşkun Karaca, Cumhuriyet University, Turkey

Chapter 5
Inequality and Rural Poverty: Innovative Agricultural Practices for Sustainable and Social Development in Kenya 84
Gladys Thuita, Riara University, Kenya
Matilda Ouma, Ministry of Agriculture, Livestock, and Fisheries, Kenya

Chapter 6
A Scale of Relative Institutional Challenge During MNC Global Expansion.................................... 98
Ehsan Derayati, Concordia University, Canada
Rick Molz, Concordia University, Canada
Gwyneth Edwards, HEC Montréal, Canada

Chapter 7
Global Labor Market, "Re-Shoring" Dynamics, and Skill Mismatch: An Exploratory Study at a Job-Specific Level.................................... 125
Filippo Ferrari, Bologna University, Italy

Chapter 8
Challenges in Creating and Sustaining an Entrepreneurial Business in Milwaukee 144
Garfield A. Plunkett, University of Phoenix, USA
Libi Shen, University of Phoenix, USA

Chapter 9
Product Sophistication: A Cross-Country Analysis.................................... 167
Fatma Nur Karaman Kabadurmus, Yasar University, Turkey

Chapter 10
Potential Changes in the Demand and Supply Sides in the Construction Industry: Emerging Concepts for the Sustainable and Innovative Economy.................................... 187
Begum Sertyesilisik, Istanbul Technical University, Turkey

Chapter 11
Determinants of Access and Utilization of Climate Services Among Vulnerable Communities: A Case Study of Isoko Communities in Delta State, Nigeria.................................... 203
Andrew Onwuemele, Nigerian Institute for Social and Economic Research, Nigeria

Chapter 12
Essence of International Environmental Law to Address the Effects of Climate Change.................. 220
Md. Mahfuzar Rahman Chowdhury, The Legal Care, Bangladesh

Chapter 13
How Unemployment May Impact Happiness: A Systematic Review.................................... 237
André Barros, Polytechnic Institute of Cávado and Ave, Portugal
Teresa Dieguez, Polytechnic Institute of Cávado and Ave, Portugal & Polytechnic Institute of Porto, Portugal
Pedro Nunes, Polytechnic Institute of Cávado and Ave, Portugal

Chapter 14
The Dragon's Footprints: The Impact of Chinese Migration and Investment in the European Union.................................... 260
Mona Chung, Deakin University, Australia
Bruno Mascitelli, Swinburne University of Technology, Australia

Chapter 15
Residents' Attitudes in Punta del Este (Uruguay): A Cluster Analysis 274
María Dolores Sánchez-Fernández, University of A Coruña, Spain
Daniel Álvarez Bassi, Catholic University of Uruguay, Uruguay
José Ramón Cardona, University of the Balearic Islands, Spain

Chapter 16
Welfare Programs as a Strategy of Promoting Employees' Economic Growth and Work Productivity 291
Chandra Sekhar Patro, Gayatri Vidya Parishad College of Engineering (Autonomous), India

Chapter 17
A Green Energy Management Framework for Software Development Firms 312
Arunasalam Sambhanthan, Curtin University, Australia

Chapter 18
The Modelling of the Economy by Means of C-V-M Matrices 329
Grigorii Pushnoi, Independent Researcher, Russia

Compilation of References 373

About the Contributors 423

Index 428

Detailed Table of Contents

Foreword xvii

Preface xix

Acknowledgment xxiv

Chapter 1
The Effect of Globalization on Economic Growth: Evidence From Emerging Economies 1
Recep Ulucak, Erciyes University, Turkey

Globalization has gathered great momentum over the past four decades and it has led to important changes in the economic, political, and cultural dynamics of countries. It is theoretically expected that globalization stimulates economic growth by leading institutional reforms, opening economies to global markets, direct and indirect foreign investments, and technology transfers. Therefore, it is crucial for emerging economies to increase economic growth. This study investigates the impact of globalization on economic growth for the panel of emerging economies by conducting second generation panel data techniques. For this purpose, employing annual data spanning from 1970 to 2014, the effects of overall KOF globalization index and three dimensions of globalization on economic growth are estimated via CUP-FM and CUP-BC estimators. Results show that overall the KOF globalization index, economic, and social dimensions of globalization have positive influence on economic growth while the effect of political dimension on economic growth is negative.

Chapter 2
The Relationship Between Globalization and Income Distribution: An Empirical Analysis in the Context of South Korea 20
Buhari Doğan, Süleyman Demirel University, Turkey
Muhlis Can, Hakkari University, Turkey

Income inequality is a major economic problem in many countries, and it is clear that numerous parameters affect income distribution. In this study, the effects of globalization on income distribution were examined in the contexts of South Korea and the Kuznets curve between 1970 and 2010. The cointegration test of the series was carried out using the Maki approach, which considers multiple structural breaks. The cointegration test indicated the series moved together in the long term. The long-term analysis indicated that globalization first reduces income inequality and then increases it in a U-shaped relationship. In the short-term analysis, it was found that the error correction term was negative and statistically significant. In this context, it is crucial that policy makers develop policies that minimize the impact of globalization on income inequality; otherwise, social and economic distortions will increase with the increase in globalization, which will cause different socioeconomic problems.

Chapter 3
Is Sustaniable Tourism a Leverage FOR Economic Development? A Critical Review 46
Hakan Sezerel, Anadolu University, Turkey
Cihan Kaymaz, Gumushane University, Turkey

Does development mean employment and social welfare, or the natural environment, ecosystem, and biodiversity? The answer to this question is sought worldwide while trying to solve the dichotomy between ecological sustainability and the development sustainability. The authors observe a series of pursuits under the names of ecological tourism, environmentally friendly tourism, and socially responsible tourism that emerge in order to overcome this dichotomy in the tourism discipline. They all merge around the common idea of offering a framework that examines economic activities for this dilemma. Meanwhile, this chapter examines the pursuits within the scope of sustainable tourism based on the assumptions of principal ecological approaches (e.g., environment protection, shallow ecology, deep ecology, and social ecology) and determines the position of sustainable tourism within these ecological approaches. It is deduced that sustainable tourism is actually sustainable at very low levels from the perspective of ecological sustainability.

Chapter 4
Selection of Renewable Energy Sources for Sustainable Development and an Economic Model Proposal for Countries 65
Alptekin Ulutaş, Cumhuriyet University, Turkey
Coşkun Karaca, Cumhuriyet University, Turkey

Meeting the energy requirements with imported fuels leads to economic and political problems in the countries. Therefore, renewable energy investments continue to grow globally as a sustainable and increasingly economically viable alternative to conventional sources of energy. This study aims to reduce the share of imported fuels in Turkey's electricity generation and to estimate the employment gain to be provided by renewable energy investments to be established instead. Approximately 900,000 jobs are created during the production, construction, operational, and maintenance phases of additional 49,448 MW capacity renewable power plants to be installed. While analyzing, the decision on how much to invest in which renewable resource is determined with respect to multi-criteria decision making (MCDM) model.

Chapter 5
Inequality and Rural Poverty: Innovative Agricultural Practices for Sustainable and Social Development in Kenya.. 84
Gladys Thuita, Riara University, Kenya
Matilda Ouma, Ministry of Agriculture, Livestock, and Fisheries, Kenya

The main purpose of this chapter was to establish the effect of innovative agricultural practices on reduction of inequality and rural poverty among sorghum farmers in Homabay County, Kenya. A multistage stratified sampling technique was used to randomly select 120 smallholder sorghum farmers. The study found that use of innovative agricultural practices has an impact on agricultural produce and, therefore, on reduction of inequality and rural poverty among farmers in Homabay County. The study thus concluded that sorghum farming has drastically reduced inequality and rural poverty in the county. The study recommends that the government should provide more support in the application of innovative agricultural practices to assist farmers have diversified portfolio of crops that generate more income to address the issue of inequality and rural poverty in Homabay County. Lastly, the research recommends further research in other innovative agricultural practices such as livestock rearing and maize growing to combat inequality and rural poverty in Homabay County.

Chapter 6
A Scale of Relative Institutional Challenge During MNC Global Expansion 98
Ehsan Derayati, Concordia University, Canada
Rick Molz, Concordia University, Canada
Gwyneth Edwards, HEC Montréal, Canada

This chapter develops a reliable and valid scale of relative institutional challenge between 40 country pairs by drawing on three measures of institutional uniqueness. The single measure can be used by researchers and practitioners to assess the relative institutional challenge that a multinational corporation (MNC) may face in the internationalization process between their home and potential host country. The value of this single scale includes (1) a more comprehensive and broad scale than three separate scales, (2) demonstrated reliability and validity, (3) a standardized measure of institutional challenge that can be used by different researchers in different research settings, and (4) a tool for practitioners that is easily applied and robust when considering alternative off-shore investment opportunities.

Chapter 7
Global Labor Market, "Re-Shoring" Dynamics, and Skill Mismatch: An Exploratory Study at a Job-Specific Level 125
Filippo Ferrari, Bologna University, Italy

Workers' capabilities and knowledge are factors that a company can use to boost its productivity. The relocation of operational activity away from industrialized nations has led to the erosion of manufacturing skills, and this fact often results in a severe skill shortage in specific local labor markets, becoming much more prominent in the case of re-shoring. Consistent with the transaction cost economics approach (TCE), the purpose of this research was to verify if students possess at least basic skills at the end of their educational path to face the labor market without economic frictions in school-to-work transition. Finally, this chapter presents a model that could be useful in order to design programs aimed to overcome the erosion of manufacturing skills and provide students with skills that companies need to deal with local labor markets successfully.

Chapter 8
Challenges in Creating and Sustaining an Entrepreneurial Business in Milwaukee 144
Garfield A. Plunkett, University of Phoenix, USA
Libi Shen, University of Phoenix, USA

Small business entrepreneurs have made important contributions to economic activities in the U.S. In recent years, there were decline and high entrepreneurial failure rates for entrepreneurs throughout the country. Specifically, the continuous challenges faced by entrepreneurs in the city of Milwaukee, Wisconsin have negatively affected job creation and the entrepreneurial process. What are the challenges faced by

Milwaukee's entrepreneurs in creating and sustaining their businesses? How have the entrepreneurial challenges affected Milwaukee entrepreneurs' experiences in creating and sustaining their businesses? What specific support might be effective in overcoming the challenges? The purpose of this study was to explore the lived experiences of 20 entrepreneurs, specifically the challenges they encountered while sustaining an entrepreneurial enterprise in the city of Milwaukee. This chapter identifies the barriers and challenges that entrepreneurs and entrepreneurial small businesses must overcome. Recommendations for government leaders, entrepreneurs, and future researchers are provided.

Chapter 9
Product Sophistication: A Cross-Country Analysis.......... 167
Fatma Nur Karaman Kabadurmus, Yasar University, Turkey

The sudden rise of countries like China and India has captured serious attention among economists. Some papers explain it with the changing structure of their product mix and construct an export sophistication index to rank countries according to their comparative advantages. By starting from the discussions on product quality, this chapter investigates whether a more rapid progression up the comparative advantage ladder or a more sophisticated export basket results in a more rapid economic expansion. For this purpose, data from 115 countries for the period 1985 to 2001 are used. The results support the positive effect of export sophistication on growth. The authors also show that when a country progresses, its growth rate increases.

Chapter 10
Potential Changes in the Demand and Supply Sides in the Construction Industry: Emerging Concepts for the Sustainable and Innovative Economy.......... 187
Begum Sertyesilisik, Istanbul Technical University, Turkey

Sustainability of the economy depends on the reduction of the environmental footprint of the supply and demand as economy relies on the production enabled by natural resources. The construction industry is one of the major industries influencing sustainable and social development. The construction industry and the built environment, however, have important environmental footprints. Therefore, the demand and supply sides in the construction industry must be transformed into more sustainable ones. Furthermore, the principles and emerging concepts of sustainable and innovative economy need to be adopted by the construction industry. Based on an in-depth literature review, this chapter focuses on the integration and impacts of the emerging concepts for the sustainable and innovative economy in the construction industry. This chapter is expected to be useful for academics, graduate and undergraduate students, researchers, policymakers, and construction industry professionals.

Chapter 11
Determinants of Access and Utilization of Climate Services Among Vulnerable Communities: A Case Study of Isoko Communities in Delta State, Nigeria.......... 203
Andrew Onwuemele, Nigerian Institute for Social and Economic Research, Nigeria

Changes in climate have caused impacts on natural and human systems. These impacts affect poor people's lives through impacts on livelihoods and the destruction of homes. In Delta State, Nigeria, the impacts of climate change are real. Adaptation has been identified as the key to reducing the impacts of climate change. However, successful adaptation depends on use of climate services. While climate services are essential to adaptation, the services do not always reach the users who need it most. This chapter analyzes factors influencing access and utilization of climate services in Delta State. The chapter utilizes the survey research while data were analyzed using both descriptive and inferential statistics. Findings show a low utilization of climate service. The determinants of access and utilization of climate services include income, educational attainments, access to ICT facilities, extension agents, and the level of local climate variability. The chapter calls for awareness creation on the importance of climate services.

Chapter 12
Essence of International Environmental Law to Address the Effects of Climate Change................. 220
Md. Mahfuzar Rahman Chowdhury, The Legal Care, Bangladesh

Environmental problems are enormous around the world and threaten the global environment. In most cases, these problems are caused by rapid growth of population and poverty. Climate change and sustainable development are inter-linked and are priority issues in the development continuum. Any adverse impact on the environment and biodiversity can cause the restriction of resources and limit available options. Concerted efforts of all the states can bring positive result to address the effects of climate change. Compliance with the treaty provision and sharing of resources and actions among the states can ensure proper utilization of resources and sustainable development.

Chapter 13
How Unemployment May Impact Happiness: A Systematic Review.. 237
André Barros, Polytechnic Institute of Cávado and Ave, Portugal
Teresa Dieguez, Polytechnic Institute of Cávado and Ave, Portugal & Polytechnic Institute of Porto, Portugal
Pedro Nunes, Polytechnic Institute of Cávado and Ave, Portugal

The wealth of an economy is traditionally measured by its level of productivity. However, countries with the highest level of productivity do not always report equal levels of happiness and general wellbeing. In fact, there is no direct relationship between both variables and sometimes less wealthy productive countries report higher levels of happiness. Recent studies and theories are trying to demonstrate that the term happiness has made its way into economics literature as the result of economist dissatisfaction who believe happiness should become a matter of study in the field. Unemployment is one of the most recently researched variables in economics and has a direct relationship with happiness. Potentially some other variables such as autonomy, reliability, and added value of happiness would help researchers to better complete economic analysis via a multidisciplinary perspective.

Chapter 14
The Dragon's Footprints: The Impact of Chinese Migration and Investment in the European Union... 260
Mona Chung, Deakin University, Australia
Bruno Mascitelli, Swinburne University of Technology, Australia

This chapter examines Chinese migration and investment into Europe and explores models of migration and investment by identifying the gap between the two. The chapter highlights the major characteristics of Chinese investment and migration into Europe by identifying and separating the investment from Chinese state-owned enterprises (SOEs) and that of private individuals. This triangulation provides scholars and policy makers with a unique scenario. The migration and investment literature has been conducted as two separate and parallel topics. A small number of studies investigate the relationship of the two as one inter-connected relationship. There is even less focus on Chinese migration and investment due to the fact that over the past decade it has been a fast-moving phenomenon because of the speed of Chinese economic development. In addition, China's different political and economic system and its unique state structure adds another layer of complexity for scholars.

Chapter 15
Residents' Attitudes in Punta del Este (Uruguay): A Cluster Analysis 274
María Dolores Sánchez-Fernández, University of A Coruña, Spain
Daniel Álvarez Bassi, Catholic University of Uruguay, Uruguay
José Ramón Cardona, University of the Balearic Islands, Spain

Homogeneity studies in recent decades have segmented residents according to their attitudes. The aim of this work is to segment the residents of Punta del Este according to their attitudes toward tourism. Recently, there have been some segmentations of residents in diver's tourist destinations in the world. Resident segmentation has been performed with a cluster analysis using the K-mean algorithm, generating three groups: enthusiastic supporters (33.1%), supporters with nuanced opinion (45.2%), and people without a formed opinion (21.7%). The profile of the groups generated is quite similar and no groups with a clear opposition to tourism have been detected. The overall assessment of the residents surveyed in this research is positive.

Chapter 16
Welfare Programs as a Strategy of Promoting Employees' Economic Growth and Work Productivity 291
Chandra Sekhar Patro, Gayatri Vidya Parishad College of Engineering (Autonomous), India

Many organizations apply the notion of employee welfare programs as a strategy of improving employee productivity, since work-related exertions could lead to deprived quality of work life for employees and a decline in performance. Welfare schemes promote economic development by increasing the efficiency and productivity with the underlying principle being making workers bestow their loyal services ungrudgingly in genuine spirit of cooperation. The welfare schemes improve the organizational relations and also enhance the productivity of the employees. The main aim of implementing the welfare measures in any organization is to secure the labor force by providing proper working conditions and minimizing its hazardous effect on the life of the employees and their family members. The chapter articulates the various employee welfare programs put into practice by the industrial and service organizations and its influence on the employees' economic growth and productivity, in both public and private sectors.

Chapter 17
A Green Energy Management Framework for Software Development Firms.................................... 312
Arunasalam Sambhanthan, Curtin University, Australia

This chapter documents a green energy management framework for software development companies. An initial framework has been constructed through analyzing the reports of large scale software development firms. The key components of the framework consist of energy sources and energy efficiency, energy-efficient heating, energy-efficient lighting, and energy-efficient cooling. These themes include a number of sub-themes and criteria therein which are used to build the green energy management framework and then utilized for constructing the research questions for further data collection. The results highlight the most efficient energy sources, efficient heating measures and technologies, efficient lighting measures, and technologies as well as efficient cooling measures and technologies. Implications for practice have been suggested at the end of the chapter.

Chapter 18
The Modelling of the Economy by Means of C-V-M Matrices 329
Grigorii Pushnoi, Independent Researcher, Russia

The classical three-sector model of the economy: 1) "the means of production", 2) "the goods for employees", and 3) "the goods consumed by other economic agents" ("luxury goods") is considered in matrix formulation. Each sector contains many industries producing the goods of these three kinds. The "transformation problem" in Marxian economics is considered in a three-sector model of the economy with simple production. The solution of this problem is based on the action of the statistical "laws of large numbers" (LLN) in the economy. The stylized facts about the economy of the United States indicate onto the existence of the following probability distributions: 1) the inverse power distribution for the elements of matrix of direct requirements and 2) the Gaussian distribution for the direct labor per the unit of goods. The action of the statistic "law of large numbers" guarantees the C-V-M matrix of the economy must be almost symmetric. The "labor value" and the "price of production" of the total product produced within each sector in this case are almost equal.

Compilation of References 373

About the Contributors 423

Index 428

Foreword

The global social inequalities continue to remain in spite of ongoing economic globalization. The rapid economic growth of China, India, Brazil and other countries has brought the global sustainability challenges to the forefront. Global sustainability involves protecting natural environment, creating healthy communities through economic growth. Global sustainability looks across national boundaries to see how finite resources are being exploited globally. It also includes man-made organizations and markets. Rapid economic, environmental and social changes can threaten sustainable social development and inequalities (Kalfagianni, 2014).

Economic models for economic growth, global sustainability and social development are context-specific and dynamic. The 'China model' of rapid economic growth is a unique model involving leadership by the authoritarian state to promote exports and infrastructure investment with co-existence of state-owned enterprises and private firms. In China, the state directed extraordinary resources into infrastructure, housing and transportation. The state-owned firms played a role in China's dealing with the global financial crisis better than the western countries.

However, the rapid economic growth in China has come with significant costs in sustainability and social development. These include income disparity, environmental pollution, human casualties, excess-capacity and rampant corruption in state-owned enterprises and moral disintegration leading to deepening social tension marked by protests and social unrest. Both the state-owned and private firms are shedding their excess capacity by laying off millions of workers. At this time, the economic growth model needs to shift from exports and investment to social development. Institutional checks on state authority and accountability are needed (Zhao, 2017). China faces a number of new structural challenges as global interest rates rise. These include shrinking labor force and constraints on property and infrastructure investments. The new economic growth model for China has to focus more on sustainability and quality, and less on capacity. The new growth will come from the advanced manufacturing and medium-to-high end consumption (Deutsche Bank, 2017).

The "Circular Economy" represents the most recent attempt to conceptualize the integration of economic activity and environmental wellbeing in a sustainable way. Circular Economy has been defined as "an economic model wherein planning, resourcing, procurement, production and reprocessing are designed and managed, as both process and output, to maximize ecosystem functioning and human well-being" (Murray et al., 2017). Each country has to follow an economic model consistent with their political and social structure to maximize social development in a sustainable way.

The governments worldwide renewed their commitments to formulating a more sustainable development goals that would eradicate poverty, halt climate change and conserve ecosystems. Different combinations of technological measures and behavioral changes could contribute to achieving a set of sustainability objectives including eradicating hunger, providing universal access to modern energy, preventing dangerous climate change, conserving biodiversity and controlling air pollution. The different pathways of achieving the set of long-term objectives and their implications for short-term action can contribute to building a comprehensive strategy to meet the SDGs by proposing near-term actions (Van Vuuren et al., 2015).

Harish C. Chandan
Argosy University, USA

REFERENCES

Deutsche Bank. (2017). *China 2018 outlook – Striving for a new growth model*. Retrieved from https://www.db.com/newsroom_news/2017/china-2018-outlook-striving-for-a-new-growth-model-en-11744.htm

Kalfagianni, A. (2014). Addressing the Global Sustainability Challenge: The Potential and Pitfalls of Private Governance from the Perspective of Human Capabilities. *Journal of Business Ethics*, *122*(2), 307–320. doi:10.100710551-013-1747-6

Murray, A., Skene, K., & Haynes, K. (2017). The Circular Economy: An Interdisciplinary Exploration of the Concept and Application in a Global Context. *Journal of Business Ethics*, *140*(3), 369–380. doi:10.100710551-015-2693-2

Van Vuuren, D. P., Kok, M., Lucas, P. L., Prins, A. G., Alkemade, R., Van den Berg, M., ... Stehfest, E. (2015). Pathways to achieve a set of ambitious global sustainability objectives by 2050: Explorations using the IMAGE integrated assessment model. *Technological Forecasting and Social Change*, *98*, 303–323. doi:10.1016/j.techfore.2015.03.005

Zhao, S. (2017). *A time of test for the China model of economic growth*. Retrieved from http://www.eastasiaforum.org/2017/01/29/a-time-of-test-for-the-china-model-of-economic-growth/

Preface

As the twenty-first century continues to roll on at an increasingly faster pace, there is a need to review current economic models and revise them to meet new global demands for developed and developing nations alike. The inputs involved are obviously numerous and include issues such as human productivity, skills gaps, education, income distribution, poverty, labor markets, climate change, a global population that is ageing rapidly, and foreign direct investment. These and other related topics are covered in this book meant for research scholars, university students, professors, and practitioners around the world to ponder new models.

Each year the World Economic Forum ranks 144 countries in terms of a global competitiveness index (GCI) which captures the fundamentals of an economy on a scale that ranges from 1 to 7. The GCI uses statistical data such as government debt and life expectancy obtained from a variety of internationally recognized agencies such as the International Monetary Fund (IMF) and the World Bank to rank nations in terms of ability to compete on a global scale. This data and other key inputs provides a solid foundation for understanding the wealth of nations and their current economic status. However, we believe it is now crucial to develop more contemporary economic models in this century for sustainable development and global stability by examining the content of the following chapters.

Chapter 1 covers the effects of globalization on economic growth via evidence from emerging countries. This study investigates the impact of globalization on economic growth for a panel of emerging economies by conducting second generation panel data techniques. By using annual data spanning from 1970 to 2014, the effects of overall KOF globalization index and three dimensions of globalization on economic growth are estimated by CUP-FM and CUP-BC estimators. Results show that overall the KOF globalization index and the economic and social dimensions of globalization have a positive influence on economic growth while the effect of political dimension on economic growth is negative.

Chapter 2 examines the relationship between globalization and income distribution via an empirical analysis in South Korea. In this study, the effects of globalization on income distribution were examined in the contexts of South Korea and the Kuznets curve between 1970 and 2010. The cointegration test of the series was carried out using the Maki approach, which considers multiple structural breaks. The cointegration test indicated the series moved together in the long term. The long-term analysis indicated that globalization first reduces income inequality and then increases it in a U-shaped relationship. In the short-term analysis, it was found that the error correction term was negative and statistically significant. In this context, it is crucial that policy makers develop policies that minimize the impact of globalization on income inequality; otherwise, social and economic distortions will increase with the increase in globalization, which will cause different socioeconomic problems.

Chapter 3 provides a critical review of sustainable tourism as a leverage for economic development. Does development mean employment and social welfare, or the natural environment, ecosystem, and biodiversity? The answer to this question is sought worldwide while trying to solve the dichotomy between ecological sustainability and development sustainability. The authors observe a series of pursuits under the names of ecological tourism, environment-friendly tourism, and socially responsible tourism. This chapters examines the pursuits within the scope of sustainable tourism based on the assumptions of principal ecological approaches. It is deduced that sustainable tourism is actually sustainable at very low levels from the perspective of ecological sustainability.

Chapter 4 offers a model proposal for countries via a selection of renewable energy sources for sustainable development. Meeting the energy requirements with imported fuels leads to economic and political problems in the countries. Therefore, renewable energy investments continues to grow globally as a sustainable and increasingly economically viable alternative to conventional sources of energy. This study aims to reduce the share of imported fuels in Turkey's electricity generation and to estimate the employment gain to be provided by renewable energy investments to be established instead. Approximately 900,000 jobs are created during the production, construction, operational and maintenance phases of additional 49,448 MW capacity renewable power plants to be installed. Analysis permits the decision on how much to invest in which the renewable resource is determined with respect to the Multi-Criteria Decision Making (MCDM) model.

Chapter 5 establishes the effect of innovative agricultural practices on reduction of inequality and rural poverty among sorghum farmers in Homabay County, Kenya. A multistage stratified sampling technique was used to randomly select 120 smallholder sorghum farmers. The study found that use of innovative agricultural practices has an impact on agricultural produce and, therefore, on reduction of inequality and rural poverty among farmers in Homabay County. Thus, sorghum farming has drastically reduced inequality and rural poverty in Homabay County. The study recommends that the government should provide more support in the application of innovative agricultural practices to assist farmers have diversified portfolio of crops that generate more income to address the issue of inequality and rural poverty in Homabay County. Lastly, the research recommends further research in other innovative agricultural practices such as livestock rearing and maize growing to combat inequality and rural poverty in the County.

Chapter 6 develops a reliable and valid scale of Relative Institutional Challenge between 40 country pairs by drawing on three measures of institutional uniqueness. The single measure can be used by researchers and practitioners to assess the relative institutional challenge that a multinational corporation (MNC) may face in the internationalization process, between their home and potential host country. The value of this single scale includes: (1) a more comprehensive and broad scale than three separate scales; (2) demonstrated reliability and validity; (3) a standardized measure of institutional challenge that can be used by different researchers in different research settings; and, (4) a tool for practitioners that is easily applied and robust when considering alternative off-shore investment opportunities.

Chapter 7 reviews an exploratory study at a job-specific level with regards to the global labor market and skills mismatch. Workers' capabilities and knowledge are factors that a company can use to boost its productivity. The relocation of operational activity away from industrialized nations has led to the erosion of manufacturing skills, and this fact often results in a severe skill shortage in specific local labor markets, becoming much more prominent in the case of re-shoring. Consistent with the Transaction Cost Economics approach (TCE), the purpose of this research was to verify if students possess at least basic skills at the end of their educational path to face the labour market without economic frictions in school-to-work transition. The chapter presents a model that could be useful in order to design programs to overcome the erosion of manufacturing skills and provide students with skills firms require to contend successfully with local labor markets.

Chapter 8 inspects the challenges in creating and sustaining an entrepreneurial business in Milwaukee, Wisconsin in the USA. Small business entrepreneurs have made important contributions to economic activities in the U.S. In recent years, there were decline and high entrepreneurial failure rate for entrepreneurs throughout the U.S. Specifically, the continuous challenges faced by entrepreneurs in the city of Milwaukee have negatively affected job creation and the entrepreneurial process. What are the challenges faced by Milwaukee's entrepreneurs in creating and sustaining their businesses? How have the entrepreneurial challenges affected Milwaukee entrepreneurs' experiences in creating and sustaining their businesses? What specific support might be effective in overcoming the challenges? The purpose of this study was to explore the lived experiences of 20 entrepreneurs specifically the challenges they encountered while sustaining an entrepreneurial enterprise in the City of Milwaukee. This chapter aims at identifying barriers and challenges that entrepreneurs and entrepreneurial small businesses have to overcome. Recommendations for government leaders, entrepreneurs, and future researchers are provided.

Chapter 9 is a cross-country analysis of product sophistication. The sudden rise of countries like China and India has attracted serious attention among economists. Some papers explain this phenomenon with the changing structure of their product mix and construct in an Export Sophistication Index to rank countries according to their comparative advantages. By starting from discussions on product quality, this chapter investigates whether a more rapid progression up the comparative advantage ladder or a more sophisticated export basket results in a more rapid economic expansion. Data from 115 countries for the period 1985-2001 are used and the results support the positive effect of export sophistication on growth.

Chapter 10 considers potential changes in the demand and supply sides of the construction industry to develop some concepts for a sustainable and innovative economy. Sustainability of the economy depends on the reduction of the environmental footprint of the supply and demand as the economy relies on the production enabled by natural resources. The construction industry is one of the major industries influencing sustainable and social development. However, this industry and the built environment have an important environmental footprint. Therefore, the demand and supply sides in the construction industry must be transformed into more sustainable ones. Furthermore, the principles and emerging concepts of sustainable and innovative economy need to be adopted by the construction industry. Based on an in-depth literature review, this chapter aims to focus on the integration and impacts of the emerging concepts for a sustainable and innovative economy to the construction industry.

Chapter 11 contributes a case study of the Isoko communities in the Delta State of Nigeria regarding the impacts of climate change on the local population. Changes in climate have caused impacts on natural and human systems which affect poor people's lives through impacts on livelihoods and destruction of homes. In Delta State, the impacts of climate change are real. Adaptation has been identified as the key to reducing the impacts of climate change. However, successful adaptation depends on use of climate services. While climate services are essential to adaptation, the services do not always reach the users who need it most. This chapter analyzes factors influencing access and utilization of climate services in Delta State. The determinants of access and utilization of climate services include income, educational attainments, access to ICT facilities, extension agents and the level of local climate variability.

Chapter 12 involves examining environmental law to address the effects of climate change. Global environmental problems are enormous and in most cases they are caused by rapid growth of population and poverty. Climate change and sustainable development are inter-linked and are considered priority issues in the development continuum. Any adverse impact on the environment and biodiversity can cause restricting of resources and limiting options. Concerted efforts of all nations can bring positive result to address the effects of climate change for sustainable development.

Chapter 13 is a systematic review of how unemployment impacts personal happiness. The wealth of an economy is traditionally measured by its level of productivity. However, countries with the highest level of productivity do not always report equal levels of happiness and general well-being. In fact, there is no direct relation between both variables and sometimes less wealthy productive countries report higher levels of happiness. Recent studies and theories are trying to demonstrate that the term happiness has made its way into economic literature as the result of economists who believe that happiness should become a matter of study in economics. Unemployment is one of the most recently researched variables in economics and has a direct relationship with happiness. Other variables such as autonomy, reliability, and added value of happiness could potentially assist researchers to better complete economic analysis via a multidisciplinary perspective.

Chapter 14 chapter examines Chinese migration and investment into Europe and explores models of migration and investment by identifying the gap between the two. The chapter highlights the major characteristics of Chinese investment and migration into Europe by identifying and separating the investment from Chinese State-Owned Enterprises (SOEs) and that of private individuals. This triangulation provides scholars and policy makers with a unique scenario. The migration and investment literature has been conducted as two separate and parallel topics. A small number of studies investigate the relationship of the two as one inter-connected relationship. There is even less focus on Chinese migration and investment due to the fact that over the past decade it has been a fast moving phenomenon due to the speed of Chinese economic development. In addition, China's different political and economic system and its unique State structure adds another layer of complexity for scholars.

Chapter 15 segment the residents of Punta del Este in Uruguay according to their attitudes toward tourism. In recent years, there have been some segmentations of residents in diver tourist destinations in the world. Resident segmentation has been performed with a cluster analysis using the K-mean algorithm, generating three groups: Enthusiastic Supporters (33.1%), Supporters with Nuanced Opinion (45.2%) and people Without a Formed Opinion (21.7%). The profile of the groups generated is quite similar and no groups with a clear opposition to tourism have been detected. The overall assessment of the residents surveyed in this research is positive.

Chapter 16 discusses welfare programs as a strategy to promote employee work productivity and economic growth. Many organizations apply the notion of employee welfare programmes as a strategy of improving the employees' productivity, since work related exertions could lead to deprived quality of work life for employees and a decline in the performance. Welfare schemes promote economic development by increasing the efficiency and productivity with the underlying principle being making workers bestow their loyal services ungrudgingly in genuine spirit of co-operation. The welfare schemes improve the organisational relations and also enhance the productivity of the employees. The main aim of implementing the welfare measures in any organisation is to secure the labour force by providing proper working conditions and minimizing its hazardous effect on the life of the employees and their family members. The chapter articulates the various employee welfare programmes put into practice by the industrial and service organisations and its influence on the employee's economic growth and productivity, in both public and private sectors.

Chapter 17 presents a green energy management framework for software development firms. An initial framework has been constructed by analyzing the reports of large scale software development firms. The key components of the framework consist of energy sources and energy efficiency, energy efficient heating, energy efficient lighting, and energy efficient cooling. These themes include a numbers of sub-themes and criteria therein which are used to build the green energy management framework and then utilized for constructing the research questions for further data collection. The results highlight the most efficient energy sources, efficient heating measures and technologies, efficient lighting measures and technologies as well as efficient cooling measures and technologies. Implications for practice have been suggested at the end of the chapter.

Chapter 18 presents a potential economic model via C-V-M matrices. The classical 3-sector model of the economy: I – the "means of production", II - "the goods for employees", and III – the "the goods consumed by other economic agents" ("luxury goods") are considered in matrix formulation. Each sector contains many industries producing the goods of these three kinds. The "transformation problem" in Marxian economics is considered in the 3-sector model of the economy with simple production. The solution of this problem is based on the action of the statistical "laws of large numbers (LLN)" in the economy. The stylized facts about the economy of the United States indicate onto the existence of the following probability distributions: (1) the inverse power distribution for the elements of matrix of direct requirements and (2) the Gaussian distribution for the direct labor per the unit of goods. The action of the statistic "law of large numbers" guarantees that C-V-M matrix of the economy must be almost symmetric. The "labor value" and the "price of production" of the total product produced within each sector in this case are nearly equal.

Fast-moving events around the world today are changing the economic, political, and social environments quicker than ever before in history. Therefore, the need to reevaluate current economic models and develop more contemporary ones is paramount to making the world a safer and happier place for all in an era of hypercompetition and dwindling natural resources. We trust this publication shall help spur serious debate and research towards that goal.

Bryan Christiansen
Global Research Society, LLC, USA

Irina Sysoeva
Independent Researcher, Russia

Alexandra Udovikina
Independent Researcher, Russia

Anna Ketova
Khabarovsk State Academy of Economics and Law, Russia

Acknowledgment

We wish to thank the editorial board members and chapter authors for their fine contributions to this book. We would also like to thank the many reviewers who took the time from their busy schedules to complete the double-blind peer review of each chapter in this book. Without their input and effort this publication would not have been possible.

Chapter 1
The Effect of Globalization on Economic Growth:
Evidence From Emerging Economies

Recep Ulucak
Erciyes University, Turkey

ABSTRACT

Globalization has gathered great momentum over the past four decades and it has led to important changes in the economic, political, and cultural dynamics of countries. It is theoretically expected that globalization stimulates economic growth by leading institutional reforms, opening economies to global markets, direct and indirect foreign investments, and technology transfers. Therefore, it is crucial for emerging economies to increase economic growth. This study investigates the impact of globalization on economic growth for the panel of emerging economies by conducting second generation panel data techniques. For this purpose, employing annual data spanning from 1970 to 2014, the effects of overall KOF globalization index and three dimensions of globalization on economic growth are estimated via CUP-FM and CUP-BC estimators. Results show that overall the KOF globalization index, economic, and social dimensions of globalization have positive influence on economic growth while the effect of political dimension on economic growth is negative.

INTRODUCTION

As a known and comprehensive definition, *globalization* is a statement that can be simply defined as interaction and integration among people who lives anywhere in the world, and, who has different culture and ethnicity. So, it has crucial effects on all of life's occasions with respect to economic, political and cultural aspects. In this regard, it refers to the growing interdependence and increasing integration among countries resulting from the increasing integration of trade, finance, consumption preferences, policies, life styles and ideas in one global marketplace (Soubbotina & Sheram, 2000).

The main contributing mechanism for globalization is economic motives that try to maximize welfare. Other types of globalization are byproducts of economic globalization. Hence, many international

DOI: 10.4018/978-1-5225-5787-6.ch001

institutions have been founded to increase economic cooperation in the wake of World War II, such as the World Bank (WB), International Monetary Fund (IMF), The Organization for Economic Co-operation and Development (OECD), European Union (EU), World Trade Organization (WTO), General Agreement on Tariffs and Trade (GATT). Much as these foundations have contributed to increase globalization, it has acquired huge dimension in parallel with increasing communication and transportation tools through technological advancement over past a few decades. Otherwise, "globalization could not have happened without extensive innovations in transport, communications, and data processing" (Ardalan, 2017).

Liberalization is a complimentary factor of this integration process as well. When considered from this point of view, it is evaluated as a process of becoming same of goods and capital market around the world in which legal limitations for foreign trade and investment are repealed (Gurgul & Lach, 2014). In this manner, economies become closer and more interrelated (Heshmati & Lee, 2010) and also interdependent. In this case, two accelerating factors of globalization are technological progress and liberalization (Soubbotina & Sheram, 2000).

Dreher (2006) deduces that economic growth is promoted through globalization by exemplifying with more globalized countries' growth process. In his example, it is clear that globalized countries show a higher growth performance while growth performance is negligible in less globalized ones. According to Mishkin (2009), globalization stimulates economic growth by leading to institutional reforms in emerging economies and advanced ones contribute to this process by opening of their markets to goods and services from them. Institutional reforms have also been crucial to explain growth differences among countries and many seminal papers stress the importance of institutions in economic growth process (Acemoglu, Johnson, & Robinson, 2004, 2001; Easterly & Levine, 2001, 2003; Hall & Jones, 1999; Rodrik, Subramanian, & Trebbi, 2004).

Thus, numerous empirical studies focus on investigating the effect of globalization on the economic variables. However, most of the literature in this field suffer from insufficiency in terms of globalization measurement since they employ just a single variable and ignore policies such as restrictions, tariffs, quotas and so on. Additionally, as claimed by Rodriguez and Rodrik (2000), using only one specific data in order to capture the effects of globalization is not reliable. Also, the effects of globalization may be overestimated owing to the use of inappropriate indicators (Pekarskiene & Susniene, 2014). Additionally, most studies ignore cross-sectional dependence in panel data models. However, cross-sectional dependence problem, if exists, may lead biasedness, inconsistency or inefficiency in panel data estimations (Sarafidis & Wansbeek, 2010, 2012).

Contrary to prevailing literature, employing second generation panel data techniques that consider cross-sectional dependence, this study aims to investigate the impact of globalization on economic growth for the panel of emerging economies since globalization has vital importance, especially, for this kind of countries' growth process (Gurgul & Lach, 2014). Another important point of this chapter is that it includes three dimensions of globalization into the panel data analyses to capture the effects of economic, social and political globalization. To the best of our knowledge, this is the first study analyzing emerging economies classified by Standard & Poor's, as well as using second generation panel data estimators such as CUP-FM and CUP-BC. The remainder of the study is organized as follows: the next section explains background of globalization in economic growth process and reviews the literature. Then, data, model, and methodologies are introduced in section 3. Empirical applications and estimation results are presented in section 4. Finally, the study is concluded.

BACKGROUND AND LITERATURE REVIEW

Based on the fundamental assumptions of liberal economic paradigm, free movement of production factors, goods and services lead to increase interaction and integration of economic policies and variables. Thus, all countries would be more advanced. Convergence hypothesis and studies, in fact for the very reason, enable us to realize how poor countries catch up the rich ones over time (Barro & Sala-I-Martin, 1992; Solow, 1956). In this convergence process, the driving force beyond doubt is globalization (LaFree, 2005; Sachs & Warner, 1995;Villaverde & Maza, 2011).

However, nations have different globalization or integration process owing to their idiosyncratic dynamics with respect to socio-economic and cultural aspects. In addition, depending on these dynamics, they have experienced different growth and development paths (Kormendi & Meguire, 1985; De Long, 1988; Grier & Tullock, 1989). More importantly, growth theories explain one of these dynamics as based on technological differences among countries. In this respect, globalization enables countries to access new technologies and opportunities (Mayer, 2000; Pekarskiene & Susniene, 2014).

Research on the determinants of economic growth has been an important part of economics literature recently (Ecevit et al., 2016; Bretschger, 2017; Thompson, 2018). In his seminal study in 1956, Robert Solow pioneered the neoclassic theory of modern economic growth by explaining the growth in an economy by technology instead of capital accumulation. Solow (1956) determines that essential source of economic growth is technology, not capital accumulation. The endogenous relation between technology and growth, however, is not explained in Solow's model. Then, new economic growth theories as known endogenous growth models try to explain how technology influences economic growth. The common characteristic of endogenous growth models is that the essential source of economic growth can be endogenously determined in the model (Leeuven, 2007). Owing to difficulties to make a general definition for technology, Romer (1986) explains technological change through learning by doing while Lucas (1988) considers human capital based on education. Extending Romer (1986), Romer (1990) uses research and development (R&D) activities and knowledge accumulation to explain how technology influences economic growth. Aghion & Howitt (1992) focus on innovation that creates new products or technologies. Grossman and Helpman (1991) underline that openness degrees of economies increase economic growth through technological improvement. Mankiw, Romer, and Weil (1992) augment the Solow model by including human capital to explain technological progress. According to these pioneering models, although physical capital is a source of economic growth in transitional period, it is not one of the essential determinants in the long run (Fischer, 2011).

From the dominant liberal view, there is no doubt that trade and investment (direct and indirect) opportunities, thus technology and innovation transfers lead to increase economic growth (Frankel & Romer, 1999). Therefore, the effect of globalization has been tested for either single country or cross-country groups using different econometric techniques and variables by many studies so far. A great majority of the previous studies, however, have focused on economic dimension of globalization by using trade, openness or FDI-related data since they are driving force of economic globalization and this dimension of globalization has obviously been crucial on the growth process of countries (Pekarskiene & Susniene, 2015). On the other hand, most of the literature in this field suffer from insufficiency in terms of globalization measurement since they employ just a single variable and ignore policies such as restrictions, tariffs, quotas and so on.

The measurement of globalization has been very important to compare and evaluate countries' status and to investigate the matter in empirical analyses. Therefore, various approaches have been attempted to develop an index containing all aspects of globalization. G-Index proposed by Randolph (2001), the KFP index proposed by Kearney (2001), the MG Index proposed by Rennen and Martens (2003), the CSGR Index proposed by Lockwood and Redoano (2005), the KOF Index proposed by Dreher (2006), Dreher, Gaston, and Martens (2008), and the NG Index proposed by Vujakovic (2010) are some of them. Samimi, Lim, & Buang (2011) made a comprehensive review for these indexes by three dimensions and they conclude that the KOF index seems best alternative in representing the three dimensions of globalization. In addition, it is convenient to make empirical analyses that require long data set since it is available on a yearly basis for 207 countries over the period 1970 – 2014. Therefore, it has become most often used index measuring globalization (Potrafke, 2015).[1] Therefore, this study gives place to studies that use comprehensive globalization index such as the KOF and others and a few pioneering papers in the literature.

As one of the pioneering papers, Sachs and Warner (1995) have provided strong evidence that income discrepancies among countries which have open economies will disappear. In their paper they use cross country analyses for the period 1970-1989 and they conclude that opening the economy and trade policies are crucial in growth process. Edwards (1998) investigates growth effect of globalization by using nine alternative openness indexes measuring openness and trade policy-induced distortions for 93 countries during 1980-1990. Results obtained from panel regression (weighted least squares) show that more open countries experienced faster productivity growth. Greenaway, Morgan, and Wright (2002) find positive impact on 69 countries' economic growth for the period 1975-1993 through dynamic panel estimation in the frame of growth equations incorporating three different liberalization indexes that involve trade, tariffs, quotas and trade reforms.

Later, KOF indices have been widely preferred as an indicator of globalization in the literature (Martens et al., 2015; Potrafke, 2015). Including the KOF indices into their analyses, Dreher (2006) finds empirical evidence that globalization promotes economic growth by conducting panel data techniques to 123 countries' 1970-2000 data. Then, Dreher et al. (2008) analyze OECD countries by performing panel data estimations for the period 1970-2000 and find evidence that globalization spurs economic growth. Choosing 29 OECD countries, Bergh and Karlsson (2010) examine the effects of government size controlling for globalization in two sample periods: 1970-1995 and 1970-2005. They apply Bayesian averaging over classical estimates (BACE) and show that globalization has positive impact on the growth during the 1970-2005.

Villaverde and Maza (2011) confirm that total globalization index, social, economic and political globalization, separately, have positively affected growth rate of 101 countries by carrying out panel data estimation methodologies for the period 1970-2005. Positive impact is verified by Rao, Tamazian and Vadlamannati (2011) for five Asian countries through panel data analyses. Using panel estimation techniques and extreme bounds analysis, 21 low-income African countries are analyzed to determine long run growth effects of globalization in relatively poor countries by Rao and Vadlamannati (2011) and the authors detect positive and significant coefficient for globalization.

Since globalization series of 23 OECD countries over the period 1970-2006 has unit root, Chang and Lee (2010) apply first generation panel cointegration and panel vector error correction model (VECM) and find significant positive impact and significant causal relationship running from each sub-indices of globalization to economic growth. Considering structural breaks, Chang, Lee, and Hsieh (2011) employ second generation panel unit root and cointegration analyses to test long run relationship between globalization and real output and panel DOLS to estimate long run coefficient of overall index of globalization and three sub-indices for G7 countries over the period 1970-2006. Their findings provide strong evidence that overall and social dimension of globalization have positive and significant coefficients. On the other hand, they found no significant long run relationship between real output and other sub-indices.

Performing panel fixed effect and weighted average least squares (WALS) approaches, Osterloh (2012) includes overall KOF index, while researching the impact of politics on economic performance in a panel of 23 OECD countries for 1971-2004, and he finds that globalization has negative impact on Gross Domestic Product (GDP) per capita. Potrafke (2012) employs panel GMM to investigate the relationship between political cycles and economic performance measuring by GDP growth for 21 OECD countries over the period 1971-2006 by including growth rate of overall KOF index and it does not turn out to be significant, while economic globalization is positive and significant.

Chang, Berdiev, and Lee (2013) perform the bias-corrected least square dummy variable model in a panel involving Azerbaijan, Armenia, Georgia, Russia, and Turkey for the period 1990-2009 to study the effects of globalization and energy exports on economic growth and they conclude that globalization is a significant determinant of economic growth. Based on panel fixed and random effect methodologies in the period 1990-2009, Gurgul and Lach (2014) examine a panel of 10 CCE economies in transition by including KOF overall and sub-indices into Cobb-Douglas growth equation and they reach statistically significant growth-stimulating effects of overall, social and economic globalization process, even though the coefficient of political dimension is statistically insignificant.

Utilizing GMM estimator for a panel of 33 OIC countries Samimi and Jenatabadi (2014) show that economic dimension of the index has positive impact on economic growth for the period 1980-2008. They also indicate that the effect differs by income level of countries and high and middle incomes get more benefit than low income ones. Asian countries are examined by Ying et al. (2014) over the period 1970-2008 through panel cointegration test and the FMOLS estimator. They employ three sub-indices of KOF index and find that economic globalization has a positive influence on economic growth. In their study, however, the coefficients of social and political globalization are found negative and insignificant respectively.

Chang et al. (2015) just investigate the cointegration relationship between GDP and KOF globalization indicators (overall and three sub-indices) by performing non-linear time-varying cointegration approach based on quantile method for G7 countries' data covering from 1970 to 2006 and they conclude that these economies become more closely integrated in the process of globalization. Separating countries by income level and using first generation non-stationary panel data techniques, Kazar and Kazar (2016) estimate coefficients of regression equations established for growth, globalization and financial development through panel dynamic OLS estimator. They include economic, social and political dimensions of KOF index and conclude that social globalization for high income non-OECD and low income countries, political globalization for high income OECD countries, economic globalization for lower middle income countries can be driving force to economic growth.

Lee et al. (2017) use non-parametric approaches to investigate the effects of insurance activities and KOF overall index on economic growth for 38 countries' data spanning 1984-2009 and they obtain negative and positive partial effects for developed countries and underdeveloped countries respectively. Following empirical results, they conclude that globalization stimulates economic growth for underdeveloped countries. Following panel fixed effect estimator for 100 developing nations spanning 1995–2013, Majidi (2017) employs KOF overall and each sub-indices to estimate the effects of each one of them on economic growth and he finds negative impacts for political globalization in upper middle income countries while other globalization types has not significant effect on economic growth. In this study, positive impacts for overall and political globalization in lower middle-income countries are obtained.

Economic and social globalization, however, have no significant effect on economic growth of lower middle-income countries.

Given the critically importance of globalization for economic growth, empirical results remain unclear or inconsistent in the light of economic literature, whereas most of the literature results find positive impact for globalization indicators. The inconsistency might stem from the papers' own different methodologies, data set and regions. Different from current literature, to the best of our knowledge, this paper focuses on a different sample and employs more powerful estimators that are relatively newly developed and have not been applied in this literature to date.

DATA, MODEL AND METHODOLOGIES

The study follows the annual data spanning from 1970 to 2014 for each country to investigate the effects of globalization indicators on economic growth. Due to importance of the issue, especially for developing economies as is underlined by Gurgul and Lach (2014), a panel of emerging economies consisting of Brazil, Chile, China, Colombia, Egypt, Hungary, Indonesia, India, Morocco, Mexico, Malaysia, Peru, Philippines, Poland, South Africa, Thailand, Turkey are selected by following Standard & Poor's Dow Jones country classification[2]. However, the Czech Republic and Russia are excluded from the sample due to data unavailability spanning from 1970 to1993. Additionally, Taiwan is not included because of no data for globalization indices. As a measurement of globalization, KOF overall and its sub-indices for economic, social and political globalization are used since it is widely preferred in the literature. Some explanations about KOF index calculations are presented in Appendix.

The models that will be estimated are established in equations 1 and 2.

$$Y_{it} = \gamma_1 K_{i,t} + \gamma_2 L_{i,t} + \gamma_3 EG_{i,t} + \gamma_4 SG_{i,t} + \gamma_5 PG_{i,t} + \varepsilon_{i,t} \tag{1}$$

$$Y_{it} = \varphi_1 K_{i,t} + \varphi_2 L_{i,t} + \varphi_3 KOF_{i,t} + \vartheta_{i,t} \tag{2}$$

Y, *K* and *L* depict real GDP per capita, real capital stock per capita and employment rate calculated as the ratio of country's total employment to the country's population respectively. These data are extracted from database of Penn World Tables. *EG*, *SG* and *PG* stand for economic globalization, social globalization and political globalization sub-indices of KOF overall globalization index respectively and they are obtained from the KOF database of the Swiss Economic Institute.

The current literature investigates the effects of each sub-indices and/or KOF overall globalization index on economic growth. However, we construct two models to estimate the coefficients separately to deal with possible collinearity problem since these series are highly correlated for most countries. Our models in equations 1 and 2 are estimated panel data techniques to consider cross-section and time dimensions. For such a sample, cross-sections should be independent, and variables should be stationary to be able to reach unbiased and efficient outcome (Baltagi, 2015). Hence, it is required to check cross correlation between the sections and stationarity properties of the variables since the time dimensions of the models are sufficiently long. Therefore, cross-section dependence (CSD) is firstly checked for each variables and models. Breusch and Pagan (1980) developed an Lagrange Multiplier (LM) test based on the average of the squared pair-wise correlation of the residuals (CD LM_1) but in case where cross section dimension is large this approach is not appropriate (Pesaran, 2004).

Pesaran (2004) proposes two tests based on average of pair-wise correlation coefficients of the OLS residuals from the individual regressions in the panel. These tests might be conducted for any fixed lag order (CD LM_2) while no a priori ordering of the cross-section units is assumed (CD). Pesaran, Ullah and Yamagata (2008) suggest, then, a bias-adjusted version of Breusch and Pagan (1980). It is also consistent when Pesaran (2004) CD test is inconsistent. As a preliminary control, CSD tests proposed by Breusch and Pagan (1980), Peseran (2004) and Peseran et al. (2008) are conducted and obtained statistics for each variable and model in equation 1 and 2 are shown in Table 1.

According to CSD test results in Table 1, the null hypothesis of "no cross-sectional dependence" is strongly rejected for all variables and models. Therefore, following applications are carried out through second generation approaches that take dependence into account. The second check is to determine whether series has unit root or not. Smith, Leybourne, Kim, and Newbold (2004) propose more powerful panel unit root test dealing with cross-correlations through bootstrap methodology. Calculating *Max**, *Min** and *WS** statistics which each one of them is modified version of Im, Pesaran and Shin (2003) IPS test and Solo (1984) LM test respectively, Smith et al. (2004) performed the test to their sample with $N=17$, $T=45$, by 5000 bootstrap replications. Within this direction, our sample coincides with their sample in terms of number of section N and time dimension T. Having performed Smith et al. (2004) procedures, the results in Table 2 are produced.

Table 2 shows that null hypothesis of unit root cannot be rejected for all variables in level. One exception is *Max** and *Min** statistics of *PG* series implying series has not unit root at the 10% significance level. Its *WS** statistic, however, does not verify them. On the other hand, the null hypothesis is rejected for all series in first difference. Therefore, estimating the models in equation 1 and 2 would yield spurious results as it is in time series analysis (Granger & Newbold, 1974) as well as panel data analysis (Phillips & Moon, 1999) even though panel data problems yielded by spuriousness results are different from time series analysis, important deviations from the basic assumptions of panel data are observed (Baltagi, 2014).

Table 1. CSD test results for variables and regression equations

High Income	CD LM_1	CD LM_2	CD	CD LM_{BA}
Y	238.355***	6.206***	-3.363***	5.385***
K	235.483***	6.032***	-3.304***	5.150***
L	160.827*	1.505*	-2.276**	11.438***
KOF	276.679***	8.530***	-4.183***	18.999***
EG	250.573***	6.947***	-4.196***	8.326***
SG	376.015***	14.553***	-4.381***	11.401***
PG	483.332***	21.060***	-3.677***	8.988***
Model 1	1501.771***	82.812***	29.041***	112.912***
Model 2	1362.858***	74.389***	22.781***	111.611***

*, **, *** denote statistical significances of 10%, 5%, 1% respectively

Table 2. Panel unit root test results

	Level			First Difference	
	Statistic	Bootstrap p-value		Statistic	Bootstrap p-value
GDP					
Max*	-0.933	0.998		-4.398	0.000
WS*	-1.081	1.000		-4.660	0.000
Min*	1.608	0.999		14.273	0.000
K					
Max*	-1.124	0.540		-2.559	0.000
WS*	-1.659	0.690		-2.835	0.000
Min*	2.301	0.795		7.068	0.000
L					
Max*	-1.117	0.997		-5.351	0.000
WS*	-1.379	0.999		-5.629	0.000
Min*	2.548	0.966		17.397	0.000
KOF					
Max*	-1.539	0.848		-5.451	0.000
WS*	-1.802	0.835		-5.756	0.000
Min*	2.785	0.913		18.601	0.000
EG					
Max*	-1.580	0.842		-5.516	0.000
WS*	-1.817	0.812		-5.798	0.000
Min*	2.927	0.866		18.880	0.000
SG					
Max*	-1.657	0.585		-5.419	0.000
WS*	-1.809	0.757		-5.708	0.000
Min*	3.123	0.694		18.381	0.000
PG					
Max*	-2.082	0.096		-5.452	0.000
WS*	-2.219	0.200		-5.793	0.000
Min*	4.934	0.064		18.653	0.000

Note: p-Values are based on 5000 replications.

In this case, cointegration relation should be investigated to determine long run equilibrium that implies linear combination of series is stationary and long run coefficients should be estimated by cointegration estimators. Before long run estimations Durbin-Hausman test proposed by Westerlund (2008) is followed to examine long run relation. This approach is based on correction of common factors across units to consider dependence. Following several steps which we couldn't track in order to save space since they require lots of procedures, they are however able to be checked from the equations 7-13 in Westerlund

(2008, pp. 199-202). Westerlund (2008) obtains the Durbin-Hausman statistics to test cointegration relation by the following formulas:

$$\sum_{i=1}^{n}\hat{S}_i\left(\tilde{\varnothing}_i-\hat{\varnothing}_i\right)^2\sum_{t=2}^{T}\hat{e}_{it-1}^2 \text{ and } DH_{panel}=S_n\left(\tilde{\varnothing}-\hat{\varnothing}\right)^2\sum_{i=1}^{n}\sum_{t=2}^{T}\hat{e}_{it-1}^2$$

where $\tilde{\varnothing}_i$ and $\hat{\varnothing}_i$ represents coefficient for one lagged series of error term obtained from the lagged regression of error term (e_{it}) through OLS and instrumental variables estimators. $\hat{S}$ depicts variance ratios calculated by Kernel estimator based on OLS residual to variance of OLS estimation. The null hypothesis of these tests states no cointegration relation. Having applied these tests, it is decided that there is long run co-movement and long run relationship among those variables if the null hypothesis is rejected. Then, long run coefficients are estimated through cointegration estimators.

Bai and Kao (2006) and Bai, Kao, and Ng (2009) suggest a new estimator of cointegration models considering cross section dependence by using common factors. Bai and Kao (2006) then follow Equation 3:

$$y_{it}=a_i+\beta' x_{it}+u_{it}, \tag{3}$$

$$x_{it}=x_{i,t-1}+\varepsilon_{it},\ u_{it}=\lambda'_i f_t+\eta_{it},$$

where λ_i and f_t are factor loadings and unobserved I(0) factors, respectively. They adapt Phillips and Hansen (Phillips & Hansen, 1990) FM-OLS estimator to observe the presence of factors as is given in Equation 4.

$$\hat{\beta}_{FM}=\left(\sum_{i=1}^{N}\sum_{t=1}^{T}\left(x_{it}-\bar{x}_i\right)\left(x_{it}-\bar{x}_i\right)'\right)^{-1} x\left(\sum_{i=1}^{N}\left(\sum_{t=1}^{T}\left(x_{it}-\bar{x}_i\right)\hat{y}_{it}^{+}-T\left(\hat{"}_{\varepsilon u}+\hat{"}_{\varepsilon f}^{+}\hat{\lambda}_i\right)\right)\right) \tag{4}$$

β coefficients estimated by FM-OLS are repeated using residuals from the FM-OLS of previous stage until convergence. This procedure is named as continuously updated fully modified (CUP-FM) estimator (Choi, 2015). Bai et al. (2009) change equation 3 to 5.

$$y_{it}=a_i+\beta' x_{it}+\lambda'_i f_t+u_{it} \tag{5}$$

$$x_{it}=x_{i,t-1}+\varepsilon_{it}$$

$$f_t=f_{t-1}+\eta_t$$

where f_t are observed or unobserved I(1) time series called stochastic trends. It is assumed that the independent variables (x_{it}) to be independent across *i*. Then they construct two estimators to account for the bias arising from endogeneity and serial correlation. One of these estimators is named CUP-FM and follows same procedure by considering model 3 instead of model 2. The other one is CUP-BC (bias corrected) estimator and it estimates asymptotic bias directly. Both are continuously updated till convergence (Bai et al., 2009). They are also consistent in the absence of endogeneity (Bai et al., 2009) since they are based on FM-OLS (Breitung, 2005). Additionally, estimation results of CUP-FM and CUP-BC are consistent and efficient since they take into account of issues of serial correlation and endogeneity, through FM-OLS procedures and the issue heteroscedasticity by using Barlett Kernel procedure (Bai et al., 2009; Kiefer & Vogelsang, 2002).

ESTIMATION RESULTS

The presence of unit root in the variables is required to follow investigation of cointegration relationship and long run coefficients by cointegration estimators. By doing so, results of cointegration test and long run coefficients are obtained and presented in Table 3.

Considering results in Table 3, no cointegration relationship can be rejected at 5% significance level by *DH_panel* and *DH_group* statistics. The first three columns in Table 3 show the results of model 1 in equation 1 which includes each sub-indices of globalization. Accordingly, CUP-FM and CUP-BC estimators reveal that the coefficients of economic and social globalization have positive sign while political globalization's is negative. Model 2 that includes only overall globalization index in addition to capital stock and employment yields positive coefficient for overall globalization index. All coefficients in table 3 are statistically significant and there is no inconsistence between CUP-FM and CUP-BC outputs. Significance of all coefficients fall within 99 percent confidence interval except CUP-BC result for γ_1 and both of results for φ_3.

These results can be interpreted that overall globalization or economic and social dimension of globalization stimulate economic growth in emerging countries. Political dimension, however, does not have an increasing effect on their growth process. Political dimension has less weight in the overall KOF index calculations and it includes international treaties as a metric. Accordingly, some international treaties or standards may restrict economic activities. For example, global warming and climate change debates have been major issue since 1980s which are also critical years in terms of globalization process. Under the guidance of United Nations many summits have been made and treaties have signed to struggle with environmental threats that require to reduce polluted production.

Hence, Dreher et al. (2008) underline that the negotiation of international environmental agreements have ambiguous positive effects on environmental quality. Therefore, such agreements may have some constraints on economic growth by leading additional costs for production. That may be why model 1 estimates negative coefficient for political globalization by CUP-FM and CUP-BC.

Taking overall globalization into consideration in model 2, it has approximately the same coefficient value with capital stock and the coefficient is greater than employment's three times more. In this regard, that overall globalization, more precisely, integration process of emerging countries to the rest of the world has substantial influence on the growth equation of emerging countries.

Table 3. Estimation Results

	Model 1			Model 2	
coefficient	*CUP-FM*	*CUP-BC*	*coefficient*	*CUP-FM*	*CUP-BC*
γ_1	0.0674[a] (2.931)	0.0569[b] (2.545)	φ_1	0.1036[a] (24.640)	0.1072[a] (25.688)
γ_2	0.0435[b] (2.239)	0.0205 (1.094)	φ_2	0.0320[a] (8.827)	0.0299[a] (8.343)
	-	-	φ_3	0.0968[b] (2.546)	0.0790[b] (2.088)
γ_3	0.0378[a] (20.560)	0.0491[a] (26.961)		-	-
γ_4	0.0231[a] (10.847)	0.0233[a] (11.389)		-	-
γ_5	-0.0126[a] (-5.972)	-0.0643[a] (-3.160)		-	-
DH_panel	-1.930[b] [0.027]			-1.979[b] [0.024]	
DH_group	-2.956[b] [0.002]			-2.240[b] [0.013]	

[a],[b], [c] denotes statistical significance at 1%, 5%, 10% respectively, t-statistics are presented in the parentheses. *DH_panel* and *DH_grup* statistics are results of Westerlund Durbin Hausman cointegration test and their p-values are in the Brackets.

CONCLUSION

Globalization has gathered great momentum over the past four decades and it has led to important changes in economic, political, and cultural dynamics of countries. In this process, two accelerating factors of globalization are technological progress and liberalization. Much as countries have globalized in different degrees, it is thought that globalization enables countries to access new technologies and opportunities. Globalization also stimulates economic growth by leading institutional reforms in emerging economics and advanced economies contribute to this process by opening of their markets to goods and services from them. Thus, employing annual data spanning from 1970 to 2014, this study aims to empirically investigate the impact of globalization on economic growth for the panel of emerging countries consisting of Brazil, Chile, China, Colombia, Egypt, Hungary, Indonesia, India, Morocco, Mexico, Malaysia, Peru, Philippines, Poland, South Africa, Thailand, Turkey by conducting second generation panel data techniques. For this purpose, the effects of overall KOF globalization index and three dimensions of globalization on economic growth are estimated.

Having conducted CUP-FM and CUP-BC estimators that consider cross-sectional dependence and that are relatively newly developed and that haven't been applied in this literature so far, all coefficients turn out statistically significant. According to the results, overall globalization index, economic and social dimensions of globalization stimulate economic growth while political dimension has not increasing effect on the growth process of emerging countries. Accordingly, countries should attach importance to integrating their economies with the world.

Negative impact of political globalization makes us think that international treaties and standards restricting pollution or dirty production sectors may lead to decrease output since especially developing countries object to international pollution abatement agreements because of their economic growth will be adversely affected. Therefore some studies investigate the effects of such agreements on the developing countries (Ellerman, Jacoby, & Decaux, 1998; Gallo, Faccilongo & Sala, 2017). They however do not consider political globalization in their studies. Therefore, making new research trying to explain the effect of political globalization on the environment and economic growth from this standpoint will help to be able to clarify negative impact of political globalization.

REFERENCES

Acemoglu, D., Johnson, S., & Robinson, J. (2004). Institutions as the Fundamental Cause of Long-Run Growth. Cambridge, MA: Academic Press. doi:10.3386/w10481

Acemoglu, D., Johnson, S., & Robinson, J. A. (2001). The Colonial Origins of Comparative Development: An Empirical Investigation. *The American Economic Review*, *91*(5), 1369–1401. doi:10.1257/aer.91.5.1369

Aghion, P., & Howitt, P. (1992). *A Model of Growth Through Creative Destruction. Econometrica* (Vol. 60). The Econometric Society. doi:10.2307/2951599

Ardalan, K. (2017). Driving force of globalization: A multi- paradigmatic look. *Research in International Business and Finance*, *41*, 480–492. doi:10.1016/j.ribaf.2017.05.005

Bai, J., & Kao, C. (2006). Contributions to Economic Analysis: Vol. 274. On the Estimation and Inference of a Panel Cointegration Model with Cross-Sectional Dependence. Academic Press. doi:10.1016/S0573-8555(06)74001-9

Bai, J., Kao, C., & Ng, S. (2009). Panel cointegration with global stochastic trends. *Journal of Econometrics*, *149*(1), 82–99. doi:10.1016/j.jeconom.2008.10.012

Baltagi, B. H. (2014). Econometric Analysis of Panel Data (5ht ed.). Wiley.

Baltagi, B. H. (Ed.). (2015). *The Oxford Handbook of Panel Data*. Oxford University Press; doi:10.1093/oxfordhb/9780199940042.001.0001

Barro, R. J., & Sala-I-Martin, X. (1992). Public Finance in Models of Economic Growth. *The Review of Economic Studies*, *59*(4), 645–661. doi:10.2307/2297991

Bergh, A., & Karlsson, M. (2010). Government size and growth: Accounting for economic freedom and globalization. *Public Choice*, *142*(1–2), 195–213. doi:10.100711127-009-9484-1

Breitung, J. (2005). A Parametric approach to the Estimation of Cointegration Vectors in Panel Data. *Econometric Reviews*, *24*(2), 151–173. doi:10.1081/ETC-200067895

Bretschger, L. (2017). Climate policy and economic growth. *Resource and Energy Economics*, *49*, 1–15. doi:10.1016/j.reseneeco.2017.03.002

Breusch, T. S., & Pagan, A. R. (1980). The Lagrange Multiplier Test and its Applications to Model Specification in Econometrics. *The Review of Economic Studies*, *47*(1), 239. doi:10.2307/2297111

Chang, C.-P., Berdiev, A. N., & Lee, C.-C. (2013). Energy exports, globalization and economic growth: The case of South Caucasus. *Economic Modelling*, *33*, 333–346. doi:10.1016/j.econmod.2013.04.027

Chang, C.-P., & Lee, C.-C. (2010). Globalization and Economic Growth: A Political Economy Analysis for OECD Countries. *Global Economic Review*, *39*(2), 151–173. doi:10.1080/1226508X.2010.483835

Chang, C.-P., Lee, C.-C., & Hsieh, M.-C. (2011). Globalization, Real Output and Multiple Structural Breaks. *Global Economic Review*, *40*(4), 421–444. doi:10.1080/1226508X.2011.626154

Chang, C.-P., Lee, C.-C., & Hsieh, M.-C. (2015). Does globalization promote real output? Evidence from quantile cointegration regression. *Economic Modelling*, *44*, 25–36. doi:10.1016/j.econmod.2014.09.018

Choi, I. (2015). Panel Cointegration. In B. H. Baltagi (Ed.), *The Oxford Handbook of Panel Data* (pp. 46–75). Oxford, UK: Oxford University Press.

De Long, J. B. (1988). Productivity Growth, Convergence, and Welfare. *The American Economic Review*, *78*(5), 1138–1154.

Dreher, A. (2006). Does globalization affect growth? Evidence from a new index of globalization. *Applied Economics*, *38*(10), 1091–1110. doi:10.1080/00036840500392078

Dreher, A., Gaston, N., & Martens, P. (2008). *Measuring Globalization - Gauging its Consequences*. New York, NY: Springer.

Easterly, W., & Levine, R. (2001). *It's Not Factor Accumulation: Stylized Facts and Growth Models. The World Bank Economic Review*. Oxford University Press; doi:10.2307/3990260

Easterly, W., & Levine, R. (2003). Tropics, germs, and crops: How endowments influence economic development. *Journal of Monetary Economics*, *50*(1), 3–39. doi:10.1016/S0304-3932(02)00200-3

Ecevit, E., Yücel, A. G., & Yücel, Ö. (2016). Are Some Taxes Better than Others for Economic Growth? An ARDL Approach for Turkey. *The Empirical Economics Letters.*, *15*(11), 1129–1136.

Edwards, S. (1998). Openness, Productivity and Growth: What Do We Really Know? *Economic Journal (London)*, *108*(447), 383–398. doi:10.1111/1468-0297.00293

Ellerman, A. D., Jacoby, H. D., & Decaux, A. (1998). *The Effects on Developing Countries of the Kyoto Protocol and Carbon Dioxide Emissions Trading* (Policy Research Working Papers). The World Bank. 10.1596/1813-9450-2019

Fischer, M. M. (2011). A spatial Mankiw–Romer–Weil model: Theory and evidence. *The Annals of Regional Science*, *47*(2), 419–436. doi:10.100700168-010-0384-6

Frankel, J. A., & Romer, D. (1999). Does Trade Cause Growth? *The American Economic Review*, *89*(3), 379–399. doi:10.1257/aer.89.3.379

Gallo, C., Faccilongo, N., & Sala, P. (2017). Clustering analysis of environmental emissions: A study on Kyoto Protocol's impact on member countries. *Journal of Cleaner Production*. doi:10.1016/J.JCLEPRO.2017.07.194

Granger, C., & Newbold, P. (1974). Spurious regressions in econometrics. *Journal of Econometrics*, *2*(2), 111–120. doi:10.1016/0304-4076(74)90034-7

Greenaway, D., Morgan, W., & Wright, P. (2002). Trade liberalisation and growth in developing countries. *Journal of Development Economics*, *67*(1), 229–244. doi:10.1016/S0304-3878(01)00185-7

Grier, K. B., & Tullock, G. (1989). An empirical analysis of cross-national economic growth, 1951–1980. *Journal of Monetary Economics*, *24*(2), 259–276. doi:10.1016/0304-3932(89)90006-8

Grossman, G. M., & Helpman, E. (1991). *Innovation and Growth in the Global Economy*. Cambridge, MA: MIT Press.

Gurgul, H., & Lach, Ł. (2014). Globalization and economic growth: Evidence from two decades of transition in CEE. *Economic Modelling*, *36*, 99–107. doi:10.1016/j.econmod.2013.09.022

Hall, R. E., & Jones, C. I. (1999). *Why Do Some Countries Produce So Much More Output Per Worker Than Others? The Quarterly Journal of Economics*. doi:10.3386/w6564

Heshmati, A., & Lee, S. (2010). Human Dimension of Globalization The Relationship Between Globalization, Economic Growth And Income Inequality. *Journal of Globalization Studies*, *1*(2), 87–117. Retrieved from http://www.sociostudies.org/journal/files/jogs/2010_2/the_relationship.pdf

Im, K. S., Pesaran, M. H., & Shin, Y. (2003). Testing for unit roots in heterogeneous panels. *Journal of Econometrics*, *115*(1), 53–74. doi:10.1016/S0304-4076(03)00092-7

Kazar, A., & Kazar, G. (2016). International journal of economics and financial issues. *International Journal of Economics and Financial Issues*, *6*(2), 578–587. Retrieved from http://www.econjournals.com/index.php/ijefi/article/view/2125

Kiefer, N. M., & Vogelsang, T. J. (2002). Heteroskedasticity-Autocorrelation Robust Standard Errors Using the Bartlett Kernel without Truncation. *Econometrica*, *70*(5), 2093–2095. doi:10.1111/1468-0262.00366

Kormendi, R. C., & Meguire, P. G. (1985). Macroeconomic determinants of growth: Cross-country evidence. *Journal of Monetary Economics*, *16*(2), 141–163. doi:10.1016/0304-3932(85)90027-3

LaFree, G. (2005). Evidence For Elite Convergence in Cross-National Homicide Victimization Trends, 1956 to 2000. *The Sociological Quarterly*, *46*(1), 191–211. doi:10.1111/j.1533-8525.2005.00009.x

Lee, C.-C., Lee, C.-C., & Chiou, Y.-Y. (2017). Insurance activities, globalization, and economic growth: New methods, new evidence. *Journal of International Financial Markets, Institutions and Money*, *51*, 155–170. doi:10.1016/j.intfin.2017.05.006

Lucas, R. E. Jr. (1988). On the mechanics of economic development. *Journal of Monetary Economics*, *22*(1), 3–42. doi:10.1016/0304-3932(88)90168-7

Majidi, A. F. (2017). Globalization and Economic Growth: The Case Study of Developing Countries. *Asian Economic and Financial Review, 7*(6), 589–599. Retrieved from https://ideas.repec.org/a/asi/aeafrj/2017p589-599.html

Mankiw, N. G., Romer, D., & Weil, D. N. (1992). A Contribution to the Empirics of Economic Growth. *The Quarterly Journal of Economics*, *107*(2), 407–437. doi:10.2307/2118477

Martens, P., Caselli, M., De Lombaerde, P., Figge, L., & Scholte, J. A. (2015). New Directions in Globalization Indices. *Globalizations*, *12*(2), 217–228. doi:10.1080/14747731.2014.944336

Mayer, J. (2000). *Globalization, Technology Transfer And Skill Accumulation In Low-Income Countries* (UNCTAD/OSG/DP/150 No. 150). Retrieved from http://www.unctad.org/en/pub/pubframe.htm

Mishkin, F. S. (2009). Globalization and financial development. *Journal of Development Economics*, *89*(2), 164–169. doi:10.1016/j.jdeveco.2007.11.004

Osterloh, S. (2012). Words speak louder than actions: The impact of politics on economic performance. *Journal of Comparative Economics*, *40*(3), 318–336. doi:10.1016/j.jce.2012.05.004

Pekarskiene, I., & Susniene, R. (2014). The Assessment of the Manifestation of Economic Globalization: The International Trade Factor. *Procedia: Social and Behavioral Sciences*, *156*, 392–397. doi:10.1016/j.sbspro.2014.11.209

Pekarskiene, I., & Susniene, R. (2015). Features of Foreign Direct Investment in the Context of Globalization. *Procedia: Social and Behavioral Sciences*, *213*, 204–210. doi:10.1016/j.sbspro.2015.11.427

Pesaran, M. H. (2004). *General Diagnostic Tests For Cross Section Dependence in Panels* (CWPE 0435 No. 1233). Academic Press.

Pesaran, M. H., Ullah, A., & Yamagata, T. (2008). A bias-adjusted LM test of error cross-section independence. *The Econometrics Journal*, *11*(1), 105–127. doi:10.1111/j.1368-423X.2007.00227.x

Phillips, P. C. B., & Hansen, B. E. (1990). Statistical Inference in Instrumental Variables Regression with I(1) Processes. *The Review of Economic Studies*, *57*(1), 99. doi:10.2307/2297545

Phillips, P. C. B., & Moon, H. R. (1999). Linear Regression Limit Theory for Nonstationary Panel Data. *Econometrica*, *67*(5), 1057–1111. doi:10.1111/1468-0262.00070

Potrafke, N. (2012). Political cycles and economic performance in OECD countries: Empirical evidence from 1951–2006. *Public Choice*, *150*(1–2), 155–179. doi:10.100711127-010-9695-5

Potrafke, N. (2015). The Evidence on Globalisation. *World Economy*, *38*(3), 509–552. doi:10.1111/twec.12174

Rao, B. B., Tamazian, A., & Vadlamannati, K. C. (2011). Growth effects of a comprehensive measure of globalization with country-specific time series data. *Applied Economics*, *43*(5), 551–568. doi:10.1080/00036840802534476

Rao, B. B., & Vadlamannati, K. C. (2011). Globalization and growth in the low income African countries with the extreme bounds analysis. *Economic Modelling*, *28*(3), 795–805. doi:10.1016/j.econmod.2010.10.009

Rennen, W., & Martens, P. (2003). The Globalisation Timeline. *Integrated Assessment*, *4*(3), 137–144. doi:10.1076/iaij.4.3.137.23768

Rodriguez, F., & Rodrik, D. (2000). Trade Policy and Economic Growth: A Skeptic's Guide to the Cross-National Evidence. In B. S. Bernanke & K. Rogoff (Eds.), *NBER Macroeconomics Annual 2000* (Vol. 15, pp. 262–338). MIT Press. Retrieved from http://www.nber.org/books/bern01-1

Rodrik, D., Subramanian, A., & Trebbi, F. (2004). Institutions Rule: The Primacy of Institutions Over Geography and Integration in Economic Development. *Journal of Economic Growth*, *9*(2), 131–165. doi:10.1023/B:JOEG.0000031425.72248.85

Romer, P. M. (1986). Increasing Returns and Long-Run Growth. *Journal of Political Economy*, *94*(5), 1002–1037. doi:10.1086/261420

Romer, P. M. (1990). Endogenous Technological Change. *Journal of Political Economy*, *98*(5), 71–102. doi:10.1086/261725

Sachs, J. D., & Warner, A. (1995). *Economic Reform and the Process of Global Integration* (Brookings Papers on Economic Activity No. 1). Retrieved from https://www.brookings.edu/wp-content/uploads/1995/01/1995a_bpea_sachs_warner_aslund_fischer.pdf

Samimi, P., & Jenatabadi, H. S. (2014). Globalization and Economic Growth: Empirical Evidence on the Role of Complementarities. *PLoS One*, *9*(4), e87824. doi:10.1371/journal.pone.0087824 PMID:24721896

Samimi, P., Lim, G. C., & Buang, A. A. (2011). Globalization Measurement: Notes on Common Globalization Indexes. *Journal of Knowledge Management, Economics and Information Technology, 1*(7), 1–20. Retrieved from https://ideas.repec.org/a/spp/jkmeit/1216.html

Sarafidis, V., & Wansbeek, T. (2010). *Cross-sectional Dependence in Panel Data Analysis* (No. 20367). Retrieved from http://mpra.ub.uni-muenchen.de/20367/

Sarafidis, V., & Wansbeek, T. (2012). Cross-Sectional Dependence in Panel Data Analysis. *Econometric Reviews*, *31*(5), 483–531. doi:10.1080/07474938.2011.611458

Smith, L. V., Leybourne, S., Kim, T.-H., & Newbold, P. (2004). More powerful panel data unit root tests with an application to mean reversion in real exchange rates. *Journal of Applied Econometrics*, *19*(2), 147–170. doi:10.1002/jae.723

Solo, V. (1984). The Order of Differencing in ARIMA Models. *Journal of the American Statistical Association*, *79*(388), 916–921. doi:10.1080/01621459.1984.10477111

Solow, R. M. (1956). A contribution to the theory of economic growth. *Source: The Quarterly Journal of Economics, 70*(1), 65–94. Retrieved from http://www.jstor.org/stable/1884513

Soubbotina, T. P., & Sheram, K. (2000). *Beyond economic growth: Meeting the challenges of global development.* World Bank. Retrieved from https://books.google.com.tr/books/about/Beyond_Economic_Growth.html?id=ZPQ1I8WuDcgC&redir_esc=y

Thompson, M. (2018). Social capital, innovation and economic growth. *Journal of Behavioral and Experimental Economics*, *73*, 46–52. doi:10.1016/j.socec.2018.01.005

Villaverde, J., & Maza, A. (2011). Globalisation, Growth and Convergence. *World Economy*, *34*(6), 952–971. doi:10.1111/j.1467-9701.2011.01359.x

Vujakovic, P. (2010). How to Measure Globalization? A New Globalization Index (NGI). *Atlantic Economic Journal*, *38*(2), 237–237. doi:10.100711293-010-9217-3

Westerlund, J. (2008). Panel cointegration tests of the Fisher effect. *Journal of Applied Econometrics*, *23*(2), 193–233. doi:10.1002/jae.967

Ying, Y.-H., Chang, K., & Lee, C.-H. (2014). The Impact of Globalization on Economic Growth. *Journal for Economic Forecasting*, (2), 25–34. Retrieved from https://ideas.repec.org/a/rjr/romjef/vy2014i2p25-34.html

ENDNOTES

1 A list of studies using this index is available at https://www.kof.ethz.ch/en/publications.html.

2 https://www.spindices.com/documents/index-policies/20140729-country-classification-consultation.pdf (01.11.2017).

APPENDIX

The KOF index covers each pillar of globalization (economic, social and political) and it is calculated by including lots of relevant data obtained various databases of international organizations. For example, economic globalization is constructed on two sub-indexes in accordance with available literature. One of them, known actual flows, employs data on trade, foreign direct investments and portfolio investments provided by World Bank, UNCTAD and IMF, respectively. The second one allows restrictions on international trade and capital movements by using hidden barriers, tariffs, taxes and controls. An index that includes 13 different types of capital controls, provided by Gwarthney et al. (2016), is employed. In this restriction index, the IMF's Annual Reports on exchange arrangements and restrictions are considered as well. The second pillar is social globalization and it is calculated through personal contacts, information flows and cultural leveling. Personal contacts are compiled by using data on international telecom traffic, number of international letters, tourism, government and workers' transfers received and paid. On the other hand, information flows are measured by interactions of people living different countries such as number of internet users, international newspapers traded and the share of households with a television set. The last and most arguable component of social globalization, namely cultural leveling, is represented by number of English songs in national hit lists or movies shown in national cinemas that originated in Hollywood.

These data, however are not available for some countries. In this case, imported and exported books are used based on the suggestion of Kluver and Fu (2004). Additionally, spread of some cultural products is accepted as part of cultural globalization like McDonald's restaurants located in a country. In this manner, the number of McDonalds and Ikea per country is considered to evaluate cultural leveling. Political dimension that covers the number of membership to international organizations, the number of embassies and high commissions in a country, the number of treaties signed between countries and the number of participation to global affairs is final calculation in KOF indexation.

Each variable used in KOF calculations is transformed to an index scored one to hundred where one is the minimum value while hundred is maximum to denote degrees of globalization. Applying principal components analysis, weights for sub-indices are decided for all years and countries after the data are converted by percentiles of the original distribution. Then, variances of the variables are compartmentalized for all sub-groups. Considering values that maximizes variation of principal component's results, the weights are re-determined so as to obtain the variation as wholly as possible. These procedures are repeated for each sub-indices to compose whole globalization index. Each component of indices and variables are shown by weights in Table 4.

Table 4. 2016 KOF index of globalization

	Indices and Variables	Weights
A.	**Economic Globalization**	**[36%]**
	i) Actual Flows	(50%)
	Trade (percent of GDP)	(22%)
	Foreign Direct Investment, stocks (percent of GDP)	(27)
	Portfolio Investment (percent of GDP)	(24)
	Income Payments to Foreign Nationals (percent of GDP)	(27)
	ii) Restrictions	(50%)
	Hidden Import Barriers	(23%)
	Mean Tariff Rate	(28%)
	Taxes on International Trade (percent of current revenue)	(26)
	Capital Account Restrictions	(23)
B.	**Social Globalization**	**[37%]**
	i) Data on Personal Contact	(33%)
	Telephone Traffic	(26%)
	Transfers (percent of GDP)	(2%)
	International Tourism	(26%)
	Foreign Population (percent of total population)	(21%)
	International letters (per capita)	(25%)
	ii) Data on Information Flows	(35%)
	Internet Users (per 1000 people)	(36%)
	Television (per 1000 people)	(38%)
	Trade in Newspapers (percent of GDP)	(26%)
	iii) Data on Cultural Proximity	(32%)
	Number of McDonald's Restaurants (per capita)	(46%)
	Number of Ikea (per capita)	(46%)
	Trade in books (percent of GDP)	(7%)
C.	**Political Globalization**	**[27%]**
	Embassies in Country	(25%)
	Membership in International Organizations	(27%)
	Participation in U.N. Security Council Missions	(22%)
	International Treaties	(26%)

Source: http://globalization.kof.ethz.ch/

Chapter 2
The Relationship Between Globalization and Income Distribution:
An Empirical Analysis in the Context of South Korea

Buhari Doğan
Süleyman Demirel University, Turkey

Muhlis Can
Hakkari University, Turkey

ABSTRACT

Income inequality is a major economic problem in many countries, and it is clear that numerous parameters affect income distribution. In this study, the effects of globalization on income distribution were examined in the contexts of South Korea and the Kuznets curve between 1970 and 2010. The cointegration test of the series was carried out using the Maki approach, which considers multiple structural breaks. The cointegration test indicated the series moved together in the long term. The long-term analysis indicated that globalization first reduces income inequality and then increases it in a U-shaped relationship. In the short-term analysis, it was found that the error correction term was negative and statistically significant. In this context, it is crucial that policy makers develop policies that minimize the impact of globalization on income inequality; otherwise, social and economic distortions will increase with the increase in globalization, which will cause different socioeconomic problems.

INTRODUCTION

Globalization has become one of the most important concepts in defining today's international economy and the change in world politics.[1] Globalization is defined as the free movement of production factors, goods, and services across country borders (Heshmati, 2004, p.1). Moreover, globalization refers to the process of comprehensive economic integration, which increases the international mobility of national

DOI: 10.4018/978-1-5225-5787-6.ch002

resources and the dependence of national economies (OECD, 2005, p.11), and, according to Held & McGrew (2008, p.72), to the transformation process that increases bonds between countries and allows social relations to converge. This process has brought the economies of countries closer to each other and strengthened economic bonds. Today, as economies and societies are intertwined, individuals and institutions have access to things they wish for faster and more economically than in the past. In this context, globalization ensures the acceleration of trade relations and the development of the global labor force, resulting in market forces that are more developed (Heshmati, 2004, p.1).

The literature highlights many positive and negative developments caused by globalization; therefore, globalization, and its effects, is a controversial subject. The most important underlying reason for the controversy arises from the viewpoint that some countries benefit from globalization, while others are significantly harmed by it (Villaverde & Maza, 2011, p.952). Nevertheless, Dreher (2006, p.1091) and many other scholars contend that the net effect of globalization on the prosperity of countries is positive. Increased globalization contributes to the rapid development of technology, the liberalization of capital circulation, and the creation and development of new investment instruments, thus creating a positive perception of globalization, particularly in the scientific community (Eroğlu & Albeni, 2002, p.61).

The phenomenon of globalization, which gained momentum in the last quarter of the 20th century, also has been examined in terms of its effects on income distribution and various additional parameters. According to the liberal view, globalization affects countries positively due to the economic advantages it provides, which can significantly contribute to the reduction of income inequality (Rao & Vadlamannati, 2011, p.795). However, globalization has numerous negative effects[2], such as increasing and spreading poverty[3], and causing social and environmental deterioration. Income distribution inequality within the context of globalization is measured using four approaches. The first three approaches involve measuring the intercountry average income differences where the populations of all countries are accepted as being equal, measuring the average of each country's national income according to the populations of the relevant country, and measuring the inequality between individuals on a global, national, and regional basis. The fourth is the vertical and horizontal inequality approach. Vertical inequality explains the inequality between individuals in different income groups, while horizontal inequality measures inequality between individuals in the same income group (Nissanke & Thorbecke, 2006, p.1340). Different indexes and coefficient methods are used to measure income distribution on the global and national scales, namely the McLoone index, the Lorenz curve, the Gini coefficient, and the Theil index. Among them, the Gini coefficient[4] is the most commonly used in the literature (Martin, 2002, p.27).

The recent increase in income inequality in many countries has led to growing concern among economists and policy makers in both developed and developing countries. Despite the technological progress, benefits of free-market-oriented reforms, and output and income growth experienced due to globalization, these benefits have not been distributed to all segments of the population in all countries. In this respect, it is essential to understand the causes of inequality and to implement policy measures to support the emergence of more equal societies (Asteriou, 2014, p.592). The aim of the study is to examine the relationship between globalization and income distribution in South Korea between 1970 and 2010 in the context of the Kuznets curve. South Korea has been selected due to the rapid development and transformation in the country in the last quarter of a century (Doğan & Can, 2016). In addition, South Korea was classified as both developing and developed country during the period study. Therefore, significant transformation in development and income levels has been achieved in the country through globalization, and the importance of globalization in this transformation is undeniable.

The rest of the chapter is organized as follows. Firstly; the KOF Index of Globalization and income distribution are discussed, and the possible effects of globalization on income distribution are examined. Subsequently, the theoretical framework of the relationship between globalization and income distribution, and the course of globalization and income distribution in the South Korean context are presented. Secondly; the studies investigating the effects of globalization on income distribution are reviewed. Finally, an econometric analysis and the findings of the study are discussed, and the paper concludes with an overview of the results.

GLOBALIZATION

Globalization is the process of worldwide socioeconomic integration, and it remains a topic of significant interest for the international economy. According to Norris (2000, p.155), globalization is a process that removes national borders; integrates national economies, cultures, technologies, and governance; and establishes complex, interdependent relationships. Moreover, globalization is a multifaceted concept with economic, social, and political aspects beyond indicators such as capital mobility (Potrafke, 2014, p.510). Particularly after the Second World War, with the rapid transformation of international trade and finance environments into open and integrated markets, the influence of globalization within the process began to attract attention (Chang, Lee, & Hsieh, 2011), and the influence of liberalism became more pronounced in the international trade and finance sectors. In the post-war era, the policies implemented to integrate markets made globalization more efficient (Chang, Lee, & Hsieh, 2011, p.421), and many countries focused on economic integration by reducing customs taxes and liberalizing their trade flows. Today, technology causes rapid development at the points of flow of information and goods and services.

With the development of telecommunications, the world entered the Information Age. Transnational relations have become much more productive, as these developments have reduced commercial operation and transportation costs (Chang, Lee, & Hsieh, 2011, p.422). Especially in 1989, with the disintegration of the Soviet Union, the bipolar world became multipolar. This situation accelerated the globalization process by stimulating regional competition (Eroğlu & Albeni, 2002, p.23). Furthermore, 20 years ago, globalization was rarely discussed, yet at the same time, at least 15% of the world population participated in global trade (Marber, 2004, p.29). However, recent interest in globalization has sparked debates on whether it benefits economic performance and various other factors (Garrett,2001; Milanovic, 2003b; Lee & Chang, 2009; Shen, 2010). Additionally, because of the economic crisis that emerged in 2007, rising income inequality has caused researchers to question the positive aspects of globalization (Potrafke, 2014, p.509). Nevertheless, when evaluated in general terms, the net effect of globalization is viewed as positive (Potrafke, 2014, p.1).

Globalization has become one of the most important topics of interest in science within the last 25 years, and numerous studies have been performed on the subject by researchers from different branches of science. Thus, globalization studies have covered aspects such as the sociological, psychological, communicative, and historical facets of the phenomenon. Nonetheless, the subject is most often approached from the economic perspective, with researchers focusing on the economic effects of globalization and examining various macroeconomic implications (Can & Doğan, 2016, p.2). Furthermore, research on global integration generally focuses on ending the obstruction of global free trade, and it highlights that countries are linked through political matters such as the environment, climate change, and international migration. In addition, the literature exposes several key questions related to globalization, such as economic and technological change, the social aspects of life, and policy issues. In other words, commercial behavior emerging from economic globalization is also based on political and social integration (Chang, Lee, & Hsieh, 2011, p.423). Thus, in this context, not only the economic aspects but also the social and political aspects of globalization are important.

Dreher (2006, p.1092) discussed the economic, social, and political measures covered by the globalization indexes and noted that economic integration progresses parallel to political and social integration over time. In this respect, the different dimensions of globalization affect each other. Keohane and Nye (2000, p.4–5) supported Dreher's opinions, specifically that:

1. Economic globalization can be characterized as long-distance goods, capital flows and services, as well as perceptions of information and market exchange companionship,
2. Political globalization can be characterized as a diffusion of government policies and,
3. Social globalization can be characterized as the spread of ideas, knowledge, images, and people.

Moreover, Dreher (2006) defined globalization as an economic, social, and political integration of each country with other countries and created four indexes related to this definition, namely the economic globalization index, social globalization index, political globalization index, and general globalization index; the latter is calculated by combining the first three.[5]With Dreher's combined index, it became possible to test the effects of different dimensions of globalization on different parameters at the same time. Known as the KOF Index of Globalization,[6] or KOF Index, this index allows for the testing of the effects of globalization both individually and as a whole (Dreher, 2006, p.1092).[7]

According to the KOF Index, globalization is a process that removes national boundaries and integrates economies, politics, and technology. In this respect, the Index covers the economic, social, and political dimensions of globalization (Samimi, 2012, p. 29). The components that form globalization are presented in Table 1.

In Table 1, each index takes a value between 0 and 100. If the self-constituent parameters of the country are at the top level, the index value will approach 100. Otherwise, the index value will be close to zero.

INCOME DISTRIBUTION

Income distribution is an interesting issue not only for economists but also for other social scientists. Income distribution is the share of people contributing to the total income in a given period (Karluk, 1996). Income distribution also refers to the share or distribution of the total income from the goods or services produced by the individuals living in a country by means of distribution to the individuals in that country (Işiğiçok, 1998). This share is crucial in economic theory, as it is an important indicator of a country's economic refinement. Income inequality is the proof that a country's income is distributed unequally and inequitably by the individuals in that country.

A plethora of studies has been conducted on the relationship between income inequality and various economic and social variables, and economic inequality can affect these variables in many ways. Social science researchers generally regard inequality in income distribution as an undesirable situation. One of the reasons for this view is its adverse effect on economic growth (Persson & Tabellini,1994). Inequality increases the distributional struggle, which can be harmful to economic growth when considered

Table 1. Components of the globalization index

Economic Globalization	*Trade and capital flows*	a) Foreign trade (percentage of GDP) b) Direct foreign investments (percentage of GDP) c) Portfolio investments (percentage of GDP) d) Revenue paid to foreign nations (percentage of GDP)
	Limitations	a) Secret import barriers b) Average tariff rate c) Taxes on international trade (percentage of current income) d) Capital account restrictions
Political Globalization		a) Embassies in the countries b) Membership in international organizations c) Participation in the UN Security Council
Social Globalization	*Personal communication*	a) Telephone traffic b) Transfers (percentage of GDP) c) International tourism d) Average cost of calling United States e) Foreign population (percentage of total population)
	Information flow	a) Telephone main lines (per 1,000 people) b) Internet servers (per person) c) Internet users (as a share of the population) d) Cable TV (per 1,000 people) e) Daily newspapers (per 1,000 people) f) Radio (per 1,000 people)
	Cultural connection	a) Number of McDonald's restaurants

Source: Dreher (2006, p.1094).

completely theoretically. In addition, it has been proven that inequality in income distribution reduces growth rates, at least in democracies (Weede, 1997).

Income distribution may change due to structural effects such as globalization and/or technological change or the worsening macroeconomic performance of the country. In that case, we can summarize the factors that determine income distribution as distribution of the labor market and labor force; production factors and the distribution of the price of these factors; the distribution of wealth; education levels; social rules and regulations; changes in world economy (globalization, technological change, etc.); and changes in the country's economy and policies (inflation, crises, budget deficits, devaluation, customizing, etc.) (Thorbecke & Charumilind, 2002).

It is inevitable for researchers to identify the same basic trends when income distribution statistics are disclosed by a particular institution in each country. However, debates among researchers over the distribution of income might create confusion, as they might use many definitions and concepts in relation to the subject. From this point of view, income inequality is a multifaceted concept, and generalizations about distribution trends might cause misleading results. The trend of income distribution depends on the income category (wage, daily wage, interest, etc.), the income distribution inequality measures (Gini coefficient, Kuznets coefficient, Lorenz curve, general entropy measures, etc.), the period analyzed, and the group studied (male, female, family, age groups, etc.). Thus, a large number of income distribution or inequality trends can be calculated; however, it is important to know which one is most robust (Burkhauser, Crews & Daly 1997). The most important question that faces researchers in this regard is undoubtedly the explanation of how inequality derives from income distribution (Sharpe & Zyblock, 1997).

Determining the causes of inequality in income distribution is challenging. Most economists were not particularly interested in the growing disparity in income distribution until the 1990s. In the economics textbooks, it is assumed that inequality and the concentration of income among the rich might have a positive effect on growth. In contrast, after the 1990s, economists began to argue that inequality might be the reason for the decline in economic growth (Person & Tabelleni, 1994; Fields, 1989).

Economists assume certain factors as reasons for inequality. Wade (2001) identified the difference in the rate of population growth in rich and poor countries, and the reduction of the real prices of non-petroleum goods by half between 1980 and 1990, which in turn affected poorer countries, as reasons. In addition, the debt trap affects equality, as especially fast-growing emerging countries are being dragged into financial crises because they borrow on less favorable terms. These crises pull them to the lower levels of the world's income hierarchy. Furthermore, technological changes have led to growing income inequality because the high added value of the technological changes experienced in the last 20 years is concentrated in developed countries rather than developing countries.

Before the First World War, inequality increased in the United States and other New World countries, while inequality decreased in European countries because many immigrants immigrated to the United States, thus increasing trade. After the Second World War, inequality increased in both the United States and other Organization for Economic Co-operation and Development countries. Similarly, inequality increased in countries such as the Four Asian Tigers, China, Mexico, and Brazil. However, according to Lindert and Williamson (2001, p.41–42), the increasing inequality in these countries was not between the new commercial regions and people in the sector, but rather between the lower income and non-commercial areas.

Among the causes of the increase in inequality in the 20th century, the importance of externalities such as technology has increased. First, technology increased the demand for skilled labor. Second, information technologies reduced the cost of auditing the performance of unqualified labor, minimized labor shrinkage, and improved efficiency, thus reducing the cost of unskilled labor. Third, as new information technologies emerged, particularly in the service sector, the labor shift and unemployment increased. Fourth, developments in information technologies made services that were not subject to trade agreements tradeable within the international market. Although this creates new jobs for the educated workforce in low-income countries, it also increases unemployment in developed countries (Cornia, 1999, p.12). In other words, globalization has created a labor movement in the medium-sized sectors where wage discrepancies are larger than in the agricultural sector, where wage discrepancies are the smallest (Milanovic, 2002, p.4).

While recessions in developing countries increase inequality, developments in economic conditions reduce inequality. In industrialized countries, contrary to the developing countries, the rapid regression in economic conditions causes wages to fall less than profits, particularly with the influence of a developed social security system. In middle-income countries, wages fall faster than GDP or capital and profits, like in developed countries, depending on whether the wages are flexible and the social security expenditures are adequate. This situation increases the extent of inequality in income distribution by lowering wage rates (Cornia, 1999, p.13).

As the effects of globalization on income distribution might vary depending on which period and concept of inequality is discussed, they might also not be precisely determined due to a lack of access to sufficient data in all countries. However, global income inequality increased from 1820 to the present day—the difference between the wealthiest country and the poorest country, which was nine times the GDP per person in 1870, increased to 45 times in 1990 (World Bank, 2006, p.56–57). According to Lindert and Williamson (2001) and Taylor (2002, p.20), a significant part of the increased income inequality derived not from the increase in inequality within the country but rather from the intercountry increase in income differences.[8] Milanovic (2002, p.3) and Ravallion (2003, p.17) concluded that openness reduces inequality in rich countries but amplifies in equality in poor countries. Nevertheless, Dollar and Kraay (2004, p.41) have shown that there is no systematic relationship between openness and inequality.[9]

Why income inequality is greater in some countries than in others is one of the most difficult problems of economic analysis (UN, 1997, p.116). The traditional answer to this problem, which has an important place in the literature of inequality, was provided by Simon Kuznets: income inequality increases during the first phase of economic development and then begins to decline. According to this hypothesis, which is named reverse U, income inequality in middle-income countries might be expected to be greater than in the least developed and industrialized countries. This situation includes a transition from an agricultural-based economy with low productivity to a high-efficiency industrial economy during the economic development process. When industrialization is completed, it is predicted that inequalities in income distribution tend to decrease.

THE EFFECTS OF GLOBALIZATION ON INCOME DISTRIBUTION

Globalization is generally defined as the free movement or transportation of goods, services, and capital over the borders of different countries. Furthermore, Western market economies involve a continuous process that is spreading effectively throughout the world. Parallel to this definition, the process of integration of the world economy has reached unprecedented levels by exceeding the pre-First World War peak. This change in the global economic environment has greatly improved the economic welfare of individuals in all world regions and, more importantly, income groups (Heshmati, 2003, p.2). Although globalization and income distribution feature prominently in the body of recent research studies, the focus seems to be on how globalization affects income inequality in the United States or Western Europe.[10] Nevertheless, some studies are concerned with how globalization affects world or international income distribution through the difference between countries and the rates of average income per capita (Milanoviç, 2003a, p.2).[11]

In light of neo-classical international trade theory (the Heckscher–Ohlin model and one of the theorems associated with Heckscher–Ohlin trade theory, namely the 1941 Stolper–Samuelson theorem), openness in the business process leads to an increase in the real and nominal profit in a country with abundant factors of production and, conversely, with scarce factors. Thus, in countries where both physical and human capital is abundant, such as developed countries, trade openness or delivery has significantly improved the real and nominal income of the owners of the two so-called production factors. In essence, this economic relationship implies that this regulation has reduced the level of inequality in developing countries and has had the inverse effect in developed countries. In summary, globalization eventually led to a decrease in inequality in less developed countries and an increase in inequality in more developed countries (Wood, 1994; Bourguignon & Morrison, 1990; Calderon & Chong, 2001; Dollar & Kraay, 2004; Hanson & Harrison, 1999; Arellano & Bond, 1991; Arellano & Bover, 1995; Barro, 2000). However, most importantly, this result contradicts the widely accepted popular view of globalization and its effects and seems to contradict the concerns expressed in the ongoing discussions regarding globalization, which is the standard theory presented by Barro (2000, p.27). The general view was firmly established when it was verified that the progress of international openness will be in the interest of the majority of the relatively indigenous inhabitants.

In the literature, income inequality is evaluated in the context of the Kuznets curve. Kuznets (1955) argued that there is a inverse U-shaped relationship between income inequality and income per capita, and Kuznets's hypothesis uses income per capita as a basis for explaining income inequality. According to Kuznets, at the beginning of economic development, income at low income levels was distributed fairly. However, afterward, as income increased, income equality also began to increase. As per capita income approached the level of industrialized countries, income distribution would grow, and inequality would decrease. However, several researchers did not support the Kuznets hypothesis (Baş, 2009, p.58),[12] emphasizing that the level of economic development varies from country to country (Papanek & Kyn, 1995; Deininger & Squire, 1998). Moreover, many parameters affect income distribution, including income level per capita, inflation rate, technical progress, and foreign direct investment (FDI).

Today, globalization is expressed by the increase of trade and FDI flows. Whether international trade leads to a decrease in the economic wealth (income, assets) of the poor or less capable people has been researched extensively. According to Stolper and Samuelson (1941), societies with relatively abundant production factors benefit from free trade, while countries with scarce factors are disadvantaged because of that. This shows that engaging in foreign trade in labor-intensive industrialized countries increases the demand for labor-intensive sectors, leading to a decrease in unemployment and a decrease in income inequality (Mah, 2003, p.158–159).

Globalization has caused a significant relationship between FDI and income inequality levels in the world and has led to an increase in FDI flows between countries, which has had a major influence on distribution outcomes in various economies. Investigations made by economists such as Mundell (1957, p.321–335) indicated that FDI in developing countries has a significant effect on reducing income distribution inequality. The main reason for this is that FDI flows from developed countries to developing countries, which leads to a general increase in capital in developing countries, which in turn means an increase in marginal physical product. Because of this increase in the marginal physical product, real and nominal wages increase, and therefore inequalities in developing countries decrease.

According to Fccnstra and Hanson (1997, p.371–393), thc inflow of FDI to developing countries has created or expanded the levels of inequality in these countries. Capital is transferred from wealthy to poor (developing) countries because it enables developed countries to outsource activities to the largely unskilled labor forces in developing countries; the opposite applies when investing in developing countries. The mass transfer of capital to developing countries has created a great demand for this qualified workforce by proportionally increasing the relative wages earned by the qualified labor force (Feenstra & Hanson, 1997). Similarly, Figini and Gorg (1999) confirmed that the growing influence of FDI, which is a product of globalization, continues to expand the inequality gap in developing countries because multinational companies promote new technologies previously unknown in developing countries and outsource activities based on cheap labor. The introduction of these new technologies leads to an initial increase in wage levels by creating a demand for highly skilled workers to use these machines, and this creates inequality and market division. This study was proven in Ireland when the 1979–1995 period was analyzed, and the evidence supported the reverse U-shaped relationship between wage inequality and the inward flow of FDI. Moreover, several studies have shown the continued expansion of inequality in income distribution in middle-income developing countries through the diffusion or transfer of technology to less developed countries because of the higher absorption capacity for new technologies (Firebaugh & Beck, 1994; Stringer, 2006; Windmeijer, 2005; Mahler, Jesuit,& Roscoe, 1999; Figini & Gorg, 1999).

Furthermore, Bergh and Nilsson (2010), using the KOF Index and the Fraser Index of Economic Liberalization, surmised that reforms supporting economic liberalization tend to increase the inequality in developed countries by confirming the results of the Stolper-Samuelson theorem. In a study conducted on middle- and low-income countries, it was found that the main reason for the increase in income inequality was social globalization, which is one of the components of the KOF Index, including the number of phone calls and the number of Internet users, among other indicators (see Table 1). In addition, Birdsall (2006) identified three reasons why globalization increases inequality. First, countries and individuals with production resources in global markets are increasing their profits. Second, in global economies, negative externalities bring new costs for weak economies. Finally, in global economies, the existing rules are favored by countries and individuals with more economic power (Birdsall, 2006, p.22).

Lindert and Williamson (2001) divided the effects of globalization on inequality into five factors. First, the income difference between the countries integrated into the world economy has been reduced, and, second, pre-1914 migration and opening up to international trade in labor-intensive countries led to a decrease in inequality in the countries involved. Third, migration in countries where labor is scarce and the process of opening up international trade led to an increase in income inequality; fourth, globalization seems to decrease income inequality when its effects at international and national level are considered; and fifth, income inequality decreases if countries integrate into a union (Lindert & Williamson, 2001, p.1–2). Moreover, in their studies on the relationship between globalization and inequality, Lindert and Williamson (2001) and O'Rourke (2001) pointed out that increasing world inequality is largely due to inequality between countries rather than inequality within countries. This implies that globalization might have different consequences in the context of inequality within the country. The direction of the effect of globalization on inequality within the country depends on the institutional structure of the country that wants to adapt to the global system. In other words, the source of inequality within the country is democracy and weak government instead of globalization, which does not exist in underdeveloped countries (Heshmati, 2004, p.3).

GLOBALIZATION AND INCOME DISTRIBUTION: SOUTH KOREA

The improvement and development of countries is directly linked to their economic, social, cultural, and political progress, and more developed countries have addressed problems related to these factors. Determining the value of progress is difficult, much like the process of making progress. Nevertheless, when countries do progress, social welfare tends to improve, which is vital for these countries. In this respect, it is important to consider East Asian countries that achieved developmental momentum. These countries—South Korea, Hong Kong, Singapore and Taiwan underwent structural transformation in the 1970s by focusing on manufacturing-oriented development rather than on the basis of agriculture (Papageorgiou & Spatafora, 2012, p.4). Three main factors supported this transformation: entrepreneurship, innovation, and learning (Nelson & Pack, 1999, p.418). These countries success and rapid growth can further be ascribed to the high levels of savings, physical capital, and infrastructure investments; government being an important determinant in the market;and allowancesfor financial flows (Stiglitz, 1996, p.151).Similarly, the shift in the labor force from low-yielding sectors to high-yielding sectors led to growth. The Four Asian Tigers countries (Hong Kong, Singapore, South Korea, and Taiwan) seem to have undergone this shift during the 1990s (McMillan, 2014, p.18–20). The subsequent increase in human capital after this success allowed these nations to capture a large share of emerging products and to use new technologies (Nelson & Pack, 1999, p.418–419).

South Korea is one of the many Asian countries that have successfully exported products, providing economic growth and significantly increasing the living standard of the population. The developmental success of the Asian Tiger countries, particularly South Korea, where the advantages of being actively involved in the globalizing economy can be seen, is remarkable. South Korea is one of the few countries that have transformed from an agricultural economy to a leading global industrial power, and it did so within a period of 40 years (OECD, 2014, p.32; Chung, 2010; Chen & Suh, 2007, p.4). The Korean economy has a multifaceted industrial structure that has shifted from light industrialization to heavy and high technology industry. The most significant factor underlying South Korea's success is the importance given to the real economy. The main reason for its success is that different sectors were supported in each period because the country realized the importance of shaping production to prevailing conditions (Aricioğlu, 2012, p.51). Following the welfare period in South Korea after the second half of the 20th century, institutional innovation increased the efficiency and legitimacy of the markets too much. The country drew its strength from the financial advances allowed by market forces and integrated through foreign capital[13].

Income distribution in the South Korean economy and the course of globalization are illustrated in Figure 1 and Figure 2.

When the index was analyzed, it was observed that South Korea's globalization index had increased over time. As shown in the diagram, the index value is above 60 after 2000, and the index reached its highest value in 2007-2008 period. Then, it proceeded around the level of 60.

When the Gini index by years is examined, it appears that income distribution in South Korea is balanced. The relationship between income distribution and globalization varies within the literature, and whether the country is classified as developed or developing determines the influence level of the relationship. Generally, an increase in globalization is predicted to increase income inequality.

Figure 1. Globalization trends in South Korea (1970–2010)

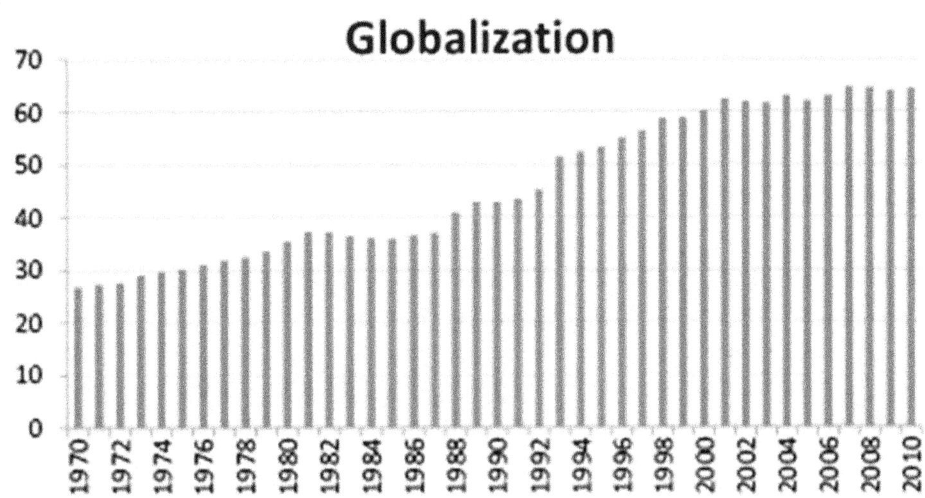

Figure 2. Income distribution in South Korea (1970–2010)

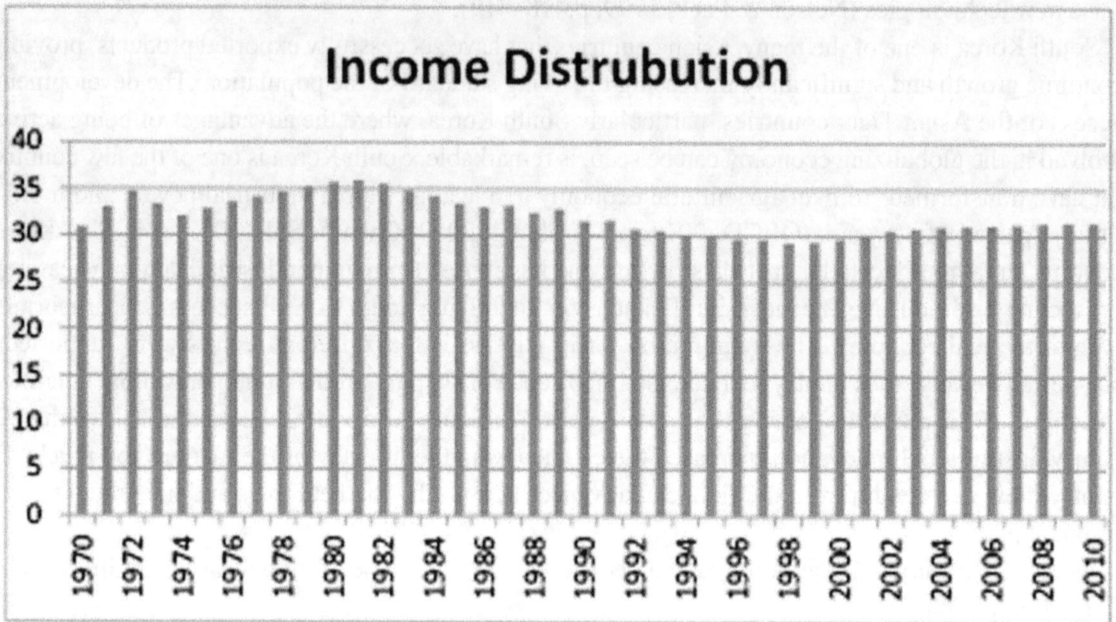

EMPIRICAL EVIDENCE

According to several studies,globalization has a positive and negative influence on income distribution. Sufficient empirical evidence exists that globalization in essence causes an increase in inequality in many countries (Beck, 2007; Dollar & Kraay, 2004; Goldberg-Koujianou & Pavcnik, 2007; International Monetary Fund, 2007a, 2007b). However, despite the wealth of studies regarding the effects of globalization on income distribution, many of them were driven by limited parameters that constitute globalization. In some studies, trade openness is considered a measure of globalization, while in others FDI is considered a measure of globalization. Barro (2000), for example, suggested that the basis for the changes in increasing income inequality is based on commercial expansion, but Paus and Robinson (1999) disagreed. When the existing body of literature is evaluated in this context, it appears that a limited number of studies comprehensively examine the effects of globalization on income inequality. Table 2 provides a summary of the literature on globalization and income inequality.

DATA AND METHODOLOGY

In this study, the impact of globalization (GLOB) on income distribution in the South Korean sample (GINI) for 1970 to 2010 was examined within the context of the Kuznets Curve. The sample period was selected because the GINI series ended in 2010. The model used in the study was formed by following Shahbaz (2015)[14]. In this context, economic growth (PGDB) and inflation (CPI) variables were included as control variables in the model. Per capita national income was used for economic growth, and consumer price index was used for inflation. The main model used in the study is as follows:

Table 2. Studies on the relationship between globalization and income distribution

Authors	Sample	Period	Parameter/s Used for Globalization	Method	Findings
Borjas & Ramey (1994)	USA	1963–1988	Trade openness (as percentage of GDP)	Engle–Granger Cointegration	A positive relationship exists between globalization and income inequality.
Wei & Wu (2001)	China	1988–1993	Trade openness	Ordinary Least Squares (OLS)	Globalization has reduced urban–rural income inequality.
Mah (2003)	Korea	1975–1995	Openness rate and FDI	OLS	Globalization in Korea does not affect income distribution, and the study provides weak evidence supporting the Kuznets hypothesis.
Lee (2006a)	14 European countries	1951–1992	Openness rate and FDI	Panel Data Analysis	Globalization first increased income inequality and then reduced it; i.e., a inverse U-shaped relationship was detected.
Lee (2006b)	China,India, Indonesia, Japan, Korea, Malaysia, Singapore,Thailand	1970–2002	Openness rate and FDI	Panel Data Analysis	Globalization first increased income inequality and then reduced it; i.e., a inverse U-shaped relationship was detected.
Dreher & Gaston (2008)	100 countries	1970–2000	KOF Globalization Index	Generalized Methods of Moments (GMM)	In the sub-sample of OECD countries, globalization had a positive and significant effect on income inequality.
Adams (2008)	62 developing countries	1985–2001	FDI, openness rate, and intellectual property rights	Panel Cointegration	Globalization clarifies 15% of the variance in income inequality; a positive relationship exists between intellectual property and openness and income inequality; and a negative relationship was detected between FDI and income inequality. As a result, globalization is not completely responsible for income inequality.
Bergh & Nilsson (2011)	79 developed and developing countries	1970–2005	KOF Globalization Index	GMM	Social globalization causes high income inequality and has a stronger influence in low- and middle-income countries.
Atif (2012)	68 developing countries	1990–2010	KOF Globalization Index	OLS	Growing globalization in developing countries has increased income inequality.
Jalil (2012)	China	1952–2009	Openness and square of outward openness, KOF Globalization Index	ARDL	Globalization first increased income inequality and then reduced it. In other words, a inverse "U"-shaped relationship was detected.
Castilho (2012)	Brazil	1987–2005	Openness (commercial liberalization)	OLS	Trade liberalization increased poverty and inequality in urban areas.
Mah (2013)	China	1985–2007	Openness rate and FDI	OLS	Globalization leads to high income inequality.
Ogunyomi (2013)	Nigeria	1986–2010	Openness rate	OLS	Economic globalization causes income inequality.
Asteriou(2014)	27 EU countries	1995–2009	Trade openness	GMM	Financial globalization increases income inequality.
Gozgor & Ranjan (2017)	140 countries	1970–2012	KOF Globalization Index	GMM	Income inequality increases with globalization.
Shahbaz (2015)	Iran	1970–2010	KOF Globalization Index	ARDL	Globalization first reduced income inequality and then increased it.
Inmee & Shi (2016)	26 developed and 52 developing countries	1990–2010	Openness	OLS	Globalization increases income inequality in developed countries and reduces it in developing countries.

$$GINI_t = \alpha_0 + \alpha_1 GLOB_t + \alpha_2 GLOB2_t + \alpha_3 PGDP_t + \alpha_4 CPI + \varepsilon_t \tag{1}$$

The GINI series, GLOB, GLOB2, PGDB, CPI, and ε_t refer to income distribution, globalization, the square of globalization, growth, inflation, and the error term, respectively. The GINI series, GLOB series, PGDB (2005 constant) series, and CPI (consumer price index) were obtained from the Standardized World Income Inequality Database, the KOF Index database, and the World Bank World Development Indicator (WDI) database, respectively. All the series were included after logarithmic transformation of the model was performed. If $\alpha_1 > 0$ and $\alpha_2 < 0$ were included in the equation, the conclusion would be reached that there is an inverse-U relationship between globalization and income inequality. If $\alpha_1 < 0$ and $\alpha_2 > 0$ occurred, the conclusion would be reached that that there is a U-shaped relationship between globalization and income inequality (Shahbaz, 2015, p.365).

The long-term relationship between the series was explored with the Maki (2012) cointegration analysis with multiple structural changes. There are four main models in Maki Cointegration Test. These are;

1. **Model 0:** There is a break in the fixed term—the trendless model.

$$y_t = \mu + \sum_{i=1}^{k} \mu_i K_{it} + \beta x_t + \upsilon_t \tag{2}$$

2. **Model 1:** There is a breakin the fixed term and the slope—the trendless model.

$$y_t = \mu + \sum_{i=1}^{k} \mu_i K_{it} + \beta x_t + \sum_{i=1}^{k} \beta_i x_i K_{it} + \upsilon_t \tag{3}$$

3. **Model 2:** There is a breakin the fixed term and the slope—the trendy model.

$$y_t = \mu + \sum_{i=1}^{k} \mu_i K_{it} + \gamma x_t + \beta x_t + \sum_{i=1}^{k} \beta_i x_i K_{it} + \upsilon_t \tag{4}$$

4. **Model 3:** There is a breakin the fixed term, the slope, and the trend.

$$y_t = \mu + \sum_{i=1}^{k} \mu_i K_{it} + \gamma t + \sum_{i=1}^{k} \gamma_i t K_{it} + \beta x_t + \sum_{i=1}^{k} \beta_i K_{it} + \upsilon_t \tag{5}$$

$K_{i,t}$ in the equation refers to the dummy variable. If the test statistics are greater than the critical value, they are $K_{i,t}$=1;otherwise, they are $K_{i,t}$=0. In the equation, γ refers to constant β refers to the time trend, and υ_t refers to the error term.

The hypotheses of Maki's (2012) multiple structural break cointegration test are;

- **H_0:** There is no cointegration between the series.

- **H_1:** There is a cointegration between the series.

In the presence of cointegrations, long-term coefficients of the series were demonstrated with the Stock and Watson (1993) dynamic least squares method (DOLS). The fracture dates obtained in the cointegration test were included in the model as a dummy variable. The short-term relationship between the series was examined based on DOLS. A delay of the error terms obtained from the long-term analyses was used in the error correction model. The related model is;

$$\Delta GINI_t = \alpha_0 + \alpha_1 \Delta GLOB_t + \alpha_2 \Delta GLOB2_t + \alpha_3 \Delta PGDP_t + \alpha_4 \Delta CPI + \alpha_5 ECT_{t-1} + \varepsilon_t \quad (6)$$

The explanatory variables within the equation are the same as in Equation 1, except ECT, which refers to the error correction term, and Δ, which refers to the difference processor. If the error correction term is negative and statistically meaningful, it indicates the presence of a mechanism that will balance the series in the event of a deviation among the series. The causality relationship between the series was examined based on the Granger causality/block exogeneity Wald test.

The realization of all the tests mentioned above depended on the results of the unit root test. The series should contain the unit root at the level and should be stable; in other words, I(1) as a result of difference operation. Accordingly, first the Augumented Dickey–Fuller (ADF) root test was implemented.

Results of the Unit Root Test

Before moving to the cointegration test between the series, it is necessary to determine what level of stationary the series are. The results obtained from the ADF unit root test are reported in Table 3.

According to the results of ADF, the level values of the series have unit roots and become stable because of the difference operation. Accordingly, it was concluded that the precondition of the Maki (2012) test was fulfilled. Thus, it was decided to move on to the cointegration test.

Cointegration Test

The Maki (2012) cointegration analysis is used to determine the relationship between the series in the presence of structural breaks. Some of the many tests used under these conditions include the Gregory and Hansen (1996), Carrion-i-Silvestre and Sanso (2006), and Westerlund and Edgerton (2006) tests. While the tests can be used for analysis in the presence of a single break, Maki's (2012) test can detect cointegration in the presence of up to five breaks. In this respect, the cointegration relationship of the series was investigated according to the four different models mentioned above and reported in Table 4.

The cointegration analysis revealed the existence of cointegration for all models. Accordingly, it was concluded that the GINI, GLOB, GLOB2, PGDP, and CPI series are cointegrated in the long term. In this direction, it was decided to switch to the DOLS analysis to determine the coefficient signs and values of the series.

Table 3. Results of the unit root test

Variables	ADF Test Statistics	Significance Level		
		1%	5%	10%
GINI	-0.95 [2]	-4.21	-3.53	-3.19
ΔGINI	-5.46*** [1]	-4.21	-3.53	-3.19
GLOB	-0.78 [0]	-4.21	-3.53	-3.19
ΔGLOB	-4.93*** [0]	-4.21	-3.53	-3.19
GLOB2	-0.93 [0]	-4.21	-3.53	-3.19
ΔGLOB2	-4.94*** [0]	-4.21	-3.53	-3.19
PGDP	-0.425 [0]	-4.21	-3.53	-3.19
ΔPGDP	-5.96*** [0]	-4.21	-3.53	-3.19
CPI	-1.95 [1]	-4.21	-3.53	-3.19
ΔCPI	-3.97** [1]	-4.21	-3.53	-3.19

Note: The fixed and trendy model was preferred in unit root detection. The values in square brackets in the ADF test indicate the stability of the variables at the levels of significance of 1% and 5%, respectively, with *** and ** the optimal delay length determined according to Schwarz Information Criteria (SIC).

Table 4. Results of Maki cointegration

Models	Statistical Value	Critical Vales			Dates of Structural Breaks[15]
		1%	5%	10%	
Model 0	-6.288**	-6.640	-6.132	-5.892	1976, 1983, 1989, 2001
Model 1	-6.820**	-7.053	-6.494	-6.220	1976, 1983, 1989, 1994, 2000
Model 2	-17.192***	-9.441	-8.869	-8.541	1974, 1979, 1984, 1997, 2003
Model 3	-10.113***	-9.433	-8.871	-8.574	1978, 1985, 1996, 2003

Note: The critical values are the critical values from the Maki (2012) Table 1. ** and *** indicate that there is a cointegration at the significance levels of 5% and 1%, respectively.

Long-Term Analysis

In the DOLS analysis, it was decided that the Maki (2012) cointegration test should be performed from the break (stable break) in Model 0. Within this context, the break dates that were detected in the corresponding model were included in the DOLS model as DU76, DU83, DU89, and DU01 dummy variables. The findings obtained from the analysis are reported in Table 5.

As a result of the DOLS analysis, all the independent variables were found to be statistically significant. The coefficient of the globalization (GLOB) series was observed to be negative, and the coefficient of the square of the globalization was observed to be positive. This shows that globalization first reduces and then increases income inequality. Thus, the findings indicate that there is a U-shaped relationship between globalization and income inequality. Moreover, it has been identified that as economic growth (PGDP) increases, income inequality decreases, and income inequality increases with an increase in inflation.

Table 5. DOLS long-term analysis

Variable	Coefficient	t-Statistics	Probability
GLOB	-4.074	-2.261	0.037**
GLOB2	1.132	2.177	0.043**
PGDP	-0.135	-2.418	0.027**
CPI	0.226	4.175	0.000***
C	5.277	3.569	0.002***
DU76	0.018	2.226	0.039**
DU83	-0.012	-1.929	0.070**
DU89	0.009	1.216	0.240
DU01	0.009	1.373	0.187

Note: The researcher aimed to solve the changed variance and autocorrelation problems within the predicted model using the Newy-West method. The R2 value of the related model was identified as 0.97, and the Jarque-Bera probability rate was identified as 0.84. *** and ** indicate 1% and 5% significance, respectively.

Short-Term Analysis (Error Correction Model)

After the long-term analysis, the short-term analysis was undertaken. This analysis was conducted to determine whether a mechanism exists to remove a deviation that appears in the series. In addition, in cases where the mechanism is working, it allows the calculation of the number of periods after which the series returns to balance. The short-term analysis was performed by including a delayed-value model of the difference between independent variables and the errors obtained in the long-term analysis. The findings are reported in Table 6.

In the error correction model, the coefficient sign of the error correction term was observed to be negative and statistically significant. That the error term is greater than one is an indication of the future of the series fluctuating in balance (Narayan & Smyth, 2006, p.339). Accordingly, it has been concluded that a mechanism exists to eliminate a deviation that emerges between the series.

Table 6. DOLS short-term analysis

Variable	Coefficient	t-Statistics	Probability
ΔGLOB	-2.184778	-0.936556	0.3649
ΔGLOB2	0.594972	0.866531	0.4008
ΔPGDP	-0.169581	-1.136451	0.2748
ΔCPI	0.217723	3.239533	0.0059***
ECTt-1	-1.465056	-2.218126	0.0436**
C	0.000513	0.116213	0.9091

Note: The researcher aimed to solve the changed variance and autocorrelation problems within the predicted model using the Newy-West method.The R^2 value of the related model was identified as 0.88, and the Jarque-Bera probability rate was identified as 0.87. ** and *** indicate 5% and 1% significance levels, respectively.

Causality Analysis Based on the Error Correction Model

Based on error correction, analysis of the causality relationship between the series was performed using the Granger causality/block exogeneity Wald test. The findings are reported in Table 7.

As a result of these investigations, it has been concluded that independent variables cause income inequality as a whole. The results include that there is "one-sided causality" from inflation (CPI) to income inequality. In general, the econometric findings support the studies of Shahbaz et al. (2015), Jalil (2012), and Deininger and Squire (1998), and several lessons should be learned from them, particularly in terms of developing countries.

CONCLUSION

Globalization has numerous economic effects, with its effect on income inequality being among the most important. In this study, the effect of globalization on income inequality between 1970 and 2010 was empirically tested in the South Korean sample in the context of Kuznets Curve. In empirical part of the study, the Maki cointegration (2012) approach, which considers multiple structural breaks was employed. The cointegration results reveal that the series are cointegrated in the long run. The long-term analysis indicated that globalization first reduces income inequality and then increases it. In other words, there is a U-shaped relationship between globalization and income inequality. In the short-term analysis, it was found that the error correction term was negative and statistically significant.

During the observation period, South Korea was both a developing and developed country. When evaluated in this context, globalization first led to a decline in income inequality. In this period, policy makers managed the globalization process well. However, after a certain point, the negative impact of globalization on income inequality shows that policy makers failed to ameliorate the negative effects of globalization. Finally, globalization continues to be a force in the current business environment and thus continues to affect the lives of individuals in every country in the world. This is largely due to the

Table 7. Causality analysis based on error correction

Dependent Variable	ΔGINI	ΔGLOB	ΔGLOB2	ΔPGDP	ΔCPI	As a Whole (Overall)
ΔGINI	-	2.459 [0.294]	2.483 [0.288]	2.789 [0.247]	13.556*** [0.001]	14.352* [0.073]
ΔGLOB	3.073 [0.215]	-	1.272 [0.529]	13.985*** [0.000]	5.245* [0.072]	18.820** [0.015]
ΔGLOB2	2.593 [0.273]	1.248 [0.535]	-	12.807*** [0.001]	4.769* [0.092]	17.355** [0.026]
ΔPGDP	0.998 [0.607]	1.421 [0.491]	1.492 [0.474]	-	6.536** [0.038]	8.456 [0.390]
ΔCPI	1.920 [0.382]	9.590*** [0.008]	10.361*** [0.005]	0.319 [0.852]	-	20.126*** [0.009]

Note: Chi2 was stated with its values. The values in square brackets express the probability values. *,**,and *** expresses the 10%, 5%, and 1% relevance levels, respectively.

prevalence of multinational companies in the global economy because of their huge power on capital, which drives globalization worldwide.

Most importantly, globalization has not fully solved the problem of income inequality, as it reduces differences in income in developing countries and increases income inequality in developed countries. In this respect, it is essential for policy makers to develop policies that minimize the impact of globalization on income inequality. Otherwise, social and economic distortions will increase with the increase in globalization, which will cause additional socioeconomic problems.

REFERENCES

Adams, S. (2008). Globalization and income inequality: Implications for intellectual property rights. *Journal of Policy Modeling*, *30*(5), 725–735. doi:10.1016/j.jpolmod.2007.10.005

Aktan, Ç. C., & Vural, İ. Y. (2002). Gelir Dağılımında adalet(siz)lik ve gelir eşit(siz)liği: terminoloji, temel kavramlar ve ölçüm yöntemleri. In C. C. Aktan (Ed.), *Yoksullukla Mücadele Stratejileri*. Ankara: Hak-İş Konfederasyonu Yayınları.

Arbache, J. S., Dickerson, A., & Green, F. (2004). Trade liberalisation and wages in developing countries. *Economic Journal (London)*, *114*(February), F73–F96. doi:10.1111/j.0013-0133.2004.00188.x

Arellano, M., & Bond, S. (1991). Some tests of specification for panel data: Monte Carlo evidence and an application to employment equations. *The Review of Economic Studies*, *58*(2), 277–297. doi:10.2307/2297968

Arellano, M., & Bover, O. (1995). Another look at the instrumental variable estimation of error components models. *Journal of Econometrics*, *68*(2), 9–51.

Arıcıoğlu, E. (2012). Kalkınma kavramına küreselleşme prespektifinden bir bakış. *Niğde Üniversitesi İİBF Dergisi*, *5*(1), 36–53.

Asteriou, D., Dimelis, S., & Moudatsou, A. (2014). Globalization and income inequality: A panel data econometric approach for the EU27 countries. *Economic Modelling*, *36*, 592–599. doi:10.1016/j.econmod.2013.09.051

Atif, S.M., Srivastav, M., Sauytbekova M., & Arachchige U. K. (2012). Globalization and income inequality: A panel data analysis of 68 countries. *MPRA Paper No:42385*.

Barro, R. J. (2000). Inequality and growth in a panel of countries. *Journal of Economic Growth*, *5*(1), 5–32. doi:10.1023/A:1009850119329

Baş, K. (2009). Küreselleşme ve gelir dağılımı eşitsizliği. *Çanakkale Üniversitesi. Sosyal Bilimler Enstitüsü Dergisi*, *18*(1), 49–70.

Beck, T., Demirgüc-Kunt, A., & Levine, R. (2007). Finance, inequality, and the poor. *Journal of Economic Growth*, *12*(1), 27–49. doi:10.100710887-007-9010-6

Bergh, A., & Nilsson, T. (2010). Do liberalization and globalization increase income inequality? *European Journal of Political Economy*, *26*(4), 488–505. doi:10.1016/j.ejpoleco.2010.03.002

Birdsall, N. (2006). The world is not flat: Inequality and injustice in our global economy. *UNU World Institute for Development Economic Research (UNU -WIDER) WIDER Annual Lecture 9.*

Borjas, G. J., & Ramey, V. A. (1994). Time-series evidence on the sources of trends in wage inequality. *The American Economic Review*, *84*, 10–16.

Bourguignon, F., & Morrisson, C. (1990). Income distribution, development and foreign trade. *European Economic Review*, *34*(6), 1113–1132. doi:10.1016/0014-2921(90)90071-6

Burkhauser, R. V., Crews, A. D., & Daly, M. C. (1997). Recounting winners and losers in the 1980s: A critique of income distribution measurement methodology. *Economics Letters*, *54*(1), 35–40. doi:10.1016/S0165-1765(96)00945-7

Calderon, C., & Chong, A. (2001). External sector and income inequality in interdependent economies using a dynamic panel data approach. *Economics Letters*, *71*(2), 225–231. doi:10.1016/S0165-1765(01)00374-3

Can, M. & Doğan, B. (2016). Küreselleşme ve enerji tüketimi ilişkisi: Türkiye örnekleminde eşbütünleşme analizi. *Maliye Dergisi, 170.*

Can, M., & Dogan, B. (2017). The effects of economic structural transformation on employment: An evaluation in the context of economic complexity and product space theory. In F. Yenilmez & E. Kilic (Eds.), *Handbook of research on unemployment and labor market sustainability in the era of globalization* (pp. 275–306). Hershey, PA: IGI Global Publishing. doi:10.4018/978-1-5225-2008-5.ch016

Carrion-I-Silvestre, J. L., & Sanso, A. (2006). Testing the null of cointegration with structural breaks. *Oxford Bulletin of Economics and Statistics*, *68*(5), 623–646. doi:10.1111/j.1468-0084.2006.00180.x

Castilho, M., Menendez, M., & Sztulman, A. (2012). Trade liberalization, inequality, and poverty in Brazilian states. *World Development*, *40*(4), 821–835. doi:10.1016/j.worlddev.2011.09.018

Chang, C., Lee, C., & Hsieh, M. (2011). Globalization, real output and multiple structural breaks. *Global Economic Review*, *40*(4), 421–444. doi:10.1080/1226508X.2011.626154

Chen, D. H. C., & Suh, J. (2007). Introduction. In J. Suh & D. H. C. Chen (Eds.), *Korea as a knowledge economy: Evolutionary process and lessons learned. WBI Development Studies*. Washington, DC: World Bank.

Chung, S. (2010). Innovation, competitiveness and growth: Korean experiences. In J. Y. Lin & B. Pleskovic (Eds.), *Lessons from east asia and the global financial crisis* (pp. 333-358). Annual Word Bank Conference on Development Economics.

Cornia, G. (1999). *Liberalisation, globalization and income distribution, UNU world institute for development economics research*. Helsinki, Finland: UNU/WIDER.

Dabour, N. (2000). The role of foreign direct investment (FDI) in development and growth in OIC member countries. *Journal of Economic Cooperation*, *21*(3), 27–55.

Deininger, K., & Squire, L. (1998). New ways of looking at old ideas: Inequality and growth. *Journal of Development Economics*, *57*(2), 259–287. doi:10.1016/S0304-3878(98)00099-6

Dluhosch, B. (1998). Globalization and European labor markets. *CEPR Discussion Paper No. 1992.*

Doğan, B. & Can, M. (2016). Küreselleşmenin büyümeye etkisi: Güney Kore örnekleminde eşbütünleşme analizi. *Çankırı Karatekin Üniversitesi İktisadi ve İdari Bilimler Fakültesi Dergisi*, *6*(2), 197-220.

Dollar, D., & Kraay, A. (2004). Trade, growth and poverty. *Economic Journal (London)*, *114*(493), F22–F49. doi:10.1111/j.0013-0133.2004.00186.x

Dreher, A. (2006). Does globalization affect growth? Evidence from a new index of globalization. *Applied Economics*, *38*(10), 1091–1110. doi:10.1080/00036840500392078

Dreher, A., & Gaston, N. (2008). Has globalization increased inequality? *Review of International Economics*, *16*(3), 516–536. doi:10.1111/j.1467-9396.2008.00743.x

Dreher, A., Gaston, N., & Martens, P. (2008). *Measuring globalization-gauging its consequences*. New York: Springer.

Eroğlu, Ö., & Albeni, M. (2002). *Küreselleşme, ekonomik krizler ve Türkiye*. Isparta: Bilim Kitabevi.

Feenstra, R., & Hanson, G. (1997). Foreign direct investment and relative wages: Evidence from Mexico's maquiladoras. *Journal of International Economics*, *42*(3-4), 371–393. doi:10.1016/S0022-1996(96)01475-4

Fields, G. S. (1989). Changes in poverty and inequality in developing countries. *The World Bank Research Observer*, *4*(2), 167–185. doi:10.1093/wbro/4.2.167

Figini, P., & Gorg, H. (1999). Multinational companies and wage inequality in the hostcountry: The case of Ireland. *Weltwirtschaftliches Archive. Review of World Economics*, *135*(4), 135–145.

Firebaugh, G., & Beck, F. (1994). Does economic growth benefit the masses? Growth, dependence, and welfare in the third world. *American Sociological Review*, *59*(5), 631–653. doi:10.2307/2096441

Goldberg-Koujianou, P., & Pavcnik, N. (2007). Distributional effects of globalization in developing countries. *Journal of Economic Literature*, *45*(1), 39–82. doi:10.1257/jel.45.1.39

Gozgor, G., & Ranjan, P. (2017). Globalization, inequality, and redistribution: Theory and evidence. *World Economy*, *40*(12), 2704–2751. doi:10.1111/twec.12518

Gregory, A. W., & Hansen, B. E. (1996). Residual-based tests for cointegration in models with regime shifts. *Journal of Econometrics*, *70*(1), 99–126. doi:10.1016/0304-4076(69)41685-7

Hanson, G., & Harrinson, A. (1999). Trade and wage inequality in Mexico. *Industrial & Labor Relations Review*, *52*(2), 271–288. doi:10.1177/001979399905200207

Haughton, J., & Khandker, R. S. (2009). *The handbook on poverty and inequality*. Washington, DC: The International Bank for Reconstruction and Development, The World Bank.

Held, D., & Mc Grew, A. (2008). *Küresel dönüşümler büyük küreselleşme tartışması*. Ankara: Phoenix Yayınevi.

Heshmati, A. (2003). *The relationship between income inequality and globalization*. Retrieved from http://www.soc.iastate.edu/sapp/globalizationoutcomes4.pdf

Heshmati, A. (2004). *The relationship between income inequality, poverty and globalisation.* IZA Discussion Paper No. 1277.

Inmee, B., & Shi, Q. (2016). Impact of economic globalization on income inequality: Devoloped economies and emerging economies. *Global Economy Journal, 16*(1), 49–61.

International Monetary Fund (IMF). (2007a). World economic outlook: Globalization and inequality. Washington, DC: IMF.

International Monetary Fund (IMF). (2007b). *Reaping the benefits of financial globalization.* Retrieved from www.imf.org/extrenal/np/res/docs/2007/0607.htm

Intriligator, M. (2004). Globalization of the world economy: Potential benefits and costs and a net assessment. *Journal of Policy Modeling, 26*(4), 485–498. doi:10.1016/j.jpolmod.2004.04.004

Işığıçok, E. (1998). Türkiye'de gelir dağılımı ve 1987-1994 gelir dağılımı araştırmalarının karşılaştırmalı bir analizi. *Uludağ Üniversitesi İ.İ.B.F. Dergisi, 16*(1), 1.

Jalil, A. (2012). Modeling income inequality and openness in the framework of Kuznets curve: New evidence from China. *Economic Modelling, 29*(2), 309–315. doi:10.1016/j.econmod.2011.10.012

Karluk, S. R. (1996). *Türkiye ekonomisi tarihsel gelişim yapısı ve sosyal değişim.* İstanbul: Beta Basım Yayım Dağıtım A.Ş.

Keohane, R. O., & Nye, J. S. (2000). Introduction. In J. S. Nye & J. D. Donahue (Eds.), Governance in a globalizing world (pp. 1-44). Brookings Institution Press.

Kuznets, S. (1955). Economic growth and income inequality. *The American Economic Review, 45*(1), 17–26.

Lee, C., & Chang, C. (2009). FDI, financial development, and economic growth: International evidence. *Journal of Applied Econometrics, 12*, 249–271.

Lee, J. (2006a). Inequality and globalization in Europe. *Journal of Policy Modeling, 28*(7), 791–796. doi:10.1016/j.jpolmod.2006.04.013

Lee, J. (2006b). Does globalization matter to income distribution in Asia? *Applied Economics Letters, 13*(13), 851–855. doi:10.1080/13504850500425352

Lindert, P. H., & Williamson, J. G. (2001). *Does globalization make the world more unequal?* NBER Working Paper 2001:8228.

Mah, J. S. (2002). The impact of globalization on income distribution: The Korean experience. *Applied Economics Letters, 9*(15), 1007–1009. doi:10.1080/13504850210149124

Mah, J. S. (2003). A note on globalization and income distribution—the case of Korea, 1975-1995. *Journal of Asian Economics, 14*(1), 157–164. doi:10.1016/S1049-0078(02)00244-0

Mah, J. S. (2013). Globalization, decentralization and income inequality: The case of China. *Economic Modelling, 31*, 653–658. doi:10.1016/j.econmod.2012.09.054

Mahler, A., Jesuit, K., & Roscoe, D. (1999). Exploring the impact of trade and investment on income inequality. *Comparative Political Studies*, *32*(3), 363–395. doi:10.1177/0010414099032003004

Maki, D. (2012). Tests for cointegration allowing for an unknown number of breaks. *Economic Modelling*, *29*(5), 2011–2015. doi:10.1016/j.econmod.2012.04.022

Marber, P. (2004). Globalization and its contents. *World Policy Journal*, *21*(4), 29–37. doi:10.1215/07402775-2005-1010

Martin, X. S. (2002). *The world distribution of income (Estimated from individual country distributions).* National Bureau of Economic Research. Retrieved from http://www.nber.org/papers/w8933

McMillan, M., Rodrik, D., & Verduzco-Gallo, I. (2014). Globalization, structural change, and productivity growth, with an update on Africa. *World Development*, *63*, 11–32. doi:10.1016/j.worlddev.2013.10.012

Milanovic, B. (1999). World Income Distribution in 1988 and 1993. The World Bank.

Milanovic, B. (2002). True world income distribution 1988 and 1993: First calculations based on household surveys alone. *Economic Journal (London)*, *112*(476), 51–92. doi:10.1111/1468-0297.0j673

Milanovic, B. (2003a). *Can we discern the effect of globalization on income distribution? Evidence from household budget surveys. International Trade 0303004*. Econwpa.

Milanovic, B. (2003b). The two faces of globalization: Against globalization as we know it. *World Development*, *31*(4), 667–683. doi:10.1016/S0305-750X(03)00002-0

Milanovic, B., & Yitzhaki, S. (2002). Decomposing world income distribution: Does the world have a middle class? *Review of Income and Wealth*, *48*(2), 155–178. doi:10.1111/1475-4991.00046

Mundell, R. (1957). International trade and factor mobility. *The American Economic Review*, *47*(3), 321–335.

Narayan, P. K., & Smyth, R. (2006). What determines migration flows from low-income to high-income countries? An empirical investigation of fiji-u.s migration 1972-2001. *Contemporary Economic Policy*, *24*(2), 332–342. doi:10.1093/cep/byj019

Nelson, R. R., & Pack, H. (1999). The asian miracle and modern growth theory. *Economic Journal (London)*, *109*(457), 416–436. doi:10.1111/1468-0297.00455

Nissanke, M., & Thorbecke, E. (2006). Channels and policy debate in the globalization–inequality–poverty nexus. *World Development*, *34*(8), 1338–1360. doi:10.1016/j.worlddev.2005.10.008

Norris, P. (2000). Global governance and cosmopolitan citizens. In J. S. Nye & J. D. Donahue (Eds.), Governance in a globalizing world (pp. 1-44). Brookings Institution Press.

O'Rourke, K. H. (2001). *Globalization and inequality: Historical trends.* NBER Working Paper 8339. Cambridge, MA: NBER.

OECD. (2005). *OECD handbook on economic globalization indicators*. Retrieved from http://www.realinstitutoelcano.org/materiales/docs/OCDE_handbook.pdf

OECD. (2014). *Industry and technology policies in Korea*. OECD Publishing.

Ogunyomi, O. O., Daisi, O. R., & Oluwashikemi, R. A. (2013). Economic globalization, income inequality and economic growth in Nigeria: A static data analysis (1986-2010). *ABC Journal of Advanced Research, 2*(2), 55–68.

Papageorgiou, C., & Spatafora, N. (2012). *Economic diversification in lic's: Stylized facts and macroeconomic implication.* IMF Staff Discussion Notes 12/13.

Papanek, G., & Kyn, O. (1995). The effect on income distribution of development. *Journal of Development Economics, 23*(1), 55–65. doi:10.1016/0304-3878(86)90079-9

Paus, E., & Robinson, M. D. (1999). Real wage performance under greater trade openness: Lessons from Latin America and Asia. *Journal of Developing Areas, 33*(2), 269–288.

Person, T., & Guido, T. (1994). Is inequality harmful for growth? *The American Economic Review, 84*(3), 600–621.

Potrafke, N. (2014). The evidence on globalization. *World Economy, 38*(3), 509–552. doi:10.1111/twec.12174

Rao, B. B., Tamazian, A., & Vadlamannati, K. C. (2011). Growth effects of a comprehensive measure of globalization with country-specific time series data. *Applied Economics, 43*(5), 551–568. doi:10.1080/00036840802534476

Rao, B. B., & Vadlamannati, K. C. (2011). Globalization and growth in the low income african countries with the extreme bound analysis. *Economic Modelling, 28*(3), 795–805. doi:10.1016/j.econmod.2010.10.009

Ravallion, M. (2003). *The debate on globalization, poverty and inequality: Why measurement matters.* The World Bank, Policy Research Working Paper 3038.

Sala-i-Martin Xavier. (2002). *The disturbing rise of world income inequality.* NBER Working Paper No. 8904.

Samimi, P., Lim, G. C., & Buang, A. A. (2012). A critical review on synthetic globalization indexes. *International Journal of Fundamental Psychology and Social Sciences, 2*(1), 28–31.

Schott, P. K. (1999). *One size fits all? Specialization, trade and income inequality.* Retrieved from http://faculty.som.yale.edu/peterschott/files/research/papers/schott_cones_103199.pdf

Shahbaz, M., Loganathan, N., Tiwari, A. K., & Sherafatian-Jahromi, R. (2015). Financial development and income inequality: Is there any financial Kuznets curve in Iran? *Social Indicators Research, 124*(2), 357–382. doi:10.100711205-014-0801-9

Sharpe, A., & Zyblock, M. (1997). Macroeconomic performance and income distribution in Canada. *The North American Journal of Economics and Finance, 8*(2), 167–199. doi:10.1016/S1062-9408(97)90006-1

Shen, C. H., Lee, C., & Lee, C. (2010). What makes international capital flows promote economic growth? An international cross-country analysis. *Scottish Journal of Political Economy, 57*(5), 515–546. doi:10.1111/j.1467-9485.2010.00529.x

Sklair, L. (1999). Competing conceptions of globalization. *Journal of World-systems Research, 5*(2), 143–163. doi:10.5195/JWSR.1999.140

Slaughter, M. J., & Swagel, P. (1997). *The effect of globalization on wages in the advanced economies.* International Monetary Fund Staff Studies for the World Economic Outlook.

Stiglitz, J. E. (1996). Some lessons from the East Asian miracle. *The World Bank Observer, 11*(2), 151–177. doi:10.1093/wbro/11.2.151

Stolper, W., & Samuelson, P. (1941). Protection and real wages. *The Review of Economic Studies, 9*(1), 58–73. doi:10.2307/2967638

Stringer, J. (2006). *Unpublished results. Foreign direct investment and income inequality in developing countries: An exploration of the causal relationship using industry level FDI data.* Document prepared for the 2006 annual Midwest Political Science Association conference.

Taylor, A. M. (2002). *Globalization, trade and development: Some lessons from history.* NBE Working Paper No:9326, November.

Thorbecke, E., & Charumilind, C. (2002). Economic inequality and its socioeconomic impact. *World Development, 30*(9), 1477–1495. doi:10.1016/S0305-750X(02)00052-9

United Nations (UN). (1997). *Trade and development Report. United Nations Conference on Trade and Development.*

Villaverde, J., & Maza, A. (2011). Globalization, growth and convergence. *World Economy, 34*(6), 952–971. doi:10.1111/j.1467-9701.2011.01359.x

Wade, R. H. (2001). The rising inequality of world income distribution. *Finance & Development, 38*, 37–36.

WDI. (n.d.). Retrieved from http://data.worldbank.org/data-catalog/world-development-indicators

Weede, E. (1997). Income inequality, democracy and growth reconsidered. *European Journal of Political Economy, 13*(4), 751–764. doi:10.1016/S0176-2680(97)00028-1

Wei, S. J., & Wu, Y. (2001). *Globalization and inequality: Evidence from within China.* NBER Working Paper No. 8611. Retrieved from http://www.nber.org/papers/w8611.pdf

Westerlund, J., & Edgerton, D. (2008). Simple tests for cointegration in dependent panels with structural breaks. *Oxford Bulletin of Economics and Statistics, 70*(5), 665–704. doi:10.1111/j.1468-0084.2008.00513.x

Windmeijer, F. (2005). A finite sample correction for the variance of linear efficient two-step GMM estimators. *Journal of Econometrics, 126*(1), 25–51. doi:10.1016/j.jeconom.2004.02.005

Wood, A. (1994). *North-South Trade, Employment, and Inequality: Changing Fortunes in a Skill-Driven World.* Oxford, UK: Clarendon Press.

Woods, N. (1998). Editorial introduction. Globalization: Definitions, debates and implications. *Oxford Development Studies, 26*(1), 5–13. doi:10.1080/13600819808424142

World Bank. (2006). *World Development Indicators.* Washington, DC: Author.

KEY TERMS AND DEFINITIONS

Gini Index: Gini index is a coefficient that shows the distribution of income and consumption expenses between households.

Globalization: Globalization is defined as the transfer or easy flow of goods, services and capital from one country to another.

Income Distribution: Income distribution is the share of people contributing to the total income in a given period.

Kuznets Curve: Graphs the hypothesis that as an economy develops, market forces first increase and then decrease economic inequality.

South Korea: A country in the southern part of the Korean peninsula.

ENDNOTES

1 This study titled "The Relationship between Globalization and Income Distribution: An Empirical Analysis in the Context of South Korea" was presented in 10th European Social and Behavioral Sciences Conference in Bosnia and Herzegovina (2016). This chapter is revised and expanded version of presented study.
For the basic definitions and approaches, see Sklair (1999) & Woods (1998).

2 See Intriligator (2004) for the negative effects of globalization.

3 See Wade (2001) regarding global integration in the world economy causing unfair income distribution between countries.

4 The Gini index is a coefficient that shows the distribution of income and consumption expenses between households; see Haughton & Khandker (2009).

5 For detailed information, see Dreher (2006, p.1094), Dabour (2000), Dreher (2008) and Rao (2011).

6 Suggested as the best index for measuring all dimensions of globalization; see Samimi (2012).

7 For studies conducted using the KOF index, see http://globalization.kof.ethz.ch/papers/.

8 Mah (2002), in a study on the effects of globalization on income distribution in Korea, concluded that increased liberalization and foreign direct capital flows tended to increase the Gini coefficient in the country; in other words, globalization increased income inequality in the country.

9 Arbache, Dickerson, & Green (2004, p.78) argued that the effects of economic liberalization on wage discrepancies and hence income inequalities in developing countries vary depending on the flexibility of the supply of qualified and unqualified labor in these countries.

10 See Slaughter & Swagel (1997), Dluhosch, (1998), and Schott (1999).

11 See Milanovic (1999); Milanovic & Yitzhaki (2002), and Sala-i- Martin (2002).

12 See Deininger & Squire, (1998).

13 See Can & Dogan (2017) for detailed information about South Asian economic history.

14 A financial development variable has also been used within the related model. However, because the financial flows included the parameter in the globalization variable, the corresponding variable model was not included to avoid the econometric multiple linear problem.

15 The structural break dates were automatically determined using Maki's Gaussian codes. The researcher hoped to perform the cointegration test in the presence of five structural breaks, but the Gaussian codes detected four breaks for Model 0 and Model 4. Consequently, the critical values of the mentioned values were tested according to four breaks, and the other two models were tested according to five breaks.

Chapter 3
Is Sustaniable Tourism a Leverage FOR Economic Development?
A Critical Review

Hakan Sezerel
Anadolu University, Turkey

Cihan Kaymaz
Gumushane University, Turkey

ABSTRACT

Does development mean employment and social welfare, or the natural environment, ecosystem, and biodiversity? The answer to this question is sought worldwide while trying to solve the dichotomy between ecological sustainability and the development sustainability. The authors observe a series of pursuits under the names of ecological tourism, environmentally friendly tourism, and socially responsible tourism that emerge in order to overcome this dichotomy in the tourism discipline. They all merge around the common idea of offering a framework that examines economic activities for this dilemma. Meanwhile, this chapter examines the pursuits within the scope of sustainable tourism based on the assumptions of principal ecological approaches (e.g., environment protection, shallow ecology, deep ecology, and social ecology) and determines the position of sustainable tourism within these ecological approaches. It is deduced that sustainable tourism is actually sustainable at very low levels from the perspective of ecological sustainability.

INTRODUCTION

Today the world questions the environmental social and cultural consequences caused by economic development on a global scale today. The concept of whether economic development may be sustained or not in the current situation preoccupies non-governmental organizations, nations, and ordinary citizens. The concept of sustainability, which we know today has been developed in parallel with the development of

DOI: 10.4018/978-1-5225-5787-6.ch003

environmental awareness since the 1970s, is offered as a remedy for the destructive impacts of economic development. Tourism, which is one of the largest economic activities in the world, is questioned based on this argument, and there is an endeavor in the literature to determine whether sustainable tourism is possible or not and arguments aimed for practice.

According to the World Tourism Organization (UNWTO, 2014), tourism has exhibited a striking growth for the past 60 years. While approximately 25 million people on the average travelled for tourism purposes in the world in 1950, this figure reached 278 million in the 1980s, 528 million in 1995, and finally 1 billion 87 million in 2013. The diversification of tourism activities, and the advertisements and incentives, have been particularly effective in increasing these figures. When we review the objectives of tourist trips, we observe that recreation and vacation activities constitute the highest proportion. A total of 52% of touristic trips are made for recreation, leisure, and holiday purposes; additionally, when reviewing the proportions of the remaining trips, health, religion, and touring activities for other purposes consume 27% of all trips. Other than these two main purposes, the proportion of trips for business and trade purposes equals 14%, followed by trips made for purposes that could not be determined equalling a share of 7%. Approximately 3.3 billion people were transported to some 50,000 different locations in 2014 (IATA, 2014).

Tourism activities constitute one of the largest industries in the world that generate revenues on a global scale and create employment in the tourism sector when seen from the perspective that brings economy to the forefront. This aspect is primarily identified by accommodation, wining-dining, entertainment, and similar activities carried out under the name of “mass tourism”. The most obvious example that may be given for mass tourism is the holidays in the all-inclusive concept offering standard products and services in which tourists generally spend most of their time at a certain accommodation facility. Besides mass tourism, alternative tourism emerges with a different understanding and is identified by alternative tourism activities where the tourists harmonize and interact with the natural, cultural, and social entities and life at the places they visit and adopt this as an experience that is different from mass tourism.

In the sustainability approach that has been in discussion in tourism research, establishment of touring policies and tourism practices since the 1980s is one of the most important components of sustainable tourism which seeks a balance between nature, social life, and cultural assets and economic gains. This approach also examines principles and practices that could also be applicable for future generations in ecological tourism (ecotourism).

In addition to the increase in the tourism phenomenon, tourism activities are supported by economic justifications and worldwide expansion of tourism areas is being encouraged. The economic benefits of the quantitative increase in tourism events in parallel with the expansion of tourism are under scrutiny today due to the ecological damages caused over the past 40 years, and there is an endeavor to generate “intermediate formulas” that would not impact economic development, but would not damage or at least cause minimal on nature. One of these intermediate formulas generated for tourism during the recent years is the concept of sustainable tourism that bears the characteristics of development literature.

Sustainable tourism, which has been developed by setting off from the damage caused by ecology by mass tourism, claims to use tourism instruments by taking ecological assets into account (Briassoulis, 2002). It aims to serve through different destinations in a certain region, as different from traditional (mass) tourism primarily with the demand to sustain development by maintaining the ecological balance. Therefore, it is believed the damages caused to ecology by mass tourism will be reduced, while significant economic opporrtunities are offered to newly established/created environments. In that sense, sustainable tourism contributes to the social welfare by creating a variety of employment opportunities and meeting the demands of different segments through the opening of new tourism areas.

Bianchi (2017) underlines the paradigm shift and discources on sustainable tourism via the political economy of tourism development. According to him, "the sustainability discource" plays a key role in overshadowing the accumulation of capital and the concerns for ecology associate with niche markets, particularly in the so-called "Third World". In the same vein, we have questioned the concepts of sustainability and sustainable economy and whether the sustainable development model is capable of offering a model that would stop the ecological crisis or is sensitive to the ecological balance within the context of tourism, which is one of the largest and fastest growing industries in the world.

The use of sustainable tourism as a leverage for economic development and capitalizing on natural and cultural resources particularly is being presented in this chapter as a new and more humanistic approach. It becomes more important to determine what the "softer", more "environment friendly" appeals of activities within the scope of sustainable tourism that prioritize local economy and observe nature as one of the stakeholders, correspond to from the environmentalist (ecologist) perspectives. Rainer (2018) emphasizes the importance of political ecology that to ascertain the "production of nature" and the consequences of capital accumulation via ecological tourism activities.

In the following sections, we have first provided a brief literature summary regarding sustainability and ecological tourism and the latter's impacts to discover responses to the questions of whether sustainable tourism is merely a "new wine in the old bottle" or an alternative for the future. Next, we have benefited from a controversy (dichotomy) on how sustainable tourism may be handled from the economist and ecologist perspectives. Finally, we have made a brief evaluation of the historical process under the headings of economism and sustainable development and ecologism and sustainable development.

SUSTAINABLE TOURISM ORIENTED POSITIONS

Sustainability means the ability to repeat the same or similar activities for an unlimited future (Bien, 2006, p. 4). We need to know the limitations of the activities that are being currently conducted. Understanding sustainable tourism aims for economic, social, and cultural sustainability and environmental sustainability. Sustainability has three dimensions: environmental, social and cultural, and economic. Environmental sustainability aims to minimize the damage on the environment and benefit from the environment in a constructive manner. Social and cultural sustainability covers activities that are conducted without damaging the social texture and culture in areas where the locals dwell. Economic sustainability expresses the economic benefits offered for the local communities by tourism activities. These three dimensions are called the "triple bottom line" (Bien, 2006; Hill & Gale, 2009, p. 8). This entails a management understanding where the natural, cultural, and economic resources forming the basis of sustainability can be turned over to the future without damage.

The concepts of social and ecological responsibility underlie the sustainable tourism understanding. The idea is to preserve and develop environmental, social, and cultural assets for the future while meeting the needs and expectations of the tourists and host destinations that are already available. In a sense, this is similar to comparing the heritage and trust concepts. When we look at nature, and the social and cultural assets as our heritage, the common responsibility of humanity remains ambiguous at individual scale since the inheritor is not known. However, the main idea here originates from the "equity principle". According to this principle, we have a responsibility to leave the world in a state that is better than how we found it to the future generations. Therefore, the idea of environmental protection supports compatible environmental usages and activities that avoid irreversible environmental damages, establishment of an environmentally acceptable tourism and collaboration in this area (Fennell & Dowling, 2003, p. 5). Tourism activities such as ecotourism appear as the concrete form of the sustainability concept in tourism.

The current tourism literature includes the destructive impacts of mass tourism (especially sun-sand-sea tourism) on the natural environment and pursuits aimed to eliminate these impacts. World Tourism Organization (EC, 2003, p. 5) anticipates that alternative tourism movements and activities will hold a 20% share in the general tourism economy in the future and there will be tendency for activities other than "sun and sea tourism". In that sense, a paradigm change becomes evident in the current tourism understanding. The factors that cause such change are listed as: a) aspiration of humans to explore and experience new places and new cultures, b) more feasible means of transportation, c) increased holiday periods, d) more active roles assumed in cultural and social activities, and e) increase in environmental awareness.

Following the basic report of the World Commission on Environment (WCED, 1987), these natural, cultural, sportive and ecological changes have started to be handled within the scope of the sustainability concept in order use the resources effectively (Krüger, 2005, p. 579; Leung et al., 2008, p. 20). Sustainable tourism has evolved into a concept that means continuous economic, social and environmental benefits in areas that are accepted to be ecologically sensitive. Ecotourism is defined as "trips that protect the environment, increase the welfare of the local community and incorporate responsibility for natural areas" (TIES, 1990). Ecotourism is also defined as "trips intended for small groups", "social responsibility tourism" (Sırakaya, et al., 1999); and ecotourism is highly interrelated with commercial activities. Ecotourism incorporates the promotion of natural life and environment protection in economic investments and at the same time the ability to integrate with other tourism activities (Wommels, 2009).

Ecotourism contributes in: a) determining the damages senselessly caused on the natural environments by tourism activities and evaluating sustainability in tourism and protecting natural areas in order to reduce these, b) increasing the role of ecotourism in tourism and distributing the revenue generated by ecotourism, in the sense of market focused industry, environment industry and job industry (Libosada, 2009, p. 391), to the local stakeholders living in a given area, c) promoting cultural and traditional assets through educated tourists (Donohoe, 2011), d) incorporating the learning experience; e) promoting conducts for responsibility to tourism industry and tourists f) emphasizing cultural identity and especially supporting local administrations and entrepreneurs to participate in the decision making processes (Wood, 2002). Another definition is the concept of socially responsible ecological tourism that "intends to preserve and enrich the natural and cultural assets in the operated region and supports the economic initiatives of the local stakeholders within that framework" (Sezerel & Çil, 2012).

The starting point of ecotourism is to observe the principles of sustainability in the economic (distribution of the revenues to the locals), social and cultural (preservation and development of social and cultural assets) and environmental (minimization of damages on nature) sense, as alterative to mass tourism. Ecotourism creates an effect that supports the preservation of biological species and ecological habitats, and integrates these with the other tourism activities, according to the view that promotes ecotourism. Many favorable aspects of this integrating effect are emphasized as the contribution in:

1. Determining the damages that have been senselessly caused on natural environments by tourism activities; ensuring sustainability in tourism to reduce these damages and protecting natural envi-

ronments (Libosada, 2009, p. 391) and distributing the revenues generated by ecotourism primarily to the local stakeholders living in a given area,

2. Promoting cultural and traditional assets through educated tourists (Donohoe, 2011),
3. Incorporating a learning experience,
4. Promoting conducts for responsibility to tourism industry and tourists,
5. Emphasizing the cultural identity and especially supporting local administrations and entrepreneurs to participate in decision-making processes (Wood, 2002).

The major environmental benefit of ecotourism is believed to be the prevention of any damages that may be caused on natural habitats that have not yet deteriorated with the view of short-term earnings. In the meantime, the impacts of ecotourism activities, supported with the above justifications, are also complicated. Therefore, we must examine the environmental impacts, social impacts and economic impacts in order to determine the impacts of ecotourism.

The development of ecotourism in a region creates impacts that are similar to the development of other tourism activities that do not qualify as ecotourism.

There is a certain change in areas where tourism develops and this especially alters the lives of the communities that have been involved with agriculture and livestock breeding for many years. One of the reasons that underlie this is the belief of tourists who come for ecotourism purposes on that ecotourism will develop only in certain specific areas. Therefore, tourists are concentrated in certain areas. This also brings along commercial concerns. For example, local administrations encourage investments in areas where ecotourism starts to develop. The reason for this is the foreign currency and tax revenues that would be generated by tourism.

Tour operators produce tours targeted for ecotourism areas and travel agencies encourage tourists who will visit ecotourism areas to travel to such areas before they are deteriorated. As a consequence of this cumulative effect, tourism causes an increased demand for transport vehicles, and the emergence of many new businesses such as the shops that are opened to sell equipment (e.g., raincoats, tents, boots) for nature-based activities. Moreover, the local communities are employed in the tourism industry to capitalize on ecotourism in the economic sense, and to contribute to their livelihoods and improve their living conditions. Local cultures evolve into tourism assets in areas where ecotourism develops and traditional production activities are replaced with seasonal commercial relations (Erdoğan, 2003, p.158).

In addition, an increase is also observed in the migration phenomenon with the dynamism of economic activities and increase in employment in areas where ecotourism develops. Many social problems emerge when the employment demand that is not managed well is combined with rapid migration. For example, the migration that has increased as a consequence of opening Kuşadası, Turkey to tourism has resulted in the growth of the construction sector, traffic problems, shanty settlement, and rapid depletion of natural resources (Aykaç, 2009, p. 30).

Another point that promotes the development of tourism is the fact that it proposes a model that could find a solution for unemployment (Erdoğan, 2003, pp.160-161). According to the positive perspective, tourism increases total welfare by helping local communities to strengthen their economic conditions, preventing young unemployment which prevents regional migrations, and distributing the generated revenues to the local communities. Nevertheless, opening ecotourism areas to use in an unplanned manner also creates numerous unfavorable consequences. First, it is necessary to establish accommodation facilities such as eco-lodges in areas where ecotourism develops as compatible with the nature of such tourism activities. The preparation of such facilities as fully compatible with nature requires certain standards and venues that cannot reach the ideal accommodation standards remain outside the focus of the tour operators. In addition, this offers advantages to major entrepreneurs who have the economic strength to make investments capable to meeting certain standards, rather than local entrepreneurs. Furthermore, we observe there are not too many economic initiatives that are indirectly related with tourism which are similar to that in mass tourism. For example, it is not possible for tourists to buy souvenirs or pay parking fees in ecotourism.

Versatile plans that will encompass all stakeholders are required to increase the revenues generated by ecotourism. The development of local travel agencies and tourist guides, establishment of food and beverage businesses based on organic products, waste management, and promotion activities constitute important cornerstones in guiding the economic revenues in a certain region to the individuals who live in that region. The researches made on ecotourism emphasize that ecotourism should be approached skeptically regarding the ability to ensure economic growth in areas where tourism activities are conducted.

The way to minimize the adverse impacts of ecotourism in the environmental, social, and cultural sense is to be careful about the bearing capacity of the region that is planned to be opened to ecotourism, to prepare policies that will protect the interests and expectations of all stakeholders involved in ecotourism by determining the ecological, social, and economic bearing capacities, and to implement these policies unwaveringly. The priorities of the dimensions that are considered in tourism also vary with the development levels of countries. This circumstance is similar to the hierarchy of need that Maslow has developed for individuals. Hence, economy rather than ecology takes priority in Third World nations. It is believed that sustainable tourism will serve economic sustainability under four headings in that sense (Ritchie & Crouch, 2006): a) Equity in the distribution of economic revenues, b) Uttilization of local manpower, c) Occupational safety, and d) Wages, salaries and fringe benefits. These demonstrate that the benefits handled under economy will be possible with balanced economic distribution to the local community and investments made on human resources.

The natural environment constitutes the nucleus of many touristic destinations. A unique environment constitutes a touristic attractiveness. People living in such areas are the primary actors in protecting such environments in general. However, the responsibility of the tourism industry, which is effective in generating economic gains and in protecting the environment, is actually more than its effectiveness in generating economic gains. Considering that each destination has unique features, characteristics such as the presence of an environment with susceptible (fragile) environmental renewability, the positive and negative viewpoints of the local community on tourism, the qualifications and adequacy of the local manpower and geographic location also constitute differences for the compatibility of the destination for tourism.

In brief, there is a unique interaction between each destination and the tourism event. Therefore, there is no scale that could measure the positive and negative impacts of tourism or a standard recipe to eliminate its negative impacts (Ritchie& Crouch, 2006, pp. 44-45). At this point, we need to mention the impacts that could arise within the sustainable tourism context.

Figure 1 shows that sustainable tourism activities develop alternative tourism, ensure the opening of new destinations and, consequently, contribute positively in the economic sense on a local and national scale. The main goal to increase employment opportunities and the national development goals are the consequences of opening new destinations. Furthermore, new destinations that are subjected to tourism activities allow the opening of new vacation areas and increase diversity. Thus, this tourism strategy offers alternative tourism opportunities to individuals who do not want to participate in mass tourism or want different vacations or trips during different months of the year, outside of mass tourism.

Sustainable tourism activities also have negative aspects as shown in Figure 1: social and ecological. These may primarily be listed as the marketization of non-capitalist venues, damage on the regional ecosystem, destruction of the region; homogenization of the region through the erosion of cultural characteristics (Urry, 1999); and deepening of exploitation relations (labor-capital conflict) by sustainable tourism. As a matter of fact, one in every 10 people in the world is working in the tourism sector today (UNWTO, 2014). The negative impacts of sustainable tourism from the social perspective include the gradual homogenization of the local texture in the new destination and subjection to market relationships, while the elimination of the natural and architectural texture and emergence of artificial areas may be listed among the negative impacts from the cultural perspective.

For example, the Uzungöl and Ayder Plateau in the Eastern Black Sea Region of Turkey has gradually started to lose its natural and architectural textures upon being opened to tourism. Concrete settlement immediately stands out in areas transformed into tourist destinations. Some of the people living in these areas are transforming their village houses into hotels, and their approach to the coming tourists is determined based on market relations. Furthermore, again citing Uzungöl and Ayder Plateau as examples, we observe that labor relations also experienced changes. Some of the local community that was involved with agriculture and livestock breeding has gravitated towards tourism once these areas have been transformed into tourism destinations.

This has resulted in the shift of a majority of the people who were once involved with agriculture to the tourism sector once tourism activities have begun, ultimately transforming labor-capital relations similar to the example in the Mediterranean city of Antalya, Turkey. In addition to the positive and negative impacts of sustainable tourism activities, there is also another dimension that is debated regarding the destruction of the ecological balance. The environmental impacts of sustainable tourism have been evaluated both as positive and negative in Figure 1.

First, the claim that it is alternative to the negative environmental impacts of mass tourism underlies the opinion that the activity has positive impacts on the environment. In fact, this claim maintains its validity when any sustainable tourism activity is compared with a mass tourism activity. Second, there are claims that sustainable development has negative environmental impacts. These claims are mainly based on the damage that will be caused on the environment by each new destination. In fact, the main point in this debate is the difference in perspectives in evaluating environmental problems.

Figure 1. Positive and negative aspects of sustainable tourism activities

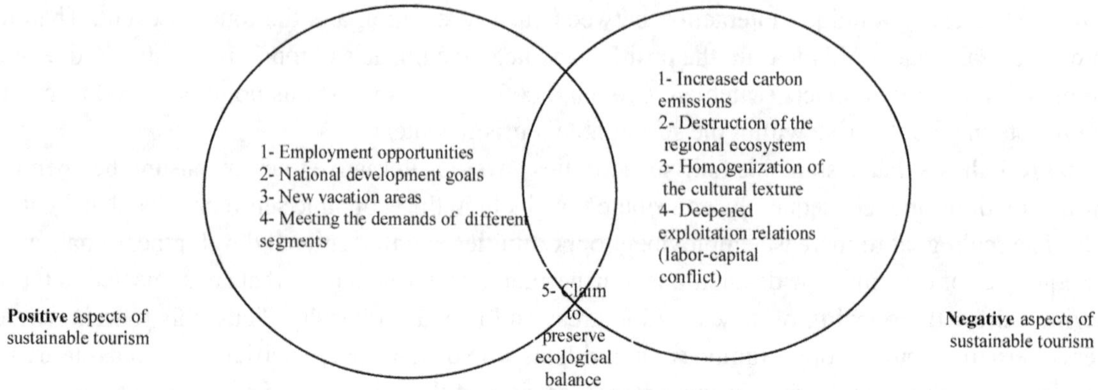

The positive aspects of sustainable tourism activities represent an economic perspective. As stated by Lewontin (2013, pp. 138-139), one of the main factors causing the emergence of the positive aspects of sustainable tourism activities to the forefront is the reduction of the actual causes of ecological problems to the mediators; in other words, confusing the causes with the mediators. The positioning made through ecological approaches for sustainable tourism activities such as preventing the destruction of ecological balance with the environment protection approach, and simultaneously increasing opportunities for development and employment, may be criticized with respect to obscuring the actual cause of the problem. This is because the mediator is being burdened with the root cause of ecological tourism problems, which inherently possess deep environmental consequences, serves a function in reorganizing the available capital areas occupied with state policies and opening areas outside of the market system by developing new strategies, since it is the "largest industry of the world" from the perspective of employment and trade (Urry, 1999, p. 237).

It becomes evident there is a need to follow a planning and policy development process that especially keeps the unique dynamics of each region at the forefront in the economic and ecological dimensions of sustainable tourism. However, there also are universal viewpoints that sustainable tourism will contribute to development Hunter (1997, p. 853; pp. 860-863) collects these theoretical comments under four headings. The first one (the very weak position) is the opinion that tourism will offer compelling development. According to this opinion, the basis of the tourism activity is the effort to meet the demands of the dominant actors such as tour operators and primarily the tourists. This process offers economic contributions to the local community especially those living in poor areas. However, the impacts of tourism aimed for the depletion of natural resources may be overlooked as compared to economic gains. This perspective is at a human focused and pragmatic, developmentalist line that is aimed to meet the demands of tourism industry at an optimal level.

The second (weak position) supports bringing tourism products to the forefront resulting I economic development. The joint efforts of the public and private sectors will be able to limit the negative impacts of tourism on the environment and will also be able to support initiatives that will provide benefits to the local community by developing the necessary infrastructure activities at each small and unique destination. This position is also human-focused and pragmatic, similar to thc first position. Howcvcr, resource protection is at the forefront in this position and there is a search to find a balance between the earnings from tourism and the negative impacts.

The third (strong position) is extremely sensitive for developing tourism activities, primarily ecotourism, in a certain area with minimal damage on the environment and culture and the bearing capacity. The difference of this approach from the second is that the former prioritizes environmental assets more than marketing opportunities in tourism and subjects the activities to strict scrutiny. It focuses on top quality nature and culture events in destinations where tourism has newly started to develop or has not yet emerged. It exhibits a stand that attaches more importance on the local community rather than the ecosystem based or individual consumers, and to the benefit of the second one between population increase and the ecosystem.

The fourth (very strong position) is the opinion that advocates the restriction of tourism activities as far as possible, and highlights environment protection. This ecology-based position promotes the protection of nature by generating policies to inhibit industrial tourism in areas where tourism has not yet emerged yet. It prioritizes other living organisms and nature and attempts to exclude economic development as much as possible.

Given the the information provided above, we believea dichotomy emerges on the basis of economism and ecologism and it would be meaningful to offer a synthesis by examining the fundamental concepts of economism and ecologism.

ECONOMISM VS. ECOLOGISM

The political, social, and economic transformations that began near the end of the 18th century have introduced the capitalist production style that is characterized by the production of commodities with commodities (Sraffa, 2010) and operates as the accumulation cycle of commodity masses. By the 20th century, the (non-capitalist) extensions remaining outside of the present market system (capitalist extension) entered a new phase called "marketization". This phase, which continued until the end of World War II and is referred to as monopolistic capitalism, is the imperialist phase in which capital has endeavored to expand beyond national borders and, therefore, had to discover new venues. The market capitalism period evolved towards the post-Fordist production/consumption style dominated by the consumers when non-liberal policies were implemented and producers became consumer-oriented starting with the 1970s. This new phase of capitalism is the new accumulation model also referred to as "late capitalism" and expands to larger and more different areas than ever before (Jameson, 2011; Harvey, 2012; Urry, 1999, p. 206).

As the output of the late capitalism phase, non-liberalism expresses the need to open new areas to solve the capital accumulation problem due to commodification and privatization (driving the village populations from their lands); in other words, the commodification of resources such as land under the care of the state and opening these to the market for capital accumulation. This expansion knows no bounds in damaging natural assets since it accelerates the gradual commodification of nature. However, the world was able to understand the damage caused on nature by capitalism only after the second half of the 20th century.

The massive deaths experienced in the 1950s as a direct consequence of air and soil pollution drew the attentions on studies related with environmental problems. By the 1970s, the fact that environmental problems reached global dimensions became public knowledge. While natural resources were deemed as fixed assets until the 1970s, the social vision following the 1970s primarily started to "predict that nature will collapse and all life on earth will come to an end" (Zizek, 2013, p. 7). The recognition of ecological problems has led to re-defining nature; however, the production style has tried to adapt to this new situation by trying to develop new techniques and discourses.

It is possible to say that two different opinions have consequently started to be debated in the extant literature. In this chapter, we separate the two different opinions as economism and ecologism and try to emphasize the importance of the social dimension that expresses the ability to sustain the social aspect in a balanced manner besides economism and ecologism (Harris, 2000; Öztürk, 2007, pp. 102-112). The economist opinion (economism) is an approach that evaluates nature as "environmental commodity" (or natural capital) from which we must produce new goods and services continuously. In this approach, environment problems are framed as an external problem and nature protection is handled with an "environment friendly" understanding (Keleş, 1998; Keleş et.al., 2012).

This viewpoint that emphasizes the relationship between the environment and economy has two fundamental problems that can be summarized as: a) the impacts of economic activities on the environmental problems, and b) he economic costs of activities that are required to be implemented against environmental problems. Meanwhile ecologism, which is the second opinion, may be explained as the effort to find solutions for the environmental problems created by humans starting with the 19th century. The limitations of the ability of nature for self-renewal are placed at the forefront in the basis of this opinion. According to ecologism, damage occurs as a consequence of exceeding this limit. In any case, ecologism is based on the need to act in compliance with the "logic of nature".

ECONOMISM AND SUSTAINABLE DEVELOPMENT

The economy-based perspective to environment problems has emerged by adding the sustainability expression to development upon entering the last quarter of the 20th century as a consequence of the inability to achieve development and to solve poverty and the impacts of environmental pollution since the available development model was not (could not be) adequate for the ecological, economic, social and political developments. The desire of the US hegemony to gain strength when the Cold War era started following World War II has caused development policies (similar to the New Deal program where the state played an effective role in the US following the 1929 crisis) to be brought on the agenda in the world. The development policies found fields of application especially through the support of the US to the Western European countries that were impoverished during the war.

Subsequently, the age of development through the state took its final form when underdeveloped countries also started to implement development policies (Esteva, 2007). Following the 1970s, the available production system started to be questioned and the classical development understanding started to be found inadequate and questioned under the pretext of excessive intervention in the markets by the state. In other words, the primary claim during that period was the need to shift to a new development model conducted through the market, where the state did not intervene in the markets. When environmental problems became global in parallel with this and reached a point where they could no longer be disguised, sustainable development started to be deemed as appropriate.

In brief, this transition following the 1970s from the classical development models conducted through the state by applying Keynesian fiscal policies started to become evident with the implementation of sustainable development policies where neoliberal policies reducing the effectiveness of the state became functional. Furthermore, the new development model reached its final form with the globalization of environmental problems and the deepening of the poverty problem in underdeveloped counties.

Hence, the environmental vision, which became popular in the society staring with the last quarter of the 20th century, added the concept of 'sustainability', which expresses the ability of anything for self-renewal and self-viability, to the development strategies in order to ensure the continuity of the current production style.

The sustainable development understanding has three components as economic, social, and environmental (ecological). Sustainable development sets off with the claim of offering a model based on the sustainability of these three components. While environmental (ecological) sustainability is intended to protect the self-reproduction ability of nature, economic sustainability sets off with the purpose of taking precautions against the depletion of the "natural capital" in order to ensure the continuity of economic activities. Meanwhile, social sustainability is based on the need to offer a balanced life to the present generations and yet to operate in order to ensure the existence of the future generations as well (Harris, 2000). However, these components associated with the sustainability expression add further ambiguities

Figure 2.Transition from development to sustainable development

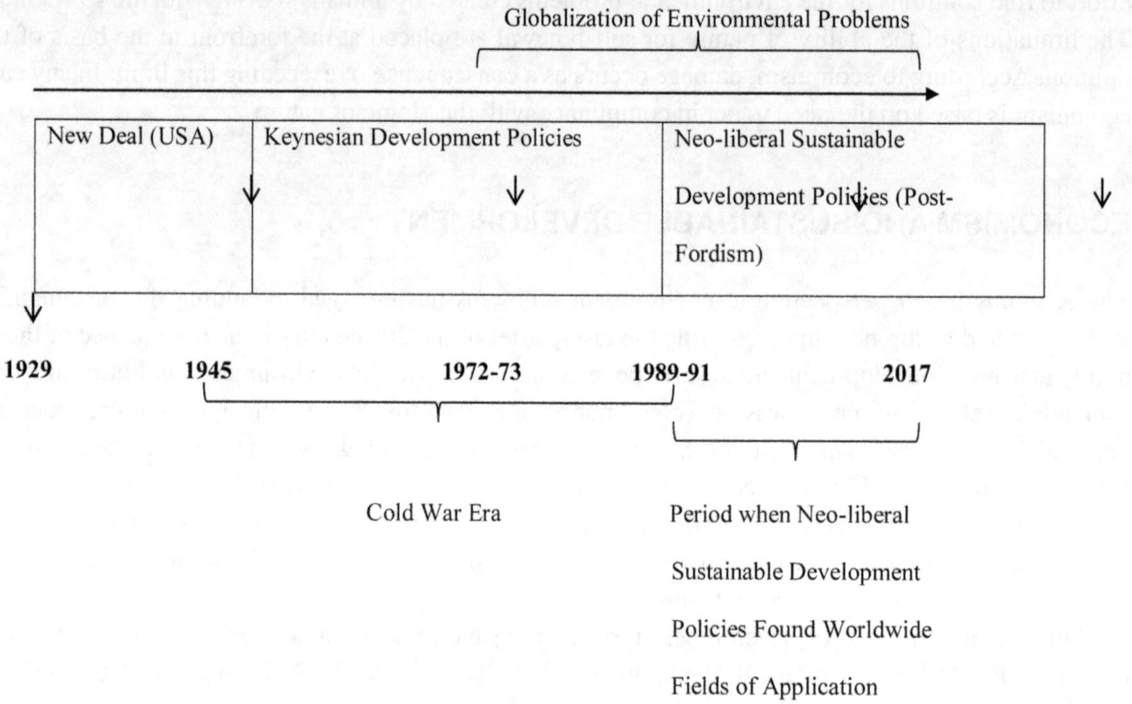

to the meaning of the development concept, because it is not possible to define what will be prioritized and what will be sustainable for everyone.

Expressions such as "integrating environment and economy in decision making" used in the report titled Our Common Future presented during the Environment and Development Commission organized by the United Nations (UN) in 1987 (1991, p. 78) indicate the need to maintain natural balance in order to solve ecological problems. However, as Lewontin (2013, pp. 138-139) mentions, a non-realistic confrontation is experienced in the sustainable development understanding because the causes and the mediators are confused.

The confusion of the causes with the mediators obscures the character of the production style that leads to ecological problems and leads to the prediction that development is not truly a problem, it is only necessary for it to acquire and environmentalist world vision and the problem will be solved. Right at this point, the environment protection approach, which claims to protect the sustainability of development by protecting nature without disturbing the natural balance, is criticized on the grounds that it would not solve ecological problems. Criticisms regarding the environment protectionism approach (sustainable development) that is believed to be unable to solve ecological problems, are especially concentrated along the axis of ecological sustainability that has already been voided by neoliberal accumulation conditions.

Sustainability, which has been formed as based on the reproduction and self-renewal ability of nature but has suffered a semantic shift after being added to the development model, has arisen from the need to sustain ecology. However, since ecological sustainability means nature - the house (oikos) where men (and other living species) live - it expresses the ability of man to maintain a possession relationship with nature in a facultative manner. In other words, if the relationship of man with nature – which is a labor relationship – is intervened in or prevented, one cannot expect ecology to be sustainable.

In short, "The sustainable development expression [is] an attempt to reconcile two concepts, one of which (development) eliminates the other (sustainability)" (Şahin, 2004). On the other hand, ecological approaches (e.g., deep ecology, social ecology) that criticize the economic perspective (environment protectionism) evaluate ecological problems from different perspectives.

ECOLOGISM AND SUSTAINABLE DEVELOPMENT

There are different approaches that criticize the environment protectionism approach, which intends to protect the environment by scientific and technological developments based on the need for technical and administrative reforms aimed for taking a variety of measures to reduce environmental problems and also to offer alternative proposals for ecological problems. First, Arne Naess (1973) has used the shallow ecology expression for environment protectionism, developed the deep ecology approach, and made a differentiation between these approaches. Naess defines the environment protectionism approach as the man-centered (anthropocentric) approach that acts on the motive of "combat against pollution and resource depletion" and is mainly intended to protect the health and welfare of the people in developed countries (Önder, 2000, pp. 147-151).

Meanwhile, deep ecology is an approach that rejects the anthropocentric viewpoint and adopts a nature-centered (ecocentric) approach and thus observes humans and other creatures as equivalents to each other. Therefore, in this approach nature has a value in itself. The spontaneity of nature (numen) indicates that man is only one of the pieces of nature. Deep ecology, which stores non-mental elements

Figure 3. Sustainability from the economism and ecologism perspectives

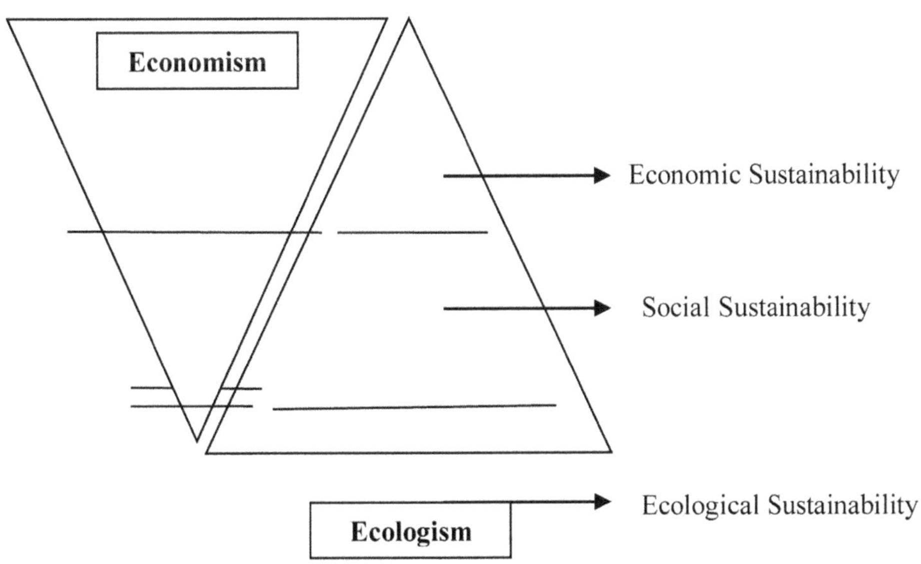

and has an idea of a mystic union with nature (İdem, 2009), thus objects to the anthropocentric environment protectionism that believes the domination of man over nature will not create problems as long as economic development is not prevented (Şahin, 2003).

However, the view of nature by the deep ecology approach observes man as any creature within the ecosystem, and positions man only as a creature that harms nature. Thus, it does not consider that man may also have his own missions for nature. The idea that man was a part of nature physically at first, started from himself (habeas corpus) and reached habeas oikos, in other words the idea that man has started from himself and used nature, is reversed in the deep ecology approach (Cangızbay, 2003, pp. 96-97).

Another ecological approach that tries to generate consistent opinions against ecological crisis is social ecology that emerges with the need to reorganize the society. Social ecology, which was developed by Murray Bookchin in the 1960s, is an approach that criticizes deep ecology setting off from the inability to see that the capacity of man to reason, devise tools, design technology, and communicate through a symbolic language may be used not only to destroy the biosphere but also for the good of the biosphere. According to Bookchin (1996a), as contrary to what deep ecology mentions, ecological problems primarily arise from society.

Therefore, the main basis of social ecology is the idea that the problems that bring the society and nature into conflict do not emerge between the society and nature, but from within social development. "The controversy and division that is perceived between the society and nature today arises from the splits in the social arena, from the controversies of men among each other." If we want to find a solution to the ecological crisis that Bookchin (1996b, pp. 44-45) has tried to express, we have to "transform the institutive, moral and spiritual changes deep down in the human society that give rise to hierarchy and dominations, not only in the bourgeois, feudal and ancient societies, or class societies in general, but right at the dawn of civilization", in his own words.

As can be seen from the above, the related literature offers alternative opinions whether the dichotomy between economism and ecologism may be reduced to a dichotomy between man and nature or not, at the expense of creating employment opportunities and generating revenues for the sustainability of development with respect to sustainable tourism. Findings on where sustainable tourism may be placed in the scheme are presented in the conclusion section.

FUTURE RESEARCH DIRECTIONS

In this chapter, we have demonstrated the economic and ecological limitations of sustainable tourism theoretically. These limitations are required to evolve for the future through variables such as bearing capacity, geographic expansion, and cultural differences. In other words, those that need to be done "before breaking the jug", as the phrase goes, must be varied beyond the limited perspective of economism. Therefore, there is a need for empirical researches that will show the interaction of both local experiences and universal theories. Tretyakova (2014, p. 424) suggests a system of dynamic indicators depending on a series of principles; namely, analyzing the constituents of the economic, ecological, and social components in an integral complex; a set of indicators that reflects the state of these components in dynamics; suitability for the practical use of the results of analysis and substantiation of sustainable development strategies and programs; methodical simplicity (i.e., the accessibility of statistical data) for analysis in the absence of large financial and time costs; dynamic balance of the eco+nomic, ecological, and social components, dynamic comparability and subordination of the indicators. Hence, the further research might include the assessment and monitoring of sustainability and the balance between ecology and economy.

CONCLUSION

As a result of reviewing the literature on economy and ecology regarding sustainability, we have obtained cores about where the concept of sustainability in tourism may be placed in the economic and ecological perspectives. In this chapter, we have tried to determine where sustainable tourism, which is one of the sustainable development strategies, is positioned within ecological sustainability in line with the arguments offered by ecological approaches (environment protectionism/shallow ecology, deep ecology and social ecology). Then, we have made an evaluation on the positive and negative aspects of sustainable tourism and its adequacy to prevent the ecological problems caused by mass tourism, and reached the conclusion that ecological sustainability can be achieved at a very low degree in the tourism discipline under the domination of the current production style, which is the main problem in this study (as shown in Figure 4).

Figure 4 shows taht sustainable tourism has a strong impact with respect to economic sustainability. The reasons for this include increases in employment and development level through the opening of new destinations. Meanwhile, sustainable tourism may not be deemed as a powerful tourism activity as compared to mass tourism. However, sustainable tourism destinations opened and close to and as alternatives for areas where mass tourism is already exercised, are quite beneficial with respect to economy both by the contribution it makes to mass tourism and the stimulation of its own internal dynamics. Li et al. (2011, p. 370) assert that ecological destruction, environmental deterioration, and resources shortage often become serious issues when development of economy is over stressed. This is particularly

Figure 4. Sustainable tourism from the economism and ecologism perspectives

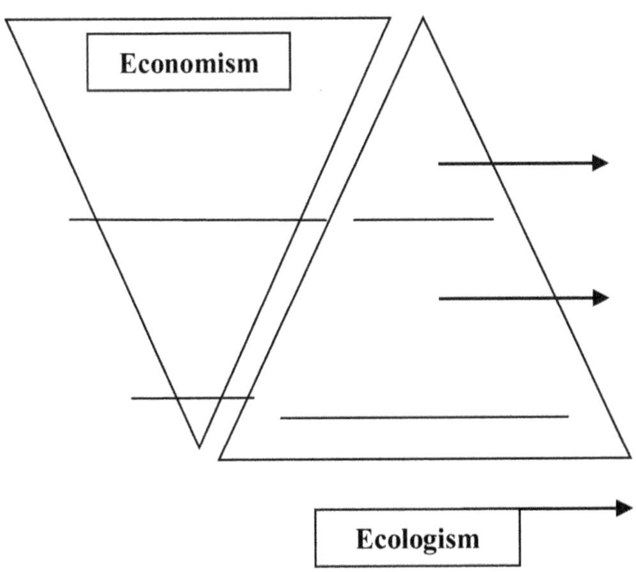

	Sustainable Tourism
Economic Sustainability	Strong
Social Sustainability	Low
Ecological Sustainability	Very Low

Ecological sustainability

true for many developing countries since rapid economic growth, decentralization, privatization, and related socio-cultural changes are leading to the emergence of a complex decision-making environment.

The reason for sustainable tourism activities to remain at a low level with respect to social sustainability, as shown in Figure 4, is due to the influence of the labor intensiveness of tourism activities and the labor force that has shifted from agriculture to tourism. Another important problem that could arise through sustainable tourism is that the sustainable tourism technique, developed as a alternative for the environmental destruction by mass tourism, will contribute even further in environmental problems, as contrary to what has been foreseen. It is possible to find the basis of this debate in ecological approaches such as deep ecology and social ecology. It is possible to explain the formulation of this problem with the Jevons paradox.

William Stanley Jevons, in his study titled the "Coal Question" that he wrote in 1865, evaluates the increase in energy consumption –coal was the largest energy resource of the time- with the increase in commodity production. In this study, Jevons, has determined that the quantity coal consumption, which would normally be expected to decrease with the development of technology (development of the steam engines), in other words the increase in the efficiency of commodity production, has actually increased on the contrary. Consequently, he has observed that coal has also continued to be consumed in increasing amounts, despite the decrease experienced in the prices of commodities as technology increased, the increase in commodity production through opening more and larger factories. What Jevons mentions is the paradox created by the effort of capitalism to develop technology (Foster, 2006).

It is quite clear that the ability of capitalism to expand underlies this problem. Paul Sweezy and Paul Baran, in the 1966 book titled "Monopolistic Capital" mentions the monopoly that is created by the ability of capitalism to expand. The steam engine, railway and automobile, which are three innovations (opening a new era) that have absorbed other capitals and created new investment opportunities, have been the guarantee for strengthening monopolization. "Each of these altered the economic geography radically by causing internal migrations and establishment of new communities. Each have necessitated or enabled the production of many new commodities and services, each have expanded the Market means of industrial products indirectly" (Şahin, 2007).

In conclusion, setting off from the Jevons paradox and monopolization through the ability of capitalism to expand, it is evident that sustainable tourism activities, offered as an alternative technique against the damage caused by mass tourism, will have more negative impacts rather than positive impacts on ecological problems in the long run because they will accelerate the carbon emission process by allowing the increase of more consumption centers and the development of the traveling sector. In addition, even if new investment opportunities are opened in line with the potentials of the regions, monopoly –which we may mention as finance capital in our day- will absorb other capitals. Acting from here, we can observe that the repetition of the available methods and instruments of global capitalism in the field of tourism will not be useful in ensuring the ecology-economy balance. In other words, it becomes evident that a developmentalism and economism weighted sustainability is not possible in the field of tourism with a reconciliatory statement. Therefore, we recommend handling unique local dynamics with a creative and ecologist perspective, rather than standard recipes.

We need an alternative development understanding that upholds local dynamics today, instead of the development understanding that is offered from the global and national scales down to the local scale. This alternative development understanding may be expressed with the different development paradigm that Rajni Kothari from India has tried to develop. The alternative development model of Kothari is based on a fundamental hypothesis which proposes to review the production system and technologies, the consumption culture and the current spatial organization once more (Dirlik, 2012, p. 131).

When we seek a different solution for sustainable tourism activities, by setting off from Kothari's hypothesis, first local development should no longer be integrated with global capitalism, as different from the present development understanding, and move away from the contester logic that accepts competition between localities as a prerequisite. Thus, the local will move away from both the obligation to compete and from the oppressive and destructive influences of global and national scales. Hence, sustainable tourism activity sites will be able to evolve into fortresses, protected from the elements of global capitalism and national development that constantly damage and destroy the nature, culture and the city at the local sclae.

However, another important point that local development must consider is the ethics understanding that necessitates the local people to disengage from their personal interest and profit focused thinking. Especially considering that one of the threats aimed for nature is the effort of the individual to maximize his personal interest, it is necessary to guide the individual to consume only as much as he actually requires.

The question of need, which necessitates sustainable tourism activity in a place with a potential and also transforms this into a risk, should be developed with an ecological awareness and ecological ethics understanding. Finally, there is the need to reorganize all sites, and primarily the local site for local development. Since sites are relatively equalitarian with each other, sustainable tourism activities may be designed in such a way that they are capable of standing on their own feet, without oppressing other sites and without competing with each other in this new organization.

REFERENCES

Aronsson, L. (2004). *The development of sustaniable tourism*. London: Thomson Learning.

Avcı, N. (2007). Turizmde taşıma kapasitesinin önemi. *Ege Akademik Bakış*, *7*(2), 485–501.

Aykaç, A. (2009). *Yeni işler, yeni işçiler: Turizm sektöründe emek*. İstanbul: İletişim Yayınları.

Bianchi, R. (2017). The political economy of tourism development: A critical review. *Annals of Tourism Research*. doi:10.1016/j.annals.2017.08.005

Bien, A. (2006). *A simple user's guide to certification for sustainable tourism and ecotourism* (3rd ed.). Washington, DC: Center for Ecotourism and Sustainable Development.

Blamey, R. K. (2001). Principles of ecotourism. In D. B. Weaver (Ed.), *Encyclopedia of Ecotourism* (pp. 5–22). New York: CABI Publishing.

Bookchin, M. (1996a). *Toplumsal Ekolojinin Felsefesi, Çev. Rahmi*. G. Öğdül, Kabalcı Yayınları, İstanbul, 197s.

Bookchin, M. (1996b). *Ekolojik Bir Toplumuna Doğru*. Çev. Abdullah Yılmaz, Ayrıntı Yayınları, İsyanbul, 300s.

Bozok, D., & Yılmaz, Ö. (2011). Turistik ürün çeşitlendirmesi. In N. Hacıoğlu & C. Avcıkurt (Eds.), Ekoturizm (2. Baskı) içinde (pp. 111-137). Ankara: Nobel Yayınları.

Briassoulis, H. (2002). Sustainable Tourism And The Question Of The Commons. *Annals of Tourism Research, 29*(4), 1065–1085. doi:10.1016/S0160-7383(02)00021-X

Cangizbay, K. (2003). *Sosyalizm ve Özyönetim: Reel Sosyalizmden Sosyalist Realiteye*. Ankara: Ütopya Yayınevi.

Çevre & Komisyonu. (1991). *Ortak Geleceğimiz*. Türkiye Çevre Sorunları Vakfı Yayını, ss. 73-102.

Çoban, A. (2002). *Çevreciliğin İdeolojik Unsurlarının Eklemlenmesi*. Siyasal Bilgiler Fakültesi Dergisi Cilt 57, Sayı 3, ss. 3-30.

Çoban, A. (2013). Çevrecilik., iç. In Gökhan Atılgan & Atilla Aytekin (Eds.), Siyaset Bilimi Kavramlar İdeolojiler Disiplinlerarası İlişkiler. Yordam Yayınları, İstanbul, ss. 455-473.

Dirlik, A. (2012). *Küreselleşmenin Sonu mu? (çev. İ. Kovacı ve V. Batmaz)*. İstanbul: Ayrıntı Yayınları.

Donohoe, H. M. (2011). Defining culturally sensitive ecotourism: A Delphi consensus. *Current Issues in Tourism, 14*(1), 27–45. doi:10.1080/13683500903440689

Erdoğan, N. (2003). *Çevre ve (Eko)turizm*. Ankara: Erk Yayıncılık.

Esteva, G. (2007). Kalkınma. Çev. Oktay Etiman, iç. Sachs,Wolsgangs (ed.), Kalkınma Sözlüğü Bir İktidar Olarak Bilgiye Giriş, Özgür Üniversite Yayınları, Ankara, ss. 17-50.

European Communities. (2003). *Using Natural and Cultural Heritage to Develop Sustainable Tourism*. Luxembourg: Office for Official Publications of The Europian Communities.

Fennell, D., & Dowling, R. K. (Eds.). (2003). *Ecotourism Policy and Planning*. Wallingford: CABI Publishing. doi:10.1079/9780851996097.0000

Fennell, D., & Weaver, D. (2005). The ecotourium concept and tourism-conservation symbiosis. *Journal of Sustainable Tourism, 13*(4), 373–390. doi:10.1080/09669580508668563

Foster, J. B. (2006). *Ekolojik Devrimi Örgütlemek*, iç. Ekolojik Felaket. *Özgür Üniversite Forumu Dergisi*, Ankara, ss. 99-108.

Harris, M. J. (2000). *Sürdürülebilir Kalkınmanın Temel Prensipleri*, Çev. Emine Özmete. Retrieved on March 28, 2015, from: http://www.sdergi.hacettepe.edu.tr/makaleler/EmineOzmet2eviri.pdf

Harvey, D. (2012). Yaratıcı yıkım olarak Neoliberalizm. *Atılım Sosyal Bilimler Dergisi, 2*(2), 67-88.

Hill, J., & Gale, T. (2009). *Ecotourism and Environmental Sustainability: Principles and Practice*. London: Ashgate Limited Company.

Hunter, C. (1997). Sustainable Tourism as an Adaptive Paradigm. *Annals of Tourism Research, 24*(4), 850–867. doi:10.1016/S0160-7383(97)00036-4

IATA. (2014). *Annual Review*. IATA.

İdem, Ş. (2009). *Toplumsal Ekoloji Nedir? Ne Değildir?* Retrieved on March 15, 2013, from: http://ecotopianetwork.wordpress.com/2009/11/17/toplumsal-ekoloji-nedir-ne-degildir-sadi-idem/

Jameson, F. (2011). *Postmodernizm ya da Geç Kapitalizmin Kültürel Mantığı, Çev. Nuri Plümer, Abdülkadir Gölcü*. Ankara: Nirengi Kitap.

Kayıkçı, M. (2012). *Çevre ve Kalkınma Söylemi, Birinci Baskı*. Ankara: Orion Kitabevi.

Keleş, R. (1998). *Kent Bilim Terimleri Sözlüğü, İkinci Basım*. Ankara: İmge Yayınları.

Keleş, R., Hamamci, C., & Çoban, A. (2012). *Çevre Politikası*. Ankara: İmge Kitabevi.

Krüger, O. (2005). The role of ecotourism in conservation: Panacea or Pandora's box? *Biodiversity and Conservation*, *14*(3), 579–600. doi:10.100710531-004-3917-4

Kuter, N., & Ünal, H. E. (2009). Sürdürülebilirlik kapsamında ekoturizmin çevresel, ekonomik ve sosyokültürel etkileri. Kastamonu Üni. *Orman Fakültesi Dergisi*, *9*(2), 146–156.

Leung, Y. F., Marion, J. L., & Farrell, T. A. (2008). Recreation ecology in sustainable tourism and ecotourism. A streghtening role. In S. F. McCool & R. N. Moisey (Eds.), *Tourism, Recreation, and Sustainability: Linking Culture and the Environment* (2nd ed.; pp. 19–38). Oxon, UK: CABI Publishing. doi:10.1079/9781845934705.0019

Lewontin, R. (2013). *Üçlü Sarmal Gen, Organizma ve Çevre, Çev. Ergi Deniz Özsoy*. İstanbul: Say Yayınları.

Li, Y. P., Huangb, G. H., Zhangc, N., & Nied, S. L. (2011). An inexact-stochastic with recourse model for developing regional economic-ecological sustainability under uncertainty. *Ecological Modelling*, *222*(2), 370–379. doi:10.1016/j.ecolmodel.2009.12.010

Libosada, C. Jr. (2009). Business or leisure? Economic development and resource protectiond-Concepts and practices in sustainable ecotourism. *Ocean and Coastal Management*, *52*(7), 390–394. doi:10.1016/j.ocecoaman.2009.04.004

Lopez, R. (2002). Evaluating ecotourism in natural protected areas of La Paz Bay, Baja California Sur, Mexico: Ecotourism or nature-based tourism? *Biodiversity and Conservation*, *11*(9), 1539–1550. doi:10.1023/A:1016887417263

Mutlu, A. (2008). *Ekoloji ve Yönetim Toplumsal Ekoloji ve Sürdürülebilir Gelişme'nin Karşılaştırılması*. Ankara: Turhan Kitabevi.

Önder, T. (2003). *Ekoloji, Toplum ve Siyaset*. Ankara: Odak Yayınları.

Orams, M. B. (2001). Types of Ecotourism. In D. B. Weaver (Ed.), *The Encyclopaedia of Ecotourism* (pp. 23–36). Wallingford, CT: CABI Publishing.

Öztürk, L. (2007). *Sürdürülebilir Kalkınma*. Ankara: İmaj Yayıncılık.

Rainer, G. (2018). Producing nature for tourism: A political ecology angle. *Annals of Tourism Research*. doi:10.1016/j.annals.2018.01.004

Ritchie, B., & Crouch, G. (2005). *The Competitive Destination A Sustainable Tourism Perspective*. Cambridge: CABI Publishing.

Şahin, Ü. (2003). *Ekolojizmi Çevrecilikten Ayırmak Yeniden Bir Düşünme Denemesi, Üç Ekoloji, Sayı 1*. Retrieved on March 27, 2015, from: http://www.ucekoloji.net/?p=89

Şahin, Ü. (2004). Bir Truva Atı Olarak Sürdürülebilir Kalkınma. *Üç Ekoloji,* Sayı 2, ss. 9-30.

Şahin, Ü. (2007). Antikapitalist Bir İklim Değişikliği Mücadelesine Doğru. *Birikim Dergisi*, Sayı 223. Retrieved on March 27, 2015, from: http://www.birikimdergisi.com/sayi/223/anti-kapitalist-bir-iklim-degisikligimucadelesine-dogru.

Sezerel, H., & Cil, A. (2012). Connecting nature, culture, and art in the context of socially responsible ecological tourism. *MMV6 Conference Proceedings*, 266-267.

Sirakaya, E., Sasidharan, V., & Sönmez, S. (1999). Redefining ecotourism: The need for a supply side view. *Journal of Travel Research, 38*(2), 168–172. doi:10.1177/004728759903800210

Sraffa, P. (2010). *Malların Mallarla Üretimi İktisat Kuramını Eleştiriye Açış, Çev. Ümit Şenesen*. İstanbul: Yordam Yayınları.

TIES. (1990). *Global Ecotourism Fact Sheet*. The International Ecotourism Society. Retrieved on June 2, 2015, from: https://ibgeographylancaster.wikispaces.com/file/view/TIES+GLOBAL+ECOTOURISM+FACT+SHEET.PDF

Tretyakova, E. (2014). Assessing sustainability of development of ecological and economic systems: A dynamic method. *Studies on Russian Economic Development*, *25*(4), 423–430. doi:10.1134/S1075700714040133

Urry, J. (1999). *Mekânları Tüketmek, Çev. Rahmi G. Öğdül*. İstanbul: Ayrıntı Yayınları.

Wallerstein, I. (1997). *Tarihsel Kapitalizm, Çev. Necmiye Alpay*. İstanbul: Metis Yayınları.

WCED. (1987). *Our CommonFuture: Report ofthe World Commission on Environment and Development*. WCED.

Weaver, D. (2001). *Ecotourism*. Milton, Australia: John Wiley & Sons, Ltd.

Weaver, D. (2006). *Sustainable tourism: Theory and practice*. Oxford, UK: Elsevier Butterworth Heinemann.

Wood, M. E. (2002). *Ecotourism: Principles, practices & policies for sustainability*. Paris: UNEP.

Zizek, S. (2013). İdeoloji Hayaleti, Çev. Sibel Kibar, iç. Slavoj Zizek (Ed.), İdeolojiyi Haritalamak, Dipnot Yayınları, Ankara.

Chapter 4
Selection of Renewable Energy Sources for Sustainable Development and an Economic Model Proposal for Countries

Alptekin Ulutaş
Cumhuriyet University, Turkey

Coşkun Karaca
Cumhuriyet University, Turkey

ABSTRACT

Meeting the energy requirements with imported fuels leads to economic and political problems in the countries. Therefore, renewable energy investments continue to grow globally as a sustainable and increasingly economically viable alternative to conventional sources of energy. This study aims to reduce the share of imported fuels in Turkey's electricity generation and to estimate the employment gain to be provided by renewable energy investments to be established instead. Approximately 900,000 jobs are created during the production, construction, operational, and maintenance phases of additional 49,448 MW capacity renewable power plants to be installed. While analyzing, the decision on how much to invest in which renewable resource is determined with respect to multi-criteria decision making (MCDM) model.

INTRODUCTION

Countries have many alternative energy sources to meet their energy demands. Currently, a total of 78.3% of the global energy demand is met by fossil fuels, while 19.2% is met by renewable energy and 2.5% by nuclear energy. Nevertheless, debates about sustainable development over the last 40 years have indicated that fossil fuels with such a high share of final energy consumption are obstacles to the development of countries. At the base of these discussions are the harmful effects of fossil fuels on the environment and human health, as well as the economic and social problems that they result in the countries.

DOI: 10.4018/978-1-5225-5787-6.ch004

The first effect of fossil fuels on the environment and human health are the harmful greenhouse gases that are revealed by the consumption of these fuels. According to the Environment Protection Authority (EPA) data, the share of fossil fuels in greenhouse gas emissions is 79.4% (EESI, 2016). Measurements made by the US Energy Information Administration (EIA) in 2014 validate these data and these measurements show a significant portion of gases, such as the carbon dioxide, methane and nitrogen gas (EIA, 2016) that constitute 97.4% of the greenhouse gas is emitted by the burning of fossil fuels (EWEA, 2008a, pp. 326-327). When it is thought that air pollution has a significant share in global environmental disasters and human deaths, it is clear how dangerous results are caused by consumption of fossil fuels according to these data.

For example, Hurricane Katrina in 2005 in the USA caused 1,836 people to lose their lives and result in US$81 billion in material damage in the country. Additionally, the World Bank data has illustrated that air pollution increases the risk of people catching many fatal diseases. According to recent estimates, about 5.5 million premature deaths worldwide have been caused by air pollution. This data indicates that one out of every 10 premature deaths is owing to air pollution (World Bank, 2016a, p. 22).

The consumption of fossil fuels has negative effects on the environment as well as on the economy. One of these is the problem of foreign trade deficit. If the countries meet their energy demands by import, the security of energy supply run into danger. Moreover, the increases in prices of oil and natural gas causes damage to the production and national output in the importer countries, leading to an increase in foreign trade deficit. The most notable example of this was the oil crisis in October, 1973, and the increase in energy prices in this period led to an increase in production costs, resulted in energy supply inflation and deterioration of macroeconomic balances in many countries.

Another problem arising in fossil fuel importer countries due to the import of energy is the employment problem which creats both economic and social costs on countries. The countries, which export fossil fuel to other nations, take employment opportunity in the steps of this process, such as extraction, processing and relocation of these sources. On the other hand, countries that do not use their own energy resources face a significant opportunity cost. Many studies investigating the relationship between import dependency ratio and unemployment show that this relationship is linear and that imports lead to unemployment (e.g., Stone et al., 2013; De Pinto, 2014; Kostecki, 2014).

Another alternative to meet energy demand is nuclear energy. These plants are preferred by the countries as they have the high energy efficiency. However, the risks of nuclear accidents, nuclear waste of high radioactivity, and the cost of safely storing nuclear energy clearly demonstrate that these plants are not a suitable source of energy for sustainable development. Countries currently desire to realize development model and it is difficult that this model continue with an energy model consisting of fossil fuels and nuclear energy due to the aforementioned reasons.

Because of the above-mentioned challenges, the aim of this study is to propose an economic model to help the development of countries. This model suggests abandoning fossil fuels and substituting renewable energy sources in meeting the energy needs of countries. The additional investments that will be made with such a transformation stimulate the national income of the country and they also solve the unemployment problem.

However, in order to run the model, it is necessary to determine how much to invest in which renewable energy source. As such, there is a need for efficiency analysis for each renewable source taking into account the technical, economic, environmental and social characteristics of renewable sources. Therefore, considering the characteristics of renewable energy resources in the study, the most appropriate renewable resource is ranked for the countries. The selection process of renewable energy sources consists of three steps. In the first step, objective data is analyzed by using criteria importance through intercriteria correlation (CRITIC) method to obtain weights of criteria. Then, complex proportional assessment (COPRAS) method is used to rank renewable energy sources.

In the final step, the effects of the investments, which is made in accordance with the ranking of renewable sources made with respect to COPRAS results, on the national income and employment of the countries are analyzed. The additional contribution to employment and national income was estimated with respect to the Jobs and Economic Development Impact (JEDI) developed by the National Renewable Energy Laboratory (NREL).

THE IMPORTANCE OF RENEWABLE ENERGY INVESTMENTS FOR TURKEY

The overall objective of energy-related policies should be ensuring sufficient, reliable and affordable energy supplies to support economic and social development, while protecting the environment. Since Turkey's energy demand and imports increase daily, producing electricity from renewable may provide huge benefits for the country. Creation of a domestic renewable energy manufacturing industry in Turkey would not only help to create a low-carbon economy and cleaner environment, but also increase the security of energy supply by reducing the dependence on imported oil and gas supplies. Such a policy drive would eventually be expected to improve the balance of payments through exporting the domestically produced renewable energy component overseas and tapping into the expanding global market for renewable energy. An additional benefit of this option would be the creation of new employment within a rising industry (Erdogdu & Karaca, 2014, pp. 82-83).

Turkey is a very vulnerable country in terms of energy as the overwhelming share of Turkey's energy requirement is met by fossil fuels, and 90 per cent of such energy must be imported. Turkey's greenhouse gas emissions were about 115 per cent higher in 2010 compared to 1990 (Figure 1). Thus, renewable energy resources are becoming more important because of increasingly restrictive environmental constraints (Karaca & Erdogdu, 2014, p. 336).

Electricity generated from fossil fuels has major negative impacts on the local environment and human health. By comparison, renewable energies would clearly appear to have a positive environmental impact, resulting from the elimination of carbon dioxide and sulfur releases. Thus, the most important gain of renewable energy utilization is the environmental benefit of displacing fossil fuel usage and the consequent reduction of the adverse environmental impacts caused by fossil fuel consumption (Erdoğdu, 2009, pp. 1367-68).

Renewable energy represents a secure domestic source of energy not subject to price fluctuations and supply uncertainties of imported petroleum and natural gas. Turkey is heavily dependent on imported energy (Erdogdu & Karaca, 2014, p. 61). In 2015, a total of 77% of the total energy supply was met by imports while the rest was domestically produced (MENR, 2016). In 2015 alone, there was a net outflow of US$71.8 billion from Turkey to the outside world due to the country's foreign trade deficit (CBRT, 2016).

Another advantage of the widespread use of renewable energy investments in Turkey is the employment increase effect of these investments. According to data from 2014, Turkey is the 80th country with the worst unemployment rate in the world (217 countries). The unemployment rate in the last 15 years shows that the average of unemployment in Turkey is over 10%. The employment contribution of renewable energy investments is quite high. Because of this feature, renewable energy investments

Figure 1. Greenhouse gas emissions in EEA-32 countries: Change 1990 - 2010
Source: UNFCCC, 2017.

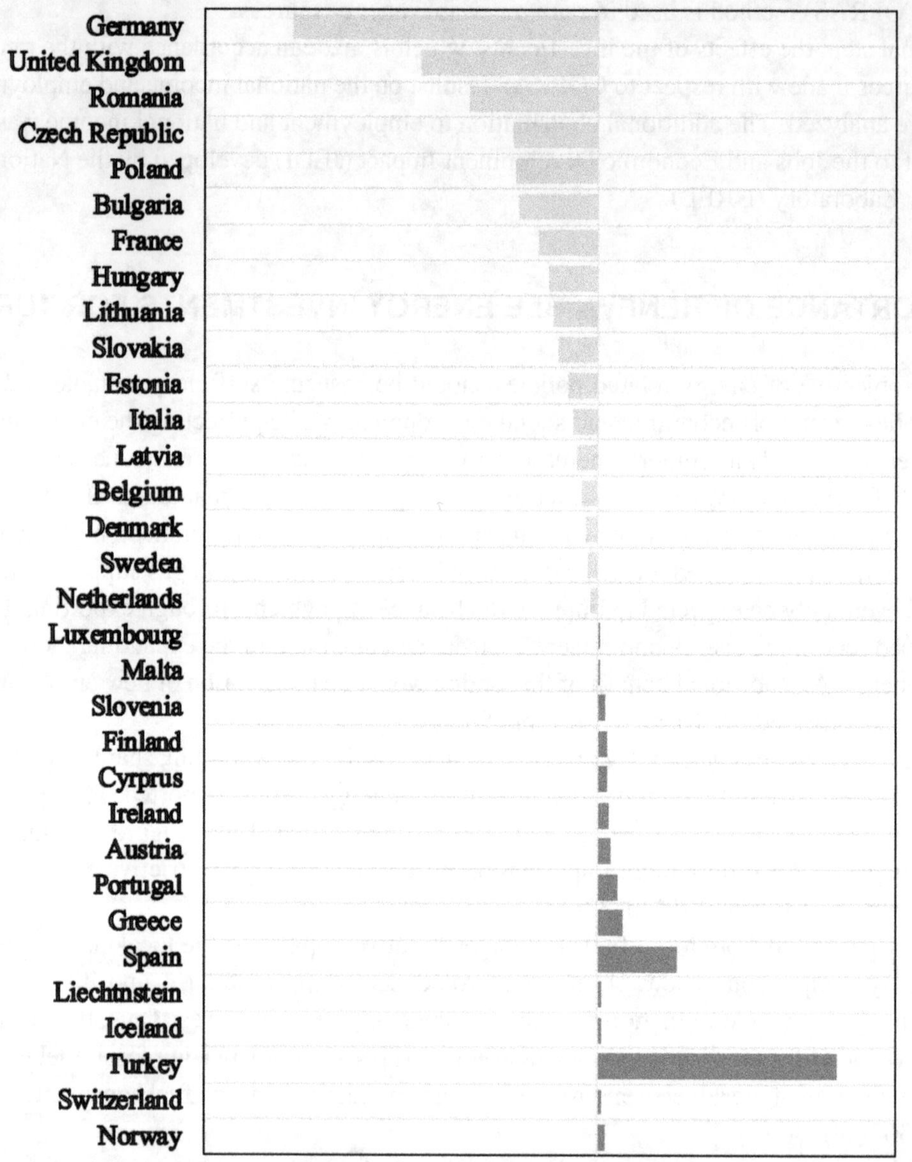

offer the opportunity to find solutions to the unemployment in the country at large. Studies by Pollin et al. (2009) in the US reveal that each US$1 million spent on the energy sector creates 5.2 jobs in oil and natural gas, while this amount is 13.3 in wind, 13.7 in solar and 17.4 in biomass.

The studies by Rutovitz and Harris (2012) also has reached a similar result. As can be seen from Figure 2, In the case of energy production with natural gas, while one person per megawatt is employed, this amount reaches 7.7 jobs in wind onshore and to 6.9 jobs in Solar PV on average. Turkey employed

Figure 2. Potential Jobs per megawatt by technology
Source: Rutovitz and Harris, 2012.

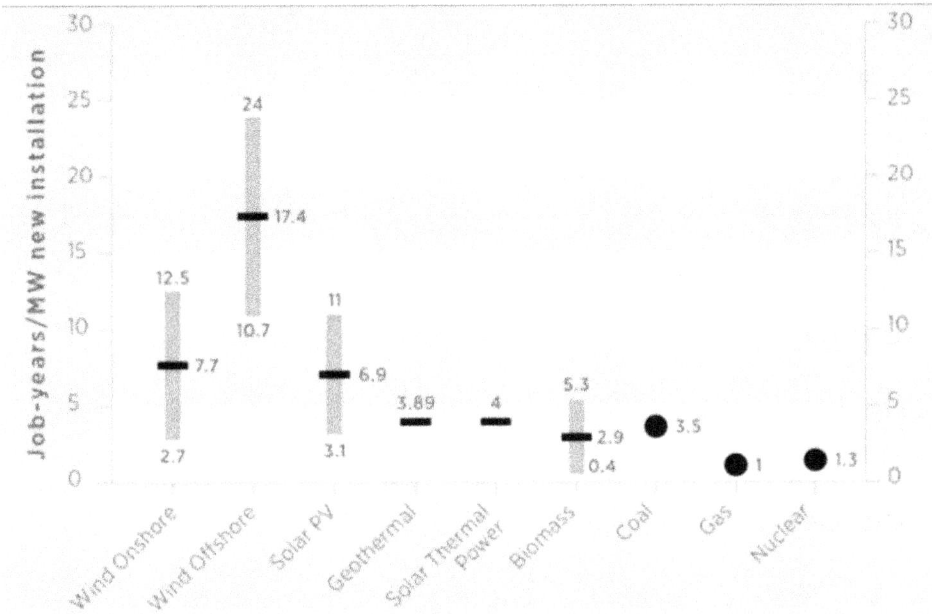

53,000 people in wind power and 16,600 in solar heating and cooling, and 12,700 in PV. Altogether, the number of people working in renewable energy totals about 94,400 (IRENA, 2017).

With the help of its local content requirements, the country is hoping to become a solar and wind manufacturing hub. Winners of a December, 2016 tender for utility-scale PV projects will be required to build panels in Turkey, and a 50% tariff on panel imports was introduced in July, 2016. In the wind sector, generators are awarded preferential feed-in tariff rates that rise with the share of local content (Hirtenstein & Ant, 2016).

CRITERIA IN THE ANALYSIS

Main Criteria Used in Analysis

Four main criteria and twenty-three sub-criteria will be used for analysis in the selection of renewable energy resources for Turkey. The main criteria considered in the analysis are technical criteria, economic criteria, environmental criteria and social criteria.

Technical Criteria

Technical criteria involving technical attributes for renewable energy sources and investments include sub-criteria, such as energy efficiency, economic potential and installed power capacity. Table 1 indicates sub-criteria of technical criteria, which are used in MCDM analysis.

Table 1. Technical criteria

	Wind	Solar	Hydro	Biomass	Geothermal
Energy efficiency [a]	2,58	0,78	2,49	4,97	5,48
Economic potential (GW/year)[b]	98	91	130	0,4	4
Operation year (year)[c]	20	30	80	30	25
Global installed power capacity (%)[d]	6,1	2,9	17,5	1,5	0,2
Capacity factor (%)[c]	30	27,4	37,1	85	90

Source: [a]TEİAŞ, 2016; [b]Görez and Alkan 2005; [c] NETL, 2013; [d] REN21, 2015.

Economic Criteria

Efficiency of renewable energy investments with respect to cost are measured by means of considering economic criteria. Table 2 demonstrates the sub-criteria of economic criteria.

Environmental Criteria

The environmental criteria consisting of sub-criteria indicate that renewable energy resources used in energy generation how much damages the environment and human health. Table 3 indicates environmental criteria.

Social Criteria

Social criteria are criteria indicating for how the investment in renewable energy sources impacts society. Table 4 shows the sub-criteria of social criteria.

METHODOLOGY

In this study, two MCDM methods (CRITIC and COPRAS) will be used to evaluate the performance of renewable energy alternatives. The CRITIC method will be used to determine the weights of criteria and the COPRAS method will be used to rank renewable energy alternatives with respect to their performance scores.

Table 2. Economic criteria

	Wind	Solar	Hydro	Biomass	Geothermal
Investment cost ($/kW)[a]	1920	4693	6300	230	3000
Fixed operation and maintenance cost ($/MW-year)[a]	24050	56780	4120	86600	164640
Electricity generation cost ($/kW-hour)[b]	0,07	0,125	0,08	0,1	0,05
LCOE electricity generation cost ($/MWs)[c]	73,6	125,3	83,5	100,5	47,8
Payoff period (year)[d]	0,9	1,85	11,8	1,92	5,7

Source: [a]NETL, 2013; [b]EİA, 2016 adapted from [c]US Energy Information Administration, 2015; [d]Kenny, Law and Pearce, 2010.

Table 3. Environmental criteria

	Wind	Solar	Hydro	Biomass	Geothermal
NO_x emission (g/MWs)[a]	26,80	94,40	17,30	959,00	12,50
CO_2 emission (gCO_2/kWs)[b]	11	41	24	230	38
CO emission (g/MWs)[a]	38,1	607	12,2	1490	25,1
SO_2 emission (g/MWs)[a]	29,9	59,2	11,2	439	3,11
Greenhouse gas emission (g/MWs)[a]	0,000168	0,00101	0,0000526	0,0345	0,0000386
Airborne particles emission (g/MWs)[a]	0,0168	0,0352	0,00527	0,325	0,00132
Lead (Pb) (g/MWs)[a]	0,000000783	0,0000173	0,000000483	0,00000181	0,00000134
Ammoniac (NH_3) (g/MWs)[a]	0,000564	0,0000664	0,00000255	0,000224	0,453
Compounds (except Methane) (g/MWs)[a]	7,24	37,6	0,597	40,5	0,442
Area Requirement m^2/kWs[c]	0,000814	0,001894	0,000189	0,00047	0,000404

Source: [a]NETL, 2013; [b]IPCC, 2014; [c]Kayakutlu and Ercan, 2015.

Table 4. Social criteria

	Wind	Solar	Hydro	Biomass	Geothermal
External costs [a]	0,19	0,6	0,54	2,01	0,2
Employment in the processes of Manufacturing-construction-installation (per MW) [b]	8,6	17,9	7,5	7,7	10,7
Employment in the processes of operation-maintenance (per MW) [b]	0,2	0,3	0,3	5,51	0,4

Source: [a]Stein, 2013, [b]Rutovitz, and Harris, 2012; Rutovitz, 2010.

CRITIC Method

The CRITIC method, which was developed by Diakoulaki et al. (1995), is generally used to obtain objective weights of criteria. This method does not need opinions of any decision-makers to obtain criteria weights and it only requires decision matrix. This enables researchers not to waste time for collecting data from decision makers.

CRITIC method can be summarized as (Madić & Radovanović, 2015):

Step 1-1: Equation 1 indicate that a decision matrix (B) involves n columns (criteria) and m rows (renewable energy alternatives).

$$B = \left[x_{ij}\right]_{m \times n} = \begin{bmatrix} x_{11} & x_{12} & \cdots & x_{1n} \\ x_{21} & x_{22} & \cdots & x_{2n} \\ \vdots & \vdots & \vdots & \vdots \\ x_{m1} & x_{m2} & \cdots & x_{mn} \end{bmatrix} \tag{1}$$

In equation 1, x_{ij} sows the performance of i th renewable energy alternative on j th criterion.

Step 1-2: The values in the decision matrix is normalized by equations 2 and 3. Beneficial criteria in the decision matrix are normalized by using equation 2 and non-beneficial criteria are normalized by using equation 3. In equations 2 and 3, r_{ij} demonstrates the normalized value of x_{ij}.

$$r_{ij} = \frac{x_{ij} - x_j^{min}}{x_j^{max} - x_j^{min}} \tag{2}$$

$$r_{ij} = \frac{x_j^{max} - x_{ij}}{x_j^{max} - x_j^{min}} \tag{3}$$

Step 1-3: Both standard deviation of criterion and its correlation between other criteria is calculated to obtain objective criteria weights. Equation 4 indicates the obtaining of criteria weights.

$$w_j = \frac{C_j}{\sum_{o=1}^{n} C_o}$$

$$j = 1, 2, \ldots n \tag{4}$$

In equation 4, w_j. indicates weight of j th criterion and C_j denotes quantity of information in j th criterion. This value can be calculated as:

$$C_j = \sigma_j \sum_{o=1}^{n} (1 - t_{jo})$$

$$j = 1, 2, \ldots n \tag{5}$$

In equation 5, σ_j demonstrates standard deviation of j th criterion and t_{jo} indicates correlation coefficient between j th criterion and o th criterion.

COPRAS Method

COPRAS method developed by Zavadskas and Kaklauskas (1996) is used to determine the performance of energy alternatives. The COPRAS method can be summarized as six steps.

Step 2-1: The first step of COPRAS is to construct the decision matrix. The decision matrix, which is considered in COPRAS, is indicated in equation 1. All values in the decision matrix are normalized by following equation.

$$x_{ij}^{*} = \frac{x_{ij}}{\sum_{i=1}^{m} x_{ij}}$$

$$j = 1,2,\ldots.n \tag{6}$$

In equation 6, x_{ij}^{*} denotes the normalized value of x_{ij}.

Step 2-2: In step 2, the normalized values are multiplied by thee weights of criteria (obtained in CRITIC method).

$$x_{ij}^{'} = x_{ij}^{*} \times w_{j}$$

$$j = 1,2,\ldots.n \tag{7}$$

In equation 7, $x_{ij}^{'}$ indicates the weighted normalized value.

Step 2-3: In step 3, beneficial and non-beneficial criteria are summed among themselves. Beneficial criteria are summed by using equation 8, on the other hand; non-beneficial criteria are summed by using equation 9.

$$S_{i}^{+} = \sum_{j=1}^{o} x_{ij}^{'} \text{ for beneficial criteria} \tag{8}$$

$$S_{i}^{-} = \sum_{j=o+1}^{n} x_{ij}^{'} \text{ for non-beneficial criteria} \tag{9}$$

Step 2-4: After step 3, the relative importance (Q_i) of each renewable energy alternative can be calculated by using the following equation:

$$Q_i = S_i^+ + \frac{\sum_{i=1}^{m} S_i^-}{(S_i^- * \sum_{i=1}^{m} \frac{1}{S_i^-})} \tag{10}$$

Step 2-5: After determining the relative importance (Q_i) of each alternative, total performance score can be obtained by the following equation:

$$T_i = \left(\frac{Q_i}{Q_{max}}\right) \tag{11}$$

Step 2-6: The total performance score of each alternative is divided by the total performance score of all the alternatives (Equation 12), therefore; share of energy alternatives in the employment (T_i^*) is calculated.

$$T_i^* = \frac{T_i}{\sum_{i=1}^{m} T_i} \tag{12}$$

APPLICATION

When starting the analysis for the selection of renewable energy resources, criteria should be divided into two types of criteria (beneficial and non-beneficial). Table 5 demonstrates beneficial and non-beneficial criteria.

After dividing into beneficial and non-beneficial criteria, the values of criteria showed in Table 1,2,3 and 4 are used in constructing decision matrix, which is used in calculations in the CRITIC and COPRAS methods. Table 6 indicates the criteria weights obtained from the CRITIC method.

These weights are transferred to COPRAS method. The results of the COPRAS method are indicated in Table 7.

According to the results of the COPRAS method, renewable energy sources are ranked as Wind >Hydro>Geothermal>Solar>Biomass with respect to their performance. Therefore, Wind energy is determined as the best renewable energy resource for Turkey. The last column in the table will be used in analysis of employment for Turkey.

Table 5. Beneficial and non-beneficial criteria

Main Criteria	Sub-criteria	Beneficial/Non-beneficial
Technical	Energy efficiency (EE)	Beneficial
	Economic potential (EP)	Beneficial
	Operation year (OY)	Beneficial
	Global installed power capacity (GC)	Beneficial
	Capacity factor (CF)	Beneficial
Economic	Investment cost (IC)	Non-beneficial
	Fixed operation and maintenance cost (FOMC)	Non-beneficial
	Electricity generation cost (EGC)	Non-beneficial
	LCOE electricity generation cost (LCOE)	Non-beneficial
	Payoff period (PP)	Non-beneficial
Environmental	NOx emission (NOE)	Non-beneficial
	CO2 emission (CO2E)	Non-beneficial
	CO emission (COE)	Non-beneficial
	SO2 emission (SO2E)	Non-beneficial
	Greenhouse gas emission (GGE)	Non-beneficial
	Airborne particles emission (APE)	Non-beneficial
	Lead (Pb) (L)	Non-beneficial
	Ammonia (NH_3) (AC)	Non-beneficial
	Compounds (except Methane)(C)	Non-beneficial
	Area Requirement (AR)	Non-beneficial
Social	External costs (EC)	Non-beneficial
	Employment in the processes of manufacturing-construction-installation (EMCI)	Beneficial
	Employment in the processes of operation-maintenance (EOM)	Beneficial

Table 6. Results of the CRITIC method

Criteria	EE	EP	OY	GC	CF	EMCI	EOM	EC	IC	FOMC	EGC	LCOE
w_j.	049	0,044	0,042	0,038	0,063	0,054	0,064	0,034	0,053	0,042	0,033	0,033
Criteria	PP	NOE	CO2E	COE	SO2E	GGE	APE	L	AC	C	AR	Sum
w_j.	033	0,057	0,037	0,035	0,034	0,036	0,038	0,036	0,042	0,057	0,039	1

Table 7. The Results of COPRAS method

Energy Alternatives	S_i^+.	S_i^-.	Q_i.	T_i.	T_i^*.
Wind	0,05164	0,04413	0,31989	1	
Solar	0,05316	0,14749	0,13342	0,41708	0,13355
Hydro	0,08617	0,07698	0,23995	0,7501	0,24019
Biomass	0,10417	0,25295	0,15097	0,47194	0,15112
Geothermal	0,05886	0,12344	0,15476	0,48379	0,15492

AN EMPLOYMENT ANALYSIS FOR TURKEY'S ENERGY POLICY

Generating electricity from renewable energy may provide huge benefits. Renewable energy investments contribute the development of economic activities in countries. The advancement in the technologies of power plants contribute to local and national economy by providing the formation of new manufacturing and service sector within local, national and international levels. In particular, using domestic components such as inverter, rotor, blade, generator and so on in making renewable energy investment would mean that Turkey gradually gains international competitiveness in the renewable energy industry (Erdogdu & Karaca, 2016, p. 62).

According to Perloff (1957), the growth rate of local industries develops much more than the national growth rate which enables the former to make these investments as the locomotives of national economy by achieving scale economy in renewable energy technologies. In this respect, production costs decrease by means of benefiting from scale economies and external economy advantages occur in labor market after all the companies providing the production with procurement concentration on determined areas (Krugman, 1990, p. 4).

Numerous studies demonstrated that countries investing in renewable energy tends to reach high level of employment. Some of the countries using this opportunity can be seen in Table 8. By making investments in renewable energies, a total of 8.1 million people could be employed worldwide in 2015.

As seen in Table 8, renewable energy investments have very high business creation capacities. By means of only solar energy investments (PV panel and heating), a total of 3.7 million people worldwide benefit from the advantage of employment. In bioenergy, this amount is about 2.9 million. China is the country that creates the most employment with renewable energy investments. There are approximately 3.5 million people in the sector in this country. However, almost 1 million employees work in the sector in the EU and Brazil.

Method

Employment opportunities appear in the processes such as, the installation of power plants, their operation and maintenance processes. Employment in these processes is divided into direct, indirect and induced employment (Erdogdu & Karaca, 2016, p. 64). In this section, such employment to be provided by renewable energy investments in Turkey will be estimated. Calculations of these estimations will be made with the JEDI (Jobs and Economic Development Impact) method developed by the National Renewable Energy Laboratory (NREL) in the US.

Table 8. Employment in the Renewable Energy Sector (year 2015, thousand)

	World	China	Brazil	USA	India	Japan	Bangladesh	European Union		
								Germany	France	Other EU Countries
Biomass	**822**	241	n.a.	152	58	n.a.	n.a.	49	48	214
Biofuel	**1,678**	71	821	277	35	3	n.a.	23	35	47
Biogas	**382**	209	n.a.		85	n.a.	9	48	4	14
Geothermal	**160**	n.a.	n.a.	35	n.a.	2	n.a.	17	31	55
Hidro	**204**	100	12	8	12	n.a.	5	12	4	31
Solar (panel)	**2,772**	1,652	4	194	103	377	127	38	21	84
Solar (heating)	**939**	743	41	10	75	0.7	n.a.	10	6	19
Wind	**1,081**	507	41	88	48	5	0.1	149	20	162
Total	**8,079**	**3,523**	**918**	**769**	**416**	**388**	**141**	**355**	**170**	**644**

Source: IRENA (2016, p. 17).

The JEDI) models are user-friendly tools estimating the economic impacts of constructing and operating power generation at the local and state levels. JEDI constructs profiles of investments during different phases of the project cycle, and it allows demonstration of employment during construction and operation phases. This enables to differentiate between local and non-local job-creation activities. Local spending results from using local labor, such as concrete pouring jobs, services, which are engineering, legal or design, materials and other components. The user can replace these default values with project-specific information, such as costs and expenditures, financing, taxes, and local share of spending (NREL, 2016).

Job estimates are expressed as Full-Time Employment (FTE)s, or job-years, as well as average annual jobs per year. One FTE job (or job-year) is full-time employment for one person for the duration of a year. Hence, three FTEs could be made up either one full-time job for three years or three full-time jobs for one year. Earnings are the total payroll costs, including wages, salary compensation, and benefits paid to labors. Economic output is the sum of all economic activities (value of production for all industry sectors) resulting from the investments in the renewable energy generation facilities (NREL, 2016).

Data Set

Electricity generation and installed power size of Turkey in March, 2017 are seen in Table 9. Accordingly, almost 67 percent of the power generation is covered by fossil fuels, while 33 percent of the power generation is provided by renewable energy sources.

As shown in Table 9, a total of 12.195.679 MW of total production is met by imported natural gas and lignite. The main focus of the study is that the electricity demand is met with domestic resources instead of imported resources. To realize this policy, renewable energy investment should be made to the extent that it meets the electricity generated by the imported resources. However, to achieve the maximum amount of employment to be provided from investments, it is necessary to use domestic resources in all processes. This assumption was accepted in the next section of the employment analysis.

Table 9. Electricity generation and installed power size of Turkey in March, 2017

	Installed Power (MW)	Contribution (%)	Power Generation (MWh)	Contribution (%)
FOSSIL SHARE	43.893	56,21%	15.994.220	67,27%
Natural Gas	25.340	32,45%	8.206.468	34,51%
Imported Coal	7.494	9,60%	3.989.211	16,78%
Lignite, Anthracite	9.899	12,68%	3.495.813	14,70%
Asphaltites, Fuel Oil	1.160	1,49%	302.728	1,27%
RENEWABLE	34.192	43,79%	7.782.470	32,73%
Hydro (Stream, dam)	26.860	34,40%	5.706.609	24,00%
Wind	5.974	7,65%	1.374.019	5,78%
Geothermal	851	1,09%	485.634	2,04%
Biomass	494	0,63%	214.179	0,90%
Solar PV	13	0,02%	2.029	0,01%
TOTAL	78.085	100,00%	23.776.690	100,00%

Source: EMRB, 2017.

Another data required for analysis is the amount of employment to be provided by renewable energy investments. Table 10 indicates the amount of employment provided by renewable energy investments. If it can be considered, the installed power capacity of each renewable energy in Table 10 is different from each other. The reason for this is that the employment calculations done by NREL are based on investments in different regions of the United States. Hence, it is possible to reach realistic employment data.

As seen in the table, in a hydroelectric power plant with 100 MW installed power, a total of 1,681 people to be get direct employment, while in the same size solar power plant this amount drops to 1,065 in the production and construction phase. In the Operation and Maintenance phase, there is a sharp decline in the number of employees together with the decrease in workload.

Table 10. Number of employment by reference capacity size

		The Phase of Production and Construction			The Phase of Operational and Maintenance (Annual)		
	Installed Capacity (MW)	Direct	Indirect	Induced	Direct	Indirect	Induced
Wind	20	108	164	68	4	1	1
Hydro (Dam)	100	1.681	391	542	13	27	9
Geothermal	12	71	47	22	8	2	3
Biomass	50	155	42	62	25	94	35
Solar PV	100	1.065	690	514	45	29	11

Source: NREL, JEDI, 2016.

Analysis: Additional Employment Estimates

The generation of electricity in Turkey with imported resources leads to significant opportunity cost in employment. Therefore, in the analysis, to meet this need, the impact on the employment of domestic investments to be made to renewable energy sources will be estimated.

As seen in Table 11, natural gas and coal power plants with an installed power of 32,834 MW are desired to be removed. It is suggested to use domestic and renewable resources instead of this electricity generation made with imported resources. However, it is noted that more installed power (49,448 MW) is needed to generate electricity equivalent to renewable energy sources (12,195,679 MWh). The reason for this is that some of the renewable energy sources have a discrete generation structure. The MCDM results on the table indicate how much each renewable energy source will have in total electricity generation in the proposed new strategy.

Another point to note in the table is the installed capacity of geothermal energy. According to MCDM results, the installed power capacity of geothermal energy is estimated as 5,087 MW. Nevertheless, the geothermal capacity for electricity generation in Turkey is 650 MW. Thus, an installed capacity of 5,087 MW, which is not possible for Turkey, was allocated to other renewable sources with respect to the MCDM results.

The installed capacity of the power plants is a significant factor affecting the amount of employment. For instance, the number of people to be employed in a power plant with a capacity of 100 MW and it with a capacity of 25 MW, which will be installed in four different regions, will demonstrate variation. In this study, an employment analysis was carried out based on the plant size, which is determined by NREL. In Table 12, the last column shows the number of planned established power plants.

Based on the installed capacity determined by NREL, it is estimated that a total of 1,368 power plants will be established in Turkey. Estimated number of employment, which are obtained through the number of plants to be established and their installed capacity, are shown in Table 13.

According to the results of the analysis, while it is provided 446,320 direct job opportunities during the production and construction phase by using domestic resources instead of imported resources in Turkey's electricity generation, this amount is realized as 13,936 per year in the phase of operational and

Table 11. The information on recommended policy

		MCDM Results (AfterGeo)	Installed Capacity (AfterGeo-MW)	Electricity generation per MW	Generation (MWh)
Removed	Natural Gas		25,340	324	8,206,468
	Imported Coal		7,494	532	3,989,211
	Total		**32,834**		**12,195,679**
Recommended	Wind	37%	18,490	230	4,252,569
	Hydro (Dam)	28%	13,869	186	2,573,965
	Geothermal	1%	650	571	371,027
	Biomass	18%	8,727	434	3,785,297
	Solar PV	16%	7,712	157	1,212,822
	Total	**100%**	**49,448**		**12,195,679**

Table 12. The number of planned power plants

	Installed Capacity (MW)	Reference Plant Size (MW)	Number of Planned Power Plants (Unit)
Wind	18,490	20	925
Hydro (Dam)	13,869	100	139
Geothermal	(5,087) 650	12	53
Biomass	8,727	50	175
Solar PV	7,712	100	77
Total	**49,448**		**1,368**

Table 13. Estimated employment rate to be provided by renewable energy investments in Turkey

			The Phase of Production and Construction			The Phase of Operational and Maintenance (Annual)		
	Installed Capacity (MW)	**Number of Plant**	**Direct**	**Indirect**	**Induced**	**Direct**	**Indirect**	**Induced**
Wind	20	925	100,217	151,249	62,959	3,891	1,365	661
Hydro (Dam)	100	139	233,146	54,230	75,173	1,819	3,733	1,244
Geothermal	12	53	3,775	2,499	1,170	425	106	159
Biomass	50	175	27,053	7,331	10,821	4,363	16,406	6,109
Solar PV	100	77	82,130	53,211	39,638	3,437	2,204	876
Total		**1,368**	**446,320**	**268,519**	**189,761**	**13,936**	**23,815**	**9,048**
Final Total				**904,600**			**46,799**	

maintenance. Indirect and induced jobs are estimated to be 458,280 during the production and construction phase and 32,863 during the operational and maintenance phase.

In all stages of production and construction, the amount of employment is estimated as 904,600. In other words, about 900,000 people are employed in the production of the parts to be used for investment and in the installation of the power plant. According to June, 2017 unemployment figures, there are 3 million 251 unemployed in Turkey. According to this data, 25% of the unemployment will be resolved by implementing of the proposed policy.

CONCLUSION

There is growing interest by governments to renewable energy investments due to the positive social and economic impacts of them. Although the effects of renewable energy investment on the employment, in particular, are increasingly gaining prominence in the global renewable energy debate, specific analytical studies and empirical evidence on this important subject remain relatively limited. Thus, this study highlights the importance of an enabling policy framework to realize the full potential for job creation within the sector and analyses the contribution of renewable energy investments to employment.

The results of the analysis demonstrate that Turkey with renewable energy investments will significantly solve the unemployment problem. According to the results of the analysis, investments in renewable energy systems are estimated to provide approximately 900,000 jobs during the production and construction phase. Additionally, annually approximately 46,000 jobs are estimated to ensue in the phase of the operation and maintenance of the power plant. These estimated figures include indirect and induced jobs providing input to sector as well as direct employees in the sector.

Thus, the appropriate mix of policies needs to be in place to ensure that value creation is maximized in Turkey. Planning for adequate skills is essential to support a rapidly growing renewable energy sector. The gap of this critical skill is already visible in many markets, where the education and training infrastructure is unable to cater to the labor demand of the sector in Turkey. Additionally, governments should support such investments while considering their external benefits. When economic and production costs are at reasonable level, the demand for imported resources will decrease. Therefore, it is expected that the employment and current account deficit of the country will be largely resolved, while the air pollution caused by fossil fuels will decrease.

REFERENCES

CBRT. (2016). *Electronic Data Distribution System, General Statistics, Central Bank of the Turkish Republic*. Retrieved on November 24, 2017, from: http://evds.tcmb.gov.tr/

De Pinto, M. (2014, January). International Trade and Unemployment – the Worker-selection Effect. *Review of International Economics*. Retrieve on September 2, 2016, from: http://ideas.repec.org/p/mar/magkse/201127.html

Diakoulaki, D., Mavrotas, G., & Papayannakis, L. (1995). Determining objective weights in multiple criteria problems: The critic method. *Computers & Operations Research*, *22*(7), 763–770. doi:10.1016/0305-0548(94)00059-H

Duygu, A. E. (2004). AB'nin enerji bağimsizliği ve sürdürülebilir kalkinma politikalarinda biyokütle enerjisinin yeri: Üye, aday ülkelerdeki araştirmalar ve uygulamalar. *Türkiye IV: Enerji Sempozyumu*, 451-480.

EESI. (2016). *Fossil Fuels*. Retrieved on January 10, 2017, from: http://www.eesi.org/topics/fossil-fuels/description

EİA. (2016). *What are greenhouse gases and how do they affect the climate*? Retrieved on January 10, 2017, from: https://www.eia.gov/tools/faqs/faq.cfm?id=81&t=11

EMRB. (2017). *Electricity Market Sector Report*. Energy Market Regulatory Board, Ankara, Turkey. Retrieved on June 2, 2017, from: http://www.epdk.org.tr/TR/Dokumanlar/Elektrik/YayinlarRaporlar/AylikSektor

Erdoğdu, E. (2009). On the wind energy in Turkey. *Renewable & Sustainable Energy Reviews*, *13*(6-7), 1361–1371. doi:10.1016/j.rser.2008.09.003

Erdoğdu, M., & Karaca, C. (2016). An Industrial Policy Recommendation for Raising Solar Energy Investments. In *Turkey and Its Possible Employment Effect", in Social and Economic Perspectives on Sustainability* (pp. 51–70). London: IJOPEC Publication.

EWEA. (2008a). Wind Energy Facts. *Environmental Issues*, 307-411. Retrieved on January 10, 2017, from: http://www.wind-energy-the-facts.org/images/chapter5.pdf

Görez, T., & Alkan, A. (2005). *Türkiye'nin Yenilenebilir Enerji Kaynakları ve Hidroelektrik Enerji Potansiyeli, III*. Mersin: Yenilenebilir Enerji Kaynakları Sempozyumu.

IPCC. (2014). *IPCC Working Group III-Mitigation of Climate Change, Annex III: Technology-Specific Cost and Performance Parameters*. Retrieved on May 9, 2017, from: https://www.ipcc.ch/pdf/assessment-report/ar5/wg3/ipcc_wg3_ar5_annex-iii.pdf

IRENA. (2016). *Renewable Energy and Jobs Annual Review 2016*. International Renewable Energy Agency. Retrieved on October 1, 2016 from: http://www.irena.org/DocumentDownloads/Publications/IRENA_RE_Jobs_Annual_Review_2016.pdf

IRENA. (2017). *Renewable Energy and Jobs Annual Review 2016*. International Renewable Energy Agency. Retrieved on November 21, 2017 from: http://www.irena.org/-/media/Files/IRENA/Agency/Publication/2017/May/IRENA_RE_Jobs_Annual_Review_2017.ashx

Karaca, C., & Erdoğdu, M. M. (2014). Sustainable Development and Turkey's Biomass Energy Potential. *Global Climate Change, Environment and Energy: Global Challenges and Opportunities to Global Stability*, 133.

Kayakutlu, G., & Ercan, S. (2015). Regional Energy Portfolio Construction: Case Studies in Turkey. In *Sustainable Future Energy Technology and Supply Chains* (pp. 107-126). Springer International Publishing.

Kenny, R., Law, C., & Pearce, J. M. (2010). Towards Real Energy Economics: Energy Policy Driven by Life-Cycle Carbon Emission. *Energy Policy*, *38*(4), 1969–1978. doi:10.1016/j.enpol.2009.11.078

Kostecki, M. (2014). International Trade and Unemployment: On the Redistribution of Trade Gains When Firms Matter by Marco de Pinto Berlin, Heidelberg: Physica-Verlag (Springer), 2012. *World Trade Review*, *13*(03), 589–591. doi:10.1017/S1474745614000172

Krugman, P. (1990). *Increasing returns and economic geography (No. w3275)*. Washington, DC: National Bureau of Economic Research. doi:10.3386/w3275

Madić, M., & Radovanović, M. (2015). Ranking Of Some Most Commonly Used Non-Traditional Machining Processes Usıng Rov And Critic Methods. *Upb Sci. Bull., Series D*, *77*(2), 193–204.

MENR. (2016). *Statistics, Balance Sheets, General Directorate of Energy Affairs*. Retrieved on November 24, 2017 from: http://www.eigm.gov.tr/tr-TR/Denge-Tablolari/Denge-Tablolari

NETL. (2013). *Power Generation Technology Comparison from a Life Cycle Perspective*. National Energy Technology Laboratory, US Department of Energy, Pittsburgh, PA. Retrieved on November 11, 2015, from: https://www.netl.doe.gov/File%20Library/Research/Energy%20Analysis/Life%20Cycle%20Analysis/Technology-Assessment-Compilation-Report.pdf

NREL. (2016). *The Jobs and Economic Development Impact (JEDI) models*. National Renewable Energy Laboratory. Retrieved on 01 October 2016, from: http://www.nrel.gov/analysis/jedi/

Perloff, H. S. (1957). Interrelations of state income and industrial structure. *The Review of Economics and Statistics*, *39*(2), 162–171. doi:10.2307/1928533

Pollin, R., Heintz, J., & Garrett-Peltier, H. (2009). *The Economic Benefits of Investing in Clean Energy: How the economic stimulus program and new legislation can boost US economic growth and employment*. Political Economy Research Institute, University of Massachusetts at Amherst.

REN21. (2016). *Renewables 2016 Global Status Report*. Renewable Energy Policy Networks for the 21st Century. Retrieved on August 4, 2017, from: http://www.ren21.net/status-of-renewables/global-status-report/

Rutovitz, J. (2010). *South African Energy Sector Jobs to 2030", Greenpeace Africa by the Institute for Sustainable Futures. University of Technology*. Sydney: Greenpeace Africa, Johannesburg.

Rutovitz, J., & Harris, S. (2012). *Calculating Global Energy Sector Jobs: 2012 Methodology. Prepared for Greenpeace International by the Institute for Sustainable Futures*. Sydney: University of Technology.

Stein, E. W. (2013). A Comprehensive Multi-Criteria Model to Rank Electric Energy Production Technologies. *Renewable & Sustainable Energy Reviews*, *22*, 640–654. doi:10.1016/j.rser.2013.02.001

Stone, S., Sourdin, P., & Legendre, C. (2013). *Trade and Labour Market Adjustment*. OECD Trade Policy Papers, No. 143. Paris: OECD Publishing. 10.1787/5k4c6spvddwj-en

TEİAŞ. (2016). *Türkiye 2015 Yılı Elektrik Üretim-İletim İstatistikleri. Türkiye Elektrik İletim A.Ş. Genel Müdürlüğü Planlama ve Stratejik Yönetim Dairesi Başkanliği Üretim Planlama ve İstatistik Müdürlüğü, Ankara*. Retrieved from http://www.teias.gov.tr/T%C3% BcrkiyeElektrik%C4%B0statistikleri/istatistik2015/istatistik2015.htm

UNFCCC. (2017). *GHG Inventories National Communications. United Nations on Climate Change*. Retrieved on January 10, 2017, from: http://unfccc.int/documentation/documents/advanced_search/items/6911.php?priref=600003580#beg

World Bank. (2016a). The Cost of Air Pollution. *World Bank Group and IHME*. Retrieved on January 10, 2017, from: http://documents.worldbank.org/curated/en/781521473177013155/pdf/108141-REVISED-Cost-of-PollutionWebCORRECTEDfile.pdf

Zavadskas, E. K., & Kaklauskas, A. (1996). Determination of an efficient contractor by using the new method of multicriteria assessment. In *International Symposium for "The Organization and Management of Construction". Shaping Theory and Practice* (*Vol. 2*, pp. 94-104). Academic Press.

Chapter 5
Inequality and Rural Poverty:
Innovative Agricultural Practices for Sustainable and Social Development in Kenya

Gladys Thuita
Riara University, Kenya

Matilda Ouma
Ministry of Agriculture, Livestock, and Fisheries, Kenya

ABSTRACT

The main purpose of this chapter was to establish the effect of innovative agricultural practices on reduction of inequality and rural poverty among sorghum farmers in Homabay County, Kenya. A multistage stratified sampling technique was used to randomly select 120 smallholder sorghum farmers. The study found that use of innovative agricultural practices has an impact on agricultural produce and, therefore, on reduction of inequality and rural poverty among farmers in Homabay County. The study thus concluded that sorghum farming has drastically reduced inequality and rural poverty in the county. The study recommends that the government should provide more support in the application of innovative agricultural practices to assist farmers have diversified portfolio of crops that generate more income to address the issue of inequality and rural poverty in Homabay County. Lastly, the research recommends further research in other innovative agricultural practices such as livestock rearing and maize growing to combat inequality and rural poverty in Homabay County.

INTRODUCTION

Inequality and poverty are recurring issues of discussion in both developing and developed countries. Kenya as a developing country is not exceptional with studies highlighting inequality and rural poverty as a rampant cause of low economic growth (The World Bank, 2008; Kenya National Bureau of Statistics, 2013). Inequality and poverty are interlinked and have an adverse effect on the economic growth of a country. In a nutshell, inequality produces poverty and affects growth and, in turn, growth counters

DOI: 10.4018/978-1-5225-5787-6.ch005

poverty (Naschold, 2015). According to the United Nations (2015) report, inequality is defined as the state of being unequal economically based either on income, rights, status, and opportunities. On the other hand, poverty is the state of human being denied choice and opportunities for human development such as fulfilling life, education, reasonable standard of living, freedom, dignity, health, and participation in the community (Gordon, 2006).

While inequality can be linked to income earned, poverty is associated with lack of access to usage of preventive services. In Nyanza, HIV/AIDS coupled with malaria and other water-borne related diseases have and continue to pose a major challenge to both infected and affected population, thus increasing the rate of poverty (The World Bank, 2008). Poor and unevenly distributed development in Kenya has been cited to contribute to the high inequality. Inequality is prevalent on those without land, employable skills and capital (Wambugu & Munga, 2009). The death of the young and active generation as a result of HIV/AIDS, leaving behind orphans who rely on old and weak grandparents also contributes to poverty. In many situations the old and weak grandparents seek assistance from the able extended families and thus the poverty cycle becomes prevalent among such families.

The significant rise in economic growth in Kenya between 2003-2006 was expected to reduce poverty although this was not the case as the inequality levels still remained high (Wambugu & Munga, 2009). Approximately 80% of the total population in Kenya lives in the rural area with recent statistics showing that the rural population has migrated to urban centres to search for white collar jobs. The majority of population living in the rural area are said to be living in poverty with most unemployed as a result of reduced production from the climate changes (The World Bank, 2008). Over 80% of Kenyan land is classified as arid and semi-arid with only 20% classified as land for productive agriculture on the basis of rainfall received. Majority of the rural population work on the family owned agricultural land without pay (Naschold, 2002). The land in Kenya is unevenly distributed in terms of size, productivity and population. Land fragmentation is becoming a common phenomenon as a result of the ever increasing population leaving less and less land for cultivation. On the other hand, in arid and semi-arid areas, production is either moderate or low and sparsely populated.

In Vision 2030, the government of Kenya intends to raise the income earned from agriculture through the use of innovative and modern agriculture. The smallholder farmers will have improved yields from the less acreage cultivated. In addition, the farm products will be commercially oriented and improved access to better marketing raising the income earned from Kes 80 billion to 90 billion of the Gross Domestic Product (GDP).

This chapter provides an overview of household inequality from international to national perspective. It also highlights on various issues, controversies and problems related to sorghum farming as it draws conclusion based on the analysis on the effect of innovative agricultural practices on reduction of inequality in Homabay County, Kenya.

BACKGROUND

Most studies identify income to be the best indicator to measure the economic well-being of households and individuals because almost all people receive an income at a pre-determined rate and time (Nimpagaritse & Culver, 2002; Tachibanaki, 2006; Jorgenson & Schreyer, 2015). Review of literature from a global perspective shows interesting trends. For instance, Japan is thought to be a country of equality. However, it is not the case as inequality exists in the field of education and employment. There is also an increased rate of unemployment (5%) as a result of weak macroeconomic state of the country over the last 15 years. Furthermore, there is more population aging resulting in wages differentials. There is also a change in family structures, where more households currently have a single parent. Last, there is stiff competition from the free market without government intervention and regulation. To address the issue of inequality then, the qualified, resourceful and productive individuals should achieve education and engage in valuable professions and jobs (Tachibanaki, 2006). Jonsson, Mood, & Bihagen (2013) contend that improved macro-economic condition reduces poverty and increase income difference thus disputing that there is a positive correlation between income gap and poverty.

Saboor, Sidd, and Hussain (2004) conducted a study in Pakistan and opined that to understand the impact of agriculture on poverty, then the nature of agricultural growth is of importance. The authors contend that agriculture has been a process negatively or positively influenced by various factors at different years. For example, the water logging, prices of agricultural products and infrastructure negatively affected the growth of agricultural output in the 1950s. The case was different in the 1960s when there were high agricultural products as a result of water resources, new seeds of wheat and rice subsidies, incentives through price support and access to credit. The high production in agricultural product at one point recorded sharp decline in poverty and at another point lead to increase in poverty. The study concludes that increase in income inequality in rural areas increased and decreased the level of poverty at 0.31 and 0.27 per cent respectively. In addition, the major factors that can address the rural poverty include redistribution of land and water resources. Lastly, to achieve in reducing rural poverty, the policies in place should also aim at controlling inequality for long sustainable growth.

According to Namara, Makombe, Hagos, and Awulachew (2007), the causes of rural poverty in Ethiopia can be identified to wide fluctuations in agricultural production emanating from drought as a result of persistent fluctuation in amount of rainfall, underdeveloped transport network, ineffective agricultural marketing channels, non-accessibility of rural households to support services and lack of the rural poor people participation in decisions affecting their livelihoods. The average land holding, high vulnerability to drought, adverse natural conditions and low productivity are the factors that contribute to the small-scale farmer to have the largest group of poor people.

The government of Ethiopia has taken drastic measures to reduce rural poverty through investing in small-scale irrigation but the situation remains that the rural people are poor. Other factors such as basic social and economic infrastructure are also considered to be the cause of the rural folk being poor. The low production from the unreliable rainfall patterns has forced the farmers to adopt innovative practices and technology to boast yields and income. First, inequality and rural poverty has significantly been reduced among the small-scale farmers through embracing irrigation and secondly diversification of crop production by adopting high value crops.

The high Gross Domestic Product recorded in India during the two time periods of 2004-2005 and 2011-2012 did not have significant impact on poverty reduction. In the years 2011-2012, rural poverty reduced at 2.32 compared to urban poverty at 1.69. The findings of the study shows that the higher reduction in rural poverty was as a result of the government initiative to invest in rural roads and agricultural research (Mahendra, 2016).

In Malawi, agriculture continues to dominate and contributes about 35% of the Gross Domestic Product (GDP). The country's rural population earns 74% of their income from crop production. The farmers are classified either as estate or smallholder agriculture with the smallholder producing mainly for subsistence needs. The rural poverty is rampant among the smallholders. To reduce rural poverty the government had to subsidize the farm inputs though evidence shows that the subsidies increases the agricultural output to the middle income groups leaving out the 20% regarded as poor. The vicious cycle of poverty hampering the lives of the poor in the rural Malawi requires the government to implement other policy measures such as social cash transfer to address the recurring situation (Chirwa & Muhome-matita, 2013). Thus, it is against this background that the study sought to establish the effect of innovative agricultural practices on reduction of inequality and rural poverty in Homabay County, Kenya.

MAIN FOCUS OF THE CHAPTER

Study Location

The study was carried out in Homabay County which lies between latitude O°15'South and O°52'South, and between longitudes 34°East and 35°East. The County covers an area of 4,267.1Km^2 inclusive of the water surface which on its own covers an area of 1,227Km^2. The County is located in South Western Kenya along Lake Victoria where it borders Kisumu and Siaya Counties to the North, Kisii and Nyamira Counties to the East, Migori County to the South and Lake Victoria and the republic of Uganda to the West. Homabay County has an estimated population of 1,177,181 persons consisting of 564,843 males and 612,338 females and a population density of about 325 persons per square km (Census, 2009; Government of Kenya, 2010). The major economic activities in Homabay County include Crop and Livestock Farming (basically staple cereals and indigenous livestock species) and fishing. It is the main sorghum growing area in Nyanza region of which the majority are small-scale farmers owning on average two hectares of land. These farmers are hardest hit by both biotic and physical constraints which are a major threat to staple food productivity.

The Kenyan government accords high priority to developing agricultural sector as an important strategy to address inequality and rural poverty. A key approach among many includes promoting uptake of innovative agricultural technologies. One of these innovative ways is growing improved sorghum varieties in Homabay County which enables resource-poor smallholder farmers to achieve higher yields and incomes and a variety of additional socio-economic benefits. Improved dwarf sorghum varieties which are drought and pest tolerant and high yielding are being promoted for their superior processing qualities that make them enjoy research, marketing and financial support from different stakeholders to increase their creation and production in the County (GoK, 2014).

Sorghum Farming

Sorghum (*Sorghum bicolor* (L) Moench) is an annual staple cereal crop grown for food, feed and processed as local brews and malted beer. Sorghum is the fifth most imported cereal grain in the world after wheat, maize, oats, and barley. In contrast to the other four mentioned cereals, sorghum is extremely drought tolerant and hardy and well adapted to the marginal eco-zones of Homabay County where other cereal crops do not grow well. Sorghum originated in Ethiopia and spread to other parts of Africa, Australia, India, Southeast Asia and the United States. The traditional tall (1.5-2 meters) varieties are low yielding; however, through research/breeding efforts short varieties and hybrids of 0.6 to 1.2 m tall are available. Growing of improved sorghum has improved livelihoods through increased productivity, incomes and food and nutrition security. In Homabay, sorghum is used as an ingredient for a wide range of indigenous foods. Many farm households rely on sorghum as a major food source during the prolonged "dry period", being the food for scarce months before the harvest of the main season crop, and is considered an important food security or famine crop because of its high satiety value.

The innovative process in sorghum farming involves mobilization of smallholder sorghum growers and formation of organized common interest groups for production, processing and marketing. Alongside grouping of farmers, a number of stakeholders have come on board and participating in the sorghum value chain with different roles. Hall (2006) contends that reinforcing the linkages and interaction between actors has been considered as key to improved efficiency and effectiveness of agriculture and rural development efforts, which are aimed at raising the level of economic performance of rural economy through increased productivity. Group membership permits farmers to acquire new knowledge and skills through training and interaction with multiple stakeholders of diverse talents with complementary skills to foster mutual learning and develop creative ideas in the sorghum value-chain.

According to Wennick and Ochola (2011), new methods of doing things result from interactions. Through groups, the farmers also attain collateral for acquisition of loans from different sources to boost sorghum production and productivity, enjoy economies of scale while purchasing farm inputs and collective marketing. The availability of ready market nationally and internationally by the giant Kenya Breweries Limited (KBL) and Kenya Seed Company and export market to hunger stricken regions such as Southern Sudan indicates the core element of the supply chain. The increased sorghum production and productivity in Homabay has enabled farmers to go into contractual farming system with many stakeholders such as Kenya Breweries Limited (KBL), Kenya Seed Company, Community Action for Rural Development (CARD), Agri-Info, Community Based Organizations (CBOs), traders, food companies and local traders and processors.

Sorghum Processing

Sorghum farming in Homabay County has opened up a platform of value chain innovation around which new income generation and human nutritional components, such as processing of composite flours, malted beer and livestock feed can be added (USAID, 2010). It therefore affords the smallholder farmers an opportunity to enter into cash economy. In Homabay, sorghum grain has traditionally been used in processing various food products and items. Sorghum absorbs flavors well hence can be used as a nutritious basis for a variety of dishes (e.g., ugali, porridge, cakes and others); feed products and local brews. Through research efforts, the dwarf sweet varieties (including *Gadam* and *sila*) sorghum has become a major raw material both in the food processing and brewing industries aimed at enhancing commercial orientation of smallholder households.

There are various companies that are dealing with purchase and processing of sorghum including Kenya Seed Company, Community Action for Rural Development (CARD) and Agri-Info. Some Community Based Organizations (CBOs) and local millers/processors also process composite flours and confectionaries from sweet sorghum and the general consumer households. With increased production and income, the farming households' food security has improved and is able to meet their financial needs. Sorghum which was traditionally regarded as "the woman's crop" in the area has become a major cash crop drawing the attention and participation of male farmers in the sorghum value chain. Sorghum growing in Homabay has become a major agri-entrepreneurship. This innovative agricultural approach has been successfully implemented and applied to farmer learning in Homabay County and has the potential to minimize/change the inequality gaps and poverty in the region.

ISSUES, CONTROVERSIES, PROBLEMS

Homabay County ranks among the poorest counties in Kenya with tremendous inequality in income distribution. Majority of the working–age population is engaged in subsistence agriculture. Physical and social infrastructure is not well developed in Homabay County. The poverty index of approximately 58% is impacted by low agricultural productivity, climate change, HIV/AIDS, and low value-addition to primary agricultural products (GOK, 2014). In Homabay County, sorghum farming is a dominant feature in the socio-economic lives of households, but smallholder sorghum farmers are found to be vulnerable to distresses such as multiple effects of climate change, trends such as changes in input supply fluctuation and market prices that threaten livelihoods and resulting into inequality and widespread poverty in the area. Other issues include HIV/AIDS, Land fragmentation, Agricultural Extension Officers, Rural-Urban migration, Climate Change and Marketing.

HIV/AIDS

The HIV/AIDS pandemic has its toll in Homabay County as it has impacted on farming systems. A number of productive resources that are used in agriculture (including human, financial, physical, social and natural) are being debilitated by HIV/AIDS related illnesses and deaths. Human capital is mainly affected through loss of labour whereas financial capital is decreased by illnesses through payment of medical bills and funeral expenses. This poses a huge constraint on the factors of production exacerbating poverty in the region. The cultural practice of wife inheritance has been the main contribution to the spread of the epidemic. The disease has resulted in a number of families with no breadwinner. The orphans left behind in many cases are infected or affected by the disease.

With the able and the energetic population killed by the disease the young orphans have no option than to rely on the able extended family members to seek for financial support. This has lowered, mainly the smallholder farmers' productive capacity hence limiting the supply of sorghum, with subsequent negative effect on incomes. The coping mechanisms of AIDS affected households include diversion of cash to medical expenses and altered patterns of production and consumption (Bechu, 1998).

Earlier studies in the County indicate that the proportion of the budget spent on health care in AIDs affected households was almost double that of households in Homabay, and that Health cost of the sick in the AIDS affected households accounts for almost 80% of the health budget. The government focus on the area, educating the widows on the dangers of embracing the cultural practices which can result to death has minimized the practice of wife's inheritance. The widows are introduced to projects that generate income thus reducing inequality and rural poverty.

Land Fragmentation

In the rural settings, the family land is sub-divided between the children and the wives, particularly among the sons. With the families becoming larger and larger, each family grabs a piece of the inherited land to construct homesteads. The land remaining for farming drastically reduces. In the long run the households are affected in terms of consumption, wealth and income. In Homabay County, land fragmentation is a common phenomenon, where most families have less than 2 acres to cultivate on. To curb the situation, the farmers have opted for crops that are drought, pest and disease resistant, high yielding, early maturing and ones that have more than one season within a year increasing the income earned from the farming.

Additionally, intensive farming approaches including productivity enhancing technologies are currently promoted in the County. The positive results expected from the new products and improved methods of farming will benefit the population and reduce inequality and rural poverty.

Agricultural Extension Officers

Initially, the government had assigned agricultural extension officers to educate the farmers. With the high population of farmers, and especially the small scale farmers, the services of the extension officers are limited and their services mainly focus on progressive and large-scale farmers. This has negatively affected the productivity of the small-scale farmers. The county government of Homabay has opted for empowerment of farmers through capacity building using different approaches and methods such as demonstrations, field days, farmer field schools (FFS), Participatory videos (PV), farmer-farmer extension, workshops and seminars among others to educate farmers on new or improved methods of farming. The small-scale farmers have immensely benefited from the county initiative and positive results showing up in terms of production and productivity.

The World Bank defines extension as "the process of helping farmers to become aware of and adopt improved technologies to enhance their production efficiency, income and welfare" (Purcell & Anderson, 1997). Farmers require appropriate knowledge and information in order to maximize their potential in production. It therefore calls for effective and innovative participatory approaches to disseminate improved technologies. A UNDP (2011) development brief on "Increasing Agricultural Productivity and Food security in Africa" indicated that access and utilization of knowledge and information plays a significant role in increasing production, productivity and incomes of smallholder farmers.

A report by the Ministry of Agriculture (GoK, 2010) indicated the effectiveness of extension services declined over the last two decades due to a sharp reduction in operational budgets and human resources in the sector ministries. Structural adjustment programmes (SAPs) of the 1980s through the 1990s imposed by the World Bank and the IMF crippled many of the extension services through introduction of reforms which included major retrenchment in the civil service and government budget rationalization programmes (Rees, Momanyi, Wekundah, Ndungu, Odondi, & Oyure, 2000), a factor that has contributed to low adoption of improved technologies in the County. The conventional extension approach has not been fully successful as evaluated and reported through numerous studies (Moris, 1994). These inefficiencies can be overcome through the use of Participatory Extension Approaches (PEAs). Extension practitioners therefore, must adapt to the realities of the new information age and learn to select the most appropriate communication channels and technologies to spur productivity.

Rural-Urban Migration

Rural-urban migration is increasingly becoming rampant especially in Kenya. The young and educated generation prefers to relocate to urban centers in search of white collar jobs. The aging parents and children left in the rural areas lack the means to cultivate the land in terms of man power. This has widened the gap of inequality between the urban and the rural population. With the aging population mainly holding on subsistence farming and the productivity levels reduced. The rural population has relatively low innovative capacity to access sources of income rendering them poor. This is due to low investment levels in rural areas of Homabay to absorb school leavers and new graduates, hence the mass flow of energetic youth and young adults particularly men to urban areas in search of wage employment. To reduce the inequality and rural poverty, the government is promoting commercial agriculture through introduction of improved crop varieties such as sweet sorghum, which generate considerable yields and income from a small piece of land and does not require much attention in terms of the amount of rainfall required.

Climate Change

Global warming has immensely shown results that are not controllable. Climate change varies from year to year and therefore the government has different measures in place tailor made for a particular situation/ context. To mitigate the multiple effects of climate change, the government has introduced variety of crops that are resistant to the harsh weather and promoted irrigation in arid and semi-arid areas. Climate change does not only manifest in form of lack or less rainfall but also so excess rainfall and upsurge in pest and disease infestation that cause damage to crops affecting the farm yields.

Marketing

Marketing agricultural commodities in Homabay County has numerous challenges including price fluctuation, inadequate of storage facilities, low of bargaining power by the producers, presence of middlemen/ brokers using unstructured marketing channels, inadequate infrastructure to link farmers to national, regional and international markets, poor governance, lack of industries and erratic weather conditions. Other issues are changes in the dominant policy environment emphasizing liberalization and state withdrawal. Agricultural policy reforms such as market liberalization has impacted on smallholder sorghum farmers in Homabay; hence, not achieving remunerative and motivating prices for sorghum products.

Inadequate credit facilities and lack of focus in the production system are other issues. Most farmers do not have strategic production/business plans to guide on timing and type of market, quantity to produce, quality and market standards required. Weak partnerships and networks in the market chain also impacts on production. Processing equipment for sorghum such as machine threshers to reduce drudgery of hand threshing which is a woman's domain. With increased sorghum production, women can no longer offer enough labour for processing sorghum.

Research Questions

1. What is the effect of innovative agricultural practices on reduction of inequality and rural poverty among sorghum farmers in Homabay County?
2. Is there a statistical significant difference between agricultural produce before and after use of innovative agricultural practices among the sorghum farmers in Homabay County?

Hypothesis

H_0: There is no statistical significant difference between agricultural produce before and after use of innovative agricultural practices among the sorghum farmers in Homabay County, Kenya.

DATA AND METHODS

Information on growers was obtained through a questionnaire in Homabay County, Western Kenya. A multistage stratified sampling technique was used to randomly select 120 smallholder sorghum farmers. The first step was to purposively select 3 Sub Counties which are major sorghum producers. These included Karachuonyo, Gwassi and Ndhiwa Sub-Counties. Secondly, four sorghum farmer groups were randomly sampled from each Sub-County, giving a total of 12 groups. Third, 10 farmers were randomly selected from each group giving a total of 120 farmers. The list of farmers was provided by Ward Agricultural Officers (WAOs).

A survey questionnaire was designed and pilot-tested using 30 purposively sampled sorghum farmers in the three sub- counties. The pilot group did not constitute the final sample that participated in the study. The questionnaire covered the 2015 and 2016 long-rain seasons (March-June) when rainfall is more reliable for sorghum growth. Chi-square test for independence was used to test the association between agricultural produce before and after use of innovative agricultural practices among the sorghum farmers in Homabay County.

Results

Demographic Characteristics

For the purpose of establishing the background information of those who participated in the study, the following demographic characteristics were considered: sex, age bracket, and size of land utilized for farming. Among those who participated in the study, the majority (60%) were females while the remaining 40% were males. Gender distribution showed that more men are embracing the farming because of the cash involved, since sorghum is being commercialized. All those who participated in the study were adults, aged above 35 years. The size of the land cultivated by the overwhelming majority (90%) of the participants ranged between 2 - 20 hectares. However, a small percentage (10%) of the farmers has started to lease bigger pieces of land.

Hypothesis

H_0: There is no statistical significant difference between agricultural produce before and after use of innovative agricultural practices among the sorghum farmers in Homabay County.

The study sought to establish whether there is a statistical significant difference between agricultural produce before and after innovative agricultural practices among the sorghum farmers in Homabay County, Kenya. The t test was used to establish whether there existed a statistical significant difference between the data on before and after innovative agricultural practices. Tables 1 and 2 show the t test results.

The T test results revealed that there was a statistical significant difference between the scores of agricultural produce before (M= 1648.8, SD = 2648.8) and after (M = 2648.8, SD = 264.8) the introduction of innovative agricultural practices among sorghum farmers in Homabay Sub county; t (119) = 29.257, p = .001 This implies that use of innovative agricultural practices has an impact on agricultural produce and therefore on reduction of inequality and rural poverty among farmers in Homabay County.

Table 1. Group statistics

	VAR00003	N	Mean	Std. Deviation		Std. Error Mean
Produce-before	1.00	120	1648.8	264.8		24.169
	2.00	120	2648.8	264.8		24.169

Table 2. Independent samples test for agricultural produce before and after use of innovative agricultural practices

		Levene's Test for Equality of Variances		t-test for Equality of Means						
		F	Sig.	T	df	Sig. (2-tailed)	Mean Difference	Std. Error Difference	95% Confidence Interval of the Difference	
									Lower	Upper
Produce before and after innovation	Equal variances assumed	.000	1.000	-29.257	238	.001	-1000.00	34.180	-1067.334	-932.666
	Equal variances not assumed			-29.257	238.000	.001	-1000.00	34.180	-1067.334	-932.666

Various innovative agricultural practices in land harrowing, fertilizers, use of chemicals, weeding and threshing have been used to improve agricultural produce and therefore, ending up in improving the quality of living among the rural poor. According to the IFDC report (2015), innovative farming technologies are critical towards improving agricultural productivity and net returns of the smallholder farmers.

Another study by the OECD (2001) on adoption of technologies for sustainable farming systems also showed that changing traditional farming practices and adopting new innovative technologies has a positive impact in Agriculture. Although debates surrounding the impact of innovative agricultural practices are numerous, especially on methodology, there is a common conclusion among them that there is a correlation between treatment variable (innovative technologies) and outcome variable (income) (Ton, 2013). Thus, it is evident that use of innovative agricultural practices has an impact on reduction of inequality among farmers.

SOLUTIONS AND RECOMMENDATIONS

Active state interventions are important in supporting critical stages of agricultural market development focusing on agricultural commodities. The agricultural policy reforms should emphasize on re-orientation of extension service towards participatory processes with the more active participation of various actors and end-users in the sorghum value-chain in Homabay County. Extension practitioners, therefore, must adapt to the realities of the new information age and learn to select the most appropriate communication channels and technologies to spur sorghum productivity.

Policy should encourage provision of inputs on credit and subsidy through interlinked arrangements intended to overcome some of the constraints on inputs. As suggested by farmers, there is a need to establish a massive sorghum processing within Homabay Country closer to farmers where they can deliver the sorghum without incurring much transportation and excess costs. This is envisaged to boost production of the commodity and hence diversified products to fetch higher incomes and reduce inequalities and poverty.

CONCLUSION

The innovative agricultural practices in Homabay County have yielded positive results in reduction of inequality and rural poverty. The farmers have adopted the farming of sorghum thus increasing productivity and fetching good prices for their produce. The study shows that there is significant association between sorghum growing and reduction of inequality among sorghum farmers in Homabay County. The increased income has positively influenced rural poverty to a greater extent. The study findings indicate that smallholder farmers' incomes have increased through innovative agricultural practices subsequently reducing the inequality and rural poverty.

FUTURE RESEARCH DIRECTIONS

The study focused on sorghum growing as an innovative platform to address inequality and rural poverty in Homabay County. There are numerous innovative agricultural practices adopted by farmers in Homabay County. The study suggests further research in other innovative agricultural practices such as livestock rearing and maize growing to address inequality and rural poverty in Homabay County.

ACKNOWLEDGMENT

The authors would like to acknowledge Riara University, Kenya and Ministry of Agriculture, Livestock and Fisheries, Kenya for provision of facilities to conduct the research. Otherwise the authors did not receive grant from any funding agency in the public, commercial, or not-for-profit sectors.

REFERENCES

Bechu, N. (1998). The impact of AIDS on the economy of the families in Cote d'Voire: Changes in consumption among AIDS affected households. In M. Ainsworth, L. Fransen, & M. Over (Eds.), *In confronting AIDS: Evidence from the Developing World*. Brussels: European Commission.

Chirwa, E. W., & Muhome-matita, M. (2013). *Agricultural Growth and Poverty in Rural Malawi*. University of Malawi.

Drimie, S. (2003). HIV/AIDS and land. Case studies from Kenya, Lesotho and South Africa. *Development Southern Africa*, *20*(5), 647–658. doi:10.1080/0376835032000149289

Gordon, D. (2006). *The concept and measurement of poverty. In Poverty and Social Exclusion in Britain.* London: The Policy Press.

Government of Kenya. (2003). *Interim Poverty Reduction Strategy Paper 2002-2003.* Nairobi, Kenya: Author.

Government of Kenya. (2007). Kenya Vision 2030. Nairobi: Ministry of Planning, National Development and Vision 2030.

Government of Kenya. (2010). *Rachuonyo District Annual Report.* Nairobi: Government printers.

Government of Kenya (2014). *Homabay County Annual Report.* Author.

Hall, A. J., Yoganand, B., Sulaiman, R. V., Rajeswari, R. S., Shambu, P. C., Naik, G. C., & Clark, N. G. (2004). *Innovations in Innovation: Reflections on Partnership, Institutions and Learning.* Patancheru, Andhra Pradesh, India: International Crops Research Institute for the Semi-Arid Tropics.

IFDC. (2015). *Promoting Agriculture Technology to Improve Productivity and Net Returns for Smallholder Farmers.* Retrieved on September 22, 2016, from: https://ifdc.org/promoting-agriculture-technology-to-improve-productivity-and-net-returns-for-smallholder-farmers/

Jonsson, J. O., Mood, C., & Bihagen, E. (2013). *Income Inequality and Poverty during Economic Recession and Growth.* GINI Discussion Paper 60.

Jorgenson, D., & Schreyer, P. (2015). *Measuring Individual Economic Well-Being and Social Welfare within the Framework of the System of National Accounts.* IARIW-OECD Special Conference. Harvard University and OECD.

Kenya National Bureau of Statistics. (2015). *Exploring Kenya's Inequality.* Nairobi: Government Printer.

Mahendra, S. (2016). *Economic Reforms, poverty and Inequality.* Mumbai: Indira Gandhi Institute of Development Research.

Namara, R. E., Makombe, G., Hagos, F., & Awulachew, S. B. (2007). *Rural poverty and inequality in Ethiopia: does access to small-scale irrigation make a difference?* International Water Management Institute.

Naschold, F. (2015). *Why inequality matters for poverty.* Briefing Paper No 2 (2 of 3), 1–6.

Nimpagaritse, F., & Culver, D. (2002). *A Broader Perspective of Measuring the well-being of Rural Farm and non-Farm Households.* Agriculture and Agri - Food Canada.

Organisation for Economic Co-operation and Development (OECD). (2001). *Adoption of technologies for sustainable farming systems: Wageningen workshop proceedings.* Retrieved on June 2, 2016, from: http://www.oecd.org/greengrowth/sustainable-agriculture/2739771.pdf

Rao, J., Midega, C., Atieno, F., Auma, J. O., Cadilhon, J. J., Mango, N., ... Wesonga, M. (2015). *A situational Analysis of agricultural production and marketing, and natural resources management in West Kenya. ILRI/Icipe Project Report.* Nairobi, Kenya: International Livestock Research Institute for the Humidtropics CGIAR Research Program.

Rees, D., Momanyi, M., Wekundah, J., Ndungu, F., Odondi, J., & Oyure, A. O. (2000). *Agricultural Knowledge and Implications in Kenya - Implications for Technology Dissemination and Development.* Agricultural Research & Extension Network Paper No.107, Overseas Development Institute. Retrieved on October 7, 2017, from: www.odi.org.uk/agren

Saboor, A., Sidd, M., & Hussain, M. (2004). Life and Social Sciences Agricultural Growth, Rural Poverty and Income Inequality in Pakistan. *Pakistan Journal of Life and Social Sciences*, *2*(2), 168–173.

Seth, O. O. (2008). *Effects of HIV/AIDS Related Illnesses and Deaths on Agricultural Production: A Case of Nyando and Kericho Districts in Kenya* (Thesis). Egerton University.

Tachibanaki, T. (2006). Inequality and Poverty in Japan. *The Japanese Economic Review*, *57*(1), 1–27. doi:10.1111/j.1468-5876.2006.00355.x

Ton, G. (2013). *Finding the real impact of agricultural innovation support.* Retrieved on February 15, 2015, from: https://www.scidev.net/global/data/opinion/finding-the-real-impact-of-agricultural-innovation-support.html

United Nations. (2015). *Inequality and the end of extreme poverty.* Oxfam Media.

USAID. (2010). *Staple Foods Value Chain Analysis: Country Report-Kenya.* USAID.

Wambugu, A., & Munga, B. (2009). *Growth, Poverty and Income Inequality in Kenya.* Nairobi: KIPPRA.

Wennick, B., & Ochola, W. (2011). Designing innovation platforms: Putting Heads Together, 396. Amsterdam: KIT Publishers.

World Bank. (2008). *Kenya Poverty and Inequality Assessment.* Economic Management Unit Africa Region.

KEY TERMS AND DEFINITIONS

Climate Change: Undesirable change in the weather pattern caused by global warming. For example, shortage of rainfall leading to drought or excess rainfall leading to damage.

County: Geographical demarcation within a country for purpose of administration. In Kenya, 47 counties were created in 2010 and effected in 2013 after the general election as per the Kenyan constitution.

Farmers: A group of people practicing agriculture within a given locality. They can either be large holders (farming cash crop) or smallholders (subsistence farming).

HIV/AIDS: It is a virus transmitted disease through sexual intercourse and blood transfusion with/from an infected person rendering a person immune system weak. The first patient in Kenya was identified in 1980s.

Income: Earnings from an economic activity and can positively or negatively change the living standards of an individual. The earnings can either be from employment or self-employment.

Land Fragmentation: It is the continuous sub-division of the family land as a result of increasing population and thus affecting the agricultural sector. It is very common in Kenya with less land classified as productive.

Population: The number of people living within a given country or region.
Sorghum: It is a widely cultivated cereal/grain for consumption by both the human and the livestock.

Chapter 6
A Scale of Relative Institutional Challenge During MNC Global Expansion

Ehsan Derayati
Concordia University, Canada

Rick Molz
Concordia University, Canada

Gwyneth Edwards
HEC Montréal, Canada

ABSTRACT

This chapter develops a reliable and valid scale of relative institutional challenge between 40 country pairs by drawing on three measures of institutional uniqueness. The single measure can be used by researchers and practitioners to assess the relative institutional challenge that a multinational corporation (MNC) may face in the internationalization process between their home and potential host country. The value of this single scale includes (1) a more comprehensive and broad scale than three separate scales, (2) demonstrated reliability and validity, (3) a standardized measure of institutional challenge that can be used by different researchers in different research settings, and (4) a tool for practitioners that is easily applied and robust when considering alternative off-shore investment opportunities.

INTRODUCTION

In recent years, the international environment has been undergoing severe change and uncertainty. As the result of changes in the political, economic, and cultural settings within international institutions, the issue of uncertainty and changes in institutional contexts have become very important. Some notable events, such as the 2008 economic recession and government changes within previously stable countries, show us that uncertainty in institutional contexts occur regardless of a country's level of development.

DOI: 10.4018/978-1-5225-5787-6.ch006

In increasingly turbulent and competitive international environments, having a comprehensive understanding of a country's institutional environment is a key element for success in international business and the specific process of internationalization. Different studies examine how environmental and institutional factors affect internationalization strategies and have highlighted the role of country conditions as a determinant of firm performance (Gaur & Lu, 2007; Khanna & Palepu, 2000; Peng, Wang, & Jiang, 2008).

One of the basic arguments in this area stems from institutional theory proposing that firms are embedded in country-specific institutional arrangements (Busenitz, Gomez, & Spencer, 2000). From the neo-institutional perspective (North, 1990; Scott, 2001), a country's institutional environment (e.g., rules, social norms, and cognitive structure) has a direct effect on firm strategies. These factors set the framework for market transactions by defining both the ''rules of the game'' (North, 1990, p. 1) and firms' legitimacy conditions (Meyer & Rowan, 1977).

Institutional theorists view the institutional environment as a key determinant for firm behavior and strategy; the relationship between institutions and firms is considered a dynamic interaction leading to different strategic choices (Kostova & Roth, 2002; Peng, 2003; Peng et al., 2008). These choices can include the level and process of innovation in a given country (Bartholomew, 1997), foreign partnership activities, differences in entrepreneurial activities (Busenitz et al., 2000), mode of entry and ownership strategies (Brouthers, 2002; Davis, Desai, & Francis, 2000; Gaur & Lu, 2007; Uhlenbruck, Rodriguez, Doh, & Eden, 2006), and strategic alliance partner selection (Hitt et al., 2004).

Drawing from institutional theory, we know that internationalized firms face institutional differences in host and home countries (Bartlett & Ghoshal, 1999; Kostova, 1999; Oliver, 1991). Several studies examine the country-specific influences on the international activities of firms at different levels. The literature on country institutional profiles, as an example, has been predominately used for explaining international management phenomena (Kostova, 1999). A segment of this research studies the advantages and disadvantages of host or home countries. From an institutional perspective, these studies explore how the institutional profile of a specific host or home country can affect international activities of the firm (Bénassy-Quéré, Coupet, & Mayer, 2007; Chan, Isobe, & Makino, 2008). Collectively, this group of studies focuses on differences in the availability of 'naturally inherited' factors of production (e.g., labor, land, capital) in host countries (Dunning, 1980, 2000) or the competitive advantages of home countries that are derived from their created capabilities (Chan et al., 2008; Porter, 1990).

Another aspect of this literature focuses on the relative institutional profiles of host and home countries (Gaur & Lu, 2007; Schwens, Eiche, & Kabst, 2011; Xu & Shenkar, 2002). Most of these studies examine the distance between the institutional environments of the home country and those of the host country. Kostova (1999) introduced the construct of institutional distance to broaden the concept of home and host country differences beyond cultural differences. This recent strand of research has been useful for explaining institutional differences and its effect on international business.

Some scholars, however, have argued that institutional distance neglects factors such as the degree and process of institutionalization (Phillips, Tracey, & Karra, 2009), and the exclusion of asymmetry and direction (Chan et al., 2008; Hakanson & Ambos, 2010; Hernández & Nieto, 2015). Phillips et al. (2009) argue that institutional distance fails to capture the difference in the level of institutionalizations, especially in developing economies where firms might encounter institutions that "while similar to the home country – are only weakly entrenched" (Phillips et al., 2009, p. 341).

The objective of our research is to capture a comprehensive view on country specific factors in relation to the internationalization process of firms. We seek to encompass a broader set of institutional dimensions to cover the gaps in existing approaches. To accomplish this goal, we conceptualize a multidimensional construct, Relative Institutional Challenge, which reflects the risks that managers face in the internationalization process.

Our chapter is structured as follows. First, we provide a literature review on our three dimensions of Relative Institutional Challenge, which include institutional distance, institutional development, and institutional uncertainty. We then present our conceptualization and development of the construct. We conclude with a discussion on the role of Relative Institutional Challenge and the Relative Institutional Challenge Index in the international business (IB) literature.

THEORETICAL GROUNDING

The role of country conditions as a determinant of firm performance is particularly important to multinational companies (MNCs) (Christmann, Day, & Yip, 2000). The literature on country attractiveness argues that a large number of country-level conditions, such as demographic, economic, and political factors, affect the potential performance and international behaviour of MNCs (Busenitz et al., 2000; Christmann et al., 2000; Kiss & Danis, 2008).

A basic premise is that "firms are embedded in country-specific institutional arrangements" (Busenitz et al., 2000, p. 994). Institutional theory suggests that organizations must adapt to their local institutional environment to survive (North, 1990; Powell & DiMaggio, 1991; Scott, 2001) and defines this environment as a system of regulatory, cognitive and normative pillars (Scott, 2001). Kostova (1999) suggests that a country's institutional environment can be characterised by its institutional profile (i.e., the three pillars), which can influence a firm's internationalization strategy (Davis et al., 2000).

The assessment of a country's institutional context may rely on a variety of economic, political, and business indicators (Chan et al., 2008; North, 1990). Some researchers examine the differences between home and host country environments as a determining factor, while others consider absolute characteristics. We argue that firms must use a comprehensive approach to understanding the impact of both home and host institutional environments.

Institutional Distance

Kostova (1999) introduced the concept of country institutional profile as a 3-dimensional construct defined "as the set of regulatory, cognitive and normative institutions in a country." (Kostova, 1999, p. 314). According to Hymer (1960), the differences between the home and host country environments cause a liability of foreignness, increasing key factors: the exchange risk of operating in a foreign country; the chance of discrimination by local authorities; and, the lack of knowledge and familiarity with the foreign market (Hilmersson & Jansson, 2012; Hymer, 1960).

Kostova (1999) describes institutional distance as "the extent of similarity or dissimilarity between the regulatory, cognitive and normative institutions of two countries" (Kostova, 1999, p. 153); a country's institutional environment includes government policies (constituting a regulatory dimension), widely shared social knowledge (a cognitive dimension), and value systems (a normative dimension). These institutional differences shape different aspects of firms' international behavior and pose risks of doing business in the host country (Xu & Shenkar, 2002). For example, higher levels of institutional distance are likely to trigger conflicting demands between gaining external legitimacy (or local responsiveness) in the host country and internal consistency (or global integration) within the MNCs' system (Bartlett & Ghoshal, 1999).

The literature generally shows the negative effects of institutional distance on firms' international performance in a host country (Bae & Salomon, 2010; Chao & Kumar, 2010; Eden & Miller, 2004). Researchers relate this negative correlation to factors such as cost of doing business abroad and liability of foreignness, as both increase with higher levels of institutional distance (Eden & Miller, 2004). As institutional distance increases, the conflicting pressures for local responsiveness and global integration become more challenging for foreign firms (Doz & Prahalad, 1991; Eden & Miller, 2004, Xu & Shenkar, 2002).

Institutional distance, however, cannot fully account for the contextualization of a country's institutional environment, only the differences between home and host countries. Phillips et al. (2009) argue that to have an appropriate understanding on institutional context, we need consider the level and state of institutionalization as well. Other researchers also argue for the need for incorporation of direction in institutional distance (Hernández & Nieto, 2015).

Institutional Uncertainty

We believe that institutional contexts must also characterize the degree and status of institutionalization in addition to the degree of institutional distance. As firms internationalize, they encounter not only institutional contexts where key institutions differ, but also contexts that are composed of institutions that are not well formalized or are under rapid change (Phillips et al., 2009). While the host country may be characterized by the absence of a given institution or set of institutions, it may also be characterized by institutions that – while similar to the home country – are only weakly rooted or face rapid change (Phillips et al., 2009).

As an indicator of level of stability in a country's institutions, we consider the construct of institutional uncertainty, which has a direct link with concepts in new institutionalism such as institutionalization, institutional change and institutional entrepreneurship (Rodrigues & Child, 2008), and therefore helps us to address the gaps diagnosed by Phillips et al. (2009).

Uncertainty is generally defined as the lack of information, knowledge and understanding (Johnston, Gilmore, & Carson, 2008); however, it has been simultaneously used to describe the state of an organizational environment and the state of the person who perceives that environment. This suggests that environmental uncertainty grows from an inability to understand changes, events, and causal relationships, coupled with an inability to predict the effect these will have on the firm; this leads to an inability to develop response options and predict consequences. We focus on state uncertainty as it is concerned with a decision maker's estimation of present and future market and market-influencing factors (Johanson & Vahlne, 1977).

Environmental uncertainty can be perceived as having two main dimensions: 1) static versus dynamic notions of the environment, and 2) complexity versus simplicity of the environment. The static-dynamic dimension considers the degree to which factors in the decision maker's environment remain the same over time or are in a continual process of change. Based on this framework, environmental uncertainty increases as an environment becomes more dynamic and more complex.

Generally, in strategic management and organization theory literature, uncertainty is referred to as the unpredictability of environmental or organizational variables that affect the decision and performance of organizations (Salancik & Pfeffer, 1978). In this research, we are interested in general environmental uncertainties and their sources, which, according to Miller (1992), include political instability, government policy instability, macroeconomic uncertainties, social uncertainties, and natural uncertainties.

Uncertainty has the effect of increasing the complexity and risk for international business (Phillips et al., 2009). The effects of institutional uncertainty of host countries on firms' internationalization behavior, such as foreign investment or equity-based entry, has been mostly considered as a negative and limiting effect in internationalization process of firms (Phillips et al., 2009). The trade-off of flexibility versus resources are of significant influence on firms' responses to institutional uncertainty. Institutional uncertainty, however, does not explain a country's level of institutional development, which may vary even for the same level of uncertainty.

Institutional Development

Contextual factors influence firm behaviour, such as host country institutions. Therefore, the characteristics of institutions in a host country should be considered (Kostova & Zaheer, 1999; Peng, 2003). Institutions have formal and informal components. Formal institutions are a set of political, economic, and contractual rules that regulate individual behavior and shape human interaction. Informal institutions are conventions, codes of conduct, and norms of behavior that come from socially transmitted information and are part of a country's cultural heritage (North, 1990).

Countries differ not only in their institutional setting, but also in their level of institutional development (Kostova & Zaheer, 1999; Miller, Lee, Chang, & Le Breton-Miller, 2009; Zaheer, Schomaker, & Genc, 2003). Institutional development is "the extent to which the economic, political, and social institutions in a host country are formally developed and are favorable for foreign affiliates," affecting the efficiency of market transactions and transformation (Chan et al., 2008, p. 1180). Each host country possesses its own economic, political and social institutions that might have different levels of development (North, 1990). These differences in levels of development create unique risks for foreign firms, as the institutions alter the costs of engaging in business activities between different host countries (Chan et al., 2008; Henisz, 2000).

Institutional development at the national level has effects in three main areas: economic institutions, political institutions and social institutions. Economic institutions involve market intermediaries such as banking systems and agents, traders, auditors, all of which impact product, capital and financial markets by reducing transaction costs (Chan et al., 2008; Khanna & Palepu, 2000). In an economically underdeveloped country, the availability and efficiency of market intermediaries and infrastructure suppliers are under question, serving as an obstacle for firms (Chan et al., 2008; Khanna & Palepu, 2000).

Political institutions also influence the institutional development on a national level. Governments are the main actors of political institutions and show their effect through policies and regulations in areas such as investment regulations, tax and tariffs and trade agreements (Chan et al., 2008; Henisz, 2000; Henisz & Zelner, 2003). The level of development in political institutions influences the extent to which laws are enforced by governments, evident in the transparency of laws, the law making processes, laws regarding intellectual property rights and the level of corruption in a country (Chan et al., 2008; North, 1990; Rodriguez, Uhlenbruck, & Eden, 2005). In general, local government policies can affect foreign firms' activities in both favourable and unfavourable ways.

Social institutions include work ethics, beliefs about commercial activities, management dynamics and accepted practices and levels of trusts, all of which affect the performance of a firm in a national context (Chan et al., 2008; Scott, 2007).

Countries with high levels of institutional development tend to have well-developed banking systems, strong public equity markets, and established venture capital industries that can provide support, such as financing for international growth (Bruton, Fried, & Manigart, 2005). They also have well-established legal traditions, systems, and effective enforcement mechanisms, which facilitate new business creation and growth, and protect investors (Bevan, Estrin, & Meyer, 2004).

Conversely, indicators of low level of institutional development include existence of strong institutional voids, weak formal institutions and lack of connection to international networks (Peng & Luo, 2000). In general, the level of institutional development in emerging economies is relatively low, due to lack of or insufficient formal institutional rules, creating institutional voids (Hitt et al., 2004; Hoskisson et al., 2000; Khanna & Palepu, 1997). These institutional voids may increase transaction costs due to the existence of imperfect markets in areas such as product, labour and financial markets. On the other hand, institutional voids bring opportunities for institutional entrepreneurship (Maguire, Hardy, & Lawrence, 2004) and may lower barriers to entry for first movers (Rodriguez et al., 2005). Some research shows that in the absence of formal institutional mechanisms, alternative informal mechanisms are replacing them (Allen, Qian, & Qian, 2005).

Relative Institutional Challenge

We argue that in addition to institutional distance, both institutional uncertainty and institutional development should be considered in the internationalization process. We therefore propose a new formative construct that can capture the following three dimensions: one, the level of development of institutional environment of the host country, representing the strength of formal institutions and infrastructures that facilitate international trade; two, the level of institutional uncertainty in the host country, representing the level of risk and unpredictability of doing business; and, three, the level of institutional distance between the home and host country, representing the degree of similarity between the two countries, affecting the degree of institutional duality (between the internal and external environments of the firm).

We label this new construct *Relative Institutional Challenge* (see Figure 1) for two reasons. First, by including institutional distance between two countries, institutional development of the host country and institutional uncertainty of the host country, the construct represents the institutional risks faced and perceived by firms. Second, in addition to taking into account the absolute perspective to country's institutional arrangements, it considers the level of similarity between home and host countries. Figure 2 shows the mathematical model.

RELATIVE INSTITUTIONAL CHALLENGE AS A FORMATIVE CONSTRUCT AND PROPER MEASUREMENT MODELS

Relative Institutional Challenge as a Formative Construct

Here, we discuss the reasons for considering the RIC as a formative construct and its appropriate measurement model. Three characteristics of a formative construct are relevant: causality, interchangeability, and validity. These three factors, based on the model presented by Robert and Thatcher (2009), are reviewed for the case of the RIC.

Figure 1. Relative institutional challenge model

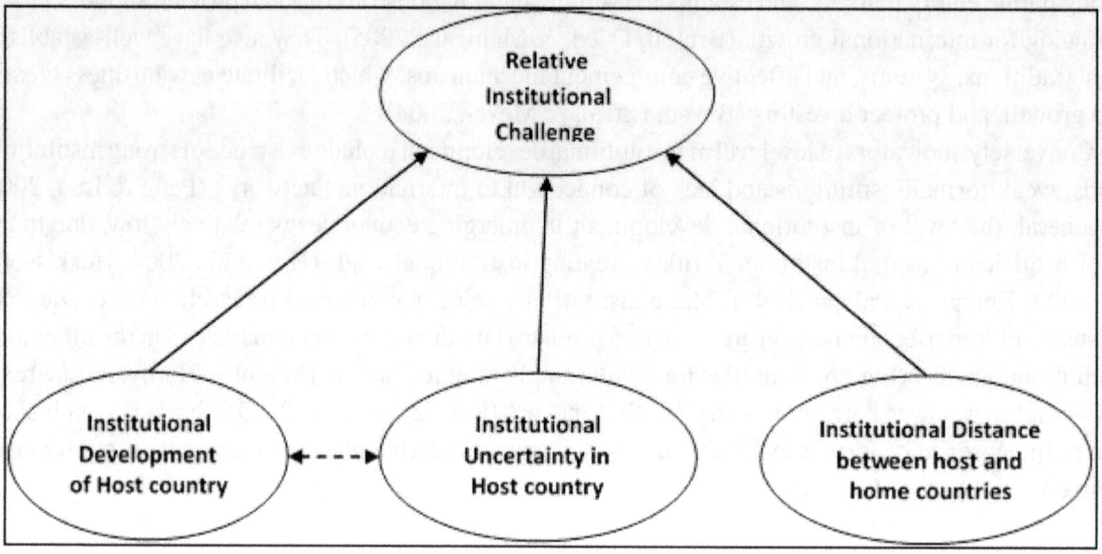

Figure 2. Mathematical model for relative institutional challenge index

$$R.I.C._{ijt} = Inst.\ Dist._{ijt} + Inst.\ Unc._{it} + Inst.\ Dev._{it}$$

i: Host country

j: Home country

t: year

$R.I.C._{ijt}$: Relative institutional challenge of country i for a firm from Country j at year t

$Inst.\ Dist._{ijt}$: Institutional distance between countries i and j at year t

$Inst.\ Unc._{it}$: level of Institutional uncertainty of country i at year t

$Inst.\ Dev._{it}$: level of Institutional development of country i at year t

Causality. The RIC is a composition of three dimensions: institutional uncertainty in the host country, institutional development in the host country, and the institutional distance between home and host country. These three dimensions are building blocks of the construct, and the change of each of them results in a change in the construct. The direction of causality is from dimensions to the construct, which is the first property of formative constructs.

Interchangeability. In the RIC, each dimension adds to other dimensions in specific ways to grasp a domain on the theoretical argument. Institutional distance adds the view on relativity and similarity in country pairs, while institutional development and institutional uncertainty give information about the state and pace of institutionalization in the host country. While institutional development and institutional uncertainty have some correlations, they represent different notions.

Validity. In a formative construct, dimensions are exogenously determined. Each dimension in the RIC is being represented by a different measurement using a different dataset. However, we expect to have some correlation between measurements of institutional distance and institutional development. To reduce the commonalities of these two constructs, we pre-screened the measures in each dataset.

This analysis shows RIC is a formative multi-dimensional construct. Based on the taxonomy of Law et al. (1998), we suggest the aggregate model is an appropriate model to use for our construct. In aggregate models, constructs are formed as mathematical functions of their dimensions, which exist at the same level of the constructs. The RIC construct is at the same level of its dimensions and encompasses a mathematical equation between the dimensions.

Measurement Model Development

Methodology. We used an aggregated model for measuring the RIC, which is composed of an algebraic addition of its dimensions. Here we explain the process and reasons for choosing specific measures for each dimension

Institutional Development in Host Country. We used the Global Competitiveness Index (GCI) for extracting measures of institutional development. The GCI has been published annually for more than three decades by the World Economic Forum to represent the level of competitiveness of nations. The Global Competitiveness Index is a comprehensive tool developed from the report to measure the microeconomic and macroeconomic foundations of national competitiveness. The GCI defines competitiveness as "the set of institutions, policies and factors that determine the level of productivity of a country" (Sala-I-Martín *et al.*, 2014, p. 4). The GCI is a weighted average of 112 indicators being grouped as 12 pillars of competitiveness, namely: Institutions, Infrastructure, Macroeconomic environment, Health and primary education, Higher education and training, Goods market efficiency, Labour market efficiency, Financial market development, Technological readiness, Market size, Business sophistication, and Innovation. The Global Competitiveness Report categorize and rank 144 countries taking into account their stages of development. The GCI is also based on main drivers of competitiveness for each country, and categorizes countries into three different types of economies: factor-driven economies, efficiency-driven economies, and innovation-driven economies (Sala-I-Martín et al., 2014).

Institutional development is not the only determinant of competitiveness; a pre-screening was done to assure the measures are representing the institutional development of a nation, not other aspects of competitiveness. With this regard, the framework for institutional development developed by Chan *et al.* (2008) was used to screen relevant indicators for each dimension of institutional development. Due to the importance of technological advancement and innovation infrastructure in national development, we added an additional category, "Innovation and Technological Development", adding two factors (technological readiness and R&D /Innovation infrastructure) to the 12 factors established by Chan *et al.* (2008). As a result, we have four main categories: Economic Institutions, Political Institutions, Social Institutions, and Innovation and Technological Development. Three experts performed pre-screening using two the following conditions: in each dimension (except GDP /capita), at least two measures were selected; and, all measures selected should represent the state of institutionalization as the main criteria for institutional development. As a result of the screening, 30 indicators were selected from the Global Competitiveness Report as shown in Table 1. These indicators were used in shaping the institutional development dimension of the RIC.

Table 1. Indicators selected from the global competitiveness report representing different dimensions of institutional development

Category	Dimensions of institutional development (Chan et al. 2008)	Indicators extracted from Global Competitiveness Report
Economic institutions	GDP per capita (in US)	• GDP/capita • Country Credit Rating • Gross National Saving, %GDP
	Distribution infrastructure	• Quality of overall infrastructure • quality of roads, railroad, ports, and air transport infrastructure • Control of international distribution
	Financial resources	• Efficiency of financial markets • Protection of minority shareholders' interests • Strength of investor protection
Political institutions	Intellectual property rights	• Property rights • Intellectual property protection
	Political system	• Diversion of Public Funds • Transparency of government policymaking
	Law and order	• Judicial independence • Favoritism in decisions of government officials
	Bureaucracy quality	• Efficiency of legal frameworks in settling disputes • Efficiency of legal framework in challenging regulations
Social institutions	Justice	• Primary education enrollment rate • Female participation in labor force
	Harassment and violence	• Business costs of crime and violence • Reliability of police services
	Corruption in government	• Public trust in politicians • Irregular payments and bribes
	Civil freedom	• Judicial independence • Legal rights index
Innovation & Technological Development	Technological readiness	• Technological adoption • Internet users
	R&D/ innovation infrastructure	• Intellectual property protection • Quality of scientific research institutions • University-industry collaboration in R&D

To test the reliability and validity of our measures, we performed a factor analysis on all factors extracted. As expected, one component with a factor loading of 18.64 emerged.

Institutional Uncertainty in Host Country. The second dimension of the RIC is institutional uncertainty in the host country. We searched for a set of indicators with a comprehensive view of uncertainty beyond just economic or political factors. We selected the Fragile States Index, a database produced by "The Fund for Peace" and published by "Foreign Policy". The index ranks 178 nations annually based on their levels of stability and the pressures they face. The Fragile States Index collects and categorizes data for every country based on 12 political, social and economic key indicators and over 100 sub-indicators. The Fragile States Index has been used previously, especially in the Economics and Public Policy fields.

To make sure that selected measures represent the desired dimension of institutional uncertainty, we repeated the same process of pre-screening previously used for Institutional Development. The purpose of the screening process was to filter indicators aligned with the definition of institutional uncertainty.

Table 2. Indicators selected from the fragile states index representing different dimensions of institutional uncertainty

Uncertainty source	Correlated dimension from Fragile State Index
Political uncertainties	• External Interventions • State legitimacy • Security Apparatus
Government Policy uncertainties	• factionalized elites
Macroeconomics uncertainties	• Poverty and economic decline
Social uncertainties	• Demographic pressures • Refugees and IDPs • Human flight and brain drain • Group grievance
Natural Uncertainties	• Demographic pressures

Three out of the 12 indicators were not chosen based on relevance of their sub-indicators to the notion of institutional uncertainty (uneven economic development, public services, human rights and rules of law). (See Table 2).

A factor analysis was performed on nine indicators for 2013 to test the validity and reliability of measures of institutional uncertainty. It was expected that all factors load in one major component. The result of the analysis shows that all the factors were loading on one major component with an Eigenvalue of 6.95.

Institutional Distance between Host and Home Countries. The last dimension of the RIC is the institutional distance between home and host countries. Institutional distance effects have been measured in different ways (e.g. Henisz, 2000). This research used Worldwide Governance Indicators (WGI), developed by World Bank, as the primary source of measuring differences between national institutions. The index measures six dimensions: 1) voice and accountability, 2) political stability and absence of violence, 3) government effectiveness, 4) regulatory quality, 5) the rule of law, and 6) control of corruption. The six aggregate indicators are based on 31 underlying data sources reporting the perceptions of governance of a vast number of survey respondents and expert assessments worldwide. WGI is a commonly used index for the international business research to study the effect of institutional environment.

To measure the institutional distance between home and host countries (showing similarity or dissimilarity of the institutional profile of two countries), the aggregated institutional index for 2013 was computed for each home and host country, and the institutional distance was brought into the analysis as an absolute value of the difference between the two.

The created database includes pairs of more than 200 countries, which, due to its size, cannot be completely presented here. Based on our methods of analysis in this dataset, the institutional distance between two countries can have a theoretical value between 0 and 30; 0 showing the absolute similarity, and 30 showing the absolute institutional difference in country institutional profiles. Table 3 shows a sample result for Institutional distance pair matrix.

Table 3. Sample of institutional distance country pair matrix

Country	ARGENTINA	BELARUS	BRAZIL	CAMEROON	CANADA	CHILE	CHINA	CUBA	ETHIOPIA	FINLAND	FRANCE	GEORGIA	GERMANY	GHANA	GREECE	HONG KONG	HUNGARY	INDIA	INDONESIA	IRAN
ARGENTINA	0.0																			
BELARUS	3.6	0.0																		
BRAZIL	1.5	5.1	0.0																	
CAMEROON	3.6	0.1	5.2	0.0																
CANADA	10.0	13.5	8.4	13.6	0.0															
CHILE	8.1	11.7	6.6	11.7	1.9	0.0														
CHINA	1.3	2.3	2.8	2.4	11.3	9.4	0.0													
CUBA	2.5	1.0	4.1	1.1	12.5	10.6	1.2	0.0												
ETHIOPIA	2.6	0.9	4.2	1.0	12.6	10.7	1.3	0.1	0.0											
FINLAND	11.1	14.7	9.6	14.8	1.2	3.0	12.4	13.7	13.8	0.0										
FRANCE	7.9	11.5	6.4	11.6	2.0	0.2	9.2	10.5	10.6	3.2	0.0									
GEORGIA	3.1	6.7	1.6	6.8	6.9	5.0	4.4	5.7	5.8	8.0	4.8	0.0								
GERMANY	9.3	12.9	7.8	12.9	0.7	1.2	10.6	11.8	11.9	1.8	1.4	6.2	0.0							
GHANA	1.9	5.4	0.3	5.5	8.1	6.2	3.2	4.4	4.5	9.3	6.1	1.3	7.4	0.0						
GREECE	3.5	7.0	1.9	7.1	6.5	4.6	4.8	6.0	6.1	7.7	4.5	0.4	5.8	1.6	0.0					
HONG KONG	9.0	12.5	7.4	12.6	1.0	0.9	10.3	11.5	11.6	2.2	1.0	5.8	0.3	7.1	5.5	0.0				
HUNGARY	4.5	8.1	3.0	8.2	5.4	3.6	5.8	7.1	7.2	6.6	3.4	1.4	4.8	2.7	1.1	4.4	0.0			
INDIA	0.5	4.1	1.0	4.2	9.5	7.6	1.8	3.0	3.2	10.6	7.4	2.6	8.8	1.3	3.0	8.4	4.0	0.0		
INDONESIA	0.2	3.4	1.7	3.5	10.2	8.3	1.1	2.4	2.5	11.3	8.1	3.3	9.5	2.0	3.7	9.1	4.7	0.7	0.0	
IRAN	4.0	0.5	5.6	0.4	14.0	12.1	2.7	1.5	1.4	15.2	12.0	7.2	13.3	5.9	7.5	13.0	8.6	4.5	3.8	0.0

Table 4. Relative institutional challenge measures

Dimension	Index	Data source	Items
Institutional Uncertainty	Fragile States Index	The Fund For Peace & Foreign Policy (Foreign Policy)	Demographic pressures, refugee and Internally Displaced persons, Group grievance, human flight and brain drain, uneven economic development*, poverty and economic decline, state legitimacy, public services*, human rights and rule of law*, Security Apparatus, factionalized Elites, external Interventions (* not used)
Institutional Development	Global Competitiveness Ranking	World Economic Forum	Institutions, infrastructure, Macro-economy, health and primary education, higher education and training, market efficiency, technological readiness, business sophistication, innovation
Institutional Distance	Worldwide Governance Indicators (WGI)	World Bank	Voice and Accountability, Political Stability and Absence of Violence/Terrorism, Government Effectiveness, Regulatory Quality, Rule of Law, Control of Corruption

Compiling Data for Relative Institutional Challenge

We compiled three different dimensions based on previously measured factors to form the aggregate Relative Institutional Challenge construct, as summarized below in Table 4.

To develop the construct, the following issues were addressed to assure homogeneity between the datasets. First, datasets are different in their representations: while institutional development and Institutional uncertainty in the host country represent the data for a country, institutional distance shows the relative information between two countries. As the RIC similarly represents the data for country pairs, it is necessary that our data for institutional development and institutional uncertainty are also represented for all possible country pairs.

Second, datasets have different scales and need to be standardized: our three different datasets have different scales with different range and different standard deviation, so we standardized all the data before compiling them.

Third, the effect direction on RIC: while institutional uncertainty and institutional distance have the same effect direction on the RIC (higher levels of both means higher levels of the RIC), institutional development shows a reverse effect (higher levels of institutional development means lower levels of RIC). We correct this effect by using a reverse scale of institutional development, where higher levels of that scale means lower levels of institutional development.

The calculated index of RIC is an index theoretically varying between -100 and 100. Negative indicators show lower levels of RIC, while the positive section represents higher levels of RIC. The RIC does not represent a symmetrical relationship. The RIC of country A as faced by a firm from country B is different from the RIC of country B as perceived by a firm from country A. After extracting data for each dimension of RIC, the results were standardized and developed for the same pairs of countries for each dimension. The standardized data were then aggregated and the index for Relative Institutional Challenge for years 2011-2013 was developed. The RIC index, calculated for the year 2013 for a set of 72 countries is included in the appendix.

DISCUSSION

The purpose of this research was to develop a valid scale of a single measure that can be useful for researchers and practitioners to assess the relative institutional challenge for a firm from a particular home country entering alternative host countries. We performed this task by developing a new construct, Relative Institutional Challenge, measuring its dimensions (institutional distance, institutional development and institutional uncertainty), and creating the Relative Institutional Challenge Index through an aggregation of these measures.

ACADEMIC IMPLICATIONS

The current study has several contributions and implications for the development of the institution-based view within the field of international business. Primarily, this study extends the understanding on the influence of country-specific factors influences in the internationalization process. We believe the RIC has numerous implications at conceptual and empirical levels. First, the theoretical development of the construct incorporates both the process and degree of institutionalization, along with direction; elements that have been missing in earlier research (Phillips et al., 2009). Second, the RIC not only captures the level of similarity or dissimilarity of country institutional environments, but also encompasses the level and pace of institutionalization. Third, the RIC adds to commonly used constructs such as institutional distance. It can be used by scholars in the fields of international business, international development, political science, and strategic management. The construct provides a reliable measure for country specific-effects from a home country perspective. Replicability of the development process and availability of the data for the Relative Institutional Challenge Index will make it possible to update it every year.

Implications for Business Practice and Policy Making

In addition to its contribution to theory and its academic implications, the RIC possesses several practical implications for groups outside the academic setting. The construct and related index can help practitioners and managers to gain a better understanding of their internationalization destination based on the comprehensive set of variables.

REFERENCES

Allen, F., Qian, J., & Qian, M. (2005). Law, finance, and economic growth in China. *Journal of Financial Economics*, *77*(1), 57–116. doi:10.1016/j.jfineco.2004.06.010

Bae, J. H., & Salomon, R. (2010). Institutional distance in international business research. *Advances in International Management*, *23*, 327–349. doi:10.1108/S1571-5027(2010)00000230020

Bartholomew, S. (1997). National systems of biotechnology innovation: Complex interdependence in the global system. *Journal of International Business Studies*, *28*(2), 241–266. doi:10.1057/palgrave.jibs.8490100

Bartlett, C. A., & Ghoshal, S. (1999). *Managing across borders: The transnational solution* (Vol. 2). Taylor & Francis.

Bénassy-Quéré, A., Coupet, M., & Mayer, T. (2007). Institutional determinants of foreign direct investment. *World Economy*, *30*(5), 764–782. doi:10.1111/j.1467-9701.2007.01022.x

Bevan, A., Estrin, S., & Meyer, K. (2004). Foreign investment location and institutional development in transition economies. *International Business Review*, *13*(1), 43–64. doi:10.1016/j.ibusrev.2003.05.005

Brouthers, K. D. (2002). Institutional, cultural and transaction cost influences on entry mode choice and performance. *Journal of International Business Studies*, *33*(2), 203–222. doi:10.1057/palgrave.jibs.8491013

Bruton, G. D., Fried, V. H., & Manigart, S. (2005). Institutional influences on the worldwide expansion of venture capital. *Entrepreneurship Theory and Practice*, *29*(6), 737–760. doi:10.1111/j.1540-6520.2005.00106.x

Busenitz, L. W., Gomez, C., & Spencer, J. W. (2000). Country institutional profiles: Unlocking entrepreneurial phenomena. *Academy of Management Journal*, *43*(5), 994–1003. doi:10.2307/1556423

Chan, C. M., Isobe, T., & Makino, S. (2008). Which country matters? Institutional development and foreign affiliate performance. *Strategic Management Journal*, *29*(11), 1179–1205. doi:10.1002mj.705

Chao, M. C.-H., & Kumar, V. (2010). The impact of institutional distance on the international diversity–performance relationship. *Journal of World Business*, *45*(1), 93–103. doi:10.1016/j.jwb.2009.04.005

Christmann, P., Day, D., & Yip, G. S. (2000). The relative influence of country conditions, industry structure, and business strategy on multinational corporation subsidiary performance. *Journal of International Management*, *5*(4), 241–265. doi:10.1016/S1075-4253(99)00015-0

Davis, P. S., Desai, A. B., & Francis, J. D. (2000). Mode of international entry: An isomorphism perspective. *Journal of International Business Studies*, *31*(2), 239–258. doi:10.1057/palgrave.jibs.8490904

Doz, Y. L., & Prahalad, C. K. (1991). Managing DMNCs: A search for a new paradigm. *Strategic Management Journal*, *12*(S1), 145–164. doi:10.1002mj.4250120911

Dunning, J. H. (1980). Towards an eclectic theory of international production: Some empirical tests. *Journal of International Business Studies*, *11*(1), 9–31. doi:10.1057/palgrave.jibs.8490593

Dunning, J. H. (2000). The eclectic paradigm as an envelope for economic and business theories of MNE activity. *International Business Review*, *9*(2), 163–190. doi:10.1016/S0969-5931(99)00035-9

Eden, L., & Miller, S. R. (2004). Distance matters: Liability of foreignness, institutional distance and ownership strategy. *Advances in International Management*, *16*, 187–221. doi:10.1016/S0747-7929(04)16010-1

Gaur, A. S., & Lu, J. W. (2007). Ownership strategies and survival of foreign subsidiaries: Impacts of institutional distance and experience. *Journal of Management*, *33*(1), 84–110. doi:10.1177/0149206306295203

Hakanson, L., & Ambos, B. (2010). The antecedents of psychic distance. *Journal of International Management*, *16*(3), 195–210. doi:10.1016/j.intman.2010.06.001

Henisz, W. J. (2000). The institutional environment for multinational investment. *Journal of Law Economics and Organization*, *16*(2), 334–364. doi:10.1093/jleo/16.2.334

Henisz, W. J., & Zelner, B. A. (2003). The strategic organization of political Challenges and opportunities. *Strategic Organization*, *1*(4), 451–460. doi:10.1177/14761270030014005

Hernández, V., & Nieto, M. J. (2015). The effect of the magnitude and direction of institutional distance on the choice of international entry modes. *Journal of World Business*, *50*(1), 122–132. doi:10.1016/j.jwb.2014.02.002

Hilmersson, M., & Jansson, H. (2012). Reducing Uncertainty in the Emerging Market Entry Process: On the Relationship Among International Experiential Knowledge, Institutional Distance, and Uncertainty. *Journal of International Marketing*, *20*(4), 96–110. doi:10.1509/jim.12.0052

Hitt, M. A., Ahlstrom, D., Dacin, M. T., Levitas, E., & Svobodina, L. (2004). The institutional effects on strategic alliance partner selection in transition economies: China vs. Russia. *Organization Science*, *15*(2), 173–185. doi:10.1287/orsc.1030.0045

Hoskisson, R. E., Eden, L., Lau, C. M., & Wright, M. (2000). Strategy in emerging economies. *Academy of Management Journal*, *43*(3), 249–267. doi:10.2307/1556394

Johanson, J., & Vahlne, J. E. (1977). The internationalization process of the firm-a model of knowledge development and increasing foreign market commitments. *Journal of International Business Studies*, *8*(1), 23–32. doi:10.1057/palgrave.jibs.8490676

Johnston, M., Gilmore, A., & Carson, D. (2008). Dealing with environmental uncertainty: The value of scenario planning for small to medium-sized entreprises (SMEs). *European Journal of Marketing*, *42*(11/12), 1170–1178. doi:10.1108/03090560810903628

Khanna, T., & Palepu, K. (1997). Why focused strategies may be wrong for emerging markets. *Harvard Business Review*, *75*(4), 41–48.

Khanna, T., & Palepu, K. (2000). Is group affiliation profitable in emerging markets? An analysis of diversified Indian business groups. *The Journal of Finance*, *55*(2), 867–891. doi:10.1111/0022-1082.00229

Kiss, A. N., & Danis, W. M. (2008). Country institutional context, social networks, and new venture internationalization speed. *European Management Journal*, *26*(6), 388–399. doi:10.1016/j.emj.2008.09.001

Kostova, T. (1999). Transnational transfer of strategic organizational practices: A contextual perspective. *Academy of Management Review*, 308–324.

Kostova, T., & Roth, K. (2002). Adoption of an organizational practice by subsidiaries of multinational corporations: Institutional and relational effects. *Academy of Management Journal*, *45*(1), 215–233. doi:10.2307/3069293

Kostova, T., & Zaheer, S. (1999). Organizational legitimacy under conditions of complexity: The case of the multinational enterprise. *Academy of Management Review*, 64–81.

Law, M., Stewart, D., & Pollock, N. (1998). *Critical review form – Quantitative studies*. McMaster University: Occupational Therapy Evidence-Based Practice Research Group.

Maguire, S., Hardy, C., & Lawrence, T. B. (2004). Institutional entrepreneurship in emerging fields: HIV/AIDS treatment advocacy in Canada. *Academy of Management Journal*, *47*(5), 657–679. doi:10.2307/20159610

Meyer, J. W., & Rowan, B. (1977). Institutionalized organizations: Formal structure as myth and ceremony. *American Journal of Sociology*, *83*(2), 340–363. doi:10.1086/226550

Miller, D., Lee, J., Chang, S., & Le Breton-Miller, I. (2009). Filling the institutional void: The social behavior and performance of family vs non-family technology firms in emerging markets. *Journal of International Business Studies*, *40*(5), 802–817. doi:10.1057/jibs.2009.11

Miller, K. D. (1992). A framework for integrated Challenge management in international business. *Journal of International Business Studies*, *23*(2), 311–331. doi:10.1057/palgrave.jibs.8490270

North, D. C. (1990). *Institutions, institutional change and economic performance*. Cambridge University Press. doi:10.1017/CBO9780511808678

Oliver, C. (1991). Strategic responses to institutional processes. *Academy of Management Review*, *16*(1), 145–179. doi:10.5465/AMR.1991.4279002

Peng, M. W. (2003). Institutional transitions and strategic choices. *Academy of Management Review*, 275–296.

Peng, M. W., & Luo, Y. (2000). Managerial ties and firm performance in a transition economy: The nature of a micro-macro link. *Academy of Management Journal*, *43*(3), 486–501. doi:10.2307/1556406

Peng, M. W., Wang, D. Y. L., & Jiang, Y. (2008). An institution-based view of international business strategy: A focus on emerging economies. *Journal of International Business Studies*, *39*(5), 920–936. doi:10.1057/palgrave.jibs.8400377

Phillips, N., Tracey, P., & Karra, N. (2009). Rethinking institutional distance: Strengthening the tie between new institutional theory and international management. *Strategic Organization*, *7*(3), 339–348. doi:10.1177/1476127009337439

Porter, M. E. (1990). The competitive advantage of notions. *Harvard Business Review*.

Powell, W. W., & DiMaggio, P. J. (1991). *The new institutionalism in organizational analysis*. University of Chicago Press.

Rodrigues, S., & Child, J. (2008). The development of corporate identity: A political perspective. *Journal of Management Studies*, *45*(5), 885–911. doi:10.1111/j.1467-6486.2007.00750.x

Rodriguez, P., Uhlenbruck, K., & Eden, L. (2005). Government corruption and the entry strategies of multinationals. *Academy of Management Review*, *30*(2), 383–396. doi:10.5465/AMR.2005.16387894

Sala-i-Martin & Schwab. K (2014). *Globabl Competitiveness Report 2014-2015*. Geneva: World Economic Forum.

Salancik, G. R., & Pfeffer, J. (1978). *The external control of organizations: A resource dependence perspective*. New York: Harper and Row.

Schwens, C., Eiche, J., & Kabst, R. (2011). The moderating impact of informal institutional distance and formal institutional Challenge on SME entry mode choice. *Journal of Management Studies*, *48*(2), 330–351.

Scott, W. R. (2001). *Institutions and organizations*. Thousand Oaks, CA: Sage Publications, Inc.

Uhlenbruck, K., Rodriguez, P., Doh, J., & Eden, L. (2006). The impact of corruption on entry strategy: Evidence from telecommunication projects in emerging economies. *Organization Science*, *17*(3), 402–414. doi:10.1287/orsc.1060.0186

Xu, D., & Shenkar, O. (2002). Institutional distance and the multinational enterprise. *Academy of Management Review*, 608–618.

Zaheer, S., Schomaker, M., & Genc, M. (2003). Identity versus culture in mergers of equals. *European Management Journal*, *21*(2), 185–191. doi:10.1016/S0263-2373(03)00013-6

APPENDIX

Relative Institutional Challenge Index Calculated for the Year 2013 for a set of 72 Countries

Table 5.

Host country / Home country	Algeria	Argentina	Australia	Austria	Azerbaijan	Belgium	Bolivia	Brazil	Bulgaria	Cambodia	Cameroon	Canada	Chile	China	Colombia	Croatia
Algeria	N.A	-8.2	-13.4	-13.1	-10.4	-13.1	1.7	-4.9	-1.7	0.4	6.7	-15.5	-8.5	-11.2	3.2	0.8
Argentina	4.1	N.A	-19.9	-19.5	-7.6	-19.6	0.3	-11.3	-8.1	4.2	13.1	-21.9	-14.9	-12.6	-3.2	-5.7
Australia	30.3	11.5	N.A	-44.8	18.6	-40.4	26.5	5.7	4.9	30.3	39.3	-48.1	-30.5	13.6	21.4	-1.1
Austria	29.8	11.1	-45.6	N.A	18.1	-40.8	26.1	5.3	4.4	29.9	38.8	-47.6	-30.9	13.1	21.0	-1.5
Azerbaijan	-0.5	-10.0	-15.2	-14.9	N.A	-14.9	-0.1	-6.7	-3.5	-0.5	8.5	-17.3	-10.3	-12.9	1.4	-1.0
Belgium	27.6	8.9	-43.4	-43.0	15.9	N.A	23.8	3.1	2.2	27.7	36.6	-45.4	-33.2	10.9	18.8	-3.7
Bolivia	1.6	-12.1	-17.3	-17.0	-10.1	-17.0	N.A	-8.8	-5.6	1.6	10.6	-19.4	-12.4	-15.0	-0.7	-3.1
Brazil	8.7	-10.1	-24.4	-24.1	-3.0	-24.1	4.9	N.A	-12.7	8.7	17.7	-26.5	-19.5	-8.0	-0.2	-10.2
Bulgaria	10.7	-8.1	-26.4	-26.1	-1.0	-26.2	6.9	-13.8	N.A	10.8	19.7	-28.5	-21.5	-6.0	1.9	-12.3
Cambodia	-1.0	-9.6	-14.8	-14.5	-11.8	-14.5	0.3	-6.2	-3.0	N.A	8.0	-16.8	-9.8	-12.5	1.9	-0.6
Cameroon	-1.0	-6.9	-12.1	-11.8	-9.1	-11.8	3.0	-3.6	-0.4	1.8	N.A	-14.2	-7.2	-9.8	4.5	2.1
Canada	30.8	12.0	-45.6	-44.4	19.1	-39.9	27.0	6.2	5.4	30.8	39.8	N.A	-30.0	14.0	21.9	-0.6
Chile	25.0	6.2	-40.7	-40.4	13.3	-40.4	21.2	0.5	-0.4	25.0	34.0	-42.8	N.A	8.3	16.2	-6.4
China	1.6	-12.2	-17.4	-17.1	-10.1	-17.1	-2.2	-8.8	-5.6	1.7	10.6	-19.4	-12.4	N.A	-0.7	-3.2
Colombia	4.9	-13.9	-20.6	-20.3	-6.8	-20.3	1.1	-12.1	-8.9	4.9	13.9	-22.7	-15.7	-11.9	N.A	-6.4
Croatia	14.9	-3.9	-30.6	-30.3	3.2	-30.4	11.1	-9.6	-10.5	15.0	23.9	-32.7	-25.7	-1.8	6.1	N.A
Denmark	33.2	14.5	-43.1	-41.9	21.5	-37.5	29.4	8.7	7.8	33.3	42.2	-46.1	-27.6	16.5	24.4	1.9
Ecuador	1.2	-11.7	-16.9	-16.6	-10.5	-16.6	-1.8	-8.4	-5.2	1.2	10.2	-19.0	-12.0	-14.6	-0.3	-2.7
Egypt	-1.3	-7.2	-12.4	-12.1	-9.4	-12.1	2.7	-3.9	-0.7	1.4	5.7	-14.5	-7.5	-10.2	4.2	1.8
Finland	34.1	15.4	-42.2	-41.0	22.4	-36.6	30.3	9.6	8.7	34.2	43.1	-45.2	-26.7	17.4	25.3	2.8
France	24.8	6.0	-40.5	-40.2	13.1	-40.2	21.0	0.2	-0.6	24.8	33.8	-42.5	-35.6	8.0	15.9	-6.6
Germany	29.0	10.2	-44.7	-44.4	17.3	-41.7	25.2	4.4	3.6	29.0	38.0	-46.7	-31.8	12.2	20.1	-2.4
Greece	13.2	-5.5	-29.0	-28.7	1.5	-28.7	9.4	-11.3	-12.2	13.3	22.2	-31.0	-24.0	-3.5	4.4	-14.8
Iceland	29.1	10.3	-44.8	-44.5	17.4	-41.6	25.3	4.5	3.6	29.1	38.1	-46.8	-31.7	12.3	20.2	-2.3
India	4.3	-14.5	-20.0	-19.7	-7.4	-19.7	0.5	-11.5	-8.3	4.3	13.3	-22.1	-15.1	-12.4	-3.4	-5.8
Iran, Islamic Rep.	1.6	-4.3	-9.5	-9.2	-6.5	-9.3	5.6	-1.0	2.2	4.3	7.9	-11.6	-4.6	-7.3	7.1	4.7
Ireland	28.3	9.5	-44.0	-43.7	16.6	-42.4	24.5	3.7	2.9	28.3	37.3	-46.1	-32.5	11.5	19.4	-3.1
Israel	17.4	-1.3	-33.2	-32.8	5.7	-32.9	13.6	-7.1	-8.0	17.5	26.4	-35.2	-28.2	0.7	8.6	-13.9
Italy	15.8	-3.0	-31.5	-31.2	4.1	-31.3	12.0	-8.7	-9.6	15.8	24.8	-33.6	-26.6	-0.9	7.0	-15.6
Japan	26.8	8.0	-42.5	-42.2	15.1	-42.2	23.0	2.2	1.4	26.8	35.8	-44.6	-34.0	10.1	17.9	-4.6
Jordan	6.9	-11.9	-22.6	-22.3	-4.8	-22.3	3.1	-14.1	-10.9	6.9	15.9	-24.7	-17.7	-9.9	-2.0	-8.4
Korea, Rep.	19.3	0.5	-35.0	-34.7	7.6	-34.7	15.5	-5.3	-6.1	19.3	28.3	-37.0	-30.1	2.5	10.4	-12.1
Kuwait	8.1	-10.7	-23.8	-23.5	-3.6	-23.5	4.3	-15.2	-12.1	8.1	17.1	-25.8	-18.9	-8.7	-0.8	-9.6
Lebanon	-0.7	-9.8	-15.0	-14.7	-12.0	-14.7	0.1	-6.5	-3.3	-0.7	8.3	-17.1	-10.1	-12.7	1.6	-0.8
Libya	6.8	0.8	-4.4	-4.1	-1.4	-4.1	10.7	4.2	7.4	9.5	13.1	-6.4	0.6	-2.1	12.3	9.8
Malaysia	14.3	-4.4	-30.1	-29.7	2.6	-29.8	10.5	-10.2	-11.1	14.4	23.3	-32.1	-25.1	-2.4	5.5	-15.9
Mexico	6.9	-11.9	-22.6	-22.3	-4.8	-22.3	3.1	-14.1	-10.9	6.9	15.9	-24.7	-17.7	-9.8	-1.9	-8.4
Morocco	4.4	-14.4	-20.1	-19.8	-7.3	-19.8	0.6	-11.5	-8.3	4.4	13.4	-22.1	-15.2	-12.4	-3.5	-5.9
Netherlands	31.9	13.1	-44.4	-43.2	20.2	-38.8	28.1	7.3	6.5	31.9	40.9	-47.4	-28.9	15.2	23.0	0.5
New Zealand	33.6	14.8	-42.7	-41.5	21.9	-37.1	29.8	9.0	8.2	33.6	42.6	-45.7	-27.2	16.9	24.7	2.2
Nicaragua	1.8	-12.3	-17.5	-17.2	-9.9	-17.3	-2.0	-9.0	-5.8	1.9	10.8	-19.6	-12.6	-14.9	-0.9	-3.4

Table 6.

Host country Home country	Algeria	Argentina	Australia	Austria	Azerbaijan	Belgium	Bolivi	Brazil	Bulgaria	Cambodia	Cameroon	Canada	Chile	China	Colombia	Croatia
Norway	33.6	14.9	-42.7	-41.5	21.9	-37.1	29.8	9.1	8.2	33.7	42.6	-45.7	-27.2	16.9	24.8	2.3
Pakistan	1.6	-4.3	-9.5	-9.2	-6.5	-9.2	5.6	-0.9	2.3	4.4	8.0	-11.5	-4.5	-7.2	7.2	4.7
Panama	9.9	-8.9	-25.6	-25.3	-1.8	-25.3	6.1	-14.7	-13.9	9.9	18.9	-27.6	-20.7	-6.9	1.0	-11.4
Paraguay	0.3	-10.8	-16.0	-15.7	-11.4	-15.7	-0.9	-7.5	-4.3	0.3	9.3	-18.1	-11.1	-13.7	0.6	-1.8
Poland	20.4	1.6	-36.1	-35.8	8.7	-35.8	16.6	-4.2	-5.0	20.4	29.4	-38.2	-31.2	3.7	11.5	-11.0
Portugal	22.1	3.3	-37.8	-37.5	10.3	-37.5	18.3	-2.5	-3.4	22.1	31.0	-39.8	-32.8	5.3	13.2	-9.3
Qatar	19.1	0.3	-34.8	-34.5	7.4	-34.6	15.3	-5.4	-6.3	19.2	28.1	-36.9	-29.9	2.4	10.3	-12.2
Romania	11.0	-7.8	-26.7	-26.4	-0.7	-26.4	7.2	-13.6	-14.4	11.0	20.0	-28.8	-21.8	-5.7	2.2	-12.5
Russian Federation	-0.6	-9.9	-15.1	-14.8	-12.1	-14.8	0.0	-6.6	-3.4	-0.6	8.4	-17.1	-10.2	-12.8	1.5	-0.9
Rwanda	7.4	-11.4	-23.1	-22.8	-4.3	-22.8	3.6	-14.6	-11.4	7.4	16.4	-25.2	-18.2	-9.3	-1.5	-8.9
Saudi Arabia	4.9	-13.9	-20.6	-20.3	-6.8	-20.3	1.1	-12.1	-8.9	4.9	13.9	-22.7	-15.7	-11.9	-4.0	-6.4
Senegal	6.5	-12.3	-22.2	-21.9	-5.2	-21.9	2.7	-13.7	-10.5	6.5	15.5	-24.3	-17.3	-10.3	-2.4	-8.0
Serbia	7.7	-11.1	-23.4	-23.1	-4.0	-23.1	3.9	-14.9	-11.7	7.7	16.7	-25.5	-18.5	-9.1	-1.2	-9.2
Seychelles	12.0	-6.8	-27.7	-27.4	0.3	-27.4	8.2	-12.6	-13.4	12.0	21.0	-29.7	-22.8	-4.8	3.1	-13.5
Sierra Leone	-0.4	-10.2	-15.4	-15.1	-12.1	-15.1	-0.3	-6.8	-3.6	-0.3	8.6	-17.4	-10.4	-13.1	1.3	-1.2
Singapore	30.0	11.2	-45.7	-45.1	18.3	-40.7	26.2	5.4	4.6	30.0	39.0	-47.8	-30.8	13.3	21.2	-1.4
Slovenia	20.6	1.9	-36.4	-36.1	8.9	-36.1	16.9	-3.9	-4.8	20.7	29.6	-38.4	-31.4	3.9	11.8	-10.7
South Africa	12.2	-6.6	-27.9	-27.6	0.4	-27.6	8.4	-12.4	-13.3	12.2	21.1	-29.9	-22.9	-4.6	3.3	-13.7
Spain	20.1	1.3	-35.8	-35.5	8.4	-35.5	16.3	-4.5	-5.3	20.1	29.1	-37.8	-30.9	3.3	11.2	-11.3
Sweden	33.5	14.8	-42.8	-41.6	21.8	-37.2	29.8	9.0	8.1	33.6	42.5	-45.8	-27.2	16.8	24.7	2.2
Switzerland	32.6	13.8	-43.8	-42.6	20.9	-38.1	28.8	8.0	7.1	32.6	41.6	-46.7	-28.2	15.8	23.7	1.2
Tunisia	5.1	-13.6	-20.9	-20.6	-6.6	-20.6	1.3	-12.3	-9.1	5.2	14.1	-22.9	-15.9	-11.6	-3.7	-6.7
Turkey	8.0	-10.8	-23.7	-23.4	-3.7	-23.4	4.2	-15.2	-12.0	8.0	17.0	-25.8	-18.8	-8.8	-0.9	-9.5
Ukraine	-0.7	-9.9	-15.1	-14.7	-12.1	-14.8	0.0	-6.5	-3.3	-0.6	8.3	-17.1	-10.1	-12.8	1.6	-0.9
United Arab Emirates	17.6	-1.2	-33.3	-33.0	5.9	-33.0	13.8	-7.0	-7.8	17.6	26.6	-35.4	-28.4	0.9	8.7	-13.8
United Kingdom	28.0	9.3	-43.8	-43.5	16.3	-42.7	24.3	3.5	2.6	28.1	37.0	-45.8	-32.7	11.3	19.2	-3.3
United States	25.5	6.7	-41.2	-40.9	13.8	-40.9	21.7	0.9	0.1	25.5	34.5	-43.3	-35.3	8.8	16.6	-5.9
Uruguay	19.6	0.8	-35.3	-35.0	7.8	-35.0	15.8	-5.0	-5.9	19.6	28.5	-37.3	-30.3	2.8	10.7	-11.8
Venezuela	4.2	-1.7	-6.9	-6.6	-3.9	-6.7	8.2	1.6	4.8	6.9	10.5	-9.0	-2.0	-4.7	9.7	7.2
Zimbabwe	4.3	-1.6	-6.8	-6.5	-3.8	-6.5	8.3	1.8	5.0	7.1	10.7	-8.8	-1.8	-4.5	9.9	7.4

Table 7.

Host country Home country	Denmark	Ecuador	Egypt	Finland	France	Germany	Greece	Iceland	Indi	Iran, Islamic Rep.	Ireland	Israel	Italy	Japan	Jordan	Korea, Rep.
Algeria	-11.4	-3.6	2.6	-21.4	-13.0	-15.6	-0.7	-12.2	-6.6	1.0	-15.5	0.8	-2.7	-14.7	-7.3	-10.7
Argentina	-17.8	-4.1	9.1	-27.8	-19.4	-22.1	-7.1	-18.6	-13.0	7.5	-22.0	-5.6	-9.2	-21.1	-13.7	-17.1
Australia	-44.0	22.1	35.2	-54.0	-34.6	-45.6	0.8	-42.3	12.8	33.6	-44.1	-6.1	-6.4	-40.3	6.9	-21.2
Austria	-43.5	21.6	34.8	-53.5	-35.0	-46.0	0.4	-42.8	12.4	33.2	-44.5	-6.5	-6.8	-40.7	6.5	-21.7
Azerbaijan	-13.2	-5.4	4.4	-23.2	-14.8	-17.4	-2.5	-14.0	-8.4	2.8	-17.3	-1.0	-4.5	-16.5	-9.1	-12.5
Belgium	-41.3	19.4	32.6	-51.3	-37.2	-45.6	-1.8	-42.1	10.2	31.0	-45.5	-8.7	-9.0	-43.0	4.3	-23.9
Bolivia	-15.3	-6.7	6.5	-25.3	-16.9	-19.5	-4.6	-16.1	-10.5	4.9	-19.4	-3.1	-6.6	-18.6	-11.2	-14.6
Brazil	-22.4	0.4	13.6	-32.4	-24.0	-26.6	-11.7	-23.2	-8.8	12.0	-26.5	-10.2	-13.7	-25.7	-14.7	-21.7
Bulgaria	-24.4	2.5	15.6	-34.4	-26.0	-28.6	-13.7	-25.2	-6.8	14.1	-28.6	-12.2	-15.8	-27.7	-12.6	-23.7
Cambodia	-12.7	-4.9	4.0	-22.7	-14.4	-17.0	-2.0	-13.6	-7.9	2.4	-16.9	-0.6	-4.1	-16.1	-8.7	-12.1
Cameroon	-10.1	-2.2	2.0	-20.1	-11.7	-14.3	0.6	-10.9	-5.3	-0.3	-14.2	2.1	-1.4	-13.4	-6.0	-9.4
Canada	-44.4	22.5	35.7	-54.4	-34.1	-45.1	1.3	-41.9	13.3	34.1	-43.6	-5.6	-5.9	-39.8	7.4	-20.8
Chile	-38.7	16.8	29.9	-48.7	-39.9	-42.9	-4.5	-39.5	7.5	28.3	-42.8	-11.4	-11.7	-42.0	1.6	-26.5
China	-15.3	-6.6	6.6	-25.3	-17.0	-19.6	-4.6	-16.1	-10.5	5.0	-19.5	-3.1	-6.7	-18.7	-11.2	-14.6
Colombia	-18.6	-3.4	9.8	-28.5	-20.2	-22.8	-7.9	-19.4	-12.6	8.2	-22.7	-6.4	-9.9	-21.9	-14.5	-17.9
Croatia	-28.6	6.7	19.8	-38.6	-30.2	-32.8	-14.6	-29.4	-2.6	18.3	-32.7	-16.4	-20.0	-31.9	-8.4	-27.9
Denmark	N.A	25.0	38.2	-56.9	-31.6	-42.6	3.8	-39.4	15.8	36.6	-41.2	-3.1	-3.4	-37.3	9.9	-18.3
Ecuador	-14.9	N.A	6.1	-24.9	-16.5	-19.1	-4.2	-15.7	-10.1	4.5	-19.0	-2.7	-6.2	-18.2	-10.8	-14.2
Egypt	-10.4	-2.6	N.A	-20.4	-12.0	-14.6	0.3	-11.2	-5.6	0.0	-14.5	1.8	-1.7	-13.7	-6.3	-9.7
Finland	-46.0	25.9	39.1	N.A	-30.7	-41.7	4.7	-38.5	16.7	37.5	-40.3	-2.2	-2.5	-36.5	10.8	-17.4
France	-38.5	16.5	29.7	-48.4	N.A	-42.7	-4.7	-39.3	7.3	28.1	-42.6	-11.6	-11.9	-41.8	1.4	-26.8
Germany	-42.7	20.7	33.9	-52.6	-35.9	N.A	-0.5	-43.5	11.5	32.3	-45.4	-7.4	-7.7	-41.6	5.6	-22.6
Greece	-26.9	5.0	18.2	-36.9	-28.6	-31.2	N.A	-27.7	-4.2	16.6	-31.1	-14.7	-18.3	-30.3	-10.1	-26.2
Iceland	-42.7	20.8	34.0	-52.7	-35.8	-46.8	-0.4	N.A	11.6	32.4	-45.3	-7.3	-7.6	-41.5	5.7	-22.5
India	-18.0	-3.9	9.2	-28.0	-19.6	-22.2	-7.3	-18.8	N.A	7.6	-22.1	-5.8	-9.3	-21.3	-13.9	-17.3
Iran, Islamic Rep.	-7.5	0.3	4.5	-17.5	-9.1	-11.7	3.2	-8.3	-2.7	N.A	-11.6	4.7	1.1	-10.8	-3.4	-6.8
Ireland	-42.0	20.0	33.2	-52.0	-36.6	-46.2	-1.2	-42.8	10.8	31.6	N.A	-8.1	-8.4	-42.3	4.9	-23.3
Israel	-31.1	9.2	22.4	-41.1	-32.8	-35.4	-12.0	-31.9	0.0	20.8	-35.3	N.A	-19.2	-34.5	5.9	30.4
Italy	-29.5	7.6	20.7	-39.5	-31.1	-33.7	-13.7	-30.3	-1.7	19.1	-33.6	-17.3	N.A	-32.8	-7.6	-28.8
Japan	-40.5	18.5	31.7	-50.5	-38.1	-44.7	-2.7	-41.3	9.3	30.1	-44.6	-9.6	-9.9	N.A	3.4	-24.8
Jordan	-20.6	-1.4	11.8	-30.6	-22.2	-24.8	-9.9	-21.4	-10.6	10.2	-24.7	-8.4	-11.9	-23.9	N.A	-19.9
Korea, Rep.	-32.9	11.0	24.2	-42.9	-34.6	-37.2	-10.2	-33.8	1.8	22.6	-37.1	-17.1	-17.4	-36.3	-4.1	N.A
Kuwait	-21.8	-0.2	13.0	-31.7	-23.4	-26.0	-11.0	-22.6	-9.4	11.4	-25.9	-9.6	-13.1	-25.1	-15.3	-21.1
Lebanon	-13.0	-5.1	4.2	-22.9	-14.6	-17.2	-2.3	-13.8	-8.2	2.6	-17.1	-0.8	-4.3	-16.3	-8.9	-12.3
Libya	-2.3	5.5	9.7	-12.3	-4.0	-6.6	8.4	-3.1	2.5	2.3	-6.5	9.9	6.3	-5.7	1.8	-1.6
Malaysia	-28.0	6.1	19.3	-38.0	-29.6	-32.3	-15.1	-28.8	-3.1	17.7	-32.2	-15.8	-19.4	-31.3	-9.0	-27.3
Mexico	-20.6	-1.3	11.8	-30.6	-22.2	-24.8	-9.9	-21.4	-10.6	10.2	-24.7	-8.4	-11.9	-23.9	-16.5	-19.9
Morocco	-18.0	-3.9	9.3	-28.0	-19.7	-22.3	-7.3	-18.9	-13.1	7.7	-22.2	-5.9	-9.4	-21.4	-14.0	-17.4
Netherlands	-45.6	23.7	36.8	-55.6	-33.0	-44.0	2.4	-40.7	14.4	35.2	-42.5	-4.5	-4.8	-38.7	8.5	-19.6
New Zealand	-46.6	25.4	38.5	-57.3	-31.3	-42.3	4.1	-39.0	16.1	36.9	-40.8	-2.8	-3.1	-37.0	10.2	-17.9
Nicaragua	-15.5	-6.4	6.7	-25.5	-17.1	-19.7	-4.8	-16.3	-10.7	5.2	-19.7	-3.3	-6.9	-18.8	-11.4	-14.8

Table 8.

Host country	Denmark	Ecuador	Egypt	Finland	France	Germany	Greece	Iceland	India	Iran, Islamic Rep.	Ireland	Israel	Italy	Japan	Jordan	Korea, Rep.
Home country																
Norway	-46.5	25.4	38.6	-57.3	-31.2	-42.2	4.2	-39	16.2	37	-40.7	-2.7	-3	-36.9	10.3	-17.9
Pakistan	-7.4	0.4	4.6	-17.4	-9.1	-11.7	3.3	-8.3	-2.6	-2.8	-11.6	4.7	1.2	-10.8	-3.4	-6.8
Panama	-23.6	1.6	14.8	-33.5	-25.2	-27.8	-12.8	-24.4	-7.6	13.2	-27.7	-11.4	-14.9	-26.9	-13.5	-22.9
Paraguay	-14	-6.2	5.2	-24	-15.6	-18.2	-3.3	-14.8	-9.2	3.6	-18.1	-1.8	-5.3	-17.3	-9.9	-13.3
Poland	-34.1	12.2	25.3	-44.1	-35.7	-38.3	-9.1	-34.9	2.9	23.7	-38.2	-16	-16.3	-37.4	-3	-31.1
Portugal	-35.7	13.8	27	-45.7	-37.4	-40	-7.4	-36.6	4.6	25.4	-39.9	-14.3	-14.6	-39.1	-1.3	-29.5
Qatar	-32.8	10.9	24	-42.8	-34.4	-37	-10.3	-33.6	1.6	22.5	-37	-17.3	-17.5	-36.1	-4.2	-32.1
Romania	-24.7	2.8	15.9	-34.7	-26.3	-28.9	-14	-25.5	-6.5	14.3	-28.8	-12.5	-16	-28	-12.4	-24
Russian Federation	-13.1	-5.2	4.3	-23	-14.7	-17.3	-2.3	-13.9	-8.3	2.7	-17.2	-0.9	-4.4	-16.4	-9	-12.4
Rwanda	-21.1	-0.8	12.3	-31.1	-22.7	-25.3	-10.4	-21.9	-10.1	10.7	-25.2	-8.9	-12.4	-24.4	-16	-20.4
Saudi Arabia	-18.6	-3.4	9.8	-28.6	-20.2	-22.8	-7.9	-19.4	-12.6	8.2	-22.7	-6.4	-9.9	-21.9	-14.5	-17.9
Senegal	-20.2	-1.8	11.4	-30.2	-21.8	-24.4	-9.5	-21	-11	9.8	-24.3	-8	-11.5	-23.5	-16.1	-19.5
Serbia	-21.4	-0.6	12.6	-31.4	-23	-25.6	-10.7	-22.2	-9.8	11	-25.5	-9.2	-12.7	-24.7	-15.7	-20.7
Seychelles	-25.7	3.7	16.9	-35.6	-27.3	-29.9	-14.9	-26.5	-5.5	15.3	-29.8	-13.5	-17	-29	-11.4	-25
Sierra Leone	-13.3	-5.5	4.6	-23.3	-15	-17.6	-2.6	-14.1	-8.5	3	-17.5	-1.1	-4.7	-16.7	-9.3	-12.7
Singapore	-43.7	21.8	34.9	-53.7	-34.9	-45.9	0.5	-42.6	12.5	33.3	-44.4	-6.4	-6.7	-40.6	6.6	-21.5
Slovenia	-34.3	12.4	25.6	-44.3	-36	-38.6	-8.8	-35.2	3.2	24	-38.5	-15.7	-16	-37.7	-2.7	-30.9
South Africa	-25.8	3.9	17.1	-35.8	-27.5	-30.1	-15.1	-26.7	-5.3	15.5	-30	-13.7	-17.2	-29.2	-11.2	-25.2
Spain	-33.8	11.8	25	-43.7	-35.4	-38	-9.4	-34.6	2.6	23.4	-37.9	-16.3	-16.6	-37.1	-3.3	-31.5
Sweden	-46.6	25.3	38.5	-57.2	-31.3	-42.3	4.1	-39.1	16.1	36.9	-40.8	-2.8	-3.1	-37	10.2	-18
Switzerland	-46.2	24.3	37.5	-56.2	-32.3	-43.3	3.1	-40.1	15.1	35.9	-41.8	-3.8	-4.1	-38	9.2	-19
Tunisia	-18.8	-3.1	10.1	-28.8	-20.5	-23.1	-8.1	-19.6	-12.3	8.5	-23	-6.6	-10.2	-22.2	-14.7	-18.1
Turkey	-21.7	-0.3	12.9	-31.6	-23.3	-25.9	-11	-22.5	-9.5	11.3	-25.8	-9.5	-13	-25	-15.4	-21
Ukraine	-13	-5.2	4.3	-23	-14.6	-17.3	-2.3	-13.8	-8.2	2.7	-17.2	-0.8	-4.4	-16.4	-8.9	-12.3
United Arab Emirates	-31.3	9.3	22.5	-41.3	-32.9	-35.5	-11.9	-32.1	0.1	20.9	-35.4	-18.8	-19.1	-34.6	-5.8	-30.6
United Kingdom	-41.7	19.8	33	-51.7	-36.8	-46	-1.4	-42.5	10.6	31.4	-45.9	-8.3	-8.6	-42.5	4.7	-23.5
United States	-39.2	17.3	30.4	-49.2	-39.4	-43.4	-4	-40	8	28.8	-43.3	-10.9	-11.2	-42.5	2.1	-26
Uruguay	-33.2	11.3	24.5	-43.2	-34.9	-37.5	-9.9	-34.1	2.1	22.9	-37.4	-16.8	-17.1	-36.6	-3.8	-32
Venezuela	-4.9	2.9	7.1	-14.9	-6.5	-9.1	5.8	-5.7	-0.1	-0.2	-9.1	7.3	3.7	-8.2	-0.8	-4.2
Zimbabwe	-4.7	3.1	7.3	-14.7	-6.4	-9	6	-5.6	0.1	-0.1	-8.9	7.4	3.9	-8.1	-0.7	-4.1
Table is wider than 6.25 inches																

Table 9.

Host country Home country	Kuwait	Lebanon	Libya	Mexico	Morocco	Netherlands	New Zealand	Nicaragua	Norway	Pakistan	Panama	Paraguay	Poland	Portugal	Qatar	Romania
Algeria	**-12.1**	**4.0**	**9.3**	**-3.0**	**-6.3**	**-15.2**	**-18.6**	**0.5**	**-16.3**	**12.0**	**-12.5**	**0.5**	**-2.8**	**-9.6**	**-24.2**	**0.1**
Argentina	-18.5	7.3	15.7	-9.4	-12.7	-21.6	-25.0	-1.3	-22.7	18.5	-19.0	1.8	-9.3	-16.0	-30.6	-6.3
Australia	-0.2	33.5	41.9	11.2	13.0	-47.7	-51.2	24.8	-48.9	44.6	-4.3	28.0	-15.6	-25.7	-34.4	6.1
Austria	-0.7	33.0	41.5	10.8	12.5	-47.3	-50.7	24.4	-48.5	44.2	-4.7	27.5	-16.1	-26.2	-34.8	5.7
Azerbaijan	-13.9	2.6	11.1	-4.7	-8.1	-16.9	-20.4	-1.3	-18.1	13.8	-14.3	-1.2	-4.6	-11.4	-26.0	-1.7
Belgium	-2.9	30.8	39.2	8.6	10.3	-45.1	-48.5	22.2	-46.2	42.0	-6.9	25.3	-18.3	-28.4	-37.1	3.5
Bolivia	-16.0	4.7	13.2	-6.8	-10.2	-19.0	-22.5	-3.4	-20.2	15.9	-16.4	-0.8	-6.7	-13.5	-28.0	-3.8
Brazil	-21.9	11.8	20.3	-10.4	-8.6	-26.1	-29.6	3.2	-27.3	23.0	-23.5	6.3	-13.8	-20.6	-35.2	-10.9
Bulgaria	-19.8	13.9	22.3	-8.4	-6.6	-28.2	-31.6	5.3	-29.3	25.0	-23.9	8.4	-15.8	-22.6	-37.2	-12.9
Cambodia	-13.5	2.7	10.7	-4.3	-7.6	-16.5	-20.0	-0.9	-17.7	13.4	-13.9	-0.8	-4.2	-10.9	-25.5	-1.2
Cameroon	-10.8	5.3	8.0	-1.6	-5.0	-13.8	-17.3	1.8	-15.0	10.7	-11.2	1.9	-1.5	-8.3	-22.9	1.4
Canada	0.2	33.9	42.4	11.7	13.4	-48.2	-51.7	25.3	-49.4	45.1	-3.8	28.4	-15.2	-25.2	-33.9	6.6
Chile	-5.5	28.2	36.6	5.9	7.7	-42.5	-45.9	19.6	-43.6	39.3	-9.6	22.7	-20.9	-31.0	-39.7	0.8
China	-16.0	4.8	13.3	-6.9	-10.2	-19.1	-22.5	-3.5	-20.3	16.0	-16.5	-0.7	-6.8	-13.5	-28.1	-3.8
Colombia	-19.3	8.0	16.5	-10.1	-12.4	-22.3	-25.8	-0.6	-23.5	19.2	-19.7	2.5	-10.0	-16.8	-31.3	-7.1
Croatia	-15.6	18.1	26.5	-4.2	-2.4	-32.4	-35.8	9.5	-33.5	29.2	-19.7	12.6	-20.0	-26.8	-41.4	-9.3
Denmark	2.7	36.4	44.9	14.2	15.9	-48.0	-54.1	27.8	-51.9	47.6	-1.3	30.9	-12.7	-22.8	-31.5	9.1
Ecuador	-15.6	4.3	12.8	-6.4	-9.8	-18.6	-22.1	-3.0	-19.8	15.5	-16.0	-1.2	-6.3	-13.1	-27.7	-3.4
Egypt	-11.1	5.0	8.3	-2.0	-5.3	-14.2	-17.6	1.5	-15.3	11.0	-11.5	1.5	-1.8	-8.6	-23.2	1.1
Finland	3.6	37.3	45.8	15.1	16.8	-47.1	-53.9	28.7	-51.8	48.5	-0.4	31.8	-11.8	-21.9	-30.6	10.0
France	-5.8	27.9	36.4	5.7	7.5	-42.2	-45.7	19.3	-43.4	39.1	-9.8	22.4	-21.1	-31.2	-39.9	0.6
Germany	-1.6	32.1	40.6	9.9	11.7	-46.4	-49.9	23.5	-47.6	43.3	-5.6	26.6	-16.9	-27.0	-35.7	4.8
Greece	-17.3	16.4	24.9	-5.8	-4.1	-30.7	-34.1	7.8	-31.9	27.6	-21.3	10.9	-18.4	-25.1	-39.7	-10.9
Iceland	-1.5	32.2	40.7	10.0	11.7	-46.5	-50.0	23.6	-47.7	43.4	-5.5	26.7	-16.9	-26.9	-35.6	4.9
India	-18.7	7.5	15.9	-9.6	-12.9	-21.7	-25.2	-1.2	-22.9	18.6	-19.1	2.0	-9.4	-16.2	-30.8	-6.5
Iran, Islamic Rep.	-8.2	7.9	5.4	0.9	-2.4	-11.3	-14.7	4.4	-12.4	8.1	-8.6	4.4	1.1	-5.7	-20.3	4.0
Ireland	-2.3	31.4	39.9	9.2	11.0	-45.7	-49.2	22.8	-46.9	42.6	-6.3	25.9	-17.6	-27.7	-36.4	4.1
Israel	-13.1	20.6	29.1	-1.6	0.1	-34.9	-38.3	12.0	-36.1	31.8	-17.1	15.1	-22.6	-29.3	-43.9	-6.7
Italy	-14.7	19.0	27.4	-3.3	-1.5	-33.3	-36.7	10.4	-34.4	30.1	-18.8	13.5	-20.9	-27.7	-42.3	-8.4
Japan	-3.8	29.9	38.4	7.7	9.5	-44.2	-47.7	21.3	-45.4	41.1	-7.8	24.4	-19.1	-29.2	-37.9	2.6
Jordan	-21.3	10.0	18.5	-12.1	-10.4	-24.3	-27.8	1.4	-25.5	21.2	-21.7	4.5	-12.0	-18.8	-33.3	-9.1
Korea, Rep.	-11.3	22.4	30.9	0.2	1.9	-36.7	-40.2	13.8	-37.9	33.6	-15.3	16.9	-24.4	-31.2	-45.4	-4.9
Kuwait	N.A	11.2	19.7	-11.0	-9.2	-25.5	-29.0	2.6	-26.7	22.4	-22.9	5.7	-13.2	-20.0	-34.5	-10.2
Lebanon	-13.7	N.A	10.9	-4.5	-7.9	-16.7	-20.2	-1.1	-17.9	13.6	-14.1	-1.0	-4.4	-11.2	-25.7	-1.5
Libya	-3.0	13.1	N.A	6.1	2.8	-6.1	-9.5	9.5	-7.3	13.2	-3.5	9.6	6.2	-0.5	-15.1	9.2
Malaysia	-16.2	17.5	25.9	-4.7	-3.0	-31.8	-35.2	8.9	-32.9	28.7	-20.3	12.0	-19.5	-26.2	-40.8	-9.9
Mexico	-21.3	10.1	18.5	N.A	-10.4	-24.4	-27.8	1.5	-25.5	21.2	-21.7	4.6	-12.0	-18.8	-33.4	-9.1
Morocco	-18.8	7.5	16.0	-9.6	N.A	-21.8	-25.3	-1.1	-23.0	18.7	-19.2	2.0	-9.5	-16.3	-30.8	-6.5
Netherlands	1.4	35.1	43.5	12.8	14.6	N.A	-52.8	26.4	-50.5	46.2	-2.7	29.6	-14.0	-24.1	-32.8	7.7
New Zealand	3.1	36.8	45.2	14.5	16.3	-47.6	N.A	28.1	-52.2	47.9	-1.0	31.3	-12.3	-22.4	-31.1	9.4
Nicaragua	-16.2	5.0	13.4	-7.1	-10.4	-19.3	-22.7	N.A	-20.4	16.1	-16.6	-0.5	-6.9	-13.7	-28.3	-4.0

Table 10.

Host country Home country	Kuwait	Lebanon	Libya	Mexico	Morocco	Netherlands	New Zealand	Nicaragua	Norway	Pakistan	Panama	Paraguay	Poland	Portugal	Qatar	Romania
Norway	3.1	36.8	45.3	14.6	16.3	-47.6	-54.4	28.2	N.A	48.0	-0.9	31.3	-12.3	-22.4	-31.1	9.5
Pakistan	-8.2	8.0	5.4	1.0	-2.4	-11.2	-14.7	4.4	-12.4	N.A	-8.6	4.5	1.1	-5.6	-20.2	4.1
Panama	-20.7	13.0	21.5	-9.2	-7.4	-27.3	-30.8	4.4	-28.5	24.2	N.A	7.5	-15.0	-21.8	-36.3	-12.0
Paraguay	-14.7	3.5	11.9	-5.6	-8.9	-17.7	-21.2	-2.1	-18.9	14.6	-15.1	N.A	-5.4	-12.2	-26.8	-2.5
Poland	-10.1	23.6	32.0	1.3	3.1	-37.8	-41.3	14.9	-39.0	34.7	-14.2	18.1	N.A	-32.3	-44.3	-3.8
Portugal	-8.5	25.2	33.7	3.0	4.7	-39.5	-43.0	16.6	-40.7	36.4	-12.5	19.7	-23.9	N.A	-42.6	-2.1
Qatar	-11.4	22.3	30.7	0.0	1.8	-36.6	-40.0	13.7	-37.7	33.5	-15.5	16.8	-24.2	-31.0	N.A	-5.1
Romania	-19.5	14.2	22.6	-8.1	-6.3	-28.4	-31.9	5.6	-29.6	25.3	-23.6	8.7	-16.1	-22.9	-37.5	N.A
Russian Federation	-13.8	2.5	11.0	-4.6	-8.0	-16.8	-20.3	-1.2	-18.0	13.7	-14.2	-1.1	-4.5	-11.3	-25.8	-1.5
Rwanda	-21.8	10.6	19.0	-11.7	-9.9	-24.8	-28.3	1.9	-26.0	21.7	-22.2	5.1	-12.5	-19.3	-33.9	-9.6
Saudi Arabia	-19.3	8.0	16.5	-10.1	-12.4	-22.3	-25.8	-0.6	-23.5	19.2	-19.7	2.5	-10.0	-16.8	-31.4	-7.1
Senegal	-20.9	9.6	18.1	-11.7	-10.8	-23.9	-27.4	1.0	-25.1	20.8	-21.3	4.1	-11.6	-18.4	-32.9	-8.7
Serbia	-22.1	10.8	19.3	-11.4	-9.6	-25.1	-28.6	2.2	-26.3	22.0	-22.5	5.3	-12.8	-19.6	-34.1	-9.9
Seychelles	-18.6	15.1	23.6	-7.1	-5.3	-29.4	-32.9	6.5	-30.6	26.3	-22.6	9.6	-17.1	-23.9	-38.4	-12.2
Sierra Leone	-14.1	2.8	11.3	-4.9	-8.2	-17.1	-20.5	-1.5	-18.3	14.0	-14.5	-1.4	-4.8	-11.5	-26.1	-1.8
Singapore	-0.5	33.2	41.6	10.9	12.7	-47.5	-50.9	24.6	-48.6	44.3	-4.6	27.7	-15.9	-26.0	-34.7	5.8
Slovenia	-9.9	23.8	32.3	1.6	3.3	-38.1	-41.6	15.2	-39.3	35.0	-13.9	18.3	-25.3	-32.5	-44.0	-3.5
South Africa	-18.4	15.3	23.8	-6.9	-5.2	-29.6	-33.1	6.7	-30.8	26.5	-22.4	9.8	-17.3	-24.1	-38.6	-12.0
Spain	-10.5	23.2	31.7	1.0	2.8	-37.5	-41.0	14.6	-38.7	34.4	-14.5	17.7	-25.2	-32.0	-44.6	-4.1
Sweden	3.0	36.7	45.2	14.5	16.2	-47.7	-54.4	28.1	-52.2	47.9	-1.0	31.2	-12.4	-22.5	-31.1	9.4
Switzerland	2.0	35.7	44.2	13.5	15.2	-48.7	-53.5	27.1	-51.2	46.9	-2.0	30.2	-13.4	-23.4	-32.1	8.4
Tunisia	-19.6	8.3	16.8	-10.4	-12.2	-22.6	-26.0	-0.3	-23.8	19.5	-20.0	2.8	-10.3	-17.0	-31.6	-7.3
Turkey	-22.4	11.1	19.6	-11.1	-9.3	-25.4	-28.9	2.5	-26.6	22.3	-22.8	5.6	-13.1	-19.9	-34.4	-10.2
Ukraine	-13.7	2.5	11.0	-4.6	-7.9	-16.8	-20.2	-1.2	-18.0	13.7	-14.2	-1.1	-4.5	-11.2	-25.8	-1.5
United Arab Emirates	-13.0	20.7	29.2	-1.5	0.3	-35.0	-38.5	12.1	-36.2	31.9	-17.0	15.2	-22.7	-29.5	-44.1	-6.6
United Kingdom	-2.5	31.2	39.7	9.0	10.7	-45.5	-48.9	22.6	-46.7	42.4	-6.5	25.7	-17.9	-28.0	-36.6	3.9
United States	-5.1	28.7	37.1	6.4	8.2	-42.9	-46.4	20.0	-44.1	39.8	-9.1	23.2	-20.4	-30.5	-39.2	1.3
Uruguay	-11.0	22.7	31.2	0.5	2.2	-37.0	-40.5	14.1	-38.2	33.9	-15.0	17.2	-24.7	-31.5	-45.1	-4.6
Venezuela	-5.6	10.5	2.8	3.5	0.2	-8.7	-12.1	7.0	-9.8	10.6	-6.0	7.0	3.7	-3.1	-17.7	6.6
Zimbabwe	-5.5	10.7	2.7	3.7	0.3	-8.5	-12.0	7.1	-9.7	10.8	-5.9	7.2	3.8	-3.0	-17.5	6.8

Table 11.

Host country Home country	Russian Federation	Rwanda	Saudi Arabia	Senegal	Serbia	Seychelles	Sierra Leone	Singapore	Slovenia	South Africa	Spain	Sweden	Switzerland	Tunisia	Turkey	Ukraine
Algeria	-2.5	-2.3	-20.3	5.6	7.4	-3.3	10.2	-21.0	-7.5	-7.1	-5.9	-18.4	-18.8	-2.8	-4.3	-4.1
Argentina	0.6	-8.8	-26.7	-0.8	1.0	-9.8	12.8	-27.4	-13.9	-13.6	-12.3	-24.8	-25.2	-9.2	-10.7	-0.9
Australia	26.8	10.9	-2.1	20.7	20.0	0.7	38.9	-53.0	-20.8	-3.5	-18.0	-51.0	-51.4	14.9	7.7	25.2
Austria	26.3	10.4	-2.5	20.2	19.6	0.3	38.5	-53.1	-21.2	-3.9	-18.4	-50.5	-51.0	14.5	7.3	24.8
Azerbaijan	-4.1	-4.1	-22.1	3.9	5.6	-5.1	8.5	-22.7	-9.3	-8.9	-7.6	-20.1	-20.6	-4.6	-6.1	-5.6
Belgium	24.1	8.2	-4.7	18.0	17.4	-2.0	36.3	-50.9	-23.5	-6.1	-20.7	-48.3	-48.7	12.3	5.1	22.6
Bolivia	-2.0	-6.2	-24.2	1.8	3.5	-7.2	10.2	-24.8	-11.4	-11.0	-9.7	-22.2	-22.7	-6.7	-8.2	-3.5
Brazil	5.1	-10.7	-23.7	-0.9	-1.6	-14.3	17.3	-31.9	-18.5	-18.1	-16.8	-29.3	-29.8	-6.7	-13.9	3.6
Bulgaria	7.2	-8.7	-21.7	1.1	0.4	-16.4	19.4	-34.0	-20.5	-20.1	-18.9	-31.4	-31.8	-4.7	-11.9	5.6
Cambodia	-3.9	-3.7	-21.7	4.3	6.0	-4.7	8.9	-22.3	-8.8	-8.5	-7.2	-19.7	-20.2	-4.1	-5.7	-5.5
Cameroon	-1.2	-1.0	-19.0	7.0	8.7	-2.0	11.6	-19.6	-6.2	-5.8	-4.5	-17.0	-17.5	-1.5	-3.0	-2.8
Canada	27.2	11.3	-1.6	21.2	20.5	1.2	39.4	-52.5	-20.3	-3.0	-17.5	-51.4	-51.9	15.4	8.2	25.7
Chile	21.5	5.6	-7.4	15.4	14.7	-4.6	33.7	-48.3	-26.1	-8.7	-23.3	-45.7	-46.1	9.6	2.4	19.9
China	-1.9	-6.3	-24.2	1.7	3.5	-7.3	10.3	-24.9	-11.4	-11.1	-9.8	-22.3	-22.8	-6.7	-8.3	-3.4
Colombia	1.3	-9.5	-27.5	-1.5	0.2	-10.5	13.5	-28.1	-14.7	-14.3	-13.0	-25.5	-26.0	-10.0	-11.5	-0.2
Croatia	11.4	-4.5	-17.5	5.3	4.6	-14.7	23.6	-38.2	-24.7	-18.8	-23.1	-35.6	-36.0	-0.5	-7.7	9.8
Denmark	29.7	13.8	0.9	23.6	23.0	3.7	41.9	-50.0	-17.8	-0.5	-15.0	-53.9	-53.0	17.9	10.7	28.2
Ecuador	-2.4	-5.8	-23.8	2.2	3.9	-6.8	9.8	-24.4	-11.0	-10.6	-9.3	-21.8	-22.3	-6.3	-7.8	-3.9
Egypt	-1.5	-1.3	-19.3	6.6	8.4	-2.3	11.2	-20.0	-6.5	-6.1	-4.9	-17.4	-17.8	-1.8	-3.3	-3.1
Finland	30.6	14.7	1.8	24.5	23.9	4.5	42.8	-49.1	-17.0	0.4	-14.2	-53.6	-52.1	18.8	11.6	29.1
France	21.2	5.3	-7.6	15.2	14.5	-4.8	33.4	-48.0	-26.3	-9.0	-23.5	-45.4	-45.9	9.4	2.2	19.7
Germany	25.4	9.5	-3.4	19.4	18.7	-0.6	37.6	-52.2	-22.1	-4.8	-19.3	-49.6	-50.1	13.6	6.4	23.9
Greece	9.7	-6.2	-19.1	3.6	3.0	-16.3	21.9	-36.5	-23.0	-20.5	-21.4	-33.9	-34.4	-2.1	-9.3	8.2
Iceland	25.5	9.6	-3.3	19.5	18.8	-0.5	37.7	-52.3	-22.0	-4.7	-19.2	-49.7	-50.2	13.7	6.5	24.0
India	0.8	-8.9	-26.9	-0.9	0.8	-9.9	12.9	-27.5	-14.1	-13.7	-12.4	-25.0	-25.4	-9.4	-10.9	-0.8
Iran, Islamic Rep.	1.4	1.5	-16.4	9.5	11.3	0.5	14.1	-17.1	-3.6	-3.2	-2.0	-14.5	-14.9	1.1	-0.4	-0.2
Ireland	24.7	8.9	-4.1	18.7	18.0	-1.3	36.9	-51.5	-22.8	-5.5	-20.0	-48.9	-49.4	12.9	5.7	23.2
Israel	13.9	-2.0	-14.9	7.8	7.2	-12.2	26.1	-40.7	-27.2	-16.3	-25.6	-38.1	-38.6	2.1	-5.1	12.4
Italy	12.3	-3.6	-16.6	6.2	5.5	-13.8	24.5	-39.1	-25.6	-17.9	-24.0	-36.5	-36.9	0.4	-6.8	10.7
Japan	23.2	7.4	-5.6	17.2	16.5	-2.8	35.4	-50.0	-24.3	-7.0	-21.5	-47.4	-47.9	11.4	4.2	21.7
Jordan	3.3	-11.5	-25.5	-2.7	-1.8	-12.5	15.5	-30.1	-16.7	-16.3	-15.0	-27.5	-28.0	-8.5	-13.5	1.8
Korea, Rep.	15.7	-0.2	-13.1	9.7	9.0	-10.3	27.9	-42.5	-29.0	-14.5	-27.4	-39.9	-40.4	3.9	-3.3	14.2
Kuwait	4.5	-11.4	-24.3	-1.5	-2.2	-13.7	16.7	-31.3	-17.8	-17.5	-16.2	-28.7	-29.2	-7.3	-14.5	3.0
Lebanon	-4.1	-3.9	-21.9	4.1	5.8	-4.9	8.7	-22.5	-9.1	-8.7	-7.4	-19.9	-20.4	-4.4	-5.9	-5.7
Libya	6.6	6.7	-11.2	14.7	16.5	5.7	19.3	-11.9	1.6	1.9	3.2	-9.3	-9.8	6.3	4.8	5.0
Malaysia	10.8	-5.1	-18.0	4.7	4.1	-15.3	23.0	-37.6	-24.1	-19.4	-22.5	-35.0	-35.4	-1.0	-8.2	9.3
Mexico	3.4	-11.5	-25.5	-2.7	-1.8	-12.5	15.6	-30.2	-16.7	-16.3	-15.0	-27.6	-28.0	-8.5	-13.5	1.8
Morocco	0.8	-9.0	-27.0	-1.0	0.7	-10.0	13.0	-27.6	-14.1	-13.8	-12.5	-25.0	-25.5	-9.4	-11.0	-0.7
Netherlands	28.4	12.5	-0.5	22.3	21.6	2.3	40.5	-51.4	-19.2	-1.9	-16.4	-52.6	-53.0	16.5	9.3	26.8
New Zealand	30.0	14.2	1.2	24.0	23.3	4.0	42.2	-49.7	-17.5	-0.2	-14.7	-54.2	-52.6	18.2	11.0	28.5
Nicaragua	-1.7	-6.5	-24.4	1.5	3.3	-7.5	10.5	-25.1	-11.6	-11.2	-10.0	-22.5	-22.9	-6.9	-8.4	-3.3

Table 12.

Host country / Home country	Russian Federation	Rwanda	Saudi Arabia	Senegal	Serbia	Seychelles	Sierra Leone	Singapore	Slovenia	South Africa	Spain	Sweden	Switzerland	Tunisia	Turkey	Ukraine
Norway	30.1	14.2	1.3	24.0	23.4	4.1	42.3	-49.6	-17.4	-0.1	-14.6	-54.1	-52.6	18.3	11.1	28.6
Pakistan	1.4	1.6	-16.4	9.6	11.3	0.6	14.2	-17.0	-3.5	-3.2	-1.9	-14.4	-14.9	1.2	-0.4	-0.2
Panama	6.3	-9.6	-22.5	0.3	-0.4	-15.5	18.5	-33.1	-19.7	-19.3	-18.0	-30.5	-31.0	-5.5	-12.7	4.8
Paraguay	-3.2	-4.9	-22.9	3.1	4.8	-5.9	8.9	-23.5	-10.1	-9.7	-8.4	-21.0	-21.4	-5.4	-6.9	-4.8
Poland	16.8	1.0	-12.0	10.8	10.1	-9.2	29.0	-43.6	-30.2	-13.4	-27.9	-41.0	-41.5	5.0	-2.2	15.3
Portugal	18.5	2.6	-10.3	12.4	11.8	-7.5	30.7	-45.3	-29.0	-11.7	-26.2	-42.7	-43.2	6.7	-0.5	17.0
Qatar	15.6	-0.3	-13.3	9.5	8.9	-10.5	27.8	-42.4	-28.9	-14.6	-27.3	-39.8	-40.2	3.7	-3.5	14.0
Romania	7.5	-8.4	-21.4	1.4	0.7	-16.6	19.6	-34.3	-20.8	-20.4	-19.1	-31.7	-32.1	-4.4	-11.6	5.9
Russian Federation	N.A	-4.0	-22.0	4.0	5.7	-5.0	8.6	-22.6	-9.2	-8.8	-7.5	-20.0	-20.5	-4.5	-6.0	-5.7
Rwanda	3.8	N.A	-25.0	-2.2	-2.3	-13.0	16.0	-30.6	-17.2	-16.8	-15.5	-28.0	-28.5	-8.0	-14.0	2.3
Saudi Arabia	1.3	-9.5	N.A	-1.5	0.2	-10.5	13.5	-28.1	-14.7	-14.3	-13.0	-25.5	-26.0	-10.0	-11.5	-0.2
Senegal	2.9	-11.1	-25.9	N.A	-1.4	-12.1	15.1	-29.7	-16.3	-15.9	-14.6	-27.1	-27.6	-8.9	-13.1	1.4
Serbia	4.1	-11.7	-24.7	-1.9	N.A	-13.3	16.3	-30.9	-17.5	-17.1	-15.8	-28.3	-28.8	-7.7	-14.3	2.6
Seychelles	8.4	-7.5	-20.4	2.4	1.7	N.A	20.6	-35.2	-21.8	-21.4	-20.1	-32.6	-33.1	-3.4	-10.6	6.9
Sierra Leone	-3.9	-4.3	-22.3	3.7	5.4	-5.3	N.A	-22.9	-9.4	-9.1	-7.8	-20.3	-20.8	-4.7	-6.3	-5.4
Singapore	26.5	10.6	-2.4	20.4	19.7	0.4	38.7	N.A	-21.1	-3.7	-18.3	-50.7	-51.1	14.6	7.4	24.9
Slovenia	17.1	1.2	-11.7	11.0	10.4	-8.9	29.3	-43.9	N.A	-13.1	-27.6	-41.3	-41.8	5.3	-1.9	15.6
South Africa	8.6	-7.3	-20.2	2.5	1.9	-17.4	20.8	-35.4	-21.9	N.A	-20.3	-32.8	-33.3	-3.2	-10.4	7.1
Spain	16.5	0.6	-12.3	10.5	9.8	-9.5	28.7	-43.3	-29.9	-13.7	N.A	-40.7	-41.2	4.7	-2.5	15.0
Sweden	30.0	14.1	1.2	23.9	23.3	4.0	42.2	-49.7	-17.5	-0.2	-14.7	N.A	-52.7	18.2	11.0	28.5
Switzerland	29.0	13.1	0.2	23.0	22.3	3.0	41.2	-50.7	-18.5	-1.2	-15.7	-53.2	N.A	17.2	10.0	27.5
Tunisia	1.6	-9.8	-27.2	-1.8	0.0	-10.8	13.8	-28.4	-14.9	-14.6	-13.3	-25.8	-26.3	N.A	-11.8	0.1
Turkey	4.4	-11.4	-24.4	-1.6	-2.3	-13.6	16.6	-31.2	-17.8	-17.4	-16.1	-28.6	-29.1	-7.4	N.A	2.9
Ukraine	-4.1	-4.0	-21.9	4.0	5.8	-5.0	8.6	-22.6	-9.1	-8.8	-7.5	-20.0	-20.5	-4.4	-5.9	N.A
United Arab Emirates	14.0	-1.8	-14.8	8.0	7.3	-12.0	26.2	-40.8	-27.4	-16.2	-25.7	-38.2	-38.7	2.2	-5.0	12.5
United Kingdom	24.5	8.6	-4.3	18.4	17.8	-1.5	36.7	-51.3	-23.0	-5.7	-20.2	-48.7	-49.2	12.7	5.5	23.0
United States	21.9	6.1	-6.9	15.9	15.2	-4.1	34.1	-48.7	-25.6	-8.3	-22.8	-46.1	-46.6	10.1	2.9	20.4
Uruguay	16.0	0.1	-12.8	9.9	9.3	-10.0	28.2	-42.8	-29.3	-14.2	-27.7	-40.2	-40.7	4.2	-3.0	14.5
Venezuela	4.0	4.1	-13.8	12.1	13.9	3.1	16.7	-14.5	-1.0	-0.6	0.6	-11.9	-12.3	3.7	2.2	2.4
Zimbabwe	4.1	4.3	-13.7	12.3	14.0	3.3	16.9	-14.3	-0.8	-0.5	0.8	-11.7	-12.2	3.9	2.3	2.5

Table 13.

Host country / Home Country	United Arab Emirates	United Kingdom	United States	Uruguay	Venezuela	Zimbabwe
Algeria	-21.4	-16.3	-14.7	-8.4	11.6	18.7
Argentina	-27.8	-22.7	-21.1	-14.8	18.0	25.1
Australia	-28.6	-44.4	-37.7	-19.5	44.2	51.3
Austria	-29.0	-44.8	-38.1	-19.9	43.7	50.9
Azerbaijan	-23.2	-18.0	-16.5	-10.1	13.4	20.5
Belgium	-31.2	-46.2	-40.3	-22.1	41.5	48.7
Bolivia	-25.3	-20.1	-18.6	-12.2	15.5	22.6
Brazil	-32.4	-27.2	-25.7	-19.3	22.6	29.7
Bulgaria	-34.4	-29.3	-27.7	-21.4	24.6	31.7
Cambodia	-22.7	-17.6	-16.0	-9.7	12.9	20.1
Cameroon	-20.1	-14.9	-13.4	-7.0	10.3	17.4
Canada	-28.1	-43.9	-37.2	-19.0	44.6	51.8
Chile	-33.9	-43.6	-42.0	-24.8	38.9	46.0
China	-25.3	-20.2	-18.6	-12.3	15.5	22.7
Colombia	-28.6	-23.4	-21.9	-15.5	18.8	25.9
Croatia	-38.6	-33.5	-31.9	-25.6	28.8	35.9
Denmark	-25.6	-41.4	-34.7	-16.5	47.1	54.3
Ecuador	-24.9	-19.7	-18.2	-11.8	15.1	22.2
Egypt	-20.4	-15.3	-13.7	-7.4	10.6	17.7
Finland	-24.7	-40.5	-33.8	-15.6	48.0	55.2
France	-34.1	-43.3	-41.8	-25.0	38.7	45.8
Germany	-29.9	-45.7	-39.0	-20.8	42.9	50.0
Greece	-36.9	-31.8	-30.2	-23.9	27.1	34.3
Iceland	-29.8	-45.6	-38.9	-20.7	42.9	50.1
India	-28.0	-22.8	-21.3	-15.0	18.2	25.3
Iran, Islamic Rep.	-17.5	-12.4	-10.8	-4.5	7.7	14.8
Ireland	-30.6	-46.4	-39.7	-21.5	42.2	49.3
Israel	-41.1	-36.0	-34.4	-28.1	31.3	38.5
Italy	-39.5	-34.4	-32.8	-26.5	29.7	36.8
Japan	-32.1	-45.3	-41.2	-23.0	40.7	47.8
Jordan	-30.6	-25.4	-23.9	-17.5	20.8	27.9
Korea, Rep.	-39.6	-37.8	-36.3	-29.9	33.2	40.3
Kuwait	-31.8	-26.6	-25.1	-18.7	22.0	29.1
Lebanon	-23.0	-17.8	-16.3	-9.9	13.2	20.3
Libya	-12.3	-7.2	-5.6	0.7	7.7	14.5
Malaysia	-38.0	-32.9	-31.3	-25.0	28.2	35.3
Mexico	-30.6	-25.5	-23.9	-17.6	20.8	27.9
Morocco	-28.1	-22.9	-21.4	-15.0	18.2	25.4
Netherlands	-27.0	-42.8	-36.1	-17.9	45.8	52.9
New Zealand	-25.3	-41.1	-34.4	-16.2	47.5	54.6
Nicaragua	-25.5	-20.4	-18.8	-12.5	15.7	22.8

Table 13.

Host Country / Home Country	United Arab Emirates	United Kingdom	United States	Uruguay	Venezuela	Zimbabwe
Norway	-25.2	-41.0	-34.3	-16.1	47.5	54.7
Pakistan	-17.4	-12.3	-10.7	-4.4	7.6	14.8
Panama	-33.6	-28.4	-26.9	-20.5	23.8	30.9
Paraguay	-24.0	-18.8	-17.3	-11.0	14.2	21.3
Poland	-38.5	-38.9	-37.4	-29.4	34.3	41.4
Portugal	-36.8	-40.6	-39.0	-27.7	35.9	43.1
Qatar	-39.7	-37.7	-36.1	-29.8	33.0	40.1
Romania	-34.7	-29.6	-28.0	-21.7	24.9	32.0
Russian Federation	-23.1	-17.9	-16.4	-10.0	13.3	20.4
Rwanda	-31.1	-25.9	-24.4	-18.0	21.3	28.4
Saudi Arabia	-28.6	-23.4	-21.9	-15.5	18.8	25.9
Senegal	-30.2	-25.0	-23.5	-17.1	20.4	27.5
Serbia	-31.4	-26.2	-24.7	-18.3	21.6	28.7
Seychelles	-35.7	-30.5	-29.0	-22.6	25.9	33.0
Sierra Leone	-23.3	-18.2	-16.6	-10.3	13.5	20.7
Singapore	-28.9	-44.7	-38.0	-19.8	43.9	51.0
Slovenia	-38.2	-39.2	-37.6	-29.1	34.5	41.7
South Africa	-35.8	-30.7	-29.1	-22.8	26.0	33.2
Spain	-38.8	-38.6	-37.1	-29.7	34.0	41.1
Sweden	-25.3	-41.1	-34.4	-16.2	47.4	54.6
Switzerland	-26.3	-42.1	-35.4	-17.2	46.4	53.6
Tunisia	-28.8	-23.7	-22.1	-15.8	19.0	26.2
Turkey	-31.7	-26.5	-25.0	-18.6	21.9	29.0
Ukraine	-23.0	-17.9	-16.3	-10.0	13.2	20.4
United Arab Emirates	N.A	-36.1	-34.6	-28.2	31.5	38.6
United Kingdom	-30.8	N.A	-39.9	-21.7	41.9	49.1
United States	-33.4	-44.0	N.A	-24.3	39.4	46.5
Uruguay	-39.3	-38.1	-36.5	N.A	33.4	40.6
Venezuela	-14.9	-9.8	-8.2	-1.9	N.A	12.2
Zimbabwe	-14.8	-9.6	-8.0	-1.7	5.3	N.A

Chapter 7
Global Labor Market, "Re-Shoring" Dynamics, and Skill Mismatch:
An Exploratory Study at a Job-Specific Level

Filippo Ferrari
Bologna University, Italy

ABSTRACT

Workers' capabilities and knowledge are factors that a company can use to boost its productivity. The relocation of operational activity away from industrialized nations has led to the erosion of manufacturing skills, and this fact often results in a severe skill shortage in specific local labor markets, becoming much more prominent in the case of re-shoring. Consistent with the transaction cost economics approach (TCE), the purpose of this research was to verify if students possess at least basic skills at the end of their educational path to face the labor market without economic frictions in school-to-work transition. Finally, this chapter presents a model that could be useful in order to design programs aimed to overcome the erosion of manufacturing skills and provide students with skills that companies need to deal with local labor markets successfully.

INTRODUCTION

In many western countries, re-shoring and back-shoring of manufacturing, assembly work, and warehousing is increasing at an unprecedented rate (Adelmann, 2013; Alderman, 2014). Behind this trend is the ability of firms to dramatically increase production without hiring new workers (Kroft, 2013), and this fact has a strong impact on global human capital value chain. In fact, the relocation of operational activity away from industrialised nations has led to the erosion of manufacturing skills (Bailey et al., 2010), and this fact often results in a severe skill shortage in specific local labour markets, becoming much more prominent in the case of back-shoring.

DOI: 10.4018/978-1-5225-5787-6.ch007

Furthermore, the loss of manufacturing capabilities might also imply the reduction of innovation competencies (Pisano & Shih, 2012). Hence, it appears very important for scholars to present a model of intervention in order to carry out training needs analysis by checking skills and knowledge and identifying gaps between skills provided by school and skills requested by firms for the same jobs. Given this scenario, current literature (Fratocchi et al., 2014) suggests that research should try to answer several traditional questions about back-shoring processes: causes of back-shoring (Why), the value chain activities involved (What), the home countries characteristics determining the back-shoring decision (Where), and the modes of entry into (and subsequently exit from) the host country (How).

However, empirical evidence on back-shoring is relatively scarce and advocates for more knowledge about its effects and about its likely evolution (Kinkel, 2014). Hence, this chapter aims to proceed focusing on the impact of back-shoring processes, especially on human resources practices. In fact, given the organizational and managerial dynamics highlighted by the empirical research on back-shoring (e.g., Campagnolo & Gianecchini, 2015; Ferrari, 2015), it seems sensible to expect that the current back-shore trend will have a strong impact on human resources management practices, especially on training and skills development.

Thus, the first purpose of this chapter is to investigate the impact of back-shoring process on skill shortage/mismatch in a local labour market in the Italian fashion sector. The aim of this chapter is also to present a model of intervention to conduct training needs analysis by checking skills and knowledge and identifying gaps between skills provided by school and skills requested by firms for the same jobs. Finally, beyond the implications on training practices, this chapter aims to predict the short-term impact which the back-shoring process is likely to have on the other human resources practices, in particular on recruitment, knowledge management, team building and team management, performance appraisal, and compensation.

This chapter contributes to current literature in a threefold manner. First, by investigating the impact of back-shoring process on skill mismatch, this chapter react to the recent call (Fratocchi et al., 2014) for a deeper comprehension of the impact of such process on the value chain.

Second, by applying the Economic Transaction Cost to the Italian context, this chapter provides an original contribution to a literature until now mainly grounded on Anglo-Saxon context.

Third, testing the Job Requirement Approach to skill mismatch, this chapter provides a suitable approach in order to investigate the skill mismatch at a firm-job-specific level, thus providing a better suited training needs analysis.

GLOBAL VALUE CHAIN AND INTANGIBLE ASSETS

This chapter is grounded on three different (and here combined) approaches to intangible assets economics: Transaction Cost Economics (TCE), School-to-Work Transition and Educational Mismatch theories (e.g. theories which provide explanations for educational and skill mismatch, such as Assignment Theory, Human Capital Theory, Institutional Theory, and Heterogeneous Skills Theory). These approaches were chosen because of their strong focus on elements like human capital and dynamics of the labour market.

Transaction Cost Economics Approach

Job specialization is a basic mechanism in organizational behaviour, and also builds on a market grounded on exchange relationships (Smith, 1973), which are necessary since every job makes a partial output that has to be exchanged in the market. However, if in a market there are few players, who also act in a situations characterized by bounded rationality, then the market itself becomes *imperfect*. Consequently, the exchange relationships value becomes uncertain, due to the scarce efficacy of the free competition among players. In an imperfect market, using a *just-in-time market* is very difficult, because the costs of negotiation (between a client and a provider) could become too expensive; furthermore, if the provider plays as a monopolist, these costs could become even higher.

In summary, when the exchange value is certain, there are no frictions (such as negotiations) and the market becomes a perfect coordination mechanism; otherwise, when the exchange value is uncertain, additional market costs arise (Coase, 1937), due to transaction costs (Tadenis & Williamson, 2012). If it's not possible to use a just-in-time market, the market doesn't work and then it's necessary to build up a hierarchy (e.g. a system of rules), in order to manage the exchanges and control players' behaviour. (Williamson, 1985).

The TCE approach analyses each transaction and assesses the economic advantage of purchasing from the market relationship (i.e., out-sourcing goods and/or services from an external provider) rather than an internal solution. Usually, core production and firm-specific know-how are provided internally by the organization itself, while raw materials and labour force are purchased in the external market because their costs are more precisely definable. When transaction management by internal organization as coordination control doesn't work, it is necessary to consider economic effects of learning: if know-how is widespread outside an organization, then it's better to purchase it in the external market, laying production costs upon the market itself.

It is necessary to consider three dimensions in describing economic transactions (Williamson, 1985): their *uncertainty*, their *frequency* and how *specific* invested resources are,, in order to minimize production costs. Regarding the last characteristic especially (i.e., *specificity*), if those resources are generic, the market provides more advantages than internal production and management; when resources become more specific, the exchange becomes bilateral and needs more negotiation between the actors, as a result management costs rise and internal production could become more profitable.

How specific a resource is, therefore, a fundamental aspect. A generic resource, in fact, is easily delivered in the market rather than a specific one, but at the same time it could be easier for a client to purchase that resource from other providers. Conversely, extremely specific resources lead to a monopoly position, and can become very expensive for the purchaser and finally they become a hazardous investment for the producer. In particular, a resource can be *human-specific:* the skills are related to a specific job in a specific firm, and they can't be applied to another job (or another firm). Human capital theory (Becker, 1964) asserts that, in the job market, skills improvement automatically leads to a value improvement (both in terms of worker's employability and organizational value).

However, TCE contributes a further point (Williamson, 1985): if skills are specific and have limited transferability (i.e. between colleagues), then they must be managed by a protection system (e.g. a contract) in order to avoid a loss of value (for the organization, of course) due to unexpected and undesirable resignations of employees.Training (the organizational process for developing skills) can provide generic or specific skills. In the former case, training for newcomers is focused on the basic skills of a job; in the latter, training for newcomers is focused on specific issues, in order to provide the best way to carry out *that* job in *that* organization. Consistent with the TCE approach, it is more profitable for an organization to purchase generic skills on a *just-in-time market* and to develop specific ones by training (Williamson, 1985). In a perfect situation, generic skills are learned at school, and specific ones through on-the-job training.

Unfortunately, educational paths often do not provide young workers with generic skills, and so organizations are forced to provide these skills to their newcomers (Ferrari & Emiliani, 2009). Hence, the cost of generic training is added on to that of the specific training. The outline (program) of a course of study, and the standard specifications of vocational profiles usually have little or negligible fit with real organizational jobs, especially in Small- and Medium-sized Enterprises (SMEs): in these firms jobs are less formally defined, and often have more (or less) *richness* (autonomy level) and a *large*r number of tasks than the standard.

Due to the ongoing elements, there arises the need to provide the actors of an educational system with proper tools for assessing and correcting vocational skills mismatch, i.e. the gap between skills possessed at the end of an educational path and skills required by the labour market. Consistent with these arguments, the aim of the research project described below has been to reduce frictions in *school-to-work transition*, reducing the skill mismatch and, in turn, reducing transaction costs due to these frictions.

School-to-Work Transition Approach

The Organisation for Economic Co-operation and Development (OECD) defines school-to-work transition as the period between the end of compulsory schooling and the attainment of full-time, stable employment (OECD, 1996a; 1998c). The failure of scholastic outcomes, high unemployment, high employee turn-over and, finally, mismatch between educational path and job attainment are common problems that can arise in this process. European occupational policies about minimum wage and job protection are rigid, and thus lead to negative performance in terms of employment rate. Hence, it's necessary to focus on educational training before school-to-work transition: in fact, there is evidence of higher wage and lower unemployment due to added training years (Card, 1995; Grubb, 1996), especially if training is vocational.

However, there is no evidence of a direct, positive correlation between vocational training and wage level; thus, the specific educational programs seem more relevant than formal degrees at the end of educational paths (Blomskog et al., 1997). Also in school-to-work transition literature, two different approaches to vocational training are proposed: general training vs. specific training.

As discussed, *human capital theory* (Becker, 1964) posits that employers, in a perfect competitive market, don't provide general skills to employees; if they are forced to do so, they choose to hire skilled employees. In small firms, training costs are negligible (or even negative: there could be a gain deriving from the exploitation of workers skills); but in larger firms (which have more complex and intensive training programs) those costs become unsustainable (Acemoglu & Pischke, 1999). Furthermore, a rigid application of National Occupational Standards in apprenticeship and a high turn-over among the apprentices themselves hinder specific training (Streeck e al., 1987).

Nonetheless, employers provide general training to their young employees, and the literature suggests two hypotheses in order to explain this. First, the *decentralized approach* (Acemoglu & Pischke, 1999) suggests that the opportunity to provide general training depends on two limits of the labour market, especially with a high unemployment rate: the situation of *monopsony* of demand, and the higher percentage of over-qualified workers than under-qualified ones (due to high intellectual unemployment).

This situation allows employers to pay lower wages, and, in turn, to invest the resulting profit in training: in fact, if the wage does not increase, then a skilled worker is more profitable for the firm. The result is that when few firms provide training to their workers (such as in the USA), the average level of skills and wages are both high; consequently, employers are forced to hire rather than to train, and workers are also encouraged to leave firms (for a better position). Conversely, when apprenticeship is widespread (such as in Germany), average skill and wage levels are quite low, reinforcing firms' decisions to train rather than hire their workers.

Second, *regulating explanation* emphasizes the role of external components in order to explain the determinants of the decision to provide general training to young workers. An important role could be played by employers' syndicates. In fact, in a perfect competition market, general training increases workers' value almost permanently, although also with advantages for the competitors. Hence, employers who are forced to pay for providing general training to their workers don't do it spontaneously; furthermore, if they do provide it, usually this is not sufficient for whole market's training needs. Therefore, the lack of coordination among employers (in order to provide general training) leads them to the choice of hiring rather than training their workers.

In this situation, employers' syndicates could organize a collective pursuit of common interests, stimulating and helping (economically and technically) their associates toward training activities rather than hiring. If employers' syndicates are unable to achieve that with their own resources, it would be strongly advisable to involve the workers' unions and/or educational systems. Decentralized and regulatory approaches can be considered complementary. In fact, in an imperfect labour market, the regulation of training policies by firms becomes easier, especially for the firms in a condition of *monopsony*. Whereas the labour market is characterized by perfect competition, firms can, in reality, decide not to pay for training.

In conclusion, because the market is never perfect, but firms are not usually in a *monopsony* condition, employers are forced to finance general training, against their interests. Alternatively, they could exploit the stock of over-skilled workers in the labour market due to the high rate of intellectual unemployment.. The problem is are workers really over-skilled, or are they only over-educated?

Educational Mismatch and Skill Mismatch Theories

The expression '*educational mismatch*' means the lack of coherence between the qualification level achieved by a worker and the level requested by a firm in order to carry out a specific job (ISFOL, 2006). The economic literature shows that this incoherence has negative effects on wages, employee turn over (Hersch, 1991), occupational choice (Viscusi, 1979), overall job satisfaction (Cabràl Vieira, 2005; Tsang & Levin, 1985) and finally employment rate (Manacorda, Petrongolo, 1999). Research suggests multiple models in order to explain those negative effects, all explanations grounded somewhat on relations between achieved qualifications and the job being conducted.

Assignment Theory (Sattinger, 1993) posits that investments in on-the-job training are justified by educational mismatch. Furthermore, Hartog (2000) underlines that *educational mismatch* could also be explained by lack of information or distortions, especially during school-to-work transition; according to this hypothesis, workers accept jobs that they are either under- or over-qualified or because they do not understand their job market.

Human Capital Theory (Becker, 1964) helps to explain the wage differential among workers with the same level of educational qualification. Different wages depend on the job itself, not the educational mismatch; in other words, in the labour market wage level is determined by job level and not by the qualification level of workers.

Institutional Theory (Thurow, 1975) posits that workers are often forced to accept low wages because job characteristics are more salient and valuable rather than workers' characteristics (e.g skills, personal traits etc.). Wage discrimination is almost always in line with the official salary scales;.(such as in Italy, CCNL - *National Labour Collective Contract*), without consideration for workers' skill level or their productivity, efficiency, effectiveness and so on.

Heterogeneous Competence Theory (Green & McIntosh, 2002; 2007), suggests that the relationship between educational and skill mismatch could be weak. The basic assumption of this theory is that, even between workers with the same qualification level, there is an considerable variance of possessed skills. Over-educated but under-skilled workers could experience difficulty in finding a job, due to their lack of competence, and could earn less than another worker with lower qualifications but more skills. (Borghans & De Grip, 2000; Buchel, De Grip, Mertens, 2003). According to this theory, and in order to overcome educational mismatch and to analyze skill-mismatch directly, Allen e Van der Velden (2001) utilized a subjective method, asking workers for a self-evaluation of their skill level. The findings confirmed Heterogeneous Competence Theory, and didn't support Institutional Theory.

Back-Shoring Dynamics and Skill Mismatch

During the 2013 Stanford Global Supply Chain Management Forum (GSCMF) symposium titled, *Reshoring: Beyond the Buzz*, attendees mentioned four key factors that are often overlooked: the impact of the overall vertical ecosystem (with an emphasis on tooling), the connecting factors between innovation and manufacturing, the automation opportunities and, finally, the strength of the manufacturing skill base. Many participants also discussed the need for influencing government policies to ameliorate regulatory, tax, and especially skill issues (for a synthesis of the Forum, see PricewaterhouseCooper LLP, 2013). In fact, literature highlights that skill mismatch can arise from structural changes in the economy, like back-shoring. Individuals lacking skills which are necessary in order to face structural change become unemployed or have to accept jobs that do not match their skill portfolios (Acemoglu & Autor, 2011).

Furthermore, literature suggests that back-shoring involves especially the most innovative and productive firms (Fratocchi et al., 2014; Kinkel, 2014), characterized by a high level of firm-specific skills. Considering the skills as a resource available on the labour market, the most suitable approach in order to evaluate the skills' purchasing costs is the *Transaction Costs Economics Theory* (TCE: Coase, 1937; Tadenis & Williamson, 2012; Williamson, 1985). Consistent with the TCE approach, it is more profitable for an organization to purchase generic skills on a *just-in-time market* and to develop specific ones by training (Williamson, 1985).

In a perfect situation, generic skills are learned at school, and specific ones through on-the-job training. Unfortunately, Italian educational paths often do not provide young workers with generic skills, and so organizations are forced to provide these skills to their newcomers (Ferrari & Emiliani, 2009). Furthermore, the skill shortage as a consequence of the back-shoring process has a negative impact on transaction costs, forcing the firm to provide generic skills to their newcomers once again. Hence, the cost of generic training is added on top of that of the specific training. Thus, the aim of this research is to answer the following research question:

RQ1: What's the impact of the back-shoring process on the skill shortage/mismatch in a local labour market?

Several studies suggest that this sill shortage (and consequent difficulties in hiring properly skilled workers) also depends on whether skills are *occupation-specific* or not (Acemoglu & Autor, 2011; Gathmann & Schönberg, 2010; Nedelkoska, Neffke, & Wiederhold, 2014; Poletaev & Robinson, 2008). However, how specific a skill is (job-specific, firm-specific or even *firm-job-specific,* that is, a skill relevant for a specific job in a specific firm), represents a prominent economical issue, both from a theoretical and methodological point of view. Therefore, to assess the skill mismatch within a labour market, a further problem arises: at what level should the skill mismatch assessment be carried out? How job-specific should the tool used in this assessment be?

A methodological problem is to assess in a reliable way the perceived skill relevance in the opinion of all involved stakeholders in the training process (managers, entrepreneurs, teachers at the vocational schools). Measuring skill mismatch is often problematic since that objective data is rarely available (Leuven & Oosterbeek, 2011; Allen & van der Velden, 2001; 2005): for instance, the type of formal qualification seldom is a reliable indicator of the possessed skills.

However, research concerning *educational mismatch* is more considerable than that on *skill mismatch,* and that could be an indicator of the difficulties that arise facing the latter phenomenon. Some authors (Allen & Van der Velden, 2005) posit the problem of selecting (and evaluating) each singular skill contained within the entire job specification against the workers' skills. Hence, two different approaches have been proposed; the first is an 'as soon as possible' objective (e.g. job description, official vocational standards etc.) the second one is more subjective, such self-evaluations carried out by the workers themselves.

However, in the extant literature, there is not complete agreement about a standard approach to skill mismatch study. Literature on how skill-mismatch can be measured is already ample (for a recent review, see Perry et al., 2014). More often, self-reports are used to measure skill mismatch. Information on self-reported skill mismatch is obtained by asking workers to what extent their skills correspond to the tasks performed at work (e.g., Allen & van der Velden, 2001; Green & McIntosh, 2007; Mavromaras, McGuinness, & Fok, 2009; Mavromaras, McGuinness, O'Leary, Sloane, & Fok, 2010). Self-report measures have the advantage of being easily implementable in a survey; thus, up-to-date information on skill mismatch can be obtained. However, self-reports are prone to bias. Respondents may have the tendency to overstate the requirements of their workplace and upgrade their position at work (see Hartog, 2000, for education mismatch).

Skill mismatch can also be measured directly which provides a more objective measure. In all direct skill mismatch measures, workers' skills are compared to skills required at their workplace. For instance, required skills can be measured using the Job Requirement Approach (JRA) (Felstead, Gallie, Green, & Zhou, 2007). However, bias can also arise from this approach if respondents overstate their skill use at work. Alternatively, required skills can be measured by obtaining a general, occupation-specific skill level (e.g., Pellizzari & Fichen, 2013).

A further problem could arise even when there is no mismatch between required skills and possessed skills. It is in fact possible that a worker does not experience a skill mismatch but the possessed skills are perceived as unimportant/useless by the firm. In this case, a problem of skill deficit or skill surplus arises (Krahn & Lowe, 1998; Schooler, 1984), with well-known undesired consequences in terms of job satisfaction, workers turn-over, wage level, and employment rate (Allen & van der Velden, 2001;

Desjardins & Rubenson, 2011; OECD, 2013). Hence, it seems necessary that a skill mismatch measuring system also considers the relevance of the job skills for the labour market. This last issue is mainly relevant for policy makers and educational managers, because the vocational training system is the first provider of suitable skills for firms, ensuring the proper skill portfolio for the student to reduce the transaction costs in school-to-work transition.

To overcome these significant limitations in skill assessment, this research applied a slightly different approach. Literature suggests that a suitable tool is the Job Requirement Approach, especially when applied at a job-specific skill level rather than in the usual, more generic way (Felstead et al., 2007; Pellizzari & Fichen, 2013; Perry et. al., 2014). In particular, such an approach shows a good fit in assessing the skill mismatch, measuring the students' self-evaluated skill level in each skill and comparing this evaluation with the skill relevance level (in the opinion of both teachers and entrepreneurs). Investigating the skill mismatch on a firm-specific level would be possible to provide a training needs analysis which can help both the implementation of local development policies and the strategic decisions at a firm level. Thus, the aim of this research is also to answer the following research question:

RQ2: Is JRA a suitable approach for assessing skill shortages/mismatch in local economies?'

The Research: An Explorative Study in the Italian Fashion Sector

This paragraph presents an outline of an exploratory research carried out in the Italian Fashion sector in a Province of the North-East. The Fashion sector was chosen for a twofold reason. First, this sector was maybe the earliest that off-shored its manufacturing processes in the 1990s (Prota & Viesti, 2007). Now, several entrepreneurs are back-shoring or declare the intention to back-shore in the near future (Merico, 2015). Second, previous research (Ferrari & Emiliani, 2009; Ferrari, 2014) has clearly shown that the most common complaint among fashion entrepreneurs is the skill mismatch which 'affects' Fashion operators when they leave school.

The Sample

This research was performed in a local labour market, analysing one job (*Fashion Operator*). The research involved a secondary school (a total of 47 questionnaires were administered to the students and 12 to their teachers), and several firms belonging to the fashion sector (a total of seven entrepreneurs/HRMs were interviewed). All the data was collected between the end of May and early June; hence, immediately before final examinations (*Qualifica Professionale*).

Data Collection

Following the JRA, the first aim of the research was to investigate and compare, for each job skill and aptitude, the relevance for the organization from the point of view of the school teachers on one side, and of the employers on the other side. In order to achieve this outcome, the research was carried out with the involvement of entrepreneurs and/or human resource managers (HRMs) to collect exhaustive data about the same jobs. These entrepreneurs and human resource managers belong to a sample of firms which are currently back-shoring their activities or wish to back-shore in the near future. The second

Table 1. Sample of tool – Fashion Operator

'In this job, how relevant are the following skills?' (0= not at all; 5= strategic)						
Job Task	**Practical Skills (to be able to...)**	**Skill Relevance**	**Theoretical Skills (to know...)**	**Skill Relevance**	**Soft Skills**	**Soft Skill Relevance**
Task 1 Machines Set up	Recognizing specific machines to be used in each production step	0 1 2 3 4 5	The production work flow of ready-made clothing: steps, activities, technologies	0 1 2 3 4 5	Goal orientation	0 1 2 3 4 5
	Understanding order descriptions in order to set up tailoring parameters	0 1 2 3 4 5	The most important sewing techniques	0 1 2 3 4 5	Accuracy	0 1 2 3 4 5
	Recognizing malfunctioning in tools and machines ...	0 1 2 3 4 5	The most important cutting techniques...	0 1 2 3 4 5	Planning	0 1 2 3 4 5

aim of the research was to compare the two relevance levels (both teachers' and entrepreneurs') with students' perception of their own skill level (*skill mismatch*).

However, by using a cross-sectional approach only it would not be clear whether consequences on skill mismatch are unique for back-shoring or whether they are more general. For instance, the same problems could arise also in industries with disruptive technologies. Furthermore, a cross sectional approach does not permit to investigate how exactly the issue of skill mismatch is related to back-shoring.

Thus, this research aimed to go beyond the mere description of the current skill mismatch, investigating if competences in firms or the educational system has been lost or what has changed. In so doing, a comparison between current job descriptions and those in use before the back-shore was started. A total of five out of seven have held an ISO-9001 certification since the 1990s, so it was possible to obtain previous version of the current job description, thus comparing required skills. All these job descriptions contain data regarding the specific job requirement, especially demanded skills and personal aptitudes; therefore, they were consistent with the overall research design.

Obviously, the structure of the job descriptions was very similar but different in details. Hence, the content has been standardized to compare the specific requested skills and aptitudes. Furthermore, an historical analysis of the educational outlines was carried out to examine if and how the content and the issues of the educational path have or have not modified and updated since the 1990s. Finally, the job description details were defined following the JRA approach in terms of: job task(s), practical skills (to be able to do something…), theoretical skills (to know something) and personal aptitude/soft skills.

Moreover, to collect data each job description was drawn up in two versions, one for teacher and employer use, the other for students. Using a self-reporting six-point scale for each practical, theoretical and aptitude/soft skill, it was possible to collect the opinions of both teachers and employers about the organizational *relevance* of that skill and aptitude (for example: 'In this job, how relevant are team work skills?' 0= not at all; 5= strategic).

Below in Table 1 is a sample of this kind of tool (Fashion operator).

Using a second version of the same self-reporting six-point scale, it was possible to collect the students' self-evaluation about the level of possessed skill (For example: 'At the end of your educational path, how do you evaluate your level of team work skills? 0= not at all, 5= maximum level). Table 2 below is a sample of this kind of tool (Fashion operator).

With this grid, a self-evaluative (hence subjective) tool was chosen instead of an objective one (like final marks for each subject), according to suggestions from extant literature (McGuinness, 2006; for

Table 2. Sample of tool – Fashion Operator

' At the end of your educational path, how do you evaluate your level of the following skills?' (0= not at all; 5= maximum level)						
Job Task	**Practical Skills (to be able to...)**	**Skill Level**	**Theoretical Skills (to know...)**	**Skill Level**	**Soft Skills**	**Soft Skill Level**
Task 1 Machines Set up	Recognizing specific machines to be used in each production step	0 1 2 3 4 5	The production work flow of ready-made clothing: steps, activities, technologies	0 1 2 3 4 5	Goal orientation	0 1 2 3 4 5
	Understanding order descriptions in order to set up tailoring parameters	0 1 2 3 4 5	The most important sewing techniques	0 1 2 3 4 5	Accuracy	0 1 2 3 4 5
	Recognizing malfunctioning in tools and machines...	0 1 2 3 4 5	The most important cutting techniques...	0 1 2 3 4 5	Planning...	0 1 2 3 4 5

a comparison between objective and subjective protocols, see ISFOL, 2006). Self-reported scales are obviously prone to bias; however, this kind of evaluation is also strongly related to self-efficacy, which in turn leads to a better job performance (Bandura, 1969; Bandura & Wood, 1989).

FINDINGS

RQ1: What's the impact of the back-shoring process on the skill shortage/mismatch in a local labour market?

For each skill, the result of the matching between entrepreneurs'/teachers' evaluations and students' self-evaluations was within a range between -100% (maximum skill shortage of a strategic skill) and +100% (maximum possession of a useless or unnecessary skill). However, in the results, only ± *30%* mismatch at the top of the scale (maximum level of relevance/possession), corresponding to two full degrees of evaluation, was considered to define the critical area. Table 3 is a sample of the data analysis regarding the soft skills: the mismatches between the relevance of each skill in the teachers' evaluation and the students' self-assessment.

The data in Table 3 shows an example of the mismatch between the relevance evaluation in teachers' perception (-0%= skill completely useless/unnecessary; +100% = strategic skill) combined with the students' self-assessment (0% = minimum possession of the skill; +100% maximum possession of the skill). The combined score -produces a result between -100 (maximum skill shortage of a strategic skill), +100% (maximum possession of a useless or unnecessary skill). Due to the six-point scale, the critical areas are less than – 66,68 and over + 66,68. For example, -64% related to 'Goal Orientation' skill means that in the sample there is a skill shortage in goal orientation among students, and at the same time this skill is considered strategic in the teachers' point of view, but the situation does not seem so critical.

In Table 4, the data shows an example of the mismatch between the relevance evaluation in both entrepreneurs' and teachers' evaluation (0%= skill completely useless/unnecessary; +100% = strategic skill). The combined score produces a result between -100% (a skill useless in teachers evaluation but strategic in entrepreneurs' evaluation) and +100% (a skill strategic in teachers evaluation but useless in

Table 3. Mismatch between relevance and skill level

Teachers vs. Students	Possession	Relevance	Mismatch
Goal orientation	16,34%	22,00%	-5,66%
Accuracy	32,68%	97,00%	-64,32%
Planning	32,68%	83,34%	-50,66%
Autonomy	32,68%	32,68%	0,00%

Table 4. Mismatch between relevance in Entrepreneurs' and Teachers' perception

Entrepreneurs (E') vs. Teachers (T')	E' Relevance	T' Relevance	Mismatch
Goal orientation	100,00%	22,00%	78,00%
Accuracy	93,00%	97,00%	-4,00%
Planning	83,34%	83,34%	0,00%
Autonomy	32,68%	32,68%	0,00%

entrepreneurs' evaluation 1). Due to the six-point scale, the critical areas are less than – 66,68 and over + 66,68, For example, 69% related to 'Goal Orientation' skill means that, in the sample, there is a strong difference in evaluation of the skill relevance between entrepreneurs and teachers.

In Table 5, the data shows an example of the mismatch between the relevance evaluation in entrepreneurs' perception (0%= skill completely useless/unnecessary; 100% = strategic skill) combined with the students' self-assessment (0% = minimum possession of the skill; +100% current maximum possession of the skill). The combined score produces a result between -100 (maximum skill shortage of a strategic skill) and +100% (maximum possession of a useless or unnecessary skill). Due to the six-point scale, the critical areas are less than – 66,68 and over + 66,68, For example, -83% related to the 'Goal Orientation' skill means that in the sample there is a strong skill shortage in goal orientation among students, and at the same time this skill is considered strategic in the entrepreneurs' point of view.

Comparing the current employers' evaluations with the job descriptions used before the back-shore, it seems that the relevance of technical skills are unchanged, instead soft skills have become much more

Table 5. Mismatch between relevance and skill level

Entrepreneurs vs. Students	Possession	Relevance	Mismatch
Goal orientation	16,34%	100,00%	-83,66%
Accuracy	32,68%	93,00%	-60,32%
Planning	32,68%	83,34%	-50,66%
Autonomy	32,68%	32,68%	0,00%

relevant/strategic for the job. Regarding technical skills, school paths also are unchanged. Twenty years ago the educational path were integrated with the so-called 'Terza area', in which soft skills were provided by HR professionals, like external trainers and counsellors. These integrated courses were often provided involving employers' associations and their learning agencies. Currently, this 'Terza area' does not exist due to the paucity of financial resources. It seems that off-shoring processes interrupted the relationships between school and firm; hence, resulting in a skill shortage of the students, mainly regarding soft skills.

In summary, it is possible to underline some results.

- Frequently, in the opinion of employers, educational outlines are characterized by unnecessary and/or useless skills rather than skill shortage. Therefore, it is fundamental to update these outlines.
- The students perceive themselves as under-skilled, both in skills and aptitude (soft skills), and they do not feel ready for the labour market.
- Soft skills (communication, teamwork, problem-solving) are almost always critical: this skills category has more relevance in employers' opinions than that of teachers, and students perceive themselves as under-skilled.

The local labour market studied in this research shows frictions in school-to-work transition. Consistent with the TCE approach (Coase, 1937; Tadenis & Williamson, 2012; Williamson, 1985), this suggests that firms involved in a back-shoring process are affected by rising costs due to transactions necessary to provide general training to their newcomers. This friction seem to be due to the off-shoring dynamics: before the off-shore process, in this local labour market firms foster the development of specific skill areas, for instance soft skills.

RQ2: Is JRA a suitable approach for assessing skill shortages/mismatch in local economies?'

Considering the model used here for skill mismatch assessment, it is possible to underline some advantages and disadvantages. This model should be tested in a real workers population: an anonymous self-reported questionnaire is likely to be prone to bias. Furthermore, students, by definition, ignore the real job in a real workplace; hence, their evaluations are based on perception rather than experience. Furthermore, self-evaluated skill level is an indicator of self-efficacy but can be prone to self-serving biases. On one side, to protect their self-esteem, students could be likely to overestimate their skill level; on the other side, to denigrate their school, they could underestimate the skill level possessed at the end of the education. Moreover, difficulty could arise with implementation of the tools for jobs which are not defined by National Occupational Standards. In this case, the job description must be realized by gathering all information involving all the stakeholders and collecting data from several sources.

However, this model is very effective in identifying the specific skills that need to be improved, and the organisational impact is extremely minimal. Furthermore, this model assesses the skill mismatch at a firm-specific level in a (local) labour market. Hence, provides a very specific level of training needs analysis. Moreover, it produces external validity of the results, due to the involvement of the stakeholders (employers). The tool is easily applied once it is prepared by the researcher.

This is a very appreciable feature, because one of the most common complaints from entrepreneurs is the difficult they find in applying tools provided by the academic world. Finally, it focuses on skills relevance as well as on skills level, it leads to a twofold positive outcome: a very specific level of training needs analysis, and at the same time it provides a priority scale for the training activities. This model also could be useful in order to design programmes aiming to overcome the erosion of manufacturing skills and provide students with skills that company need to deal with global markets.

CONCLUSION

These findings suggest a need for an extensive re-organization and/or overhaul of educational outlines to modify the real standard. First, it is necessary to insert soft skills in learning activities (communication; problem-solving; teamwork and customer care) and utilize different teaching methods (e.g., cooperative learning). Second, it seems to be necessary to provide final-year students with early orientation and assessment paths to improve their self-esteem and self-efficacy.

A third practical implication is a suggestion for policy makers. A widespread application of contract-like apprenticeship is desirable to reduce economic costs arising from general training. Although, of course, the content and the outlines of this training should really provide basic skills to apprentices and not follow a standard so far removed from reality. Finally, findings underline the gap between school and the labour market. Usually, teachers' skills and knowledge are obsolete, unnecessary and even useless. Hence, it should be mandatory for teachers themselves to complete a stage (work placement) every year to update their own skills.

BACK-SHORING PROCESS AND HUMAN RESOURCES MANAGEMENT PRACTICES: MANAGERIAL IMPLICATIONS AND FUTURE RESEARCH

This initial evidence suggests this trend will almost definitively involve firms in the short-term future, especially for those firms which have showed organizational behaviours aimed at the internationalization and de-localization of activities in the past. Literature suggests that back-shoring involves firms whose activities are affected by strong interdependencies and complementarities (Berry, 2014). This fact necessarily leads to an integration of the human resources capabilities of the overall value chain.

The current back-shoring dynamics will probably result in, for some companies, the co-location of strategic, R&D and manufacturing activities side-by-side. The geographical integration of organizational functions that have been separated in the past can result in advantages in innovation (Alcacer & Delgado, 2014), but could also lead to weaknesses in human resources management practices. The back-shore process on one hand entails a re-definition of some well-established managerial practices, and on the other hand the enactment of practices so far overlooked.

A weakness could arise from the *knowledge sharing and knowledge management* practices needed to ensure organizational reliability and innovation both for SMEs and larger enterprises. These human resources practices appear to be fundamental in a situation characterized by the integration of different organizations, capabilities and territories. For the SMEs, despite their smaller size (which seems to make knowledge sharing easier), this kind of firm seems to pay scarce attention to this organizational strategic factor (Ferrari, 2015a). If this strong limitation is to be confirmed by future research among the firms involved in the back-shore process, this fact could lead to an emerging problem of reliability and innovation (Ferrari, 2015b). For the larger firms, it seems that, quite counter-intuitively, the mere adoption of a knowledge management system without a specific reward system could even lead to a 'de-skilling' of the involved workers, and resistance to implementation (Tasking & van Bunnen, 2015).

The geographical integration of different organizational functions and jobs that have been separated in the past (manufacturing, R&D, strategic management, sales force and so on), shapes the inter-organizational relationship into collective and multi-contents teamwork. The relevant socio-psychological literature provides copious evidence supporting the fact that this *teambuilding process* is fragile and with an uncertain outcome (Quaglino et al., 1992). The geographical integration of separated organizational functions and jobs can result in advantages in innovation (Alcacer & Delgado, 2014), but could also result in competition and dysfunctional behaviours among team members. Future research should investigate if these dysfunctional processes affect the integration as a consequence of the organizational re-location.

Finally, with the aim of integration and innovation in mind, *performance appraisal and compensation* practices should add to the standard performance indicators (absenteeism, productivity, efficiency, effectiveness, quality, customer care) a 'dashboard' of indicators aimed to also evaluate the *Organizational Citizenship Behaviours* (OCB), due to the fact that, as is well known, these kinds of behaviours are strongly related to innovation and knowledge sharing (Cohen-Carash & Spector, 2001). As a consequence, the focus of the performance appraisal system should shift from equality to merit; furthermore, regarding the compensation system, it seems necessary to balance rewards and incentives at an individual level (in order to foster job performance) with rewards and incentives at a team/collective level (in order to foster a sense of belonging and OCB).

In conclusion, the initial empirical evidence allows scholars to depict a challenging future scenario, characterized by several factors which threaten firms involved in a back-shoring process, at least at the human resources management level. It seems that especially SMEs will be forced to develop a *managerialization* process to ensure the necessary outcomes in innovation and reliability.

LIMITATIONS AND FUTURE DEVELOPMENT

Due to the explorative nature of this research, and sample limitation, findings are not fully generalizable. Future research should investigate if and at which extent to make the ongoing operator accountable for the handover outcome has a positive impact on the handover process.

REFERENCES

Acemoglu, D., & Autor, D. (2011). *Skills, Tasks and Technologies: Implications for Employment and Earnings.* NBER Working Paper No. 16082.

Acemoglu, D., & Pischke, J. (1999). Beyond Becker: Training In Imperfect Labour Markets. *Economic Journal (London), 109*(453), 112–142. doi:10.1111/1468-0297.00405

Adelmann, B. (2013). America's Reshoring of Jobs is Accelerating. *The New American.* Retrieved on August 3, 2014, from: http://www.thenewamerican.com/economy/markets/item/16616-thanks-to-america-s-fracking-boom-and-skilled-laborforce-the-re-shoring-of-jobs-is-accelerating

Alcacer, J., & Delgado, M. (2014). Spatial organization of firms and location choices through the value chain. *Management Science*, *62*(11), 3213–3234. doi:10.1287/mnsc.2015.2308

Alderman, L. (2014, January 3). Unemployed in Europe Stymied by Lack of Technology Skills. *New York Times*. Retrieved on September 22, 2017, from: http://www.nytimes.com/2014/01/04/business/international/unemployed-in-europe-hobbled-by-lack-oftechnology-skills.html?emc=eta1kills

Allen, J., & Van Der Velden, R. (2001). Educational Mismatches Versus Skill Mismatches: Effects On Wages, Job Satisfaction, And On-The-Job Search'. *Oxford Economic Papers*, *3*(3), 434–452. doi:10.1093/oep/53.3.434

Allen, J., & Van Der Velden, R. (2005). *The Role Of Self-Assessment In Measuring Skills*. Paper For The Jacobs Foundation Conference Interdisciplinary And Cross-National Perspectives On Skill Formation And The Reform Of Vocational And Professional Training, Marbach, Switzerland.

Bailey, D. A., de Ruyter, A., Michie, J., & Tyler, P. (2010). Globalisation and the Auto Industry. *Cambridge Journal of Regions, Economy and Society*, *3*(3), 367–382. doi:10.1093/cjres/rsq021

Bandura, A. (1969). Social-learning theory of identificatory processes. In D. A. Goslin (Ed.), *Handbook of socialization theory and research*. Chicago: Rand McNally.

Bandura, A., & Wood, R. E. (1989). Effect of perceived controllability and performance standards on self-regulation of complex decision-making. *Journal of Personality and Social Psychology*, *56*(5), 804–814. doi:10.1037/0022-3514.56.5.805 PMID:2724068

Becker, G. (1964). *Human Capital: A Theoretical And Empirical Analysis With Special Reference To Education*. New York: Columbia University Press.

Berry, A. (2014). Global Integration And Innovation: Multicountry Knowledge Generation Within Mncs. *Strategic Management Journal*, *35*(6), 869–890. doi:10.1002mj.2140

Blomskog, S., & Schroder, L. (1997). Labour Market Entry, Vocational Training And Mobility In The Young Workforce In Sweden 1950-91. In S. Blomskog (Ed.), *Essays On The Functioning Of The Swedish Labour Market*. Stockholm: Swedish Institute For Social Research.

Borghans, L., & De Grip, A. (2000). *The Overeducated Worker? The Economics Of Skill Utilization*. Cheltenham, UK: Edward Elgar.

Büchel, F. & Mertens, A. (2003). Overeducation In Europe. Cheltenham, UK: Edward Elgar.

Cabral Vieira, J. A. (2005). Skill Mismatches And Job Satisfaction. *Economics Letters*, *89*(1), 39–47. doi:10.1016/j.econlet.2005.05.009

Campagnolo, D., & Gianecchini, M. (2015). *Oltre le ragioni: tempi e distanza nei processi di reshoring delle imprese italiane*. Padova: Padova University Press.

Card, D. (1999). The Causal Effect Of Education On Earnings. In O. Ashenfelter & D. Card (Eds.), *Handbook Of Labour Economics, 3*. Amsterdam: Elsevier. doi:10.1016/S1573-4463(99)03011-4

Coase, R. H. (1937). The Nature Of The Firm. *Economica*, *4*(11), 386–405. doi:10.1111/j.1468-0335.1937.tb00002.x

Cohen-Charash, Y., & Spector, P. E. (2001). The role of justice in organizations: A meta-analysis. *Organizational Behavior and Human Decision Processes*, *86*(2), 278–321. doi:10.1006/obhd.2001.2958

Desjardins, R., & Rubenson, K. (2011). *An Analysis of Skill. Mismatch Using Direct Measures of Skills.* OECD Education. Working Papers, No. 63. Paris: OECD Publishing.

Felstead, A. (2007). *How "smart" are Scottish jobs? Summary evidence from the Skills Surveys, 1997-2006.* Glasgow, UK: Futureskills Scotland Expert Briefing.

Ferrari, F. (2015). *'Re-Shoring' and Skill Mismatch. Training Needs Analysis in School-to-Work Transition.* Paper to the 27th Annual Meeting of the Society for the Advancement of Socio-Economics, London School of Economics and Political Science, London, UK.

Ferrari, F. (2015a). *The back-shoring process and its impact on Human Resources Management practices. First empirical evidence and some issues for the future research agenda'.* Paper for the AIB Conference 'Breaking up the global value chain: Possibilities and consequences', Milano, Italy.

Ferrari, F. (2015b). *Knowledge Sharing in Family Business Transmission. Bad News From Italian SMEs.* Paper to the International Conference on Organizational Knowledge, Learning and Capabilities (OLKC), Milan, Italy.

Ferrari, F., & Emiliani, E. (2009). *Le Competenze E Il Mercato Del Lavoro. Un'analisi Dei Fabbisogni Formativi Tra Scuola E Impresa.* Roma: Carocci.

Fratocchi, L., Di Mauro, C., Barbieri, P., Nassimbeni, G., & Zanoni, A. (2014). When manufacturing moves back: Concepts and questions. *Journal of Purchasing and Supply Management*, *20*(1), 54–59. doi:10.1016/j.pursup.2014.01.004

Gathmann & Schönberg. (2010). How General Is Human Capital? A Task-Based Approach. *IZA DP No. 3067.*

Green, F., & Mcintosh, S. (2002). *Is There A Genuine Underutilization Of Skills Amongst The Over-Qualified?* Skope Research Paper, 30.

Green, F., & Mcintosh, S. (2007). Is There A Genuine Underutilization Of Skills Amongst The Over-Qualified? *Applied Economics*, *39*(4), 427–439. doi:10.1080/00036840500427700

Grubb, D. (1996). *Learnings To Work: The Case For Reintegrating Job Training And Education.* New York: Russel Sage Fundation.

Hartog, J. (2000). Over-Education And Earnings: Where Are We,Where Should Se Go? *Economics of Education Review*, *19*(2), 131–147. doi:10.1016/S0272-7757(99)00050-3

Hersch, J. (1991). Education Match And Job Match. *The Review of Economics and Statistics*, *73*(1), 140–144. doi:10.2307/2109696

Isfol. (2006). *Organizzazione, Apprendimento, Competenze.* I Libri Del Fse.

Kinkel, S. (2014). Future and impact of backshoring—Some conclusions from 15 years of research on German practices. *Journal of Purchasing and Supply Management*, *20*(1), 63–65. doi:10.1016/j.pursup.2014.01.005

Krahn, H., & Lowe, G.S. (1998). *Literacy Utilization in Canadian Workplaces. Ottawa and Hull: Statistics*. Canada and Human Resource Development Canada.

Kroft, S. (2013). Are Robots Hurting Growth? "60 Minutes – CBS Television. *CBS News*. Retrieved on June 2, 2016, from: http://www.cbsnews.com/8301-18560_162-57601121/are-robots-hurtingjob-growth

Leuven, E., & Oosterbeek, H. (2011). Overeducation and Mismatch in the Labor Market. In Handbook of the Economics of Education. Elsevier Science. doi:10.1016/B978-0-444-53444-6.00003-1

Manacorda, M., & Petrongolo, B. (1999). Skill Mismatch And Unemployment In Oecd Countries. *Economica*, *66*(262), 181–207. doi:10.1111/1468-0335.00164

Mavromaras, K., McGuinness, S., & Fok, Y. (2009). *Overskilling dynamics and education pathways*. Institute for the Study of Labor (IZA), Discussion Paper 4321.

Mavromaras, K., McGuinness, S., O'Leary, N., Sloane, P., & Fok, Y. (2010). The problem of overskilling in Australia and Britain. *Manchester School*, *78*(3), 219–241. doi:10.1111/j.1467-9957.2009.02136.x

McGuinness, S. (2006). Overeducation In The Labour Market. *Journal of Economic Surveys*, *20*(3), 387–418. doi:10.1111/j.0950-0804.2006.00284.x

Merico, C. (2015). *L'imprenditore va all'estero? La sua banca lo accompagna*. Milano: Selpress.

Nedelkoska, L., Neffke, F., & Wiederhold, S. (2015). Skill mismatch affects life-long earnings. *Policy Brief, proceedings of LLLight'in'Europe research project*. Retrieved on November 11, 2017, from: www.lllightineurope.com/publications

OECD. (1996). Transition From School To Work. In *Education At A Glance: Analysis*. Paris: OCED.

OECD. (1998). *Thematic Rewiew Of The Transition From Initial Education To Working Life: Interim Comparative Report*. Paris: OCED.

OECD. (2013). *First International Report on PIAAC* (Vol. 1). Paris: OECD Publishing.

Pellizzari, M., & Fichen, A. (2013). *A new measure of skills mismatch: Theory and evidence from the survey of adult skills (PIAAC)*. OECD Social, Employment and Migration Working Papers 153. Paris: OECD Publishing.

Perry, A., Wiederhold, S., & Ackermann-Pieket, D. (2014). How Can Skill Mismatch be Measured? New Approaches with PIAAC. *Methods, Data, Analyses, 8*(2), 137-174.

Pisano, G. P., & Shih, W. C. (2012). *Producing Prosperity: Why America Needs a Manufacturing Renaissance*. Boston: Harvard Business Review Press.

Poletaev, M., & Robinson, C. (2008). 2008). Human Capital Specificity: Evidence from the Dictionary of Occupational Titles and Displaced Worker Surveys, 1984-2000. *Journal of Labor Economics*, *26*(3), 387–420. doi:10.1086/588180

Prota, F., & Viesti, G. (2007). *La delocalizzazione internazionale del made in Italy*. Università di Bari, Cerpem.

Quaglino, G. P., Casagrande, S., & Castellano, C. (1992). *Gruppo di lavoro, lavoro di gruppo*. Milano: Cortina Editore.

Sattinger, M. (1993). Assignment Models Of The Distribution Of Earnings. *Journal of Economic Literature*, *31*, 851–880.

Schooler, C. (1984). Psychological effects of complex environments during the life span: A review and theory. *Intelligence*, *8*(4), 259–281. doi:10.1016/0160-2896(84)90011-4

Smith, A. (1973). *Indagine Sulla Natura E Le Cause Della Ricchezza Delle Nazioni*. Milano: Isedi.

Soskice, D. (1994). Reconciling Markets And Institutions: The German Apprenticeship System. In L. M. Linch (Ed.), *Training And The Private Sector*. Chicago: University Of Chicago Press/Nber.

Streeck, W. (1987). The Role Of The Social Partners. In *Vocational Education And Training In The Federal Republic Of Germany*. Berlin: Cedefop.

Tadelis, S., & Williamson, O. E. (2012). *Transaction Cost Economics*. Retrieved on May 9, 2014, from: Http://Ssrn.Com/Abstract=2020176

Tasking, L., & van Bunnen, G. (2015). Knowledge Management Through the Development of Knowledge Repositories: Towards Work Degradation, New Technology. *Work and Employment*, *30*(2), 158–172. doi:10.1111/ntwe.12049

Thurow, L. C. (1975). Generating Inequality: Mechanisms Of Distribution. In *The U.S. Economy*. New York: Basic Books. doi:10.1007/978-1-349-15723-5

Tsang, M. C., & Levin, H. (1985). The Economics Of Overeducation. *Economics of Education Review*, *4*(2), 93–104. doi:10.1016/0272-7757(85)90051-2

Viscusi, W. K. (1979). Job Hazards And Workers Quit Rates: An Analysis Of Adaptive Workers Behavior. *International Economic Review*, *20*(1), 29–58. doi:10.2307/2526415

Williamson, O. E. (1985). L'economia Dell'organizzazione: Il Modello Dei Costi Di Transazione. In R. C. D. Nacamulli & A. Rugiadini (Eds.), *Organizzazione & Mercato*. Bologna: Il Mulino.

KEY TERMS AND DEFINITIONS

Back-Shoring: Reinsertion of shores beneath a stripped concrete slab after the original formwork and shoring has been removed from a small section. Unlike reshoring, back-shoring keeps the slab from supporting its own weight or the weight of existing loads above it until the slab attains full strength.

Educational Mismatch: The lack of coherence between the qualification level achieved by a worker and the level requested by a firm in order to carry out a specific job.

Job Requirements Approach: Method of analysis based on the qualification that a worker must have in order to be suitable for a certain job.

Re-Shoring: The practice of transferring a business operation that was moved overseas back to the country from which it was originally relocated.

School-to-Work Transition: Process involving students to *transition* successfully into the economy, either through paid employment with a business or self-employment.

Skill Mismatch: Situation in the labor market where the level of skills of individuals does not match the level of skills required in the jobs (see Gap, Overskilling, Underskilling, Overqualification, Underqualification). Mismatches could be vertical (when the level of skills or education is more or less than the level of skills or education required to perform a job), horizontal (when the type of education or skills is not appropriate for the current job, but the level of education or skills matches the requirements of the job) or geographical (where the workers with types and levels of skills or education required are based in a country or region different from where such skills are needed).

Transaction Cost Economics: Analyses each transaction and assesses the economic advantage of purchasing from the market relationship (i.e., out-sourcing goods and/or services from an external provider) rather than an internal solution.

Chapter 8
Challenges in Creating and Sustaining an Entrepreneurial Business in Milwaukee

Garfield A. Plunkett
University of Phoenix, USA

Libi Shen
University of Phoenix, USA

ABSTRACT

Small business entrepreneurs have made important contributions to economic activities in the U.S. In recent years, there were decline and high entrepreneurial failure rates for entrepreneurs throughout the country. Specifically, the continuous challenges faced by entrepreneurs in the city of Milwaukee, Wisconsin have negatively affected job creation and the entrepreneurial process. What are the challenges faced by Milwaukee's entrepreneurs in creating and sustaining their businesses? How have the entrepreneurial challenges affected Milwaukee entrepreneurs' experiences in creating and sustaining their businesses? What specific support might be effective in overcoming the challenges? The purpose of this study was to explore the lived experiences of 20 entrepreneurs, specifically the challenges they encountered while sustaining an entrepreneurial enterprise in the city of Milwaukee. This chapter identifies the barriers and challenges that entrepreneurs and entrepreneurial small businesses must overcome. Recommendations for government leaders, entrepreneurs, and future researchers are provided.

INTRODUCTION

Creating and sustaining entrepreneurial small businesses is important for the U.S. economy. Entrepreneurial small businesses are the engines of growth that create jobs, opportunities, and financial support for many communities (Yang, 2012). Successful entrepreneurial undertakings provide a speedy increase in economic activities and growth (Nelson & Quick, 2009). As Mach and Wolken (2006) manifested, entrepreneurial small businesses were responsible for about 50% of production and created over 70% of

DOI: 10.4018/978-1-5225-5787-6.ch008

net new jobs annually. Despite their size, entrepreneurial small businesses have all the needs of larger businesses.

A crucial factor facing entrepreneurial small business leaders in the first few years of business is a deficiency in leadership (Collins, 2005). People being involved in the entrepreneurial process are required to create, discover, and execute leadership that is cognizant of the reality in the environment, yet many do not possess the right leadership skills (Kouzes & Posner, 2003). Information on how to start and sustain a business is crucial because entrepreneurial leaders are constantly dealing with issues and challenges (e.g., finding additional revenue sources, the lack of suitable and qualified workers, the rising cost of energy, the rising cost of healthcare, and limited access to capital) (Jones, 2010). How leaders choose to deal with those issues and challenges will ultimately determine their future and that of the organization (Jones, 2010).

The major problem was that many small business entrepreneurs have confronted challenges due to a decline in entrepreneurial activities resulting in high entrepreneurial failure rate in the U.S. (Foley & Zimmer, 2014; Gee, 2013; GEM, 2016; SBA, 2012). Specifically, the continuous challenges faced by entrepreneurs in the City of Milwaukee have resulted in fewer opportunities for potential and established entrepreneurs (MMAC, 2012; SBA, 2014). Although entrepreneurship has its importance and growing recognition on economic growth and development, limited empirical data exist regarding to the sustainability of small entrepreneurial businesses and the lived experiences of the individuals who started these entrepreneurial businesses in the City of Milwaukee. The purpose of this empirical phenomenological study was to explore the lived experiences of 20 entrepreneurs, especially the challenges they faced due to a decline in entrepreneurial activities while they were creating and sustaining an entrepreneurial business in the City of Milwaukee.

BACKGROUND

Milwaukee is the largest city in both size and population in the US state of Wisconsin. The latest census data showed a population of 595,047 residents, and the median income for the City of Milwaukee is $35,958 (U.S. Census Bureau Data, 2016). The demographics of Milwaukee included Black (40%), White (39%), Hispanic (17%), Asian (3.5%), and American Indian (0.5%). Milwaukee has the reputation for being one of the most segregated cities in America; African Americans dominate the north side, Caucasians dominate the east side, and the south side is largely Hispanic (Causey, 2014; Denvir, 2011; Kulling, 2014; Tidmarsh, 2014; WUWM/ Milwaukee Public Radio, 2013). Milwaukee has earned a reputation for precision manufacturing. Milwaukee is a major supplier of industrial controls, steel, foundry parts, and mining machinery (MMAC, 2012). The city is the home headquarters to five Fortune 500 companies: (a) Harley-Davidson, (b) Manpower, (c) Johnson Controls, (e) Northwestern Mutual, and (f) Rockwell Automation (MMAC, 2012). In 2014, the American Institute for Economic Research (AIER) ranked the Milwaukee area number 12 on the mid-size metro-scale for being one of the best college cities (AIER, 2014).

In retrospect, Milwaukee started out as a trading post in the early 1800s when three white settlers (i.e., Slomon Juneau, Byron Kilbourn, and George Walker) arrived (Gurda, 1999). These Milwaukee's founding fathers helped turn the swamp into the city of Milwaukee, and each man settled in a different place along the river called Juneautown, Kilbourntown, and Walker's Point (Gurda, 1999). From the 1930s to the 1960s, Milwaukee was a major industrial city making a wide variety of machinery products

(Milwaukee History and Timeline, 2011). “Sprawling complexes turned out engines, tractors, electrical equipment, controls, mining shovels, and automobile frames; people seeking jobs and opportunity flocked to the machine shop of the world” (Milwaukee History and Timeline, 2011, para. 6).

Milwaukee’s industrial success continued well into the 20th century and was a magnet for European immigrants, primarily from Germany, Poland, Italy, and Ireland. “As Milwaukee matured, immigrants from Mexico and African-Americans from the southern states found decent-paying factory work in Milwaukee” (Milwaukee History and Timeline, 2011, para. 7). Entrepreneurial businesses in Milwaukee have made important contributions to the City’s development by employing and providing opportunities for many of the city’s residents (MMAC, 2012). To protect the interest of and the sustainability of small enterprise, small business received its official recognition from the U.S. Congress in 1953 when Congress enacted “The Small Business Act” (SBA, 2012). Within the Act, Congress affirmed its support for small businesses, and stated that it would assist, guide, and protect small businesses to support and maintain open trade that would work to reinforce the U.S. economy (SBA, 2012). The Small Business Administration’s primary responsibility is to supervise, advocate, and safeguard the interests of small business operators (SBA, 2012).

Milwaukee’s decline started in the manufacturing industry in the early 1970s and continued into the year 2000. The decline was magnified by competitions from outside the United States, and manufacturing had lost over 77,000 jobs in early 2000s (MMAC, 2012). The loss was particularly painful and detrimental to the city because manufacturing represented the bulk of jobs in Milwaukee. Despite many initiatives to effect growth, production in the city remains low resulting in high unemployment rate for many of the city residents (MMAC, 2012). Milwaukee was also ranked fourth worst in the nation with 27% of low income population. Milwaukee was the only city in the State of Wisconsin to make the top 50 lists for low-income population (U.S. Census Bureau Data, 2014).

The latest recession of 2007-2009 was devastating for entrepreneurial small businesses. Job loss was approximately 60% (SBA, 2014). Entrepreneurial small businesses faced many challenges the years following the recession. Some of the challenges included less than adequate sales, inadequate employment, and limited access to capital (SBA, 2014). In 2014, Milwaukee was ranked the top ten poorest cities in the United States based on U.S. Census Bureau Data. Similar to New York and Atlanta, city leaders in Milwaukee have tried to implement programs to jump-start entrepreneurial actives, but despite the measures, entrepreneurial activities in Milwaukee have fallen short of expectations. Mayborne (2012) noted that “out of 21 comparable areas, the Milwaukee area ranked the seventh lowest in new business starts per capita and the fifth lowest for venture capital investment” (para,1).

In 2015, there were over 40,000 registered small businesses, representing 97% of all employers and employing 51% of the private-sector workforce in Milwaukee. Despite a large number of entrepreneurial small businesses in the city, entrepreneurial activities have been relatively stagnant in some sectors while declining others (Kauffman Foundation, 2015). The stagnation and decline in entrepreneurial activities have been detrimental to the Milwaukee’s economy. In fact, a total of 44% of entrepreneurial small businesses failed within the first four years of operation; the challenges are great and the sustainability is critical (SBA, 2014). In its latest 2015 report, the Kauffman Foundation Index, which tracks entrepreneurship in the 40 largest metro areas in the U.S., ranked Milwaukee second to last for entrepreneurial activities with Pittsburgh following (kauffmanindex.org, 2015).

Since the City of Milwaukee was ranked one of the poorest cities in the nation based on Kauffman Foundation (2015), information from this study may interest city leaders and policy makers as well as serve as a blueprint for potential entrepreneurs who create jobs in the City of Milwaukee. Identifying what leads to sustainability is significant because as entrepreneurial small businesses activities decline in some U.S cities, so does the prosperity that come with those businesses. Understanding the challenges entrepreneurs encounter in Milwaukee and having the right resources to support them might help establish effective strategies and preventative actions to mitigate risks and business failures for entrepreneurs.

LITERATURE REVIEW

Entrepreneur: Definition, Classification, and Theories

The word "entrepreneur" derived form the Latin words "entre" (stay afloat), and "prendes" (to seize, know, or take) (Price, 2006). French-Irish Economist Jean-Baptiste Say (1767-1832) coined the term "entrepreneur" in his book *Treatise on Political Economy* in 1800 and stated that the entrepreneur shifted economic resources out of an area of lower and into an area of higher productivity (Skousen, 2009). In *the Theory of Economic Development,* Schumpeter (1982) praised entrepreneurship and claimed the entrepreneur as the driver of change. The improvement and modification in a country come from the work of entrepreneurs. "The fundamental impulse that sets and keeps the capitalist engine in motion comes from the new consumer goods, the new methods of production or transportation, the new markets, the new forms of industrial organization that capitalist enterprise create" (Schumpeter, 1942, p. 83).

Entrepreneurs can be divided into three different categories: (a) managing, (b) innovating, and (c) controlling entrepreneurs (Evans, 1949). Managing entrepreneurs manage the everyday aspect of organizing the resources needed to pursue the various opportunities that create wealth (Evans, 1949); innovating entrepreneurs represents 10-15 percent of all entrepreneurs with the primary objective to discover better ways of delivering products or services; and controlling entrepreneurs direct the flow of what comes and goes (Evans, 1949). The main difference among them is the ability of the innovative entrepreneurs to establish new companies or businesses that offer a set of distinctive value to the marketplace (Dyer, Gregersen, & Christensen, 2012).

"Born to be, or trained to be" is the big question often asked of many entrepreneurs. Some aspects of the "Great Man" theory suggested that leaders are born rather than trained, and that great individuals are the shapers of history rather than being shaped by the history (Jogulu & Wood, 2006). Turak (2013) believed that entrepreneurs are enterprising people; "Success emerges from the active push of individuals, rather than the passive pull of environmental forces acting on them" (para, 2). Entrepreneurs seek to create change and exploit on the changes as an opportunity (Drucker, 1993). Entrepreneurs are fearless innovators and creators of products and services (Harding, 2006; Shaoming, Stough, & Jackson, 2009). In emerging economies where the failure rate is much higher for entrepreneurs than those of developed economies, individuals are still driven to become entrepreneurs despite the odds stacked against them (De Villiers-Scheepers, 2012). Potential entrepreneurs in emerging economies are optimists who view their success as a way to upward mobility and a way to enhance economic development for their country (De Villiers-Scheepers, 2012).

Entrepreneurship: Definition, Classification, and Theories

The first person to highlight the importance of entrepreneurship in production was British economist Alfred Marshall (1842–1924). In *Principles of Economics*, Marshall (1920) noted that the production factors in an organization are land, labor, and capital, but those factors would not reach full utilization without the involvement of entrepreneurship. Entrepreneurship is "the act and process by which societies, regions, organizations, or individuals identify and pursue business opportunities to create wealth" (George & Zahra, 2002, para. 2).

Three types of entrepreneurship (i.e., technological, geographical, and sociological) have driven the process. Technological entrepreneurship is responsible for developing and bringing new technologies to the marketplace; the geographical entrepreneurship focuses on moving products across boundaries; and the sociological entrepreneurship searches for new ways to repackage and sell existing products before others catch on (Thurow, 2000). Since the 1990s, entrepreneurship and its association with economic growth have gained increasing importance. Economists, politicians, and business leaders have recognized the pivotal role the entrepreneurship has played in the creation of small businesses in market driven economies (Cuevas, Carrasco, & Soriano, 2009; Hebert & Link, 2006; Shaoming, Stough, & Jackson, 2009). Entrepreneurship is the primary vehicle for reducing poverty and moving countries forward economically (GEM, 2015). Entrepreneurship leads to upward mobility, and upward mobility leads to prosperity (Nelson & Quick, 2009).

Despite the importance of entrepreneurship on market driven economies, researchers and scholars have struggled to come up with an accepted modern theory of entrepreneurship. While the struggle remains, Alvarez (2005) raised three dominant theories in the work: (a) the discovery of opportunity and recognition, (b) the creation that focuses on individual entrepreneurs, and (c) the decision-making context. The discovery theory revealed that opportunities are objective, and entrepreneurs are risk bearing; the creation theory assumes that opportunities are subjective and entrepreneurs are ordinary people who have a high tolerance for uncertainty; and the decision-making context theory revealed that opportunities are discovered through market analysis, learning and hypothesis testing (Alvarez, 2005).

Entrepreneurial Activities in the United States

Since its formation as a country in 1776, the United States has been a nation of entrepreneurs, and entrepreneurship has become the emblem of business tenacity and achievement (Bygrave & Zacharakis, 2008). The United States economy has been driven primarily by entrepreneurship after the overtaking of Great Britain in 1890 as the world's largest economic country (Bygrave & Zacharakis, 2008). Cornelius Vanderbilt (1794-1877), Andrew Carnegie (1835-1919), Henry Ford (1863-1947), John D. Rockefeller (1837-1937), and Thomas Edison (1847-1931) were some early-noted successful entrepreneurs.

In the early to mid-1900s, the United States went through challenging times (e.g., the stock market crash of 1929 and the U.S. entry into World War II) which brought about decline in entrepreneurial activity (Bygrave & Zacharakis, 2008). There was an increased in entrepreneurial activities after World War II; the increase continued into the late 1960s and 1970s, which was described as the entrepreneurial revolution (Bygrave & Zacharakis, 2008). The revolution was further enhanced in the early 1990s when the United States economy experienced a new breed of entrepreneurs and unexpected phenomenal growth in the digital age (Bygrave & Zacharakis, 2008).

In the 1990s, technology became widespread, thus organizations and people became more reliant on the use of technology. The use of technology had a profound effect on society, and it has become an added factor to the factors of production (Shane, 2008). According to Drucker (1993), "The traditional factors of production land, labor, and capital have not disappeared; but they have become secondary" (p.42). Researchers have theorized that technology is the main driver of entrepreneurship activities in many organizations and countries and would continue to do so in the future (Hoque et al., 2006; Jones, 2010; Mital & Seshadri, 2007; Shane, 2008).

The emergence of the digital age ushered in a new phase of entrepreneurship in the United States that gave rise to the use of personal computers fueled by the internet, in which people have greater access to information and created a new gateway for entrepreneurs to start new businesses without a huge amount of startup capital (Harding, 2006). Some noted American companies were created because of the internet, including Yahoo, Uber, Google, eBay, Twitter, Facebook, Netflix, and Amazon. These companies have collectively generated billions of dollars for investors and have contributed greatly to the American economy by providing tax revenues to the government and jobs for thousands of Americans (Christensen, 2012; Mital & Seshadri, 2007; Shane, 2008)

In recent years, a good percentage of older Americans have made a significant contribution to entrepreneurship by becoming job creators instead of job seekers. Starting in the early 2000s, the United States witnessed a surge in Baby Boomers (those born between 1946 and 1965) who were getting involved in entrepreneurial activities (Rogoff, 2007). Small businesses started by older adults in the U.S. represented more than 40% of all new businesses created in the last ten years (SBA, 2013). In 2012, people over 55 years old started 23.4% of all new businesses (Matthews, 2014). This contribution showed a positive and promising sign for continued entrepreneurship in the U.S.

Sustainability and Entrepreneurship

Sustainability is "the ability to generate long-term value throughout mutually beneficial relationships with its business and socio-political stakeholders" (Zegarowski, 2007, p. 53). Information regarding sustainability is a fast-growing business for large organizations and an increasing amount of small and medium size businesses (Kimberly, Thomas, & James, 2012). Various studies have shown that many companies have embraced sustainability, while other companies have not yet to do so. For those who have not yet embraced sustainability, it is imperative that they embraced it quickly (Kimberly, et al, 2012).

Creating sustainability requires leaders to understand internal factors relevant to sustainability that will create change over time (Ollin & Vej, 2012). As Ollin and Vej (2012) described, "It is apparent that more attention needs to be paid to the meaning of the sustainability construct in business, and to internal aspects triggering and enabling companies to embark on a sustainability path" (para, 2). Originally, business sustainability was considered a cost reduction and risk management measure, but sustainability is being viewed as a source of innovation and growth for entrepreneurial businesses since the late 1990s (Webb et al., 2012).

Sustainability is not limited to any particular organization. It has been a growing concern that has affected businesses of all sizes (KPMG International, 2012). In 2012, KPMG International identified 10 forces that threaten business sustainability: (a) material and resource scarcity, (b) population growth, (c) food security, (d) volatility in energy and fuel security, (e) water scarcity, (f) water shortages, (g) increase in wealth and growth in the middle class, (h) increase in urbanization, (i) climate change, and (j) ecosystem decline. Leaders and organizations that are not equipped to deal with sustainability issues should increase knowledge in the various areas of sustainability (KPMG International, 2012). Small business enterprise should invest in sustainability strategies to protect and increase opportunities, and these strategies should be viewed as a necessity rather than an option (KPMG International, 2012).

Small business leaders should recognize and embrace sustainability to improve and sustain their organizations. Dressen (2009) asserted that leaders who develop sustainability practices for their small businesses are less likely to face pressure from external stakeholders. Sustainability requires having the right people in the organization because people are a source of organizational strength. Having the right people will mean the difference between growth and decline (Jones, 2010). Sustaining the business in the long run requires leaders to develop learning and knowledge in sustainability practices that will become part of the organization's culture (Kimberly et al., 2012). Essentially, sustainability is pivotal to the entrepreneurial process.

INNOVATION AND ENTREPRENEURSHIP

Innovation and entrepreneurship are closely linked. Innovation is taking an idea, and making it into something tangible that creates value, and this is a critical factor in organizational growth, and ultimately survival (Hui & Idris, 2009; Merriam, 2006; Shane, 2009). Innovation plays a vital role in the creation of opportunities. Innovation is the sustaining factor for the world economy and a tactical priority for every organization (Dyer et al., 2012). Innovation helps society move forward and become better by creating or improving products (Gem, 2011). Innovation leads to greater stability and is quickly becoming the corner stone in national economic policy; in countries like Canada, Australia, and the United Kingdom, political leaders have instituted policies that help spur development in innovation (Tidd & Bessant, 2009).

Entrepreneurship is the capacity with willingness to develop, organize, manage, and assume the risk of a business enterprise (Merriam, 2006; Shane, 2009). Blending both entrepreneurship and innovation creates an opportunity for entrepreneurs to develop new business ideas, improve business conditions, and search for new ways to improve the overall effectiveness of the business (Shane, 2010). Organizations that want to benefit the most from innovation need to have an innovation strategic in place because having the right innovation strategy leads organizations to experiment and take risks (Borgelt & Falk, 2007). Leaders who fail to take on the necessary risk will only block innovation strategies in an organization (Borgelt & Falk, 2007). Moreover, having the right innovation strategy will help the organization plan, design, create, develop, produce market innovative products, and services and processes (Maital & Seshadri, 2007).

In many instances, the survival for some organizations depends on innovation, and surviving on innovation is a matter of how quickly those organizations can make changes, introduce new technologies, and find new ideas or make the most out of existing ideas (Shane, 2010; Jones, 2010). Small business entrepreneurs are no exceptions to the rules of innovation. In a speedy environment, entrepreneurs cannot afford to spend time on outdated business methods and practices; entrepreneurs must continuously seek out the new, the diverse and unimaginable ways of doing business. Small and medium size organizations may lack the necessary resources and tools to innovate quickly. This means that leaders in organizations that are slow to innovate need to become more creative. Leaders who lack the necessary resources for a full-scale roll out, but are willing to initiate innovation, should utilize an incremental approach that garners small wins that ultimately build confidence and commitment (Kouzes & Posner, 2003). Embracing innovation lead to organizational success in a volatile and competitive marketplace (Madrid-Guijarro, Garcia, & Van Auken, 2009). Small business leaders and new entrepreneurs who do not value innovation and innovative alliances may find it difficult to compete in the future (Madrid-Guijarro et al., 2009).

To compete effectively and gain an innovative advantage, some companies have formed innovative alliances. Rosenfeld (2014) presented the Innovation Strengths Preference Indicator® (ISPI™), which is a tool combining three different psychological axes into a single indicator to highlight an individual's predispositions toward a certain type of innovation and how they prefer to interact with others (Rosenfeld, 2014). In Innovation Orientation™ (iO™), there are four orientations: "Overall ISPI™ (the total for Ideation, Risk, and Process); Ideation (the approach for generating new ideas); Risk (the approach for taking risks); and Process (the approach for establishing and following processes)" (Rosenfeld, 2014, p.44). The Innovation Orientation Modifiers™ (iOM™) consisted of control, relationship, networking, Input, flow, passion, output, and energy (Rosenfeld, 2014). Rosenfeld (2014, p. 48) illustrated that,

Innovation leaders must be comfortable with understanding and identifying differences between people. You must be "bilingual" in your ability to communicate, listen to, and be heard by builders, pioneers, and differing iOM™s. You must appreciate and positively recognize the strengths of all people and realize that they are not interchangeable.

These indicators help business leaders to consider how they prefer to innovate and how they prefer to innovate with others.

FOCUS OF THE CHAPTER: THE STUDY

Methodology

The aim of this chapter was to explore the lived experiences and challenges of 20 Milwaukee entrepreneurs through their journey of creating and sustaining a small entrepreneurial business. A qualitative method with a phenomenology design was used to conduct the study. One central question and three sub-questions guided this study. The central research question for this study was: *What are the lived experiences and challenges of Milwaukee entrepreneurs through their journey of creating and sustaining an entrepreneurial business?* Three sub-questions were: (a) what are the challenges faced by Milwaukee's entrepreneurs in creating and sustaining their businesses? (b) How have the entrepreneurial challenges affected Milwaukee entrepreneurs' experiences in creating and sustaining their businesses? and (c) What specific support might be effective in overcoming the challenges?

Twenty participants in Milwaukee were selected for the interviews based on the following criteria: (1) Participants' skill sets and experiences were relevant to creating and sustaining a small business enterprise in the City of Milwaukee; (2) the business must be a registered small business entity whose operations are within the city limits of Milwaukee, and (3) the participants must have been in business for at least five years. Ten interview questions were used to solicit their responses on the challenges they had while running their businesses in Milwaukee. NVivo 11 was used to process interview data. The findings were as follows.

RESULTS

The perceptions of the participants' experiences in creating and sustaining a business were positive, negative, and mixed. The major challenges experienced through the journey of creating and sustaining the entrepreneurial business included (a) the economy recession, (b) shortage of funding, (c) lack of government support, (d) lack of accessing to capital, (e) work-life imbalance, (f) finding people to work with, (g) receiving payment for services, (h) finding new customers, (i) additional overhead cost, and (j) lack of skills on bookkeeping. The specific support that would be most effective and helpful to entrepreneurs in Milwaukee involved knowledge, skills, education, leadership, planning, and opportunity. The major challenges experienced by other entrepreneurs in Milwaukee were diversity, segregation, and business location. The personal views on entrepreneurship being an agent for change in Milwaukee covered contribution to economic and social development.

Seven significant emergent themes were identified in the study: (a) mixed perceptions of the entrepreneurial experiences, (b) challenges and stress factors, (c) the need for knowledge, skills and education, (d) negative perception and attitude (e) diversity, segregation, and business location (f) the need for leadership, planning, and opportunity, and (g) entrepreneurship contribution to economy and social development. In the following, the significant emergent themes were discussed.

Mixed Perceptions of the Entrepreneurial Experiences

Fifteen participants (75%) had mixed perceptions; three participants (15%) had negative perceptions; and two participants (10%) had positive perceptions of the entrepreneurial experiences. Most participants felt that they were never fully prepared to deal with the down side of business and there was no clear sign that the economy was getting much better even though the recession ended a few years ago. Some participants believed that Milwaukee is not a very encouraging place for entrepreneurs, and the business might be closed in a year if the trend continues without any improvement to the bottom line. However, a few participants believed that it is a good place for doing business; working hard to overcome the challenges helped them become a better businessperson; and successful experience is a direct result of hardworking and a positive outlook on life. One optimistic participant pointed out that the ongoing construction projects in Milwaukee, estimated by the City of Milwaukee to be worth over one billion dollars.

Challenges and Stressors

The majority of the participants in the study expressed some types of challenges while operating a business in the City of Milwaukee. Nineteen participants (95%) regarded the economy depression and lack of funding as stressors. Thirteen participants (65%) described the lack of access to capital for business improvement as a stressor. Eleven participants (55%) indicated government policies and the lack of support as stressors. Eight participants (40%) identified work-life imbalance as a challenge; seven participants (35%) expressed receiving payment for service as a challenge; and seven participants (35%) endorsed finding new customers as a challenge. Six participants (30%) expressed additional overhead cost as stressor. Five participants (25%) identified finding people to work with as a stressor, and one participant (5%) endorsed book keeping as a stressor.

The Need for Knowledge, Skills, and Education

Knowledge, expertise and skills are needed to perform a particular task in an efficient manner. Eleven participants (55%) described the need of leadership, planning, and opportunity; six participants (30%) expressed the need for knowledge, skill, and education to do business. About ten participants (50%) expressed the lack of trained and educated people as one of the issues that they had to deal with. In other words, many people seeking employment lack the basic education, work ethic, and were not committed to showing up on time as well as working for 40 hours. Some business owners had to turn away many individuals who were seeking employment because they did not have the required licenses or educational training to work in the business.

In order to get the required licenses, the individuals would need to go through 1,600 hours of training. In-house training was offered by some entrepreneurs despite the frustration and challenges of not being able to find people who were properly trained and ready to work. Education was not stressed as a priority in Milwaukee for years, because plenty of jobs were available in the manufacturing sectors, and manufacturing jobs only required a person to have certain skills. As manufacturing declined, individuals were left holding skills that were obsolete.

Negative Perception and Attitude

The participants' negative perceptions of city crimes and attitude were another theme of the study. Some participants indicated that their businesses have suffered greatly from the perception of crime that was pervasive in Milwaukee and found it difficult to attract potential customers from the suburbs because of the crime and the perception of crime in the City of Milwaukee. For example, the potential guests to the hotel from outside of Milwaukee are always concerned about their safety at the hotel because of the news and reports on crime on the streets of Milwaukee. Due to the crime in the central city, potential renters have refused to live in certain areas. The auto dealership has suffered greatly because of the perception of crime in the City of Milwaukee as well. Research has shown that the problem is real; according to a Fox 6 report aired on February 23, 2016, Milwaukee was in the top 30 lists of crime-infested cities in the nation, thus making the city one of the most dangerous places in the United States.

Diversity, Segregation, and Business Location

Eight participants (40%) expressed concern about the lack of diversity in the City of Milwaukee, and the need for greater inclusion. The lack of diversity has caused a divide in the City of Milwaukee, and the divide runs deep. Milwaukee is classified as one of the most segregated cities in the United States as stated earlier. The demographics showed that the north side of Milwaukee had about 85% of African Americans, and the north side of Milwaukee has never recovered from the industrial downturn of the 1980s. One participant pointed out that the latest recession only exacerbated the problem, and the root of the crime problem plaguing the north side of the City. Another participant who operated the charter school expressed that the lack of diversity has prevented him from attracting a diverse group of students to his school. The other participant noted that segregation in Milwaukee has prevented her from getting greater exposure for her artwork. Segregation has caused certain area in Milwaukee to be "redlined" and this has had a detrimental effect on some neighborhoods, especially on real estate business in Milwaukee. Segregation has caused some areas and the people in those areas to left behind. Five participants perceived the location of their respective businesses as a problem; the location is a hindrance to attracting customers from the outer suburbs.

The Need for Leadership, Planning, and Opportunity

Ten participants (50%) viewed leadership as an important element in the process. Several participants expressed that there is a need of leadership, and some entrepreneurs in Milwaukee needed additional training in the area of leadership. On the external side, about 75% of the participants' expressed negative satisfaction with the leadership from the city government of Milwaukee. One participant emphasized that leaders at the government level in Milwaukee need to recognize that times have changed, and their leadership should focus on removing red tapes and getting business to see themselves as partners in the development process.

If entrepreneurship is to become the catalyst for growth in Milwaukee, city leadership will have to assume a prominent roll. The city leaders need to present a vision of where the city is headed and stop preying on business. While other cities have shown tremendous growth, Milwaukee has remained stagnant, and the stagnation has to do with city leaders not having a clear plan on how to get the city moving. City leaders could do a lot more to encourage businesses; city leaders need to tell us where Milwaukee is headed.

Additionally, a few participants explained the need for planning. One participant emphasized that, "we started the business more as passion and without having a proper business plan to guide the process, as the business evolved we had to figure out how to manage the next step." A proper business plan in place to guide the business is essential. One participant articulated that his business would not have survived if he did not step up as a leader and create a proper business plan. Many participants viewed entrepreneurship as an opportunity for them to be independent. One participant indicated that owning her own small business has given her the opportunity of a lifetime because she loves being her own boss. Another participant expressed gratitude for the opportunity of owning and operating a business for 22 years. The other participant stressed that he welcomed the opportunity to be his own boss, and to be able to operate a business with his wife as a partner.

Entrepreneurship Contribution to Economic and Social Development

The entrepreneurship contribution to economic and social development was endorsed by 19 participants (95%). Creating an entrepreneurial base would be most beneficial for economic and social development in the city of Milwaukee. A participant responded, "Education is the key building block for any society to advance, so without a proper educational base Milwaukee will not advance." Confidence in entrepreneurship contributed to economic and social development. "Milwaukee is a city of entrepreneurs, and that was key to Milwaukee's success in the past; moving forward will require the help of entrepreneurs," said a participant. The other participant emphasized that, "more entrepreneurship would be great for Milwaukee's development, there are too many unemployed people around just been wasted, entrepreneurship would be helpful in getting these individuals more productive."

ISSUES, CONTROVERSIES, PROBLEMS

Based on the findings, the entrepreneurs in Milwaukee have encountered several challenges. There were internal and external problems. The internal problems came from the entrepreneurs themselves, for example, work-life imbalance, finding the right people to work with, receiving payment for the services, finding new customers, paying additional overhead cost, and having issues with the bookkeeping. The external challenges came directly from the City of Milwaukee and the environment surrounding the operations. Table 1 presented the internal and external challenges that the entrepreneurs in Milwaukee experienced.

Table 1. Internal and external challenges

Internal	External
Work-life balance (40%)	Downturn of economy (95%)
Finding new customers (35%)	Lack of funding (95%)
Receiving payment for services (35%)	Lack of access to the capital (65%)
Additional overhead cost (30%)	Lack of support from the government (55%)
Finding the right people to work with (25%)	
Bookkeeping and accounting (5%)	

INTERNAL PROBLEMS

Work-Life Imbalance

Eight participants expressed the failure of working less and spending more time with family. For instance, some participants intended to work about 30 hours each week in the business, but they were doing about 70 hours per week, and this has created stress for the families. Some participants had to be in the office from 6:00a.m. to 9:00 p.m., so they had to cut family time. Others have spent many days and nights working in the facility because staff members would call in sick or no show. Maintaining a work-life balance is challenging.

Finding New Customers

Seven participants expressed the difficulty to find new customers. They believed there is a need for new customers to drive sales in the business. However, many reasons contributed to not having new customers, for example, the economy, the environment, the price of the products, etc. Finding new customers is not an easy task for them.

Receiving Payment for Services

Seven participants expressed not being able to collect payment on outstanding invoices has been a burden on the bottom line. Small businesses rely on the payment to develop marketing plans, to pay the ren, to pay employees' salaries, to purchase materials, and to update the facilities. Without payment from the services on time, the business will run slow or not run well.

Additional Overhead Cost

Six participants expressed having to deal with additional overhead cost after moving away from one business to another. The cost included employees' salary, workers' compensation, rental for the building, and increased utilities. The participants have to deal with extra cost every time someone moves out as well.

Finding the Right People to Work With

Five participants identified finding people to work with as an issue. Certain jobs are too large for the business to manage and thus require a partner. Finding a partner has proven to be more difficult than expected. Instead of creating partnership and working together, many people have adopted "Me first mentality" and would rather failed than collaborating with someone else. A lack of cohesion and trust among people in Milwaukee were the problem.

Bookkeeping and Accounting

Only one participant endorsed book keeping as an issue. The participant expressed having problem with the bookkeeping or accounting for business, while the entrepreneur had no knowledge about bookkeeping and accounting.

The **internal** challenges have forced entrepreneurs to examine the roles and readiness of leaders to develop skills, to develop business capabilities, to seek opportunities, to be creative and develop innovative processes. Internally, entrepreneurs are challenged by the necessity to create and align human capital with the vision of the organization. Creating a compelling vision that is transmittable is necessary for business improvement and sustainability. The internal problems need to be solved to help their businesses prosper.

EXTERNAL PROBLEMS

The Downturn of Economy

Nineteen of the 20 participants reported the downturn of the economy as a problem. Since the last economic downturn that began in 2007 in the U.S., Milwaukee has not recovered. Based on the United States Census Bureau Report of 2015, Milwaukee economy has shown sign of decline with poverty on the increase. In fact, the Milwaukee economy was in bad shape before the last recession; many manufacturing jobs were lost. The Milwaukee economy could be the worst in Wisconsin compared to the neighborhood cities that have abundant jobs.

Lack of Funding

Nineteen participants reported the lack of funding an issue. Funding took two forms (i.e., funding for starting up and funding to maintain the business); both seemed to be of equal concern for the participants. Some participants indicated that most lending institutions are not willing to loan money to businesses that are not yet proven or well established in Milwaukee. This situation makes securing funding a challenging and difficult task. Some participants reflected that even though a proper business plan was in place, it was difficult to secure funding from a bank to start the business.

To get the business started, a participant exhausted personal savings and a bonus check received from the previous job and acquired additional funding from family members. The problem is that the government did not support it and the bank did not help. Lack of funding or lack of access to the funding prevented entrepreneur from acquiring the necessary equipment. Hence, growing the business was slow. Without some additional funding, some businesses may be forced to close its doors because they do not have enough funds to operate for another year.

Lack of Access to the Capital

The lack of access to capital for business improvement was endorsed by 13 participants. The years following the recent financial meltdown were very difficult for businesses because raising the required capital for building improvement was rather difficult. Several local banks rejected people's applications for loans with varied reasons. One rejection letter noted, "The bank did not have the appetite for the risk." The project finally got off the ground when the participant secured capital from a private lender in Atlanta. The participant articulated that acquiring capital from a private lender was not difficult, but the capital usually comes at a higher cost. One participant expressed challenge in raising capital when it was time to improve the car lot; because of a shortage in capital, resurfacing of the parking lot was placed on hold. Another participant expressed frustration when she was not able to raise enough capital to replace three roofs. The participant reported that being denied bank loans because the intended properties for collateralization were all underwater; the appraised value of the properties was less than what she owed the bank.

Lack of Support From the Government

Lack of government support and policies were endorsed by 11 participants. The government (i.e., local, county, state and federal) contributed to the challenges the entrepreneurs faced. A participant expressed that Milwaukee has been struggling for a while and the leaders at city hall does not know how to fix the problem, and the matters are only getting worst despite many discussions. Leaders at the state level have no real desire to help Milwaukee because of politics. When the subject of government leadership was raised, leadership at the City of Milwaukee was only concerned with raising money off the back of businesses because businesses are constantly being nickel and dimed by the City of Milwaukee. The leaders have discussed issues about moving the city forward, but to date the City has not moved advanced.

One participant stated the government is the biggest impediment to Milwaukee's solutions. For example, the Wisconsin State government has tried to undermine the City of Milwaukee by imposing new laws, which required City employees to live within the boundaries of the city. Since the removal of the home rule, more than 900 City employees have moved out of the City of Milwaukee. Some of the people who were relocated were the customers of the businesses. All the participants who raised this issue agreed that leaders at the city level lacks vision. City leaders need to promote and sell the City of Milwaukee and provide a compelling vision and a road map of where the city is heading.

In a word, the business climate in the city has presented several external challenges for entrepreneurs. The problems consisted of low governmental support, limited access to funding, lack of qualified workers, a high degree of poverty, crime, and a lack of leadership insight pertaining to solutions on fixing problems. If the city wants to grow and provide opportunities for its residents, structural changes must occur. Removing the barriers would create tremendous opportunities for existing and budding entrepreneurs.

SOLUTIONS AND RECOMMENDATIONS

Innovation Promotes Entrepreneurship

To solve the aforementioned problems, entrepreneurs need to recognize the relationship between entrepreneurship and innovation. Innovation plays a vital role in the creation of opportunities. Innovation is the sustaining factor for the world economy and a tactical priority for every organization (Dyer et al., 2012). "Innovation acts as the well spring for long- term economic growth; business that are lacking in innovation won't keep pace because they lack the fuel to generate new growth" (Mayborne, 2012, para, 3). According to Jones (2010), "cultures based on entrepreneurial norms and values are more likely to encourage innovation than a culture that is conservative and bureaucratic because entrepreneurial values encourage people to learn how to respond and adapt to a changing situation" (p. 13).

Entrepreneurs should have the concept of innovation because it allows them to identify additional revenue, finding connections, generate growth, and add benefits to the existing products and services. Small business entrepreneurs are no exceptions to the rules of innovation. As Schmidpeter and Weidinger (2014) pointed out, "businesses will play a key role when it comes to making our societies more sustainable. Only through innovation, new business models and the creativity and imagination of entrepreneurs will we use all the capacities necessary to tackle world challenges" (p.33).

Optimism Helps Entrepreneurship

People involve in entrepreneurship faces many different challenges. With a failure rate of 44% in the first four years of operation, starting a business is a daunting prospect for many would be entrepreneurs (SBA, 2012). People involved in entrepreneurship require a great level of optimism to be successful. In this study, many participants have negative or mixed perceptions of the businesses. Individuals who are pessimistic are less likely to take up the entrepreneurship challenges or to cope with difficult situations. To deal with the problems, entrepreneurs must be optimists who use critical thinking skills and task-oriented styles to tackle the difficulties. When there is a problem, there is a solution.

In face of a difficulty in business or life situations, those entrepreneurs should be optimists who adjust to life transitions, who seek for help, and who focus on strategies to tackle the issues. For example, to reach work-life balance, store hours could be adjusted or more employees can be hired. Store policies can be changed to receive payment for services to avoid late payment. Delivery trucks can be obtained to deliver goods to new customers in other location if finding customers is an issue. Bookkeeping can be learned, and accountant can be hired, if there is an issue. Changing the attitude from pessimism to optimism is important for entrepreneurs.

Leadership Is the Key

In all organizations, large or small "everything rises or falls on leadership" (Maxwell, 2005; p. 233). Leadership is vital in creating and operating a new entrepreneurial business because of the many challenges that have to be overcome before success is possible. In a newly formed entrepreneurial business, leadership is essential for creating and deploying the organization's strategic plans; leadership is even more critical during organizational changes because creating and sustaining the organization's growth depends on the active role of the leaders (Emale, 2010; Kayemuddin, 2012). In a competitive entrepreneurial business environment, leaders must exhibit flexibility, adaptability, accepting of new conditions, open to alternatives, and be prepared to take greater risks, leaders who are risk averse will find it difficult to seek new conditions and alternatives (O'Toole, 1996).

Recommendations for Business Leaders

Overcoming challenges are not easy, but there are steps leaders can take to mitigate the problem (Strazewski, 2010). First, business leaders must seek knowledge because knowledge is crucial and vital to the long-term success of any organization (Braunerhjelm, Audretsch, & Carlsson, 2010). Second, business leaders need to create energy in the people following them (Braunerhjelm et al, 2010; Bueno & Tubbs, 2004). Leaders who lack energy are less likely to energize those who follow them. Business leaders should first energize themselves and then the people who surround the leaders (Clawson, 2003). Clawson (2003) posited that if an organizational energy is low, the energy could increase; but to increase energy, leaders need to apply change in the work environment.

Clawson (2003) used the term change quotient (CQ) to illustrate that change quotient individuals confront challenges through learning and applying new skills, and are much easier to adapt to a rapidly changing business environment, because they view the challenges as opportunities to learn rather than as threats. Individuals who are not change quotient will have a hard time identifying signs that are necessary for change (Clawson, 2003). Leaders who articulate an inspirational vision can persuade followers to internalize attitudes and beliefs that will later offer as a source of intrinsic motivation to carry out the mission of the organization in the future (Yukl, 2010).

Recommendations for Government Leaders

There are several recommendations for government leaders to help improve the existing conditions for entrepreneurs. Government leaders in Milwaukee should take a closer look at the business environment in which entrepreneurs are operating. The majority of the participants in the study expressed the economy recess and shortage of funding to be their two biggest challenges. About 50% of the participants reported that the lack of government support and government policies were a hindrance to entrepreneurial activities. With this observation, government leaders should seek to implement laws and policies to support entrepreneurial activities. The development of city agencies to act as supporters for entrepreneurs in Milwaukee is needed. The agency would lend support and guidance to individuals who need assistance navigating the complex entrepreneurial process.

The agency could act as an intermediary where entrepreneurs and people looking for work are connected. Leaders at the state and city level can create a special funding source for entrepreneurs in the City of Milwaukee. The funding source should not be confused with the existing loans provided by the Small Business Association; it should be viewed as an investment in the City of Milwaukee's future rather than as an expense. Cities that lend support to their entrepreneurs are likely to do well in the future.

Recommendations for Entrepreneurs

The entrepreneurial process is full of risk, and there is no absolute guarantee that individuals will be successful in their endeavors. With this in mind, entrepreneurs in the City of Milwaukee should take a closer look at the ventures they have created and make a conscious decision if the venture is viable.

Decision-making is an essential process that the entrepreneurs must contend with on daily basis; the way a person chooses to make a decision could mean success or failure for the business (Christensen, 2012). The effectiveness of a decision depends greatly on the knowledge of the person making the decision (Jones, 2010). In order to ensure success in the decision-making process, entrepreneurs are encouraged to follow seven essential steps in decision-making: (1) identify the decision, (2) collect the information, (3) identify the alternatives, (4) weigh the evidence, (5) choose among alternatives, (6) take action, and (7) review the decision (Hussung, 2017).

Based on the findings, the participants listed several issues that can only be addressed by entrepreneurs themselves. First, entrepreneurs must have a proper business plan that lays out specific goals and objectives. A plan that has built in contingencies that will offset unforeseen problems is needed. Another recommendation for entrepreneurs is training and knowledge development. Without comprehensive knowledge of the requirements to be successful, experts in the field of entrepreneurship recommends that small business leaders take leadership courses and seek information on how to start, lead, and sustain a business (Bygrave & Zacharak, 2008).

Entrepreneurs should seek training programs that will aid them in developing the necessary skills to overcome present and potential challenges. Entrepreneurs in Milwaukee do not venture too far from their home base. The entrepreneurs should look at markets and opportunities outside their comfort zones. Some participants expressed that potential customers will not come to them because of the perception of crime. If potential customers will not come, then entrepreneurs need to find a way of getting to the customers. This could be in the form of online purchase or phone orders, and the products could then be delivered directly to the customers.

FUTURE RESEARCH DIRECTIONS

The findings from the study provide a unique opportunity for other researchers to broaden the field of the entrepreneurship as it pertains to the City of Milwaukee. Milwaukee is a unique case and the researcher believed that further study is warranted to uproot some of the causes that are preventing Milwaukee from advancing. Future researchers can take a deeper look at some of the structural problems facing Milwaukee and try to address them through the lenses of the residents. Even though several participants mentioned segregation, but the purpose of this study was not to investigate issues relating to segregation. Future researchers can investigate if there is any correlation between segregation and low entrepreneurship output. Future researchers can also examine the role of leadership as it pertains to the entrepreneurial development, and offer some suggestions that are substantive to bring about changes. This study adopted a qualitative method with a phenomenological design. Future researchers can use other types of research methods and designs to gain more profound results across cities and states.

CONCLUSION

In this study, the participants identified several features for creating and sustaining a business: (a) leadership, (b) purpose, (c) creativity, (d) passion, (e) innovation, and (f) the desire to be more. The participants believed that people are driven by purposes – the purpose to create, the purpose to discover, and the purpose to shape their future. While some people venture into the field of entrepreneurship to satisfy a personal need, others do so with the hope of solving problems and contributing to the economy. The vast majority of participants in the study view entrepreneurship as vital to the growth and the development of the City of Milwaukee. This finding was in alignment with the views of several researchers in the field. Entrepreneurship and its association with economic growth have garnered increasing importance; economists, politicians, and business leaders have recognized the pivotal role entrepreneurship has played in the creation of small businesses in market driven economies (Cuevas, Carrasco & Soriano, 2009; Herbert & Link, 2006; Shaoming, Stough, & Jackson, 2009).

The major challenges that the participants addressed included economy recession, shortage of funding, lack of government support, lack of access to capital, work-life imbalance, finding people to work with, receiving payment for services, finding new customers, additional overhead cost, and lack of skills on bookkeeping. Some of the challenges are internal and others are external. The internal problems are related to the operations of businesses in which entrepreneurs have greater control over and must find solutions to help mitigate those problems. The external problems are associated mainly with the city of Milwaukee and the economic realities on the ground that the government leaders can help. A majority of the participants indicated that the challenges provided valuable lessons from which they have learned a great deal. Whether positive or negative, participants' perceptions have a direct relation on how the participants viewed and choose to overcome challenges.

In recent years, many cities in the Midwest and throughout the United States have witnessed major entrepreneurial decline that has threatened the viability of those cities (Washington Post, 2013). Since 2010, a total of 36 cities and municipalities throughout the United States have filed for bankruptcy protection due partly to a decline in entrepreneurial activities. Some of these cities included Jefferson County, Alabama; Stockton, California; Boise County, Idaho; Mammoth Lakes, California; Harrisburg, Pennsylvania; San Bernardino, California; and Central Falls Rhode Island (PBS.org, 2014).

What specific support might be effective in overcoming the challenges? The participants believed that the most effective and helpful support for entrepreneurs to overcome challenges in Milwaukee consisted of business knowledge, skills, education, leadership, planning, and opportunity. The business leaders and the entrepreneurs need government leaders' support to help solve the problems. On the surface, one might assume that the majority of the participants were just complaining; however, when compared and contrast to other information found in the literature, the participants' views are valid. There is a direct correlation between prosperous cities and high level of entrepreneurship. In other words, leadership, innovation, and optimism are all required to sustain successful entrepreneurship.

It is apparent that entrepreneurship plays a significant role in growing economies, creating prosperity, and uplifting people out of poverty. Leadership is needed in the government to support entrepreneurial businesses in Milwaukee. Business leaders have embraced greater participation in entrepreneurship as a possible solution to economic and social problems, and have implemented policies to foster entrepreneurial success (Foley & Zimmer, 2014; Gee, 2014; Harris, 2013; NewYork.gov, 2014; Pew Charitable Trust, 2013). The implementation of policies to foster greater entrepreneurial success has produced mixed results given that some entrepreneurs and cities have prospered, while others are still struggling (Foley & Zimmer, 2014; Minniti, 2008; Pew Charitable Trust, 2013). While there are a few bright spots especially in the area of construction, the economic realities on the ground does not show signs of improvement. More efforts and cooperation from government leaders are appreciated.

REFERENCES

Alvarez, S. A. (2005). Theories of entrepreneurship: Alternative assumptions and the study of entrepreneurial action. *Foundations and Trends in Entrepreneurship, 1*(3), 105–148. doi:10.1561/0300000003

American Institute for Economic Research. (2014). *2015-2016 Top college destinations ranked*. Retrieved on April 22, 2017, from: https://www.aier.org/american-institute-economic-research-unveils-2014-2015-ranking-best-us-cities-college-students

Bygrave, W., & Zacharakis, A. (2008). *Entrepreneurship*. Hoboken, NJ: Wiley.

Causey, J. E. (2014). *No shock, Milwaukee metro area has the worst segregation*. Retrieved on November 11, 2016, from: http://www.jsonline.com/news/opinion/no-shock-milwaukee-metro-area-has-the-worst-segregation-b99233242z1-252332071.html

Clawson, J. G. (2003). Level three leadership: getting below the surface (3rd ed.). Pearson Prentice Hall.

Collins, J. (2005). *Good to great and the social sector*. New York: Harper Business.

De Villiers-Scheepers, M. (2012). Antecedents of strategic corporate entrepreneurship. *European Business Review, 24*(5), 400–424. doi:10.1108/09555341211254508

Denvir, D. (2011). *The ten most segregated urban area in America*. Retrieved on June 2, 2015, from: http://www.salon.com/2011/03/29/most_segregated_cities/slide_show/10

Dressen, E. (2009). *Sustainability and business: A narrative and annotated bibliography.* Retrieved on August 5, 2011, from: http: //www. web.ncf.ca/ct976

Dyer, J., Gregersen, H., & Christensen, C. M. (2012). *The Innovator's DNA: Mastering the Five Skill of Disruptive Innovators*. Boston: Harvard Business Review Press.

Emale, J. M. (2010). An examination of how conglomerates impact small-medium enterprises in their relationship. *Dissertation Abstracts International, 71*(5), 138A. (UMI No. 3407430)

Evans, G. H. Jr. (1949). The entrepreneur and economic theory: A historical and analytical approach. *The American Economic Review, 39*, 336–348. Retrieved from http://www. AEAweb.org

Foley, T., & Zimmer, B. (2014, July 10). How to fix our cities. *CNN*. Retrieved on May 9, 2017, from: http://www.cnn.com/2014/07/10/opinion/foley-zimmer-fix-cities/

Gee, D. J. (2014, October 26). Millennials embrace our renaissance. *Buffalo News*. Retrieved on October 7, 2017, from: http://www.buffalonews.com/columns/denise-jewell-gee/millennials-embrace-our-renaissance-20141026Millennials embrace our renaissance

Gee, J., Loewenthal, D., & Cayne, J. (2013). Phenomenological research: The case of Empirical Phenomenological Analysis and the possibility of reverie. *Counselling Psychology Review, 28*(3), 52–62.

George, G., & Zahra, S. A. (2002). Culture and its consequences for entrepreneurship. *Entrepreneurship: Theory and Practice*. Retrieved on March 2, 2017, from: http://www. Entrepreneur.com/trade journals/article/91971828_1.html

Global Entrepreneurship Monitor (GEM). (2015). *Executive Report.* Retrieved on February 7, 2017, from: http://www.gemconsortium.org/download/1300236130815/GEM_Global_15.pdf

Global Entrepreneurship Monitor (GEM). (2016). *2016 Global Report.* Retrieved on February 7, 2017, from: http://www.gemconsortium.org/report/49812

Gurda, J. (1999). *The Making of Milwaukee.* Milwaukee, WI: Milwaukee County Historical Society.

Harding, R. (2006). Entrepreneurs: The world's lifeline? *Business Strategy Review, 17*(4), 4–7. doi:10.1111/j.0955-6419.2006.00425.x

Harris, M. (2013, November 24). U.S. cities still struggling, but it doesn't seem so dire in Minneapolis. *Minneapolis Post.* Retrieved on May 3, 2016, from: http://www.minnpost.com/cityscape/2013/11/us-cities-still-struggling-it-doesn-t-seem-so-dire-minneapolis

Hebert, R. F., & Link, A. N. (2006). Historical perspectives on the entrepreneur. *Foundations and Trends in Entrepreneurship, 2*(4), 261–408. doi:10.1561/0300000008

Hussung, T. (2017, February 10). *7 steps of the decision-making process.* Retrieved on July 22, 2017, from: https://online.csp.edu/blog/business/decision-making-process

Jones, R. (2010). *Organizational Theory, Design, and Change* (6th ed.). New York: Prentice Hall Pearson Education, Inc.

Kayemuddin, M. D. (2012). Leadership in small business in Bangladesh. *International Journal of Entrepreneurship,* 1625-1635.

Kimberly, J. W., Thomas, H. T., & James, H. T. (2012). *Small business sustainability: What is the CPA's Role?* Retrieved on January 29, 2016, from: http://www.ijbssnet.com/journals/Vol_3_No_12_Special_ Issue June_2012/1.pdf

Kouzes, J. M., & Posner, B. Z. (2003). *Leadership the challenge* (3rd ed.). San Francisco, CA: Jossey-Bass.

KPMG International. (2012, February 15). Expect the Unexpected: Building Business Value in a Changing world. *KPMG.* Retrieved on December 22, 2017, from: http: //www.kpmg.com/global/en/ issuesandinsights/ articlespublications/ages/buildingbusiness-value.aspx

Kulling, M. (2014). *Tackling Milwaukee's racial and economic disparity.* Retrieved on April 22, 2016, from: http:// www.milwaukeemag.com/article/7152014TacklingMilwaukeesRacialandEconomicDisparity

Mach, T. L., & Wolken, J. D. (2006). Financial Services Used by Small Businesses: Evidence from the 2003 Survey of Small Business Finance. *Federal Reserve Bulletin.* Retrieved on August 2, 2016, from: http://www.federalreserve.gov/pubs/bulletin/2006/smallbusiness/default.htm

Marshall, A. (1920). *Principles of economics* (8th ed.). London: Macmillan and Co., Ltd. Retrieved on April 4, 2017, from: http://www.econlib.org/library/Marshall/marP.html

Matthews, S. (2014). *Older American Shun Retirement at 65 for risky startups.* Retrieved on December 2, 2016, from: http://www.bloomberg.com/news/2014-01-08/older-americans-shun-retirement-at-65-for-risky-startups.html

Mayborne, B. (2012). *Does Milwaukee have what it takes to fuel new growth?* Retrieved on May 9, 2017, from: http://www.mmac.org/wcnews/NewsArticle

Milwaukee History and Timeline. (2011). *Milwaukee county historical society*. Retrieved on October 11, 2016, from: www.https//milwaukee history. net

Minniti, M. (2008). The role of government policy on entrepreneurial activity: Productive, unproductive, or destructive? *Entrepreneurship Theory and Practice*, *32*(5), 779–790. doi:10.1111/j.1540-6520.2008.00255.x

MMAC. (2012). *Demographic and Economic Profile - Metro Milwaukee*. Milwaukee, WI: Metropolitan Milwaukee Association of Commerce.

Nelson, D. L., & Quick, J. C. (2009). *Organizational behavior: Science, the real world, and you*. Mason, OH: Southwestern Cengage Learning.

Ollin, K., & Vej, J. (2012). Sustainability in business: Understanding meanings, triggers and enablers. *Journal of Strategic Marketing*, *20*(7), 625–641. doi:10.1080/0965254X.2012.711347

Pew Charitable Trust. (2013). *Pew Report: Cities Hit Late by Great Recession, Still Struggling to Rebound*. Retrieved on June 22, 2016, from: http://www.pewtrusts.org/en/about/news-room/press-releases/2013/11/11/pew-report-cities-hit-late-by-great-recession-still-struggling-to-rebound

Price, R. (2006). *Entrepreneurship* (5th ed.). Dubuque, IA: McGraw-Hill/Dushkin.

Rogoff, E. G. (2007). Opportunities for entrepreneurship in later life. *Generations (San Francisco, Calif.)*, *31*, 90–95.

Rosenfeld, R. B. (2014). Innovation and entrepreneurship: The invisible cycle. In *Sustainable entrepreneurship: Business success through sustainability* (pp. 39–50). New York: Springer Heidelberg.

SBA. (2012). What is a small business? *United States Small Business Administration*. Retrieved on November 12, 2016, from: http://www.sba.gov/size/

SBA. (2014). Small Business, Big Impact: Celebrating Our Country and Small Businesses. *United States Small Business Administration*. Retrieved on April 8, 2017, from: http://www.sba.gov/

Schmidpeter, R., & Weidinger, C. (2014). Linking business and society: an overview. In *Sustainable entrepreneurship: Business success through sustainability* (pp. 1–10). New York: Springer Heidelberg.

Schumpeter, J. A. (1942). *Capitalist, socialism, and Democracy*. New York: Harper and Brothers.

Schumpeter, J. A. (1982). *The theory of economic development: An inquiry into profits, capital, credit, interest, and the business cycle* (Rev. ed.). Edison, NJ: Transaction.

Shane, S. (2008). *Technology Strategy for Managers and Entrepreneurs* (1st ed.). Upper Saddle River, NJ: Pearson.

Shaoming, C., Stough, R., & Jackson, R. (2009). Measuring and building high-quality entrepreneurship: A research prospectus. *Innovation: The European Journal of Social Sciences*, *22*, 329–340. doi:10.1080/13511610903399088

Skousen, M. (2009). *The Making of Modern Economics: The Lives and Ideas of the Great Thinkers*. New York: M E Sharpe.

Thurow, L. C. (2000). *Building Wealth: The New Rules for Individuals, Companies and Nations in a Knowledge Base Economy*. New York: HarperCollins.

Tidd, J., & Bessant, J. (2009). *Managing innovation: Integrating technological, market and organizational change* (4th ed.). Hoboken, NJ: Wiley.

Tidmarsh, K. (2014). *Milwaukee: The most segregated and Polarized place in America*. Retrieved on September 9, 2016, from: http://www.governing.com/topics/politics/gov-milwaukee-most-segregated-polarized-place.html

U.S. Census Bureau Data. (2014). *Population Reports U.S. Department of Commerce Economics and Statistics Administration*. U.S. Census Bureau. Retrieved on April 9, 2015, from: https://www.census.gov/content/dam/Census/library/ publications/2015/demo/p60-252.pdf

U.S. Census Bureau Data. (2016). *Population Report, city of Milwaukee*. Retrieved on January 4, 2017, from: https://www.census.gov/quickfacts/fact/table/Milwaukeecitywisconsin/RHI125216

Webb, K. J., Hodge, T. G., & Thompson, J. H. (2012). Small Business Sustainability: What is the CPA's Role? *International Journal of Business and Social Science*, *3*(12), 1–7.

Weidinger, C., Fischler, F., & Schmidpeter, R. (2014). *Sustainable entrepreneurship: Business success through sustainability*. New York: Springer. Retrieved on April 22, 2016, from: https://www.researchgate.net/profile/Mara_Baldo/publication/300155089_Sustainable_Entrepreneurship_Next_Stage_of_Responsible_Business/links/57481dc608ae2301b0b9680b/Sustainable-Entrepreneurship-Next-Stage-of-Responsible-Business.pdf

WUWM, Milwaukee Public Radio. (2013). *New ranking: Milwaukee still country's most segregated metro area*. Retrieved on May 3, 2017, from: http://www.wuwm.com/post/new-ranking-Milwaukee-still-countrys-most-segregated-metro-area

Yukl, G. (2010). *Leadership in organizations* (7th ed.). Upper Saddle River, NJ: Pearson Prentice Hall.

Zegarowski, G. (2007). Corporate sustainability after Sarbanes-Oxley linking social political initiatives and small and medium-sized enterprise resources. *International Journal of Disclosure and Governance*, *4*(1), 52–58. doi:10.1057/palgrave.jdg.2050043

KEY TERMS AND DEFINITIONS

Entrepreneur: An individual who establishes, organizes the process, assumes uncertain financial risks for a business enterprise with the hope of generating profit, and creating growth.

Entrepreneurship: A dynamic process of establishing a business or businesses with the intent of creating meaningful opportunities for individuals or groups.

Innovation: The action or process of successfully generating, and implementing new or novel ideas, which introduce new products, processes or strategies to the market.

Leadership: The act or process of creating the environment where others are willing to follow.

Organizational Culture: The shared norms, values, and beliefs of members of an organization

Small Business: The independently owned firms with fewer than 500 employees and is not dominant in the industry where the business operates.

Sustainability: The ability or capacity for a process, strategy, or idea to maintain or sustain itself at a certain rate or level for a specified or unspecified period.

Chapter 9
Product Sophistication: A Cross-Country Analysis

Fatma Nur Karaman Kabadurmus
Yasar University, Turkey

ABSTRACT

The sudden rise of countries like China and India has captured serious attention among economists. Some papers explain it with the changing structure of their product mix and construct an export sophistication index to rank countries according to their comparative advantages. By starting from the discussions on product quality, this chapter investigates whether a more rapid progression up the comparative advantage ladder or a more sophisticated export basket results in a more rapid economic expansion. For this purpose, data from 115 countries for the period 1985 to 2001 are used. The results support the positive effect of export sophistication on growth. The authors also show that when a country progresses, its growth rate increases.

INTRODUCTION

Production of new goods is at the core of sustained growth. The classic endogenous growth model of Lucas (1988) suggests that product-specific learning should involve modeling the continuous introduction of new goods. Similarly, Stokey (1989) develops a general equilibrium model in which the introduction of new and better products is an integral part of the growth in a learning-by-doing process. In this line of thought, Lall (2000a) sees the incorporation of new technologies into manufacturing and services as the main tool to compete in liberalized markets for both developing and developed countries. The author believes raising the long-term rate of growth requires a structural shift into more advanced technologies since technology-intensive activities are growing faster than other activities. In another article, Lall (2000b) gives the example of Turkey in which he claims that Turkey faces two aspects of difficulty in expanding and diversifying its export base. First, Turkey is a high-wage nation but it has to compete with low-wage countries in low technology products. Secondly, it has to compete against high-technology European firms, but Turkey is a technologically lagging economy.

DOI: 10.4018/978-1-5225-5787-6.ch009

A large and growing body of literature has investigated how larger economies increase exports. While some assume that big economies export more in size but not in variety, others believe that they produce and export more range of goods. Vertical differentiation models, such as those by Flam and Helpman (1987) and Grossman and Helpman (1991), feature a quality margin, namely richer countries produce and export higher quality goods (Hummels & Klenow, 2004).

For developing countries like India and China, the factor-endowments model falls short of explaining their growth success. For example, the information technology sector in India is one of the key sectors. However, India ranks low in other high-tech sectors, and is relatively well-endowed with unskilled rather than with skilled workers (Hausmann & Rodrik, 2003). Kwan (2002) proposes a method to measure the level of advancement of a country's export structure based on the weighted average of the level of sophistication of the products composing it, and take China as a special case. Rodrik (2006) also finds that China's export basket is more sophisticated than what would be expected for a country at its income level[1].

Hausmann et al. (2007) argue that it is better to specialize in products which bring higher growth than specializing in others. They propose an index called PRODY that ranks traded goods in terms of their productivity, by taking a weighted average of the per capita income of the countries exporting a product, where the weights reflect the revealed comparative advantage of each country in that product. Then, the income/productivity level that corresponds to a country's export basket which measures the productivity level associated with a country's specialization pattern is calculated using the first index (this second index is named EXPY).

Building on these, Hausmann and Klinger (2006) discuss the two dominant approaches in determining what drives growth – the varieties model (Romer, 1988) which uses Dixit-Stiglitz production functions and the quality ladders model (Aghion-Howitt, 1992; Grossman-Helpman, 1991), which assumes a degree of homogeneity across products that eliminates the possibility to capture the impact of initial specialization. The mentioned article develops these two approaches and develop a new *proximity* measure. They suggest that changes over time in the revealed comparative advantage of individual nations are associated with the pattern of relatedness across products. As countries change their export mix there is a strong tendency to move towards related goods rather than to goods that are less related. For successful structural transformation, existing exports must have many close high value-added goods in the product space.

Recent studies continue to focus on the role of structural transformation to promote economic growth. Innovation, which leads to the introduction of sophisticated products is at the heart of our understanding of why some countries remain poor. Thus, this chapter aims to examine the linkages of product sophistication and economic growth. Our main contribution is to analyze whether a more rapid progression up the comparative advantage ladder or a more sophisticated export basket results in a more rapid economic expansion. To the best of our knowledge, this is the first paper that addresses this question.

To answer this, we use the aforementioned the EXPY index of Hausmann et al. (2007) and the ESI of Desroches et al. (2006). We find that if the country starts with exporting higher quality products, it will achieve higher growth rates. We also find evidence of a positive effect of change in ESI rank on growth as expected but the coefficient is insignificant. We also choose an emerging country, Turkey, and compare it with its competitors in the export market using these two indices.

The remainder of the chapter proceeds as follows. Section 2 reviews growth literature in terms of new goods and product quality. Section 3 presents empirical analysis findings. Section 4 is devoted to Turkey in light of the above discussions. Section 5 concludes the chapter.

LITERATURE SURVEY

Lall (2000a) shows that advanced technologies and innovation are the engine of trade led growth. In his analysis of the 50 most dynamic exports in the world during the period 1980-1996, medium- and high-technology products account for a full 75 per cent by value. Within these exports, high technology products (e.g., fine chemicals, electronics, aircraft and precision instruments) grow the fastest, followed by medium-technology products such as machinery, chemicals, and simple electronics and transport equipment.

According to the author, technology intensive products offer better growth prospects than others due at least to the following:

- Activities with the rapid product or process innovation generally enjoy faster growing demand as compared to technologically stable activities.
- Technology-intensive activities are less vulnerable to entry by competitors compared to low technology activities where scale, skill and technology requirements are low.
- Ceteris paribus, technology-intensive activities lead to faster growth in capabilities and higher quality capabilities. They offer higher learning potential and greater opportunity for the continued application of science to technology.
- Capabilities in technology-intensive activities are more attuned to technological and market trends, and so are more flexible and responsive to changing competitive conditions.
- A technology-intensive structure is likely to have larger spillover benefits to other activities and to the national technology system (Lall, 2000a, p. 11).

Easterly and Levine (2001) emphasize the role of factors other than factor accumulation. They point to the fact that growth is highly unstable over time, while factor accumulation is more stable. This fact hints the role of "something else" in explaining variations in economic growth. The authors recommend economists pay more attention to residual determinants of growth and income such as technology and externalities.

Brecher, Chen, and Choudri (2002) introduce international technological differences into the 3-sector Findlay-Komiya and 2-sector Oniki-Uzawa-Stiglitz models of open-economy growth with optimal saving. They believe the reason behind trade is technological superiority rather than factor abundance. Schott (2003) uses product-level US trade data to show that countries use their endowment advantage to produce vertically superior varieties. There is a positive association among within product unit values, exporter capital, and skill abundance. Exporter production techniques are also consistent with factor-proportions specialization within products.

Following Schott (2003), Hwang (2006) finds "the vertical distance a country has to the frontier" by calculating the percentage difference between its own unit value and that of a frontier country (best producer of the good) or group of countries. He concludes that countries which enter sectors with long quality ladders will catch up to the frontier rapidly compared to those that do not. Hummels and Klenow (2004) also highlight the importance of technology in understanding the differences in economic performance of developed and developing countries. They analyze what is behind the larger exports of advanced economies through extensive margin (wider set of goods), intensive margin (larger quantities) and higher quality margin. They find the extensive margin accounts for around 60% of the greater exports of larger economies. In addition, richer countries export higher quantities at higher prices. Their estimated show that quality differences could be the cause of around 9% of country differences in real income per worker.

To test the view above, Schott (2006) examines the relative "sophistication" of China's exports to the United States along two dimensions. First, he compares China's export bundle to those of the relatively skill- and capital abundant members of the OECD as well as to similarly endowed U.S. trading partners. Then, prices within product categories are examined to determine if China's varieties command a premium relative to its level of development. He finds that China's export bundle increasingly overlaps with that of more developed countries, rendering it more "sophisticated" than countries with similar relative endowments. On the other hand, its exports sell at a substantial discount relative to its level of Gross Domestic Product (GDP) and the exports emanating from the OECD.

Lall, Weiss, and Zhang (2006) also developed a "sophistication index" and suggest that having high per capita incomes is not a guarantee of a sophisticated export structure. Countries may become rich without building advanced industrial skills and capabilities; doing this requires specific strategies. Gaglio (2017) surveys the literature on the measures of export performance. There are three new measures: export sophistication (following Lall et al., 2006; Hausmann et al., 2007), product space (following Hidalgo et al., 2007), and economic complexity (following Hausmann and Hidalgo, 2009, 2011).

The first measure mentioned above is developed by Hausmann, Hwang, and Rodrik (2007). The authors argue that it is better to specialize in products which bring higher growth than specializing in others. Basically, they suggest that attempts to reshape the production structure by the classical approach, which say that a country's fundamentals determine relative costs and the patterns of specialization, would fail. As an alternative, they propose an index that ranks traded goods in terms of their productivity, by taking a weighted average of the per capita GDPs of the countries exporting a product, where the weights reflect the revealed comparative advantage of each country in that product.

Then, the income/productivity level that corresponds to a country's export basket is calculated using the first index which measures the productivity level associated with a country's specialization pattern. Their theoretical model indicates that growth is the result of transferring resources from lower-productivity activities to the higher-productivity goods identified by the entrepreneurial cost-discovery process. Empirical findings suggest that type of goods in which a country specializes has important implications for subsequent economic performance. Therefore, ceteris paribus, an economy is better off producing goods that richer countries export.

Xu and Lu (2006) use the same EXPY index to examine the product sophistication of Chinese exports. For Desroches, Francis, and Painchaud (2006) both institutions and trade determine long-run comparative advantage and affect growth. They construct an export sophistication index (ESI) to rank countries according to their comparative advantages and then relate it to institutional quality. The authors suggest China and India continue to improve the quality of their institutions so that trade will magnify the benefits of institutional reform.

Concentrating on the role of institutions in expanding product varieties, Sheng and Yang (2016) show that two institutional reforms, namely relaxing foreign ownership controls and improving contract enforcement will increase new product introduction.

The second new sophistication measure, product space, is constructed by Hausmann and Klinger (2006). They stress that a country's opportunities for structural transformation will be affected by the structure of the product space in its neighborhood. They develop an outcomes-based measure of the relatedness between pairs of products using cross-country export data, which shows the broad relationships of both factor endowments and technological sophistication. They find that a country's current location in the product space significantly affects its opportunities for future productive transformation. Gourdan and Monjon (2016) use data for China over the period 2002-2012 and show the importance of increased government support for sophisticated high-technology products. This policy was especially implemented during 2009 to mitigate the economic crisis.

Bayudan-Dacuycuy and Lim (2017) is another application of product space framework for ASEAN (Association of Southeast Asian Nations) and developed Asian countries including Korea and China. The authors construct Hausmann et al. (2007)'s PRODY and EXPY for the years 2000-2006. Their analysis indicate that less-developed Asian economies may catch-up with their more developed neighbors with correct government policies that target greater innovation rates.

The third and final new measure is based on economic complexity. Hausmann and Hidalgo (2009, 2011) determine productive capabilities of countries using the method of reflections. A country's productivity depends on finding new products (*product innovation*) and the diversity of non-tradable capabilities. According to this, a more diversified country can develop more complex products. Recently, Petralia et al. (2017) have analyzed countries' patterns of technological development and shown that well-performing countries tend to have a productive structure oriented towards the production of more complex and valuable technologies. Another recent contribution is Audretsch et al. (2017) who developed a new measure for product maturity and argue that developing countries need to switch to invention of new products to be competitive and to join advanced economies in the technology frontier.

REGRESSION RESULTS

Data and Methodology

To investigate whether a more rapid progression up the comparative advantage ladder or a more sophisticated export basket results in a more rapid economic expansion, we estimate the following model.

$$avg.growth - \alpha$$

$$(avg.growth) = \alpha + \log PCGDP_{1985} + ESI_{1985} + u \tag{1}$$

where avg. growth is measured by $\dfrac{\sum_{t=1985}^{2001} \dfrac{Y_{t+1} - Y_t}{Y_t} * 100}{number.of.years}$, *PCGDP* is Gross Domestic Product per capita (constant 2000US$) (World Development Indicators), *ESI (1985)* is initial Export Sophistication Index (ESI) value, *ESI (2001)* is ESI 2001 value. Per capita growth is calculated with GDP per capita (constant 2000 US dollars) data from World Development Indicators. We use ESI data from 115 countries for the years 1985 and 2001 obtained from Desroches et al. (2006, Appendix 1).

The index is calculated as follows:

The first step in this brief analysis is to create for each three-digit SITC (Standard International Trade Classification) code, what Kwan (2002) refers to as a product sophistication index (PSI). This index measures, for each classification, the exporting country's expected per capita GDP. For example, handicrafts tend to be exported by countries with low levels of GDP and hence have low PSI numbers, while high-tech medical equipment is generally exported by countries with high income levels and hence have a high PSI numbers. Having calculated this number for each commodity, we then calculate for each country an export sophistication index (ESI), which is the mean PSI value of its exports (Desroches et al., 2006, p. 233)

We also test whether countries that move more rapidly in the quality ladder have an advantage over the others. We use the following model.

$$(avg\ growth) = \alpha + \log PCGDP_{1985} + change\ in\ ESI\ rank\ 1985 - 2001 + u \quad (2)$$

where *ESI Rank* is a given country's rank in the ladder of comparative advantage (Appendix 1, Desroches, Francis and Painchaud, 2006) and change in ESI rank is measured by $\frac{Rank\ ESI_{1985} - Rank\ ESI_{2001}}{Rank\ ESI_{1985}} * 100$.

If the country's rank is increasing (e.g., the rank falls from 10 to 20), the coefficient will be a negative value. For the reverse case, it will be positive. The expectation is a positive coefficient as it indicates higher comparative advantage leading to higher growth. Table 1 presents findings for both models. As expected, initial GDP per capita has a negative effect on growth although the coefficient is insignificant. We also see that initial ESI has a positive and significant effect on growth. This suggests that if the country starts with exporting higher quality products, it will achieve higher growth rates.

For the second model, we again see that initial GDP per capita has a positive effect on growth; i.e., initially richer countries have higher growth rates. We also find evidence of a positive effect of change in ESI rank on growth as expected but the coefficient is insignificant.

Explanatory Data Analysis for Turkey

EXPY Analysis

Table 2 shows the top 10 export goods of Turkey for the years 1996, 2005, and 2016. We see that the export structure has changed in the last two decades, with the automotive sector becoming the leader while the textile sector keeping its importance. Is this change in the structure helpful for economic growth? Where is Turkey in terms of export sophistication? What are the implications in terms of EXPY index?

To address these questions, we turn to the calculation of PRODY and EXPY (Hausmann et al., 2007). First, the productivity level associated with product *k* is found.

$$PRODY_k = \sum_j \frac{\left(x_{jk}/X_j\right)}{\sum_j \left(x_{jk}/X_j\right)} Y_j$$

Here, the numerator is the value-share of the commodity in the country's overall export basket. The denominator aggregates the value-shares across all countries exporting the good. Hence the index repre-

Table 1. Regression findings

	(Model 1)	(Model 2)
VARIABLES	avg_85_0	avg_85_0
lny	-0.110	0.389**
	(0.275)	(0.187)
esi_1985	0.000194**	
	(8.18e-05)	
Change in ESI rank		0.00253
		(0.00420)
Constant	-0.317	-1.627
	(1.609)	(1.558)
Observations	113	113
R-squared	0.083	0.039
F test	0.00837	0.109
Standard errors in parentheses		
*** p<0.01, ** p<0.05, * p<0.1		

Table 2. Top 10 exports of Turkey

Export by chapters	1996	2005	2016
Vehicles Other Than Railway Or Tramway (87)	6	1	1
Boilers, machineries and mechanical appliances (84)	7	4	2
Precious stones, precious metals, pearls (71)	38	12	3
Knitted and crocheted goods (61)	1	2	4
Electrical machinery and equipment (85)	4	3	5
Iron and steel (72)	3	5	6
Non knitted and crocheted goods (62)	2	6	7
Plastic and articles (39)	18	11	8
Articles of iron and steel (73)	13	7	9
Edible fruits and nuts, peel of melons or citrus fruits (8)	5	9	10

Source: TUIK[2]

sents a weighted average of per-capita GDPs, where the weights correspond to the revealed comparative advantage of each country in good *k*. Then, the productivity level associated with country *i*'s export basket, $EXPY_i$, is calculated as

$$EXPY_i = \sum_i \left(\frac{x_{il}}{X_i} \right) PRODY_l$$

Figure 1 shows that the distribution of Turkey's EXPY is not symmetric and is skewed to left, thus lower values.

According to data from the Turkish Institute of Statistics (TUIK), Turkey's exports to the European Union (EU) constitute 48% of the total exports. Additionally, for the year 2016, the EU's top five exporters are China, the USA, Switzerland, Russia, and Turkey[3], where Japan ranks the 6th. These five countries can be taken as competitors in the EU market. Figure 2 provides the line graph of EXPY over time for Turkey and Competitors in the EU Market.

For the period 1992-2003, the ranking of EXPY medians in descending order is Switzerland (19582.41), Japan (18174.105), US (16935), China (13464.715), the Russian Federation (122275.285), and Turkey (11636.265). We can see that Turkey's productivity level associated with its specialization pattern has increased only a little, surpassing its closest competitor-Russian Federation in the last few years. Additionally, except Turkey and China, the productivity levels are decreasing. Figure 3 shows box-plots for Turkey and its competitors.

EXPY values differ significantly between Turkey and its competitors in the EU market. Turkey has the lowest productivity level, while Switzerland has the highest (Figure 3). In addition, it has the smallest range of EXPY values, which shows that its productivity level has not changed much, while Russian Federation has the largest dispersion. From the calculations made in SPSS, we know that all these

Figure 1. Box-Plot of Turkey's EXPY (1992-2003)
Source: Haussman et al. (2007)

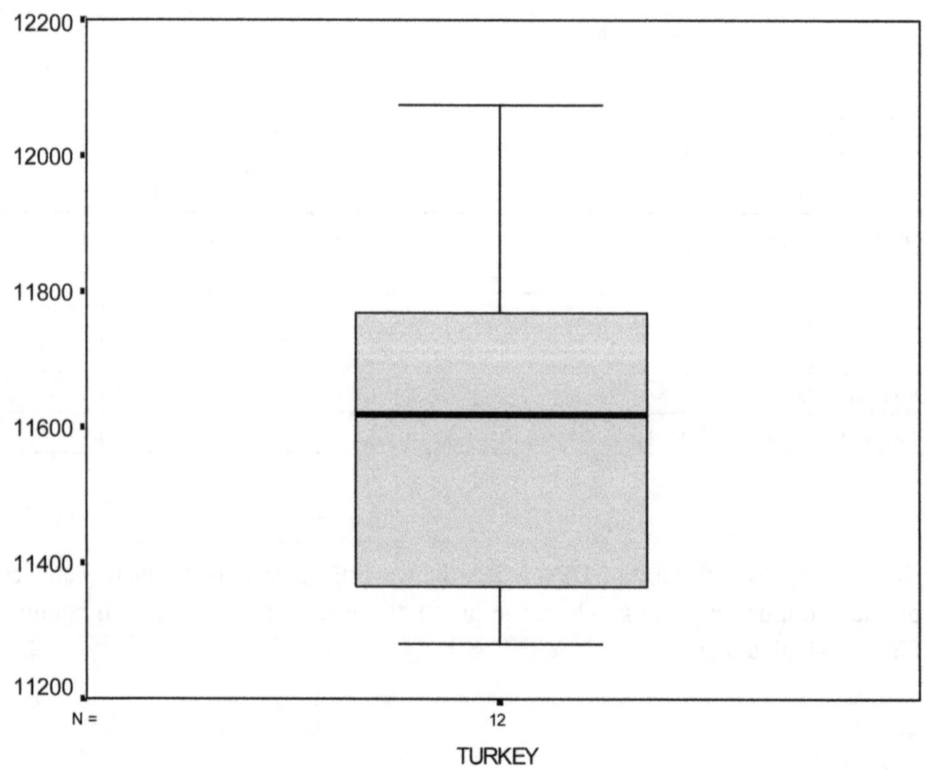

Figure 2. EXPY over time for Turkey and competitors in the EU market (1992–2003)
Source: Haussman et al. (2007)

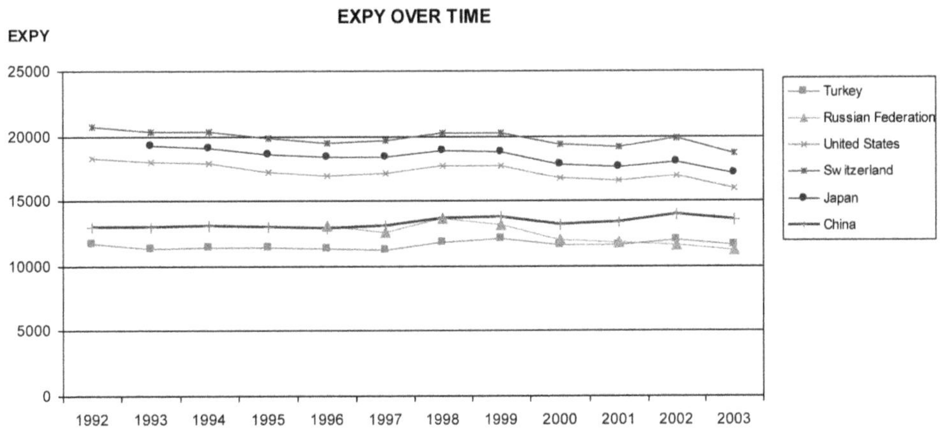

countries except the Russian Federation have negative skewness values, indicating that the distribution is skewed to the left.

Looking at a list of countries in Figure 4, we see that the range of EXPY has declined over time; the countries converge in terms of EXPY. For the year 2003, the first five are Switzerland, Ireland, Iceland, Finland, and Germany. The median value has not changed much for these countries, and over time the distribution has become more symmetric.

Figure 3. Box-Plot for Turkey and its competitors
Source: Haussman et al. (2007)

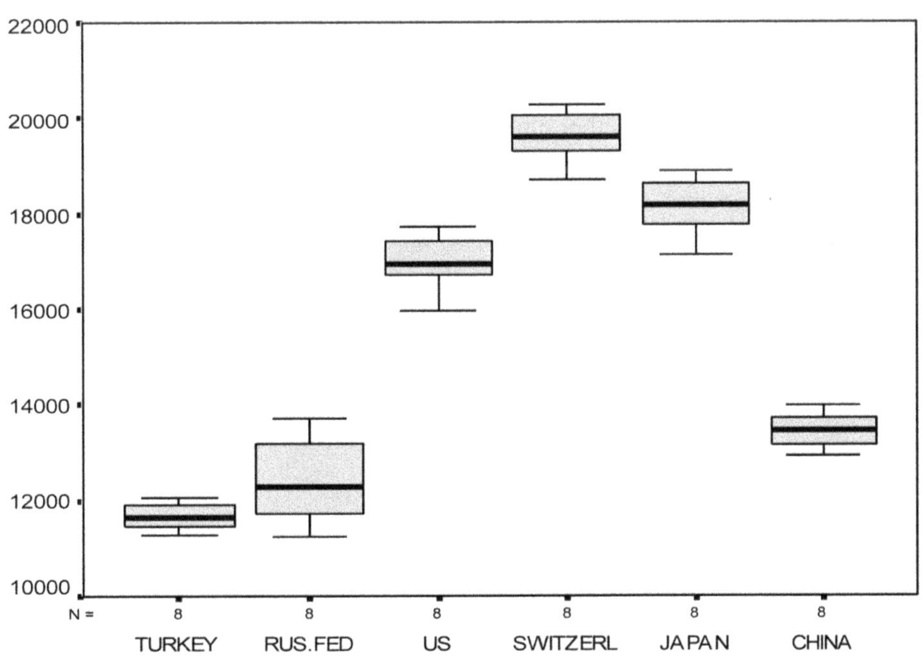

Figure 4. Box-Plot for EXPY over time (39 countries)
Source: Haussman et al. (2007)

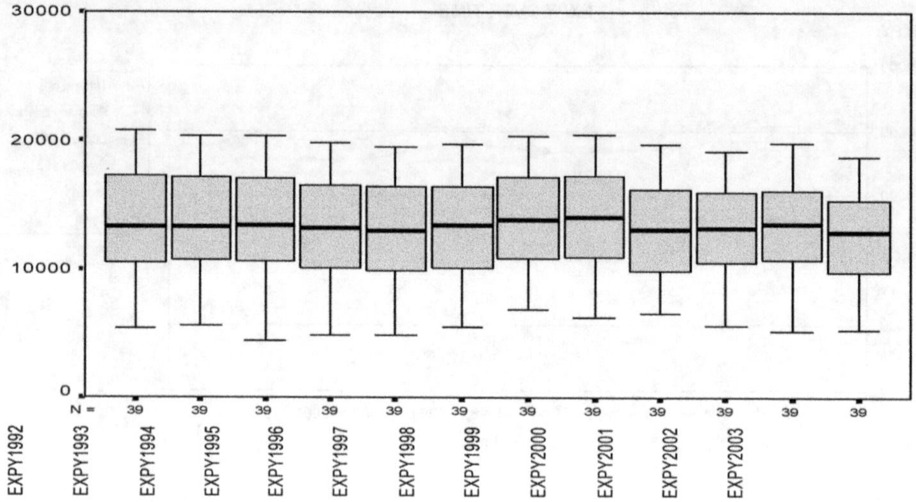

ESI Analysis

We now turn to Export Sophistication Index (ESI) values. Figure 5 shows ESI (1985) and ESI (2001) for 113 countries. The ESI has increased although the dispersion has not changed much. This suggests that exports of countries have become more sophisticated. Figure 6 confirms our finding above that export sophistication and economic growth has a positive relationship. In addition, we can conclude that those countries exporting more sophisticated goods grow more.

ESI values for Turkey and its competitors in the EU market also show that Turkey is behind them. Switzerland is still the leader with China having similar export sophistication level. Turkey's ranking for 1985 and 2001 are 36 and 52 respectively, while China's ranking has changed from 55 to 41. Values for respective years are given in Table 3.

Finally, we compare Turkey with other emerging economies. Table 4 gives the rank of the first 20 emerging economies for the last five years. They are found according to eight dimensions (market size, market growth rate, market intensity, market consumption capacity, commercial infrastructure, economic freedom, market receptivity and country risk) that are chosen to represent the market potential of a country. Turkey ranks 37 in 2017. In Figure 7, the emerging economies include Argentina, Brazil, Chile, China, Colombia, Egypt, Hong Kong, Hungary, India, Israel, Malaysia, Mexico, Pakistan, Peru, Philippi, South Africa, Thailand, and Turkey. Turkey seems to have lower export sophistication compared to other emerging markets.

Figure 5. Box-Plot for ESI (1985) and ESI (2001)
Source: Desroches et al. (2006)

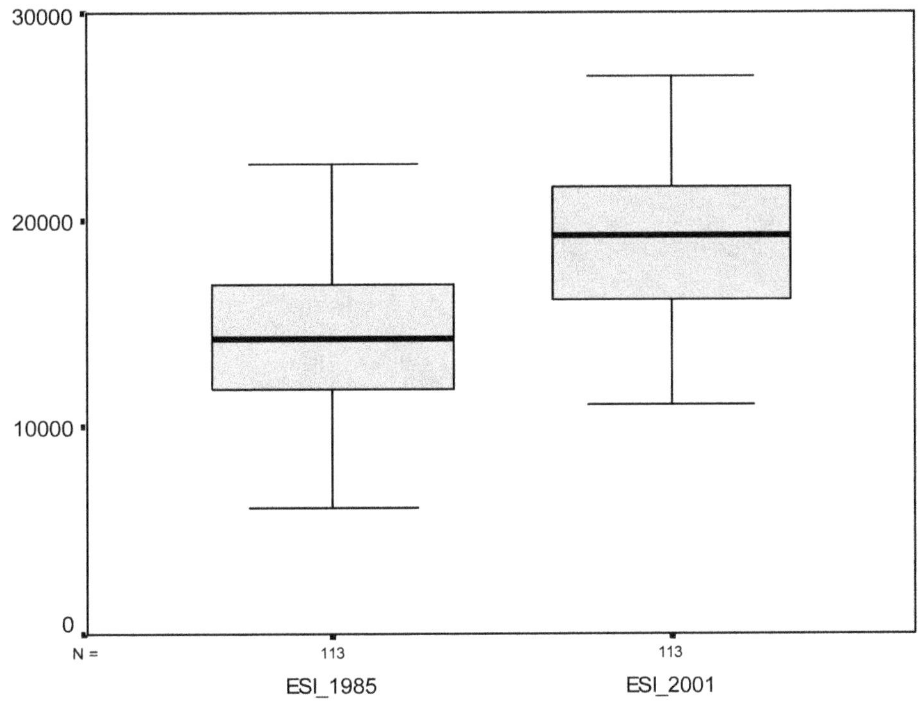

CONCLUSION

Growth miracle countries like China and India have obtained much attention recently. Their success is mostly explained by their structure of exports (i.e., sophistication level). Sophistication level is related with the basis of growth models – technology. When countries expand their product mix and continuously target new and better products, their chances of economic growth increase. Thus, innovation, which leads to the introduction of sophisticated products is at the heart of our understanding of why some countries remain poor.

In this study we analyze the relationship of product sophistication and growth relationship by using Export Sophistication Index of 113 countries. The regression findings indicate that the level of export sophistication has a positive effect on growth. There is also a slight evidence related with the countries' ranking in the comparative advantage ladder. When a country is climbing the ladder, its growth rate increases.

Figure 6. ESI (1985) vs. average growth (113 countries)
Source: Desroches et al. (2006)

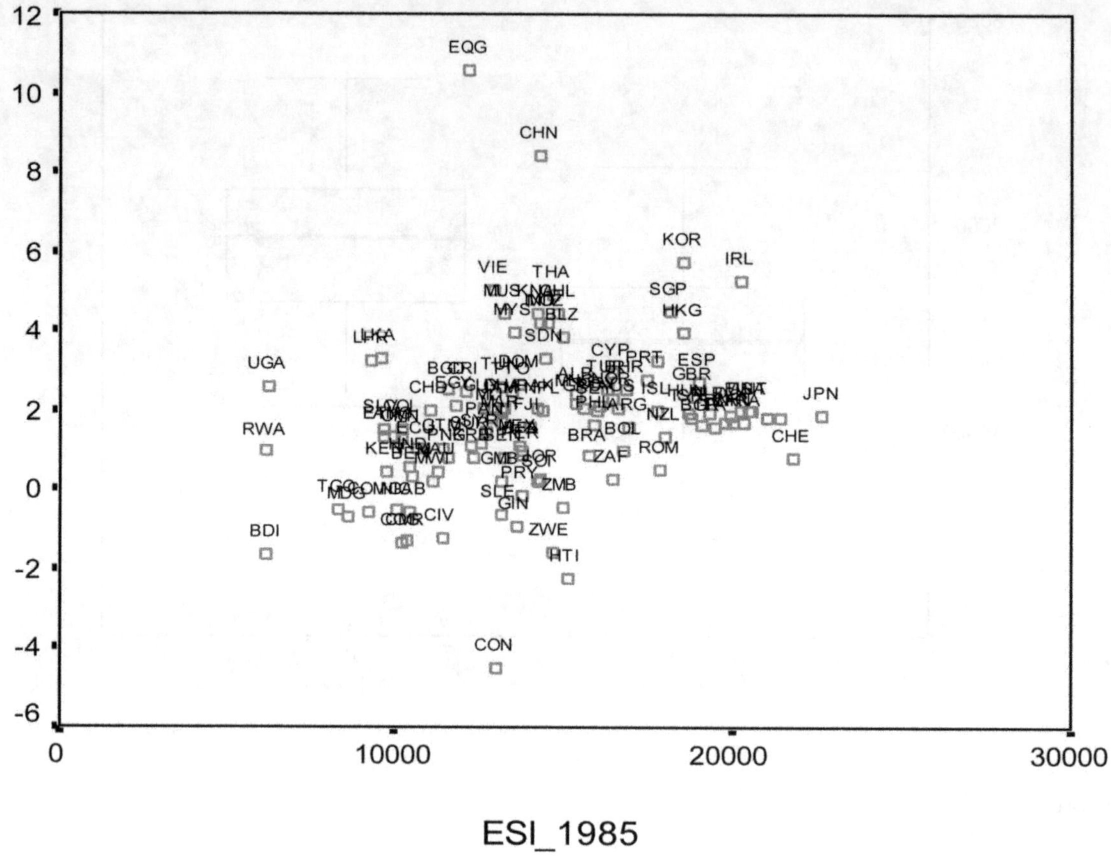

Table 3. ESI (1985) and ESI (2001) for 113 countries

	ESI_1985	ESI_2001
World_median	14246	19203
Turkey	16370	19560
USA	20,511	25,198
Switzerland	21,789	26,933
China	14,901	19,802
Japan	22,650	26,089

Source: Desroches et al. (2006)

*Table 4. List of Emerging Markets-2017**

Country	2017	2016	2015	2014	2013
	Rank	Rank	Rank	Rank	Rank
China	1	1	1	1	3
Hong Kong	2	2	2	2	2
India	3	4	4	7	9
Canada	4	6	6	4	-
Japan	5	5	5	3	-
Singapore	6	3	3	5	1
Germany	7	7	7	6	-
United Kingdom	8	8	9	9	-
Qatar	9	9	8	27	-
Switzerland	10	10	10	8	-
South Korea		11	11	11	10
Belgium	12	15	16	18	-
Netherlands	13	13	15	17	
United Arab Emirates	14	12	12	13	-
France	15	14	13	11	-
Australia	16	16	14	12	-
Ireland	17	23	24	23	-
Norway	18	17	17	14	-
Austria	19	18	19	16	-

* Some of the countries do not have ranking before 2014 because those countries were added to MPI in 2014. Source: https://globaledge.msu.edu/mpi/yeartoyear

Figure 7. ESI (1985) vs. average growth for emerging economies
Source: Desroches et al. (2006)

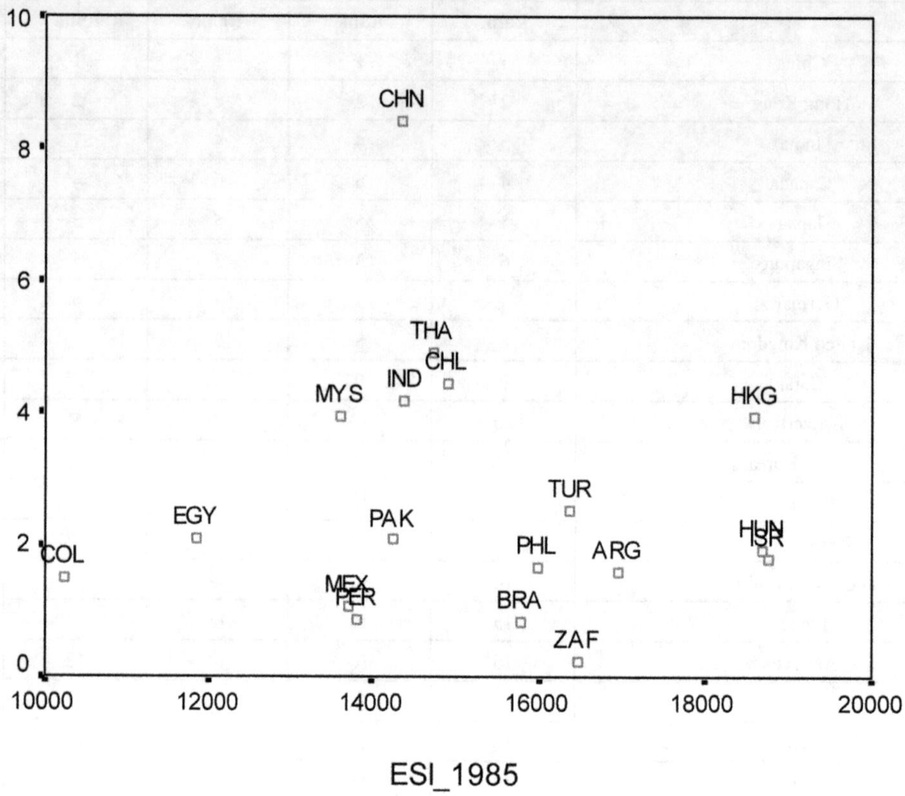

We also draw implications for Turkey. Turkey is much behind its competitors in the EU market in terms of EXPY as the country's productivity level is low. In terms of ESI, Turkey remains behind its competitors. Its rank in comparative advantage ladder has fallen between 1985 and 2001. Our findings suggest that if Turkey increases its export sophistication level, it will move to the upper ranks and will benefit from higher growth advantages.

REFERENCES

Audretsch, D., Sanders, M., & Zhang, L. (2017). International product life cycles, trade and development stages. *The Journal of Technology Transfer*, 1–44.

Bayudan-Dacuycuy, C., & Lim, J. A. Y. (2017). Export Sophistication, Export-Led Growth and Product Space: Evidence from Selected Asian Economies. *Journal of Asian and African Studies*, *52*(1), 3–20. doi:10.1177/0021909614560241

Brecher, R. A., Chen, Z., & Choudhri, R. A. (2002). Absolute and Comparative Advantage, Reconsidered: The pattern of international trade with optimal saving. *Review of International Economics, Vol*, *10*(: 4), 645–656. doi:10.1111/1467-9396.t01-1-00355

Desroches, B., Francis, M., & Painchaud, F. (2006). Growth and Integration: The Emergence of China and India and the Implications for Canada. *ASSA Conference Paper*.

Easterly, W., & Levine, R. (2001). *It's Not Factor Accumulation: Stylized Facts and Growth Models*. Central Bank of Chile, Working Papers, No:164.

Gaglio, C. (2017). Trade Liberalization and Export Performance: A Literature Review. *Revue d'Economie Politique*, *127*(1), 25–46. doi:10.3917/redp.271.0025

Gourdon, J., Monjon, S., & Poncet, S. (2016). Trade policy and industrial policy in China: What motivates public authorities to apply restrictions on exports? *China Economic Review*, *40*, 105–120. doi:10.1016/j.chieco.2016.06.004

Hausmann, R., & Hidalgo, C. A. (2011). The network structure of economic output. *Journal of Economic Growth*, *16*(4), 309–342. doi:10.100710887-011-9071-4

Hausmann, R., Hwang, J., & Rodrik, D. (2007). What you export matters. *Journal of Economic Growth*, *12*(1), 1–25. doi:10.100710887-006-9009-4

Hausmann, R., & Klinger, B. (2006). *The Evolution of Comparative Advantage: The Impact of the Structure of the Product Space. Center for International Development and Kennedy School of Government*. Harvard University.

Hausmann, R., & Rodrik, D. (2003). Economic development as self-discovery. *Journal of Development Economics*, *72*(: 72), 603–633. doi:10.1016/S0304-3878(03)00124-X

Hidalgo, C. A., & Hausmann, R. (2009). The building blocks of economic complexity. *Proceedings of the National Academy of Sciences of the United States of America*, *106*(26), 10570–10575. doi:10.1073/pnas.0900943106 PMID:19549871

Hummels, D., & Klenow, P. J. (2004). *The Variety and Quality of a Nation's Exports.* NBER Working Paper, No:8712.

Hwang, J. (2006). *Introduction of New Goods, Convergence and Growth.* Harvard University.

Kwan, C. H. (2002). *The Rise of China and Asia's Flying-Geese Pattern of Economic Development: An Empirical Analysis Based on US Import Statistics.* Nomura Research Institute Working Paper, No:52.

Lall, S. (2000a). *Skills, Competitiveness and Policy in Developing Countries.* QEH Working Paper Series, No: 46

Lall, S. (2000b). *Turkish Performance in Exporting Manufactures: A Comparative Structural Analysis.* QEH Working Paper Series, No:47.

Lall, S., Weiss, J., & Zhang, J. (2006). The "Sophistication" of Exports: A New Trade Measure. *World Development, 34*(2), 222–237. doi:10.1016/j.worlddev.2005.09.002

Lu, J., & Xu, B. (2006). The Impact of Foreign Firms on the Sophistication of Chinese Exports. *ASSA Conference Paper.*

Lucas, R. E. Jr. (1998). On the Mechanics of Economic Development. *Journal of Monetary Economics, 22*(1), 3–42. doi:10.1016/0304-3932(88)90168-7

Petralia, S., Balland, P. A., & Morrison, A. (2017). Climbing the ladder of technological development. *Research Policy, 46*(5), 956–969. doi:10.1016/j.respol.2017.03.012

Rodrik, D. (2006). *What's So Special about China's Exports?* NBER Working Paper, No:11947.

Schott, P. K. (2003). Across-Product versus Within-Product Specialization. In *International Trade*. Yale School of Management and NBER.

Schott, P. K. (2006). *The Relative Sophistication of Chinese Exports.* NBER Working Paper, No: 12173.

Sheng, L., & Yang, D. T. (2016). Expanding export variety: The role of institutional reforms in developing countries. *Journal of Development Economics, 118*, 45–58. doi:10.1016/j.jdeveco.2015.08.009

Stokey, N. L. (1989). Learning by Doing and the Introduction of New Goods. *Journal of Political Economy, Vol, 96*(:4), 701–717.

TUIK. (2017). *Turkish Statistical Institute.* Retrieved on July 26, 2017, from: http://www.turkstat.gov.tr

ENDNOTES

1 However, Lu and XU (2006) show that China's exports are mainly from costal provinces where per capita GDP levels are much higher.

2 http://www.turkstat.gov.tr

3 http://trade.ec.europa.eu/doclib/docs/2006/september/tradoc_122530.02.2017.pdf

APPENDIX

Table 5.

Country Name	Country	ESI 1985	ESI 2001	Rank 1985	Rank 2001	Change
Albania	ALB	15,446	15,492	42	95	–53
Angola	ANG	9,957	13,765	104	109	–5
Argentina	ARG	16,952	20,831	29	39	–10
Australia	AUS	16,646	20,942	32	37	–5
Austria	AUT	20,537	24,956	5	8	–3
Bahrain	BHR	16,863	19,227	30	58	–28
Bangladesh	BGD	11,552	13,082	89	113	–24
Belgium-Luxemburg	BLX	19,978	24,253	11	11	0
Belize	BLZ	15,031	17,108	46	75	–29
Benin	BEN	10,501	17,988	96	70	26
Bolivia	BOL	16,830	19,327	31	57	–26
Brazil	BRA	15,786	21,361	40	34	6
Bulgaria	BGR	19,120	20,083	15	46	–31
Burkina Faso	BFA	13,846	19,382	61	55	6
Burundi	BDI	6,168	13,197	114	112	2
Cameroon	CMR	10,361	16,352	99	86	13
Canada	CAN	20,062	23,745	10	16	–6
Chad	CHD	11,027	17,954	94	71	23
Chile	CHL	14,901	19,802	47	51	–4
China	CHN	14,348	20,468	55	41	14
Colombia	COL	10,222	18,292	102	66	36
Comoros	COM	9,231	12,580	110	114	–4
Congo (Dem.Rep.of)	CON	13,013	17,357	77	73	4
Congo (Republic of the)	COG	10,226	14,347	101	104	–3
Costa Rica	CRI	12,099	20,908	86	38	48
Côte d'Ivoire	CIV	11,396	19,035	91	62	29
Cyprus	CYP	16,465	23,681	35	17	18
Denmark	DNK	19,765	23,816	12	14	–2
Dominican Rep.	DOM	13,731	17,262	64	74	–10
Ecuador	ECU	10,670	16,159	95	87	8
Egypt	EGY	11,848	19,006	87	63	24
El Salvador	SLV	9,636	20,345	107	42	65
Equatorial Guinea	EQG	12,172	14,034	85	106	–21
Ethiopia	ETH	9,702	16,941	106	79	27

continued on following page

Table 5. Continued

Country Name	Country	ESI 1985	ESI 2001	Rank 1985	Rank 2001	Change
Fiji	FJI	14,033	16,148	59	88	–29
Finland	FIN	20,220	24,723	9	9	0
France	FRA	20,370	25,079	7	7	0
Gabon	GAB	10,456	13,895	97	108	–11
Gambia	GMB	13,228	17,022	72	77	–5
Germany	DEU	21,407	25,698	3	4	–1
Ghana	GHA	13,258	20,047	70	48	22
Greece	GRC	15,643	20,068	41	47	–6
Guatemala	GTM	11,470	18,606	90	64	26
Guinea-Bissau	GIN	13,651	16,130	66	89	–23
Guyana	GUY	12,654	17,010	81	78	3
Haiti	HTI	15,172	14,341	44	105	–61
Honduras	HND	10,420	16,726	98	81	17
Hong Kong	HKG	18,597	21,726	20	30	–10
Hungary	HUN	18,698	23,521	19	19	0
Iceland	ISL	17,769	21,840	27	29	–2
India	IND	14,376	19,192	54	60	–6
Ireland	IRL	20,230	25,846	8	3	5
Israel	ISR	18,767	22,634	18	23	–5
Italy	ITA	19,461	23,369	13	21	–8
Jamaica	JAM	13,173	14,967	76	98	–22
Japan	JPN	22,650	26,089	1	2	–1
Jordan	JOR	14,381	19,354	53	56	–3
Kenya	KEN	9,716	16,713	105	82	23
Kiribati	KRB	12,380	20,121	83	43	40
Korea (Republic of)	KOR	18,562	23,632	21	18	3
Lao People's Dem. Rep.	LPR	9,293	15,599	109	93	16
Madagascar	MDG	8,572	13,578	111	110	1
Malawi	MWI	11,140	13,211	93	111	–18
Malaysia	MYS	13,609	21,997	67	27	40
Mali	MLI	12,913	19,823	79	49	30
Malta	MLT	17,819	23,290	25	22	3
Mauritania	MAU	11,263	14,380	92	102	–10
Mauritius	MUS	13,281	14,583	69	100	–31
Mexico	MEX	13,705	22,522	65	25	40
Mongolia	MNG	15,407	15,407	43	96	–53
Morocco	MAR	13,207	15,933	74	90	–16

continued on following page

Table 5. Continued

Country Name	Country	ESI 1985	ESI 2001	Rank 1985	Rank 2001	Change
Mozambique	MOZ	14,576	19,398	50	54	–4
Nepal	NPL	14,459	16,362	52	85	–33
Netherlands	NLD	19,336	23,953	14	13	1
New Zealand	NZL	18,047	23,517	23	20	3
Nicaragua	NIC	10,051	18,272	103	67	36
Norway	NOR	16,476	18,085	33	69	–36
Oman	OMN	10,228	15,818	100	91	9
Pakistan	PAK	14,252	16,602	57	83	–26
Panama	PAN	12,757	19,420	80	53	27
Papua-New Guinea	PNG	11,598	15,534	88	94	–6
Paraguay	PRY	13,808	20,481	63	40	23
Peru	PER	13,810	19,120	62	61	1
Philippines	PHL	15,986	22,537	39	24	15
Portugal	PRT	17,466	21,505	28	32	–4
Romania	ROM	17,892	19,203	24	59	–35
Rwanda	RWA	6,131	11,022	115	115	0
Senegal	SEN	13,238	18,409	71	65	6
Seychelles	SEY	16,010	16,768	38	80	–42
Sierra Leone	SLE	13,183	20,107	75	45	30
Singapore	SGP	18,174	24,083	22	12	10
Solomon Islands	SOI	14,271	18,122	56	68	–12
South Africa	ZAF	16,474	21,000	34	36	–2
Spain	ESP	19,015	23,798	16	15	1
Sri Lanka	LKA	9,584	13,935	108	107	1
St. Kitts and Nevis	KNA	14,246	21,562	58	31	27
Sudan	SDN	14,465	14,358	51	103	–52
Suriname	SUR	12,302	14,439	84	101	–17
Sweden	SWE	21,049	25,194	4	6	–2
Switzerland	CHE	21,789	26,933	2	1	1
Syrian Arab Republic	SYR	12,619	14,743	82	99	–17
Thailand	THA	14,725	21,241	48	35	13
Togo	TGO	8,288	15,677	112	92	20
Trinidad and Tobago	TTO	13,473	20,118	68	44	24
Tunisia	TUN	13,210	16,479	73	84	–11
Turkey	TUR	16,370	19,560	36	52	–16
Uganda	UGA	6,218	17,777	113	72	41
United Kingdom	GBR	18,893	24,585	17	10	7

continued on following page

Table 5. Continued

Country Name	Country	ESI 1985	ESI 2001	Rank 1985	Rank 2001	Change
United States	USA	20,511	25,198	6	5	1
Uruguay	URY	16,099	21,432	37	33	4
Vietnam	VIE	12,970	15,384	78	97	–19
Zambia	ZMB	15,035	19,821	45	50	–5
Zimbabwe	ZWE	14,717	17,095	49	76	–27

Source: Desroches et al. (2006)

Chapter 10
Potential Changes in the Demand and Supply Sides in the Construction Industry:
Emerging Concepts for the Sustainable and Innovative Economy

Begum Sertyesilisik
Istanbul Technical University, Turkey

ABSTRACT

Sustainability of the economy depends on the reduction of the environmental footprint of the supply and demand as economy relies on the production enabled by natural resources. The construction industry is one of the major industries influencing sustainable and social development. The construction industry and the built environment, however, have important environmental footprints. Therefore, the demand and supply sides in the construction industry must be transformed into more sustainable ones. Furthermore, the principles and emerging concepts of sustainable and innovative economy need to be adopted by the construction industry. Based on an in-depth literature review, this chapter focuses on the integration and impacts of the emerging concepts for the sustainable and innovative economy in the construction industry. This chapter is expected to be useful for academics, graduate and undergraduate students, researchers, policymakers, and construction industry professionals.

INTRODUCTION

Climate change, caused by the human activities and their production and consumption patterns, resulted in the deterioration of the world's living conditions [changes in the precipitation rates, increase in the temperature and sea levels, melting ice in the poles as well as increased frequencies and magnitudes of disasters (e.g., floods, hurricanes)]. Climate change's adverse affects can cause disasters (e.g. floods, etc.) which can destruct the production process and failure in the supply chain. Therefore, managers and business leaders have started to consider climate risk as a business risk in their companies' investment

DOI: 10.4018/978-1-5225-5787-6.ch010

decisions and in their efforts for enhancing resilience of their supply chain. Furthermore, deteriorated nature causes scarcity in production factors. Humanity's environmental footprint both with respect to production and consumption patterns needs to be more sustainable so the world's living conditions can be regenerated. Efforts for reducing environmental footprint of the production processes started to change production patterns. Sustainable production and consumption patterns do not only contribute to the sustainability of the world's resources, but also to the sustainability of the production and economy due to their dependence on nature for the majority of the production factors. Sustainable development requires achievement of the long–term goals of sustainability: a balanced socio–ecological system (Bibri 2013, 2015; Bibri & Krogstie, 2017, p. 192).

Production and consumption models are being transformed from a linear economy to a circular economy (Yuan et al., 2006; Gómez, González, & Bárcena, 2017) which relies on the cradle-to-cradle cycle principle. Circular economy enables zero waste, synergy among businesses, efficiency in the resource usage, reduction in the environmental footprint, reduction in the costs, and increase in the competitiveness of the participated companies. The circular economy is fostered by the eco-industrial development and eco-industrial parks which are important for the sustainable development and for reducing environmental footprint of the production processes (Sertyesilisik & Sertyesilisik, 2016, p. 6) which ensure circular economy (Gómez, et al., 2017).

Sustainability performance of the production processes can be enhanced by sustainability innovation which can lead to dematerialization as well as to the emergence of environmental friendly products and production processes substituting the non-sustainable ones. Sustainability innovation can contribute to the competitiveness of the companies as it can contribute to the reduction in the production cost focusing on the value creation as well as to the sustainable and lean performance of the production process. Dematerialization and sustainability innovation can act like lean tools and enhance the lean performance of the supply side. Innovation is important for the economic development. According to Schumpeter, innovation accepted/absorbed by the economic system can contribute to the economic development (Brouwer, 1991, p. 58). Furthermore, Schumpeter emphasized the role of the business leaders stating that the entrepreneur, as the 'agent of innovation', can cause 'creative destruction' as a result of their innovations which can make exiting ideas, skills, technologies etc. obsolete (Ziemnowicz, 2010, p. 1173). Innovation fosters smart economy enabled by the smart production contributing to the sustainability and efficiency performance of the production processes. Smart production is IT- and innovation-based production. The circular economy can be enhanced by smart production. For example, eco-industrial parks are getting smarter with the help of new technologies and innovations as well as through bio-inspired multi-agent systems (Gómez, et al., 2017). Smart eco-industrial parks can further enhance competitiveness of the companies operating in these parks. The shift in the eco-industrial parks towards more smart ones is an example for the shift in the economy towards smarter and innovative one. Competition levels among companies has reached to the global hypercompetition level, especially due to the globalization, accelerated rate of innovations in all industries, and transformation in the economy towards a circular, sustainable, smart, innovative and resilient one. Even locally operating companies cannot isolate themselves from global competition. Global hypercompetition and changes in the production technologies changes the skills needed from the human resources fostering global skills' gap which results in unemployment. There is a lack of human resources equipped with the skills and knowledge needed to cope with the contemporary expectations of the industries.

The construction industry is one of the main industries contributing to the countries' GDP (gross domestic product) and employment rates as well as to the countries' development providing the infrastructure needed. The construction industry plays an important role in the sustainable development, economy, and resilience of the society with the help of its production/construction processes and its outputs (e.g., construction materials, built environment). The construction industry's resilience is vital for the disaster resilience of the society and for the rapid recovery of the society from the disasters. The construction industry can play important role in fulfillment of the sheltering need of the society in the post-disaster phase. The construction industry's sustainability performance, however, needs to be improved (e.g., carbon footprint, water footprint) due to the construction process, and its outputs throughout their lifecycle (e.g. operation and maintenance, and demolition phases).

The construction industry relies on natural resources (e.g., materials, sand, water) and causes emission of greenhouses gases (e.g., CO_2 emission in the inbound activities, construction, material production). As with all other industries, the construction industry cannot isolate itself from the changes in the economy and in other industries. The demand and supply sides of the construction industry are being transformed through the adaptation of the principles and emerging concepts of the sustainable and innovative economy. This chapter focuses on the integration and impacts of the emerging concepts for the sustainable and innovative economy to the construction industry.

BACKGROUND

Industrial revolutions have changed the production speed, cost, processes, and supply chains as well as the way in which companies are operating. Throughout history there have been various industrial revolutions. The post-industrial economy of mass production has been transformed into the knowledge economy in the 1990s and to the digital economy in the 2000s (Berdykulova, Sailov, Kaliazhdarova, & Berdykulov, 2014, p. 1287). Today, we witness the fourth industrial revolution. Dai (2006, pp. 3-9) suggested the development of the nanotechnology as the start of the fourth industrial revolution. Despite the fact that this development has been an important one, the beginning of the fourth industrial revolution (Industry 4.0) is accepted to be the intensified digitisation in the production and the emergence of the digital value chain (Oesterreich & Teuteberg, 2016, p. 122). This shift in the industrial revolutions requires the companies to adopt themselves to the changing demand and supply conditions as well as the countries to adopt their human resources to the changes in the skills demanded by the industries.

Companies which failed to adopt themselves to the industrial revolution could not survive. Similarly, countries failing to adopt themselves and their human resources to the industrial revolutions could not become fully developed countries. The global economy is in the transformation of becoming a circular, sustainable, smart, innovative and resilient entity. Sustainability and innovativeness are interrelated as enhancing sustainability performance of the economy can be fostered by the innovative solutions and innovations. Innovations can foster new opportunities for employment and production. Innovative technology and creative ideas are the main pillars for creative economy as they can foster creation of value and economic growth (Sung, 2015, pp. 89-91).

The shift in the economy towards the creative economy is expected to be the end of the chase-and-imitate economic model (Sung, 2015, p. 89). Sustainable and innovative economy is fostered by Information and Communications Technology (ICT). ICT has become a key factor of production in the digital economy (Berdykulova, et al., 2014, p. 1287) as the digital transformation enables the companies to create value and to gain competitive advantages (Solis, 2017; Pagani & Pardo, 2017). The shift towards digitization can change the decision on the technology type which will be used in the production process as the trade-off between labor intensive and capital intensive production is transformed into the trade-off among labor intensive, capital intensive and information intensive production as ICT and IT became production factors.

Companies can enhance their competitiveness and increase their profits in case they learn how to use their companies' information to create new products and services as information has economic value enabling them to create the wealth of information (Garifova, 2015, p. 738). For this reason, the new information economy necessitates a new measurement tool instead of the GDP (Quiggin, 2014, p. 142). As the economy is being transformed into an information and innovation based economy, GDIII (Gross domestic information and innovation impact) and GDIIV (Gross domestic information and innovation value) can be introduced as the new tools in addition to the GDP for more accurate assessment of the economic performance of a nation. GDIII can be described as the impact of the domestically produced information and innovation. GDIIV can be described as the value of the domestically produced information and innovation.

Changes in the economy influences innovation, supply, and demand characteristics. Industries are transformed due to the changing needs, competition, policies, and technologies. The speed of these changes has been accelerated especially due to the intensified competition and innovation in the industries as well as due to the shift in the economy towards sustainable, circular, innovative, smart, and resilient economy. The construction industry is one of the main industries experiencing change. The construction industry and its outputs (e.g., the built environment, materials) have started to witness changes and to be transformed into smart, sustainable, innovative and more resilient ones. The construction industry's demand and supply characteristics influence the characteristics of the cities and their environmental footprint.

Cities are expected to hold 66% of the world's population by 2050 (United Nations, 2015), and they have become centers for the global economy (Zhuhadar, Thrasher, Marklin, & de Pablos, 2017, p. 273). Cities started to experience a transition towards smart and sustainable ones in accordance with the transformation in the construction industry. City networks [e.g., Covenant of Mayors, CIVITAS, CONCERTO and Green Digital Charter] have been established to enhance energy efficiency and to reduce carbon footprint of the cities (Ahvenniemi, Huovila, Pinto-Seppä, & Airaksinen, 2017, p. 234).

Cities are becoming smart and smart cities are becoming smarter. The smart city is a tool for fostering economic growth, environmental quality, quality of life, social equity, well-being and social development, facilitated by collaborative dialogue and innovations in technology enabling efficiency gains, cost savings and economic development (Albino et al., 2015; Bibri & Krogstie, 2017, p. 193; Foth, Hudson-Smith, & Gifford, 2016; Sarma & Sunny, 2017, p. 1; Zhuhadar, et al., 2017, pp. 274-281). Transformation of the cities into smarter ones is a revolutionary change (Bhowmick et al., 2012) requesting ICT and GeoICT (Geoinformation and Communication Technology) to be embedded to the operations, functions, designs, and services of the smarter cities (Aina, 2017, p. 49; Bibri & Krogstie, 2017, p. 192) as well as to be integrated with top-down and bottom-up approaches to the development of the cities (Aina, 2017, p. 49). Furthermore, the climate change and the increase in the frequencies of disasters fosters the need for disaster resilient built environment and construction industry. All these transformations in the cities reveal the fact that the demand and supply sides of the construction industry are changing.

CHANGES IN THE DEMAND AND SUPPLY SIDES OF THE CONSTRUCTION INDUSTRY

Changes in the Demand Side of the Construction Industry

The demand side of the construction industry is influenced mainly by customer preferences and value perception. Customers' preferences for a particular product and their value perception are influenced by their purchasing power, sensitivity for and consciousness of the environment, living styles, taste, education, and culture as well as by the effectiveness of the advertisement, availability of the substitutes, innovations, and elasticity of demand for particular product. The characteristics of demand for construction is influenced by the purchasing power of the potential customers. Unemployed people's purchasing power is diminished. Unemployment rates throughout the world are increasing, especially among the young generations due to the global skills gap and changes in the production factors. For example, the shift towards the fourth industrial revolution reduces the demand for labor workforce which is being replaced by technology. The purchasing power of the people is expected to be reduced especially due to the reduced food resources and collapse in the food chain as a result of the climate change as people are expected to be able to fulfil their primary needs (e.g., food) at higher price levels than ever before.

The demand characteristics for construction is shaped by the customers' awareness of environmental friendly products, their consciousness about the need for reducing their environmental footprint and their perception that they can contribute to the fight against climate change in case they change their consumption habits and preferences. All human beings can act as change agents for sustainability in their purchasing decisions. For this reason, formal and informal education are important as they can enhance people's consciousness about the state-of-the-art of the world's living conditions and climate change as well as about their role in the fight against climate change when they make a purchasing decision.

Potential customers' living styles, taste, education, and culture influence each other and the characteristics of demand for construction due to these factors' influence on design as well as on the elasticity of demand for a certain product. Furthermore, advertisements can influence potential customers' purchasing decision making them aware of the properties of the product and influencing their perception of the product. Green marketing efforts can increase demand for sustainable products and production processes. Elasticity of demand for a particular product is expected to increase the bargaining power of the potential customers. Elasticity of demand for particular product can be influenced mainly by the availability of substitutes or by the innovations introducing new products acting as substitutes of a particular product or causing a particular product to become obsolete. For example, smart and sustainable construction materials can concur the market of the non-smart and non-sustainable construction materials.

Even if there is no substitute for the sheltering as the demand is inelastic due to its vitality for the human beings' primary needs, there will be more substitutes for particular construction materials as a result of innovations. As innovation rates are being accelerated in the construction industry, the customers' bargaining power for construction materials is expected to be increased as they will be able to make their purchasing decisions under the availability of more product types. Furthermore, advertisements and marketing efforts can influence the elasticity of demand as they can influence the taste of the potential customers.

The characteristics of demand for the construction industry is influenced by the increase in the frequencies and magnitudes of the disasters due to climate change. The need for more resilient built environment influences the demand for resilient built environment. Change in the built environment and transformation of the cities into smart ones are changing the role of the customers. The customers tend to be no longer on the demand side only but also on the supply side as they can contribute to the co-evolution and co-design of smart cities with the help of the social media and internet of things. In smart cities "*... citizens effectively function as co-designers of urban initiatives ... the design process becomes more agile*" (Gardner & Hespanhol, 2017). Similarly, managers and urban management of the smart cities are supported by the social media fostering the usage of the ICT for urban management issues (e.g., crowd and safety management, alert systems for emergency cases, e-democracy) (Kourtit, Nijkamp, & Steenbruggen, 2017, p. 19). Furthermore, citizens started to demand for services instead of owing the cars or other facilities and equipment as smart cities enabled emergence of the "*... 'sharing economy' urban service providers such as Uber2 (for car sharing) or AirBnB3 (for short term accommodation rentals).*" (Gardner & Hespanhol, 2017). This demand for flexibility has been started to be observed in the design of the buildings. For example, the construction firm Nef introduced unfolding office and apartments concept enabling its customers who own an office or apartment in one of this company's projects to rent additional rooms (e.g., meeting rooms) in the same building or in another project of this company. Change in the demand for more sustainable, smart, and resilient built environment reveals the customers' role in fostering innovation in the construction industry and in transforming the construction industry.

Changes in the Supply Side of the Construction Industry

Characteristics of the supply is influenced by the changes in the characteristics of demand as well as by the sustainability innovation, competition in the market, laws and regulations, government policies (such as carbon taxes, etc.) and the emerging new concepts (e.g., circular economy, virtual water). Furthermore, benchmarking from other industries and adopting these changes to a particular industry (e.g., adaptation of lean principles to the construction process) fosters the change. Companies' survival depends on their adaptation to the changing trends, changes in the demand, in economy, production techniques and factors.

Competition in the construction industry is being intensified and competitiveness factors are being changed. Intensified competition leads to the intensified innovation efforts (e.g., for reducing cost, enhancing sustainability and lean performance of their production process) of the companies so they can increase or maintain their competitive advantage. Companies' innovation efforts can support their competitive advantage and enable them to influence the trends and competition rules in the construction industry as well as to adopt to the changes in the demand in case their innovation efforts are successful. Innovation in the built environment is needed to reduce the environmental footprint of the built environment as well as to adapt the built environment to the climate change and to the changes in the world's living conditions. Technological developments enable creation of value in cities and new business models (Díaz-Díaz, Muñoz, & Pérez-González, 2017, p. 1).

There is a transition towards a low-carbon economy (Foxon, 2011; Hall & Foxon, 2014, p. 601). Projects (e.g., the Climate Neutral Urban Districts) enabling collaboration among the cities can contribute to the promotion of innovative technologies to reduce the carbon footprint of the cities (Gardner & Hespanhol, 2017) and to influence the supply characteristics. Innovations can result in dematerialization, reduced environmental footprint, reduced cost, and reduced production time. Innovations can introduce new products substituting the products having environmental footprint. "Increasing competitiveness implies economic change through the introduction of new technologies and new methods of production as well as the development of new skills" (Kadar, Moise, & Colomba, 2014, p. 1083).

Digital innovations can make a difference with respect to the: smart living, smart governance, smart economy, smart environment, smart people and smart mobility (Giffinger & Pichler-Milanović, 2007). The capability of the companies to make innovations necessitates "*... knowledge infrastructure, a highly skilled labor force, creative workplaces, business models built with ... customers and ... global supply chains (Graham, 2016; Haidine, Aqqal & Ouahmane, 2016).*" (Zhuhadar, Thrasher, Marklin, & de Pablos, 2017, p. 275).

Innovation in the construction industry transforms the supply side. The construction material industry is being transformed and the competition in the construction material market is being intensified due to the innovation in smart, sustainable and nano materials. The construction material industry is expected to be transformed at a higher rate, as the cities and built environment are becoming more smart, sustainable and resilient. Smart cities can be accomplished with the help of smart materials which include sensors and IT. Similarly, the efforts for reducing the environmental footprint of the humanity, of the built environment and of the construction industry as well as for increased customers' awareness for the need for sustainable built environment and the sustainable buildings and material labeling can foster the demand for smart and sustainable construction materials. Furthermore, resilience of the construction materials gain importance as the frequencies and magnitudes of the disasters are increasing due to the climate change. As the nano materials are more resilient compared to the non-nano materials, the demand for the nano materials can be increased. For these reasons, the market for construction materials is expected to shift towards smart, sustainable, and nano materials. This transformation of the supply side can act as a treat for the companies failing to adopt themselves to these changes as they can lose their market share. The materials having at least one of the characteristics of smart, sustainable and nano can be substitutes of the construction materials which do not possess these properties.

Changes in the characteristics of supply influences the business models. Establishment of smart cities or trend for enhancing the smart performance of the cities result in the emergence of new business models in the construction industry due to the changing role of the stakeholders in these processes. Smart cities require new business models (Bélissent, Mines, Radcliffe, & Darashkevich, 2010; Mulligan & Olsson, 2013; Díaz-Díaz, Muñoz, & Pérez-González, 2017) as the stakeholders (e.g., the private sector) assume a more active role in the project, especially through the data they generated via social media, crowd sourcing etc. (Zygiaris, 2013; Koppenjan & Enserink, 2009; Ndeto, 2009; De Rosario, Martín, Pérez, & Martínez, 2013; Bakıcı, Almirall, & Wareham, 2012; Díaz-Díaz, et al., 2017, pp. 3-4). Smart cities, with the help of the ICTs enable the society to create intellectual capital, and wealth through the direct democracy of their participatory governance open up, add value to and construct." (Deakin, 2014; Aina, 2017). Furthermore, networked cities (e.g., Open and Agile Smart Cities) can share their experiences in their co-design initiatives and facilitate their citizens' participation in the design (Gardner & Hespanhol, 2017). The marketing process is enhanced by ICT which enables the companies to have access to the detailed marketing data on potential customers as well as to develop personalized and tailor-made marketing strategies (Sarma & Sunny, 2017, p. 7).

The supply chain and production processes in the construction industry both for the construction material production and for the construction processes are influenced by the contemporary trends and innovations in other industries. For example, the construction industry is expected to be affected by Industry 4.0 which intensified digitization of the value chain (including tendering, briefing, design, planning, construction, usage and maintenance phases), and of the production as well as introduced new technologies (e.g., Internet of Things/Internet of Services, modularization; product-lifecycle-management;

augmented reality/virtual reality/mixed reality; 3D printing/additive manufacturing; mobile computing; social media, robotics; big data; cloud computing) (Oesterreich & Teuteberg, 2016, pp. 122-136). Production processes and supply chains can become more flexible due to the agility of Industry 4.0. Companies can enhance their competitive advantage with the help of optimum balance of the local and global production as well as adopting lean and agile principles to their entire supply chain.

Supply chains in the construction industry need to be resilient to disasters and climate risks. Construction companies and construction material producers must establish strategies for enhancing resilience of their supply chains both in their local and global operations so that their production processes do not fail in case of disasters. Global or international supply chains tend to become more vulnerable due to the disasters which can destruct the production process and cause failure in the supply chain. Resilience of the supply chains in the construction industry can further enhance resilience of the community and contribute to their recovery process in the post-disaster phase.

The smart construction process and material production process as well as intensified competition and the globalization in production/construction activities and markets can increase the need for the supply chains to be transformed into virtual ones. Virtual supply chains are supported by the ICT and internet. Internet changed the speed of connection between people and business as well as the competition levels enabling rivals to challenge markets and supply chains (Davies, 2015; Zhuhadar, et al., p. 275). The supply side in the construction industry is expected to be influenced by the potential changes in the accounting system as it is expected to be transformed so that it includes the cost of the nature and of the water footprint as well as carbon taxes. This change in the accounting system can have an impact on the increase in the cost of the companies which have environmental footprint. For example, carbon tax is expected to contribute to the sustainability performance of the production processes as carbon tax will increase the cost of the companies having carbon footprint. For this reason, carbon tax can encourage the companies to reduce their carbon footprint so that they can enhance their competitiveness. Similarly, inclusion of the cost of the water footprint/virtual water of the production process and of the products in this new accounting system, can introduce the virtual water as one of the factors affecting the competitiveness of the companies. Virtual water is the amount of water needed for the production of an output starting from raw material extraction. Calculation of the virtual water of the production process and of the product is important for the understanding of their sustainability performance. Water is one of the main ingredients of the production process. Industrialization is influenced by and depends on the availability of water as production processes are water intensive. For example, "*In Europe, as much as 40% of the total water abstraction is destined for industrial use (Eurostat, 2015)*" (Wärmark, 2015, p.2).

The construction industry began to assess not only the sustainability performance of its outputs via building assessment tools (green and sustainable building certificates such as LEED, BREEAM, etc.) and material assessment tools (green and sustainable material labels) but also the performance of its production process with respect to its environmental footprint. For example, the Civil Engineering and Environmental Quality Assessment and Award Scheme (CEEQUAL) considers the water footprint as an important criterion for choosing building materials (Wärmark, 2015, p.2-9). Wärmark's (2015, p.i) study revealed steel as a water intensive product whereas fill material as a material having low water consumption. Furthermore, as the reduction in the environmental footprint is expected to become a competitive advantage due to its influence on the cost, the construction material industry can benchmark from other industries and adopt the smart eco-industrial parks system establishing smart eco-industrial zones for construction material manufacturing. The environmental footprints' effects on the cost, competitiveness and on the sustainability of the environment contribute to the trend for regenerative production/construction processes and products/constructions/construction materials. "Regenerative characteristics refer to the capacity to achieve net positive development contributing to the regeneration of nature" (Sertyesilisik, 2016). To enhance their competitive advantage and to outperform their rivals, companies can enhance their sustainability performance going beyond sustainability so that they can look for having regeneration performance both in their production processes and in their products (e.g., regenerative built environment).

Construction companies aiming to construct regenerative constructions need to perform regenerative construction project management which changes the construction project management (with respect to the "... feasibility and processes; designers', project managers' and communities' roles; scope, complexity, and focus of construction project management; contracts; supply chain and material industry") and which introduces new concepts (e.g. 'life-cycle revenue'; 'life-cycle regenerative revenue'; 'total life-cycle regenerative cash flow'; 'regeneration index') (Sertyesilisik, 2016).

SOLUTIONS AND RECOMMENDATIONS

The transformation of the global economy towards a circular, sustainable, smart, innovative one and the fourth industrial revolution influence the construction industry which is experiencing global hypercompetition and changes in the demand and supply characteristics. Change in the construction industry is happening at an accelerated speed due to the various factors (e.g., innovation, globalisation, changing production factors). Competition rules and competitive advantage factors in the construction industry are expected to be changed and new investment requirements as well as new skills are expected to play important role in the competitiveness.

Innovation and ICT technologies as well as ability to cope with uncertainty and agility became important competitive advantage factors. Adaptation of the construction industry to the changes in the demand and in the economy depends on the human resources' capacity, skills, and knowledge. Strategic importance of attracting and retaining human resources equipped with the skills needed for the smart and innovative production tends to be increased. The speed of change is expected to increase further due to the global hyper competition and new technologies as the construction industry cannot isolate itself from the developments and changes in other industries. For example, the construction industry is expected to witness a transformation into the industry 4.0 which is more IT and innovation based and which increases agility and uncertainty. Ability of the companies to cope with increased uncertainty and agility emerges as a key competitive advantage.

Innovations influence the competitiveness in the construction industry and can introduce new substitutes and/or new companies to the marketplace. New substitutes introduced to the market can influence the elasticity of demand affecting and increasing the bargaining power of the buyers/customers due to the increased product options available for them in the market. Innovations can further influence the bargaining power of the suppliers affecting their workload in case they can exploit the opportunity for taking part in the production of these new products as well. Therefore, considering today's economy, innovation needs to be added to the Porter's Five Forces framework which emphasises the role of the buyers and their bargaining power, suppliers and their bargaining power, potential entrants and their threat as well as substitutes and their threats in the competitive rivalry (Porter, 1980).

Sustainability performance of firms in the construction industry is becoming one of their key competitive advantages, especially due to the expected changes in the accounting system covering cost of the environmental footprint (e.g., water footprint, carbon footprint) and potential changes in the taxes (e.g., carbon taxes). These changes can be fostered by the innovations and environmental footprint assessment of the production/construction process. They can encourage companies and their entire supply chain to reduce their environmental footprints.

The value chain of construction companies and of the construction material producers tends to be changed to include creation of value, information, smart and innovative production processes and products. Porter's value chain within an organisation emphasised that the profit margin depends on the effectiveness of the primary activities and secondary activities (Porter, 1985). Porter (1985)'s generic value chain needs to be updated with the contemporary and future needs (Sertyesilisik, 2016, pp. 62-63). Similarly, Porter's (1990, 1998) "Diamond Framework", which defines factors influencing the competitive advantage of the companies working internationally, can be redefined embedding contemporary factors (e.g., sustainability perspective *adding future generations requirements as outside factor and sustainability as main factor*) (Sertyesilisik, 2016, p. 72).

The production technology used and the change in the production towards smarter one determine the employment characteristics and the skills the employees need to be equipped with. The shift towards a knowledge-based economy requires the future workforce/professionals (Davies, 2015) to have higher education and to possess skills, creativity, and innovation capacities (Anthopoulos, Janssen, & Weerakkody, 2016; Zhuhadar, et al., 2017, p. 275). Unemployment tends to increase especially among the young generations not equipped with the skills and knowledge needed in the smart, sustainable, circular and innovative economy. In other words, the growing global skills gap tends to increase the unemployment. Global hyper competition among the companies can affect their competition for attracting and retaining skilled and innovative human resources. For this reason, the workforce equipped with the necessary skills, however, can have more high bargaining power due to the job offers and the growing global skills gap.

The global skills gap problem can be solved via changes in the education at all levels. STEM (science, technology, engineering and mathematics) education and STEAM (science, technology, engineering, art, and mathematics) are one of the main strategies for training the future generations complying with the business requirements of the future. For example, in the USA, the Presidential Memorandum for the Secretary of Education released on the 25 September 2017 focuses on strategies for increasing access to High-Quality STEM Education and announced allocation of at least US$200 million in grant funds per year to promote STEM education. The US administration in 2014 allocated US$3.1 billion for STEM education (Hom, 2014). Furthermore, the U.S. Senate and House of Representatives have legislative actions (e.g., America RISING Act of 2017, Computer Science Career Education Act of 2017) to foster the STEM education (the STEM Education Coalition website). Similar efforts are observed in other developed countries. The United Kingdom plans to graduate 100,000 STEM majors annually by 2020 (Hom, 2014).

Based on the changes in the industries and in the economy, the curriculums of the universities and higher education institutes need to be updated so future professionals are equipped with the required skills needed by organizations. University curriculum needs to equip the students with the knowledge and skills needed in the emerging technologies (e.g. Mobile, 3D-Printing, IoT/Sensors, Big Data, Robotics – Drone, Renewable energy) (Grimaldi & Fernandez, 2017). Even the business administration professionals need to be familiar with the technological language as they will need to decide on the IT subject (Feld & Stoddard, 2004; Grimaldi & Fernandez, 2017).

FUTURE RESEARCH DIRECTIONS

Adaptation of the construction industry as well as its demand and supply sides to the changes in the sustainable and innovative economy is an inescapable transformation of the construction industry. The importance of this topic is expected to increase further with the time as construction industry plays an important role in the economy of the countries and in their development as well as in the well-being of the society. Future research is recommended to be conducted on:

- The ways of fostering STEM/STEAM education for fostering innovation in the construction industry
- Identifying potential benchmarking areas from other industries so that sustainability and resilience performance of the construction industry can be enhanced
- Benchmarking from other industries so that construction industry can be adapted to the industry 4.0
- The ways of enhancing innovation capability in the construction industry
- Developing strategies for establishment of the smart eco-industrial parks for the production of the construction materials.
- Developing strategies needed for reducing environmental footprint of the construction industry and for enhancing resilience of the construction supply chain.

CONCLUSION

This chapter focused on the changes in the demand and supply sides in the construction industry. Humanity's unsustainable production and consumption patterns caused climate change and environmental conditions' degradation. As the world cannot regenerate itself at the rate it is being deteriorated by the human beings, the economy is being adversely affected as production relies on the resources obtained or extracted from nature. Production processes and supply chains need to become resilient due to the adverse climate conditions or disasters. Furthermore, production processes and supply chains need to have enhanced sustainability performance. Circular and sustainable economy is a solution for reducing environmental footprint of the production processes. In addition, firm competitiveness can be influenced by their environmental footprint due to the expected changes in the taxation to cover the carbon taxes and due to the expected changes in the cost calculations covering the cost of the virtual water. Innovations have been intensified as they act like a tool for companies to enhance their competitive advantage as well as to reduce their cost and environmental footprint.

Innovations and developments in IT have fostered the fourth industrial revolution which is based on smart production. Transformation of the economy into a circular, sustainable, smart and resilient one has influenced the demand and supply sides' characteristics of the construction industry. This transformation caused global skills gap due to the scarcity of the human resources compatible in dealing with the requirements of the contemporary production techniques and economy.

Construction companies cannot isolate themselves from global hypercompetition. Construction processes are expected to be shaped based on the decision with respect to the trade-off among labor-intensive, capital-intensive, and information-intensive production. Construction and production processes are expected to be transformed by the fourth industrial revolution. Innovation and information are becoming important competitive advantage factors for the construction companies.

Construction material manufacturing companies are expected to shift their production to the smart eco-industrial zones to enhance their competitive advantage. Built environment and construction materials are becoming more smart, sustainable, resilient and innovative. Demand for smart, sustainable, resilient and innovative built environment and construction materials is increasing. Customers' role as purchaser has been enriched as cities becoming smarter and ICT intensive enabling the citizens to contribute to the governance via e-democracy. This chapter is expected to be useful for the researchers, academics, undergraduate and post-graduate students as well as to the professionals in various disciplines.

REFERENCES

Ahvenniemi, H., Huovila, A., Pinto-Seppä, I., & Airaksinen, M. (2017). What are the differences between sustainable and smart cities? *Cities (London, England)*, *60*, 234–245. doi:10.1016/j.cities.2016.09.009

Aina, Y. A. (2017). Achieving smart sustainable cities with GeoICT support: The Saudi evolving smart cities. *Cities (London, England)*, *71*, 49–58. doi:10.1016/j.cities.2017.07.007

Albino, V., Berardi, U., & Dangelico, R. M. (2015). Smart Cities: Definitions, dimensions, performance, and initiatives. *Journal of Urban Technology*, *22*(1), 3–21. doi:10.1080/10630732.2014.942092

Anthopoulos, L., Janssen, M., & Weerakkody, V. (2016). Smart service Portfolios: Do the cities follow standards? *Proceedings of the 25th International conference companion on world wideWeb: International world wide web conferences steering committee*, 357-362. 10.1145/2872518.2888618

Bakıcı, T., Almirall, E., & Wareham, J. (2012). A smart city initiative: The case of Barcelona. *J. Knowl. Econ.*, *4*(2), 135–148. doi:10.100713132-012-0084-9

Bélissent, J., Mines, C., Radcliffe, E., & Darashkevich, Y. (2010). *Getting Clever About Smart Cities: New Opportunities Require New Business Models*. Cambridge, MA: Forrester Research.

Berdykulova, G. M. K., Sailov, A. I. U., Kaliazhdarova, S. Y. K., & Berdykulov, E. B. U. (2014). The Emerging Digital Economy: Case of Kazakhstan. *Procedia - Social and Behavioral Sciences, 109*, 1287 – 1291.

Bhowmick, A., Francellino, E., Glehn, L., Loredo, R., Nesbitt, P., & Yu, S. (2012). *IBM intelligent operations center for smarter cities*. Armonk, NY: IBM International Technical Support Organization.

Bibri, S. E. (2013). *ICT for sustainable urban development in the European InformationSociety: A discursive investigation of energy efficiency technology* (Master Thesis). School of Culture and Society, Malmö University.

Bibri, S. E. (2015). *The shaping of Ambient Intelligence and the Internet of Things: Historico-epistemic, socio-cultural, politico-institutional and eco-environmental dimensions*. Berlin: Springer-Verlag. doi:10.2991/978-94-6239-142-0

Bibri, S. E., & Krogstie, J. (2017). Smart sustainable cities of the future: An extensive interdisciplinary literature review. *Sustainable Cities and Society*, *31*, 183–212. doi:10.1016/j.scs.2017.02.016

Brouwer, M. (1991). *Schumpeterian puzzles – technological competition and economic evolution*. Ann Arbor, MI: University of Michigan Press.

CIVITAS. (2018). Retrieved on January 30, 2018, from: http://www.civitas.eu

CONCERTO. (2017). Retrieved on November 11, 2017, from: http://concerto.eu/concerto/

Covenant of Mayors. (2017). Retrieved on September 23, 2017, from: http://www.covenantofmayors.eu/index_en.html

Dai, L. (2006). Chapter 1 From conventional technology to carbon nanotechnology: The fourth industrial revolution and the discoveries of C60, carbon nanotube and nanodiamond. In Carbon Nanotechnology. Elsevier B.V.

Davies, B. (2015). *Internet of everything - Powering the smart campus & the smart city*. Armonk, NY: IBM Institute for Business Value.

De Rosario, A., Martín, A., Pérez, M., & Martínez, A. (2013). *Are the Smart Cities the most democratic?: The Spanish Case*. *EGPA Annu. Conf.*, Edinburgh, UK.

Deakin, M. (2014). Smart cities: The state-of-the-art and governance challenge. *Triple Helix*, *1*(7), 1–16.

Díaz-Díaz, R., Muñoz, L., & Pérez-González, D. (2017). Business model analysis of public services operating in the smart city ecosystem: The case of SmartSantander. *Future Generation Computer Systems*, *76*, 198–214. doi:10.1016/j.future.2017.01.032

Feld, C. S., & Stoddard, D. B. (2004). Getting IT Right. *Harvard Business Review*. Retrieved on December 12, 2013, from: http://www.scopus.com/inward/record.url?eid=2-s2.0-1542320698&partnerID=tZOtx3y1

Foth, M., Hudson-Smith, A., & Gifford, D. (2016). *Smart cities, social capital, and citizens at play: A critique and a way forward*. Research Handbook on Digital Transformations.

Foxon, T. J. (2011). A co-evolutionary framework for analysing a transition to a sustainable low carbon economy. *Ecological Economics*, *70*(12), 2258–2267. doi:10.1016/j.ecolecon.2011.07.014

Gardner, N., & Hespanhol, L. (2017). *SMLXL: Scaling the smart city, from metropolis to individual*. City, Culture and Society.

Garifova, L. F. (2015). Infonomics and The Value of Information in The Digital Economy. *Procedia Economics and Finance 23*, 738–743. 10.1016/S2212-5671(15)00423-2

Giffinger, R., & Pichler-Milanović, N. (2007). *Smart Cities: Ranking of European Medium-Sized Cities*. Academic Press.

Gómez, A. M. M., González, F. A., & Bárcena, M. M. (2017). Smart eco-industrial parks: A circular economy implementation based on industrial metabolism. *Resources, Conservation and Recycling*, *xxx*, xxx–xxx.

Graham, G. (2016). Smart cities and operations management. *Production Planning and Control*, *27*(6), 431–432. doi:10.1080/09537287.2016.1147100

Green Digital Charter. (2015). Retrieved on February 20, 2016, from: http://www.greendigitalcharter.eu

Grimaldi, D., & Fernandez, V. (2017). The alignment of University curricula with the building of a Smart City: A case study from Barcelona. *Technological Forecasting and Social Change*, *123*, 298–306. doi:10.1016/j.techfore.2016.03.011

Haidine, A., Aqqal, A., & Ouahmane, H. (2016). Evaluation of communications technologies for smart grid as part of smart cities. In *Proceedings of the Mediterranean conference on information & communication technologies 2015* (pp. 277-285). Berlin: Springer. 10.1007/978-3-319-30298-0_29

Hall, S., & Foxon, T. J. (2014). Values in the Smart Grid: The co-evolving political economy of smart distribution. *Energy Policy*, *74*, 600–609. doi:10.1016/j.enpol.2014.08.018

Hom, E. J. (2014). *What is STEM Education?* Retrieved on May 9, 2015, from: https://www.livescience.com/43296-what-is-stem-education.html

Kadar, M., Moise, I. A., & Colomba, C. (2014). Innovation Management in the Globalized Digital Society. *Procedia: Social and Behavioral Sciences*, *143*, 1083–1089. doi:10.1016/j.sbspro.2014.07.560

Koppenjan, J., & Enserink, B. (2009). Public–private partnerships in urban infrastructures: Reconciling private sector participation and sustainability. *Public Administration Review*, *69*(2), 284–296. doi:10.1111/j.1540-6210.2008.01974.x

Kourtit, K., Nijkamp, P., & Steenbruggen, J. (2017). The significance of digital data systems for smart city policy. *Socio-Economic Planning Sciences*, *58*, 13–21. doi:10.1016/j.seps.2016.10.001

Mulligan, C. E. A., & Olsson, M. (2013). Architectural implications of smart city business models: An evolutionary perspective. *IEEE Communications Magazine*, *51*, 80–85. doi:10.1109/MCOM.2013.6525599

Ndeto, J. (2009). Innovative financing mechanisms for municipal solid waste management in secondary cities of ethiopia: The case of Arba Minch city. *IUP J. Infrastruct.*, *7*, 79–102.

Oesterreich, T. D., & Teuteberg, F. (2016). Understanding the implications of digitisation and automation in the context of Industry 4.0: A triangulation approach and elements of a research agenda for the construction industry. *Computers in Industry*, *83*, 121–139. doi:10.1016/j.compind.2016.09.006

Pagani, M., & Pardo, C. (2017). *Industrial Marketing Management*. doi:10.1016/j.indmarman

Porter, M. E. (1980). *Competitive Strategy: Techniques for Analyzing Industries and Competitors*. New York: Free Press.

Porter, M. E. (1985). *Competitive Advantage: Creating and Sustaining Superior Performance*. Free Press.

Porter, M. E. (1990). *The competitive advantage of nations*. New York: Free Press. doi:10.1007/978-1-349-11336-1

Porter, M. E. (1998). *The competitive advantage of nations*. New York: Free Press, MacMillan. doi:10.1007/978-1-349-14865-3

Quiggin, J. (2014). National accounting and the digital economy. *Economic Analysis and Policy*, *44*(2), 136–142. doi:10.1016/j.eap.2014.05.008

Sarma, S., & Sunny, S. A. (2017). Civic entrepreneurial ecosystems: Smart city emergence in Kansas City. *Business Horizons*.

Sertyesilisik, B. (2016). Embedding Sustainability Dynamics in the Lean Construction Supply Chain Management. *YBL Journal of Built Environment*, *4*(1), 62–63. doi:10.1515/jbe-2016-0006

Sertyesilisik, B. (2016). A preliminary study on the regenerative construction project management concept for enhancing sustainability performance of the construction industry. *International Journal of Construction Management*. DOI: 10.1080/15623599.2016.1222665

Sertyesilisik, B., & Sertyesilisik, E. (2016). Eco industrial Development: As a Way of Enhancing Sustainable Development. *Journal of Economic Development, Environment and People*, *5*(1), 6–27. doi:10.26458/jedep.v5i1.133

Sertyesilisik, B., & Sertyesilisik, E. (2017). Ways of Fostering Green Economy and Green Growth. In W. L. Filho, D. M. Pociovalisteanu, & A. Al-Amin (Eds.), *Sustainable Economic Development. World Sustainability Series*. Cham: Springer. doi:10.1007/978-3-319-45081-0_3

Solis, B. (2017). *The definition of digital transformation*. Retrieved on December 22, 2017, from: http://www.briansolis.com/2017/01/definition-of-digital-transformation/

Sung, T. K. (2015). The creative economy in global competition. *Technological Forecasting and Social Change*, *96*, 89–91. doi:10.1016/j.techfore.2015.04.003

The STEM Education Coalition. (2017). Retrieved on January 3, 2018, from: http://www.stemedcoalition.org/stem-ed-coalition-activities/legislation/

The White House Office of the Press Secretary. (2017). *Presidential Memorandum for the Secretary of Education*. Retrieved on November 7, 2017, from: https://www.whitehouse.gov/the-press-office/2017/09/25/memorandum-secretary-education

United Nations. (2015). *World urbanization prospects*. New York: Department of Economic and Social Affairs. Retrieved on January 1, 2017, from: http://esa.un.org/unpd/wup/Publications/Files/WUP2014-Report.pdf

USA Department of Education Office of Innovation and Improvement. (2016). *STEM 2026 A vision for innovation in STEM education*. Retrieved on February 22, 2017, from: https://innovation.ed.gov/files/2016/09/AIR-STEM2026_Report_2016.pdf

Wärmark, K. (2015). Assessment of water footprint for civil construction projects. The Department of Aquatic Sciences and Assessment, Swedish University of Agricultural Sciences (SLU) UPTEC W15 018, Digitally published at the Department of Earth Sciences, Uppsala University, Uppsala.

Weiller, C., & Neely, A. (2013). *Business Model Design in an Ecosystem Context*. Cambridge, UK: University of Cambridge.

Zhuhadar, L., Thrasher, E., Marklin, S., & de Pablos, P. O. (2017). The next wave of innovation-Review of smart cities intelligent operation systems. *Computers in Human Behavior*, *66*, 273–281. doi:10.1016/j.chb.2016.09.030

Ziemnowicz, J. (2010). *Joseph A. Schumpeter and Innovation*. Retrieved on April 11, 2017, from: https://link.springer.com/content/pdf/10.1007/978-1-4614-3858-8_476.pdf

Zygiaris, S. (2013). Smart city reference model: Assisting planners to conceptualize the building of smart city innovation ecosystems. *J. Knowl. Econ.*, *4*(2), 217–231. doi:10.100713132-012-0089-4

KEY TERMS AND DEFINITIONS

Circular Economy: Economy aiming to reduce environmental footprint of the production processes enabling eco-industrial development fostered by the eco-industrial zones where the companies share their experiences and use their outputs in their production processes.

Dematerialization: Dematerialization is about decreasing the amount of the material used in the product without scarifying from the quality. Innovation can enhance dematerialization. Dematerialization can result in enhanced quality, reduced cost, and reduced environmental footprint. It can act as a competitive advantage for the companies and its impact's magnitude can grow with the quantities produced.

Elasticity of Demand: Degree of changes in the willingness of the potential customers to buy a particular product due to the changes in the product's price.

Gross Domestic Information and Innovation Impact: Gross domestic information and innovation impact is the impact of the domestically produced information and innovation.

Gross Domestic Information and Innovation Value: Gross domestic information and innovation value is the value of the domestically produced information and innovation.

Information Intensive Production: The decision on the technology type used in the production process is shifted from the trade-off between labor intensive and capital-intensive production to the trade-off among labor intensive, capital intensive and information intensive production as ICT and IT became production factors.

Resilient Supply Chain: Supply chain which can continue performing its functions and fulfilling its duties despite of the disasters or adverse conditions.

Sustainable Economy: Sustainable economy is the economy having zero adverse impacts to the environment and fostering next generation's survival and the nature's regeneration.

Chapter 11
Determinants of Access and Utilization of Climate Services Among Vulnerable Communities:
A Case Study of Isoko Communities in Delta State, Nigeria

Andrew Onwuemele
Nigerian Institute for Social and Economic Research, Nigeria

ABSTRACT

Changes in climate have caused impacts on natural and human systems. These impacts affect poor people's lives through impacts on livelihoods and the destruction of homes. In Delta State, Nigeria, the impacts of climate change are real. Adaptation has been identified as the key to reducing the impacts of climate change. However, successful adaptation depends on use of climate services. While climate services are essential to adaptation, the services do not always reach the users who need it most. This chapter analyzes factors influencing access and utilization of climate services in Delta State. The chapter utilizes the survey research while data were analyzed using both descriptive and inferential statistics. Findings show a low utilization of climate service. The determinants of access and utilization of climate services include income, educational attainments, access to ICT facilities, extension agents, and the level of local climate variability. The chapter calls for awareness creation on the importance of climate services.

INTRODUCTION

In recent decades, changes in climatic conditions have caused impacts on natural and human systems on all continents and across the oceans (IPCC, 2014). These impacts affect poor people's lives directly through impacts on livelihoods, reductions in crop yields, destruction of homes and indirectly through increased in food prices and food insecurity. These impacts also exacerbate other stressors in the envi-

DOI: 10.4018/978-1-5225-5787-6.ch011

ronment with negative implications for livelihoods especially those that rely on natural resources such as agriculture. According to the Nigerian Meteorological Agency [NIMET] (2008), which is the agency charged with the responsibility of providing climate information, Nigeria's climate is already changing based on the assessment of the Nigerian climate over the period 1941 to 2000. The report noted the following changes in climatic condition of Nigeria over the period:

- **Rainfall:** The report demonstrated that during the period 1941 to 2000, the combination of late onset and early cessation shortened the length of the rainy season in most parts of the country. Between 1941 and 2000, annual rainfall decreased by 2-8 mm across most of the country, but increased by 2-4 mm in a few places (e.g., Port Harcourt) (NIMET, 2008).
- **Temperature:** Furthermore, it shows that from 1941 to 2000, there was evidence of long-term temperature increase in most parts of the country. The main exception was in the Jos area, where a slight cooling was recorded. The most significant increases were recorded in the extreme north-east (Maiduguri), extreme northwest (Sokoto) and extreme southwest (Ibadan), where average temperatures rose by 1.4-1.9oC (NIMET, 2008). With respect to climate change future projection in Nigeria, several scenario analyses have been done by the Climate Systems Analysis Group (CSAG) at the University of Cape Town in South Africa, Department for International Development (DFID) and the Maplecroft Company. Using statistical downscaling method to extrapolate the empirical data of about 40 meteorological stations in the Nigeria, CSAG suggest a general trend of rising temperature from 2.0 – 2.2OC from south to north for the period 2046 – 2065, with a much more rapid increase in the range of 3.5 – 4.5OC at the end of the 21st century.

In view of the projected climate disruption precipitated by high levels of Greenhouse Gases (GHG) emissions, adaptation is seen as a necessary strategy at all scales to mitigate the impacts of climate change. Hallegatte et al. (2015) notes that between today and 2030, good climate-informed development will give the best chance for warding off increases in poverty due to climate change. This clearly demonstrates the importance of climate services in climate change adaptation. Climate services are scientifically based information and products that enhance users' knowledge and understanding about the impacts of climate on their decisions and actions (American Meteorological Society, 2015).

Climate services deliver data, statistical analyses, tools, and other information resources about historical weather patterns and expected future climate conditions including temperature and precipitation scenarios, sea-level changes and their potential impacts on agriculture, infrastructure, health, and other sectors (USAID, 2013). It has been shown to be useful in planning various activities that depend on climate information. In the agriculture sector, farmers are able to select more effective planting times, and choose the most appropriate crops for the coming season. In the health sector, it is used in designing early warning systems to improve surveillance on diseases affected by climate conditions (such as Malaria, Dengue Fever, and so forth) and help mitigate against the suffering resulting from weather extremes such as heat waves and winter cold, and urban smog events (Nyenzi & Malone, 2005; Ayubu, Malongo, Siza, & Respickius, 2012). In the construction industry, planners and engineers use long-term climate forecasts to decide where buildings should be sited as floodplains move, or how to design bridges to ensure they can withstand increasingly heavy storms (McMichael *et al* 2003; Patz, 2002).

While climate information services are essential to help address extremes climatic events in a changing climate, the information does not always reach the users who need it most (WMO, 2006; Suarez, 2009; Onwuemele, 2013). Tall et al. (2012) noted that climate services had been previously underutilized for several reasons. These include the existence of information gap between critical stakeholders in the use of climate services, cultural barriers reinforced by difficulties in changing from a mindset of disaster response to preparedness and early action, lack of sufficient funding from donor agencies, too much technicality attached to provided climate services which limits ability of final users to properly decode them, and non-salience and reliability of provided information. The above issues emphasize the fact that in many instances, despite some previously relayed climatic services, preparedness of people to ensure mitigation of any welfare losses as a result of climatic hazards is often limited (Suarez, 2009; Tall et al., 2012).

As noted previously, the Nigerian Meteorological Agency (NMET) has the mandate to provide climate services, Apart from NMET, academic institutions such as universities, non-governmental organizations and research institutions are other main sources of climate services in Nigeria (Onwuemele, 2013). Despite the availability of these institutions and their services, the devastating impacts emanating from climate related hazards such as flooding in the last decade cast doubts in the accessibility and utilization of climate services by vulnerable communities in the study area.

One region in Nigeria that is vulnerable to climate change is Isoko land in the Niger-Delta. Isoko communities are noted for high agricultural activities but highly vulnerable to climate change impacts especially flooding and suffered severe impacts during the 2012 flood disaster in Nigeria (Onwuemele, 2013). The factors determining the level of access and utilization of climate services among vulnerable communities in Isoko land have not been fully investigated. It is on this premise that this study aims at identifying the factors influencing access and utilization of climate services among vulnerable communities in Isoko land in Delta state, Nigeria.

Goal and Objectives of the Study

The goal of this chapter is to identify the factors influencing access and utilization of climate services among vulnerable communities in Isoko land of Delta State, Nigeria. The specific objectives are to:

1. Identify the socio-economic characteristics of the respondents in the study area
2. Determine the awareness level of climate services among the respondents and their sources of information
3. Ascertain the extent of utilization of climate services among the respondents
4. Determine the socio-economic variables influencing access to climate services among vulnerable communities in the study area
5. Proffer policy recommendation to improve access to climate services

Hypothesis of the Study

There is no significant relationship between the socio-economic characteristics of respondents and their accessibility and utilization of climate service in Isoko land Delta State, Nigeria.

CONCEPTUAL FRAMEWORK AND LITERATURE REVIEW

A climate service is a decision aide derived from climate information that assists individuals and organizations in society to make improved ex-ante decision-making (Tall, 2013). A climate service requires appropriate and iterative engagement to produce a timely advisory that end-users can comprehend and which can aid their decision-making and enable early action and preparedness. Climate services need to be provided to users in a seamless manner and, most of all, need to respond to user requirements (Hellmuth et al., 2011). Climate services are essential for adaptation to climate variability and change.

In 2009, the World Climate Conference 3, attended by more than 2, 500 participants from more than 150 countries, including 13 Heads of State and Government and 81 Ministers, decided to establish a Global Framework for Climate Services (GFCS) to strengthen the production, availability, delivery, and application of science -based climate prediction and services. This only attests to the importance of climate services to successful climate change adaptation and sustainable development. Climate services include the use of simple information like historical climate data sets as well as more complex products such as predictions of weather elements on monthly, seasonal or decadal timescales, also making use of climate projections according to different greenhouse gas emission scenarios (World Meteorological Organization, 2011).

Various applications of climate services have been identified to include helping farmers to determine which crops to plant or whether to reduce livestock numbers if a drought is forecast, helping engineers to make decisions on where to invest in disaster mitigation measures such as dams, where to locate buildings, which construction methods to use and how much heating and cooling is needed for critical infrastructure, helping in the health sectors when and where disease outbreaks are likely to occur, helping water engineers to guide major investment decisions relating to long-term water management such as whether and where to build new reservoirs, among others (World Meteorological Organization, 2011).

The framework of analyses of determinants of access and utilization of climate services is based on the Ziervogel, (2004) framework for assessing how forecast information is integrated into decisions. It begins with the premise that people are not always optimizing and rational and so idealized decision-making models will never be achieved (Clark & Marshall 2002). By implication, households in vulnerable communities will not all make the same decisions in the same way and in isolation (Weber & Sonka 1994). It therefore builds on the notion of 'bounded rationality'. It holds that the decisions people make are shaped by limited knowledge, cognitive capacity, resources and the structure of the environment in which decisions occur (Simon, 1957).

These factors are seen as filters in determining what the response to new information will be. Fischhoff (1994) identified four steps for addressing the problem of forecast integration into household decision making. The first step is the delivery or dissemination of the forecast. If the household receives the forecast, the second step occurs where filters are applied that either encourage or discourage further consideration of the forecast. The filters may include the importance placed on the forecast by households, household's available resources, seasonal forecast conflicts or alignment with household's traditional climate forecasts and local environmental indicators.

Other filters might be a function of the perceived options that exist for responding to the forecast that are based on the history of decision making, the perceived riskiness of using the information and the success or failure of past decisions (Weber & Sonka 1994). If the filters allow for the forecast to be adopted, then in Step 3 decisions need to be made on how to use the information. Finally, in Step 4 the impact of the decisions made in response to the forecast are assessed. These can be positive, negative or no impact. The results from Step 4 (the impacts) become one of the filters for future years. The numerous constraints associated with accessing and utilization of the forecast can be broadly separated into problems of forecast delivery and problems with using the forecast.

The first problems are those of dissemination, include the mechanisms for delivery, the timing, and the message that is conveyed. The credibility of the forecast, built on the accuracy of past forecasts and the forecast communicators' reputation, can also restrict uptake (Patt 2000; Patt & Gwata 2002). Thus, socio-economic and physical environments are underlying filters that affect how households will access and utilize new information about the climate. Currently, the primary source of climate data is observation by ground-based weather stations across the continent. The main strength of these station observations is that they give the true measurements of the climate variable of interest.

However, in many parts of Africa stations are sparse, declining in number, and unevenly distributed. For example, while the World Meteorological Organization (WMO) recommends a minimum of one rainfall station for every 15 to 25 km depending on geography, the current station coverage in Africa is a small and declining fraction of this requirement. Compounding this problem, the distribution of existing stations is uneven, with most located in cities and towns along major roads. As a result, coverage tends to be worse in rural areas, exactly where livelihoods may be most vulnerable to climate variability and climate change (International Research Institute for Climate and Society, 2016).

Several scholars have over the years examined the applications and impacts of climate services in diverse sectors. One of the most widely reported application of climate services was Cyclone Phailin, which tore through the Indian states of Odisha and Andhra Pradesh on October 18, 2013. It was the equivalent of a category 5 hurricane as strong as Hurricane Katrina, which devastated the US Gulf Coast in 2005 with a death toll of 1,836 (Federal Emergency Management Agency, 2005). Due to climate services utilization by the Indian Government which led to the evacuation of more than 800,000 people from coastal areas, the casualties figures were as low as 21; however, that number was far fewer than the 10,000 people who died in a storm in the same area in 1999 (United Methodist Committee on Relief (UMCOR), 2013).

In his study, Ritchie et al. (2004) found that the use of streamflow forecasts significantly increases the amount of water available for instream flows/environmental purposes in the Murray-Darling River Basin in Australia, while maintaining the amount of water needed by irrigators. Similarly, Steinemann (2006) examined the use of seasonal precipitation forecasts by water resource managers in Georgia to decide whether to pay farmers to suspend irrigation in forecasted drought years. Results indicates that the economic benefits associated with the use of these forecasts included US$100 –350 million in mitigated agricultural losses in state-declared drought years and US$5–30 million in savings to the state in non-drought years.

In the energy sector, studies have demonstrated the value of short -term and seasonal forecasts. For instance, Hamlet et al. (2002) found that the use of stream flow forecasts increases energy production from major Columbia River hydropower dams by 5.5 million MWh/year, resulting in an average increase in annual revenue of approximately US$153 million per year. Additionally, the Block (2011) study shows that the use of forecasts to manage hydropower operations in Ethiopia produces cumulative decadal benefits ranging from US$1 to US$6.5billion, compared to a climatological (no forecast) approach. In the transportation sector, the use of climate services also results in increased revenues and voided costs for transportation industries and/or public agencies. Frei et al. (2012) found that the use of meteorological information by the road transportation sector in Switzerland generates an economic benefit of $56.1 to $60.1million per year in reduced government spending, and an additional $14.2 to $25.3 million per year in value added.

Stewart et al. (2004) found that improved short-term precipitation forecasts can help road supervisors improve their allocation of resources and their efficiency in snow removal activities on the New York Thruway. In disaster risk management, studies show that climate services help lower the social and economic costs of extreme events, including floods and hurricanes, Hallegatte (2012) estimated that in Europe, hydro-meteorological information and early warning systems save several hundreds of lives per year, and avoid between US$596 million and US$3.5 billion of disaster asset losses per year.

In the above review, there is increasing recognition that climate service has a central role in attaining sustainable development of nations. Summarily, while several scholars have examined the benefits of the utilization of climate services, there are little or no studies examining the determinants of access to climate services which is one of the preconditions for application and utilization of climate services especially in a developing country such as Nigeria. This is the *raison de etre* of the present study.

MATERIALS AND METHOD

Description of the Study Area

Location: The Isoko land of Delta State in the Niger-Delta is defined as the geographical unit situated between Latitudes 5⁰, 13', 05'' and 5⁰, 37', 55'' north of the equator, and between Longitudes 6⁰, 03', 20'' and 6⁰, 26', 45'' east of the Greenwich Meridian (Figure 1). The area is bounded in the west by Ughelli North and Ughelli South Local Government Areas of Delta State, in the north by Ndokwa West Local Government Area and in the east by Ukwani Local Government Area. It is bounded in the south by Patani Local Government Area and in the Southeast by River Focados. Politically, the Isoko area of Delta State is made up of two Local Government Areas, namely: Isoko North and Isoko South

Based on the 2006 censuses, Isoko land had a total population of 371,867 made up of 186,211 males and 185,656 females (NPC, 2007). Primary economic activities include farming, fishing, oil mining, sand mining and lumbering. Secondary activities include modern manufacturing and oil refining. Tertiary activities include services such as banking, communication, marketing and transportation services.

The Physical Background

1. **Relief and Drainage:** Isoko land is located on a flood plain with a network of rivers. The area is made up of two distinct relief zones. They are the River Flood Plain zone, which comprises the upper riverine plain that extends from the lower River Niger towards upper Bomadi axis and the poorly drained transitional lower riverine plain. This zone is characterised by a swampy terrain with some small rivers forming tributaries of the River Niger.The second zone is the higher well-drained plain in the north. This zone extends to the River Ase, which drains into the Focados River. This zone covers the northern part of the region.
2. **Climate:** The region experiences high rainfall and high relative humidity most of the year. Isoko land has an average annual rainfall of about 1200-4500mm. The climate is humid equatorial and is marked by two distinct seasons, the Dry and Rainy seasons which is influenced by two air masses, namely, the South Monsoon Trade Wind associated with moisture and which blows across the

Figure 1. Map of Isoko land

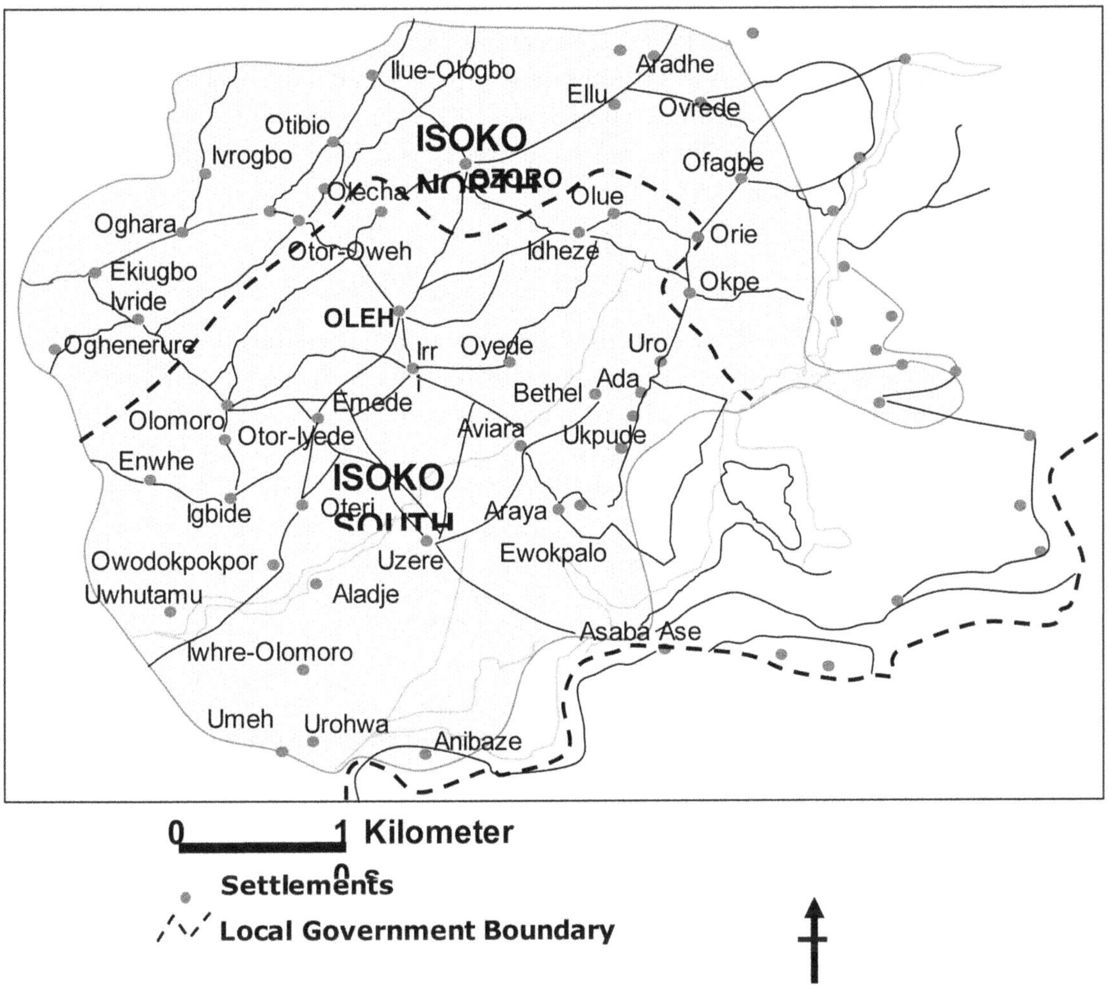

Southern Atlantic Ocean. The other wind is the Northeast Trade Wind from the Sahara Desert associated with Harmattan. The Dry season lasts from about November to April and is significantly marked by the cool "harmarttan" dusty haze from the north-east winds. The Rainy season spans from May to October with a brief dry spell in August. Temperature increases from the south to the north. Average daily temperature is about $30^{0c.}$

The cross-sectional survey design was adopted for the study. The population of the study consists of household heads in Isoko communities in Delta State. Eight communities (Uzere, Umeh/Erohwa, Olomoro, Irri, Otibio, Orie, Ofagbe, Ovrede) were randomly selected from a list of communities in Isoko land. Thirty (30) copies of structured questionnaire were randomly administered to each of the selected community. A total of two hundred and forty (240) copies were administered in all. Data for the study were obtained through the questionnaire administration.

In addition, content analysis was carried out on key official documents of NMET which is the officially recognized climate services agency in Nigeria. Both descriptive and inferential statistics were employed in the analysis of the data that were collected. Objectives 1, 2, 3 and 5 were achieved using mean, frequency distribution and percentages, while logistic regression was employed to analyse the relationship between the socio-economic characteristics of farmers and their accessibility to climate services (objective 4). Both the descriptive and inferential statistics were performed by the use of Statistical Packages of the Social Sciences (SPSS).

Model Specification

Binary choice models are commonly used when outcomes are divided into two categories. For this study, the logit model, which is one type of binary choice model, was adopted which produced the t-ratios that were compared with t-critical values to test the hypothesis of the study, which states that there is no significant relationship between the socio-economic characteristics of farmers and their accessibility to climate services. Logit regression analysis is a unit/multivariate technique that allows for estimating the probability that an event occurs or not, by predicting a binary dependent outcome of a set of independent variables. For instance, if a linear probability model is given as:

$$P_i = E\left(Y = 1 \mid X_i\right) = \beta_1 + \beta_2 X_i . \quad (1)$$

where X is the explanatory variable and $Y = 1$ means that the outcome is positive, while 0 imply otherwise. A representation of equation (1) given as in equation (2) below is the (cumulative) logistic distribution function, where the value of Z_i ranges from $-\infty$ to $+\infty$; and $\mathrm{P_i}$ ranged between 0 and 1;.

$$\mathrm{P_i} \text{ is non-linearly related to } \mathrm{Z_i} \left(\text{i.e.} P_i X_i\right) E\left(Y = 1 \mid X_i\right) = \frac{1}{1 + \exp\left[-\left(\beta_1 + \beta_2 X_i\right)\right]} = \frac{1}{1 + \exp\left(-\dot{Z}_1\right)}$$

(2)where $Z_i = \beta_1 + \beta_2 X_i$.

The logistic distribution in equation (2) satisfied the two conditions required for a probability model. The two conditions are (i) as X increases, $P_i = E\left(Y = 1 \mid X_i\right)$ increases but never steps outside the 0-1 interval and (ii) the relationship between P_i and X_i is non-linear, that is, it approaches zero at slower rates as X_i get small and approaches one at slower rates as X get very large.

Rearranging and taking natural log of equation (3) will result in:

$$L_i = \ln\left[P_i / \left(1 - P_i\right)\right] = Z_i = \beta_1 + \beta_2 X_i \quad (3)$$

L in equation (3) is called the logit, it is the log of odds ratio that is linear in X and also in the parameters.

The dependent variable for this study is the access to climate services from the Nigerian metrological Servicers (NMET). The dependent variable, access to climate services, is a dummy variable which takes the value of 1 if respondents have access or 0 if otherwise. The independent explanatory variables include:

$\mathrm{X_1}$ =Age (measured in years)

X_2 = sex (dummy variable, 1 for male, 0 for female)
X_3= Marital status (dummy variable, married=1, single =0)
X_4= Education level (Number of years spent in school)
X_5= Income (Naira)
X_6= household size (Number of people in household)
X_7= Access to electricity (yes=1; No=0
X_8= location of respondents whether urban or rural (Urban=1; Rural 0)
X_9=membership of cooperatives (membership of association=1; not a member=0)
X_{10}=access to extension agents (having access =1 no access=0)
X_{11}=access to ICT (having access to ICT=1; no access=0)
$X_{12.}$ = Participation in workshops and conferences (participation=1; no participation =0)
X_{13} = level of local climate variability (Highly variable =1; little variability)

RESULTS AND DISCUSSION

The result shows that the majority (66.3%) of the respondents were males while average age of the respondents is 46 years of age. Result further shows that 76.5 per cent of the respondents are married with an average household size of 5.8. Results also indicate that respondents are fairly literate as about 44.4 per cent of the respondents had primary education, 16.8 per cent had secondary educational qualification and 22.4 per cent of the respondents had tertiary educational qualification while 16.3 per cent of the respondents had no formal educational qualification.

Income is generally low as 16.3 per cent of the respondents earned about N10,000 ($27.7) per month. The mean income of households in the sampled population is N25, 561 per month. If poverty is defined globally as living below the equivalent of US$1.00 per capita / day, then given an average household size of 5.8 at an exchange rate of N360 to a dollar, the average family will need to earn about N62, 640 (US$174) to live above the poverty line. The implication of this is that the people in the study area are living below the poverty line which is one of the major factors contributing to low adaptation and vulnerability to climate change impacts.

Awareness, Access and Utilization of Climate Services

Adequate knowledge and awareness of the existence of climate services is one of the preconditions for accessing and utilization of climate services for climate change adaptation practices. Hence, the chapter attempt to determine the extent of awareness of climate services among vulnerable households in the study area. Figure 2 shows that the majority (60.0%) of the respondents are not aware of the existence of climate services in the study area. Only 30 per cent of the respondents are aware of the existence of climate services. Climate services awareness is much needed for public access and utilization of climate services in planning for adaptation to climate change impacts among vulnerable communities. In this regard, public education is critical in raising levels of awareness of the existence and importance of climate services among vulnerable population.

Despite the importance of climate services in climate change adaptation among vulnerable communities, only 31.2% of the respondents in the study area are using climate services in planning for adaptation while the majority noted that they are not using climate services (Figure 3). The above findings

Table 1. Socioeconomic characteristics of respondents

Variables	No. of Respondents	Percentage
Sex:		
Male	130	66.3
Female	66	33.7
Age in Years:		
21-30	19	9.7
31-40	49	25.0
41-50	40	20.4
51-60	51	26.0
61-70 Mean =46.07 Years	37	18.9
Marital Status:		
Married	150	76.5
Single	20	10.2
Divorced	12	6.1
Separated	1	0.5
Widowed	13	6.6
Household Size (No. of Persons):		
1-3	32	16.3
4-6	97	49.6
7-9	36	18.5
10 -12 Mean =5.8 persons	31	15.6
Education Level (No. of years spent in School):		
0(No formal education)	32	16.3
1-6	87	44.4
7-12	33	16.8
13-18 Mean =9.6 Years	44	22.4
Income of Respondents Per Month Per Household:		
1000- 10, 000	33	16.9
11, 000-20, 000	54	27.4
21, 000-30, 000	52	26.4
31, 000-40, 000	15	7.8
41, 000-50, 000	10	5.2
51, 000-60,000 Mean Income = N25, 561	32	16.3

Source: Field Survey, 2017

Figure 2. Awareness of the existence of climate services

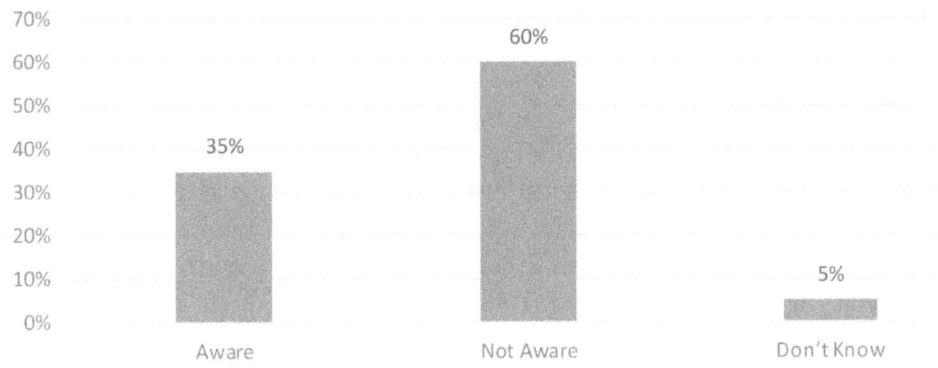

not only confirm the fact that there is poor access to climate services, but it also indicates that there is poor utilization of climate services in the study area. This finding is supported by Tall *et al.* (2012) who indicate that there is gross underutilization of climate services particularly in the developing countries including Nigeria. Among the reasons advanced are the absence of sustained dialogue between climate services providers and end users and the information provided by climate services providers was largely incomprehensible to decision maker/disaster manager (Onwuemele, 2013; Onwuemele, 2014).

Sources of Climate Information in Nigeria

Results indicate that the Nigerian Meteorological Agency (NIMET) has the mandate to monitor weather and climate in Nigeria and provide meteorological information for sustainable development and safety of life and property in the country. Therefore, in response to this mandate the Agency produces the rainfall prediction annually and presents it as the Seasonal Rainfall Prediction (SRP) in the first quarter of every year. Apart from NIMET, academic institutions such as universities, non-governmental organizations and research institutions are other main sources of climate information in Nigeria.

Some institutions created by the government such as Special Climate Change Unit (SCCU) within the Federal Ministry, Building the Nigerian Response to Climate Change (BNRCC), Nigerian Environmental Study/Action Team, among others also help in the dissemination of climate information. Some

Figure 3. Usage of climate services by respondents

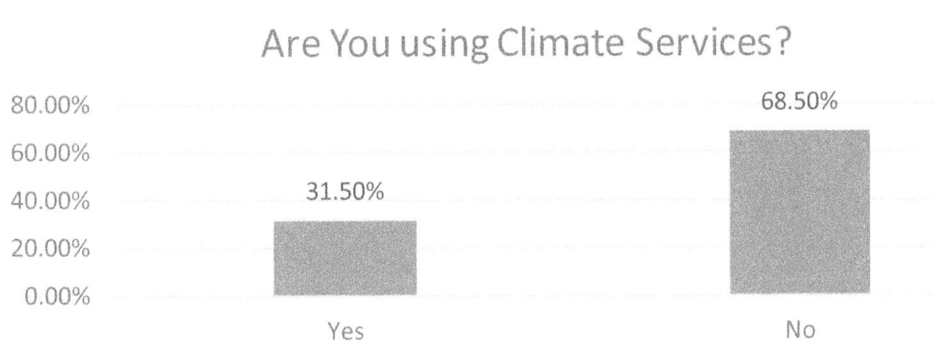

academic institutions have special centres dedicated to the provision of climate information such as the Centre for Climate Change and Fresh Water Resources at Federal University of Technology Minna and Centre for Energy, Research and Development at Obafemi Awolowo University Ile -Ife; and Abubakar Tafawa Balewa University, Bauchi, respectively.

The study further examines the formats for the dissemination of climate information in Nigeria. It is crucial to note that the format is a major factor that influences end-users' ability to comprehend any information. Results indicate that the main formats are text, audio and digital or images. The text format is in English language while the audio is usually sound produce from speakers. While English language is the official text format in Nigeria, however, the literacy level of the local communities is a major determinant of their ability to interpret the text. Table 3 shows the main channels of climate change communication in Nigeria.

Table 2 indicates three main channels of climate change communication including mass media comprising television and radio. The second channel is the print media which includes newspapers, brochures, posters and pamphlets. The last channel is the electronic media including internet and short message services (sms) support services. As noted by Lwoga et al, (2010), the use of ICT including internet, mobile phones, emails, community radio, TV, telecenters, computers are not fully utilized by community. What is obvious from the above table is the fact that the present channels of climate change communication lack indigenous or traditional content and thus at variance with the information sharing and communication strategies of households in the region as noted in Table 2. The implication of this is that local community in the study area will lack access to climate information since climate services are not disseminated through community channels.

It is instructive to note that in 2013, Nigeria's National Framework for Application of Climate Services (NFACS) was produced in line with World Metrological Organizations (WMO)'s Global Framework for Climate Services (GFCS) which aims at increasing access to weather and climate services especially by the most vulnerable communities who need it the most, while also improving their understanding to ensure more effective application of the information. The above finding only shows that there is need for more effort on the part of government in promoting access and utilization of climate services in Nigeria.

Determinants of Access and Utilization of Climate Services

Climate services, which provide timely, tailored information and knowledge to decision makers are seen as an important part of improving our capacity to manage climate-related risk. The aim of climate services is to provide people and organizations with timely, tailored climate-related knowledge and information that they can use to reduce climate-related losses and enhance benefits, including the protection of lives, livelihoods, and property. Amongst the challenges faced by vulnerable communities in Isoko land is inaccessibility to climate services. This section sought to identify the determinants and constraints to

Table 2. Channels of climate change communication in Nigeria

Channels of Climate Change Communication	Media
Mass Media	TV, Radio
Print media	Pamphlets, newspapers, brochures, posters
Electronic media	Internet, sms support services

access to climate services among vulnerable households in Isoko land in Delta State. The result of the logit regression is presented in Table 3.

The estimated values of education level (X_4), income (X_5) access to electricity (X_8), access to extension agents (X_{10}) access to ICT facilities (X_{11}) and level of local climate variability (X_{13}) significantly contributed to the probability of having access and utilization of climate services. It is of interest to note that age (X_1), gender (X_2), marital status (X_3) household size (X_6) membership of cooperative (X9), participation in workshops and conferences (X_{12}), do not significantly contribute to the likelihood of having access and utilization of climate services in the study area.

The estimated coefficient of educational level (0.549) was significant at 0.05 level of significance and its exp(b) value of 1.732 suggests that as number of years of school of the respondents increases, the odds of having access to climate service and utilization of climate services by respondents also increases. The estimated coefficient of income (0.438) was at 0.05 level of significance and its exp(b) value of 1.549 implies that as people get more income, the odds of having access to climate service and utilization of climate services by respondents increase (Table 3). The estimated coefficient of access to electricity (0.316) was also significant at 0.05 level of significance and its exp(b) value of 0.729 implies that as access to electricity increases, the odds of accessing climate service and utilization of climate services by respondents increase.

The estimated coefficient of access to extension facilities (1.545) was significant at 0.05 level of significance and its exp(b) value of 4.689 implies that those that have access to extension facilities stand a better chance of about 4.7 times odd of having access to climate services and utilization of climate services than those that do not have access to extension facilities. The estimated coefficient of access to ICT facilities (0.373) was significant at 0.05 level of significance and its exp(b) value of 1.452 implies that the more ICT facilities at the disposal of the respondents, the more likely the increase in odd of having access to climate services and utilization of climate services. The estimated coefficient of level of local climate variability (0.639) was significant at 0.05 level of significance and its exp(b) value of 0.528 implies that as the variability of local climate increases, the odd of having access to climate services and utilization of climate services increases.

The above finding is supported by Oyekale (2015) study which reveals that the probabilities of having access to weather forecasts significantly increased with access to formal education, farm income and previous exposure to climatic shocks. It is also glaring from the result that the predictors included in the model could only account for between 24 per cent and 37.3 per cent of the variance in determining the access to climate services and utilization of climate services as suggested by Hosmer and Lemeshow (0.24), Cox and Snell (0.276) and Nagelkerke (0.373).

CONCLUSION

While the impact of climate change on local community such as the study area is well acknowledged by scholars and vulnerable communities themselves, adaptation has been identified as the key to reducing the impacts of climate change on vulnerable populations. Adaptation is a process by which strategies to moderate, cope with, and take advantage of, the consequences of climate events are enhanced, developed and implemented. However, successful adaptation depends on the intelligent use of climate information services. While climate information services are essential to help address extremes climatic events in a changing climate, the information does not always reach the users who need it most. Ensuring the

Table 3. Logistic regression results of factors influencing farmer's perception of climate change

		B	S.E.	Sig.	Exp(B)
Step 1[a]	Age (X_1)	-.524	.683	.443	.592
	Sex (X_2)	.026	.368	.944	1.026
	Marital Status (X_3)	-.073	.539	.892	.930
	Education (X_4)	.549	.465	.03**	.1.732
	Income (X_5)	.231	.083	.016**	.729
	Household size (X_6)	-16.364	4397.976	.997	.000
	Access to electricity (X_7)	.316	.239	.048**	.729
	Location of respondents (X_8)	-.386	.457	.398	.680
	Membership of cooperatives (X_9)	-19.082	3753.700	.996	.000
	Access to extension agents (X_{10})	1.545	.790	.020**	4.689
	Access to ICT (X_{11})	0.373	1.125	.051**	1.452
	Participation in workshops (X_{12})	-17.112	3123.611	.896	.0123
	Level of local climate variability (X_{13})	0.639	.817	.019**	0.528
	Constant	42.500	5782.081	.994	2.863

Source: Authors compilation, 2017

availability of, and access to, high-quality climate services tailored to address the vulnerability of local communities is a necessity in the study area.

This chapter identified the factors that determines access and utilization of climate information services in a vulnerable population. In the light of the findings, the chapter made the following recommendation.

1. There is the need for the local authority to implement more awareness and campaign programme to raise awareness on the importance of climate services for success climate change adaptation at the community level.
2. It is also important to for local authority to increase community access to electricity, extension facilities and ICT facilities to enhance their access and utilization of climate services.

REFERENCES

AMS. (2015). *Climate Services. A Policy Statement of the American Meteorological Society*. Retrieved on May 30, 2017 from: https://www.ametsoc.org/ams/index.cfm/about-ams/ams-statements/statements-of-the-ams-in-force/climate-services1/

Ayubu, J. C., Malongo, R. S. M., Siza, D. T., & Respickius, C. (2012). Understanding Farmers Information Communication Strategies for Managing Climate Risks in Rural Semi-Arid Areas, Tanzania. *International Journal of Information and Communication Technology Research, 12*(2), 45–58.

Block, P. (2011). Tailoring Seasonal Climate Forecasts for Hydropower Operations. *Hydrology and Earth System Sciences*, *15*(4), 1355–1368. doi:10.5194/hess-15-1355-2011

Clark, G. L., & Marshall, J. (2002). *Decision-making: models of the real-world and expertise*. Paper presented at National Association of Pension Funds, Edinburgh, UK.

Fischhoff, B. (1994). What forecasts (seem to) mean. *International Journal of Forecasting*, *10*(3), 387–403. doi:10.1016/0169-2070(94)90069-8

Frei, T. (2009). Economic and Social Benefits of Meteorology and Climatology in Switzerland. *Meteorological Applications*, n/a. doi:10.1002/met.156

Hallegatte, S. (2012). *A Cost-Effective Solution to Reduce Disaster Losses in Developing Countries: Hydrometeorological Services, Early Warning, and Evacuation*. Policy Research Working Paper Series 6058. Washington, DC: The World Bank.

Hallegatte, S., Bangalore, L., Bonzanigo, M., Fay, T., Kane, U., Narloch, J., … Vogt-Schilb, A. (2015). *Shock Waves: Managing the Impacts of Climate Change on Poverty*. Climate Change and Development Series. Washington, DC: World Bank. doi:.10.1596/978-1-4648-0673-5

Hamlet, A. F., Huppert, D., & Lettenmaier, D. P. (2002). Economic Value of Long-lead Streamflow Forecasts for Columbia River hydropower. *Journal of Water Resources Planning and Management*, *128*(2), 91–101. doi:10.1061/(ASCE)0733-9496(2002)128:2(91)

Hellmuth, M. E., Mason, S. J., Vaughan, C., van Aalst, M. K., & Choularton, R. (Eds.). (2011). A Better Climate for Disaster Risk Management. Columbia University.

International Research Institute for Climate and Society. (2016). The enacts approach: Transforming climate services in Africa one country at a time. IRI Technical Note No. IRI-TR/05/1.

IPCC. (2014). *Climate Change 2014: Impacts, Adaptation, and Vulnerability. Part A: Global and Sectoral Aspects. Contribution of Working Group II to the Fifth Assessment Report of IPCC*. Cambridge, UK: Cambridge University Press.

Lwoga, E.T., Ngulube, P., & Stilwell, C. (2010). Understanding indigenous knowledge: Bridging the knowledge gap through a knowledge creation model for agricultural development. *SA Journal of Information Management, 12*(1). DOI: 10.4102ajim.v12i1.436

McMichael, A. J., Campbell-Lendrum, D. H., Corvalan, C. F., Ebi, K. L., Githeko, A., Scheraga, J. D., & Wooward, A. (2003). *Climate Change and Human Health- Risks and Responses*. Geneva: World Health Organization.

NIMET (2008). *Nigeria Climate Review Bulletin 2007*. Nigerian Meteorological Agency.

NPC (National Planning Commission). (2004). *Meeting everyone's needs*. Abuja, Nigeria: National Economic Empowerment and Development Strategy.

Nyenzi, B., & Malone, L. (2005). *Challenges of Climate Prediction and its Application to the Agriculture Sector*. Retrieved on May 20, 2017, from: https://www.wmo.int/pages/.../mod5_climate_pred_apps_ag_sector.doc

Onwuemele, A. (2013). *Understanding Information Communication Strategies among Farmers for Effective Utilization of Climate Research and Forecast in the Niger-Delta, Nigeria*. Paper Presented at the African Climate Conference, Arusha, Tanzania.

Onwuemele, A. (2014). Access And Utilization of Climate Services Among Vulnerable Communities in Nigeria: A Case Study of Isoko Communities in Delta State. *Journal of Environmental Issues & Agriculture in Developing Countries*, *6*(2-3), 15–24.

Onyekale, A. S. (2015). Access to Risk Mitigating Weather Forecasts and Changes in Farming Operations in East and West Africa: Evidence from a Baseline Survey. *Sustainability*, *7*(11), 14599–14617. doi:10.3390u71114599

Patt, A. (2000). *Communicating probabilistic forecasts to decision makers: a case study of Zimbabwe. Belfer Center for Science and International Affairs (BCSIA) Environment and Natural Resources Program, Kennedy School of Government*. Cambridge, MA: Harvard University.

Patt, A., & Gwata, C. (2002). Effective seasonal climate forecast applications: Examining constraints for subsistence farmers in Zimbabwe Global Environmental Change. *Human and Policy Dimensions*, *12*(3), 185–195. doi:10.1016/S0959-3780(02)00013-4

Patz, J. A. (2002). A human disease indicator for the effects of recent global climate change. *Proceedings of the National Academy of Sciences of the United States of America*, *99*(20), 12506–12508. doi:10.1073/pnas.212467899 PMID:12271143

Ritchie, J. W., Zammit, C., & Beal, D. (2004). Can seasonal climate forecasting assist in catchment water management decision-making? A case study of the Border Rivers catchment in Australia. *Agriculture, Ecosystems & Environment*, *104*(3), 553–565. doi:10.1016/j.agee.2004.01.029

Steinemann, A. C. (2006). Using Climate Forecasts for Drought Management. *Journal of Applied Meteorology and Climatology*, *45*(10), 1353–1361. doi:10.1175/JAM2401.1

Stewart, T. R., Pielke, R. Jr, & Nath, R. (2004). Understanding user Decision Making and the Value of Improved Precipitation Forecasts: Lessons from a case study. *Bulletin of the American Meteorological Society*, *85*(2), 223–235. doi:10.1175/BAMS-85-2-223

Suarez, P. (2009). *Linking climate knowledge and Decisions: Humanitarian Challenges*. The Pardee Papers 7.

Tall, A. (2013). *What do we mean by Climate Services?* Intergovernmental Board on Climate Services. Retrieved on June 2, 2015, from: https://library.wmo.int/opac/doc_num.php?explnum_id=3224

Tall, A., Mason, S. J., van Aalst, M., Suarez, P., Ait-Chellouche, Y., Diallo, A. A., & Braman, L. (2012). Using Seasonal Climate Forecasts to Guide Disaster Management: The Red Cross Experience during the 2008 West Africa Floods. *International Journal of Geophysics*, *2012*, 12–25. doi:10.1155/2012/986016

UMCOR. (2013). *Disaster Risk Preparedness Saves Lives in India*. Retrieved on July 15, 2014, from: http://www.umcor.org/UMCOR/Resources/News-Stories/2013/October/1018-Disaster-

USAID. (2013). *Climate Services: Better Information for Climate-Resilient Decision Making*. Retrieved on May 30, 2017, from: http://pdf.usaid.gov/pdf_docs/PA00KJWS.pdf

Weber, E., & Sonka, S. (1994). Production and pricing decisions in cash-crop farming effects of decision traits and climate change expectations. In B. Jacobsen, D. Pedersen, J. Christensen, & P. Rasmussen (Eds.), *Farmers' decision making – a descriptive approach* (pp. 203–218). Copenhagen: European Association of Agricultural Economists.

WMO. (2006). Climate Information for Development Needs: An Action Plan for Africa, Report and Implementation Strategy. GCOS 108, WMO/TD No. 1358, Geneva

World Meteorological Organization (WMO). (2011). *Climate Knowledge for Action: a Global Framework for Climate Services–Empowering the Most Vulnerable: the Report of the High-level Taskforce for the Global Framework for Climate Services*. World Meteorological Organization.

Ziervogel, G. (2004). Targeting seasonal climate forecasts for integration into household level decisions: The case of smallholder farmers in Lesotho. *The Geographical Journal*, *170*(1), 6–21. doi:10.1111/j.0016-7398.2004.05002.x

Chapter 12
Essence of International Environmental Law to Address the Effects of Climate Change

Md. Mahfuzar Rahman Chowdhury
The Legal Care, Bangladesh

ABSTRACT

Environmental problems are enormous around the world and threaten the global environment. In most cases, these problems are caused by rapid growth of population and poverty. Climate change and sustainable development are inter-linked and are priority issues in the development continuum. Any adverse impact on the environment and biodiversity can cause the restriction of resources and limit available options. Concerted efforts of all the states can bring positive result to address the effects of climate change. Compliance with the treaty provision and sharing of resources and actions among the states can ensure proper utilization of resources and sustainable development.

INTRODUCTION

Environmental problems are enormous around the world and the same are threatening the global environment. In most cases, such problems are caused by the rapid growth of population and poverty. The uncontrolled growth of urbanization and industrialization, expansion and massive intensification of agriculture, and the destruction of forests are the root causes of environmental crises around the world. Major environmental issues include forest and agricultural degradation of land, resource depletion, environmental degradation, poor public health, loss of biodiversity, loss of resilience in ecosystems, livelihood security for the poor. The increasing rate of population in comparison to the resources availability aggravates the environmental problems. Lack of resources in developing countries causes obstacles in providing proper sanitation and clean water facilities to the public.

People are indiscriminately destroying the forests for managing their fuel and furniture as being necessitated by the overpopulation. Because of continuous growth of population, the governments cannot afford their citizens with adequate food, shelter, employment and other necessary amenities for a decent

DOI: 10.4018/978-1-5225-5787-6.ch012

livelihood. Again, the growth and expansion of the industries affect the environment for emission of greenhouse gases.

Global processes such as climate change inflict the consequences of behaviors that originate at great distances in time and space and necessitate coordinated cross-scale efforts that exceed the national economic and political capacities of poor states (Pelling, 2003). Climate change and sustainable development are inter-linked and priority issues in the development continuum. Any adverse impact on the environment and biodiversity can cause restricting the resources and limiting the options.

Sustainability: Inevitable for the Planet

Practically speaking, the issue of environmental protection is a serious concern for the sake of human survival. Global warming is unequivocal and almost certainly caused by recent human activities that have increased greenhouse gas (GHG) emissions (IPCC, 2007). The risks associated with climate change are real and at the same time highly uncertain. For instance, rising sea levels due to climate change could threaten coastal settlements with floods and storm surges. Vulnerability to the risks associated with climate change may increase the ongoing social and economic challenges. Particularly, the societies dependent on resources like agriculture and fisheries in developing countries may be exposed to severe vulnerabilities. People are engaged in effectively addressing the challenges associated with climate change and sustainable development for the sustenance of humans and other living beings in the planet.

The relationship among the natural environment, population distribution, and economic growth is inevitable. Rapid growth of population severely affects the natural resources and environment, and thereby, causes the environmental degradation. Environmental deterioration caused by the overpopulation posits the challenge of sustainable development. The availability of natural resources accelerates the process of socio-economic development and transforms a society or a nation far better. Sustainability relates to the human security. Human security has been conceptualized as: the traditional areas of military/strategic security; economic security; health care priorities; and environmental security that is primarily determined by the complex interactions between human populations and the source and sink functions of their host ecosystems (United Nations, 2000).

The World Commission on Environment and Development rightly opined, sustainable development can be pursued more easily when population size is stabilized at a level consistent with the productive capacity of the ecosystem. Sustainability arose in the 1980s to dissolve the conflicts between environmental and economic values (Dryzek, 2013) and became popular to link the environment with development (Bosselmann, 2008). The issue of sustainability demands intra-generation and inter-generation equity. The debate on sustainable development has put emphasis on social well-being, economic growth and environmental protection with special attention to environmental protection over the others. Maintaining balance and priority of aims during decision making is recognized internationally.

Sustainability includes the social, economic and environmental considerations. The principle of sustainable use has traditionally been associated with conservation of natural resources so as to prolong their exploitation (Sands & Peel, 2012). Any adverse impact on the environment and biodiversity can cause restricting the resources and limiting the options. Hence, developing new products, maintaining health of the lives would be critical, and eventually, the future generations might face obstacles in addressing problems.

It is well-agreed that the concept of sustainability has developed into a new socio-economic paradigm (United Nations, 1993). It encompasses a wide range of human activities related to the use of resources, including natural, human and financial, implying long-term continuity and ability to carry on with these activities indefinitely (Marinova & Raven, 2006). According to the UN Commission for Sustainable Development, sustainability has four dimensions: social, economic, environmental and institutional (UN CSD, 1996).

SUSTAINABILITY AND DEVELOPMENT

National security is a very popular notion and concerned with the international peace and security. The security in the 1960s was no longer simply an issue of external aggressors but also one of internal threats to stability. While national security concerns were being dominated by the threat to a state's borders and sovereignty, the environment began to take its place within the security agenda in the 1970s at the time the Club of Rome published *The Limits to Growth (*Meadows, Randers, Meadows, & Behrens, 1972*).* Alexandre Timoshenko articulates security cannot only be political or military; it must be as well ecological, economical, and social. It must ensure the fulfillment of the aspirations of humanity as a whole. Thus, the necessity of a secure environment for the survival of mankind was duly stressed in the report.

There is an essential connection between social justice and the environment (Kassiola, 2002) that casts the essence of environmental policy. Proper application of policy and regulation in respect of environmental sustainability can help earning benefits of sustainable development. The Court of Justice of the European Union (EU) has, to a certain extent, demonstrated willingness to engage in balancing exercises where commercial economic interests are involved (Hamlyn, 2015). In fact, a balancing decision making among social, economic, and environmental aspects renders development.

In 1950s and 1960s, unsustainable resource exploitation and population increases severely affected the environmental sustainability. The utilization of natural resources pursuant to the national policies became a key concern for the nation states for their economic development. In 1977, Lester Brown published a World Watch Paper under the title of *Redefining National Security* in which he criticized the militarization of the world economy and opined that the emerging threat for the mankind would be their relationship with nature.

In the 1980s, the theme of unsustainable environmental exploitation gathered pace leading to the World Conservation Union's World Conservation Strategy in 1980 (World Conservation Union, 1980) and the formation and reports of the World Commission on Environment and Development. Brundtland Report of the commission put an emphasis on an integrated approach and subsequently it became known as sustainable development.

Resources Scarcity

There is a close connection between the environmental degradation and scarcity of the resources. Population growth, spread of diseases, deforestation and soil erosion, water depletion, air pollution, rising sea levels, overcrowded regions like the Nile Delta and Bangladesh will cause tensions among the states. Population size has an intimate correlation with environmental problems such as global warming, acid rain, depletion of the ozone layer, vulnerability to epidemics, and exhaustion of soils and groundwater. The effects of an ever-growing population puts pressure on the economy and creates scarcity of ocean fishing resources, agricultural production, loss of nature and biological diversity. Because the existence of nature and mankind are inter-dependent, loss of nature and biological diversity meant a threat for the survival of humans in the planet.

The uneven spread of the natural resources around the globe generates conflicts among the states. The unsustainable exploitation of resources creates scarcity in domestic and international arena. This eventually brings environmental insecurity within and across the states. Instance can be taken from Canada and Spain in 1995 in the Turbot War to control fishing off the Atlantic Coast (Brown, Crawford, & Campeau, 2008).

Over the years, energy security has become an issue for state security. Many states are dependent on foreign energy sources and this reliance sometimes creates confusion among the states and worsens the relationships. Lack of access to clean and potable water can impact the rights to life as well as the rights to health and to adequate food. According to General Comment 15 of the Committee on Economic, Social and Cultural Rights, the human rights to water entitles everyone to sufficient, safe, acceptable, physically accessible and affordable water for personal and domestic uses.

Thus, the notion of water security indicates physical and economical access to the quality and available water. The largest usage of water is in agriculture sector across the globe though rising temperature may hamper irrigation worldwide and this may force many to find alternative employment for survival. Because water resources are a security concern, river basins like Nile, Jordan, Euphrates, Colorado have been a matter of disputes for decades. Riparian states are constantly engaged in clashes over sharing of resources.

Due to resources constraint, people will be put in a vulnerable situation and agricultural productivity will be decreased for the rise of temperature. The impacts of climate change will bring resources scarcity and population movements, eventually leading to conflict.

Climate Change and Security

The climate change-induced impacts are putting the countries in an unstable situation. Due to the rising sea level, internal displacement of people has been a commonplace. The increased frequency, scale, and intensity of floods, drought, and hurricanes will undoubtedly hit hardest in developing countries and it will be delayed to respond to those natural disasters. Estimates of millions of people displaced by climate-induced weather events are causing anguish in many states for an influx of climate migrants and the resulting stress that this would place on their economies, existing ethnic or political tensions, and their general ability to cope (Myers, 2005). The incidence of heavy rainfall may cause water-borne and vector-borne diseases in the regions.

Because of the spread of diseases, changes in biosphere, temperature, seasonal conditions, and water salinity, many species will lose their survival in the planet. Maintenance of biodiversity is essential for the lives on earth. Climate change is the sole aggravating factor for the most environmental problems and the same are the security concerns. Countries in the continents are engaged in warfare. The incidences of warfare cause ecological insecurity in addition to the human insecurity as they damage to agriculture and livelihood and at the same time destroy the environment. Additionally, warfare depletes already scarce water, food, and energy resources.

The issue of the Arctic due to the effects of climate change is quite alarming. All the five coastal states surrounding the Arctic; namely, Canada, Russia, the United States, Denmark, and Norway are concerned on the environmental, energy, and military security issues with control of the continental shelf and its abundant oil and gas resources, new fishing areas, and navigable routes. In 2009, the US

Geological Survey estimated that the Arctic contains around 13 percent of the world's 'undiscovered' oil and about 30 percent of the world's undiscovered gas (Brown, Crawford, & Campeau, 2008). The militarization of the Arctic region may cause environmental security concerns despite their reassurance of resolving continental shelf claims by virtue of a peaceful resolution through the UN Convention on the Law of the Sea (LOSC).

The exploration and exploitation of oil and gas reserves, over fishing or shipping accident in the Arctic may cause pollution and potentially create environmental security issues. Apprehending the threat to Arctic wildlife from increased traffic and resource exploitation, the World Wildlife Fund (WWF) argued, the oil spills would be virtually impossible to clean up and any spill would cause irreparable long-term damage (World Wildlife Fund, 2009). With the increase of temperature due to the climate change certain species of fishes in the Arctic will decline; thus, the waters will be opened up to greater fishing fleets and there will be a greater potential for over-exploitation.

The Antarctic area poses many environmental security concerns as the warming Arctic Oceans, albeit the Antarctic Treaty System (ATS) provides for more comprehensive environmental governance. Some states are interested to establish their claims in it while others criticize their standing, and therefore, the relationship among the states, to some extent, indicate security of the states is at stake.

The Antarctic ecosystem is being threatened for tourism. Pollution and marine shipping incidents are already a reality for the Antarctic as numbers of cruise ship accidents and oil tanker accidents took place in it. The Japanese whaling in seas around Antarctica could have serious repercussions in certain species and is arguably in violation of international law obligations under the International Convention for the Regulation of Whaling.

Environmental security includes the minimization of any harm to the ecosystems that are vital to the maintenance of biological viability and human survival. In this sense, any environmental pollution or degradation could arguably fall within the notion of environmental security. Indeed, in an early version of the International Law Commission's 1996 Draft Article on State Responsibility, the commission included a provision relating marine pollution to an international crime.

The marine ecosystem faces many threats to its health and viability, including from oil spills, nuclear and hazardous waste transport and dumping, fishing, and algal blooms. While the legal regimes for vessel source pollution are strict, it is the land-based sources of pollution that account for the greatest percentage of marine pollution but that still engender less comprehensive regulation. Vast areas of the oceans are suffering from plastics pollution, so-called 'ocean garbage patches' or 'plastic/trash vortexes,' which contain millions of tons of plastic bags, packaging, and other items.

Climate change can act as a threat to instability in some of the most volatile regions of the world, and it presents significant national security challenges for the United States (CNA Corporation, 2007). Due to climate change effects, there will be a series of disputes and the states will be embroiled in resource allocation exploitation and the United Nations may have to employ more efforts for negotiating and peace keeping efforts.

International Environmental Law

Climate change continues to dominate international environmental efforts, and thereby, the issues of sustainability and development. Environmental law continues to change and evolve, as new regulations are adopted and existing rules are amended or challenged in courts or interpreted by agencies. Therefore, the international community is experiencing many areas of relevant international legal activity as well as the breadth and complexity of international development and economic activity.

The key international environment instruments in respect of climate change issues are the UNFCCC and the Kyoto Protocol that invoke the principles of inter- and intra-generational equity, Common But Differentiated Responsibilities (CBDR), the precautionary principle, the rights of all parties to sustainable development, and the need to promote a supportive and open international economic system.

The obligation of not to causing environmental harm is widely viewed as an extension of the general international norm that prohibits a state from using its territory, or allowing others to use its territory, in a way that can harm the interests of another state. Despite the significant progress that international treaties have made on certain issues, such as regulation of the ozone layer, treaties do have particular weaknesses in effectively regulating environmental issues. States can too easily make reservations or derogations in respect of obligations as inserted in the treaty provisions that might go against the interest of individual member state(s). Therefore, the binding force or effectiveness of the treaties raises serious concern for the member states as indiscriminate activities of a single or a group of states can bring catastrophic effects for the people across the countries.

The treaty negotiations are the primary international approach to addressing climate change while the slow pace of treaty negotiations has been frustrating. Growing number of countries have integrated emission trading schemes into their national climate policies, and regional arrangements have been established to combat climate change. The essence of a functional environmental law regime for a sound global economic order has been a demand of time. Compliance with the principles as including the principle of Common But Differentiated Responsibility (CBDR) has been an urgent concern for the existence of humans and their environment in the planet.

Historical Background

International environmental law has developed through bilateral and multilateral negotiation of treaties and "soft law" instruments such as declarations and plans of action. It can be traced back to 1351 as to the conclusion of a fishery treaty between England and Castile. Subsequently, the significant development was initiated with the emergence of 1893 Pacific Fur Seal Arbitration[1] and Trail Smelter Arbitration[2]. The principle developed in Trail Smelter Arbitration is pivotal to prevent transboundary environmental harm and subsequently the same became as settled principle of customary international law. Initially, international environmental law treaties concerned protection of interests of particular states, rather than the environmental protection in common. In the late 1990s, serious concerns were expressed about growing evidence of environmental degradation that prompted to realize that environmental degradation was closely linked to unsustainable levels of economic development and population growth.

The United Nations General Assembly articulated, ...effective measures to preserve natural resources, flora and fauna should be taken at the earliest possible moment simultaneously with economic development, including industrialization, and urbanization (United Nations General Assembly, 1962). United Nations Conference on the Human Environment (UNCHE) in Stockholm in 1972 aroused an understanding that development and environmental issues are clearly inter-dependent.

In addition to UNCHE in Stockholm in 1972, the 1992 United Nations Conference on Environment and Development (UNCED) in Rio de Janeiro, the World Summit on Sustainable Development (WSSD) in Johannesburg in 2002 were significant events for the development of international environmental law and adoption of the notion of rights to development and protection of the environment. The Stockholm meeting produced a number of significant outcomes including the establishment of UNEP and the adoption of the Stockholm Declaration (UNCHE, 1972) setting out 26 Principles and an Action Plan containing 109 recommendations.

The Bruntland Report in 1987 emphasized on the need to ensure "sustainable development" that meets the needs of the present without compromising the ability of future generations to meet their own needs. The Brundtland Report led to the UNCED (the Earth Summit) in Rio de Janeiro in Brazil in 1992. The Earth Summit adopted three non-binding instruments: the Rio Declaration, the UNCED Forest Principles, and Agenda 21. In addition, the Convention on Biological Diversity and the UN Framework Convention on Climate Change were opened for signature at the Earth Summit.

Following the Earth Summit, the existence of several key principles of international environmental law including the precautionary principle, the "polluter pays" principle, common but differentiated responsibility, sustainable development reflect environmental and development concerns.

UNFCCC began to hold Conference of the Parties to address the adverse consequences of climate change. States gathered in Berlin, Germany for holding the 1st Conference of Parties from 28 March to 7 April 1995.

Essence of International Environmental Law

Despite the 1992 UN Framework Convention on Climate Change and the 1997 Kyoto Protocol, the GHG emissions continue to rise worldwide. A series of annual UNFCCC meetings could not make adequate progress. In December, 2014 The UNSG (United Nations Secretary General)'s Synthesis Report proposed six essential elements to help frame and communicate the sustainable development agenda: dignity, people, prosperity, planet, justice, and partnership. The report also argued, success of the Post-2015 Agenda will depend on community ownership and participation, the community seen as including civil society, responsible business, and governments.

Broadly speaking, climate change impacts on economics and agriculture; water; ecosystems and biodiversity; human health; coast regions; and, forced migration and conflict. A two-degree rise in global temperature will conclusively cost approximately one per cent of the world's total gross domestic product to mitigate effects (A Bad Climate for Development, 2009) of climate change. The direct impacts of climate change on developing economies include the loss of human lives, livelihoods, assets and infrastructure through extreme climatic events while the indirect impacts list inability of the poor to engage in non-agricultural sectors during simultaneously increasing both poverty and nullifying any potentially positive outcomes from macro-economic policies, trader and private sector investment (Richards, 2003).

Alternative development paths will affect future climate change, and in turn, climate change will have an impact on prospects for sustainable development (IPCC, 2001). Adaptation reduces the impact of climate stresses on human and natural systems, while mitigation lowers potential greenhouse gas emissions (Munasinghe). The study estimates that global adaptation costs range from around US$25 billion a year to well over US$100 billion by 2015-2030 (Frankauser, 2009) and the cost is likely to increase in the next years. Concerted efforts for improvement in the adaptation and mitigation scheme can render success in addressing the effects of climate change and in garnering benefits of sustainable development.

Article 4 of the UNFCCC enunciates that states parties would consider their common but differentiated responsibilities and their specific priorities to cooperate in the development and implementation of adaptation measures including transfer of technologies. Moreover, Article 10 of the Kyoto Protocol pledged to cooperate in the development, application, transfer and diffusion of environmentally sound technologies, in particular to developing countries. States need to integrate environmental consideration in planning, designing, implementing development projects for the sake of sustainability of the global environment and well-being of the humans. Article 4 of the UNFCCC specifically articulates, all the parties have responsibilities to make and implement plans for adapting to any human-induced climate change. Moreover, the developed countries shall assist developing countries to meet the costs of adapting to any adverse effects of climate change.

International Environmental Law: A Practical Look

International environmental law is a body of law comprised of global treaties, conventions, regulations and policies developed for the protection of the environment and natural resources. Specifically speaking, international environmental law began to develop as a system of rules since the 1970s and, initially, it was limited to state responsibility for trans-boundary harm, resource allocation and addressing demands of cross-border jurisdiction. Over the past few decades, there has been a rapid development of binding international agreements concerning environmental protection at both global and regional levels. The continued evolution of international environmental law is vital to global efforts to identify and respond to shared problems (Carlarne, 2014). In fact, the international environmental law has limited applicability and the same affects core development issues: poverty, water scarcity, disease, regional and political instability, global health (Walsh, 2009) that necessitates a restructuring of the foundations of modern economies, especially the energy systems.

Lack of implementation of international environmental law is a common place. For instance, the US signed the Kyoto Protocol but never ratified it; therefore, the country is not bound to comply with the quantified emission reduction commitments. Though the larger developing countries such as Brazil, China and India are parties to the Kyoto Protocol, they did not take appropriate steps on binding emissions targets of their own, pursuant to the CBDR principle. As a result, the Kyoto Protocol covered only 27 per cent of current global energy-related CO2 emissions in 2012, likely to be now even less (Rajamani, Brunnée & Doelle, 2012).

The international environmental treaties do not have any binding force. States can too easily make reservation or derogation in respect of obligation if anything goes against their interest. Furthermore, in order to take these treaties into effect, certain number of ratification being required and the same causes delay for the application of treaty provisions. Because treaties take several years to negotiate, they cannot respond quickly to the emerging environmental challenges, nor adequately protect the environment even when treaties or customary laws apply. They also lack to bind certain states whose involvement is vital to resolve specific issues.

Although numerous multilateral treaties are designed to address atmospheric and transboundary pollution, none are concentrated on the reduction of GHG emissions (Current Legal Challenges in Climate Change Justice, 2014). The international environmental instruments like the 1979 Geneva Convention on Long-range Transboundary Air Pollution, the 1985 Vienna Convention for the Protection of the Ozone Layer and its Montreal Protocol on Substances that Deplete the Ozone Layer provide international frameworks to tackle global atmospheric pollution. However, these international instruments have limited scope in terms of the reduction of the human-induced effects of climate change. For example, the 1979 Geneva Convention – the purpose of which is to prevent, reduce and control transboundary air pollution – does not provide concrete commitments to specific reductions in air pollution (Birnie., Alan., & Redgwell, 2009).

The adaptation strategies and technological and financial capacities of the states differ significantly to address the effects of climate change. Expertise and resources are more concentrated on the developed states while the developing states lag far behind. Due to the absence of expertise and resources, there is a lack of availability of information in relation to the expected impacts and potential responses to climate change in developing countries.

The UNFCCC and other international treaties have been constrained to effectively address the global mitigation and prevention of disastrous effects of climate change. On the other hand, many compliance problems emanate for weaknesses in economic, regulatory and technical capacity issues. Enforcement of these issues depends on the free-will of the states to treat as precautionary principle. Hence, due to the absence of binding force on the states, pollution and environmental degradation being frequently caused due to non-compliance with the environmental regulation as the international environmental treaties do not have any binding force to compel the states to abide by the treaty provisions. Thus, the affected states do not have that much scope to seek and avail relief.

Both the Polar Regions have seen an increase in bio-prospecting (the search for commercially exploitable organisms) in recent years (Lohan & Johnston, 2005) with Antarctica raising interesting issues regarding the ownership of biological resources and the sharing of scientific information for the ATS (Antarctic Treaty, 1959). Convention on the Conservation of Antarctic Marine Living Resources, 1980 encompasses all living organisms in the Southern Ocean, and, therefore, the Antarctic environmental protection regime demonstrates its worth.

RECENT DEVELOPMENT

Responding to carbon emission scheme can bring sustainable changes for the lives and environment. Stern Review rightly puts, cost of unabated climate change on the global economy will equate to a loss of at least 5% of global gross domestic product (GDP) each year, potentially rising to 20%. In contrast, a shift to a low-carbon pathway would benefit the economy by US$2.5 trillion a year, with markets for low-carbon technologies worth at least US$500 billion per year by 2050. Avoiding the worst impacts of climate change would require an investment of only 1-2% of global GDP per annum (Stern 2007).

Warming of the climate system is unequivocal, and since the 1950s, many of the observed changes are unprecedented over decades to millennia (IPCC, 2014). Again, atmospheric concentrations of carbon dioxide, methane, and nitrous oxide have increased to levels unprecedented in at least the last 800,000 years. Human influence on the climate system is clear from the increasing greenhouse gas concentrations in the atmosphere, positive radiative forcing, observed warming, and our current understanding of the climate system. Carbon dioxide concentrations have increased by over 40% since pre-industrial times, primarily from fossil fuel emissions, and from net land-use change emissions (IPCC, 2014). Singapore may experience 'climate departure' as soon as 2028 (i.e. the year when the coolest annual temperatures are predicted to exceed the warmest annual temperature recorded in a 1960-2005 baseline period) (Mora et al., 2013) and may cause sea level rise.

U.S. Climate Science Special Report: Fourth National Climate Assessment termed the current period as the warmest in the history of modern civilization clearly mentioning that human activities, especially emissions of greenhouse gases, are the dominant cause of observed warming since the mid-20th century and the current trend might cause a global sea level rise of up to 2.4 metres by the end of the century, an increased incidence of drought and flooding, more frequent wildfires, and devastating storms (Wuebbles et al., 2017). The IPCC Fourth Assessment Report in 2007 warned that due to the disintegration of global ice-sheets, notably Greenland and Western Antarctica might cause near-term sea level rise to coastlines and low-lying islands.

The UN World Meteorological Organization (WMO) reported that 2016 was the warmest year on the instrumental record, with the yearly rise in atmospheric carbon dioxide in 2016, at 3.1 ppm, was 50% higher than the previous 10-year average (World Meteorological Organization Greenhouse Gas Bulletin, 2017). As per the latest data from the WMO, 2017 was shaped up to be the third warmest year on the instrumental record, meaning that 17 out of the 18 warmest years in the instrumental record will have all occurred in the 21st Century (Obbard, 2017).

The United Nations Emission Gap Report, in its 2017 review of global carbon emissions, reported that the emissions gap between the national pledges under the PCA to cut carbon emissions and the actual reductions needed to keep temperature rise below 2oC of warming is now "alarmingly high". Coal combustion in China contributed to 2oC rise of carbon emission in 2017(Global Carbon Project, 2017) while reluctance of USA adds negative impacts on the carbon emission trajectory worldwide. Inaction of the global leaders and states concerned simply reveal the observation that time is simply running out to keep warming well below 2oC under the PCA let alone 1.5oC.

The United Nations-led 21st Conference of the Parties (COP-21) to the United Nations Framework Convention on Climate Change held at Paris in December, 2015 agreed on some important issues that form the basis of inspiration to address the effects of climate change.

The PCA established specific actions and targets for the world to reduce greenhouse gases emissions, to mitigate and adapt to climate change, and to finance efforts to alleviate impacts in developing countries. As of November, 2017, a total of 195 countries have signed the PCA, and 169 have become a party to it. Signatory countries pledge to limit global mean temperature rise to below 2oC and make strong efforts to keep the rise to no more than 1.5oC. However, states should concentrate more on achieving carbon mission targets for a sustainable world.

States concerned unanimously agreed to enhance capacities of global response to climate change, and therefore, limit global temperature increase to well below 2 degrees Celsius, possibly to 1.5 degrees. They also agreed to communicate their nationally determined contribution (NDCs) every five years and provide information necessary for clarity and transparency reflecting gradual progress with the NDCs (i.e., successive NDC will represent a progression than the previous NDC). COP-21 also asked the developed countries to take the lead by undertaking economy-wide reduction targets, while developing countries were urged on enhancing their mitigation efforts, and subsequently move toward economy-wide targets considering the typical circumstances of a given country with the aspiration of a low carbon future for the planet.

Recently, 23rd Conference of the Parties (COP23) concluded on 20 November 2017 in Bonn, Germany. Global leaders gathered in the meeting with a view to determining how best to implement the goals of the Paris Climate Agreement (PCA) of COP21 held in December, 2015. The standing of the U.S. in COP-23 was not cooperative rather its plan of withdrawal from Paris Climate Agreement cast the light of despair and uncertainties while the global temperatures are still rising, and carbon emissions have resumed upward trend. A global transformation to low-carbon technologies has now become embedded as an economic and environmental imperative.

Thus, despite the U.S. withdrawal from the PCA, the intended changes will pave the way forward to a safer world with economic prosperity and environmental sustainability. In response to the U.S. stance on coal, several countries including Canada, the United Kingdom and Mexico responded at COP23 by forming a new global alliance to move away from unabated coal combustion.

RECOMMENDATION

The growth of the global economy made us more dependent on one another. Due to this inter-dependence among the states, the issue of environmental problems creates the concerns for fundamental human security, health, and well-being (Carlarne, 2014). These days, the focus of international environmental law is preventative and precautionary, to manage environmental risk and protect the environment on a global level (Birnie, Alan, & Redgwell, 2009). Climate change adds to the list of stressors that challenge our ability to achieve the ecologic, economic and social objectives that define sustainable development (Yohe et al., 2007). Therefore, reducing vulnerability to current climatic variability can effectively reduce vulnerability to increased hazard risk associated with climate change (Goklany, 2007).

The pressure on food, agriculture, habitation, and thereby, the whole livelihood being hampered due to the catastrophic effects of climate change. Due to climate change, there will be a reduction on the natural stress tolerance of the environment. Thus, climate change will require an increasing level of protection and prevention through enforcement of environmental law. In fact, there is a dividing line between the countries in respect of the concentration of resources and distribution of climate actions, an impediment for climate justice. Henceforth, unless there is a shared understanding on burden-sharing, it will not be possible to create a legitimate global commitment regime (Rajamani, Brunnée, & Doelle, 2012).

Measures need to be taken for the effective regulation of the LOSC; the 1973–8 International Convention for the Prevention of Pollution by Ships (MARPOL Convention) and the soft law instruments of environmental governance of the Arctic Council, including the Arctic Environmental Protection Strategy is a necessity. Alongside to the ATS, the other conventions like the Convention on Biological Diversity, the MARPOL Convention, the Whaling Convention, and the LOSC can help saving the Antarctica from being vulnerable.

Renewed efforts to create a new instrument (hard or soft law) for wartime applicability that deals specifically with protection for spaces of environmental or natural significance is a necessity to ensure greater environmental security in the future (Diplomatic Conference on the Reaffirmation and Development of International Humanitarian Law Applicable in Armed Conflicts, 1975).

Lack of control on deforestation might cause threats for the planet. The existing international framework for regulating states' maritime borders under UNCLOS may not be designed to deal with changing borders due to sea level rises (Maas & Alexander, 2010). There are complex inter-relationships and feedbacks between human driving forces and impacts, on one hand, and climate- and sea level-induced changes and effects on the other (IPCC, 1996). The climate-related impacts in coastal areas include loss and salinization of agricultural land, potential changes in the intensity of tropical cyclones and the reduction of productivity in coastal and oceanic fisheries. Integrated coastal zone management (ICZM) is an iterative and evolutionary process for achieving sustainable development by developing and implementing a continuous management capability that can respond to changing conditions, including the effects of climate change (Bijlsma *et al.*, 1996). ICZM can offer appropriate solution to address the climate change effects on coastal areas. The disputes involving water resources can be resolved pursuant to the provision of 1966 Helsinki Rules on the Uses of the Waters of International Rivers, the 1992Convention on the Protection and Use of Trans-boundary Watercourses and Lake-Shore by devising any other suitable mechanisms.

To effectively address the issues of climate change, the international community needs to strengthen the legally binding commitments and compliance under the existing UNFCCC and undertake a much broader response to meet the exigencies. Co-ordination needs to be developed between climate policies and policies relating to the internally displaced persons, biodiversity and development. In case sustainability is applied to policy and regulation, compliance with the same would bring positive outcome leading to a balancing coordination of development and exploitation of resources.

The dissemination of information is urgently required for effective and affirmative action and, therefore, it is necessary to develop concrete legal obligations to facilitate the transfer of adaptation technology among the states. The ATS and the Convention on Biological Diversity should simultaneously regulate for access to resources and their proper uses. At the same time, there should be an arrangement for environmental impact assessment and close monitoring of such activities to ensure the maintenance of this unique environment.

CONCLUDING REMARKS

According to the Brundtland Commission (1987) report, sustainable development meets the needs of the present without compromising the ability of future generations to meet their own needs. In case the impacts of climate change continue in absence of the active response of the states, sustainability of the planet and common good of the future generations likely to be frustrated. In the inter-dependent world, climate induced environmental changes can be an issue of collective and regional concerns for the sustainability of mankind. It would be a quite logical approach for the modern states to incorporate the environment in the security agenda to prevent the likely instability. There would be changes in the variability of climate, and changes in the frequency and intensity of some extreme climate phenomena. The regional changes in climate, particularly increases in temperature, have already affected a diverse set of physical and biological systems in many parts of the world.

Global climate change, the depletion of the ozone layer, desertification, deforestation, the loss of the planet's biological diversity and the trans-boundary movements of hazardous wastes and chemicals are the environmental problems that touch the nations adversely affecting the lives and health of their people. These are long-term effects on people and societies for generations. Concerted efforts on the part of the international community need to be taken at the earliest to effectively address these global environmental challenges. Immediate action on energy efficiency and non-fossil-fuel energy sources need to be taken to avoid the severe negative impacts of climate change on human society and on ecosystems.

The ability of human systems to adapt and cope with climate change depends on factors such as wealth, technology, education, information, skills, infrastructure, access to resources, and management capabilities. The states can enhance their adaptive capabilities by using those resources. The developing countries do not have that much of adaptive capacities alike to that of the developed countries, and thereby, the developing countries are more vulnerable to damages caused by the climate change phenomena. Because the climate change effects put pressure on the economy and the developing countries have limited resources and capacities, there is an extreme need for a functioning legal and regulatory framework for a balancing economic order across the globe.

There is a misconception among the policy makers that addressing climate change might take away a huge resources and major development constraints like poverty and hunger may not be given appropriate attention. On the face of the practical scenario, there is a need to integrate climate change responses into sustainable development strategies. Decision makers engaged in climate change policy, planning, and implementation at all levels should have access to research on population trends, climate change and development.

States around the world are on the continuous efforts to reduce carbon emission to minimize the effects of climate change. On the other hand, inaction of some powerful states increases the potential of environmental degradation and catastrophic effects of climate change. In view of achieving common good for the people of every corner of the planet and their environment, states adopted COP21 with the hope of ensuring a better future with green environment. The U.S. stand on COP23 in respect of non-compliance with the carbon emission does not bear a good message for the rest of the world.

As human population is increasing and the trend is set to continue while the existence of the humans and the ecosystems are at stake, it is imperative to undertake integrated programs for strengthening technical capacity of the local experts and continuous monitoring and evaluation of the programs. Knowledge about climate-change adaptation and sustainable development can be translated into public policy through processes that generate usable knowledge from national and international bodies that offer credible and legitimate information to policymakers through transparent multi-disciplinary processes (Lemos & Morehouse, 2005).

Strong political will and public commitment to promoting sustainable development is needed, focusing simultaneously on economic growth, social progress, environmental conservation and adaptation to climate change (World Bank, 1998). The involvement of both public and private sector is imperative for coordination in respect of economic, social and climate change perspectives. Initiative undertaken by the government of the United Kingdom is quite laudable as it has enacted the Climate Change Act with binding requirements to reduce emissions domestically by 80% by 2050.

REFERENCES

A Bad Climate for Development. (2009, September 17). *The Economist.* Retrieved on September 30, 2017, from: http://www.economist.com/node/14447171

Antarctic Treaty. (1959). *Article I (2).*

Bijlsma, L., Ehler, C. N., Klein, R. J. T., Kulshrestha, S. M., McLean, R. F., Mimura, N., ... Warrick, R. A. (1996). Coastal zones and small islands. In R. T. Watson, M. C. Zinyowera, & R. H. Moss (Eds.), *Climate Change 1995: Impacts, Adaptations, and Mitigation of Climate Change: Scientific-Technical Analyses. Contribution of Working Group II to the Second Assessment Report of the Intergovernmental Panel on Climate Change* (pp. 289–324). Cambridge, UK: Cambridge University Press.

Birnie, P., Boyle, A., & Redgwell, C. (Eds.). (2009). *International Law and the Environment* (3rd ed.). London: Oxford University Press.

Bosselmann, K. (2008). *The Principle of Sustainability: Transforming Law and Governance*. Farnham, UK: Ashgate.

Brown, O., Crawford, A., & Campeau, C. (2008, June). *Environmental Change and the New Security Agenda: Implications for Canada's Security and Environment, International Institute for Sustainable Development.* Retrieved on September 29, 2017, from: http://www.iisd.org/PUBLICATIONS/pub.aspx?id=975

Brundtland Commission. (1987). *Our Common Future: Report of the World Commission on Environment and Development.* Oxford, UK: Oxford University Press.

Carlarne, C. (2014). Delinking International Environmental Law. *Michigan Journal of Environmental & Administrative Law*, *4*(1), 1-62. Retrieved on September 25, 2017, from: http://repository.law.umich.edu/mjeal/vol4/iss1/1/

Corporation, C. N. A. (2007). *National Security and the Threat of Climate Change.* Retrieved on September 22, 2017, from: http://www.npr.org/documents/2007/apr/security_climate.pdf

Current Legal Challenges in Climate Change Justice. (2014). *Achieving Justice and Human Rights in an Era of Climate Disruption.* London: International Bar Association. Retrieved on September 28, 2017, from: https://www.ibanet.org/PresidentialTaskForceClimateChangeJustice2014Report.aspx

Dryzek, J. (2013). *The Politics of the Earth: Environmental Discourses* (3rd ed.). London: Oxford University Press.

Frankauser, S. (2009). *The costs of adaptation.* Grantham Research Institute and Centre for Climate Change Economics and Policy. London: London School of Economics. Retrieved on September 17, 2017, from: http://www.lse.ac.uk/GranthamInstitute/wp-content/uploads/2014/02/WorkingPaper7.pdf

Global Carbon Project. (n.d.). *Carbon Budget 2017.* Retrieved on November 20, 2017, from: http://www.globalcarbonproject.org/carbonbudget/index.htm

Goklany, I. M. (2007). Integrated strategies to reduce vulnerability and advance adaptation, mitigation and sustainable development. *Mitigation and Adaptation Strategies for Global Change.* Retrieved on September 20, 2017, from: http://citeseerx.ist.psu.edu/viewdoc/download?doi=10.1.1.167.857&rep=rep1&type=pdf

Hamlyn, O. (2015). Sustainability and the Failure of Ambition in European Pesticides Regulation. *Journal of Environmental Law*, *0*, 1–25. Retrieved from http://discovery.ucl.ac.uk/1469006/7/Sustainability%20and%20the%20Failure%20of%20Ambition%20in%20European%20Pesticides%20Regulation.pdf

IPCC. (1996). Climate Change 1995: Impacts, Adaptations, and Mitigation of Climate Change: Scientific-Technical Analyses. Contribution of Working Group II to the Second Assessment Report of the Intergovernmental Panel on Climate Change. Cambridge, UK: Cambridge University Press.

IPCC. (2001). *Climate Change: Third Assessment Report.* London: Cambridge University Press.

IPCC. (2007). *Climate Change: Synthesis Report, Fourth Assessment Report of the Intergovernmental Panel on Climate Change*. London: Cambridge University Press.

IPCC. (2014). *Climate Change 2014: Synthesis Report. Contribution of Working Groups I, II and III to the Fifth Assessment Report of the Intergovernmental Panel on Climate Change* (R. K. Pachauri & L. A. Meyer, Eds.). Geneva, Switzerland: IPCC.

Kassiola, J. (2002). Why Environmental Thought and Action Must Include Considerations of Social Justice. In M. Gillroy & J. Bowersox (Eds.), *The Moral Austerity of Environmental Decision Making Sustainability, Democracy, and Normative Argument in Policy and Law*. Duke University Press.

Lemos, M. C., & Morehouse, B. J. (2005). The co-production of science and policy in integrated climate assessments. *Global Environmental Change*, *15*(1), 57–68. doi:10.1016/j.gloenvcha.2004.09.004

Lohan, D., & Johnston, S. (2005). *Bio-prospecting in Antarctica*. United Nations University and Institute of Advanced Studies Report. Retrieved on September 27, 2017, from: http://www.ias.unu.edu/binaries2/antarctic_bioprospecting.pdf

Maas, A., & Carius, A. (2010). *Territorial Integrity and Sovereignty: Climate Change and Security in the Pacific and Beyond.* Academic Press.

Marinova, D., & Raven, M. (2006). Indigenous knowledge and intellectual property: A sustainability agenda. *Journal of Economic Surveys*, *20*(4), 587–606. doi:10.1111/j.1467-6419.2006.00260.x

Meadows, D. H., Randers, J., Meadows, D. L., & Behrens, W. W. (1972). *The Limits to Growth: Report for the Club of Rome's Project on the Predicament of Mankind*. New York: Universe Books.

Mora, C., Frazier, A. G., Longman, R. J., Dacks, R. S., Walton, M. M., Tong, E. J., ... Giambelluca, T. W. (2013). The projected timing of climate departure from recent variability. *Nature*, *502*(7470), 183–187. doi:10.1038/nature12540 PMID:24108050

Munasinghe, M. (n.d.). *Analysing the Nexus of Sustainable Development and Climate Change: An Overview.* Sri Lanka: Munasinghe Institute for Development (MIND).

Myers, N. (2005, May). *Environmental Refugees: An Emergent Security Issue.* Thirteenth Economic Forum, Prague, Czech Republic.

Obbard, J. (2017). APCEL Climate Change Adaptation Platform COP23 Bonn, Germany: The U.S. Stands Alone. Asia Pacific Centre for Environmental Law. National University of Singapore.

Obbard, J. (2017, December 12). *APCEL Climate Change Adaptation Platform COP23 Bonn, Germany: The U.S. Stands Alone.* Asia Pacific Centre for Environmental Law. National University of Singapore. Retrieved on January 15, 2018, from: https://law.nus.edu.sg/apcel/cca/COP23%20Bonn,%20Germany%20%20The%20U.S.%20Stands%20Alone.pdf

Official Records of the Diplomatic Conference on the Reaffirmation and Development of International Humanitarian Law Applicable in Armed Conflicts. (1975). Retrieved on September 15, 2017, from: Doc. CDDH/III/275 at 360.

Pelling, M. (2003). Paradigms of risk. In M. Pelling (Ed.), *Natural Disaster and Development in a Globalizing World*. New York: Routledge.

Rajamani, L., Brunnée, J., & Doelle, M. (2012). Introduction: The role of compliance in an evolving climate regime. In L. Rajamani, J. Brunnée, & M. Doelle (Eds.), *Promoting Compliance in an Evolving Climate Regime*. London, UK: Cambridge University Press. doi:10.1007/978-1-4614-1433-9_1

Richards, M. (2003). *Poverty Reduction, Equity and Climate Change: Global Governance Synergies or Contradictions?* London: Overseas Development Institute.

Sands, P., & Peel, J. (2012). *Principles of International Environmental Law* (3rd ed.). London: Cambridge University Press. doi:10.1017/CBO9781139019842

Stern, N. H. (2007). *The Economics of Climate Change: The Stern Review*. Cambridge, UK: Cambridge University Press. doi:10.1017/CBO9780511817434

UNCHE. (1972). *Declaration of the UN Conference on the Human Environment, Stockholm, 5–16 June 1972*. Report of the UN Conference on the Human Environment, UN Doc.A/CONF.48/14.

UNCSD. (1996). Indicators of sustainable development—Framework and methodologies. New York: UNCSD.

United Nations. (1993). Results of the Earth Summit 1992. New York: UN.

United Nations. (2000). *We the Peoples: The Role of the United Nations in the 21st Century*. New York: UN. Retrieved on September 20, 2017, from: www.un.org/millennium/sg/report/key.htm

United Nations General Assembly. (1962). *Economic Development and the Conservation of Nature*. G.A. Resolution 1831 (XVII), UN GAOR, 17th Session, Supp. no. 17, UN Doc. A/RES/1831 (XVII).

Walsh, B. (2009). Q&A: The U.N.'s Ban Ki-Moon on Climate Change. *TIME*. Retrieved on September 25, 2017, from: http://content.time.com/time/specials/packages/article/0,28804,1929071_1929070_1947173,00.html

World Bank. (1998). *Protecting Our Planet: Securing Our Future*. Washington, DC: Author.

World Conservation Union. (1980). *World Conservation Strategy: Living Resource Conservation for Sustainable Development*. Gland, Switzerland: International Union for Conservation of Nature.

World Meteorological Organization Greenhouse Gas Bulletin. The state of Greenhouse Gases in the Atmosphere Based on Global Observations through 2016. (2017). Retrieved on January 10, 2018, from: https://library.wmo.int/opac/doc_num.php?explnum_id=4022

World Wildlife Fund. (2009). *Arctic Still Unprepared for Major Oil Spill Twenty Years after Exxon Valdez*. Retrieved on August 30, 2017, from: http://arcticfocus.com/2009/03/23/wwf-arctic-still-unprepared-for-major-oil-spill-20-years-after-exxon-valdez/

Wuebbles, D. J., Fahey, D. W., Hibbard, K. A., Dokken, D. J., Stewart, B. C., & Maycock, T. K. (Eds.). (n.d.). USGCRP, 2017: Climate Science Special Report: Fourth National Climate Assessment (vol. 1). U.S. Global Change Research Program. doi:10.7930/J0J964J6

Yohe, G. W., Lasco, R. D., Ahmad, Q. K., Arnell, N. W., Cohen, S. J., Hope, C., . . . Perez, R. T. (2007). Perspectives on climate change and sustainability. In Climate Change 2007: Impacts, Adaptation and Vulnerability. Contribution of Working Group II to the Fourth Assessment Report of the Intergovernmental Panel on Climate Change. Cambridge, UK: Cambridge University Press.

ENDNOTES

1 Pacific Fur Seal Arbitration settled a dispute between the United States and the United Kingdom for the protection of fur seals in the Bering Sea from overexploitation. Award of the arbitration developed the notion that consent of the concerned states is imperative for the conservation of living resources as they have the rights to assert even if it is outside their jurisdiction.

[2] Trail Smelter Arbitration developed the principle that no state has the right to use or permit the use of its territory in such a manner as to cause injury by fumes in or to the territory of another or the properties or persons therein.

Chapter 13
How Unemployment May Impact Happiness: A Systematic Review

André Barros
Polytechnic Institute of Cávado and Ave, Portugal

Teresa Dieguez
Polytechnic Institute of Cávado and Ave, Portugal & Polytechnic Institute of Porto, Portugal

Pedro Nunes
Polytechnic Institute of Cávado and Ave, Portugal

ABSTRACT

The wealth of an economy is traditionally measured by its level of productivity. However, countries with the highest level of productivity do not always report equal levels of happiness and general wellbeing. In fact, there is no direct relationship between both variables and sometimes less wealthy productive countries report higher levels of happiness. Recent studies and theories are trying to demonstrate that the term happiness has made its way into economics literature as the result of economist dissatisfaction who believe happiness should become a matter of study in the field. Unemployment is one of the most recently researched variables in economics and has a direct relationship with happiness. Potentially some other variables such as autonomy, reliability, and added value of happiness would help researchers to better complete economic analysis via a multidisciplinary perspective.

INTRODUCTION

Unemployment has always been one of the most interesting study variables for economists. This may be justified due the fact that, for most Portuguese families, employment is the main income generator. In fact, it has a considerable social significance and greatly contributes for people's integration in society. Losing one's job has strong negative repercussions, not only on the individual's well-being and quality of life, but also on the social, economic and politic impact it has on society. However, and despite nowa-

DOI: 10.4018/978-1-5225-5787-6.ch013

days unemployment is a tremendously trivial subject, it is imperative to mention that only few studies pass beyond number analysis and overlook the lives, frustrations, sense of revolt and inability to fulfil life projects felt by the unemployed population.

Psychology and psychiatrics have been the main responsible areas for the study of happiness, even though they were initially more concerned in reducing pain rather than increasing pleasure. Economists don´t usually consider the concept of happiness on their researches and argues that economic study variables should be material, quantifiable and related with objective realities. Nonetheless, it is important to mention that in the last year's studies connecting unemployment with happiness raised a lot and most of them also conducted by economists (Caleiro, 2011).

It is not easy to distinct the impacts of unemployment on people's well-being without studying happiness. While the importance of happiness emerges, several economists are trying to bring new ideas to economic analysis, widening their action spectrum. Several economic models fail because don´t consider a holistic approach and do not consider that all the interrelated elements of the system exercise an influence on dynamic behavior which may explain change and complexity in the system over time (Bala et al., 2017). Consequently, a different approach is required to study economics where happiness may be a possible key study variable. The present research aims to understand and analyze not only the relationship between soaring unemployment levels with the levels of happiness, but also its impacts on the daily lives of unemployed individuals.

LITERATURE REVIEW

This research is structured around three sections. The first section will explain the pertinence of the happiness topic, pointing out the reasons why it was chosen. It will feature a brief reflection about the importance of happiness and meaning of happiness in accordance with several points of view, namely from many different authors and economists. It also analyses the term happiness and the relation between money and happiness. The second section will deal with unemployment, namely with its relevance and evolution in terms of both unemployment rates and unemployment protection policies in Portugal. The third and last section will connect happiness with unemployment, concluding with some empirical studies performed with the goal to assess the impact of unemployment on the levels of happiness.

HAPPINESS

The Importance of Happiness

Economics should be responsible for individual happiness, analyzing how it is affected by economic growth, unemployment and inflation. However, and despite the evolution of economics, the concept of welfare remains related with wealth, income, consumption and production (Mota, 2009). Nonetheless, many economists do not agree with this *status quo* and argue that it is needed to introduce new analysis methods, new models and notions of welfare.

Welfare is commonly associated as a synonym of wealth. Through times it has been acknowledged that wealth is just one part of welfare, but economists have not been totally aware of this (Bruni, 2004). Amartya Sen (2000), probably one of the most acclaimed economists, made harsh critics to standard economic models, building an entirely new theoretical reasoning that concluded with the creation of a new economic school of thought: the capabilities approach.

This new economic school of thought constitutes one of the most important attacks ever made to the orthodox welfare economy (Mota, 2009). Amartya Sen symbolizes economists like Bernard van Praag, E. J. Mishan, Fred Hirsch, George Akerlof, Kenneth Galbraith, Richard Easterlin, Richard Layard, Tibor Scitovsky and Yew-Kwang Ng, among others, who attempted to bring new input to the science of economics, mainly due to their concern with the lack of reality and practical use of many economic models, as well as with some of their predictions. These same economists argue that usually economic analysis ignore several vital aspects namely justice, morality, reciprocity and every type of immaterial questions like environmental concerns, labour pressures or daily stress (Mota, 2009). Hence, it becomes particularly important to highlight the fact that happiness can be scientifically reliable. Moreover, the importance of happiness in modern days is so undeniable that it is stated in the U.S. Declaration of Independence as an inalienable right, compared to life and freedom (Frey & Stutzer, 2002).

Psychology, sociology, and neurology are examples of disciplines where happiness is currently being seriously studied. Psychology is probably the leading "science of happiness' having started this kind of analysis early during the 1960s, long time ago before economics (Mota, 2009). Economics was one of the last disciplines which considered the study of happiness, as it has a strong trend to tangible and objective aspects. Nonetheless, the high level of subjectivity associated to it makes the theme complex and sometimes generates disregards. What seems relevant is the fact that psychology and psychiatrics have recently changed their stance on the happiness of individuals, replacing the focus on studying and relieving pain, for focus on increasing the individual's level of pleasure and satisfaction.

Nonetheless, some studies analyzed the interrelations between some economic variables; namely, unemployment and happiness. Those studies, among others, originated interesting results as they allowed economists to question economic concepts, premises and theories that were considered irrefutable until then. Faced with these results, economists are now realizing that economic growth on its own does not increase the level of welfare once one has reached a certain level of wealth.

Happiness: What Does It Mean?

Averill and More (2000) concluded that when individuals are questioned about examples of emotions, or about the main goals they wish to achieve, most of them replies "happiness". Happiness is also the most frequent answer about what they prefer for their offspring, having as possible choices fame, fortune or happiness. Since the ancient times many philosophers like Aristotle (B.C. 350) have been questioned about happiness' meaning and even nowadays there is no consensus as to its definition. The term has a huge indiscriminate use with concepts as life satisfaction and welfare. Generally, it is assumed that, in 1950, psychologists started paying more attention to positive emotions and welfare instead of focus on diminishing pain and suffering. And for sustaining this fact, Diener and Suh (1999) claimed there were 17 times more psychological articles and studies on negative emotional states than those researching positive emotional states. Most of the studies on happiness have been conducted by psychologists such as Abraham Maslow, Adrian White, Ken Wilber, Lester, Martin Seligman, Van Hoorn and Wilson, among others. All of them regarding happiness from many different perspectives.

The assessment of happiness can be performed at many levels and about the most complex realities. However, regardless of what level and reality it relates, there will always be a greater focus on its three main dimensions i) Objectivity; ii) Physiological activation; and iii) Reason *versus* Emotion (Niza, 2007):

- The first dimension refers to the assessment of an individual's degree of happiness by an outside observer. It is expected that, considering the technological advances, namely in neurology using techniques, it is possible to more accurately account for the values of objective happiness (Kahneman, Diener, & Schwarz, 1999). "The ultimate data for the judgment are, of course, subjective experiences." (Kahneman et al., 1999, p. 8);
- Equally, the subjective evaluation concerns the evaluation of the degree of happiness of the individual has of his/her own happiness. The level of physiological activation refers to the internal feeling of physiological excitement. Even though many regard joy as the leading exponent of happiness, there are those who defend that the higher goal is to achieve serenity and contentment;
- Last, the dichotomy reason *versus* emotion is related to the doubt if happiness is an emotional or a cognitive component (Schwarz & Strack, 1999). In fact, some authors claim that individuals achieve their life satisfaction, which corresponds to the cognitive component standing point (Diener & Lucas, 1999), while others believe the true answer to happiness can only be achieved by getting answers from the individual's emotional component.

From the three dimensions of happiness, objectivity is the only one that sparks less debate among researchers, as they practically agree that individual should be the one in charge of evaluating his/her own level of happiness (Mota, 2009). Happiness can be defined as an overall appreciation of an individual's life as a whole; it means the way each one values the life that is being lived (Theodossiou, 1998, Radcliff, 2001; Blanchflower & Oswald, 2004; Helliwell, 2006; Veenhoven, 2006; White, 2007). It is always important to have in mind that happiness is correlated with several factors namely personality traits, demography, institutional and/or economics. For these reasons, the search for happiness has always been present, but nowadays people are more responsible for their own happiness because they have more alternatives and choices regarding what they want for their lives and are more aware of the possibility to achieve happiness (Da Silva, 2011, p. 182).

Relationship Between Money and Happiness

The relationship between money and happiness has been studied for scientists for several decades and their findings are that money buys happiness, but it buys less than most people think (Dunn, Gilbert, & Wilson, 2011). "Either an adverse situation from an economic standpoint is not incompatible with a favorable situation from an emotional point of view' (Caleiro, 2011 p. 1). Even though most people believe that there is a strong positive relationship between increase in the available amount of money and levels of happiness. Nonetheless, these same people are unable to answer a few questions like: i) Why having more money does not make us happier?; ii) If money allows people to do what they want, shouldn't they be pleased when they spend it?; iii) If money can buy happiness, then, why do not buy it?

A possible answer to the first two questions is that not everything that makes people happy is for sale, since achieving happiness depends on a set of dimensions for which there is not a market, namely affective and family relations, inner peace, and so on. As such, it is important to remember the effects of adaptation and comparison. Referring adaptation, "in Psychology, the current trend is called the fixed-point theory, per which each individual has his/her own fixed point of happiness or welfare due to both genetic characteristics and personality." (Da Fonseca, 2004: 16). When it comes to the comparison effect, "people are led to believe that the use of certain goods depends on other people's goods" (*idem, ibidem:* 17). These facts allow stating that human beings become quite limited when they believe whatever is in the market will satisfy them in the search for happiness. Regarding the third question, a possible explanation lies in the fact that people do not properly use money.

These answers allow one to conclude that people are not fully aware of the sources of happiness that control the nature of their daily activities (Vohs & Baumeister, 2011), and most people do not know the most basic scientific facts sustaining happiness (*idem*, 2011). Thus, it is likely that many people are not aware of the existence of scientific studies about happiness, nor of the conclusions one can draw from them. Even though certain behaviours are in line with scientific studies but people are not aware of such fact.

It seems pertinent to admit that money is an opportunity for happiness. An opportunity that sometimes people waste: people generally think that money will bring them happiness but in fact it will not. Last, a surprising reaction deserves to be pointed out: when people are asked to assess their lives, the ones with most economic power tend to claim they are happier than those with less economic power. However, when the same people are asked about how happy they are/feel now, there is practically no difference between the answers given by richer or poorer people. This leads to believe that money provides people satisfaction when thinking about it, but not when using it (Diener et al., 2010).

Historical Context of the Relationship Between Happiness and Economics

It is difficult to establish this contextualization as there are many different perspectives involved. They report a different reality, depending on the assumed initially point of view. There have always been, and remain, many different points of view which, in certain aspects, appear to be antagonistic. This apparent contradiction may be explained by the use, interpretation and importance that each author grants to the word happiness. Economics has always been ruled by an exhaustive and rigorous analysis in its arguments, examining only material realities, and many times overlooking the possible inter-relation with other realities and implicit subjectivity. Several models were created and, with some many changes worldwide, those same models seem to be incomplete and might lead to erroneous conclusions, negatively influencing policies and put in danger sustainability, something sometimes irreversible.

What appears to be worthy of mention is the creation of different extreme stances. The word economics is commonly connected with the material aspect of societies, for which one is not surprised to find that something so subjective and complex as happiness is not a clear concern for economics and, in correlation, for economists. The first known author who used the expression "pubblica felicità' was the italian Ludovico Antonio Muratori in 1749 (Niza, 2007). The most representative author of that time was Napolitan Antonio Genovesi, for whom economics was mostly a theory of social relationships that should regulate a society that would prioritize the enjoyment of interpersonal relations rather than the production of material goods (Bruni, 2004). Later in France, Condorcet, Malthus, Rousseau and Sismondi were some of the researchers who studied happiness and emphasised it in a manner not previously done.

In 1759, Adam Smith published "Theory of Moral Sentiments", where for the first-time economics is seen granting the individual a *status* never experienced, by using a relational approach to the former (Niza, 2007). In 1796, Adam Smith wrote "The Wealth of Nations", a work that became a landmark, symbolizing the advances that happiness made in the world of economics. Additionally, Thomas Malthus and David Ricardo had an important role. Nevertheless, Thomas Malthus, emphasised, in his 1978 book, "An Essay on the Principle of Population", that the relation between happiness and wealth was not as linear as Adam Smith had put it: Thomas Malthus perceived it as a much more complex topic and accused economists of not accepting happiness in their field of study as were subjective and difficult to quantify.

Supporting these arguments, in 1789 Jeremy Bentham, an advocate of "Utilitarism", presented an important work, "An Introduction to the Principles of Morals and Legislation", claiming that individuals were characterized as being ruled by pleasure and pain, hence social happiness would be nothing but the aggregation of individual happiness (Denis, 2000).

In 1945, Lionel Robbins defended that utility was something that could only happens in the mind of everyone, being therefore totally subjective and impossible to measure. Economists focused on quantifiable behaviours could not predict economic behaviours.

In addition, by applying the Pareto principle economists were ready to move forward analysing economic models without having to compare levels of individual utility. Henceforward, psychology and every other science related with individual preferences were dismissed by the economic science, bringing upon the so-called Ordinal Revolution, producing a deep impact on economic theories. Economists were completely reluctant to accept what was subjective: economics was a positive science that could only deal with objective facts. This made individual happiness and, more specifically, questions such as how economic decisions affect their happiness, be disregarded for being outside the scope of the study of economics.

In 1973, Tibor Scitovsky managed to incorporate in his work "The Place of Economic Welfare in Human Welfare", the word happiness in his economic analyses. Other authors like Richard Easterlin, Richard Layard and Yew-Kwang Ng. also analysed and studied the topic and, despite their different perspectives they all perceived that happiness is an opportunity to richer and improve their analyses and should be incorporated in economics as a concept that can be important to human happiness. Scitovsky dedicated an entire section of his 1976 book, "The Joyless Economy - The Psychology of Human Satisfaction" to the analysis of the relationships between economic growth, income and happiness. He also differentiated two psychological needs: stimulus and comfort, as they produce different sentiments: stimulus promotes joy- pleasure; comfort creates joylessness-boredom.

His thesis sustains that economic growth was more likely to promote comfort than stimulus, and maybe this is the reason why his research was always very much focused on studying certain ways to reduce the high levels of restlessness and discomfort. However, eliminating negative emotions only represented half of it, as the rest pertained to the construction of positive emotions. Regardless of how one sees this phenomenon, these four authors, especially Scitovsky, believed it was necessary for economics to classify subjectivity, namely in happiness, with the purpose of building a better economic theory. Therefore, happiness first appeared directly in economic analyses not by accident, but instrumentally: it fitted the interests of those economists who thought that the immaterial side of life was important, or even that happiness was the main goal of all individuals and societies, and who were dissatisfied with economic models and policy prescriptions.

UNEMPLOYMENT

The Importance of Unemployment

Unemployment is a major life event which can have a devastating impact on people's lives. It affects not just the unemployed individuals, but also family members and the wider community. The Impact of unemployment, can be long-lasting. As unemployment becomes more long-term, its impact becomes more far reaching, often affecting living standards in retirement. The loss of income by the parents can damage the prospects of the next generation.

Quite apart from the personal impact, unemployment is a loss of valuable productive resources to the economy. The impact of job loss in rural and regional areas flows through the local community damaging businesses as family expenditure is reduced. Further damage to local communities may result from people leaving in search of work.

Unemployment is often analyzed as a social reality that is completely apart from individuals and its impact on their lives: personal histories, singular and irreducible. Moreover, unemployment constitutes one of the most visible manifestations of what has been happening in the world of labour, for it represents a form of an underuse of work, with profound consequences in many aspects of society (Gorz, 1988; Castel, 1995; Beck, 2000; Caleiras, 2011). Unemployment is posing more and more problems to Governments since it erodes the base of funding and increases the search for public support (Esping-Anderson, 1996).

Unemployment: What Does It Mean?

In very generic terms, unemployment represents a certain stance in a social structure; in this case, it represents the labour market. In the beginning of the 18th century the terms unemployed and unemployment did not exist. Other terminologies were used like "poor", "indigent" or "beggars", as a reference to the deprivation of the means to survive and not necessarily to the deprivation of work, as unemployment appears as a recent "invention" (Castel, 1995). The term "lack of work" is directly related with the emergency of the "wage earning society" (*idem*, 1995). Also noteworthy is the fact that up until the early 19th century, "chômeur" was a French word used to absorb numerous situations including a day off, breaks or interruptions, in a context of personal and non-juridical bonds of work contracts; the meaning of unemployment was not experienced as it is today as for individuals their reinstatement were certain (Demazière, 2006).

This reality suffered a deep change with the development of the wage relation and formalization of labour: for most individuals, work is, inside its all activities, the one that occupies the greatest part of their lives (Giddens, 2004). Consequently, the concept of career itself underwent major modifications and it becomes ever more pressing for individuals to be dynamic, responsible and proactive to tackle everyday demands, namely in the professional area (Santos *et al.*, 2010). This behaviour by the individual is particularly important since work has taken a determining role both in welfare and in psychological health and in the construction of an identity, constituting a crucial element of the individual's integration in the community (Jahoda, 1982; Nogueira & Ferreira, 2007; Blustein, 2005). Instilled by the combination of the Industrial Revolution with Liberal Revolutions, that is how institutionalized labour contracts emerged (as known today), which, from then on, meant dissolving a contract implied the end of the bond between employee and employer permanently, treating this period of break as unemployment (Silva, 2009).

This new reality conjured a new professional category, which by the end of this process had established unemployment as an institutionalized and assimilated category that penetrated the normal conceptions of labour and unemployment (Demazière, 2006). It was the 1929 Great Depression that certainly grabbed Governments' attention towards the need to measure unemployment. This concern for quantification raises two questions, which will be analysed henceforward: i) what does unemployment mean? and ii) who should be counted as unemployed? In 1984, Eugène Freyssinet (Caleiras, 2011) defined the unemployed population, distinguishing it from the inactive population (see Figure 1).

Figure 1. Composition of total population
Source: Adapted from Eugène Freyssinet, 1984, p. 14 apud Caleiras 2011

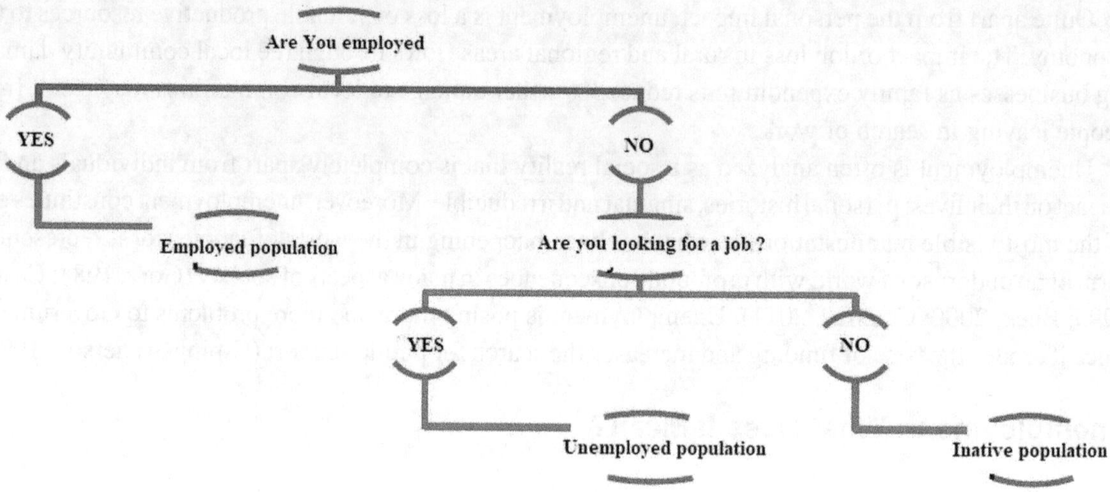

Per Eugène Freyssinet, to identify unemployed workers one must answer two key questions: the first consists in knowing whether the individual is employed. If the answer is positive, that worker will be accounted for in the employed population; if the answer is negative, the individual may be looking for a job or not. If the individual is not looking for a job he/she will be considered an integrating part of the inactive population: retired, domestic workers, students, etc. If, on the other hand, the individual is looking for a job, then he/she will integrate the unemployed population (Freyssinet, 1984). This approach causes trouble in obtaining an objective definition of the unemployed population: if the answer to the first question (do you have a job?) is objective, the second however (are you looking for a job?) incorporates a highly subjective dimension, for which it becomes difficult to answer it accurately.

In 2000, Guy Standing (Caleiras, 2011) adds one more variable to the two already presented. Standing believes that, apart from the condition of being jobless, the behaviour of looking for a job, there also must be a need for income. But, and regardless of how we analyse it, the definition may be controversial, in the sense that, according to the author, it is possible for an individual to be looking for a job without really want to get one but because of the needed income. Standing questioned the need to simultaneously fulfil the three stated criteria. This shows how, as in the previous case, the answer can be implicitly subjective, for which it is not easy to obtain unanimity in its definition.

The definition by the *Bureau International du Travail* (BIT) claims that "to be categorized as unemployed one must not have worked one single hour during the week the information is gathered, must be actively searching for a job and immediately available for one" (Gautié, 1998, p. 78). This definition presents some extremely vague criteria: how can one accurately define to be "actively searching" and "immediately available"? Despite its limitations, this is the definition that assists the base for the concepts put forward by the Portuguese National Statistics Institute (PNSI) and by the Portuguese Institute of Employment and Vocational Training (PIEVT): the two major sources of statistic information on unemployment in Portugal (Caleiras, 2011).

PIEVT, whose main mission, unlike the PNSI, is to act as an intermediary between labour supply and demand in Portugal, considers an unemployed worker as the "candidate that is enrolled in an Employment Centre (EC), that is jobless, looking for a job, immediately available and able to work" (IEFP). The category of "enrolled unemployed worker" encompasses everyone enrolled in the EC, who is jobless, actively looking and available for jobs, also including candidates previously in the condition of inactive (students, domestic workers and those retired, for example), or partial disability pensioners, if still capacitated for work and with a proactive attitude towards looking for it (*idem*, 2011). Per the established system, the problem occurs when many of the unemployed workers are not possible to be accounted for as such category, especially in the case of unemployed workers who are attending vocational training or are involved in other measures designed to fight unemployment.

However, some individuals are accounted for as employed workers even when, by lack of another option, they are working part-time. These conventions, the one by PNSI or PIEVT, rest on the principle of the so-called perfect division of the total population in three categories: employed, unemployed and inactive. However, it is not possible to unequivocally include everyone in one of these three categories. This lack of precision is further emphasised by the overlaps that in fact exist between the categories and through the dynamic approaches that illustrate the transitions and complexity of the flows which connect them (Figure 2).

Based on the analysis performed, illustrated in Figure 2, it is possible to conclude that one of the main reasons why it is difficult to define and measure unemployment is the fact that there are significant stripes of population that fall in intermediate positions between employment, unemployment and inactivity. Due to their quantitative and qualitative importance, there are five identified situations that must be mentioned: informal work, underemployment (part-time work, voluntary or involuntary), available inactive, discouraged inactive and employment policies, particularly vocational training.

Regarding informal work, this represents an aspect that is clearly escaping the statistic records. Despite being a complex reality, it can be said this is a professional activity, singular or secondary, practised outside legal, regulatory or conventional obligations, lucrative and continuous. It appears to be more common in southern countries, as Portugal, where informal work includes a very heterogeneous set of activities, ranging from unpaid domestic work to jobs performed without any legal context for the Internal Revenue Service (individual income tax) or Social Security, not excluding undeclared work side by side with declared work (Grazia, 1983, *apud* Caleiras, 2011).

From a logical point of view, assigning an informal worker to the active population is undisputable. One does work. But what happens in practical terms? If one adds declared work to informal work, the situation seems simple: fruit of the declared activity, assumingly the main one, the worker is classified as employed; in case of the individual does not work, he/she is classified as inactive or unemployed, depending on, as previously mentioned, if is looking for a job or not. If the individual is enrolled in an employment centre and is looking for a job, that individual is unemployed; if he/she is not looking for a job, he/she is classified as inactive. This is how informal work is, as can be seen in the figure above, at a crossroads, at the intersection between employment, unemployment and inactivity. As such, informal work introduces a new area of uncertainty that cannot, in truth, be overlooked. The problem is, once again, measuring its importance.

Correspondingly, comes the moment to analyse underemployment, the case of part-time work, whether voluntary or involuntary. The notion of employment often refers to the idea of a position occupied by a worker full-time, although this is not always the case, as for example when talking about short-term contracts or seasonal work. But when referring to part-time work, on the other hand, it is understood work that is carried out in a shorter schedule than usual. Thus, it makes sense to determine if this is a voluntary or involuntary situation. In the first situation, the worker may be between employment and inactivity, whereas in the second situation the worker may be placed between employment and under-employment, as observed in Figure 2.

It is worth mentioning the pertinence of the distinction between voluntary and involuntary situations. In many cases, the worker is out of options faced with the lack of more satisfying alternatives. Thus, the question of voluntarism is as if non-existing and is nothing more than a form of adapting to the labour market. Last, there are the cases of the available inactive workers, of the discouraged inactive workers and the employment policies, particularly vocational training. As previously mentioned, the notion of unemployment requires workers to be immediately available to perform a job. Such demands cause certain categories to fall out of the statistics, transferring them to the inactive population: the cases of workers enrolled in several employment centres who cease to actively search for a job due to consecutive failure.

From an official stance, these workers have not been due diligent in the search for a job and, thus ceasing to be considered unemployed workers and then classified as inactive, either available or discouraged. However, this behaviour results more from the conditions of the labour market, which is unable to (re)absorb them. These workers constitute an unusable work force and are relegated to inactivity, without the possibility to accurately measure its volume. They are placed, then, in the intersection between inactivity and unemployment.

Figure 2. Overlap between employment, inactivity and unemployment
Source: Adapted from Eugène Freyssinet, 1984: 19 apud Caleiras 2011

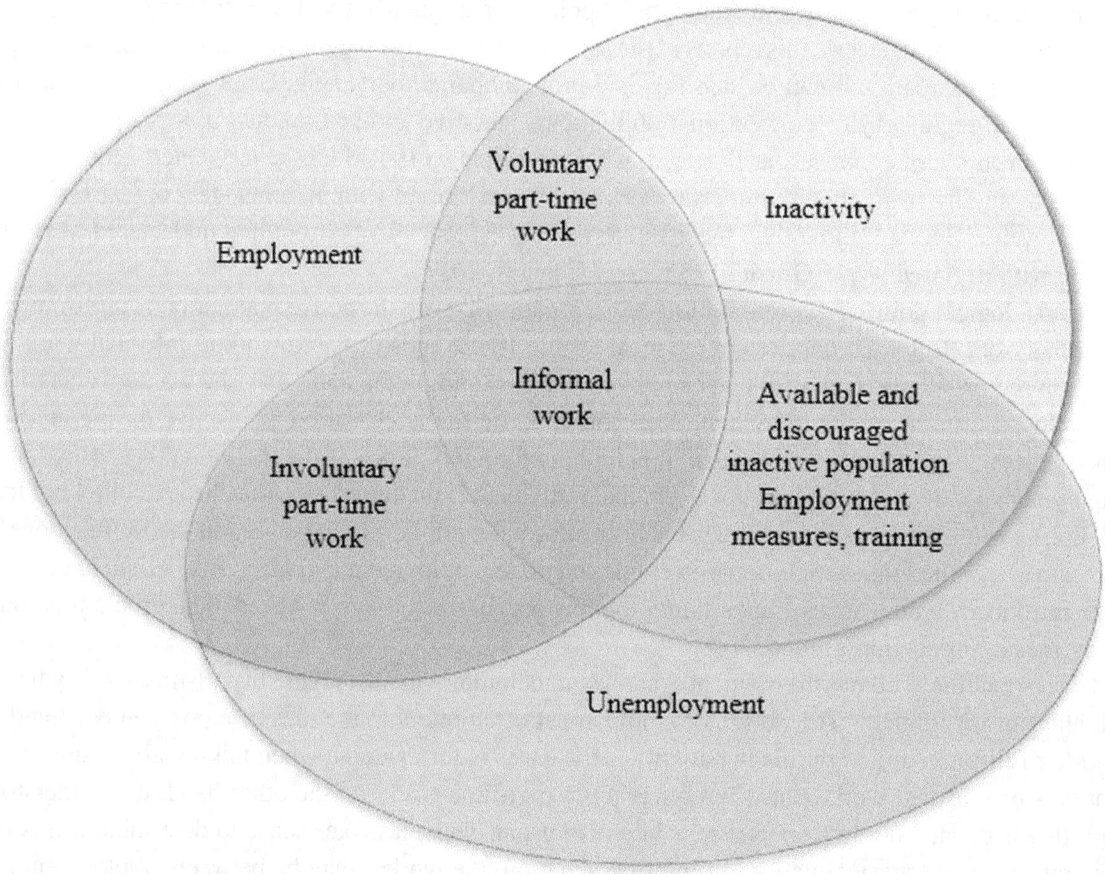

Figure 3. Active, inactive and informal workers
Source: Own elaboration

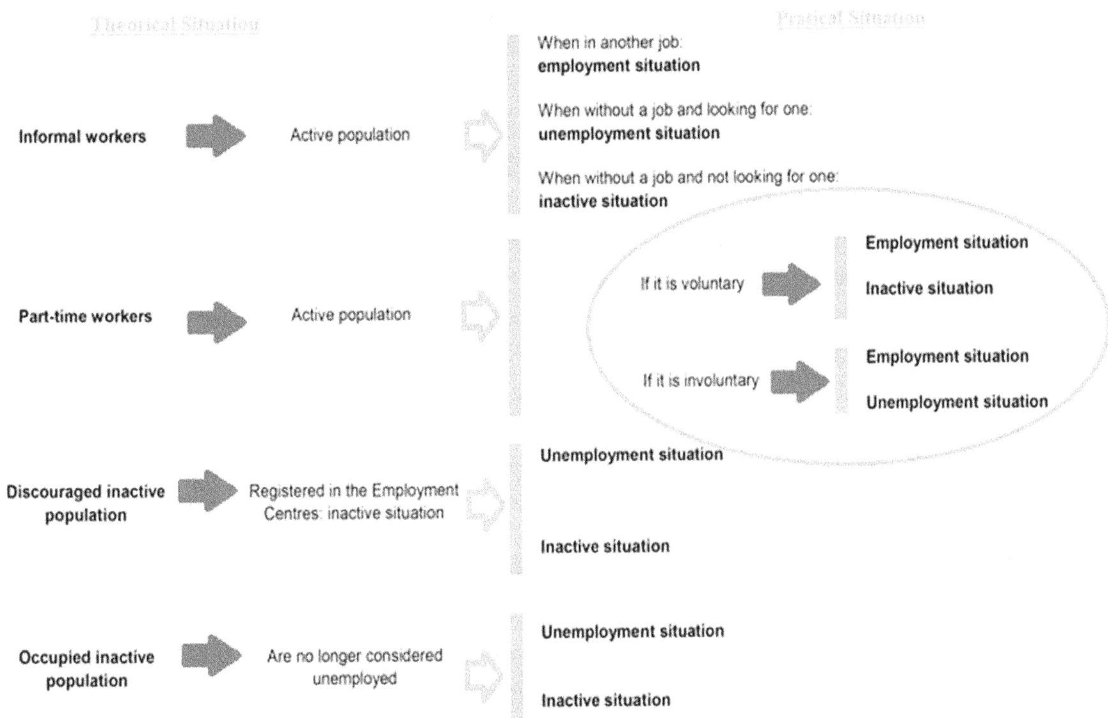

Another example results from the development of the so-called active policies for employment. The multiplication of these devices, as vocational training for example, are a positive element of the employment policy regarding the known insufficiency or inadequacy of the qualifications. Their almost "mechanic" consequences on reducing the numbers of unemployment cannot, however, be ignored. Following the argument that the integration of these policies makes the worker unavailable to accept an immediate job, the unemployed workers involved, for example in vocational training, will cease to be considered unemployed. But if the unemployed worker is in training it is because he/she is actively trying to improve his/her qualifications to then improve his/her chances to find a job. Vocational training, like other policies, is part of the search and (re)insertion trajectories of the labour market. Therefore, the declassification from unemployed seems to have an almost fictional character. In fact, it is not inactivity or employment, which eventually puts these trainees in a limbo between unemployment and inactivity.

In short, one can say that the statistic breakdown of the population in occupied active workers, unemployed and inactive workers present a high risk of leading to reductive conceptions of unemployment. On the one hand, by being a closed breakdown, it ignores the overlapping of the three categories. On the other hand, the adoption of a restrictive definition of unemployment with a simple difference between resources and work force needs leads to forget about the amplitude of the intersections that constantly occur in the evolution of the labour market, between situations of employment, unemployment and inactivity, especially during the past years (Figure 3).

In conclusion, and for purposes of this chapter, one can define unemployment (Freyssinet, 1984; Gorz, 1988; Scott, 1994; Castel, 1995; Beck, 2000; Standing, 2000; Giddens, 2004; Hespanha, 2007;

Caleiras, 2011) to underuse work, with deep consequences in several aspects of society, representing a certain position regarding a social structure: the labour market. The concept of unemployment is intrinsically connected to poverty and refers to a group of individuals who: i) share a condition: not having a job, ii) assume a certain behaviour: actively looking for a job; iii) have a need: income; and iv) are immediately available to work.

Unemployment Protection Policies in Portugal

Today, the Portuguese regime for unemployment protection includes a series of monetary allowances, which consist of the following: i) Unemployment benefits (UB): an allowance based on the principle of social insurance, of an amount proportional to the income being received before unemployment and with a tenure date; ii) Social unemployment income (SUI): corresponds to a fixed amount allowance with a less demanding tenure date than the UB and subject to a condition of resources. Besides the initial SUI, it is possible to obtain a subsequent SUI, as soon as the UB ends if like with UB the condition of resources is verified; and, iii) Social Integration Income (SII): a differential monetary allowance, subject to the condition of resources and the compliance with an integration contract, aimed not only at those who are enrolled in employment centres.

In the 1990s, there was a major period of stability in Portugal in terms of the eligibility requirements for unemployment benefits. Until then, the last reform (1989) had significantly widen the coverage of these benefits, defining a tenure date that ruled steadily until 2003 (figure 4). In 1999 the "partial unemployment income" was created, which could accumulate with part-time work, thus introducing a greater flexibility to this allowance. In 2003, the Program for Social Protection and Employment (PSPE) made eligibility for unemployment benefits easier through a significant reduction in the tenure date. These changes were in force until 2006 when, after an agreement between the Government and social partners, the tenure date for eligibility for unemployment benefits was reduced again, keeping, however, a more favourable tenure date than the one in force before 2003.

Because of the economic crisis that started in 2008, the levels of unemployment rose at a frightening rate and, in 2010, eligibility requirements for unemployment benefits became more flexible again. In Portugal, as the temporary measures ended, there was a reposition of the previous eligibility conditions in 2011. However, in 2012 the eligibility requirements were made easier once more by reducing the mandatory minimum period of contributions, as established in the financial assistance program. Aside from the fact that the Portuguese labour market does present a specific group of characteristics namely traditionally high unemployment rates, particularly in women, and high weight of low income workers, it has also been suffering extremely accelerated transformations especially in the last decade (Dornelas, Ministro, Ribeiro Lopes, & Albuquerque, 2011).

Through the data presented above, it is demonstrated that the unemployment rate has reached overwhelming and worrying levels in the European Union, where Portugal appears as one of the most affected countries, mostly in the youth population aged 15-24 who, besides being unemployed, cannot envision any prospects of (re)instating the labour market. Furthermore, it is of note that a big part of this youth population holds superior qualifications, which seems to indicate that holding a university degree no longer guarantees entering the labour market or obtaining a stable job.

However, unemployment never leaves anyone indifferent, in most cases being negatively experienced, triggering feelings of discouragement, anguish, self-deprecation and, even uselessness, together with notions of injustice and anger. From a social point of view, the consequences can also be felt through a

Figure 4. Evolution of the eligibility criteria for unemployment benefits: Tenure date in Portugal between 1990 and 2012
Source: adapted from Silva et al., 2012: 143-144.

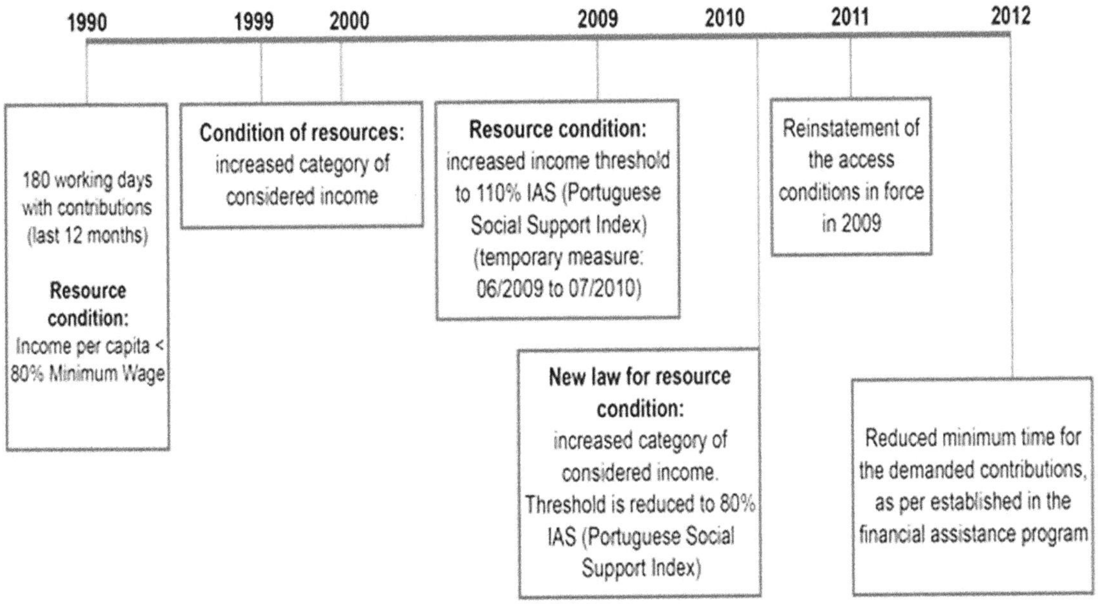

fall in taxes revenue, namely taxes coming from the unemployed workers if employed, aside from the increase in public expenditure with unemployment benefits.

This is a context in which, together with the rising long duration unemployment, exposes and compromises the future of today's and future unemployed population, specially the persistently overly exposed segment: the Youth. Even though one is not foreseeing significant gaps in their social protection, lately due to the existence of the social minimum support; it is likely the field of unemployment protection will witness the phenomenon of a very expressive youth unemployment segment that will be scarcely protected and with little or no possibility to find a job that can fit the principle of dignified work.

RELATIONSHIP BETWEEN HAPPINESS, ECONOMICS AND UNEMPLOYMENT

Relationship Between Happiness and Economics

Upon what has been previously mentioned, the prejudice of economics towards the study of happiness has been losing traction, as it now assumes a higher level of interest.

The results obtained and consequent analysis show that the level of happiness is related with economic aspects, but mostly with other factors that can take on an even greater relevance: a relevance that results from the necessary contextualization of the factors perceived by individuals and populations as important for their levels of happiness (Caleiro, 2011).

However, authors have not always been clear and objective about their studies, as the analysis is usually rather implicit in some studies. The Abraham Maslow hierarchy of needs (1970), also known

Figure 5. Abraham Maslow Pyramid of Needs
Source: adapted from Roseiro, 2009: 14.

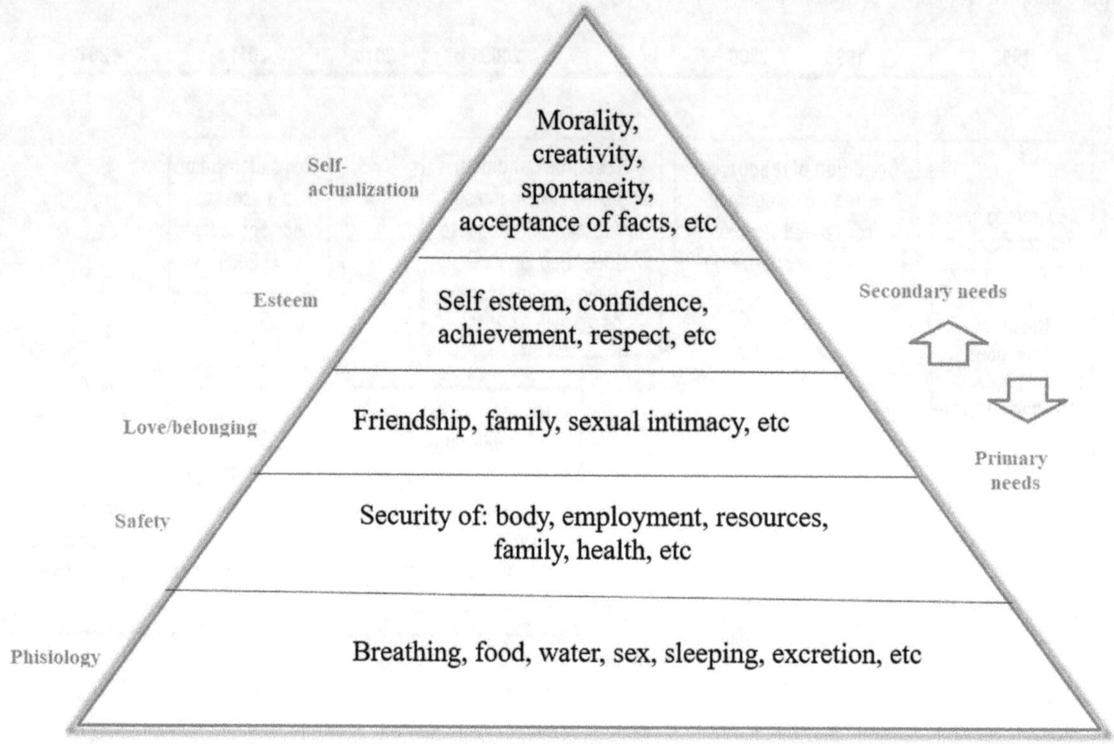

as the Maslow pyramid (Figure 5) is an example. Happiness is intimately associated with the Maslow pyramid, as the author was interested in understanding and hierarchically defining individuals' needs, which would give them a sense of satisfaction and fulfilment and, consequently, happiness.

Maslow's Pyramid of Needs is based on two principles: i) the principle of dominance, which determines that if a basic need is not fulfilled, it will influence the individual's behaviour, in the sense that the superior level needs will not consequently exert influence nor motivate the individual; and ii) the principle of emergency, which determines that any level of need of the pyramid will emerge as significantly motivating only if the inferior level needs are already satisfied (Koten, 2013). Thus, it is possible to state that, in some cases, an individual does not have to satisfy the top of the pyramid needs to feel completely fulfilled and, consequently, happy. Naturally, Abraham Maslow's pyramid of needs is not safe from criticism: workers' needs vary from country to country, according to the hierarchical position in a company and its dimension.

Moreover, the needs modify throughout time, according to the situations and comparisons individuals make between theirs and others' needs, which gives a static character to the theory and one of its biggest limitations (Porter, 1963; Hall & Nougaim, 1968; Ivancevich, 1969). Other points of view claim it is possible that a person can feel fulfilled, by the type of job performed, for example, without however obtaining total satisfaction from social needs, due to poor work premises (Porter, 1963; Manolopoulos, 2006). Nevertheless, this is the most well-known theory about motivation, which can be attributed to the theory's intuitive logic, which could be easier to understand (Ferreira, Demutti & Gimenez, P 2010).

In addition, Ken Wilber (1997, 2000) developed an integral psychology combination (Figure 6) of a coherent spiritual philosophy and an abstract psychological theory. Wilber established that all aspects

Figure 6. Ken Wilber, Integral Model
Source: Adapted from Wilber, 2000

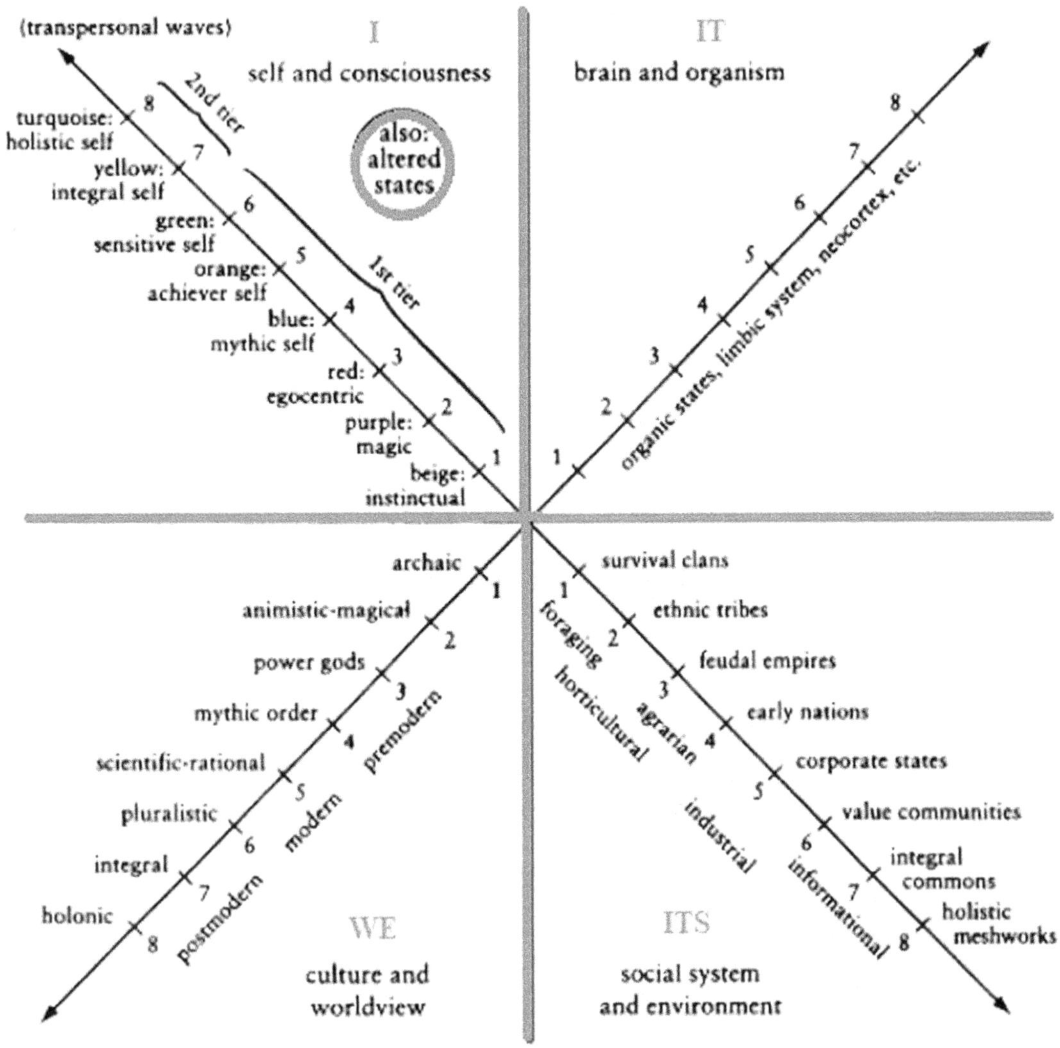

of our living and working environment have an internal (subjective values and motives) and external (objective, measurable behaviour and manifestations) dimension at both the individual and collective levels. By looking at reality from these four dimensions, it becomes clear that development presents an integral and coherent whole.

Regarding the relation between happiness and economics, there are several studies that demonstrate that a country's productivity level is not perfectly related with the level of happiness, which in turn is associated with the levels of satisfaction or quality of life (Ferreira et al., 2010). Moreover, reality shows that, in times of economic crisis, the level of happiness can increase (*idem*, 2010). Even though there are many factors associated with happiness (Theodossiou, 1998; Radcliff, 2001, Steel and Deniz, 2002, Blanchflower & Oswald., 2004; Helliwell, 2006), like personality, contextual, demographic, institutional or economic factors. This section will only analyse one single economic factor: unemployment.

Relationship Between Happiness and Unemployment

Unemployment is one of the most interesting economic variables for economists (Caleiro, 2011), as there are authors who claim that "'The experience of unemployment is one of the most significant causes of unhappiness." (Chadi, 2014, p. 1111). Consequently, more and more analyses are beginning to emerge on its relations with happiness. Interestingly, the fact that the importance of unemployment can be perceived by a study conducted by Wolfers (2003) which concluded that unemployment has 4.7 times a bigger impact on the level of happiness than inflation (Caleiras, 2011). For a better understanding, there is a question one must ask: are unemployed individuals really unhappy? It might be a common knowledge that being unemployed makes people unhappy. However, in accordance with the economic point of view that emphasizes the market equilibrium, unemployment is voluntary. In this sense, people who choose to leave their jobs, this mean the voluntary unemployed individuals, considering that everything else remains equal, should be happier than the employed ones or, at least, there should be no difference in their degree of happiness (Ohtake, 2012).

If, on the other hand, the employed people are happier than the unemployed people, taking the income level and all the other conditions as constant, the assumption by economics that people become voluntarily unemployed needs to be modified (idem, 2012). Unemployment causes a major fall in happiness, and even for those in work the quality of work can cause major variations in happiness (Helliwell, Layard, & Sachs, 2017). It is important to point out that, taking into consideration the budget constraints, it is better to create more jobs than to compensate the unemployed with the purpose of improving their level of happiness (Ohtake, 2012).

Nonetheless, several authors such as Abraham Maslow, Adrian White, Lester, Van Hoorn, and Wilson Martin Seligman (Mota, 2009) have proven not only the relevance of happiness for economics, but also the negative effects that unemployment has on the level of happiness, even when all the other analysed factors remain constant.

Empirical Studies on the Impact of Unemployment of the Levels of Happiness

Regarding the way that economics studies how unemployment affects people's happiness, there are strong critics to the way studies are made, as happiness is usually measured by using data from surveys that often ask '(…) to what extent are you currently feeling happy?' (Ohtake, 2012, p. 60.). Usually people's answers are measured on a scale ranging from 0 to 10 – where 0 means "very unhappy" and 10 "very happy". One of the accusations is that this question is simultaneously poor and vague as it not allows for an exact assessment of the individual's degree of happiness. Other comment is that it does take into consideration the reasons for the answers (Ohtake, 2012). Faced with the growing importance of happiness and studies around it, it is likely that the future is searching towards a standardization of happiness measuring methods and a definition of the concept.

This research analysed nine studies: each one of them features specific characteristics that represent an added value to the analysis of the effects unemployment has on the level of happiness (Figure 7). These nine studies were used based on the following criteria: i) seniority: the oldest study (1994), as it is a reference and it is mentioned in all the other analysed studies; ii) impact factor: the article that could have the biggest impact factor; and iii) specificity and adjustment to needs: the specificity of each study, in line with what is intended with this section, as well as the asset that each one represents, avoiding repetitions in the analyses and extracted conclusions.

Faced with the analysis of the results, it is important to reiterate the main conclusion: unemployed people are clearly unhappier than employed people. But one should not overlook the context in which these analyses and studies are inserted, as well as the several factors that may contribute to worsen or weaken the negative relationship between these two variables.

A special alert is given to Portugal, considering the high youth unemployment rates that the country is facing, a problem that can bring upon serious consequences for the labour market in the near future. Young people throughout their school careers and high qualifications have high aspirations and expectations regarding the value of all its educational degree's diplomas for employability. However, due to the recent economic crisis, these aspirations and expectations, socially nurtured by the school and the family, are largely frustrated. Because of it Portuguese youth is living hard professional insertion processes and is most likely to suffer from low self-esteem, social exclusion or a "wage scar. Something which in the long run turns out to have negative implications for society (Dieguez & Fonseca, 2016).

Last, it will be important to understand that the cost of unemployment extends well beyond the pecuniary ones, as the non-pecuniary costs today assume on a greater importance when compared with the pecuniary ones. Thus, it can be concluded that to raise peoples' level of happiness, it is more effective to create jobs than to redistribute the budget among the unemployed.

SOLUTIONS AND RECOMMENDATIONS

Given that everything seems to indicate there is a negative relationship between happiness and unemployment, it is essential that policies are set up to address these issues. Concerning happiness, it is advisable to promote initiatives that keep people occupied and motivated. Volunteer action and social entrepreneurship are highly recommended, with the advantage that people without jobs will feel useful and integrated in the community. About unemployment, in addition to policies oriented to encourage companies employing people in this situation, it is desirable to help people re-enter the labor market through professional training oriented to the profile and soft skills of the individual. Policies should be geared both towards quantity and quality of employment to support worldwide wellbeing.

FUTURE RESEARCH DIRECTIONS

As far as future research is concerned in the sense of developing and further researching the study of happiness, it is predictable that Happiness continues to assume an ever more relevant role in economics. This premise is based not only on the increasing importance given by science to the study of happiness, but also on the fact that happiness is becoming a more multidisciplinary study. This multidisciplinary aspect of happiness, together with the greater scientific engagement, support the prediction that the study of happiness will not be abandoned, unlike what happened in the 1990s.

The continuous improvement and development of technology, mostly in its interaction with neurology, make it possible to believe in its greater involvement, which may, in the future, allow to assess and objectively compare the levels of happiness of individuals, both qualitatively and quantitatively. Richard Thaler, the 2017 Nobel prize winner has given economists new insights into human psychology and new frameworks for understanding and predicting economic outcomes. Moreover, cognitive abilities, self-control, and motivation can vary significantly across different individuals, as human behave in complex ways (Benjamin, Stoker, & Suri, 2013).

Figure 7. Summary of the analysed studies on the influence of the unemployment rate on individuals' levels of happiness
Source: Clark and Oswald (1994); Winkelmann and Winkelmann (1998); Blanchflower and Oswald (2004); Böckerman and Ilmakunnas (2005); Eichhorn (2013); Chadi (2014); Helliwell and Hung (2014); Mikucka (2014); Van der Meer (2014).

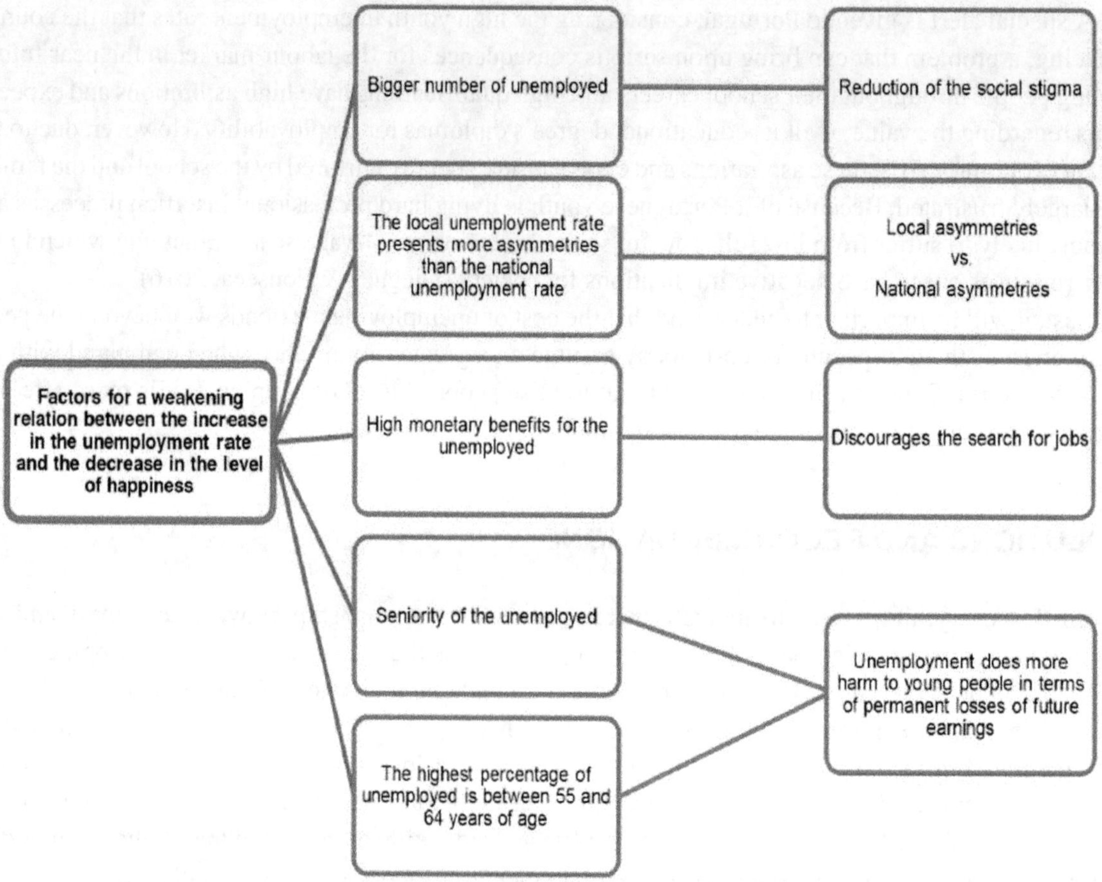

CONCLUSION

Even though the results of the investigation have already been presented throughout this paper, a global analysis of the results allows reinforcing some conclusions. Happiness is now a topic that has been gaining a growing interest for all players, in all areas, including researchers in the economic sciences. The relationship between happiness and money is positive, being possible to go as far as claiming that money buys happiness; however, it buys less than most people think, not only because people sometimes do not use it adequately, but also because there are several dimensions providing happiness for which there are no market and are unable to be acquired.

Throughout the world, employed people evaluate the quality of their lives much higher than those who are unemployed. The clear importance of employment for happiness emphasizes the damage that unemployment can do. Individuals' happiness adapts very little over time to being unemployed and that past spells of unemployment can have a lasting impact even after regaining employment.

Rising unemployment negatively affects everyone, even those still employed. These results are obtained at the individual level, but they also come through at the macroeconomic level, with national unemployment levels being negatively correlated with average national wellbeing across the world. Unemployment constitutes one of the most interesting analysis variables for several economists, as they argue that being employed, as far as the worker is concerned, represents much more than the simple income received for the performed work.

The relationship between the increase in the unemployment rate and levels of happiness is clearly negative, substantially affecting the people involved. Nonetheless, the negative relationship between the unemployment rate and the levels of happiness may be diminished or increased depending on the context of the studies, as well as the several factors that condition individuals, namely gender, marital status, age, local and national unemployment rates, given monetary support by the state to the unemployed, labor stability and literary qualifications. As a possible solution for this problem, and considering the evidence, one can claim it is more effective to create jobs than to redistribute the budget among the unemployed.

REFERENCES

Averill, J. R., & More, T. A. (2000). Happiness. In M. Lewis & J. M. Haviland (Eds.), *Handbook of emotions* (2nd ed.; pp. 663–676). New York: Guilford Publications.

Bala, B. K., Arshad, F. M., & Noh, K. M. (2017). System Dynamics: Modelling and Simulation. Springer International Publishing AG.

Beck, U. (2000). *The brave new world of work*. Cambridge, UK: Polity Press.

Benjamin, M., Stoker, K., & Suri, T. (2013). The Economics of Slums in the Developing World. *Journal of Economics Perspectives*, *27*, 187-210.

Blanchflower, D.G., & Andrew, J. O. (2004). Well-being over time in Britain and the USA. *Journal of Public Economics*, *88*.

Blustein, D. (2005). *The psychology of working. A New Perspective for Career Development, Counselling, and Public Policy*. LEA.

Böckerman, P., & Ilmakunnas, P. (2005). *Elusive effects of unemployment on happiness*. Discussion Paper no. 47. Helsinki Center of Economic Research.

Bruni, L. (2004). The "Happiness Transformation Problem" in the Cambridge Tradition. *European Journal of the History of Economic Thought*, *11*(3), 433–451. doi:10.1080/0967256042000246494

Caleiras, J. M. A. (2011). *Para além dos números — as consequências pessoais do desemprego* (PhD Thesis). Faculty of Economics of Coimbra, University of Coimbra, Portugal.

Caleiro, A. (2011). *Desemprego e Felicidade em Portugal*. Working Papers no. 2011_05, Department of Economics & CEFAGE-UE, University of Évora, Portugal.

Castel, R. (1995). *Les Métamorphoses de la Question Social: Une Chronique du Salariat*. Paris: Fayard.

Chadi, A. (2014). Regional unemployment and norm-induced effects on life satisfaction. *Empirical Economics, 46*(3), 1111–1141. doi:10.100700181-013-0712-7

Clark, A. E., & Oswald, A. J. (1994). Unhappiness and Unemployment. *Economic Journal (London), 104*(424), 648–659. doi:10.2307/2234639

Da Fonseca, A. F. (2004). A ciência em busca da verdadeira felicidade! *FidelidadESPÍRITA Magazine*, 18.

Da Silva, R. B. C. (2011). *Valores e Felicidade no século XXI: um retrato sociológico dos Portugueses em comparação europeia* (PhD Thesis). Sociology Department, University Institute of Lisbon, Portugal.

Demazière, D. (2006). *Uma abordagem sociológica sobre a categoria desemprego in: desemprego, trajectórias, identidade, mobilizações*. São Paulo: SENAC, Work and Society Series.

Denis, H. (2000). *História do Pensamento Económico*. Lisbon: Horizonte.

Dieguez, T., & Fonseca, J. (2016). Sustainable Entrepreneurship Lab, II. *Jornadas de Educação para o Empreendedorismo em Portugal*, 281-294.

Diener, E. (2000). Subjective wellbeing: The science of happiness a proposal for a national index. *The American Psychologist, 55*(1), 34–43. doi:10.1037/0003-066X.55.1.34 PMID:11392863

Diener, E., Weiting, N., Harter, J., & Arora, R. (2010). Wealth and happiness across the world: Material prosperity predicts life evaluation, whereas psychosocial prosperity predicts positive feeling. American Psychological Association.

Diener, E., Diener, M., & Diner, C. (1995). Factors predicting the subjective well-being of nations. *Journal of Personality and Social Psychology, 69*.

Diener, E., & Lucas, R. (1999). *Personality and subjective well*-being. In D. Kahneman, E. Diener, & N. Schwarz (Eds.), *Well-being: The Foundations ofHedonic Psychology*. New York: Russel Sage Foundation.

Diener, E., & Suh, E. (1999). National differences in subjective well-being. In D. Kahneman, E. Diener, & N. Schwarz (Eds.), Well-being: The Foundations of Hedonic Psychology. New York: Russel Sage Foundation.

Dornelas, A., Ministro, A., Ribeiro Lopes, F., Albuquerque, J. L., Paixão, M., & Santos, N. C. (2011). *Emprego, Contratação Colectiva de Trabalho e Protecção da Mobilidade Profissional em Portugal*. Portugal's Office of Strategy and Planning, Ministry of Labour and Social Solidarity.

Dunn, E. W., Gilbert, D. T., & Wilson, T. D. (2011). If money doesn't make you happy, then you probably aren't spending it right. *Journal of Consumer Psychology*. Retrieved on June, 2014, from http://www.wjh.harvard.edu/~dtg/DUNN%20GILBERT%20&%20WILSON%20(2011).pdf

Eichhorn, J. (2013). Unemployment needs context: How societal differences between countries moderate the loss in life-satisfaction for the unemployed. *Journal of Happiness Studies, 14*(6), 1657–1680. doi:10.100710902-012-9402-y

Esping-Andersen, G. (1996). After the Golden Age? Welfare State Dilemmas in a Global Economy. In G. Esping-Andersen (Ed.), *Welfare States in Transition. National Adaptations in Global Economies*. London: Sage. doi:10.4135/9781446216941.n1

Ferreira, A., Demutti, C. M., & Gimenez, P. (2010). *A Teoria das Necessidades de Maslow: A Influência do Nível Educacional Sobre a sua Percepção no Ambiente de Trabalho.* In the XIII Seminar in Administration.

Frey, B. S., & Stutzer, A. (2002). What can economists learn from happiness research? *Journal of Economic Literature*, *40*(3).

Freyssinet, J. (1984). *Le Chômage*. Paris: La Découverte.

Gautié, J. (1998). *Coût du Travail et Emploi*. Paris: La Découverte.

Giddens, A. (2004). *Sociologia*. Lisbon: Calouste Gulbenkian Foundation.

Gorz, A. (1988). *Métamorphoses du Travail: Quête du Sens. Critique de la Raison Économique*. Paris: Galilée.

Hall, D. T., & Nougaim, K. E. (1968). An examination of Maslow´s need hierarchy in a organizational setting. *Organizational Behavior and Human Performance*, 3.

Helliwell, J., Layard, R., & Sachs, J. (2017). *World Happiness Report*. Retrieved on September, 2017, from: http://worldhappiness.report/ed/2017/.

Helliwell, J. F. (2006). Well-being, social capital and public policy: What's new? *Economic Journal (London)*, *116*(510), C34–C45. doi:10.1111/j.1468-0297.2006.01074.x

Helliwell, J. F., & Huang, H. (2014). New measures of the costs of unemployment: Evidence from the subjective well-being of 3.3 million Americans. *Economic Inquiry*, *52*(4), 1485–1502. doi:10.1111/ecin.12093

Hespanha, P. (2007). É o desemprego fonte de pobreza? O impacto do desemprego e do mau emprego na pobreza e exclusão social no Distrito de Coimbra. *EAPN Journals*.

Ivancevich, J. M. (1969, August). Perceived need satisfactions of domestic versus overseas managers. *Journal of Applied Psychology*, *54*.

Jahoda, M. (1982). *Employment and unemployment: A social-psychological analysis*. Cambridge, UK: Cambridge University Press.

Kahneman, D., Diener, E., & Schwarz, N. (1999). *Well-Being: Foundations of Hedonic Psychology*. New York: Russel Sage Foundation.

Koten, M. M. L. (2013). *A Motivação do Trabalho dos Funcionários Públicos do Ministério da Justiça de Timor-Leste* (Master's Thesis). University of Minho, Braga, Portugal.

Manolopoulos, D. (2006). What motivates R&D professionals? Evidences from decentralized laboratories in Greece. *International Journal of HRM*, *11*(4).

Maslow, A. (1970). *Motivation and Personality*. New York: Harper and Row.

Mikucka, M. (2014). Does individualistic culture lower the well-being of the unemployed? Evidence from Europe. *Journal of Happiness Studies*, *15*(3), 673–691. doi:10.100710902-013-9445-8

Mota, G. A. L. (2009). *Three Essays on Happiness in economics. Exploring the usefulness of subjective well-being data for the economic analysis of welfare* (PhD Thesis). School of Economics and Management, University of Porto, Portugal.

Niza, C. F. (2007). *Economia da Felicidade e política social: contributos da ciência comportamental para orientação da acção pública com vista ao desenvolvimento humano* (Master's Thesis). School of Economics and Management, Technical University of Lisbon, Portugal.

Nogueira, S., & Ferreira, J. A. (2007). *A Realidade Psicossocial dos Sem-Abrigo: Breve Contributo para a sua Caracterização. Portuguese Pedagogy Magazine.*

Ohtake, F. (2012). Unemployment and Happiness. Japan Labor Review, 9(2).

Porter, L. W. (1963, April). Job Attitudes in Management: II. Perceived importance of needs as a function of job level. *Journal of Applied Psychology, 47.*

Radcliff, B. (2001). Politics, markets, and life satisfaction: The political economy of human happiness. *American Political Science Review, 95.*

Roseiro, A. H. (2009). *Factores Psicossociais de Motivação nos Cientistas. Um estudo de caso no Instituto Gulbenkian de Ciência* (Master's Thesis). School of Economics and Management, University of Lisbon, Portugal.

Santos, E., Ferreira, J., Albuquerque, C., Almeida, H., Mendonça, M., Silva, C., & Almeida, J. (2010). Desemprego: experiências de transição. *Psychologica, 52*(2).

Schwarz, N., & Strack, F. (1999). Reports of subjective well-being: Judgmental processes and their methodological implications. In D. Kahneman, E. Diener, & N. Schwarz (Eds.), *Well-being: The foundations of Hedonic Psychology*. New York: Russell Sage Foundation.

Scott, J. (1994). *Poverty and wealth: citizenship, deprivation and privilege*. New York: Longman Sociology Series.

Sen, A. (2000). *Development as Freedom*. Oxford, UK: Oxford University Press.

Silva, M. M. (2009). *O Mosaico de Desemprego* (PhD thesis). School of Philosophy and Human Sciences, State University of Campinas.

Silva, P. A. (1998). O RMG e a nova questão social. *Portugal, Society and Work, 3.*

Silva, P. A. (2002). O modelo de welfare da Europa do Sul: reflexões sobre a utilidade do conceito. *Portugal, Sociology, Problems and Practices, 38.*

Silva, P.A., & Pereira, M.T. (2012). As políticas de proteção no desemprego em Portugal. *Portugal, Sociology, Problems and Practices, 70*, 133-150.

Standing, G. (2000). *Unemployment and Income Security*. Discussion Paper Prepared for Geneva 2000: Follow-up to the World Summit on Social Development, Programme on Socio-Economic Security Papers no 3. Geneva, ILO.

Steel, P., & Deniz, S. O. (2002). Personality and happiness: A national-level analysis. *Journal of Personality and Social Psychology*, *83*.

Theodossiou, I. (1998). The effects of low-pay and unemployment on psychological well-being: A logistic regression approach. *Journal of Health Economics*, *17*(1), 85–104. doi:10.1016/S0167-6296(97)00018-0 PMID:10176317

Van der Meer, P. H. (2014). Gender, Unemployment and Subjective Well-Being: Why Being Unemployed Is Worse for Men than for Women. *Social Indicators Research*, *115*(1), 23–44. doi:10.100711205-012-0207-5

Veenhoven, R. (2006). Quality of life research. In C. D. Bryant & D. L. Peck (Eds.), *Handbook of 21st Century Sociology*. New York: Sage.

Vohs, K. D., & Baumeister, R. F. (2011). What's the use of happiness? It can't buy you money. *Journal of Consumer Psychology*, *21*, 139-141.

White, A. (2007). A Global Projection of Subjective Well-being: A Challenge to Positive Psychology? *Psychtalk*, *56*, 17–20.

Wilber, K. (1997). An integral theory of consciousness. *Journal of Consciousness Studies*, *4*(1), 71–92.

Wilber, K. (2000). *Integral psychology: Consciousness, spirit, psychology, therapy*. Boston: Shambhala.

Winkelmann, L., & Winkelmann, R. (1998). *Why Are the Unemployed So Unhappy? Evidence from Panel Data. Economica*. The London School of Economics and Political Science.

Wolfers, J. (2003). Is Business Cycle Volatily Costly? Evidence from Surveys of Subjective Well-Being. *International Finance*, *6*.

KEY TERMS AND DEFINITIONS

Frustration: A deep chronic sense or state of insecurity and dissatisfaction arising from unresolved problems or unfulfilled needs.

Individualist: One that pursues a markedly independent course in thought or action.

Individuals: Individuals as the only ones responsible for themselves, as their welfare is almost exclusively dependent on their individual success.

Quality of Life: How good or bad a person's life is.

Utilitarianism: A doctrine that the useful is the good and that the determining consideration of right conduct should be the usefulness of its consequences; specifically: a theory that the aim of action should be the largest possible balance of pleasure over pain or the greatest happiness of the greatest number.

Utility: Something useful or designed for use.

Wage Scar: To have in the future an income below the average income of people with equivalent training and experience which may induce a passive attitude and lack of social participation.

Well-Being: The state of being happy, healthy, or prosperous.

Chapter 14
The Dragon's Footprints: The Impact of Chinese Migration and Investment in the European Union

Mona Chung
Deakin University, Australia

Bruno Mascitelli
Swinburne University of Technology, Australia

ABSTRACT

This chapter examines Chinese migration and investment into Europe and explores models of migration and investment by identifying the gap between the two. The chapter highlights the major characteristics of Chinese investment and migration into Europe by identifying and separating the investment from Chinese state-owned enterprises (SOEs) and that of private individuals. This triangulation provides scholars and policy makers with a unique scenario. The migration and investment literature has been conducted as two separate and parallel topics. A small number of studies investigate the relationship of the two as one inter-connected relationship. There is even less focus on Chinese migration and investment due to the fact that over the past decade it has been a fast-moving phenomenon because of the speed of Chinese economic development. In addition, China's different political and economic system and its unique state structure adds another layer of complexity for scholars.

INTRODUCTION

The continued economic growth and prowess of China in the global economy provides new manifestations and traditional ways of economic analysis and models, which quickly become redundant. China initially began as a major low cost global exporter and quickly became the key trading partner of dozens of nations. Each year since 2004, soon after entering the World Trade Organization in 2001, China's export driven economy became every nation's "favourite son" providing cheap and often poor-quality products but scooped up by global consumers at export rates of unprecedented levels. For more than a decade China had been a magnet to multinationals to engage in joint ventures and investment in China

DOI: 10.4018/978-1-5225-5787-6.ch014

and as such producing products at low cost. It took little time before the political and economic leaders in China realised that this approach was but an entry strategy and not a long-term one and that China needed to have a multipronged approach to economic engagement in the world. In changing its approach, it sought to encourage the need for greater focus on internal consumption for its own market as well as decreasing its tendency of being the workshop of the world. While its inward investment policy had been successful, less attention was given to its outward investment strategy. Moreover with the development of a middle class in China, Chinese external migration was receiving greater facilitation and for the first time since 1949 many Chinese began travelling and in some cases also migrating for short or longer periods of time. Some of this migration accompanied Chinese capital, which was spreading, to all corners of the world.

The term 'foreign direct investment' (FDI) is based on the internationally accepted definition of FDI, which does not include portfolio investment but, rather, the goal of long term engagement overseas and having an influence on the management of a company (OECD 2008). The phenomenon of Europe is abbreviated as primarily being the European Union of 28-member states though much of the analysis is focused on the main states of Europe, which include Germany, UK, France, Italy and Spain.

This paper seeks to address the new phenomenon of Chinese migration and investment in the European Union. It addresses the gap in the literature on this relationship and activity and examines relevant migration and investment models, which incorporate migration alongside the movement of capital from China. The paper examines the history of Chinese migration to Europe and then moves to the current three categories of migration: investments, professional migration and the illegal route. It explores the relevant question of drivers, policies and trends, which have been serving as the push-pull factors of Chinese migration investments. The paper also explores the structured and less structured manner in which Chinese labour and capital have moved into contemporary Europe.

MIGRATION

Literature on migration to Europe but a decade ago made scant mention of China as a source country yet more recently it has become mainstream King (2012). Chinese migration to all corners of the world is not a new phenomenon but its nexus with outward investment is. While many Chinese in this era of rapid economic development have followed outward investment to the African continent for reasons of access to resources, migration to Europe in parallel to its outward investment is a recent phenomenon. Chinese investment levels into Europe is still relatively low but increasing as is its migration. This combination of investment and migration is sure to redefine the European political, economic, cultural and societal landscape. What is different, which does not follow any preordained theories, is a relationship among migration of citizens, private investments and state investments. Migration investment theory in general only covers migrants and their private investment in the non-Chinese scenario.

During the global financial crisis and its European manifestation, Chinese outwards investment became significant and unmistakable. When previously Chinese investment may have been in alignment with the commercial presence of Chinese goods, the new migration and investment was high profile and buyouts of major international brand names and in some cases of strategic sectors such as automotive became common. The Chinese presence was as equal and strategic as any investment from the US or any other developed economy. Things in this regard had changed for good.

Migration is not a new phenomenon nor is there an overarching and widely accepted theory of migration, which provides a platform for understanding all of its facets and characteristics. While not the view of all, one scholar posits the view that no theory is capable of explaining the complexity of the migratory process "and nor will there ever be" (King 2012: 24). Theories of migration prior to the early 1960s focused mostly on domestic or internal migration. Moreover, with the development of human capital models in the late 1950s, migration began receiving greater attention from theorists. Bodvarsson & Van den Berg (2013) point out that the early understanding of international migration laid out that "the incentive to migrate is driven purely by international differences in the average returns to labour and human capital in the source and destination countries" (2013: 40).

Some scholars have addressed the specific migration outward investment nexus. Navaretti et al (2007: 2) provide a useful point of departure in their "complementarity" of FDI and migration "when these two phenomena move in the same direction (i.e. immigration and inward FDI)". While the case of outward investment and migration from China is a unique relationship, it does have some comparison to the concept of "networking" whereas Navaretti et al (2007:2) note: "Migrants may indeed favour investment in their destination country from firms of their country or origins. Chinese and Indian diasporas in the west have most likely been induced by the recent surge of FDI from these countries". Casella and Rauch (2002), add to this notion that organized migrant networks also bring together opportunistic behaviour of their members. Schuller & Schuler-Zhou (2013) in addressing the Chinese diaspora in Germany claim that:

The existence of the Chinese diaspora can facilitate Chinese OFDI in Germany in two ways. First members of the diaspora set up business in Germany and undertake investment themselves. Second, they build bridges between the Chinese and German business community by working for Chinese or German companies...

China and the European Community (EC) established official relations in 1975 although a number of member states of the EC had established bilateral relations earlier. The UK established diplomatic relations with China in 1950 and France did so in 1964 under de Gaulle. West Germany followed the Nixon initiative after his visit with Mao Tse-Tung, and establishing diplomatic relations with China in 1972 along with the US (Congress Library 2014). The first Head of State visit from a Western European nation was French President Pompidour's visit to China in 1973 followed two years later with a reciprocal visit by the then Vice Premier Deng Xiao Ping to France. China's view up until the mid-1970s considered the European Union as a hostile capitalist entity was now in contrast to that of the Soviet Union, which saw the EC as merely the economic pillar of NATO (Erik, Hoffmann, Laird and Fleron 1991). A trade agreement between China and the EC was signed in 1978.

In 1980, China was included in the list of countries eligible for the Community's Generalised System of Preferences (of which it has since become one of the ten leading beneficiaries). Trade relations progressed to such an extent that the 1978 agreement proved to be inadequate and was superseded in 1985 by a broader agreement on economic and trade cooperation. Relations continued to improve; this was reflected in a 1987 agreement to set up a centre for the application of biotechnology in agriculture and medicine. Efforts to encourage investments for mutual benefit were also made. Meetings at ministerial level became more frequent and in 1988, the Commission opened a delegation in Beijing. The EU (then called the EC) had just reached the membership level of nine members with the entry of the UK, Denmark and Ireland.

CHINESE MIGRATION TO EUROPE

Chinese migration to Europe is a relatively new phenomenon starting as early as the Opium War 1839-41 when China was forced to open itself to the West (Latham & Wu 2013). The early migration of that period was driven by essentially two factors. On the one hand better economic conditions and return; and secondly forced migration seeking better economic conditions.

The initial Chinese migration was through the coolies trading system, which resulted in Chinese labour settling in Europe (Pieke 2004). The next wave of Chinese emigrants came after the Second World War. These included mostly Hong Kong Chinese migrating to Europe and especially to the UK thorough out the 1960s, 1970s and into the 1980s (Latham & Wu 2013). This movement from Hong Kong to the UK was largely due to *quid pro quo* from the 99-year leasing concession of Hong Kong to the UK from 1898 following a series of treaties between the Qing government and Western countries (Chang 2013). Most Chinese from mainland China were restricted from travelling outside of China from 1949 after the establishment of People's Republic of China.

The new momentum of Chinese emigration especially from mainland China only emerged after the open-door policy in 1978 (Chung 2008). The new phenomenon of Chinese migration to Europe as a consequence of the new openness occurred along three different lines. These included Investment migration (Cai & Clacher 2009); Student migration (Qu, Zhang, Luo & Li 2011) and professional migration (Iredale 2001). The third form, different from the other two forms, was smaller due to reasons related to (host) migration policies and language and skill restrictions. The other two migration categories have been growing in the last decades. This paper will however primarily focus on investment migration:

Throughout the 1950s, 1960s and 1970s, Europe's Chinese migration system had remained profoundly parochial. A handful of sending areas specialised in European migration and the flows that they generated often had little to do with the global trends in Chinese migration. Changes in the global Chinese migration system rapidly caught up with the continent in the 1980s and 1990s. (Pieke 2004)

Chinese migrants have traditionally preferred Southeast Asian countries as their destination, where about 80 per cent of the estimated 25 million overseas Chinese (Huaqiao 华侨) are currently living. People of Chinese descent living in Hong Kong, Macao and Taiwan are not included in this figure by the Chinese government, as they are not counted as being Huaqiao. Population statistics of Chinese living in the European Union, however, often mix up these different groups. The US and certain European countries are now becoming the other popular destinations for migrants from China (Latham & Wu 2013: 15).

Chinese emigration in 2010/2011 of 3.8 million was the second largest in the world after Mexico (OECD-UNDESA 2013). Although small by percentage, the Chinese emigration to Europe has grown rapidly in the past three decades (Latham & Wu 2013). Moreover, it was growing at rates much higher than the global growth rate. Chinese investment for the purpose of emigration, especially into Europe, is a relatively new phenomenon for reasons alluded to. China was relatively closed off to the world until 1979 when the open door policy (Chung 2008) approach was launched and encouraged. The open-door policy saw China undergo phenomenal economic growth of historical proportions and part of this growth was reflected in the outwards investment activities now possible for China due to the availability of capital in Chinese possession.

Chinese migration and investment by private individuals from mainland China until 1979 had been restricted by government controls. Later after the reforms, because of the relaxation of these rules, the

Chinese government made outwards investment possible and less restrictive. Further, wealth accumulation by private individuals after some levels of privatisation became more commonplace and as such individual wealth now became an investment possibility. This was in the backdrop of a fear and distrust, as occurred in the 1950s, of unexpected retaliation by government to expropriate private assets but much has happened since then to allay these fears. Finally a distinct aspect of Chinese investment (OFDI) are the SOE investments which have resulted in some substantial scale projects developed around the world. The Chinese State has a large amount of foreign currency and therefore seeks to diversify its investment outwards. Strategically, China is seeking markets and resources internationally and Europe offers a large and valuable market potential.

The recent European economic down turn has placed Europe in a position requiring capital injection into its economy. The availability of Chinese capital lured European governments to compete with each other to attract Chinese investment in order to bring in this much needed capital for economic activities. This in turn has provided acceptance and even welcoming of China into the European economic scenario including changes of a political and cultural kind.

This Chinese investment into Europe started in real terms in the 1990s by a group of Chinese coming into Germany mostly via Eastern Europe. The Chinese reforms and opening up policy triggered a new wave of migration by students, both with the assistance of government scholarships as well as through self-funding. In the case of Germany, after the Tiananmen Square incident of 1989, many Chinese decided to seek permanent residence in Germany. The new generation of migrants (called Xinyimin 新移民) commute between China and Europe, and are spread across different cities and regions in Germany and have quality housing conditions and pursue attractive working activities instead of looking for the solace of close ethnic communities (Yü-Dembski 2005: 48-51). These groups of migrants in contrast to those that fit into the traditional concept of the diaspora, from (mainland) China, and coming to Germany in the 1990s were characterized by their belonging to transnational communities.

Literature on migration is in abundance (Castles & Miller 2009: Castles 2010; King 2012), though little of it explores in any systematic way why Chinese migrate to Europe and the drivers behind it. Yü-Dembski (2005) and Latham & Wu (2013) have made initial attempts to address this trend. Nonetheless, some empirical findings suggest that migration to Europe by the Chinese occurs in three major ways. The first of these is through investment channels (private and SOEs), a second manner is professional and student migration and the third and last manner is through illegal routes. For the purpose of this paper, the first two channels are the avenues explored by this paper.

CHINESE INVESTMENT

Chinese outward investment has only begun to accelerate rapidly in the recent years even though China has been a major driver for world economic growth for some time. Along with the role of government policies, some of this private capital accumulation has to do with the Chinese having the highest saving rate in the world and as such many Chinese households deposit large sums of capital into bank accounts. In comparison, Western households tend to put their capital into investments such as real estate, shares and other investment opportunities. Until recently, the government made it a norm not to promote OFDI especially for private investors. This has changed significantly.

Although growing rapidly and drawing much attention internationally, Chinese investment into the EU is still in its infancy in the overall scheme but is growing at record levels. According to one report:

Chinese investment into Europe is at record levels. With 153 separate investments worth $18bn last year [2014] Europe has emerged as one of the top destinations for Chinese foreign investment globally. (Baker McKenzie 2015)

Moreover, this has been a re-affirmed trend beginning in large measure around 2009 encouraged by the bargain sales in the middle of the European economic crisis, many refer to as the Eurozone sovereign debt crisis. Chinese investment has stretched across many sectors such as food, agriculture and automotive sectors especially in the UK, Italy and the Netherlands.

China has been a major recipient of FDI especially in the last decades. However, a change occurred in the mid-2000s when Chinese demand sent global commodity import prices soaring and state-owned enterprises began venturing abroad in large numbers. The push for natural resource investments boosted Chinese outward FDI from less than $US2 billion in 2004 to $US364 billion by the end of 2011. Chinese OFDIs do not overall follow the same pathways indicated in the investment models in the literature. Due to the fact that Chinese SOEs may have access to capital, not only for the amounts required for making overseas acquisitions, but do so at times at below market price. The state owned system which allows Chinese firms access to vast amounts of capital, often not in proportion to the size of the firm is an unsettling characteristic. Kolstad and Wiig (2012) in their investment approach found that Chinese OFDI had a correlation with the presence of weak institution countries with rich natural resources. This would not fit the European scenario well nor would it account for the growing Chinese migration following this investment. At the end of 2012, China's investment into the EU was ninth in order of importance in the world after the US, Switzerland, Canada, Brazil, Russia, Australia, Hong Kong and Singapore totalling 118 billion Euros (Eurostat 2014).

Investment migration in to Europe has become a major focus of interest (Spaan et al 2005) and especially since the GFC in 2008. Overseas Foreign Direct Investment (OFDI) from China to Europe between 2005-2009 increased 6.6 times outstripping the total average OFDI growth by 4.6 times (Latham & Wu 2013). The focus on Chinese OFDI assumes two major categories: investment from SOEs (State owned Enterprises) or investment from private sources. These characteristics are distinctly Chinese though both forms of investment are very specific. Investments from Chinese SOEs are unique and have no equivalents in the world especially given their extensive and widespread nature in the Chinese economy. Moreover, these investments have alluded scholars, which have sought to investigate them (Peng 2012). Fundamentally, SOEs are state owned enterprises, which mean they do not comply with the normal market trends or patterns and the majority of overseas investment transactions are from SOEs (Luedi 2008).

There is a major lack of data and analysis in this particular area (Buckley et al 2008) because MOFCOM (Ministry of Commerce) and SAFE (State Administration of Foreign Exchange) are the only two official sources that publish Chinese OFDI research. Research in this area is still in its early days. The private investments have the need to follow a normal market performance theory. The initial drive of the investments is usually migration rather than business and this area experiences little data availability.

CHINESE INVESTMENT INTO THE EU

Chinese outwards investments are driven overall by trade facilitation and natural resources although this investment is undergoing maturity and is evolving, seeking operating platforms, brands and technology in developed economies· Moreover, Chinese migration is growing rapidly due to push and pull factors (Pieke and Speelman 2013). These factors are:

1. Government policies from both China and EU countries;
2. State-owned enterprise (SOE) reform;
3. The rapid growth of international trade between China and Europe;
4. The strong growth of the Chinese people's income and consumption;
5. The unequal distribution of wealth and the benefits of economic reform in China;
6. The establishment of key niche economic sectors;
7. The development of illegal immigration routes;
8. The relaxation of immigration policies in key European countries;
9. Extensive family networks, often reaching across several European countries; and
10. The internationalisation of higher education.

The major link between Chinese migration and Chinese outwards investments is economic reform, growth of the Chinese economy, increased income and foreign currency reserves. The reform of SOEs in the late 1990s lead to the redundancy of tens of millions of SOE employees. Many after losing their jobs went abroad, many to Europe to seek employment (Pieke and Speelman 2013). After the GFC, cash-strapped European governments are actively bringing out policies to attract Chinese investors[1] especially in the after math of the Eurozone crisis (Chung and Mascitelli 2013). Country governments compete to make their immigration policy attractive in ways, which can include:

1. Setting low outlay minimum investments;
2. Allowing family members to be a part of the application;
3. Relaxing or having no minimum stay;
4. Setting a wide variety of investments options such as a simple real estate investment;
5. Promising permanent residencies and citizenships in short period of time; and
6. Free travel or EU residence treatment within EU.

Researching into the Chinese OFDI, two major policies stand out in recent years in China as having acted as major triggers for Chinese MNEs, particularly SOEs, to go overseas. The first development was the 'Go abroad' policy introduced by President Jiang in March 2000 which is believed to have been a major catalyst for many Chinese MNEs, particularly those belonging to state owned enterprises, to venture offshore and 'experience' international competition (Buckley & Freeman1998). These MNEs did so with the political and financial support of the Chinese Government. Because of the strong government endorsement, Chinese investment in many parts of the world, including in Australia's resource sector, has attracted a certain amount of suspicion and concern.

The second Chinese Government policy which acted as an incentive to 'go abroad' was the overseas investment by Chinese nationals under the title of the Qualified Domestic Institutional Investor (QDII) Scheme implemented in 2005 (MOC 2005). Under this scheme, it became easier for Chinese nationals to undertake foreign portfolio investments in equities and equity funds. Although the role of proactive government policies in influencing FDI is not new, its use by governments of developing countries to encourage outward FDI is new. While portfolio investments are different from FDI, this policy was an indication of the Chinese Government's proactive role in increasing China's investment in foreign businesses and, broadly speaking, to encourage domestic capital investment overseas. In more recent years, MOFCOM has a range of policies, which are administrated by local governments to also encourage private investors to participate in OFDI, which amongst other things helps to balance the foreign currency reserve of the country and reduce the pressure of acquiring more US treasury bonds. China is today one of the largest holders of these bonds.

The government SOEs are more focused on the outward investment venture and less focused on the migration aspect when it comes to OFDI. On the other hand, private investors tend to be more concerned about the migration aspect as well as the actual outward investment. As such, they examine countries with better migration policies also to attract more private Chinese investors. Kolstad & Wiig (2012) found that much of the SOE outward investment is undertaken in institutionally weak and unstable countries. In Europe, Chinese OFDI is highly concentrated within EU countries with the UK, France, Germany and Denmark as the top four investment locations (OECD-UNDESA 2013). Over 50 per cent of OFDI made by the Chinese are from SOEs in number terms and while private investors make up the remaining 50 per cent, their investments are smaller in value compared to those made by the SOEs (Qu et al 2011). These SOE acquisitions in EU are also more active in industrial products, materials, and energy and power. As discussed earlier, regarding the lack of data available on this topic, official figures do not always present the real picture of Chinese OFDI. The Chinese SOEs often invest in major projects which can involve large sums of money but it can actually misrepresent the real picture of total Chinese OFDI.

PROFESSIONALS AND STUDENTS

China as a new emerging economic player globally has become a major sender of new migrants to Europe. The Chinese skilled migration (including students studying abroad) is attributed to the global expansion of economic, scientific and technological, as well as cultural and educational exchanges. The development of skilled migration is also a result of an increase in the educational investment made by the Chinese following the continuous increase in China's economic strength and growth in personal income (Zhang 2003). This new phenomenon is different from any previous migration activities.

Overall, EU migration policies are less purposely built for skilled labour. According to the OECD, in 2006 only 26 per cent of incoming migrants were highly-skilled, in contrast to North America where 66 per cent of immigrants were highly-skilled (Qu et al 2011). Migration of low-skilled workers comes mostly from neighbouring European countries primarily from Eastern Europe (Cai & Cacher 2009) while highly-skilled workers to the EU have been drawn most notably from Africa (Clegg & Voss 2012).

Skilled migrants remit strategically to keep potential unskilled migrants at home. This is because potential employers do not observe migrants' productivity and thus pay them a wage equal to the average productivity of the group. All EU countries today have laws regulating minimum wage which ensure that immigrant workers are paid on equal terms along local workers.

In the 1990s, Chinese SOE companies in construction played this role by tendering for labour contracts in many parts of the world especially in the Middle East. These contracts were strictly controlled by the government agencies that workers were only recruited on the basis that they were politically "safe" meaning they would not become illegal migrants.

Iredale (2001) argues that national policies and bilateral and multilateral agreements (e.g. like in the EU) were becoming important in facilitating the flow of highly skilled labour. There policies are serving as 'lubricators' to speed up desired industry-motivated movements. In Australia, the 2012 Knight Review is a fine example of this argument.

In the past three major groups of migrants have been the major drivers of migration to Europe. These are: Group A – linguistic and colonial links; Group B – Geographic proximity; and Group C – Political/

Humanitarian. Highly-skilled immigrants make up 34.4 per cent, 19.3 per cent and 26.1 per cent in each of the groups respectively (Katseli et al 2006).

In the 1950s, the Chinese export of labour was an organised as well as a political and economic exercise by the Chinese government in which a large portion were sent to Africa as highly-skilled professionals including scientists, engineers, doctors and teachers. Many of these emigrants eventually settled in the countries they were sent to (Zhang 2003). These government-organised movements of labour, in more recent years, have included students, and have mostly been focused on Europe and America. Professional migration has been following a very similar pattern in terms of destination. The most attractive European destinations are: the United Kingdom, Germany, France, Italy, Holland, Spain and Switzerland. The number of skilled or labour migrants is lower than that of student and professional migration mostly due to labour market barriers and immigration policies of host countries (Zhang 2003).

As a more prominent group, Chinese students studying overseas are dominating the international student market. The growth rate and development trend in Europe especially in the UK has been remarkable. China has become the second largest country of non-EU students studying in the UK. Not only the UK but other EU universities recognise the growth and needs of Chinese students. Even those non-English speaking countries are very actively developing courses and degrees taught only in English to satisfy the needs of Chinese students as they don't usually have sufficient European language skills such as French, German and Spanish. The rate of growth however has been very attractive each year (Zhang 2003). For Germany, Chinese students make up one of the major sources of students and ultimately migration (Giese 2003).

Despite the rapid economic growth in China, in many respects it still lags behind Europe economically, scientifically and technically. In addition, Chinese skilled migrants are also attracted to Europe by its history, culture, scientific and technological advances and research opportunities. The more recent changes in the migration and employment policies certainly adds another dimension. Chinese studying abroad in recent years has become an important avenue in pursuing migration. Research has shown dramatic increase in Chinese emigration to Europe especially in the category of the self-supported (Zhang 2003).

Interestingly the overall numbers of highly skilled Chinese academics and professionals migrating to Europe are around the same as those coming from other European, Japanese, Russian and US destinations. Noticeably the quality in terms of qualifications is not as high as those overseas, which in turn has caused significant issues of "brain drain" for China, which in turn has consequences for the international competitiveness (Spaan et al 2005).

Chinese skilled labour with Chinese cultural knowledge is increasingly in demand in Europe due to the ever-growing trade relationship between them. The trade relationship between China and Europe has increased dramatically since the open-door policy in 1978 and since 2011, China has been EU's largest trading partner China, surpassing the US in 2011, to become EU's largest trading partner. This certainly increased the need for the China-Europe relationship and called for more demand on more highly-skilled Chinese professionals to perform, facilitate, operate and manage the China-Europe relationship.

Overall, the highly-skilled Chinese migrants are still targeting the United States as their number one destination where over 50 per cent of these migrants go to the US. Nonetheless, the professional migration of Chinese to Europe is on the rise. There is no doubt that the "brain drain" is a problem for China but like any other strongly developing nation, the "brain drain" is to be expected. In more recent years, the Chinese government has launched a number of initiatives in the attempt to attract the foreign-trained professionals to return to China.

THE IMPACT OF CHINESE INVESTMENT AND MIGRATION

Though the presence of Chinese migrants to all corners of the globe has provoked curiosity in the host countries, often they are seen as a 'mysterious community' (Nieto 2003) by the locals thereby creating some integration issues, the new Chinese migration with investment have invoked a different reaction. The growing trend of Chinese private investment combined with migrating to the location of the investment and using investment as the vehicle are not only current but growing. Student migration has been one of the largest export services for many Western countries such as the UK, Australia, and the US. Among all the international students, the Chinese are the largest in number and continuing to register growth.

Overall, the scale of Chinese investment into Europe is not yet significant in percentage terms (Clegg & Voss 2012) but this growing relationship is causing European firms to look at China for the greatly needed investment capital. Nonetheless, three major areas of impact through Chinese migration investments have been identified. 1. Some European governments are seriously looking at their migration policies in order to appear more attractive to Chinese investment. 2. Migration by Chinese investors in turn is making some impact on these European countries and their cultures (Latham & Wu 2013). 3. The new migrants end up making a significant economic impact on the local European economy.

EU governments have ceased the opportunities to attract Chinese investments by moderating their migration policies. This is especially so for those cash striped countries. For instance, Greece promised a 5-year renewable resident visa to those who spend Euro 250,000. Cyprus had a program, which required Euro 300,000; Spain and Portugal both offered Euro 500,000 got 'golden visas'. The Spanish Golden visas did not even require a minimum stay, and could be renewed up to 5 years along with free travel throughout the Schengen visa countries in Europe (La Vida Spain 2013). In addition, the stagnation of the European domestic market plays an important role too while availability of investment capital, rising domestic labours costs, and saving of transports costs seem to be less important or not relevant according to a CCPIT survey (CCPIT 2010).

Chinese investment and migration has dramatically increased the inbound tourism into EU. Especially with the geographical location of the EU countries, Chinese tourists would frequent as many countries as they could on each trip. As a result, a large number of Chinese tourist companies (state owned and private one) have been growing over the years. As a part of Chinese cultural habits, many bring gifts home and create great curiosity about this exciting western location. Hiring Chinese-speaking shop assistants is just one of the many changes occurring in European cities especially where Chinese tourists flood in and not surprisingly, where there are strong brand names. Tourism is another area where Chinese new migrants are providing fellow Chinese migrants as a bridge for greater levels of engagement (Latham & Wu 2013).

Economically the Chinese migrants created impact in many areas. The increasing number of Chinese tourists for instance lifted the demand and consumption on luxury goods in many of the European countries to a level that major fashion houses would not be able to survive without the Chinese visitors. Chinese tourists would make shopping as their top priority when visiting Europe that they would cancel visits to museum, galleries and even shortening business meetings. As a result, some luxury brands had to create restriction on Chinese consumer purchases in order to keep up with the demand as well as maintaining its brand value.

The new migration trend also changed ethic Chinese in host countries economically. The traditional model of restaurant business has begun to change. In Spain due to the large numbers of Chinese in large cities such as Madrid and Barcelona, this forced some Chinese to open Chinese restaurants in smaller regional towns (Xu 1999). In some cases, they also began to exploit other opportunities such as manufacturing and personal services instead of the traditional Chinese restaurants. New shops selling Chinese goods, mostly low prices, opened everywhere. In some places such as in Spanish and Italian cities, Chinese grocery stores and imported goods stores spring up one after the other. There can be as many as four or more similar type shop in the same street within 50 meters distance. These shops are usually supported by manufacturers owned by relatives in China, usually in leather and textile manufacturing (Xu 1999). They minimise costs by stocking the shops with stock directly from factories in China without having to pay for the stock. They run these businesses with family member, without a normal wage, opening long and flexible hours outside the shopping mall hours. All these benefits them from making a reasonable life in European countries such as Spain (Xu 1999).

In Germany, there is no difference in terms of patterns that Chinese migrant business and employment pursue especially in the catering trade namely family restaurants. This started to change in the 1990s. By mid-2001 the ethnic services industry already accounted for 6 per cent of employment with Chinese travel agencies as a typical example of the change (Giese 2003). The growth of Chinese-German business connections particularly in the fields of electrical engineering and automobiles convinced German enterprises to rely highly on qualified ethnic Chinese.

These changes also opened up new opportunities and demand for Chinese to work in many of these positions. For instance, in the leather goods manufacturing sector, it is almost entirely filled by Chinese workers in France and Italy. This created further demand for Chinese goods along with Chinese migrants (Latham & Wu 2013). Only a very small number would qualify at the professional level such as lawyers, university lecturers, musicians, engineers, doctors, translators and artists (Xu 1999). In Italy for instance, Chinese migrants from Wenzhou and Qingtian started with small manufacturing shops and soon after expanded into the supply chain. In the fashion sector, *Made in Italy* is increasingly occupied by Chinese investment migrants (Latham & Wu 2013).

As another form of investment, property investment and purchases are being noticed in a range of big European centres like London, Paris and Milan as well as in other European cities. These investments are raising the costs of these assets and drawing more and more discussion on the presence and ownership of Chinese investment. In some locations, this is causing levels of apprehension and concern for the locals. More importantly, Clegg and Voss (2012) found, new Chinese migrants are establishing new niche sectors in these European countries. In addition to tourism, in France and Italy, the Chinese have a presence in fashion and leather goods markets with not only Chinese investments but also a high level of Chinse labours/workers. Unfortunately some serious levels of social unrest have occurred.

The main pulling factors are market potential, access to natural resources, access to skilled labour resources and to advanced technology and R&D, acquisition of established brands and presence of Chinese firms. England and France are the two largest recipients of Chinese migrants in Western Europe followed by the Netherlands and in the past 20 years, in particular Italy has experienced some growth from a Chinese presence. Due to historical reasons, several of the Eastern European countries, such as Russia, Hungary, are also popular among for instance is one of the other pull factors for all European countries (Xu 1999).

The major change in investments is aptly reflected in literature and art works in the Chinese society. 'Wenzhouren yi jia', for instance, is a Chinese soap telling stories of Chinese migrants in Italy. Investments and business was the main theme reflecting how different they are in their ways of doing business and how these have affected the local community and cultures.

CONCLUSION

The presence of China, Chinese and Chinese investment in the European Union will assume greater levels of penetration and simultaneously a changing panorama of human and economic blending into the European continent. China is seeking to reach all corners of the globe and the EU is a prime location for this expansion. Chinese students will remain a strong source of Chinese private migration into EU especially through major European institutions, which are now better geared and equipped with English courses and degrees. Investment into the EU will not only occur through SOEs but increasingly through the presence of private investors supported by a willing presence of more global travelling Chinese. Some of this growing presence will be enhanced by the proposed Free Trade Agreement, under discussion between the EU and China, but it is China's desire to softly spread its wings across the globe in both economic and people terms. All of these developments will further promote the parallel development of Chinese migration and investment into the EU, which will see a greater Chinese presence in the EU through people and capital.

REFERENCES

Baker & McKenzie. (2015). *Chinese investment into Europe hits record high in 2014*. Retrieved from http://www.bakermckenzie.com/news/Chinese-investment-into-Europe-hits-record-high-in-2014-02-11-2015/

Bodvarsson, O. B., & Van den Berg, H. (2013). *The economics of Immigration: Theory and Policy*. New York: Springer Sciences and Business Media. doi:10.1007/978-1-4614-2116-0

Buckley, P., & Freeman, N. J. (Eds.). (1998). *Vietnam's Country Funds: An Emerging Investment Vehicle*. New York: St. Martin's Press.

Cai, C., & Clacher, I. (2009). Chinese Investment Goes Global: The China Investment Corporation. Journal of Financial Regulation and Compliance, 17(1), 9-15.

Casella, A., & Rauch, J. (2002). 2002, Anonymous market and group ties in international trade. *Journal of International Economics*, *58*(1), 19–47. doi:10.1016/S0022-1996(01)00160-X

Castles, S. (2010, January). 2010, Understanding global migration: A social transformation perspective. *Journal of Ethnic and Migration Studies*, *36*(10), 1565–1586. doi:10.1080/1369183X.2010.489381

Castles, S., & Miller, M. (2009). *The age of migration, International population movements in the modern world* (4th ed.). New York: Guildford Press.

CCPIT. (2010). *Survey on Current Conditions and Intention of Outbound Investment by Chinese Enterprises*. China Council for the Promotion of International Trade.

Chang, J. (2013). *Empress Dowager Cixi: The Concubine Who Launched Modern China*. London: Jonathan Cape.

Chung, M. (2008). *Shanghaied: Why Foster's Could Not Survive China*. Melbourne: Heidelberg Press.

Chung, M., & Mascitelli, B. (2013). Caught up in the Eurozone Crisis: The Case of Australia and China. *Journal of Modern Accounting and Auditing*, *9*(3), 416–426.

Clegg, J., & Voss, H. (2012). *Chinese Overseas Direct Investment in the European Union*. Europe China Research and Advice Network.

Congress Library. (2014). *Recognising the People's Republic of China: The experience of Japan, Australia, France and West Germany*. Reprint from the collection of the University of Michigan Library, USA.

Erik, P., Hoffmann, E., Laird, R. F., & Fleron, F. (1991). *Soviet Foreign Policy: Classic Issues in Soviet Foreign Policy: From Lenin to Brezhnev*. Transaction Publishers.

Eurostat. (2014). *Foreign Direct Investment*. Retrieved from http://ec.europa.eu/eurostat/web/-structural-business-statistics/global-value-chains/fdi

Giese, K. (2003). New Chinese Migration to Germany: Historical Consistencies and New Patterns of Diversification within a Globalized Migration Regime. *International Migration (Geneva, Switzerland)*, *41*(3), 155–182. doi:10.1111/1468-2435.00245

Iredale, R. (2001). The Migration of Professionals: Theories and Typologies. *International Migration (Geneva, Switzerland)*, *39*(5), 7–24. doi:10.1111/1468-2435.00169 PMID:19186395

Katseli, L., Lucas, R., & Xenogiani, T. (2006). *Policies for Migration and Development: A European Perspective*. OECD. doi:10.1787/20771681

King, R. (2012). Toward a new map of migration to Europe. *International Journal of Population Geography, Wiley Interscience*, *8*(2), 89–106. doi:10.1002/ijpg.246

Kolstad, I., & Wiig, A. (2012). What determines Chinese outward FDI? *Journal of World Business*, *47*(1), 26–34. doi:10.1016/j.jwb.2010.10.017

La Vida Spain. (2013). *Spain Approves Immigration Residency Visa for 500,000 Euro Property Investment*. PR Newswire.

Latham, K., & Wu, B. (2013). *Chinese immigration to the EU, New Trends, dynamics and implications*. Europe China Research and Advice Network. Retrieved from http://eeas.europa.eu/china/docs/-division_ecran/ecran_chinese_immigration_into_the_eu_kevin_latham_and_bin_wu_en.pdf

Luedi, T. (2008). China's Track Record in M&A. *The McKinsey Quarterly*, 3.

MOC. (2005). *Statistical Bulletin of China's Outward Foreign Direct Investment*. Beijing, China.

Navaretti, G., de Simone, G., & Sembenelli, A. (2007). *Migration and Foreign Direct Investment: A review of the literature*. Centro Studi Luca d'Agliano.

Nieto, G. (2003). The Chinese in Spain. *International Migration (Geneva, Switzerland)*, *41*(3), 215–237. doi:10.1111/1468-2435.00247

OECD. (2008). *OECD Benchmark Definition of Foreign Direct Investment* (4th ed.). Retrieved from http://www.oecd.org/daf/inv/investmentstatisticsandanalysis/40193734.pdf

OECD-UNDESA. (2013). *World Migration in Figures*. OECD.

Peng, M. (2012). The Global Strategy of Emerging Multinationals from China. *Global Strategy Journal*, *2*(2), 97–107. doi:10.1002/gsj.1030

Pieke, F. (2004). *Chinese Globalization and Migration to Europe*. The Center for Comparative Immigration Studies.

Qu, J., Zhang, Y., Luo, K., & Li, M. (2011). *Annual Report on Overseas Chinese Studies*. Beijing: Social Sciences Academic Press.

Schuller, M., & Schuler-Zhou, Y. (2013). Chinese investment strategies and migration – Does Diaspora matter? A case study on Germany. MPC Migration Policy Centre, 2013/08.

Song, M. (2003). Choosing Ethnic Identity. Blackwell Publishing Ltd.

Spaan, E., van Naerssen, T., & Hillmann, F. (2005). Shifts in the European Discourses on Migration and Development. *Asian and Pacific Migration Journal*, *14*(1-2), 35–69. doi:10.1177/011719680501400104

Xu, S. (1999). *Xibanya Huaqiao Huaren Xiehui Ji Lu Xi Huaren Shetuan Qingkuang [The State of Affairs between the Association of Chinese in Spain and the Sino-Spanish Community]. In Everybody Has a Chinese Heart*. Hangzhou: Zhejiang Renmin.

Yü-Dembski, D. (2005). Huaqiao – Geschichte der Auslandschinesischen in Deutschland. von Groeling.

Zhang, G. (2003). Migration of Highly Skilled Chinese to Europe: Trends and Perspective. *International Migration (Geneva, Switzerland)*, *41*(3), 73–97. doi:10.1111/1468-2435.00242

Chapter 15 Residents' Attitudes in Punta del Este (Uruguay): A Cluster Analysis

María Dolores Sánchez-Fernández
University of A Coruña, Spain

Daniel Álvarez Bassi
Catholic University of Uruguay, Uruguay

José Ramón Cardona
University of the Balearic Islands, Spain

ABSTRACT

Homogeneity studies in recent decades have segmented residents according to their attitudes. The aim of this work is to segment the residents of Punta del Este according to their attitudes toward tourism. Recently, there have been some segmentations of residents in diver's tourist destinations in the world. Resident segmentation has been performed with a cluster analysis using the K-mean algorithm, generating three groups: enthusiastic supporters (33.1%), supporters with nuanced opinion (45.2%), and people without a formed opinion (21.7%). The profile of the groups generated is quite similar and no groups with a clear opposition to tourism have been detected. The overall assessment of the residents surveyed in this research is positive.

INTRODUCTION

Tourism mainly depends on the goodwill of the local residents. The support of the local population is essential for the development of the tourism sector (Fredline, Deery, & Jago, 2013; Sharpley, 2014; Stylidis & Terzidou, 2014; Tovar & Lockwood, 2008; Vargas, Plaza, & Porras, 2009). It is a well-known fact that tourism developers and entrepreneurs should take into account the local community if they wish to achieve sustainable tourism (e.g., Ap & Crompton, 1998; Byrd, Bosley, & Dronberger, 2009; Gursoy, Chi, & Dyer, 2010; Nunkoo & Ramkissoon, 2012) as the reaction of the local residents is extremely

DOI: 10.4018/978-1-5225-5787-6.ch015

important (Williams & Lawson, 2001). The investigation of local residents´ reaction and attitude towards tourism is a key element in the correct planning of tourism. If the reason for the support or opposition on behalf of the residents is known, development can be adapted to minimize negative impacts and maximize positive impacts (Williams & Lawson, 2001).

A wide range of investigations have focused their work on measuring attitudes and evaluating their relationship with perceived impacts (e.g., Almeida, Balbuena, & Cortés, 2015; Andereck & Nyaupane, 2011; Brida, Chiappa, Meleddu, & Pulina, 2014; Frleta, 2014; Gursoy, Chi, & Dyer, 2009; Nepal, 2008; Nunkoo & Gursoy, 2012; Sharma & Dyer, 2009; Vargas, Porras, & Plaza, 2014).

However, the majority of the investigations which have been carried out do not analyze the heterogeneous nature of the studied population as one of their objectives. It should be noted that it is logical to consider that there is significant heterogeneity in the attitudes of residents due to various personal factors: working or not working in the sector, being from the region or not, educational and cultural levels, personal values, etc. Investigations which have sought to segment residents according to their attitudes towards tourism (e.g., Ali, Hussain, Nair, & Nair, 2017; Brida, Osti, & Barquet, 2010; Del Chiappa, Lorenzo-Romero, & Gallarza, 2016; Del Chiappa, Presenza, & Yücelen, 2016; Fredline et al., 2013; Garau, Díaz, & Gutiérrez, 2014; Gon, Osti, & Pechlaner, 2016; Lundberg, 2015; Monterrubio & Andriotis, 2014; Ribeiro, Valle, & Silva, 2013; Sinclair-Maragh, Gursoy, & Vieregge, 2015; Vareiro, Remoaldo, & Ribeiro, 2013; Ven, 2016; Weaver & Lawton, 2013) have repeatedly demonstrated this idea by revealing groups which are very supportive of tourism in comparison to other groups who are less enthusiastic or clearly opposed to the development of this sector (Sharpley, 2014).

Knowing and understanding the heterogeneity of residents 'attitudes is very important to understand the possible effects of the actions taken by managers to improve residents' attitudes, since the same action can have different effects on different people. For several decades the analyzes of this heterogeneity were scarce, but in recent years there have been increases in the works that seek to segment residents according to their attitudes toward tourism. The result is an increase in case studies that should serve as a basis for creating theoretical models, but the theoretical contributions in this regard are very few (e.g., Ramon & Serra, 2015).

The objective of this investigation is to segment the residents from Punta del Este and Maldonado according to their attitudes towards tourism, and increase the information available on the different types of residents that may exist according to their attitudes towards tourism. It is worth mentioning that Punta del Este is part of the Department of Maldonado and is the main tourist destination for sun and beach tourism in the Eastern Republic of Uruguay and one of the main destinations in South America. Most of the tourist demand for this destination is from Argentina. Punta del Este is considered one of the most exclusive Health Spas in South America. The segmentation carried out by the K-means algorithm has made it possible to create three groups with clear profiles. It clearly highlights that there are different opinions regarding tourism in Punta del Este though none are clearly opposed to the tourism sector. There is a predominant stance of support towards the tourism sector although with varying degrees of nuance.

BACKGROUND

The segmentation of the population into groups is based on the idea that people and their perceptions are not homogeneous. The objective of this segmentation is to describe a population in relation to certain phenomena through their congregation in homogeneous groups. In addition to analyzing the average responses of the whole population, the average responses of population groups or communities with low internal variability and high variability between groups are also analyzed in this case study (Williams & Lawson, 2001). Different variables are used to be able to define the segments which make up the society, the most common being demographics.

Investigations usually undertaken on the attitudes of the local residents consider the local population as a homogeneous mass and focus on the average response under the influence of variables that are considered to have the capacity to alter the same responses (e.g., Brida et al., 2014; Frleta, 2014; Presenza, Del Chiappa, & Sheehan, 2013; Vargas et al., 2014). There are models which describe the evolution of the attitudes of residents such as Doxey (1975) and Butler's (1980). However, in these cases it is considered that attitudes are homogeneous at a given time and variable in time. When considering factors such as age, language, time of residence and the distance in relation to tourist areas, it is not surprising to observe some differences (Belisle & Hoy, 1980). It should be pointed out that studies which treat residents in a homogeneous manner act in this way because their objective is to study relationships which cause direct or indirect effect on the determination of attitudes and opinions.

The diversity of opinions from the local community should be recognized to ensure better management of the tourist destination although several authors support the theory that local residents are positively predisposed to tourist models that are necessary for the economic development of a community (Jurowski, Uysal, & Williams, 1997; Lankford & Howard, 1994; Um & Crompton, 1987). Segmentation is a feasible approximation to the ideal situation which is the analysis of the specific attitudes of each individual. In recent decades there have been some empirical studies which sought to segment residents with the purpose of detecting different groups according to their attitude towards the tourist. One of the first segmentations, which included a sample of 123 individuals, is a study which was carried out in the peninsula of Sleat (Skye Island), in Scotland (Brougham & Butler, 1981).

Five groups were identified in the investigation carried out by Davis, Allen and Cosenza (1988): the "Lovers" (20%), the "Haters" (16%), the "Cautious Romantics" (20%), the "In-Betweeners" (18%) and the "Love 'em for a Reason" (26%). The authors determined that sociodemographic variables are not statistically significant when excluding birthplace (born in Florida or not) and knowledge about the impacts of the industry on Florida. Canan and Hennessy (1989) found substantial differences between the residents which were grouped according to their attitude towards tourism development in Moloka'i (Hawaii). Schroeder (1992) states there are three groups in his investigation on Flagstaff (Arizona). The work of Ryan and Montgomery (1994) in Bakewell (England) is based on that of Davis et al. (1988) in Florida and uses a very small sample. Three groups are identified: the "Enthusiast" (22%), the "Somewhat Irritated" (24%) and the "Middle-of-the-Roaders" (54%). The authors determine that the socio-demographic variables are not statistically significant when excluding those with children in the family and the time residing in the area.

In the investigation undertaken by Evans (1993) which uses data from New Zealand, four groups are identified: the "Lovers" (20%) who are married, middle aged, employed and have a high level of income. This group belongs to the Pakeha (New Zealanders descendants of Europeans); the "Haters" (11%) are a large proportion of people who are widowed, divorced, separated, unemployed, retired and non-Pakeha (Maori or ethnic groups of the Pacific); the "Controlled" (32%) are mainly people who are married, retired, employed and Pakeha; the "Selfish"(37%) are people characterized by being, mainly men, young, single, students and non-Pakeha. In this case there are statistically significant differences in relation to the socio-demographic variables of individuals in the different groups. Ryan, Scotland,

and Montgomery (1998) found three groups of residents in Rangitikei (New Zealand): the "Moderate Enthusiasts" (42.5%), the "Extreme Enthusiast" (17.5%) and the "Cautious Supporters" (40%).

The investigation carried out by Williams and Lawson (2001) analyses the attitudes of residents in ten New Zealand cities (Auckland, Blenheim, Christchurch, Hokitika, Kaikoura, Napier, Queenstown, Rotorua, Taupo and Whangarei). In their study they found four groups of residents according to their attitude towards tourism: the "Lovers" (45%) are married people who have property and greater wealth than the group of the "Cynics"; the "Cynics" (10%) is older people who have less disposable income. There is a lower proportion of married people and homeowners in this group than the rest of the sample; the "Taxpayers" (25%) are characterized as residents who have been living in the area for less than two years; the "Innocents" (20%) are people who live in areas with very little tourism. Thyne and Lawson (2001) conducted a study on the Southern Lakes Region, New Zealand. A sample of 1094 valid surveys was used and four groups were found: the "Lovers" (14%), the "We Miss Out" (40%), the "Self-Interest Supporters" (30%) and the "Critics" (16%).

Two destinations were compared in the Madrigal (1995) study, a rural destination (Sedona) whose tourism is based on nature and craftsmanship and an urban destination (York). In both destinations the same three groups appear: the "Haters" (31%), the "Lovers" (13%) and the" Realists" (56%). The "Realists" are the "Silent majority" show no interest in participating in debates on tourism planning. This study finds greater differences between the groups than the cities.

The study of Fredline and Faulkner (2000) refers to an event, the Gold Coast Indy Car Race (Australia), and determines five groups of residents in relation to their attitude towards the event: the "Ambivalent Supporters (Cautious Romantics)" (29%) who live far from the area affected by the event; the "Haters" (15%) who are made up of the elderly residents and who are opposed to the continuity of the event. This group has lived in the region for more than 20 years; the "Realists" (24%) who work in tourism or in sectors with tourism dependence; the "Lovers" (23%) who are defenders and enthusiasts of the event; the "Concerned for a Reason" (9%) who show concern for certain elements. Weaver and Lawton (2013) found four groups in the Gold Coast: "Supporters" (15.0%), "Conditional Supporters" (33.0%), "Conditional Opponents" (33.6%) y "Opponents" (18.4%).

Tamborine Mountain (Queensland, Australia) can be considered in the development phase of the life cycle model described by Butler (1980). The following are the three groups found in the investigation undertaken by Weaver and Lawton (2001): "Supporters" (27%), "Opponents" (22%) and "Neutrals" (51%). The "Opponents" are older and have resided in the region for longer than the rest of the groups. The reason for their arrival to the region is linked to the search for a quiet place to live

The investigation conducted by Fredline et al. (2013) analyzes the perception of the residents towards the Formula 1 Grand Prix in Australia in two different moments. Five groups of resident were found: "Very negative" (7.77% before and 2.34% later), "Negative" (14.08% before and 7.31% later), "Unconcerned" (40.29% before and 60.82% later), "Positive" (26.70% before and 19.88% later) y "Very positive" (11.17% before and 9.65% later). The study showed a tendency towards moderation in both positive and negative attitudes.

Brida et al. (2010) found four different groups in their study on the small community of Folgaria (Italy): the "Environmental Supporters" (40%) who agree with the positive economic and sociocultural impacts and the negative environmental impacts; the" Development Supporters" (27%) who agree with the positive impacts of tourism and disagree with the negative impacts; the "Protectionists" (14%) who agree with the negative impacts on the environment and disagree with the positive impacts; the "Ambivalents" (18%) who show an ambiguous stance in relation to socio-economic and environmental impacts.

Four groups were found in the investigation carried out by Presenza et al. (2013) in Termoli (Italy): the "Activists" (38.9%) who have a great attachment to the community; the "Disenchanted" (23.6%) who are skeptical about the virtues of tourism; the "Opposers" (19.7%) who are opposed to tourism, and the "Favourers" (17.8%) who favour tourism the most. Del Chiappa et al. (2016b) found four groups of residents in Olbia (Sardinia, Italy), in relation to the FIA World Rally Championship: "Supporters", "Neutrals", "Enthusiasts but culturally and environmentally concerned" and "Critics". Gon et al. (2016) analyzed nautical tourism and the attitudes of the residents towards this offer in destinations on the Italian Adriatic coast. Three main positions towards this sector were found: "Supporters" (51%), "Cautious" (29%) and "Sceptics" (20%).

Five groups were found in the study conducted by Aguiló and Rosselló (2005) in the Balearic Islands (Spain): the "Development Supporters" (11%), the people who firmly believe that thanks to tourism there are more economic opportunities and that the overall balance is positive; the "Prudent Developers"(26%) who believe that thanks to tourism there are more job opportunities although they recognize that tourism has created a major change in the local culture; the "Ambivalent and Cautiou "(24%) who present a fairly neutral opinion when assessing the positive and negative effects of tourism. Though they approve of the general balance of tourism, their valuation is below average; the "Protectionists" (20%) are the group which emphasize the negative aspects of tourism and believe that the global balance is negative; the "Alternative Developers" (18%) are supporters of new projects and the organization of events.

Garau et al. (2014) compared Tenerife and Majorca. They are two destinations with great tourist development. A sample of 487 residents from Tenerife and 584 residents from Majorca was used to conduct a cluster analysis on three groups. The "Positive" (39.7%) who see tourism as an activity that creates a high amount of benefits. This group is more numerous in Tenerife (42.3%) than in Mallorca (37.7%). The "Cautious" (27.6%) who do not value the benefits and costs generated, however, they consider tourism to be a necessary economic activity. There is a higher percentage of this group in Tenerife (31.7%) than in Majorca (24.3%). The "Critics" (32.5%) consider the benefits of tourism to be unimportant and costly. Critics are more abundant in Mallorca (38.1%) than in Tenerife (26.0%). In Tenerife there are more individuals with positive perceptions rather than negative perceptions whereas in Majorca there is a balance between both types of perception.

Recently, Del Chiappa et al. (2016a) analyzed the perception of the impacts of cruise tourism among residents in the city of Valencia. Three groups with different profiles were found: "Pessimists", "Cautious Supporters" and "Optimists".

Studies have also been carried out in other countries in the world, as in Greece (Andriotis & Vaughan, 2003), Portugal (Vareiro et al., 2013), Cape Verde (Ribeiro et al., 2013), Mexico (Monterrubio & Andriotis, 2014), Sweden (Lundberg, 2015), Cambodia (Ven, 2016), Malaysia (Ali et al., 2017), among others. In a study conducted in Crete using a sample of 194 households, Andriotis and Vaughan (2003) detected three groups: the "Advocates" (42.5%), the "Socially and Environmentally Concerned" (39.5%) and the "Economic Sceptics" (18%). In Guimarães (Portugal), Vareiro et al. (2013) found three groups: the "Sceptics" (19%) who are very concerned about the negative impacts; the "Moderately Optimistic" (40%) who perceive both the negative and the positive impacts of tourism and the "Enthusiasts" (42%) who notice the positive impacts but not the negative impacts. In Cape Verde, Ribeiro et al. (2013) found three groups: the "Optimistic" (55.6%) who are very positive; the "Rational" (17.6%) who recognize the benefits and costs of tourism and the "Indifferent" (26.8%) who give tourism a low valuation and do not show interest in the tourism sector. In the study carried out by Monterrubio and Andriotis (2014) on the spring break in Acapulco (Mexico), three groups were found: the "Supporters" (26.1%) who have a high valuation of the benefits of tourism; the "Ambivalents" (41.4%) who are not sure of the benefits and costs, and the "Realistics" (32.5%) who recognize the costs and benefits. Lundberg (2015) compared three tourist destinations in Western Sweden, finding four different groups with different proportions in each destination: "Development Supporters", "Prudent Developers", "Ambivalent/Cautious" and "Skeptics". Four positions of residents in relation to ecotourism were detected in a study in Cambodia (Ven, 2016): "Absolute Supporter" (69%), "Beneficiary Supporter" (14%), "Concerned Supporter" (11%), and "Ambivalent" (6%). There are no clear opinions on behalf of the residents opposing tourism in this case. Ali et al. (2017) analyzed a mature Malaysian beach resort destination and found three different groups: "Optimists", "Favorers" and "Nay-Sayers".

The various revised cluster analyses are characterized by using slightly different methodologies in different destinations. However some similarities can still be seen in the results obtained. The studies detect the repeated presence of two groups: tourism defenders and tourism detractors. Both groups continuously appear although in different quantities.

The "Supporters" represent percentages of the population which oscillate between 10% in mature and overcrowded destinations and 50% in the areas which are in the early stages of tourism development They are "Lovers" of Davis et al. (1988), Evans (1993), Fredline and Faulkner (2000), Madrigal (1995) Thyne and Lawson (2001) and Williams and Lawson (2001), the "Enthusiast" of Ryan and Montgomery (1994), the "Supporters" of Monterrubio and Andriotis (2014), Weaver and Lawton (2001, 2013), Gon et al. (2016) and Del Chiappa et al. (2016b), the "Development Supporters" of Aguiló and Rosselló (2005), Brida et al. (2010) and Lundberg (2015), the "Favorers" of Presenza et al. (2013), the "Optimists" of Ribeiro et al. (2013), Del Chiappa et al. (2016a) and Ali et al. (2017), the "Absolute Supporter" of Ven (2016), etc. This group is characterized by giving enormous importance to the positive impacts generated by the sector and minimizing the negative impacts. They also receive or expect to receive important tourism benefits.

The "Detractors" represent percentages that oscillate between 10% in emerging destinations and 30% in mature and overcrowded destinations. They are "Haters" of Davis et al. (1988), Evans (1993), Fredline and Faulkner (2000), and Madrigal (1995), the "Somewhat Irritated" of Ryan and Montgomery (1994), the "Opponents" of Weaver and Lawton (2001, 2013), the "Cynics" of Williams and Lawton (2001), the "Critics" of Thyne and Lawson (2001) and Del Chiappa et al. (2016b), the "Protectionists" of Aguiló and Rosselló (2005) and Brida et al. (2010), the "Opposers" of Presenza et al. (2013), the "Pessimists" of Del Chiappa et al. (2016a), the "Skeptics" of Lundberg (2015), the "Nay-Sayers" of Ali et al. (2017), etc. This group places greater importançe on the negative impacts and do not consider that they receive any benefits from the tourism sector except costs. In general, they would prefer tourism development to be less or even null.

Apart from these two groups which are always present, the various studies undertaken detect between one to three groups which are more difficult to compare. Parallelisms are difficult to perform due to variations in the methodology used. For example, the set of variables used in each study differs considerably; the statistical methodologies used are similar but not the same, etc. (Fredline & Faulkner, 2000). In addition, there are important differences between the regions studied. These intermediate groups are usually characterized by a less clear stance towards tourism than in the two previous groups but always tend towards positive general opinions.

In highly consolidated and crowded tourist destinations, individuals with high perceptions of both positive and negative impacts and who recognize the dependence on the sector for the region are usually one of the most important groups in volume. They are aware that the resident population is dependent on tourism. The fact that they are highly in agreement with the negative and positive impacts posed has led some authors to refer to them as "Realist" (Fredline & Faulkner, 2000; Madrigal, 1995).

In regions with scarce tourist development or large areas without the presence of tourism there are more or less large groups of people who express confusing answers which in many cases conceal a lack of firsthand knowledge of the sector due to the lack of contact with it (e.g., Aguiló & Rosselló, 2005; Brida et al., 2010; Davis et al., 1988; Del Chiappa et al., 2016a; Fredline & Faulkner, 2000; Garau et al., 2014; Lundberg, 2015; Ryan & Montgomery, 1994; Thyne & Lawson, 2001; Ven, 2016; Weaver & Lawton, 2001; Williams & Lawson, 2001). Finally, it is worth mentioning that some studies detect a group of individuals who are characterized by responding in a personal way and not a social way as in the other groups. They are people who value tourism development in relation to what they receive and what they give in exchange as an individual, and do not take into account the global effects on the society or the region (e.g., Aguiló & Rosselló, 2005; Andriotis & Vaughan, 2003; Davis et al., 1988; Evans, 1993; Fredline & Faulkner, 2000; Ryan et al., 1998; Thyne & Lawson, 2001; Ven, 2016; Williams & Lawson, 2001). In many cases they have just arrived in the region to work in the sector and with little integration in the local community.

Based on the analysis of the repetition of certain guidelines in existing studies, Ramon and Serra (2015) proposed the existence of five groups of residents whose influence in society will depend on the specific destination to be analyzed:

- **The Enthusiastic Supporters:** This group of people has a more favorable opinion, since they enormously value the positive impacts and underestimate the negative impacts of tourism. They tend to lose influence in society when development advances in favor of Supporters with Nuanced Opinions and those that are Critical;
- **The Supporters with a Nuanced Opinion:** This group may not be present at the beginning, but it increases its presence with tourism development. The opinions expressed by this group are positive but nuanced by the recognition of negative impacts;
- **The Interested Supporters:** In this case these are people who support tourism for personal interests. They are usually immigrants who came to the region for economic reasons and who have been living there for a short period of time and have no attachment to the local community;
- **The Critics:** They tend to be people who do not directly perceive the benefits that tourism brings, but do perceive the costs, and consider the cultural change and the loss of capacity of decision-making on the future of the region very serious;
- **The people Without a Formed Opinion:** This is the largest group at the beginning of tourism development, but as time goes by it reduces because the population continually increases its involvement in the tourism sector. In mature destinations, this group is nonexistent or insignificant in that there is an enormous knowledge of the sector that turns these individuals into Critics or Supporters, in their various aspects.

However, Ramon and Serra (2015) indicate that the five groups do not have to appear. Enthusiastic Supporters and Critics are normally found, but the other three groups may or may not appear.

GROUPS OF RESIDENTS IN PUNTA DEL ESTE

Methodology

The data used, which was obtained between March and August 2016, is made up of a sample of 420 residents from Punta del Este. To achieve the highest level of representativeness of the sample, the demographic parameters of the collated questionnaires were checked to solve potential bias in the composition of the sample. The questionnaire used contained items with five-point Likert scales for responses and a set of socio-demographic questions (Table 1). The maximum margin of error allowed was 4.88% given a level of confidence of 95%.

Resident segmentation has been performed using a multivariate statistical technique consisting of a cluster analysis using the K-means algorithm, in particular the statistical software SPSS 20. The nine variables used in the K-means analysis are: Economic Benefits, Social Benefits, Cultural Benefits, Environmental Benefits, Economic Costs, Social Costs, Cultural Costs, Environmental Costs and Overall Assessment. These variables are constructs composed of items measured by a five-point Likert scale, with 1 "total disagreement", 3 "indifferent" and 5 "total agreement". Economic Benefits, Social Benefits,

Table 1. Socio-demographic profile of the sample

	Frequency	%
Sex:		
Man	230	54.76%
Woman	190	45.24%
Age:		
Less than 25	104	24.76%
From 25 to 34	67	15.95%
From 35 to 44	81	19.29%
From 45 to 54	80	19.05%
From 55 to 64	49	11.67%
65 or more	39	9.29%
Level of studies:		
No Studies	8	1.90%
Primary Studies	39	9.29%
Secondary Studies	177	42.14%
University Studies	196	46.67%
Birthplace:		
In the region	181	43.10%
Outside the region	239	56.90%
Works in Tourism:		
Yes	243	57.86%
No	177	42.14%

Source: own elaboration.

Cultural Benefits and Environmental Benefits measure four different types of positive impacts. Economic Costs, Social Costs, Cultural Costs and Environmental Costs measure four different types of negative impacts. Finally, Overall Assessment measures the attitude of residents towards tourism development.

A cluster analysis is a multivariate statistical technique that seeks to understand the heterogeneity of a set of elements in relation to one or more variables. Cluster analysis allows segmenting an initial set of elements into groups that are internally homogeneous but heterogeneous with each other. There are several mathematical techniques to carry out this objective and one of the most used at present is the K-means. The segmentation is an approximation to the ideal objective that would be to take into account the peculiarities and differences of each individual belonging to the set object of study.

Results

Punta del Este and Maldonado carry an enormous weight in tourism within their economic activity making it difficult not to perceive the impacts it generates. As a result there is a high degree of agreement with the economic benefits (average score of 4.23) and a clearly positive General Valuation of tourism (average score of 4.06). The degree of accordance with the environmental benefits (average of 3.35) and social benefits (average of 3.28) is lower, while there is no clear position in relation to the cultural benefits (mean of 3.08). The residents believe that tourism generates benefits for the community but they are also aware of the costs they generate, especially of the economic costs (average of 4.11), but also of the social costs (average of 3.33) and the environmental costs (average 3.19). In relation to the cultural costs they show a slight disagreement (average of 2.91).

In the cluster analysis, using the K-means algorithm, three groups with clearly defined profiles have been obtained and the average perceptions are shown in Table 2: Enthusiastic Supporters (33.1%), Supporters with Nuanced Opinion (45.2%) and people Without a Formed Opinion (21.7%). The three groups show different postures towards tourism but the fact that none of them has positions which are clearly contrary to the sector stands out. There are few significant differences in the demographic profile of the generated groups (Table 3), but these differences can help explain the attitudes of the members of each group.

The three groups generated in the segmentation have been described by carrying out an ANOVA analysis and cross tabulation with the demographic variables. The demographic differences which are significantly different based on Chi-Square statistic are indicated in Table 3. Therefore in relation to the three groups generated it should be pointed out that:

- **The Enthusiastic Supporters (33.10%):** This group shows the highest level of accordance with the various types of tourism-generated benefits, especially with the economic benefits: increased revenue for public administrations (4.70), more employment opportunities (4.69), more investment opportunities (4.67), increased business opportunities (4.66) and higher income for residents (4.53). In the case of social, environmental and cultural benefits, the average values of the various items fluctuate between 3.99 and 4.26. There is clear agreement on all points. In relation to costs, this group disagrees with the social, cultural and environmental costs, but shows a high level of agreement with economic costs, specified in the increase in prices of various goods and services (Table 2). The overall valuation of tourism development is the most positive of the sample with the average values of the items above 4.44 in all cases. It is the group with more people born outside the region, specifically 69.8% (in the total of the sample it counts for 56.9%). It is also the

Table 2. Average values of the items

Variables and Items	Total Sample	Without a Formed Opinion (21.7%)	Enthusiastic Supporters (33.1%)	Supporters With Nuanced Opinion (45.2%)
Economic benefits:				
• Tourism generates many job opportunities for residents.	4.350	3.912	4.691	4.311
• Tourism generates numerous business opportunities for residents and small businesses.	4.195	3.648	4.662	4.116
• Tourism generates greater investment opportunities in towns.	4.264	3.791	4.669	4.195
• Tourism generates higher income for the Administration and local organisms.	4.293	3.758	4.698	4.253
• Tourism makes it possible to have a significant increase in the income levels of residents.	4.048	3.451	4.532	3.979
Social benefits:				
• Thanks to tourism residents have a better and more varied leisure and entertainment offer.	3.741	3.044	4.259	3.695
• Thanks to tourism basic services are better.	2.967	2.286	3.590	2.837
• Thanks to tourism there are better public services.	2.855	2.165	3.425	2.768
• Tourism promotes the restoration and conservation of historical heritage.	3.274	2.275	4.000	3.221
• Tourism improves the quality of infrastructure and public works.	3.555	2.769	4.108	3.526
Cultural Benefits:				
• Tourism promotes the conservation of local culture.	3.062	2.275	3.619	3.032
• Tourism enhances the conservation of local traditions.	3.000	2.374	3.489	2.942
• Tourism enhances the cultural identity of citizens.	3.167	2.626	3.604	3.105
Environmental Benefits:				
• Tourism encourages the protection of natural spaces.	3.379	2.725	4.029	3.216
• Tourism turns natural resources into a source of income for residents.	3.652	3.022	4.029	3.679
• Tourism is less polluting than other economic activities.	3.429	2.868	3.892	3.358
• Tourism encourages respect for the environment.	2.936	2.528	3.468	2.742
Economic Costs:				
• Tourism has made prices and the cost of living rise.	4.076	3.286	4.122	4.421
• Tourism has led to an increase in the cost of housing and land.	4.136	3.582	4.259	4.311
Social Costs:				
• Tourism has increased the levels of citizen insecurity.	3.119	2.846	2.561	3.658
• Tourism has increased the inconvenience to residents.	3.548	2.934	3.094	4.174
Cultural Costs:				
• Tourism hinders the enjoyment of public spaces by overcrowding them.	3.269	2.835	2.719	3.879
• Tourism has caused residents to feel like foreigners in their own town.	2.817	2.418	2.144	3.500
• Tourism has generated a negative effect on local culture.	2.588	2.560	2.007	3.026
• Tourism has generated conflicts between visitors and residents.	2.969	2.659	2.417	3.521
Environmental costs:				
• Tourism causes serious environmental pollution problems.	3.057	2.934	2.439	3.568
• Tourism causes the loss of local ecosystems.	3.002	2.736	2.496	3.500
• Tourism consumes excessive natural resources.	3.319	2.802	2.849	3.911
• Tourism has caused the saturation of some natural spaces.	3.362	2.857	2.921	3.926
General Assessment:				
• Tourist development has been very beneficial for the town and its inhabitants	4.093	3.648	4.489	4.016
• Tourism should continue to be promoted as a fundamental part of the town.	4.300	3.967	4.741	4.137
• Tourist activity is beneficial for residents' daily life.	3.988	3.681	4.540	3.732
• Thanks to tourism we have a better quality of life.	3.848	3.473	4.446	3.590

Source: own elaboration.

group with more people working in the tourism sector (69.1%) and well above the average of the

Table 3. Demographic variables with significant differences amongst groups

	Total Sample		Without a Formed Opinion (21.7%)		Enthusiastic Supporters (33.1%)		Supporters with Nuanced Opinion (45.2%)	
	Freq.	**%**	**Freq.**	**%**	**Freq.**	**%**	**Freq.**	**%**
Birthplace:								
Maldonado or Punta del Este	181	43.1%	43	47.3%	42	30.2%	96	50.5%
Outside Maldonado and Punta del Este	239	56.9%	48	52.8%	97	69.8%	94	49.5%
Works in the tourism sector:								
Yes	243	57.9%	43	47.3%	96	69.1%	104	54.7%
Not	177	42.1%	48	52.8%	43	30.9%	86	45.3%
Monthly family net income:								
< $ 30.000	88	21.0%	20	22.0%	15	10.8%	53	27.9%
$ 30.001- $ 50.000	138	32.9%	39	42.9%	42	30.2%	57	30.0%
$ 50.001 - $ 100.000	120	28.6%	26	28.6%	40	28.8%	54	28.4%
> $ 100.000	74	17.6%	6	6.6%	42	30.2%	26	13.7%
The effect of a crisis on income:								
It would decrease a lot	102	24.3%	16	17.6%	48	34.5%	38	20.0%
It would decrease	167	39.8%	39	42.9%	55	39.6%	73	38.4%
It would not change	149	35.5%	35	38.5%	35	25.2%	79	41.6%
It would increase	2	0.5%	1	1.1%	1	0.7%	0	0.0%

Source: own elaboration

sample (57.9%). The family income of the members of this group is greater than in the other two groups, highlighting that 30.2% of them are in the highest section of income. The higher presence of people working in the tourism sector implies that it is the group whose income would be most affected by a crisis in the tourism sector (Table 3);

- **The Supporters with a Nuanced Opinion (45.24%):** This is the largest group, representing about half of the sample, and is characterized by showing accordance with most of the benefits and costs. Their valuations of the benefits are inferior to those made by the Enthusiastic Supporters, being clearly positive in the case of the economic benefits (averages of four or higher), slightly positive in the case of social and environmental benefits and ambiguous towards cultural benefits. This group is the only one that is clearly in accordance with all types of costs (economic, social, environmental and cultural). Despite its high levels of accordance with the various negative impacts posed, this group shows a clearly positive general valuation of tourism (Table 2). The demographic profile of the members of this group is similar to the average of the sample and would be among the other two groups in the demographic variables with significant differences amongst groups (Table 3). It can be considered that this group is, in a way, the most "rational" as they are aware of the various impacts generated by tourism, both positive and negative;

- **The people Without a Formed Opinion (21.67%):** Show a positive general valuation of tourism development, but only show clear accordance with the benefits and economic costs. In relation to the other impacts (social, cultural and environmental) they show disagreement with both the benefits and the costs. This may be because it is the group with fewest people working in the tourism sector (47.3%). Ambiguous or slight disagreement responses would indicate that this group is made up of people with less contact and involvement in tourism. These ambiguous responses show a lack of "information" on the sector.

It is very striking that no group is detected as being clearly contrary to the tourist activity, proving that it is possible for a destination to exist without significant opposition groups, as was seen in some previous studies (Andriotis & Vaughan, 2003; Del Chiappa et al., 2016a; Ryan et al., 1998; Ven, 2016). The groups detected showed very similar demographic profiles and, therefore, the demographic variables would not be a good element for the prediction of the residents' attitudes of Punta del Este.

SOLUTIONS AND RECOMMENDATIONS

Out of the various impacts, it is the benefits and economic costs which are most recognized by the residents of Punta del Este. This indicates that tourism generates jobs, business opportunities and attracts investments, but it also causes a very important increase in prices. The image of tourist destinations makes it possible to create a differentiation amongst them which therefore allows for the increase in prices parallel to the prestige of the destination. A great increase in prices is very common in many tourist destinations but it causes problems as the destination loses competitiveness and attractiveness for the issuing markets as they offer the same at higher prices. As for residents, they lose purchasing power if salaries are not increased in the same proportion. All this causes deterioration in the quality of life of the local population and the risk of there being a crisis in tourism in the future. It is necessary to raise awareness in the various agents involved (administration, associations, trade unions, businessmen, residents, etc.) of the importance of moderating price increases, since the immediate benefit of higher prices can produce a future crisis by losing tourists to more economic destinations.

The benefits and cultural costs are the least recognized by the residents of Punta del Este. The fact that the majority of tourists who arrive are from Argentina, a country with minimal cultural differences with Uruguay, would explain the low perception of cultural impacts. This situation is very different from what happens in regions like Europe or Asia, where there are important cultural differences (language, traditions, gastronomy, etc.) amongst the different countries and even between regions of the same country. As there are no significant cultural differences between the resident population, immigrants and tourists, there are no changes in local culture brought on by tourism development. In this case it can be seen that the cultural similarity of people arriving in a region with its residents may not only be useful in the case of economic immigrants, by facilitating their integration, but also in the case of tourists, by avoiding an imitation effect that destroys local cultural elements. This raises as a priority option, in sun and beach tourist destinations, promoting the issuing markets that are most culturally similar to the local culture of the region whenever possible.

FUTURE RESEARCH DIRECTIONS

One of the most interesting results of this segmentation is that a group which is clearly critical with the sector, or, at the very least, without a clear positive overall assessment is not detected. The scarcity of studies with this result makes it interesting to continue analyzing various tourist destinations, especially in parts of the world with fewer previous studies, looking for new cases with this feature. The analyses that should be carried out would be segmentations, but also causal studies that would seek to explain the motives of the segmentations.

These new studies would make it possible to determine which characteristics make it possible to avoid the existence of groups which are critical towards tourism, improving the model proposed by Ramon and Serra (2015). There is room to consider that it is only the Enthusiastic Supporters who always appear in tourist destinations, as they are the promoters of that tourism development, while the rest of groups would only appear in some cases and depending on past and present tourist development, in addition to the characteristics of the local society and the majority of tourists.

It is widely accepted that the positive opinions of residents are fundamental for tourism development. Moreover, managers, public and private, must take into account the attitudes and opinions of residents in their decisions. The main implication of the results of this chapter for managers is that they must keep in mind the composition of society in their decisions, mainly in communication with residents. In the medium term, the managers must carry out actions aimed at turning the Without a Formed Opinion into Enthusiastic Supporters or, if at all, into Supporters with Nuanced Opinion, avoiding the formation of a group of Critics with the tourist activity. The nonexistence of a critical group is something very exceptional that has occurred in this case. Normally, the critics are the main brake to the actions taken by the managers of the tourist destinations and the companies of the sector. For this reason, it is very important that there be a pedagogy work on tourism, clearly explaining the positive and negative elements to avoid the growth of Critics with tourism.

CONCLUSION

The assessment made by residents of Punta del Este and Maldonado is positive, showing high degrees of accordance with the economic benefits and the overall positive appraisal of tourism development. There is also agreement with the social and environmental benefits and economic costs, indicating the existence of a clear problem of high prices in the region.

None of the three groups generated with the K-means analysis have positions clearly contrary to tourist development, but there is a risk that in the future, if the negative impacts increase, a group of residents critical with the sector could appear and initiate opposition to tourism and entrepreneurs. Although there are no big differences amongst the three groups, there seems to be a lot of people from outside the destination in the group of Enthusiastic Supporters who work in the tourism sector and have higher income than the average. On the contrary, in the group of people Without a Formed Opinion there are more people who do not work in the tourism sector and therefore have a less intense knowledge of it.

The example of Punta del Este demonstrates that there is no clear relationship between the most common demographic variables and attitudes towards tourism and there can be tourist destinations without groups which are contrary to the sector.

REFERENCES

Aguiló, E., & Rosselló, J. (2005). Host community perceptions: A cluster analysis. *Annals of Tourism Research*, *32*(4), 925–941. doi:10.1016/j.annals.2004.11.004

Ali, F., Hussain, K., Nair, V., & Nair, P. K. (2017). Stakeholders' perceptions & attitudes towards tourism development in a mature destination. *Tourism (Zagreb)*, *65*(2), 173–186.

Almeida, F., Balbuena, A., & Cortés, R. (2015). Resident's attitudes towards the impacts of tourism. *Tourism Management Perspectives*, *13*, 33–40. doi:10.1016/j.tmp.2014.11.002

Andereck, K. L., & Nyaupane, G. (2011). Exploring the nature of tourism and quality of life perceptions among residents. *Journal of Travel Research*, *50*(3), 248–260. doi:10.1177/0047287510362918

Andriotis, K., & Vaughan, R. D. (2003). Urban residents' attitudes toward tourism development: The case of Crete. *Journal of Travel Research*, *42*(2), 172–185. doi:10.1177/0047287503257488

Ap, J., & Crompton, J. L. (1998). Developing and testing a tourism impact scale. *Journal of Travel Research*, *37*(2), 120–130. doi:10.1177/004728759803700203

Belisle, F. J., & Hoy, D. R. (1980). The perceived impact of tourism by residents: A case study in Santa María, Colombia. *Annals of Tourism Research*, *7*(1), 83–101. doi:10.1016/S0160-7383(80)80008-9

Brida, J. G., Chiappa, G. D., Meleddu, M., & Pulina, M. (2014). A comparison of residents' perceptions in two cruise ports in the mediterranean sea. *International Journal of Tourism Research*, *16*(2), 180–190. doi:10.1002/jtr.1915

Brida, J. G., Osti, L., & Barquet, A. (2010). Segmenting Resident Perceptions towards Tourism - a Cluster Analysis with a Multinomial Logit Model of a Mountain Community. *International Journal of Tourism Research*, *12*(5), 591–602.

Brougham, J. E., & Butler, R. W. (1981). A segmentation analysis of resident attitudes to the social impact of tourism. *Annals of Tourism Research*, *8*(4), 569–590. doi:10.1016/0160-7383(81)90042-6

Butler, R. W. (1980). The concept of a tourist area cycle of evolution: Implications for the management of resources. *The Canadian Geographer*, *24*(1), 5–12. doi:10.1111/j.1541-0064.1980.tb00970.x

Byrd, E. T., Bosley, H. E., & Dronberger, M. G. (2009). Comparisons of stakeholder perceptions of tourism impacts in rural eastern North Carolina. *Tourism Management*, *30*(5), 693–703. doi:10.1016/j.tourman.2008.10.021

Canan, P., & Hennessy, M. (1989). The growth machine, tourism and the selling of culture. *Sociological Perspectives*, *32*(2), 227–243. doi:10.2307/1389099

Davis, D., Allen, J., & Cosenza, R. M. (1988). Segmenting local residents by their attitudes, interests and opinions toward tourism. *Journal of Travel Research*, *27*(2), 2–8. doi:10.1177/004728758802700201

Del Chiappa, G., Lorenzo-Romero, C., & Gallarza, M. (2016a). Host community perceptions of cruise tourism in a homeport: A cluster analysis. *Journal of Destination Marketing & Management*. doi:10.1016/j.jdmm.2016.08.011

Del Chiappa, G., Presenza, A., & Yücelen, M. (2016b). Profiling residents based on their perceptions and attitude toward sport event: Insights from the FIA world rally championship. *Tourismos*, *11*(5), 26–51.

Doxey, G. V. (1975). A causation theory of visitor-resident irritants: methodology and research inferences. *Conference Proceedings: Sixth Annual Conference of Travel and Tourism Research Association*, 195-198.

Evans, T. R. (1993). *Resident's perceptions of tourism in selected New Zealand communities: a segmentation study (Master's dissertation)*. Dunedin: Dept. of Commerce, University of Otago.

Fredline, E., & Faulkner, B. (2000). Host community reactions: A cluster analysis. *Annals of Tourism Research*, *27*(3), 763–784. doi:10.1016/S0160-7383(99)00103-6

Fredline, L., Deery, M., & Jago, L. (2013). A longitudinal study of the impacts of an annual event on local residents. *Tourism Planning & Development*, *10*(4), 416–432. doi:10.1080/21568316.2013.779314

Frleta, D. S. (2014). Island destinations' tourism offer-tourists' vs. residents' attitudes. *Tourism and Hospitality Management*, *20*(1), 1–14.

Garau, J. B., Díaz, R. J., & Gutiérrez, D. (2014). Residents' perceptions of tourism impacts on island destinations: A comparative analysis. *International Journal of Tourism Research*, *16*(6), 578–585. doi:10.1002/jtr.1951

Gon, M., Osti, L., & Pechlaner, H. (2016). Leisure boat tourism: Residents' attitudes towards nautical tourism development. *Tourism Review*, *71*(3), 180–191. doi:10.1108/TR-07-2016-0025

Gursoy, D., Chi, C. G., & Dyer, P. (2009). An examination of locals' attitudes. *Annals of Tourism Research*, *36*(4), 715–734. doi:10.1016/j.annals.2009.06.003

Gursoy, D., Chi, C. G., & Dyer, P. (2010). Locals' attitudes toward mass and alternative tourism: The case of Sunshine Coast, Australia. *Journal of Travel Research*, *49*(3), 381–394. doi:10.1177/0047287509346853

Jurowski, C., Uysal, M., & Williams, R. D. (1997). A theoretical analysis of host community resident reactions to tourism. *Journal of Travel Research*, *36*(2), 3–11. doi:10.1177/004728759703600202

Lankford, S. V., & Howard, D. R. (1994). Developing a tourism impacts attitude scale. *Annals of Tourism Research*, *21*(1), 121–139. doi:10.1016/0160-7383(94)90008-6

Lundberg, E. (2015). The level of tourism development and resident attitudes: A comparative case study of coastal destinations. *Scandinavian Journal of Hospitality and Tourism*, *15*(3), 266–294. doi:10.1080/15022250.2015.1005335

Madrigal, R. (1995). Residents' perceptions and the role of government. *Annals of Tourism Research*, *22*(1), 86–102. doi:10.1016/0160-7383(94)00070-9

Monterrubio, J. C., & Andriotis, K. (2014). Social representations and community attitudes towards spring breakers. *Tourism Geographies*, *16*(2), 288–302. doi:10.1080/14616688.2014.889208

Nepal, S. (2008). Residents' attitudes to tourism in central British Columbia, Canada. *Tourism Geographies*, *10*(1), 42–65. doi:10.1080/14616680701825123

Nunkoo, R., & Gursoy, D. (2012). Residents' support for tourism: An identity perspective. *Annals of Tourism Research*, *39*(1), 243–268. doi:10.1016/j.annals.2011.05.006

Nunkoo, R., & Ramkissoon, H. (2012). Power, trust, social exchange and community support. *Annals of Tourism Research*, *39*(2), 997–1023. doi:10.1016/j.annals.2011.11.017

Presenza, A., Del Chiappa, G., & Sheehan, L. (2013). Residents' engagement and local tourism governance in maturing beach destinations. evidence from an Italian case study. *Journal of Destination Marketing & Management*, *2*(1), 22–30. doi:10.1016/j.jdmm.2013.01.001

Ramón, J., & Serra, A. (2015). Segmentando residentes según sus actitudes: Revisión de la literatura. *PASOS: Revista de Turismo y Patrimonio Cultural*, *13*(4), 837–848.

Ribeiro, M. A., Valle, P. O., & Silva, J. A. (2013). Residents' attitudes towards tourism development in Cape Verde islands. *Tourism Geographies*, *15*(4), 654–679. doi:10.1080/14616688.2013.769022

Ryan, C., & Montgomery, D. (1994). The attitudes of Bakewell residents to tourism and numbers in comunity responsive tourism. *Tourism Management*, *15*(5), 358–369. doi:10.1016/0261-5177(94)90090-6

Ryan, C., Scotland, A., & Montgomery, D. (1998). Resident attitudes to tourism development-A comparative study between the Rangitikei, New Zealand and Bakewell, United Kingdom. *Progress in Tourism and Hospitality Research*, *4*(2), 115–130. doi:10.1002/(SICI)1099-1603(199806)4:2<115::AID-PTH105>3.0.CO;2-7

Schroeder, T. (1992). Host community perceptions of tourism's impacts: A cluster analysis. *Visions in Leisure and Business*, *10*(4), 43–48.

Sharma, B., & Dyer, P. (2009). An investigation of differences in residents' perceptions on the Sunshine Coast: Tourism impacts and demographic variables. *Tourism Geographies*, *11*(2), 187–213. doi:10.1080/14616680902827159

Sharpley, R. (2014). Host perceptions of tourism: A review of the research. *Tourism Management*, *42*, 37–49. doi:10.1016/j.tourman.2013.10.007

Sinclair-Maragh, G., Gursoy, D., & Vieregge, M. (2015). Residents' perceptions toward tourism development: A factor-cluster approach. *Journal of Destination Marketing & Management*, *4*(1), 36–45. doi:10.1016/j.jdmm.2014.10.001

Stylidis, D., & Terzidou, M. (2014). Tourism and the economic crisis in Kavala, Greece. *Annals of Tourism Research*, *44*, 210–226. doi:10.1016/j.annals.2013.10.004

Thyne, M., & Lawson, R. (2001). Research Note: Addressing tourism public policy issues through attitude segmentation of host communities. *Current Issues in Tourism*, *4*(2-4), 392–400. doi:10.1080/13683500108667895

Tovar, C., & Lockwood, M. (2008). Social impacts of tourism: An Australian regional case study. *International Journal of Tourism Research, 10*(4), 365–378. doi:10.1002/jtr.667

Um, S., & Crompton, J. L. (1987). Measuring resident's attachment levels in a host community. *Journal of Travel Research, 26*(1), 27–29. doi:10.1177/004728758702600105

Vareiro, L. M. C., Remoaldo, P. C., & Ribeiro, J. A. C. (2013). Residents' perceptions of tourism impacts in Guimarães (Portugal): A cluster analysis. *Current Issues in Tourism, 16*(6), 535–551. doi:10.1080/13683500.2012.707175

Vargas, A., Plaza, M. A., & Porras, N. (2009). Understanding residents' attitudes toward the development of industrial tourism in a former mining community. *Journal of Travel Research, 47*(3), 373–387. doi:10.1177/0047287508322783

Vargas, A., Porras, N., & Plaza, M. A. (2014). Residents' attitude to tourism and seasonality. *Journal of Travel Research, 53*(5), 581–596. doi:10.1177/0047287513506295

Ven, S. (2016). Residents' participation, perceived impacts, and support for community-based ecotourism in cambodia: A latent profile analysis. *Asia Pacific Journal of Tourism Research, 21*(8), 836–861. doi:10.1080/10941665.2015.1075565

Weaver, D. B., & Lawton, L. J. (2001). Resident perceptions in the urban-rural fringe. *Annals of Tourism Research, 28*(2), 439–458. doi:10.1016/S0160-7383(00)00052-9

Weaver, D. B., & Lawton, L. J. (2013). Resident perceptions of a contentious tourism event. *Tourism Management, 37*, 165–175. doi:10.1016/j.tourman.2013.01.017

Williams, J., & Lawson, R. (2001). Community issues and resident opinions of tourism. *Annals of Tourism Research, 28*(2), 269–290. doi:10.1016/S0160-7383(00)00030-X

KEY TERMS AND DEFINITIONS

Attitude: Psychological process by which an individual evaluates a particular element in a favorable or unfavorable way based on perceptions and beliefs.

Cluster Analysis: A statistical technique that makes it possible to divide a sample into various internally homogeneous and heterogeneous groups.

Haters: People with a position which is clearly contrary to the subject in question.

Perception: The way in which people interpret the elements that surround them.

Resident: A person who lives and works in a town or region the greater part of the year.

Supporters: People with a clearly favorable position to the subject in question.

Tourist: A person that remains for a short period of time in a town or region for leisure or work purposes.

Chapter 16
Welfare Programs as a Strategy of Promoting Employees' Economic Growth and Work Productivity

Chandra Sekhar Patro
Gayatri Vidya Parishad College of Engineering (Autonomous), India

ABSTRACT

Many organizations apply the notion of employee welfare programs as a strategy of improving employee productivity, since work-related exertions could lead to deprived quality of work life for employees and a decline in performance. Welfare schemes promote economic development by increasing the efficiency and productivity with the underlying principle being making workers bestow their loyal services ungrudgingly in genuine spirit of cooperation. The welfare schemes improve the organizational relations and also enhance the productivity of the employees. The main aim of implementing the welfare measures in any organization is to secure the labor force by providing proper working conditions and minimizing its hazardous effect on the life of the employees and their family members. The chapter articulates the various employee welfare programs put into practice by the industrial and service organizations and its influence on the employees' economic growth and productivity, in both public and private sectors.

INTRODUCTION

The concept of employee welfare deals with all activities that the employers are involved in which are directed towards providing employees with certain facilities and services in addition to salaries and wages (Tweddle, Battle, & Torjman, 2013). These welfare facilities are essential for the organisations growth as they have a close association with the employees' productivity. Employee welfare schemes increases the organizational productivity, promotes motivation, promotes healthy organizational relations, maintain organizational peace and reduces labour turnover. Welfare programmes serve as a means for employee motivation and increases not only the effectiveness of the workforce but also creativity

DOI: 10.4018/978-1-5225-5787-6.ch016

in solving unique organizational challenges. This will eventually lead to attainment of higher levels of economic performance and high service delivery in an organization (Lagat, 2012).

In today's competitive economy, business organizations need to focus explicitly on providing the welfare facilities to the employees as it results in their satisfaction towards the organisation and it results in improved quality of work life (Patro, 2012). Employees are a valuable resource that may contribute in several different ways to an organization's activities if the organization gives them an appropriate chance. Welfare programme is a globally broad concept referring to a state of living of an individual or a group, in a desirable relationship with the total environment - ecological, economic and social. Employee welfare includes both social and economic content of welfare. Social welfare is primarily concerned with the solution of various problems of the weaker section of society like prevention of destitution and poverty. It aims at social development by such means as social legislation, social reforms, social service, social work or social action (Luthans and Sommer, 2005).

Employee welfare is considered one of the corporate commitments to demonstrate care for employees at all levels, underpinning their work and the environment in which it is performed (Srinivas, 2013). Employees are directly influenced by nature and quality of welfare services offered because they compare themselves with their counterparts in other organizations. Organizations should, therefore, bear in mind that for them to achieve their objectives, employee welfare services should be adequately competitive and focused towards solving real needs of employees. Most of the private organisations rarely provide overall competitive packages of employee welfare benefits, which results in low productivity, retention and may eventually lead to high rate of employee turnover (PWC, 2013).

Lack of such welfare benefits not only de-motivate employees, but also results in a high rate of employee turnover, low workplace productivity and affect the overall efficiency and performance of the non-academic staff in private universities (Ernst & Young, 2014).

The success of the employees' welfare programmes depends on the approach which the organization has considered. An organization should have a policy that guides provision of such welfare programmes to employees which include medical facilities, sanitary, accommodation of workers, amenities and industrial social security measures, training and education facilities, HIV and AIDS risk reduction and counselling (Harika, 2012).

Park (2015) argues that work environment should be comprised of issues such as working hours, employment policy, workers' health and welfare, workplace design and the general conduct of workers at the workplace. Employee welfare programmes in both developed and developing society have an impact not only on the workforce but also on the facets of human resources (Mishra & Bhagat, 2007). Welfare schemes should be implemented by all the organisations, whether public sector or private sector and industrial or service sector, as it raises the morale of employees, reduce the risk and insecurity, eliminates absenteeism, and improves the quality of living, which would go a long way in achieving the goals of an organisation. The very logic behind providing welfare schemes is to create efficient, healthy, loyal, and a satisfied labour force for the organization.

In the competitive environment, private sector organizations play a major role in the overall development of the national economy. Therefore, it is essential to focus on the welfare measures which enhance the employees quality of work life and also helpful in increasing the organizations productivity. Generally, in the public sector the funds are organized and provided either by central or state government. Therefore, they are able to provide the welfare measures effectively to their employees without any hesitation (Patro, 2015). In the private sector, large scale organizations can pool more funds and provide the welfare facilities as effectively as public sector organizations provide to their employees. But, small scale organizations may have limited funds, so they may not be able to take care of the welfare facilities effectively compared to the public sector. The chapter presents a comparison of the various welfare measures put into practice in both the industrial and service sector in contrast with public and private sector organisations. Furthermore, the chapter also highlights the areas that the management of these organizations needs to consider for improvement in welfare facilities in enhancing the productivity of employees.

BACKGROUND

The chapter provides an extensive background discussion in the area of implementation of employee welfare programmes to develop a thorough understanding of the conceptual constructs and empirical research. Wainaina (2014) studied the relationship between wellness programs and employee job satisfaction and found that the programs boosted employees' satisfaction levels. Maslach, Leiter, and Jackson (2012) stated that welfare schemes include some or all of the amenities provided in or near the organization and related to the working and living conditions. These facilities include canteens and nourishment facilities, transport arrangements, recreational services, housing schemes, education and training of employees, pension, bonus, medical facilities, childcare facilities, personal counselling, and so forth. Welfare schemes are a means to improve the productivity and efficiency of the employees. The employers are motivated to provide these facilities if it favourably affects their prosperity, profits and public image.

Binoy, Joseph, and Raju (2009) points out that the structure of a welfare state rests on its social security fabric. Government, employers, and trade unions have accomplished much to promote the betterment of workers' conditions. Kumar and Yadav (2002) study the satisfaction level from labour welfare schemes in sugar factories revealed the overall satisfaction level of workers from labour welfare schemes was low in both the private and state sugar factories. Furthermore, the workers in both sectors ranked the four labour welfare schemes such as housing scheme, medical scheme, followed by education and recreation schemes. Kuria (2012) studied on the effects of employee welfare programmes on job satisfaction of employees within the flower industry and established the effects of employee welfare programs on job satisfaction of employees in organizations within the flower industry.

Resma and Basavraju (2013) stated the employee welfare is a comprehensive term including various services, benefits and facilities offered to employees of the organization. Robinson, Sparrow, Clegg, and Birdi (2006) identified the key behaviours which were found to be associated with employee engagement. The behaviours included belief in the organisation, desire to work to make things better, understanding of the business context and the bigger picture, being respectful of and helpful to colleagues, willingness to go the extra mile, and keeping up to date with developments in the field. Satyanarayna and Reddi (2012) stated that the overall satisfaction levels of employees about welfare measures in the organization cover are satisfactory.

However, a few are not satisfied with welfare measures provided by the organization. The study suggested that existing welfare measures may be further improved. Such welfare measures enrich the employee standard of living and their satisfaction levels. Muruu, Were, and Abok (2016) demonstrated employee welfare schemes as those measures that aim at promoting physical, psychological and general well-being of the working class. The basic aim of welfare schemes in an industry is to improve the living and working conditions of the employee and their families because the employee's well-being cannot be achieved in isolation of the employee from his family. Patro and Raghunath (2016) found that the multiple facets of employee welfare facilities such as education facilities, medical facilities, retirement benefits and others facilities are indicative of the employees' efficiency in both public and private sector organizations. The management should concentrate on welfare facilities outside the work place also, so as to increase the quality of work life of the employees.

A welfare officer can be appointed to solve all the problems of the employees and maintain good relation between the employees and employer. Mishra and Bhagat (2007) found the police service provides essential service to the public in Kenya and thus their labour welfare activities need to be addressed just the same. Welfare services may be provided for matters concerning employees in terms of supplementing the income of the workers by providing services such as housing, medical assistance, canteens and recreation facilities. Indiatsy (2011) made a comparative analysis on the effects of social welfare facilities on employee motivation and found that the facilities provided by the organisation are a strong motivational element that has helped retain employees in the job for a long time and boosting their productivity.

According to Priti (2009), the role of welfare activities is to promote economic development by increasing efficiency and productivity with the underlying principle being making workers give their loyal services ungrudgingly in genuine spirit of co-operation and the general well-being of the employee. Manzini and Gwandure (2011) argued that the concept of employee welfare has been used by many organisations as a strategy of improving productivity of employees especially in the mobile industry since work related problems can lead to poor quality of life for employees and a decline in performance. It is argued that welfare services can be used to secure the labour force by providing proper human conditions of work and living through minimizing the hazardous effect on the life of the workers and their family members. Patro (2012) found that the employees are the assets of every organisation. The needs of the employee must be satisfied to meet the goals of the organisation. Any organisation would be effective only when there is high degree of co-operation between the employees and their management.

A research study in different organisations by Parul and Ashokkumar (2013) concluded in terms of proving that the different welfare provisions provided to the employees working in an organisation under the 1948 Factories Act have a positive relation with employee satisfaction after analyzing the correlation between these two factors. The reason behind this result is that these are the factors that lead to satisfaction and if these facilities are not present sometimes leads to dissatisfaction. Nanda and Panda (2013) stated the Rourkela Steel Plant has adopted a better kind of welfare activities which create an effective working environment and thus better productivity. There are different kinds of welfare schemes like medical allowance, death relief fund, insurance, housing, transportation, and recreation club facilities, etc., are provided by the company to the employees to maintain better industrial relations.

Patro (2016), in a comparative analysis of welfare measures in industrial and service organisations with reference to public and private sector found that an employees' welfare, is the key dimension to smooth employer-employee relationship. These welfare facilities improve the employees' morale and loyalty towards the management thereby increasing their happiness, satisfaction and performance.

EMPLOYEE WELFARE PROGRAMMES

Implementing necessary employee welfare programmes have become a key factor for the overall growth and development of any organization. The organizations provide welfare measures to their employees to increase their efficiency and reduce absenteeism. Voluntary efforts for the welfare of the employees by the management may reduce the thought of government and others parties intervention in future. Organizations provide welfare facilities to their employees to keep their motivation levels high (Tiwari, 2011). The employees' welfare schemes can be classified into two categories viz., statutory and non-statutory welfare schemes. The statutory schemes are those schemes that are compulsory to provide by an organization as compliance to the laws governing employee health and safety. In India, these provisions are provided in Industrial Acts like Factories Act 1948, the Dock Workers Act (Safety, Health and Welfare) 1986 and the Mines Act 1962. The statutory welfare measures include the provisions such as, drinking water facilities, facilities for sitting, first aid appliances, latrines and urinals, canteen facilities, spittoons, proper lighting and ventilation, washing places, changing rooms, rest rooms, and so forth.

The non-statutory welfare measures differ from organization to organization and from industry to industry. The non-statutory welfare schemes may includes personal health care, flexi-time, employee assistance programs, grievances policy, maternity and adoption leaves, medi-claim insurance scheme, employee referral schemes, etc. These welfare measures are not obligatory to implement but these schemes may enhance the satisfaction level of the employees and augment the quality work life of the employees. The Factories Act 1948, as amended by the latest amendment in 1987, makes elaborate provisions in relation to health, safety, and welfare of employees, provisions regarding working hours including weekly hours, daily hours, weekly holidays, regarding employment of young persons, annual leaves with wages and provision regarding employment of women and young persons.

In this act, the provisions are also made in connection with first aid appliances along with a room are to be maintained in every organization. The Government has been empowered to make rules necessitating that in any organization wherein more than two hundred fifty workers are ordinarily employed, canteens, shelters, and restrooms shall be provided and maintained for the use of employees. Finally, the Act makes provision for the employment of Welfare Officer in manufacturing organizations and service oriented organizations also. Thus, it is clear that the Act makes very elaborate and unambiguous provisions regarding the minimum welfare standards to be followed by the management. But laying down the standards alone is not enough; it must also to be ensured that these provisions are implemented successfully, and non-implementation leads to dissatisfaction of the employees working in the organizations.

SIGNIFICANCE OF PROMOTING WELFARE ACTIVITIES

Employees are the primary assets of every organization, so employee needs must be satisfied to meet the goals of the organization. Any organization is effective only when there is a high degree of co-operation between the employees and their management. The welfare facilities go a long way stimulating interest in the employees to produce their full capacity and pay a good return to management in the long-term. Although it is a costly procedure for companies, it is nonetheless needed as it helps in the overall development of the employees (Patro, 2017). Employee welfare is very comprehensive and embraces a multitude of activities of employers, state, trade unions and other agencies to help workers and their families in the context of their industrial life. Employee welfare covers an ample field and connotes a state of well-being, happiness, satisfaction, protection and enlargement of human resources and also helps to motivation of worker. The fundamental propose of employee welfare is to enrich the life of employees and to remain them joyful and conducted that helps to development of organization (Choudhary, 2017).

There are certain reasons for which the employee welfare programmes are gaining greater importance in the development of the organizations and promoting employees' economic growth and productivity. In most of the organizations, even today the employees are not united into a class. Keeping in view the numbers, the employee union movement is still in its infancy. Even if the employee unions exist, there is a lack of enlightened leadership, and there is no unity between these unions themselves. In absence of properly organized employee union the workers can neither, place their demands effectively before the employer, nor can they think clearly and systematically of their own interests. Therefore, it is essential that the welfare of employees be efficiently looked after by the employers and the Government.

As the percentage of trained employees are very low, it is necessary to have training facilities for such a vast labour force. Healthy recreation is also at a priority and the efficiency of employees' are diminished by energy being employed in all kinds of undesirable channels. Hence, it is essential that recreation and enjoyment of a healthy kind be provided to the employees. In some organizations the employees are more restless and do tendentious towards frequent migration because life in the town does not provide for his needs, and the atmosphere in general does not suit. Additionally, due to an inadequate level of wages the employees cannot comfortably settle down in one place. This may, in turn, also give rise to absenteeism. This workers migratory tendency can be curbed by providing him with adequate facilities and conditions, and this also shows a positive effect over the absenteeism in the factory.

The welfare programmes motivate the employees and maintains efficiency and productivity. As welfare of worker at work place will improve not only their efficiency, but also improve their willingness to perform their work involving themselves with organizational goals. In India, many of the organizations are not using welfare concept properly at their workplace. The industrialists compel the employees to work in uncomfortable and adverse conditions. Their uncomfortable conditions lead to serious damages to workers. Therefore, promotion of employees welfare programmes is must in the identity premises.

BENEFITS OF EMPLOYEE WELFARE PROGRAMMES

Employee welfare includes the programmes that benefit the employees working in the organisation. Although it is a costly procedure for the companies, yet it is needed as it helps in the overall growth of the employees:

1. **High Competence:** The welfare programmes act as a morale booster for the employee. When the employees get an appreciation for what they do, it helps in increasing the work efficiency of the employees. When the work done is lauded by the management, it proves productive to both the organisation as well as the employees. If the work done by the employees is not appreciated, the output might not come as expected. Therefore, it is essential to practice employee welfare programmes in the organization;
2. **Morale Boost Up:** The employees work only when they are motivated to do the work. If the company wishes to get 100 percent output, then the company has to put in little efforts to encourage the employees. No one else would deliver the expected results. Therefore, in order to boost the morale of the employees, it is essential to offer employee welfare measures;
3. **Build a Competitive Edge:** Competition is essential if the organisations want its employees to work well. In order to form a competitive environment at the work place, the company must provide employees with opportunities. The competitive edge in the work environment can only help

in getting the required work from the employees. Therefore, if the healthy work environment or the healthy competition is required within the organization, it is vital to provide employees with welfare schemes;

4. **Obtain Well-timed Results:** If the companies want the employees to give the result on time or deliver the work in time, there needs to be some extra effort by the company, so as to encourage the employees to give timely work. This can be done only when the employees are encouraged apart from praising their work and are promoted with some welfare schemes. If the extra work is expected from the employees, they should also be given extra benefits, only then the timely results could be expected by the company;
5. **Improved Industrial Relations:** When the employees are satisfied with the welfare measures provided by the organisations it results in good industrial relations also. Not just the work output is good, but also the amiable relations are built by the employees when encouraged through various schemes. Therefore, various employee schemes are essential to make employees work in a better manner in the company;
6. **Better Mental and Moral Health:** The employees when given different facilities at work will improve the mental and moral health, as well as helps in becoming a good citizen. The growth of an employee is equivalent to the development of the organisation. Therefore, if the companies want to grow, they must help employees with their growth;
7. **Social Benefits:** The employees also get various social benefits which are also advantageous to the company. The social benefits increase the productivity, production as well as the work efficiency of the employees. The good quality work by the employees also helps in increasing the remuneration. Finally, this helps in increasing the standard of the employees which is appreciated and accepted by everyone, indeed;
8. **Helps in Overall Growth:** The welfare schemes are a motivating factor to the employees and helps in enhancing the overall growth and productivity of the employees. Both the common organizational goal and the personal goals are easily achieved by the employees, which benefits not just the company but also the members working in the organization;
9. **Retention of Employees:** The organisations train the employees to get better results. But, if the employees leave the company early, it affects not just the employees but also the company. So, the company has to get some schemes to retain the employees for a longer time period and that is only possible with the employee welfare programs. The employees would not even think of leaving the company, if they will get the required share of appreciation.

The benefits of employee welfare programmes are more direct to the employees than the company. However, it is important for the company to generate various employee welfare schemes.

DRAWBACKS OF EMPLOYEE WELFARE

As every coin has two sides, similarly the employee welfare also has its drawbacks. The schemes, however, help the employees more than the organisations. This is because whatever is the scheme bought by the company must be funded by the company itself. Therefore, this is the reason why the employee welfare schemes are a great disadvantage too. Some of the drawbacks of employee welfare are discussed:

1. **Welfare Schemes Become the Driving Force to Work:** Neither the money nor the schemes should be the driving force to work for the employees. The employees must be motivated through the work done by others. A competitive environment should be the driving force for the employees to work. Only then the expected work can be delivered by the employees;
2. **Financial Burden for the Company:** The company gets burdened financially as more the employees, more the budget will be required by the company to equally distribute the schemes among the employees working within an organization. Therefore, in order to equally distribute the schemes among the employees, it is essential for the company to have proper a financial budget in order to provide employees with the required schemes;
3. **Maintain a Competitive Edge in the Market:** To remain in the market and to keep oneself in the edge, it is essential to keep good employee welfare policy so as to attract maximum skilled employees within the organization. Every company needs skilled workers to work so that they get better output. In order to do the same, the company will have to have an edge over the welfare schemes too;
4. **Difficult to Keep Everyone Happy:** As in an organization the plans chosen are such that are benefited for majority of the employees but some or few employees will not be satisfied with the current chosen policy and with the amount they have to pay for their portion. The packages chosen by the organization are often not too delightful and are meant more for their personal benefit. Plans are often changed every year in different organizations and business which hinders the growth of employee in the company as the insurance plans get along on the annual basis gets affected;
5. **Legalization and Authentication Curse:** Often the benefits create concerns regarding legal complaints against both the employees and the organization on breaking certain policy intentionally or unintentionally. On breaking up of the specific policy and not paying the retention carries legal fees that need to be submitted to get out of trouble which at times becomes troublesome;
6. **It can Make People Dependent:** By allowing people to receive money while unemployed, it can encourage a feeling of dependence. This would create a number of less motivated workers who are used to receiving financial support without doing anything and develop the habit to prolong the process for as long as possible, which would cause their skills to deteriorate;
7. **Difficulty in Switching:** Switching often becomes very difficult to manage and company loses many employees if proper actions are not being taken. The major disadvantage associated with it is that the more the employees in the organization will be, the more the company need to pay to the insurance company to manage the account of different employees;
8. **Difficult to Maintain:** Additional department needs to be established in a company to properly manage the plans in the organization which will turn in hiring additional employees. Some health insurance packages also include help from a lawyer to make sure that the employees are covered and legal fees and other such expenses are added easily. Law suits are again a curse for the organization. Law suits are sometimes extremely expensive and take great amount of time to keep it away from any business. Even if the suit makes it to the court, it can be very expensive to pay the legal feel and pay off the fines for its settlement.

Though welfare programs cannot sustain to help people in the long- term, they are still very crucial in lending assistance to those who really need it. However, there are also definite disadvantages to them. Welfare would still be viable to continue as long as it serves its functions.

WELFARE SCHEMES IN FIVE YEAR PLANS

Employee welfare schemes have gained much importance in the 5-year plans.

In the First Five Year Plan (1951-1956), the Government took considerable effort for the welfare measures of the labour classes of society. During this period, important Acts such as the Plantations Labour Act of 1951, the Employees Provident Fund Act of 1952, and the Mines Act of 1952 were implemented. A subsidy was provided for housing scheme for worker was documented and implemented in 1952. Various state governments also formulated and implemented certain Acts as legislation on housing for labour class (i.e., the Bombay Housing Board Act of 1948, the Madhya Pradesh Board Act of 1950, the Hyderabad Labour Housing Act of 1952, etc).

The Second Five Year Plan (1956–1961) provided impetus for further welfare measures and legislation for labour. New laws were also established to ensure welfare measure for merchant seamen and motor transport workers. The employee's state insurance scheme, 1948 was implemented and to cover more employees in the factories. A comprehensive scheme of Dock workers (safety, health and welfare) scheme was formulated in 1961. In 1959, the state government of Assam passed an act labour working in tea plant known as the Assam Tea Plantation Labour Employee's Welfare Fund Act. In 1956, a New Plantation Labour Housing Scheme was enacted which has provision of a certain amount of loan to be provided for construction of houses for labours. The second five year plan period also witnessed quite a large number of enactments in accommodation and housing by various state governments as labour welfare measures.

The Third Five Year Plan (1961-66) emphasized the requirement of more efficient and effective implementation of various statutory labour welfare provisions and legislation. The plan also talked about establishment of co-operative credit organisations and consumer's stores for industrial workers, and stressed on the role of trade unions and voluntary organizations in managing such co-operatives organisations. There has been enactment of the legislative provisions during this plan period which include the Apprentices Act, 1961; Iron-Ore Mines Labour Welfare Cess Act, 1961; Maternity Benefit Act, 1961 And Payment of Bonus Act, 1965. During this period, co-operative housing organisation also started to make amends gradually.

The Fourth Five Year Plan (1969–1974) was more about the expansion and implementation of the Employees' State Insurance (ESI) Act to provide health related facilities to the families of insured worker as well as labourers working in shops and commercial establishments. To protect the contract labour from exploitation government passed, the Contract Labour Regulation and Abolition Act of 1970. Provision of this Act compels contractors to undertake welfare activities for of contractual workers. In 1972, the Government enacted an important statute as the Payment of Gratuity Act, 1972 (bonuses) for the welfare of retiring industrial employees.

The Fifth Five Year Plan (1974–1979) witnessed the additional provisions for labour welfare in a number of areas. For encouraging the provision of industrial safety, safety cells were established in various states of the country. This 5-year plan period also covered: (1) new additional requirements for the most of the existing training institutions, such as the Central Training Institutes for Instructors, the Foreman Training Institute, and Central Staff Training and Research Institute; (2) strengthening and expansion of the Advanced Training Institute throughout the country; (3) Extension of the Apprenticeship Training Programme; (4) Development and establishment of Vocational Training in Women's Occupations; and (5) all other kinds of schemes related to research, surveys and studies to be undertaken by various organisations and institutes.

The Sixth Five Year Plan (1980–1985) was more about effective implementation of the welfare measures of prior legislative enactments, and extension of coverage of Act such as the Employees Provident Fund, Employees' State Insurance Scheme and the Family Pension Scheme. Special scheme also were developed and implemented by State Governments for the welfare of agricultural labour, artisans (skilled craftsmen), leather workers, fishermen, handloom weavers and other unorganised sector workers.

The Seventh Five Year Plan (1985–1989) focussed on enhancement in working conditions of informal sector worker both in the rural areas and also in the urban areas. This plan period witnessed certain major initiative for working women. Thus during this period the stress was on improvement in capacity development, efficiency and productivity.

The Eighth Five Year Plan (1992–1997) witnessed government stressing on the importance of reforms in industrial and trade policies. This five year plan put great emphasis on resource mobilisation from public enterprises. In this period, the great work had been on the aspect of enhancement for the quality of labour work, productivity, skills development, working conditions, provisions for welfare measures and the social security, especially to those working in the unorganised sectors without any socioeconomic security.

The Ninth Five Year Plan (1997–2002) emphasized the enhancement of labour welfare measures, increasing productivity through skills development, and also the adequate provisions were taken for social security of workers. Governmental institutions and resources were directed towards skill development, knowledge sharing on new job opportunities, monitoring and evaluation of working conditions for labour class, creation of industrial harmony through development of infrastructure for better industrial relations, and insurance policy for labour against illness, injury and unemployment and their families.

The Tenth Five Year Plan (2002–2007) given more weight on improving the working conditions, better industrial relations, proper enforcement of Labour Legislations and welfare measures, and also launching various schemes for the welfare activities for all industrial workers and their families. The Labour Department (GoI) worked on implementation mechanism of about two dozen of labour statutes. Their goal was not only in terms of economic benefits (such as minimum wages, overtime, bonuses, etc.) to workers, but also to provide them adequate health and safety facility at the workplace.

The Eleventh Five Year Plan (2007–2012) talked about unemployment and underemployment issue, the promotion and generation of regular wage employment opportunities and addressing the continuing problems of workers employed in unorganised sector all over the country.

The Twelfth Five Year Plan (2012–2017) is more about skill building as an instrument to improve the effectiveness and contribution of labour to the overall production. It has also made skill development as an important agenda for the Governments at Centre as well as States. In this regard, various challenges on skill development identified. Enactments and scheme such as Mahatma Gandhi National Rural Employment Guarantee Act (MGNREGA), Swarnjayanti Gram Swarozgar Yojana (SGSY) and National Rural Livelihood Mission (NRLM) to restructure and strengthened the various employment promotion schemes for the bottom of the pyramid. For enhancing living conditions of the workers and to accomplish higher productivity with higher efficiency, skill development through training is most importance.

Manpower development through skill development will provide adequate manpower of appropriate skills and quality to various sectors is fundamental for express socioeconomic development of country and its people.

OBJECTIVES OF THE CHAPTER

The main objectives of the chapter are:

1. To identify the various welfare programmes put into practice in the industrial and service sectors of both public and private sector organizations;
2. To compare the satisfaction level of employees' on the welfare programmes and also analyzes its influence on their growth and productivity;
3. To suggest measures for improving the overall welfare amenities in both the industrial and service sector organizations.

METHODOLOGY

The present chapter is an enquiry into the employee welfare programmes put into practice by different industrial and service sector organisations with reference to both the public and private sector in the Visakhapatnam city, and the satisfaction level achieved by the employees working in these organisations. The presented data are collected from both the primary and secondary sources. The secondary data was collected from various published sources such as, books, news paper publications, journals, company magazines, official websites of various industrial and service sector organisations, and some other sites are also searched to collect the relevant data.

The primary data was collected from the respondents by distributing questionnaires, through personal interviews, and direct personal observation. The information was collected from the employees who are working in different public and private sector organisations such as industrial organisations (manufacturing, automobile, and others) and service organisations (educational institutions, health centres, software companies, administrative, and financial institutions), individually and taken their views and suggestions. The questionnaire was distributed to 400 employees' personally to know their views regarding the satisfaction level on the execution of welfare schemes from different organizations.

For the purpose, a total of 160 valid and completed questionnaires are selected from various organizations out of which 80 respondents are from Industrial organisations and 80 respondents from Service organisations (both include 40 employees each from Private sector and Public sector). The collected data is used to compare the opinion regarding the satisfaction of the employees on the provision of welfare measures.

To analyze the responses of the employees on implementation of the welfare schemes, a 5-point rating scale technique is used. The scale ranges from Excellent (5), Good (4), Satisfactory (3), Poor (2), and Not In-force (1). The statistical technique mean and standard deviation is used for analyzing the collected data and tabulated wherever necessary, so as to draw inferences based on findings, suggestions and conclusions on employee welfare schemes.

RELATIVE STATISTICAL ANALYSIS

The employees of different industrial organisations and service organizations related to both public and private sector were enquired whether they are satisfied with the various welfare schemes put into practice in their organizations. Based on the questionnaire survey, a relative analysis and interpretation is made on various welfare schemes implemented in these organisations. For the purpose of both, statutory and non-statutory welfare measures are considered. Six important statutory welfare measures are identified, such as canteen and store facilities, medical and health benefits, drinking water and sanitary facilities, restroom and locker facility, workmen compensation, and safety measures. And eight non-statutory welfare schemes such as housing and quarter facilities, educational benefits, transport allowances or facilities, retirement benefits, recreational facilities, grievance settlement forums, retention polities, and other allowances and facilities are identified for collecting the opinion of the employees along with their suggestions. The results and findings regarding the employee welfare programmes that influence the employee's productivity are discussed in the chapter.

The relative analysis of statutory and non-statutory employee welfare measures implemented in industrial organisations with reference to both public and private sector organisations are shown in Table 1.

It is observed that almost all the statutory welfare programmes are implemented in both the public and private sector. The respondents are more satisfied with the provision of 'drinking water and sanitary facilities (μ=4.04)' followed by 'safety measures (μ=3.60)' and 'canteen facilities (μ=3.59)'. The respondents are less satisfied with 'workmen compensation (μ=3.15)' facility provided by the organisations. In the case of both public and private sectors, the statutory welfare measure 'drinking water and sanitary facilities' scored highest mean value of 4.08 and 4.00 respectively. In the public sector, the respondents are satisfied with all the statutory welfare programmes put into practice in their organisations. In the

Table 1. Comparison of welfare programmes in industrial organisations

Factor Perception	Public Sector		Private Sector		Total	
	Mean	Std. Deviation	Mean	Std. Deviation	Mean	Std. Deviation
Statutory Welfare Programmes						
Canteen & Store Facilities	3.48	0.954	3.70	0.848	3.59	0.907
Medical and Health Schemes	3.98	0.763	2.95	1.078	3.46	1.063
Drinking Water & Sanitary Facilities	4.08	0.652	4.00	0.712	4.04	0.681
Rest Room & Locker Facility	3.73	0.871	3.30	0.848	3.51	0.883
Workmen Compensation	3.63	0.973	2.68	1.088	3.15	1.134
Safety Measures	3.75	0.864	3.45	0.870	3.60	0.877
Non-Statutory Welfare Programmes						
Housing/Quarter Facilities	3.80	0.933	1.80	0.906	2.80	1.359
Educational Benefits	3.88	0.753	2.55	1.231	3.21	1.215
Transport Allowances/ Facilities	3.50	0.981	3.38	0.946	3.44	0.963
Retirement Benefits	4.18	0.632	1.78	0.993	2.98	1.462
Recreational Facilities	2.83	1.188	2.03	0.993	2.43	1.163
Grievance Settlement Forums	2.90	1.026	2.75	0.974	2.83	1.000
Retention Policies	3.85	0.828	2.90	1.074	3.38	1.068
Other Allowances /Facilities	3.58	0.952	2.43	1.003	3.00	1.133

Source: Primary Data

private sector, the respondents are having low satisfaction regarding 'workmen compensation (μ=2.68)' and 'medical and health schemes (μ=2.95)'.

Regarding the non-statutory welfare programmes in the public sector almost all employees' responded positively, whereas in the private sector many of them responded that these facilities are satisfactory in their organisations. The highly satisfied welfare scheme is 'transport allowances/facilities' with mean value of 3.44 followed by 'retention policies (μ=3.38)' and 'educational benefits (μ=3.21)'. The low significant factor is provision of recreational facilities (μ=2.43). In public sector, 'retirement benefits' scored highest mean value of 4.18 and the lowest is 'provision of recreational facilities' with a mean of 2.83. In the case of private sector, the most satisfied welfare measure is 'transport allowances/facilities' with mean value of 3.38.

The respondents are less satisfied with the provision of 'retirement benefits (μ=1.78)' and 'housing/quarter facilities (μ=1.80)'. Thus, it can be concluded that the public sector employees are more satisfied when compared to the private sector employees. The management's of private sector need to put much effort to implement better welfare schemes to their employees as it enhances the work productivity. The public sector can also focus on the better implementation of the non-statutory welfare programmes in their organisations.

The relative analysis of statutory and non-statutory employee welfare measures implemented in service organisations with reference to both public and private sector organisations are shown in Table 2.

In service organisations, it is observed that almost all the statutory welfare programmes are implemented in both public and private sectors and the respondents are also satisfied with these facilities. The

Table 2. Comparison of welfare programmes in service organisations

Factor Perception	Public Sector		Private Sector		Total	
	Mean	Std. Deviation	Mean	Std. Deviation	Mean	Std. Deviation
Statutory Welfare Programmes						
Canteen & Store Facilities	3.53	0.871	3.65	0.858	3.59	0.864
Medical and Health Schemes	3.88	0.682	3.13	1.036	3.50	0.952
Drinking Water & Sanitary Facilities	3.80	0.753	3.78	0.826	3.79	0.788
Rest Room & Locker Facility	3.68	0.938	3.13	0.905	3.40	0.960
Workmen Compensation	3.70	0.719	2.80	1.216	3.25	1.093
Safety Measures	3.65	0.828	3.38	0.919	3.51	0.883
Non-Statutory Welfare Programmes						
Housing/Quarter Facilities	3.80	0.786	1.85	0.969	2.83	1.315
Educational Benefits	3.60	0.922	2.50	1.102	3.05	1.154
Transport Allowances/ Facilities	3.73	0.927	3.48	1.006	3.60	0.973
Retirement Benefits	4.10	0.668	1.90	0.739	3.00	1.308
Recreational Facilities	2.60	1.327	2.20	1.174	2.40	1.265
Grievance Settlement Forums	3.10	1.051	2.68	1.111	2.89	1.099
Retention Policies	3.70	0.933	2.70	1.036	3.20	1.103
Other Allowances/ Facilities	3.43	1.003	2.35	0.969	2.89	1.121

Source: Primary Data

respondents are highly satisfied with the provision of 'drinking water and sanitary facilities (μ=3.79)' followed with 'canteen facilities (μ=3.59)' and 'safety measures (μ=3.51)'. The respondents are less satisfied with 'workmen compensation (μ=3.25)' provided by the organisations. In the case of public sector, the respondents are satisfied with all the statutory welfare programmes put into practice in their organisations. The highly significant factor is 'medical and health schemes' with a mean value of 3.88 and the lowest satisfied factor is 'safety measures (μ=3.65)'.

In the private sector, the respondents are having less satisfaction compared to public sector. The respondents are highly satisfied with the statutory measure 'drinking water and sanitary facilities (μ=3.78)' and low satisfaction regarding 'workmen compensation (μ=2.80)'. The non-statutory welfare programmes are fully implemented in the public sector and in case of private sector these schemes are not fully operational. The highly significant welfare measure is 'transport allowances/facilities' with mean value of 3.60 followed by 'retention policies (μ=3.20)' and 'educational benefits (μ=3.05)'. The low significant factor is recreational facilities (μ=2.40). In public sector, 'retirement benefits' scored highest mean value of 4.10 followed with 'housing/quarter facilities (μ=3.80)' and 'transport allowances/facilities (μ=3.73)'.

The lowest satisfied welfare measure is 'recreational facilities' with a mean of 2.60. In the case of private sector, the most satisfied welfare measure is 'transport allowances/facilities' with mean value of 3.48. The respondents are less satisfied with the facilities of 'housing/quarter facilities (μ=1.85)' and 'retirement benefits (μ=1.90)'. Thus, from the comparative analysis it can be concluded that the private sector employees are not much influenced when compared with the public sector employees. The management's need to improve these welfare programmes, as it helps in increasing the productivity of the employees. A comparison on satisfaction level of the employees on the implementation of the statutory and non-statutory welfare programmes in both the industrial and service organisations is shown in Table 3.

The employees of both industrial and service organisations are almost satisfied with the statutory welfare programmes put into practice in their organisations. It can be observed that the respondents are more satisfied with the 'drinking water and sanitary facilities (μ=3.91)' followed by 'canteen and store facilities (μ=3.59)' and 'safety measures (μ=3.56)'. The respondents are less satisfied with the 'workmen compensation (μ=3.20)' provided by the organisations. In both the industrial and service sectors, the respondents are highly satisfied with the 'drinking water and sanitary facilities (μ=3.79 and 4.04 respectively)' provided by their organisations. The low satisfied factor is 'workmen compensation' with the mean values of 3.25 and 3.15, respectively.

Regarding the implementation of non-statutory welfare programmes, both the industrial and service sector employees are not much satisfied. Many employees responded that these schemes are not implemented in their organisations. The highly significant welfare measure is 'transport allowances/facilities' with mean value of 3.52 followed by 'retention policies (μ=3.29)' and 'educational benefits (μ=3.13)'. The low significant factor is recreational facilities (μ=2.41). In the case of both industrial and service sector organisations, 'transport allowances/facilities' scored highest mean value of 3.60 and 3.44, followed by 'retention policies (μ=3.20; 3.38)' and 'educational benefits (μ=3.05; 3.21)'. The lowest satisfied welfare measure is 'recreational facilities' with a mean of 2.40 and 2.43 respectively.

Thus, from the comparative analysis it can be concluded that the service sector employees are much satisfied than the employees' industrial organisations. However, the managements of both the industrial and service sectors need to further improve the non-statutory welfare programmes for enhancing the workers economic growth and work productivity. A comparison on the satisfaction of the employees with the implementation of the statutory and non-statutory welfare programmes in both the public and private sector organisations is shown in Table 4.

Table 3. Comparison of welfare programmes in industrial and service organisations

Factor Perception	Industrial Organizations		Service Organizations		Total	
	Mean	Std. Deviation	Mean	Std. Deviation	Mean	Std. Deviation
Statutory Welfare Programmes						
Canteen & Store Facilities	3.59	0.864	3.59	0.907	3.59	0.884
Medical and Health Schemes	3.50	0.952	3.46	1.063	3.48	1.008
Drinking Water & Sanitary Facilities	3.79	0.788	4.04	0.681	3.91	0.746
Rest Room & Locker Facility	3.40	0.960	3.51	0.883	3.46	0.922
Workmen Compensation	3.25	1.093	3.15	1.134	3.20	1.113
Safety Measures	3.51	0.883	3.60	0.877	3.56	0.880
Non-Statutory Welfare Programmes						
Housing/Quarter Facilities	2.83	1.315	2.80	1.359	2.81	1.335
Educational Benefits	3.05	1.154	3.21	1.215	3.13	1.186
Transport Allowances/ Facilities	3.60	0.973	3.44	0.963	3.52	0.970
Retirement Benefits	3.00	1.308	2.98	1.462	2.99	1.385
Recreational Facilities	2.40	1.265	2.43	1.163	2.41	1.213
Grievance Settlement Forums	2.89	1.099	2.83	1.000	2.86	1.050
Retention Policies	3.20	1.103	3.38	1.068	3.29	1.088
Other Allowances/ Facilities	2.89	1.121	3.00	1.133	2.94	1.127

Source: Primary Data

The analysis shows that almost all the respondents are satisfied with the statutory welfare programmes practiced in both the public and private sector organisations, whereas they are less satisfied with the non-statutory welfare programmes. With regards to the statutory welfare measures, it can be observed that the respondents are more satisfied with the 'drinking water and sanitary facilities (μ=3.91)' followed by 'canteen and store facilities (μ=3.59)' and 'safety measures (μ=3.56)'. The respondents are less satisfied with the 'workmen compensation (μ=3.20)' provided by the organisations. In both the public and private sectors, the respondents are highly satisfied with the 'drinking water and sanitary facilities (μ=3.94 and 3.89 respectively)' provided by their organisations.

The low satisfied factor is 'canteen & store facilities' with a mean of 3.50 in the case of public sector and 'workmen compensation' with the mean values of 2.74 in the case of private sector. The satisfaction of respondents with regard to the implementation of non-statutory welfare programmes in both the public and private sector reveals that they are not much satisfied. Many employees retort that these schemes are not implemented in their organisations. The highly significant welfare measure is 'transport allowances/ facilities' with mean value of 3.52 followed by 'retention policies (μ=3.29)' and 'educational benefits (μ=3.13)'. The low significant factor is recreational facilities (μ=2.41). In the case of both public organisations, 'transport allowances/facilities' scored highest mean value of 4.14, followed by 'educational benefits (μ=3.80)' and 'retention policies (μ=3.78)'.

The lowest satisfied welfare measure is 'recreational facilities' with a mean of 2.71. With regard to private organisations, 'transport allowances/facilities' got highest rating of 3.43, followed by 'retention

Table 4. Comparison of welfare programmes in public and private sector

Factor Perception	Public Sector		Private Sector		Total	
	Mean	Std. Deviation	Mean	Std. Deviation	Mean	Std. Deviation
Statutory Welfare Programmes						
Canteen & Store Facilities	3.50	0.911	3.68	0.851	3.59	0.884
Medical and Health Schemes	3.93	0.723	3.04	1.057	3.48	1.008
Drinking Water & Sanitary Facilities	3.94	0.715	3.89	0.777	3.91	0.746
Rest Room & Locker Facility	3.70	0.903	3.21	0.879	3.46	0.922
Workmen Compensation	3.66	0.853	2.74	1.152	3.20	1.113
Safety Measures	3.70	0.845	3.41	0.893	3.56	0.880
Non-Statutory Welfare Programmes						
Housing/Quarter Facilities	3.80	0.860	1.83	0.935	2.81	1.335
Educational Benefits	3.74	0.850	2.53	1.165	3.13	1.186
Transport Allowances/ Facilities	3.61	0.958	3.43	0.975	3.52	0.970
Retirement Benefits	4.14	0.649	1.84	0.875	2.99	1.385
Recreational Facilities	2.71	1.261	2.11	1.087	2.41	1.213
Grievance Settlement Forums	3.00	1.040	2.71	1.042	2.86	1.050
Retention Policies	3.78	0.883	2.80	1.057	3.29	1.088
Other Allowances/ Facilities	3.50	0.978	2.39	0.984	2.94	1.127

Source: Primary Data

policies (μ=2.80)' and 'grievance settlement forums (μ=2.71)'. Thus, from the comparative analysis it can be concluded that the public sector employees are much satisfied than the employees' of private sector. However, the management of private sector organisations need to further improve the non-statutory welfare programmes for enhancing the workers economic growth and work productivity.

Consequently, the relative analysis clearly states that in the case of industrial organisations or service organisations, both the public sector and private sector employees are equally satisfied with implementation of the welfare programmes in their organisations. The managements' of these organisations need to put much effort to improve the welfare schemes put into practice in their organisations as it enhances the employees' economic growth and work productivity, also increases the overall efficiency of the organisations.

MEASURES TO ENHANCE WELFARE PROGRAMMES

The organisations should make pragmatic efforts to enhance the employees' work life and job satisfaction to increase their overall economic growth and work performance. Based on the comparative analysis and suggestions given by various respondents of industrial and service sector, certain measures can be enacted for further improvement in practicing of welfare programmes in the organisations that could be extremely useful for the management of both the public and private sector organisations to increase the organisational efficiency:

1. The management should update the employees about the different welfare schemes adopted in their organizations and suggest them how to make use of these facilities;
2. The employers need to concentrate on the facilities provided to the employee's outside the work place like quarters, medical benefits, etc., which helps in having better quality of work life;
3. The private sector whether industrial or service organizations need to improve the welfare schemes implemented in their organizations;
4. Proper incentives, allowances, promotions, etc., should be worked out that will fulfill the ambitions and aspirations, which will go a long way in elevating their level of job satisfaction;
5. The management should conduct stress reducing events like yoga and meditation for the employees;
6. The employers of private sector organizations need to identify the needs of their employees and provide necessary welfare schemes that will influence them in getting job satisfaction;
7. Improvements should be initiated in the field of grievance handling, rest room facilities, service awards, and other motivating facilities in both the sectors;
8. Necessary steps must be initiated to conduct job training programmes, seminars and workshops to update and enhance the knowledge of the employees;
9. A welfare officer can be appointed to solve all the problems of the employees and maintain good relation between the employees and employer;
10. The private sector organizations must take initiative to provide retirement benefits for their employees;
11. The private sector organizations must try to initiate necessary steps to provide subsidized canteen and store facilities to their employees;
12. The public and private sector organizations have to provide separate restrooms for both male and female employees;
13. Both the public and private sector organizations must set up a reading room or library for employees to make use of their leisure time and enhance their knowledge;
14. The management can think of formulation of a problem solving committee including the employees and administration, for the better solution of the welfare problems of the employees;
15. The organizations can appoint a welfare officer to solve all the problems of the employees and maintain good relationship between the employee, employer and other departments.

The welfare programmes should be properly implemented by the industrial and service organizations of both private and public sectors. These measures would make an immense contribution towards increasing the welfare, well-being and job satisfaction of employees working in these organisations.

FUTURE RESEARCH DIRECTIONS

Organizations should take necessary steps to solve the welfare problems of the employees and take certain measures, so that the employee can perform more effectively. New schemes and facilities should be added to existing ones to improve the efficiency and quality of work life of the employees by the management of all organizations. This chapter is expected to help other researchers to consider various welfare programmes that influence the employee's performance and overall organizational productivity. Furthermore, research with regards to other industrial and service sector organizations can be considered as provision of welfare schemes has become important in every type of organization.

CONCLUSION

Welfare facilities play an important role in managing the Human Resources in any organisation. The organizations whether private or public sector and industrial or service organisations need to practice the welfare programmes for better employee productivity and organisational development. A satisfied employee is the key element, who acts as the organization's ladder for success. Welfare helps in keeping the morale and motivation of the employees high, so as to retain the employees for longer duration. The thought of employee welfare has been used by many organizations as a strategy of improving the employee's productivity, especially in the private sector, since work related problems can lead to poor quality of life for employees and decline in employees work performance. The welfare programmes improve the employees' morale and loyalty towards the management thereby increasing their happiness, satisfaction and also their productivity.

The relative analysis states that the overall satisfaction of employees on both statutory and non-statutory welfare schemes in the industrial organisations with regard to public sector is good and in private sector is satisfactory. However, in service organisations, the private sector employees are not satisfied with implementation of welfare schemes in their organizations when compared with the public sector employees, who are more than satisfied with these welfare programmes. Therefore, it is suggested that the existing welfare programmes may be improved further as they enrich the employee's standard of living and their satisfaction levels. The private sector organisations has to take necessary efforts to find out what the employees want and practice those welfare schemes for the successful growth development of the organization. An employee welfare facility is the key dimension to smooth employer-employee relationship. The organisations need to take necessary steps to solve these problems and overcome the challenges, so that the employees can do their work more effectively.

REFERENCES

Binoy, J., Joseph, I., & Raju, V. (2009). Labour Welfare in India. *Journal of Workplace Behavioral Health*, *24*(1&2), 221–242.

Choudhary, S. (2017). Employee welfare: A scheme of wise investment. *International Journal of Advanced Education and Research*, *2*(1), 1–6.

Ernst & Young. (2014). *Financial report 30 June 2014 (and interim financial report for the half-year ended 31 December 2014). Endeavour Managed Investment Scheme*. Retrieved on November 13, 2017, from: http://www.ey.com/Publication/vwLUAssets/EY-endeavour-managed-investment-scheme/$FILE/ey-endeavour-mis-2014.pdf

Harika, V. (2012) *Theories of Labour Welfare*. Retrieved on November 13, 2017, from: http://www.scribd.com/doc/52987735/2/THEORIES-OF-LABOURWELFARE

Indiatsy, C. M. (2011). *Comparative analysis on the effects of social welfare facilities on employee motivation in Pan African Papermills and Mumias sugar company*. Doctoral dissertation.

Kumar, S., & Yadav, S. S. (2002). Satisfaction level from labour welfare schemes in Sugar Factories of Gorakhpur Division. *Indian Journal of Economics*, *83*, 171–190.

Kuria, P. N. (2012). *The effects of employee welfare programmes on job satisfaction of employees within the flower industry in Kenya.* Doctoral dissertation.

Lagat, A. C. (2012). *Contribution of Trade Unions in the Promotion of Employee Satisfaction: The Case of the UASU Egerton University Chapter, Kenya* (Unpublished Master of Human Resource Management Dissertation). Egerton University, Njoro, Kenya.

Luthans, K. W., & Sommer, S. M. (2005). The impact of high performance work on industry-level outcomes. *Journal of Managerial Issues*, 327–345.

Manzini, H. S., & Gwandure, C. (2011). The Provision of Employee Assistance Programmes in South African Football Clubs: A Case Study. *Journal of Social Sciences*, *27*(2), 75–83. doi:10.1080/09718923.2011.11892908

Maslach, C., Leiter, M. P., & Jackson, S. E. (2012). Making a significant difference with burnout interventions: Researcher and practitioner collaboration. *Journal of Organizational Behavior*, *33*(2), 296–300. doi:10.1002/job.784

Mishra, S., & Bhagat, M. (2007). *Principles for successful implementation of labour welfare activities.* From police theory to functional theory. Retrieved on October 26, 2017, from: https://www.tesionline.com/intl/indepth.jsp?id=575

Muruu, R. W., Were, S., & Abok, M. A. (2016). Effects of Welfare Programmes on Employee Satisfaction in the Public Sector: A Case of the Public Service Commission. *Strategic Journal of Business & Change Management*, *3*(4), 1607–1633.

Nanda, N., & Panda, J. K. (2013). Challenges and effectiveness of industrial relation environment in Indian Industries study on Rourkela Steel Plant. *International Journal of Financial Services and management Research, 2*(6), 163-174.

Park, K. (2015). *A Study on the Effect of Company Welfare Forms on Workers Satisfaction* (Doctoral dissertation). Kounggi University, Korea. (in Korean)

Parul, P. B., & Ashokkumar, M. (2013). Provision of Welfare under Factories Act and Its Impact on Employee Satisfaction. *Journal of Business Management & Social Sciences Research*, *2*(2), 57–69.

Patro, C. S. (2012). Employee Welfare Activities in Private Sector and Their Impact on Quality of Work Life. *International Journal of Productivity Management and Assessment Technologies*, *1*(2), 18–29. doi:10.4018/ijpmat.2012040102

Patro, C. S. (2015). Employee Welfare Measures in Public and Private Sectors: A Comparative Analysis. *International Journal of Service Science, Management, Engineering, and Technology*, *6*(1), 22–37. doi:10.4018/ijssmet.2015010102

Patro, C. S. (2016). A Study on Adoption of Employee Welfare Schemes in Industrial and Service Organisations: In Contrast with Public and Private Sectors. *International Journal of Service Science, Management, Engineering, and Technology*, *7*(2), 16–33. doi:10.4018/IJSSMET.2016040102

Patro, C. S. (2017). Espousal of Welfare Schemes: A Means for Employees' Satisfied Work Life with Reference to Pharmaceutical Companies. *International Journal of Asian Business and Information Management*, *8*(3), 36–51. doi:10.4018/IJABIM.2017070103

Patro, C. S., & Kamakula, M. K. R. (2016). A Take on Employee Welfare Facilities and Employees' Efficiency. *International Journal of Asian Business and Information Management*, *7*(3), 54–70. doi:10.4018/IJABIM.2016070104

Priti, S. (2009). *Employee Welfare*. Retrieved on October 20, 2017, from: http://www.citehr.com/176307employee-welfare.html#ixzz1zTZ8HheC

PWC. (2013). *PwC's NextGen: A global generational study*. Retrieved on November 13, 2017, from: https://www.pwc.com/gx/en/hr-management-services/pdf/pwc-nextgen-study-2013.pdf

Reshma, S., & Basavaraj, M. J. (2013). Employee welfare measures in mining industry–A study with reference to statutory welfare measures in NMDC, Donimalai Iron Ore Mine, Bellary district. *EXCEL International Journal of Multidisciplinary Management Studies*, *3*(7), 157–164.

Robinson, A., Sparrow, P., Clegg, C., & Birdi, K. (2006). Forecasting Future Competency Requirements: A Three Phase Methodology. *Personnel Review*, *36*(1), 65–90. doi:10.1108/00483480710716722

Satayanarayan, M. R., & Reddi, R. J. (2012). Labour welfare measure in cement industries in India. *International Journal of Physical and Social Sciences*, *2*(7), 257–254.

Srinivas, K. T. (2013). A Study on Employee Welfare Facilities adopted at Bosch Limited, Bangalore. *Research Journal of Management Science*, *2*(12), 7–11.

Tiwari, P. (2011). Impact of selected HRM practices on perceived employee performance: An empirical study. *Global Management Journal*, *3*(1/2), 37–43.

Tweddle, A., Battle, K., & Torjman, S. (2013). *Welfare in Canada 2012*. Caledon Institute of Social Policy.

Wainaina, A. (2014). *Factors affecting perception on job performance in the Kenya financial sector A case study of an international bank with substantial operations in Kenya* (Doctoral dissertation). United States International University-Africa.

KEY TERMS AND DEFINITIONS

Employee Productivity: It is an assessment of the efficiency of an employee or a group of employees.

Industrial Sector: The industrial sector (secondary sector) of the economy is one that makes finished products which can then be utilized viz. construction and manufacturing industry. This sector includes companies involved with aerospace and defense, industrial machinery, tools, lumber production, construction, waste management, manufactured housing, cement and metal fabrication.

Labor Welfare: It includes overall welfare facilities designed to take care of wellbeing of employees and in order to increase their living standard.

Mutual Welfare: Mutual welfare is a corporate enterprise undertaken by the workers themselves or their organizations called trade unions.

Private Sector: The private sector is the part of a country's economic system that is run by individuals and companies, rather than the government. It usually comprises of organizations run by individuals and groups who seek to generate and return a profit back to its owners.

Public Sector: The public sector is that portion of an economic system that is controlled by national, state or provincial, and local governments. It usually comprises of organizations that are owned and operated by the government and exist to provide services for its citizens.

Service Sector: The part of a country's economy that is made up of businesses that provide services. It includes the companies, organizations, and activities in an economy that provide services such as banking, transport, tourism, etc. rather than manufacturing goods.

Statutory Welfare: The statutory schemes are those schemes that are compulsory to provide by an organization as compliance to the laws governing employee health and safety.

Voluntary Welfare: Voluntary welfare includes all those activities which employers undertake for their employees on voluntary basis. These differ from organization to organization and from industry to industry.

Chapter 17
A Green Energy Management Framework for Software Development Firms

Arunasalam Sambhanthan
Curtin University, Australia

ABSTRACT

This chapter documents a green energy management framework for software development companies. An initial framework has been constructed through analyzing the reports of large scale software development firms. The key components of the framework consist of energy sources and energy efficiency, energy-efficient heating, energy-efficient lighting, and energy-efficient cooling. These themes include a number of sub-themes and criteria therein which are used to build the green energy management framework and then utilized for constructing the research questions for further data collection. The results highlight the most efficient energy sources, efficient heating measures and technologies, efficient lighting measures, and technologies as well as efficient cooling measures and technologies. Implications for practice have been suggested at the end of the chapter.

INTRODUCTION

Green energy management is an area worth pursuing in the context of rapidly changing energy aware society. Energy usage that relates to CO_2 emissions is predicted to increase from 188 million tons in 2010 to 720.5 million tons in 2050 (Al-Amin, Rasiah, & Chenayah, 2015). While energy usage is an increasing area of concern, it is evident that the management of energy in a greener manner is much more critical than energy savings. Green energy engineering is an emerging new field that will find ideas and for the progress of green energy approach (Oncel, 2017). Beside this background, there is lack of research in terms of assessing and benchmarking green energy management initiatives in software development firms. Particularly, research dealing with the analysis and construction of green energy management related frameworks for software development firms has not been a documented research phenomenon.

DOI: 10.4018/978-1-5225-5787-6.ch017

LITERATURE REVIEW

The organisational challenge for ensuring sustainability has been eased by a number of frameworks and concepts which aims to support organisations in their effort to ensure and implement sustainability measures in their decision making. A framework is defined as a set of conceptual elements organised in a way, the reader could get a more structured understanding of the phenomenon. This research systematically reviews the existing literature on business sustainability frameworks. Having incorporated a multiplicity in industry focus in the framework analysis, the literature review is presented in terms of the industries.

The section below analyses the business sustainability frameworks from differing domains. The frameworks for indicator set (the set of measurement criteria for assessing sustainability in those particular industries have been progressively evolving over time. The role of framework has been documented to be changed from the organisation of a core set of indicators to providing a sound basis to facilitate the formulation of exhaustive indicator sets and to ensure the selection of a core coherent set of indicators in a particular system. Thus, two types of frameworks are been distinguished by the following (Van Cauwenbergh et al., 2007):

1. **System Based Frameworks:** Primarily providing systematic indicators describing the key attributes (general functional processes) of a system as a whole (i.e., productivity, resilience, stability etc.);
2. **Content Based Disciplinary Frameworks:** Providing specific indicators that characterise single parts (related to specific functions or processes) of the system concern (e.g., supply of quality air function, air flow buffering function).

Both these approaches of conceptualisation have been identified as giving a good structure to derive indicators, it is inevitable to review and classify the existing business sustainability frameworks into these two broad themes in order to derive some insights. Whilst, the system based approaches are more conceptual and provides a valid foundation for deriving indicators which could be used for evaluation, it only facilitates the qualitative evaluation parameters. On the contrary, the content based disciplinary frameworks provide a quantitative foundation for evaluation parameters.

In addition to these classification approaches, the industry based frameworks have become inevitable to measure the industry relevant sustainability parameters. For an example supply of quality air function, air flow buffering function are two important indices to measure the environmental sustainability of agricultural systems, whilst the transport route and truck loading are specific indicators for the sustainability of manufacturing sector. Therefore, an industry based approach has been adapted for classifying the sustainability frameworks in the course of this research exercise. Arguably, there are documented criticisms with regard to the lack of research in terms of developing frameworks for assessing the economic, social and institutional aspects of sustainability (Labuschagne, Brent, & Van Erck, 2005).

Manufacturing

Business sustainability in a manufacturing environment is a paramount concern for businesses. A study (Høgevold & Svensson, 2012) explored the sustainability of a chair manufacturer in Norway. The authors have applied a case study approach to investigate the efforts of business sustainability in the demand and supply chain networks of a Norwegian office chair producer. The study indicates that business sustainability is a manyfold concept in which has much more to offer than just simple efforts. In fact, business sustainability covers a whole spectrum of efforts such as actors, resources and activities. In addition to this, the business sustainability and the demand and supply chain network is becoming a criterion in the decision-making process of customers across industries. Climate change and the global worming are the indicative factors which make business sustainability as paramount in the current society. The extreme weather condition, which makes troublesome effects on the global damage, is considered to be another alarming factor which makes sustainability more critical. The research presented infers results solely based on one case study, which could be criticised as a major weakens of this study.

Although the case study approach allows pattern matching in the data from a limited number of cases, it is not acceptable to have strong conclusions simply on the study undertaken based on one case. In addition to the methodological constraint, the research also fails to address the multifaceted dimensions of business sustainability such as the social, economic and industrial functions. The current study could be criticised for limiting its focus to only the environmental dimension whilst the other dimensions such as social, economic and industrial sustainability are well emphasised by the United Nations Environment Program (UNEP) (Labuschagne et al., 2005).

E-Learning

Managing the e-learning system is a critical factor for sustainability. Failure of e-learning systems which are jointly managed by industry-university partnership is a common observable issue, which could cause long term threat for sustainability. Why these kinds of e-learning systems fail is a paramount question. Mitigation mechanisms for e-learning system failure are almost absent in the present literature. A study (Demirkan, Goul, & Gros, 2010) investigated a potential solution for this, ending up with a reference model for sustainable e-learning service systems. The research indicates that one of the primary bottlenecks for sustainable e-learning is the lack of viable partnership covering wide range of enterprises and institutions. An avenue for bridging this gap has been suggested, bringing together many partners and stakeholders which could give access to more resources and core competencies for learners.

The research concludes with the proposal of a reference model which aims at sustainable e-learning service systems. The model covers both basic and advanced sustainability capabilities that integrating the partner, application, faculty, student and e-learning service system infrastructure issue. The model could also serve as a guide in managerial decision making related to setting up and sustaining a joint industry - university e-learning service system. The outcome of the research is predominantly based on the failure factors outlined by Keegan et al. (2007) which overlooks the strategic and managerial reasons for e-learning system failure. A balance between strategic and technical factors is essential to construct a comprehensive model.

In addition, the study does not cover a comprehensive review of e-learning business model sustainability; instead overly emphasise on the system perspective than of business perspective. Whilst, the operational and technical failure factors outlined in the table 3 could be successfully resolved through implementing effective project management practices (i.e., effective utilisation of cost and time, effectively managing all nine knowledge areas of project management), the strategic reasons outlined in the table 3 could have a definitive effect on the long-term sustainability of the e-learning service systems. Hence, there needs to be more focus and concentration on strategic and managerial aspects in order to make the overall business model of the e-learning providers sustainable.

SAFE: A Hierarchical Framework for Assessing the Sustainability of Agricultural Systems

Sustainable agriculture involves the management and utilisation of agricultural systems to maintain biological diversity, productivity, regeneration capacity, vitality and the ability to function without compromising the present and future needs – all these would lead towards significant ecological, economic and social functions at the local, national and global levels without harming the other ecosystems. The implementation of sustainable agriculture is still an open question. Van Cauwenbergh et al. (2007) investigated a framework for assessing the sustainability of agricultural systems. The research embarks on a number of assessment tools such as Life Cycle Assessment (LCA), Cost Benefit Analysis (CBA), Environmental Impact Assessment (EIA) and sustainability standards with Principles, Criteria and Indicators (PC & I). Whilst these tools are identified for using the same indicators, the procedures adapted for assessment and the fields of application have been noted for variability.

There are a number of agro-environmental indicators been designed for the evaluation of the sustainability of agro-ecosystems. However, the researchers argue that defining an appropriate set of indicators for sustainable development is a difficult task. In fact, defining too few indicators might lead to a state where crucially important developments might get escaped from attention, while defining too many indicators could lead towards difficulty in data collection and processing at a reasonable cost. Thus, the difficulty relies on coming up with an essential set of indicators for assessing the sustainability.

This challenge has been tackled by early researchers through using intuitive judgement of experts familiar with the particular discipline. Relatively fewer efforts have been documented in terms of developing a content based framework for PC & I for sustainable agriculture. The framework elements are based on the functions of agro-ecosystems as developed by (de Groot, Wilson, & Boumans, 2002). The key distinguishing factor of the SAFE framework is its holistic approach in covering many aspects of agro-environmental systems which address the drawbacks of many previous frameworks of this kind. A number of complications involved in developing a content based framework for agro-ecosystems have been covered in this framework. For example, the problems involved in indicator selection, scale problems for implementing such frameworks and the lack of reference values for testing sustainability issues are some of the notable issues addressed by this framework.

Sustainability Framework for Bioenergy Systems

Sustainability of Bioenergy Systems is an important concern due to the environmental impacts and social concerns involved in this type of businesses. Elghali et al. (2007) investigated an approach to developing a methodology to establish a sustainability framework for the assessment of bioenergy systems to provide practical advice for policy makers, planners and the bioenergy industry. The sustainability indices of the bioenergy industry vary between stakeholders. For example, the reduction of carbon emission and environmental impact reduction are some national level concerns, while the job creation, income improvement, the local environment and regional development are the main concerns of local communities. In fact, the triple bottom line approach plays a major role in deciding indices relevant for assessment in each criterion.

Some of the key issues for the development of a sustainable bioenergy sector include:

- Environmental impacts (not limited to GHG emissions) over the full fuel cycle;

- The potential for biomass to reduce GHG emissions in different sectors, including heat, electricity and transport fuels;
- Security and stability of bioenergy supply chains, using both domestic and imported fuels;
- The potential for innovation to lead to more competitive and secure bioenergy chains;
- Pathways for the introduction of bioenergy at different scales into different sectors;
- Social impacts and public acceptance of bioenergy systems;
- Policy measures to promote bioenergy, including policies in the agricultural and waste sector.

A Capability Maturity Framework for Sustainable ICT

The IT Capability maturity framework is a high-level process framework to measure and assess the environmental impact of the IT functions of an organization. The framework aims at addressing four key actions of a Sustainable ICT (SICT) practice in an organization:

- Define the scope and goal of SICT;
- Understand the current SICT capability maturity level;
- Systematically develop and manage the SICT capability building blocks;
- Assess and manage SICT progress over time.

These key actions are discussed in detail to derive IT capability maturity building block grid. The grid consists of four categories; namely, strategy and planning, process management, people and culture, and governance. Strategy and planning includes the specific objectives of SICT and its alignment with the organization's overall sustainability strategy, objectives and goals. This section focuses on the strategic alignment of business strategy as well as the sustainability strategy. Process management includes the aspects such as sourcing operation and disposal of ICT systems, as well as the provisions of systems based on sustainability objectives and the reporting of performance. The people and culture section deals with the common sustainability language and vocabulary used across the organization to leverage a common understanding. However, this section fails to include the people and cultural aspects such as the contribution of multicultural workforce towards organizational sustainability in diversified markets and the team and corporate culture of the organization which contribute towards the sustainability of the organization.

Green ICT Framework

The framework developed at RMIT University, known as the Connection Research-RMIT Green ICT Framework, categorizes four main pillars of Green ICT known as Lifecycle, End User, Enterprise, and Enablement. The framework breaks each of these further downs into several sub components. The Framework is given below for more details. The framework reviews the use of ICT in business sustainability which could be applied to any industry which utilises ICT as a strategic enabler in their day-to-day business. However, the framework has failed to incorporate the elements which are common to any industry, that contribute towards the sustainability of the overall business. For example, the elements such as the production cost, production wastage and emissions could be elements which are common to any domain in terms of sustainability, which is lacking in the existing framework.

Integrated Sustainability Framework for IT

The integrated sustainability framework for IT covers both today and tomorrow in terms of both internal and external elements (Dao, Langella, & Carbo, 2011). The specificity of this framework relies on its emphasis on balancing the people factor with profit factor. Primarily the theoretical basis of this framework is on the best use of IT, HRM and Supply Chain resources in getting the best use of the organization's sustainability capabilities that will eventually leads towards increased sustainability value and competitive advantage. However, an observable drawback in this framework could be noted with regard to its reduced emphasis on the planet aspect – which has been given more prominence in the contemporary Green IT literature. Thus, it could be argued that this framework does not satisfy all three dimensions of triple bottom line.

Impact Assessment Framework for Green IT

The environmental impact of ICTs is another concern. Raju et al. (2013) proposes a holistic impact assessment framework for Green ICT. The paper discusses the growing concern in environmental sustainability as the opening note. Increased energy consumption and greenhouse gas effect are identified as the possible contributors towards global warming. It is argued that the IT could both increase and decrease energy consumption. The reasons are not well-documented in the paper which proposes a holistic impact assessment framework to contextualize, analyze, and measure the environmental and economic effects of using ICT.

The framework is promised to be integrating the high-level policy, standardization, and industrial issues. Furthermore, the authors propose the observation of effects of ICT at different levels ranging from personal level to a national/global level. The holistic framework encompasses the environmental effects of ICT of all nature, which includes the effects which are positive and negative as well as the effects of direct and indirect nature. The direct effects are defined to be the activities related to the ICT products and services themselves and the indirect effects refers to the ICTs affecting other products and services which are outside the ICT sector. The model is clustered into different components such as high level contextual components, applied components and use case descriptions.

The Knowledge Gap

There is an overabundance of research and industry focus on the use of ICT for business sustainability. A Green ICT Framework for understanding and measuring Green ICT- a framework which has been developed at the RMIT University, Australia to measure the Green ICT in businesses (Philipson, 2010). The framework developed at the RMIT University, known as Connection Research-RMIT Green ICT Framework, categorizes four main pillars of Green ICT known as Lifecycle, End User, Enterprise and Enablement. This research has been further extended by Molla and Cooper (2010) which embarks on a Green IT Readiness framework.

The readiness framework encompasses the five important properties of the previous framework; namely, attitude, policy, practice, technology and governance. A research and consultancy initiative called ICT Sustain Review has incorporated this framework into their consultancy framework (Pete Foster, 2007). However, this framework is looking at the use of ICT in business sustainability, which could be applied to any industry which utilizes ICT as a strategic enabler in their day-to-day business. The framework has failed to incorporate the elements which are common to any industry, that contribute towards the sustainability of the overall business.

However, Hilty and Lohmann (2013) reports an annotated bibliography of conceptual frameworks in ICT for Sustainability which details the researchers conducted in the ICT for sustainability knowledge space thus far. The paper reports on the conceptual frameworks covered so far in this knowledge domain, but lacks to outline the application oriented frameworks on this domain which are contextual to specific industries. Furthermore, Donnellan, Sheridan, & Curry (2011) reported a research analyzing the Sustainable ICT Capability Maturity Framework. However, this is a maturity model to assess the ICT capability in enabling sustainability in any organization, but not a model to assess the sustainability of ICT organizations.

Another study conducted by the InfoDev looks at the sustainable and replicable ICT incubators in Sub-Saharan Africa (Ana Carrasco, 2013). However, this study has less relation to the sustainability measurement of ICT Businesses. In contrast, Bin Ismail (2008) argues the knowledge of the managers of businesses has a major impact of utilizing the ICT for sustainable competitive advantage. In fact, the knowledge could differentiate the effective use in ICT for sustainability. However, this research has been conducted for Small and Medium enterprises, which heavily relies on the Owner / Manager for all IT executions, whilst the larger organizations have consultants and specialist professionals working on ICT decisions and executions. Thus, this study could be noted for its limitation to only looking at a smaller scope of Malaysian SMEs which pose issues with the generalizability of findings to a global context where large multinational organizations are much represented in the population compared to SMEs.

On the other hand, Thongmak (2013) examined a systematic framework for Sustainable ICT in developing countries. The research has investigated how developed countries and developing countries could work together in tacking the sustainability related issues using ICT as a tool for empowerment. However, the research lacks to specifically look at the Business sustainability angle, instead overly emphasizing the sustainability of nations. It could be argued that business sustainability is paramount concern in ensuring national sustainability. Therefore, it is essential to address the business sustainability concerns first in order to achieve the stated concerns with regard to national sustainability in this framework.

However, Zhang and Fielden (2011) propose a framework for Sustainable Economic ICT strategy. The paper looks at the role of ICT in absorbing the economic and environmental sustainability of nations, but lacks to have a business perspective in it. The following are a number of frameworks reviewed from the literature in detail to give contextual relevance to this research project. A recent report published by International Telecommunication Union (2012) on a environmental sustainability toolkit for organizations highlights the increasing demands of sustainability measures to be taken by organizations which was backed by many other web based and business oriented resource / practice related concerns such as the Australian Sustainability Conference (Australian Sustinability Conference, 2012).

In addition, the Australian Government's ICT Sustainability plan for 2010-2015 outlines a number of environmental standards in ICT procurement (Australian Government, 2010). This is an example for the expectations of government in terms of environmental sustainability measures taken by the individual organizations. Thus, this research, which aims to look at the ICT Business Sustainability in relation to Australia, could be argued to be a novel, substantial, scholarly and timely contribution to the existing body of knowledge in this area of science.

METHODOLOGY

The methodology used for building and validating the framework uses a mixed method approach. A content analysis method with quantitative data collection technic has been used for transcribing and surveying the green energy management practices of organizations. Ten large scale software development companies were selected from one country (India) and the sustainability reports of those ten firms were downloaded and subjected to content analysis. The country's leadership in software export has been taken into consideration when selecting the country for report sampling. The list of standards that are documented in the reports were compiled based on a rigorous analysis of the reports.

A number of quantitative and qualitative research questions were formulated based on the framework built as part of the report analysis. An online qualitative survey based data collection approach has been conducted using the online survey design platform. The sample size has been set out to be at 79 while the samples includes responses from software development professionals from countries such as Sri Lanka, India and Australia. The organizations that are included in the study include businesses that produces software as a service as well as offshore software development firms that have the development centers in Sri Lanka and India.

A five-point Likert scale used to establish the scaling criteria for the efficiency of green energy management criteria includes: 5 = Most efficient, 4 = efficient, 3 = Average, 2 = not efficient, 1 = least efficient. Each of the elements depicted in the table 1 has been subjected to measurement using these scales. A descriptive statistical analysis has been done for the data collected based on each framework components and the results has been presented in tables 2 - 9 of this article.

FRAMEWORK

The framework depicted in Table 1 consists of four distinct components such as energy sources and energy efficiency, energy efficient heating, energy efficient lighting strategies and technologies as well as energy efficient cooling strategies and technologies. This section briefly summarizes the sub-components of green energy frameworks that are developed as part of this study. The first component consisting of energy sources and energy efficiency has two sub components such as primary energy supply from renewable energy sources as well as the types of energy efficiency. This component categorizes the types of energies available from a number of sources such as grid, captive and local renewable energy sources. The energy efficiency types categorized under this component includes thermal, electrical, fuel and solar energies.

The second component consists of energy efficient heating measures and technologies. The heating measures consist of electrical heating, solar water heating and LPG heating. The heating technologies covered in this component includes dust collector heater, solar water heater as well as combustion space heater. The third component covers energy efficient lighting strategies and technologies. This section includes elements such as energy efficient office lighting, energy efficient street lighting, energy efficient factory lighting, voltage optimization, lighting automation and lighting optimization. Energy efficient cooling strategies and technologies is the fourth component that includes elements such as office cooling, data center cooling, product cooling, cooling efficiency enhancement and cooling automation.

Table 1. Green Energy Management Framework

Category	Description	Criteria
Energy Sources & energy efficiency	Primary energy supply from renewable energy sources	Grid: hydro, thermal, wind, solar, nuclear
		Captive: biomass, thermal
		Local renewable sources: wind, solar
	Types of energy efficiency	Thermal energy efficiency (i.e. water heating energy efficiency)
		Electrical energy efficiency (i.e. office energy efficiency)
		Fuel energy efficiency (i.e. vehicle energy efficiency)
		Solar energy efficiency (i.e. lighting energy efficiency)
Energy efficient heating	heating measures	Electrical heating / urban electric heating
		Solar water heating / solar thermal heating
		LPG gas heating
	heating technologies	Dust collector heater
		solar water heater
		combustions space heater / portable space heaters
Energy efficient lighting strategies & technologies		Energy efficient office lighting (i.e. Solar PV peripheral lighting systems, Light Emitting Diodes - LED, Compact Fluorescent Lamps-CFL, energy efficient light fixtures)
		Energy efficient street lighting (i.e. CFL lamps, metal halide energy server panel / Sodium Vapor lamps)
		Energy efficient factory lighting (i.e. mercury vapor lamps)
		Voltage optimization (i.e. voltage transformers, voltage stabilizers)
		Lighting automation (i.e. wireless battery less sensors for automatic sensing and light switching)
		Lighting optimization (i.e. high masts light towers with double circuits, transparent sheets and sky light panels)
Energy efficient cooling strategies & technologies		Office Cooling (i.e. Air Conditioning, HVAC, Radiant Cooling, Furnace Cooling)
		Data Centre Cooling (i.e. Air Conditioning, Radiant Cooling, Furnace Cooling)
		Product Cooling (i.e. Refrigerators, Vapor Absorption Machine / Chillier Refrigerators, Radiant Cooling, Reverse Osmosis Plants, Furnace Cooling, Water Cooling)
		Cooling Efficiency Enhancement (i.e. Temperature Sensitive Products, Capacity Rationalization, Cold aisle Containment)
		Cooling Automation (i.e. Temperature and Humidity Sensors, Product Ambiance Sensors, Product Cooler Location Sensor Technologies)

RESULTS AND DISCUSSION

This section presents and analyses the results obtained through data collection. The results presented in Table 2 depict the descriptive statistics derived for energy sources. The hydroelectric, thermal, and solar has the highest mean values according to the employee ratings. Wind, nuclear and biomass energy

Table 2. Descriptive Statistics of Primary Renewable Energy Sources

Wind		Solar		Biomass		Hydroelectric		Nuclear		Thermal	
Mean	1.151899	Mean	1.405063	Mean	1.050633	Mean	1.594937	Mean	1.139241	Mean	1.493671
Standard Error	0.203896	Standard Error	0.23248	Standard Error	0.191425	Standard Error	0.234565	Standard Error	0.205202	Standard Error	0.234118
Median	0	Median	0	Median	0	Median	0	Median	0	Median	0
Mode	0	Mode	0	Mode	0	Mode	0	Mode	0	Mode	0
Standard Deviation	1.81227	Standard Deviation	2.06633	Standard Deviation	1.701423	Standard Deviation	2.08486	Standard Deviation	1.823874	Standard Deviation	2.080886
Sample Variance	3.284323	Sample Variance	4.269718	Sample Variance	2.894839	Sample Variance	4.346641	Sample Variance	3.326517	Sample Variance	4.330088
Kurtosis	-0.11323	Kurtosis	-0.92228	Kurtosis	0.04239	Kurtosis	-1.27269	Kurtosis	-0.26	Kurtosis	-1.2599
Skewness	1.23972	Skewness	0.975104	Skewness	1.281053	Skewness	0.715937	Skewness	1.206272	Skewness	0.784339
Range	5	Range	5	Range	5	Range	5	Range	5	Range	5
Minimum	0	Minimum	0	Minimum	0	Minimum	0	Minimum	0	Minimum	0
Maximum	5	Maximum	5	Maximum	5	Maximum	5	Maximum	5	Maximum	5
Sum	91	Sum	111	Sum	83	Sum	126	Sum	90	Sum	118
Count	79	Count	79	Count	79	Count	79	Count	79	Count	79

types are the least rated energy sources according to the mean values derived from employee ratings. The standard deviation of all the above categories are much more than 0. Therefore, the ratings are not closer to the mean value in most of the cases. In most cases, the standard deviation is above 1.5 which means most of the values are much far away from the mean value in the graph.

The results presented in Table 3 depict the descriptive statistics derived for the types of energy efficiency. According to the mean values, electrical and solar efficiency types are the highly rated energy efficiency types. Thermal and fuel efficiency types are rated to be next to the electrical and solar efficiency types according to the mean values. The standard deviation for all these categories are far above 0, meaning the ratings of almost all these types are much more far away from the mean value.

The results presented in Table 4 depicts the descriptive statistics for heating measures and technologies. Electrical heating and solar water heating has the highest mean value for heating measures while LPG gas heating is rated to be below these two categories. The mean value for the solar water heater is rated to be the most rated heating technology while combustion space heater and dust collector heater are rated to be below the solar water heater. According to the standard deviations derived for these categories, almost all variable has a standard deviation which is much higher than 0. This means most of the ratings in these categories are far away from the mean.

The results presented in Table 5 depict the descriptive statistics for energy efficiency lighting strategies. Energy efficient office lighting and energy efficient street lighting have the highest mean values for energy efficient lighting measures. Energy efficient factory lighting, voltage optimization, lighting optimization and the lighting automation have the lowest mean values. The standard deviations show that energy efficient street lighting and energy efficient office lighting has the ratings scattered quite more widely from the mean value.

The results presented in Table 6 and 7 depict the energy efficient lighting technologies used in the software development firms. The mean values show that LED lights, CFL lights, Solar PV peripheral lighting systems and voltage stabilizers has the highest mean values. Energy efficient light fixtures, metal halide energy server panel, sodium vapor lamps, mercury vapor lamps, voltage transformers, wireless battery less sensors, high masts light towers with double circuits and transparent sheets sky light panels

Table 3. Descriptive Statistics of Energy Efficiency Types

Thermal Efficiency		Electrical Efficiency		Fuel Efficiency		Solar Efficiency	
Mean	1.379747	Mean	1.455696	Mean	1.341772	Mean	1.417722
Standard Error	0.228811	Standard Error	0.227026	Standard Error	0.216854	Standard Error	0.232542
Median	0	Median	0	Median	0	Median	0
Mode	0	Mode	0	Mode	0	Mode	0
Standard Deviation	2.033715	Standard Deviation	2.017853	Standard Deviation	1.927441	Standard Deviation	2.066879
Sample Variance	4.135995	Sample Variance	4.07173	Sample Variance	3.715028	Sample Variance	4.27199
Kurtosis	-0.88318	Kurtosis	-1.13804	Kurtosis	-0.96133	Kurtosis	-1.02975
Skewness	0.966636	Skewness	0.810623	Skewness	0.89779	Skewness	0.911197
Range	5	Range	5	Range	5	Range	5
Minimum	0	Minimum	0	Minimum	0	Minimum	0
Maximum	5	Maximum	5	Maximum	5	Maximum	5
Sum	109	Sum	115	Sum	106	Sum	112
Count	79	Count	79	Count	79	Count	79

are rated below in terms of mean values. According to the standard deviation, the LED lights, CFL lights and Solar PV peripheral lighting systems have a higher standard deviation while the other technologies has a lower standard deviation.

Table 8 depicts the descriptive statistics of the cooling measures used by the organizations. The office cooling and data center cooling have higher mean value. Product cooling, cooling efficiency enhancement

Table 4. Descriptive Statistics of Heating Measures and Technologies

Electrical Heating		Solar Water Heating		LPG Gas Heating		Dust Collector Heater		Solar Water Heater		Combustion Space Heater	
Mean	1.481013	Mean	1.405063	Mean	1.253165	Mean	1.075949	Mean	1.43038	Mean	1.21519
Standard Error	0.235492	Standard Error	0.227541	Standard Error	0.21123	Standard Error	0.197987	Standard Error	0.226945	Standard Error	0.209844
Median	0	Median	0	Median	0	Median	0	Median	0	Median	0
Mode	0	Mode	0	Mode	0	Mode	0	Mode	0	Mode	0
Standard Deviation	2.093095	Standard Deviation	2.022432	Standard Deviation	1.877453	Standard Deviation	1.759751	Standard Deviation	2.017129	Standard Deviation	1.865138
Sample Variance	4.381045	Sample Variance	4.09023	Sample Variance	3.52483	Sample Variance	3.096722	Sample Variance	4.068809	Sample Variance	3.478741
Kurtosis	-1.15267	Kurtosis	-0.91369	Kurtosis	-0.70786	Kurtosis	0.248701	Kurtosis	-1.00553	Kurtosis	-0.607
Skewness	0.840698	Skewness	0.933471	Skewness	1.017476	Skewness	1.344278	Skewness	0.887772	Skewness	1.064396
Range	5	Range	5	Range	5	Range	5	Range	5	Range	5
Minimum	0	Minimum	0	Minimum	0	Minimum	0	Minimum	0	Minimum	0
Maximum	5	Maximum	5	Maximum	5	Maximum	5	Maximum	5	Maximum	5
Sum	117	Sum	111	Sum	99	Sum	85	Sum	113	Sum	96
Count	79	Count	79	Count	79	Count	79	Count	79	Count	79

and cooling automation has a lower mean value. According to the standard deviation, office cooling and data center cooling has a higher value. Product cooling, cooling efficiency enhancement and cooling

Table 5. Descriptive Statistics of Heating Measures and Technologies

Energy Efficient Office Lighting		Energy Efficient Street Lighting		Energy Efficient Factory Lighting		Voltage Optimization		Lighting Automation		Lighting Optimization	
Mean	1.658228	Mean	1.468354	Mean	1.278481	Mean	1.291139	Mean	1.177215	Mean	1.265823
Standard Error	0.245628	Standard Error	0.230599	Standard Error	0.220601	Standard Error	0.214798	Standard Error	0.202034	Standard Error	0.206758
Median	0	Median	0	Median	0	Median	0	Median	0	Median	0
Mode	0	Mode	0	Mode	0	Mode	0	Mode	0	Mode	0
Standard Deviation	2.183188	Standard Deviation	2.049612	Standard Deviation	1.960748	Standard Deviation	1.909167	Standard Deviation	1.795718	Standard Deviation	1.837702
Sample Variance	4.76631	Sample Variance	4.200909	Sample Variance	3.844531	Sample Variance	3.64492	Sample Variance	3.224602	Sample Variance	3.37715
Kurtosis	-1.45291	Kurtosis	-1.16016	Kurtosis	-0.65951	Kurtosis	-0.82295	Kurtosis	-0.44229	Kurtosis	-0.88802
Skewness	0.66406	Skewness	0.816512	Skewness	1.053527	Skewness	0.965395	Skewness	1.103626	Skewness	0.931375
Range	5	Range	5	Range	5	Range	5	Range	5	Range	5
Minimum	0	Minimum	0	Minimum	0	Minimum	0	Minimum	0	Minimum	0
Maximum	5	Maximum	5	Maximum	5	Maximum	5	Maximum	5	Maximum	5
Sum	131	Sum	116	Sum	101	Sum	102	Sum	93	Sum	100
Count	79	Count	79	Count	79	Count	79	Count	79	Count	79

automations has a lower standard deviation value. This means these measures have scattered ratings around the mean value of the former two (e.g., office cooking, data center cooling).

Tables 9 and 10 depict the descriptive statistics of cooling related technologies of the organizations. HVAC system and refrigerators does have a higher mean value than other cooling technologies. The standard deviation shows that these two technologies are scattered more widely across the mean values than the other technologies.

The qualitative results obtained through this research are presented in Tables 11 and 12. The qualitative results pertaining to the energy efficiency and temperature control measures of the organizations shows there are three types of measures taken forward by the organizations. The measures include technological measures, managerial / organizational measures and general measures. The technological measures are the types of measures that are intended to reduce energy wastage and increase energy efficiency through the use of technologies such as the usage of low energy electrical units. The managerial measures include measures that are intended for energy efficiency through managerial and business measures such as appropriate tender selection and cost efficiency. The general measures include elements such as waste reduction as well as compliance to standards and policies.

CONCLUSION AND MANAGERIAL IMPLICATIONS

The results presented in this chapter validate a framework for assessing and benchmarking green energy management in software development firms. The main components of the framework include energy sources and energy efficiency, temperature control measures (heating and cooling) as well as lighting strategies. According to the ratings the mean values of the energy conservation measures / technologies has been presented in the results section. The electrical and solar efficiency types are the highly rated energy efficiency types. Thermal and fuel efficiency types are rated to be next to the electrical and solar efficiency type. Electrical heating and solar water heating are rated to be the highest heating measures while LPG gas heating is rated to be below these two categories. The Solar water heater is rated to be

Table 6. Descriptive Statistics of Lighting Measures and Technologies

Solar PV Peripheral Lighting System		LED Lights		CFL Lights		Energy Efficient Light Fixtures		Metal Halide Energy Server Panel		Sodium Vapor Lamps	
Mean	1.443038	Mean	1.658228	Mean	1.481013	Mean	1.265823	Mean	1.240506	Mean	1.151899
Standard Error	0.23403	Standard Error	0.236883	Standard Error	0.227071	Standard Error	0.210646	Standard Error	0.211035	Standard Error	0.202298
Median	0	Median	0	Median	0	Median	0	Median	0	Median	0
Mode	0	Mode	0	Mode	0	Mode	0	Mode	0	Mode	0
Standard Deviation	2.080106	Standard Deviation	2.105463	Standard Deviation	2.018255	Standard Deviation	1.872259	Standard Deviation	1.875723	Standard Deviation	1.798066
Sample Variance	4.326842	Sample Variance	4.432976	Sample Variance	4.073353	Sample Variance	3.505355	Sample Variance	3.518338	Sample Variance	3.233041
Kurtosis	-1.09994	Kurtosis	-1.5106	Kurtosis	-1.22141	Kurtosis	-0.69208	Kurtosis	-0.60938	Kurtosis	-0.55958
Skewness	0.876233	Skewness	0.592857	Skewness	0.772347	Skewness	0.997044	Skewness	1.052161	Skewness	1.083391
Range	5	Range	5	Range	5	Range	5	Range	5	Range	5
Minimum	0	Minimum	0	Minimum	0	Minimum	0	Minimum	0	Minimum	0
Maximum	5	Maximum	5	Maximum	5	Maximum	5	Maximum	5	Maximum	5
Sum	114	Sum	131	Sum	117	Sum	100	Sum	98	Sum	91
Count	79	Count	79	Count	79	Count	79	Count	79	Count	79

Table 7. Descriptive Statistics of Lighting Measures and Technologies

Mercury Vapor Lamps		Voltage Transformers		Voltage Stabilizers		Wireless Battery Less Sensors		High Masts Light Towers with Double Circuits		Transparent Sheets and Sky Light Panels	
Mean	1.088608	Mean	1.278481	Mean	1.443038	Mean	1.291139	Mean	1.240506	Mean	1.21519
Standard Error	0.196686	Standard Error	0.214635	Standard Error	0.221929	Standard Error	0.224405	Standard Error	0.2156	Standard Error	0.217441
Median	0	Median	0	Median	0	Median	0	Median	0	Median	0
Mode	0	Mode	0	Mode	0	Mode	0	Mode	0	Mode	0
Standard Deviation	1.748185	Standard Deviation	1.907722	Standard Deviation	1.972548	Standard Deviation	1.994556	Standard Deviation	1.916294	Standard Deviation	1.932654
Sample Variance	3.056151	Sample Variance	3.639403	Sample Variance	3.890944	Sample Variance	3.978254	Sample Variance	3.672184	Sample Variance	3.735151
Kurtosis	-0.21008	Kurtosis	-0.93105	Kurtosis	-1.21284	Kurtosis	-0.79223	Kurtosis	-0.7046	Kurtosis	-0.59177
Skewness	1.205318	Skewness	0.953191	Skewness	0.775925	Skewness	1.017863	Skewness	1.049061	Skewness	1.108095
Range	5	Range	5	Range	5	Range	5	Range	5	Range	5
Minimum	0	Minimum	0	Minimum	0	Minimum	0	Minimum	0	Minimum	0
Maximum	5	Maximum	5	Maximum	5	Maximum	5	Maximum	5	Maximum	5
Sum	86	Sum	101	Sum	114	Sum	102	Sum	98	Sum	96
Count	79	Count	79	Count	79	Count	79	Count	79	Count	79

the most rated heating technology while combustion space heater and dust collector heater are rated to be below the Solar water heater.

Energy efficient office lighting and energy efficient street lighting are the highest rated energy efficient lighting measures. Energy efficient factory lighting, voltage optimization, lighting optimization and the lighting automation are the lowest rated energy efficiency measures of the organizations. LED lights, CFL lights, Solar PV peripheral lighting systems and voltage stabilizers are the highest rated lighting measures. Energy efficient light fixtures, metal halide energy server panel, sodium vapor lamps, mercury vapor lamps, voltage transformers, wireless battery less sensors, high masts light towers with double circuits and transparent sheets and sky light panels are rated to be at lowest level. The office cool-

Table 8. Descriptive Statistics of Cooling Measures and Technologies

Office Cooling		Data Centre Cooling		Product Cooling		Cooling Efficiency Enhancement		Cooling Automation	
Mean	1.78481	Mean	1.670886	Mean	1.443038	Mean	1.202532	Mean	1.35443
Standard Error	0.250718	Standard Error	0.241521	Standard Error	0.219724	Standard Error	0.204921	Standard Error	0.2192
Median	0	Median	0	Median	0	Median	0	Median	0
Mode	0	Mode	0	Mode	0	Mode	0	Mode	0
Standard Deviation	2.228434	Standard Deviation	2.146682	Standard Deviation	1.952952	Standard Deviation	1.821381	Standard Deviation	1.948293
Sample Variance	4.96592	Sample Variance	4.608244	Sample Variance	3.814021	Sample Variance	3.317429	Sample Variance	3.795846
Kurtosis	-1.60482	Kurtosis	-1.47862	Kurtosis	-1.07908	Kurtosis	-0.69165	Kurtosis	-0.92666
Skewness	0.548955	Skewness	0.624551	Skewness	0.8136	Skewness	1.023412	Skewness	0.913611
Range	5	Range	5	Range	5	Range	5	Range	5
Minimum	0	Minimum	0	Minimum	0	Minimum	0	Minimum	0
Maximum	5	Maximum	5	Maximum	5	Maximum	5	Maximum	5
Sum	141	Sum	132	Sum	114	Sum	95	Sum	107
Count	79	Count	79	Count	79	Count	79	Count	79

Table 9. Descriptive Statistics of Cooling Measures and Technologies

HVAC		Radiant Cooling		Furnace Cooling		Refrigerators		Vapor Abortion Machine		Reverse Osmosis Plants		Temperature Sensitive Products	
Mean	1.594937	Mean	1.392405	Mean	1.227848	Mean	1.556962	Mean	1.265823	Mean	1.164557	Mean	1.177215
Standard Error	0.244059	Standard Error	0.219481	Standard Error	0.211599	Standard Error	0.235413	Standard Error	0.220434	Standard Error	0.207323	Standard Error	0.206011
Median	0	Median	0	Median	0	Median	0	Median	0	Median	0	Median	0
Mode	0	Mode	0	Mode	0	Mode	0	Mode	0	Mode	0	Mode	0
Standard Deviation	2.169243	Standard Deviation	1.95079	Standard Deviation	1.880735	Standard Deviation	2.092397	Standard Deviation	1.959257	Standard Deviation	1.842729	Standard Deviation	1.831067
Sample Variance	4.705615	Sample Variance	3.805583	Sample Variance	3.537163	Sample Variance	4.378124	Sample Variance	3.838689	Sample Variance	3.395651	Sample Variance	3.352808
Kurtosis	-1.39453	Kurtosis	-1.08099	Kurtosis	-0.60363	Kurtosis	-1.27234	Kurtosis	-0.70678	Kurtosis	-0.35796	Kurtosis	-0.49205
Skewness	0.710367	Skewness	0.841219	Skewness	1.060742	Skewness	0.749161	Skewness	1.043644	Skewness	1.151738	Skewness	1.09382
Range	5	Range	5	Range	5	Range	5	Range	5	Range	5	Range	5
Minimum	0	Minimum	0	Minimum	0	Minimum	0	Minimum	0	Minimum	0	Minimum	0
Maximum	5	Maximum	5	Maximum	5	Maximum	5	Maximum	5	Maximum	5	Maximum	5
Sum	126	Sum	110	Sum	97	Sum	123	Sum	100	Sum	92	Sum	93
Count	79	Count	79	Count	79	Count	79	Count	79	Count	79	Count	79

ing and data center cooling are the highest rated cooling measures. Product cooling, cooling efficiency enhancement and cooling automation are rated to be at lowest level. HVAC system and refrigerators does have a higher mean value than other cooling technologies.

The key implications for managerial practice include that organizations make use of the highly rated energy efficiency measures and technologies to the highest possible level. The overutilization of efficient resources is to be avoided to ensure that the organizations loses the sustainable utilization at a longer run. In addition, the organizations could do an alignment of effective measures with efficient technologies. For example, the effective cooling measures could be aligned with efficient cooling technologies to leverage maximum efficiency through cooling efforts of the organizations. Organizations could also focus on the utilization of efficient technologies to mitigate the energy wastage caused through any organizational mismanagement such as unclear goals for energy usage projected on a yearly basis and cost-based budgeting.

Table 10. Descriptive Statistics of Cooling Measures and Technologies

Capacity Rationalization		Cold Aisle Containment		Temperature and Humidity Sensors		Product Ambient Sensors		Product Cooler Location Sensor Technologies		Sand Cooling	
Mean	1.151899	Mean	1.101266	Mean	1.240506	Mean	1.088608	Mean	1.101266	Mean	1.113924
Standard Error	0.207838	Standard Error	0.205092	Standard Error	0.214846	Standard Error	0.200769	Standard Error	0.198661	Standard Error	0.203816
Median	0	Median	0	Median	0	Median	0	Median	0	Median	0
Mode	0	Mode	0	Mode	0	Mode	0	Mode	0	Mode	0
Standard Deviation	1.847303	Standard Deviation	1.822895	Standard Deviation	1.909592	Standard Deviation	1.784476	Standard Deviation	1.765735	Standard Deviation	1.811554
Sample Variance	3.412528	Sample Variance	3.322947	Sample Variance	3.646543	Sample Variance	3.184356	Sample Variance	3.117819	Sample Variance	3.281727
Kurtosis	-0.34983	Kurtosis	-0.32522	Kurtosis	-0.59188	Kurtosis	-0.15359	Kurtosis	-0.33839	Kurtosis	-0.23333
Skewness	1.161009	Skewness	1.201214	Skewness	1.074204	Skewness	1.238221	Skewness	1.161275	Skewness	1.206707
Range	5	Range	5	Range	5	Range	5	Range	5	Range	5
Minimum	0	Minimum	0	Minimum	0	Minimum	0	Minimum	0	Minimum	0
Maximum	5	Maximum	5	Maximum	5	Maximum	5	Maximum	5	Maximum	5
Sum	91	Sum	87	Sum	98	Sum	86	Sum	87	Sum	88
Count	79	Count	79	Count	79	Count	79	Count	79	Count	79

LIMITATIONS AND FUTURE RESEARCH DIRECTIONS

The key objective of the work reported in this article is to build and validate a framework for assessing and benchmarking green energy related initiatives in software development firms. The research has built a framework through content analysis and validate that with a survey research. The key limitations of this research are discussed herein and suggestions have been made for possible extensions of this research.

The key limitation of this study is the relatively less number of sample responses recorded in the research. In most cases the standard deviation is quite widely spread away from the mean value, this shows that the widespread standard deviation could influence the findings of this study. The mode and median values shows that most of the ratings are close to 0. This means the quality responses recorded for this study are significantly less than half of the respondents. Does this cause issues with the validity of the conclusions? It is often the case that the measurable in this research were often related to people's experiences. A claim recorded by Jacob Nielsen, a usability expert, suggests the responses could be acceptable to make conclusions with lesser samples in studies that deals with experiences types such as user experience (Nielsen, 2014). In fact, the experience of a technology or an organizational phenomenon cannot vary among participants in a controlled environment. Therefore, it is concluded that having less number of responses is not something that could influence the quality of findings.

Future research is warranted on identifying relationship between the variables associated with each component of the framework. For example, the relationship between organizational factors such as the size of the organization / employee hierarchy with the ratings on energy sources / energy efficiency is a potential future research direction for the research documented in this article. Likewise, the research documented in this article has a number of research avenues each of which extends the research by looking at the relationship between a set of variables associated in the framework such as the temperature control measures and energy efficient lighting strategies and technologies.

REFERENCES

Al-Amin, A. Q., Rasiah, R., & Chenayah, S. (2015). Prioritizing climate change mitigation: An assessment using Malaysia to reduce carbon emissions in future. *Environmental Science & Policy*, *50*, 24–33. doi:10.1016/j.envsci.2015.02.002

Ana Carrasco. (2013). *A Model for Sustainable and Replicable ICT Incubators in Sub-Saharan Africa | infoDev*. Retrieved on May 3, 2015, from: http://www.infodev.org/articles/model-sustainable-and-replicable-ict-incubators-sub-saharan-africa

Australian Government. (2010). *Australian Government ICT Sustainability Plan 2010 - 2015 - Overview*. Retrieved on May 3, 2015, from: http://www.environment.gov.au/resource/australian-government-ict-sustainability-plan-2010-2015-2

Australian Sustinability Conference. (2012). *Australian Sustainability*. Retrieved on May 3, 2015, from: http://blog.australiansustainability.com.au/

Dao, V., Langella, I., & Carbo, J. (2011). From green to sustainability: Information Technology and an integrated sustainability framework. *The Journal of Strategic Information Systems*, *20*(1), 63–79. doi:10.1016/j.jsis.2011.01.002

de Groot, R. S., Wilson, M. A., & Boumans, R. M. (2002). A typology for the classification, description and valuation of ecosystem functions, goods and services. *Ecological Economics*, *41*(3), 393–408. doi:10.1016/S0921-8009(02)00089-7

Demirkan, H., Goul, M., & Gros, M. (2010). A Reference Model for Sustainable E-Learning Service Systems:Experiences with the Joint University/Teradata Consortium. *Decision Sciences Journal of Innovative Education*, *8*(1), 151–189. doi:10.1111/j.1540-4609.2009.00250.x

Donnellan, B., Sheridan, C., & Curry, E. (2011). A Capability Maturity Framework for Sustainable Information and Communication Technology. *IT Professional*, *13*(1), 33–40. doi:10.1109/MITP.2011.2

Elghali, L., Clift, R., Sinclair, P., Panoutsou, C., & Bauen, A. (2007). Developing a sustainability framework for the assessment of bioenergy systems. *Energy Policy*, *35*(12), 6075–6083. doi:10.1016/j.enpol.2007.08.036

Hilty & Lohmann. (2013). An Annotated Bibliography of Conceptual Frameworks in ICT for Sustainability. In *ICT4S 2013: Proceedings of the First International Conference on Information and Communication Technologies for Sustainability, ETH Zurich, February 14-16,2013* (pp. 288–300). Academic Press. 30010.3929/ethz-a-007337628

Høgevold, N. M., & Svensson, G. (2012). A business sustainability model: A European case study. *Journal of Business and Industrial Marketing*, *27*(2), 142–151. doi:10.1108/08858621211197001

International Telecommunication Union. (2012). *Toolkit on environmental sustainability for the ICT sector*. Retrieved on May 9, 2015, from: http://www.itu.int/dms_pub/itu-t/oth/4B/01/T4B010000060001PDFE.pdf

J. W. O., & Bin Ismail, H. (2008, June 1). *Sustainable Competitive Advantage through Information Technology Competence: Resource-Based View on Small and Medium Enterprises*. Retrieved from http://shdl.mmu.edu.my/2912/

Keegan, D., Lossenko, J., Mazar, I., Michels, P. F., Paulsen, M. F., & Rekkedal, T. (2007). *E-learning initiatives that did not reach targeted goals (MegaTrends)*. Bekkestua, Norway: NKI Publishing House.

Labuschagne, C., Brent, A. C., & Van Erck, R. P. G. (2005). Assessing the sustainability performances of industries. *Journal of Cleaner Production*, *13*(4), 373–385. doi:10.1016/j.jclepro.2003.10.007

Molla, A., & Cooper, V. (2010, September 13). Green IT Readiness: A Framework and Preliminary Proof of Concept. *AJIS. Australasian Journal of Information Systems*, *16*(2). doi:10.3127/ajis.v16i2.545

Nielsen, J. (2014). *When to Use Which User-Experience Research Methods*. Retrieved on August 18, 2017, from: https://www.nngroup.com/articles/which-ux-research-methods/

Oncel, S. S. (2017). Green energy engineering: Opening a green way for the future. *Journal of Cleaner Production*, *142*, 3095–3100. doi:10.1016/j.jclepro.2016.10.158

Pete Foster. (2007). *The ICT Sustainability Index - The ICT Sustinability Framework*. Retrieved on May 3, 2015, from: http://www.ictsustain.com/the-ict-sustainability-index.html

Philipson. (2010). *A Green ICT Framework - Understanding and Measuring Green ICT. Connection Research Green Paper*. Retrieved from http://www.computersite.com.au/wp-content/uploads/2015/02/A_Green_ICT_Framework_CR.pdf

Raju, A., Lindmark, S., Delaere, S., & Ballon, P. (2013). A Holistic Impact-Assessment Framework for Green ICT. *IT Professional*, *15*(1), 50–56. doi:10.1109/MITP.2012.119

Thongmak, M. (2013). A Systematic Framework for Sustainable ICTs in Developing Countries. *International Journal of Information Technologies and Systems Approach*, *6*(1), 1–19. doi:10.4018/jitsa.2013010101

Van Cauwenbergh, N., Biala, K., Bielders, C., Brouckaert, V., Franchois, L., Garcia Cidad, V., ... Peeters, A. (2007). SAFE-A hierarchical framework for assessing the sustainability of agricultural systems. *Agriculture, Ecosystems & Environment*, *120*(2–4), 229–242. doi:10.1016/j.agee.2006.09.006

Zhang, B. Q., & Fielden, K. (2011). Sustainable Economic ICT Strategy: A Proposed Framework. *All Sprouts Content*. Retrieved on May 9, 2015, from: http://aisel.aisnet.org/sprouts_all/443

Chapter 18
The Modelling of the Economy by Means of C-V-M Matrices

Grigorii Pushnoi
Independent Researcher, Russia

ABSTRACT

The classical three-sector model of the economy: 1) "the means of production", 2) "the goods for employees", and 3) "the goods consumed by other economic agents" ("luxury goods") is considered in matrix formulation. Each sector contains many industries producing the goods of these three kinds. The "transformation problem" in Marxian economics is considered in a three-sector model of the economy with simple production. The solution of this problem is based on the action of the statistical "laws of large numbers" (LLN) in the economy. The stylized facts about the economy of the United States indicate onto the existence of the following probability distributions: 1) the inverse power distribution for the elements of matrix of direct requirements and 2) the Gaussian distribution for the direct labor per the unit of goods. The action of the statistic "law of large numbers" guarantees the C-V-M matrix of the economy must be almost symmetric. The "labor value" and the "price of production" of the total product produced within each sector in this case are almost equal.

INTRODUCTION

The Three-sector model of the economy was first formulated in the second volume of "Capital" (Marx, 1885; ch.20). Later many economists, beginning with Tugan-Baranovsky (1906) and Bortkiewicz (1907), used this model for consideration of the "problem of transformation" of "labor values" into "prices of production". Marx has formulated the following two rules of this transformation in the third volume of the "Capital" (Marx, 1894; ch.9):

- **The First Rule of Transformation:** The aggregate profit in the economy accumulated for example during the year equals the aggregate surplus value created by the labor of employees;
- **The Second Rule of Transformation:** The "value" (embodied labor in the money form) of the aggregate product produced during the year equals to its price of production. Bortkiewicz (1907a; 1907b) in 1907 has considered the transformation of the "labor values" into the "prices of production" using the three-sector model of the economy with simple production. He discovered

DOI: 10.4018/978-1-5225-5787-6.ch018

that Marx's transformational rules could not be performed simultaneously in the economy with arbitrary structure. Only one rule of transformation can be performed in the general case: either the sum of the profits equals to the aggregate surplus value or the price and the value of aggregate output are equal. Bortkiewicz concluded about logical inconsistence in Marx's theory. Therefore, the "transformation problem" was created.

This discouraging result shattered confidence in the Marx's "labor theory of value". Later many scientists came to the same conclusion (Sweezy, 1949; Meek, 1956; Samuelson 1957, 1971; Medio, 1972; Steedman, 1977; Abraham-Frois (1979); Itoh, 1980) and now a majority of economists are convinced that Marx's theory is internally inconsistent. Numerous attempts have been undertaken to solve this problem. Morishima and Caterhores (1975) have assumed the Marxian algorithm of transformation is only the first step of the iterative process. Shaikh (1977, 1984) has assumed that the solution of this problem can be obtained as a result of sequence of iterations of the Marx's transformation algorithm.

Sweezy (1949) has assumed that the problem can be solved if, in reality, "values" and "prices of production" are connected by a nonlinear relation. Lipietz (1982), Dumenil (1980, 1983), and Foley (1982) have offered a so-called "new interpretation" of "transformational rules" – the so-called "new solution". Freeman (1996), Kliman and McGlone (1999), and Kliman (2007) have offered "temporal single-system interpretation" (TSSI) in which "output prices" and "input prices" can differ in each period because the real economy is not the equilibrium dynamical system. Kalyuzhnyi (2014) proposed solution based on nontrivial interpretation of "spheres of production" as complexes of industries producing only the goods of final consumption.

Despite the elegance of many ideas offered for the solution of this problem, among theorists there is currently not a consensus. Moseley (1999), Fine et al. (2004), Mariolis (2006), and a number of other authors criticize the "new solution" because it differs from the initial statement of this problem and comprises the implicit tautology. Laibman (2004), Roberto (2004), and Park (2009) recently have put forward serious objections against the TSSI-approach to a solution of the transformation problem. Therefore, the transformation problem remains unsolved in modern Marxian economics.

We consider the Three-sector model of the economy with simple production. The model of simple reproduction assumes the performance of the certain balance conditions in economy. These are conditions when the supply and the demand are equal in each sector of the economy. We argue in this chapter that Bortkiewicz' problem statement does not consider the action of statistical "law of large numbers" which guarantees the almost-symmetry of the $C-V-M$ matrix. Consequently, the set of the solutions in Bortkiewicz' paper is wider than it is possible in any real market economy with simple production.

Bortkiewicz's solutions, which do not satisfy the "transformation rules" describe the economy in which the statistical "law of large numbers" is violated. If this statistical law is working properly, the $C-V-M$ matrix of the economy is almost symmetric, and the "value" of the product of each sector equals to its "price of production". The chapter is structured as follows: the second part contains mathematical formalization of the "transformation problem" in the $C-V-M$ model of the economy with simple production. The necessary and sufficient condition for the solution of "transformation problem" in this model is formulated as the following theorem.

The Theorem about the existence of the solution of the "transformation problem" in the $C-V-M$ model of the economy with simple production.

The solution of the "transformation problem" exists in the only case when the $C-V-M$ matrix in prices of production is symmetric.

Part II of this chapter contains the proof of this Theorem. Parts III and IV of this chapter contain the description of the economy with numerous industries. These industries produce three kinds of goods: I – the "means of production", II – the "goods consumed by employees", and III – the "goods consumed by all other economic agents" ("luxury goods"). "Labor value" (and the "price of production") of the output of each sector is the sum of the "values" (the "prices of production") of products of industries of this sector.

The total sum of prices of products produced within each sector almost equals the product of mean value of terms in this sum and the number of terms of summation. The difference between the factual values of elements of the $C-V-M$ matrix and the values calculated via multiplication of the mean value and the quantity of industries within the sector tends to zero when the quantity of industries tends to infinity. This is the consequence of the statistical "law of large numbers". The analysis of stylized facts for the economy of the United States demonstrates the existence of statistic distributions for the following economic values: the expenditures of direct labor per the unit of goods (the Gaussian distribution) and the direct material expenditures (elements of matrix of direct requirements) per the unit of goods (the inverse power law distribution). If the mean values of these distributions are equal in the different sectors of the economy, the $C-V-M$ matrix is almost symmetric. These theoretical conclusions can be illustrated by means of computer computations of $C-V-M$ matrices. The differences between $C-V-M$ matrix in values and $C-V-M$ matrix in prices become negligible if the quantity of industries in each sector of the economy tends to infinity.

The existence of these statistical distributions and the action of statistical "law of large numbers" explain why both rules of transformation are almost fulfilled in the real economy. The structure of the $C-V-M$ matrix is almost symmetric due to the influence of these factors. The "labor values" and the "price of production" of the total product produced within each sector is almost equal subject to appropriate choice of the unit of measurement of the labor. These findings open new possibilities for researches of $C-V-M$ structures of real economic systems. Stylized facts can be used for the construction of the $C-V-M$ models of real economies.

The paper does not consider the economy with the expanded production but the simple production is nothing like the partial case of the expanded production with zero rate of growth. If the economy develops with a small rate of growth (this assumption is fulfilled for the majority of developed countries which grow with the rate ~ 2-4% per year), the deviation of the $C-V-M$ model of a growing economy from the $C-V-M$ model of the economy with zero rate of growth is negligible. Consequently, the main conclusions concerning the $C-V-M$ model of the economy with simple production are correct also in the $C-V-M$ model of expanded production. In particular, the "labor value" and the "price of production" of the total product produced in any sector of the $C-V-M$ model of expanded production almost equal.

"TRANSFORMATION PROBLEM" IN THE THREE-SECTOR MODEL OF THE ECONOMY WITH SIMPLE PRODUCTION

Mathematical formulation of "transformation problem" in the $C-V-M$ model.

The standard form of the $C-V-M$ model of the economy with simple production is depictured in Figure 1 and Figure 2.

We use standard designations of Marxian economics:

Figure 1. The $C-V-M$ model of the economy in value-form

	C	V	M	W
I – "means of production"	$C_1 = k_1V_1$	V_1	$M_1 = mV_1$	$W_1 = C_1 + V_1 + M_1$
II – "goods for employees"	$C_2 = k_2V_2$	V_2	$M_2 = mV_2$	$W_2 = C_2 + V_2 + M_2$
III – "luxury goods"	$C_3 = k_3V_3$	V_3	$M_3 = mV_3$	$W_3 = C_3 + V_3 + M_3$
Sum:	$C = \sum_{n=1}^{3} C_n$	$V = \sum_{n=1}^{3} V_n$	$M = \sum_{n=1}^{3} M_n$	

Figure 2. The $C-V-M$ model of the economy in price-form

	$\tilde{C}$	$\tilde{V}$	P	W
I – "means of production"	$\tilde{C}_1 = \tilde{k}_1\tilde{V}_1$	$\tilde{V}_1$	$P_1 = r\cdot(\tilde{C}_1 + \tilde{V}_1)$	$\tilde{W}_1 = \tilde{C}_1 + \tilde{V}_1 + \tilde{P}_1$
II – "goods for employees"	$\tilde{C}_2 = \tilde{k}_2\tilde{V}_2$	$\tilde{V}_2$	$P_2 = r\cdot(\tilde{C}_2 + \tilde{V}_2)$	$\tilde{W}_2 = \tilde{C}_2 + \tilde{V}_2 + \tilde{P}_2$
III – "luxury goods"	$\tilde{C}_3 = \tilde{k}_3\tilde{V}_3$	$\tilde{V}_3$	$P_3 = r\cdot(\tilde{C}_3 + \tilde{V}_3)$	$\tilde{W}_3 = \tilde{C}_3 + \tilde{V}_3 + \tilde{P}_3$
Sum:	$\tilde{C} = \sum_{n=1}^{3} \tilde{C}_n$	$\tilde{V} = \sum_{n=1}^{3} \tilde{V}_n$	$P = \sum_{n=1}^{3} P_n$	

C: The "labor value" of the constant capital.
$\tilde{C}$: The "price of production" of the constant capital.
V: The "labor value" of variable capital.
$\tilde{V}$: The "price of production" of variable capital.
M: The "surplus value".
$\tilde{M}$: The "price of production" of "luxury goods".
P: The profit.
$k_n = C_n : V_n$: The composition of the capital in value-form.
$\tilde{k}_n = \tilde{C}_n : \tilde{V}_n$: The composition of the capital in price-form.
$m = M : V$: The "rate of surplus value".
$r = P : (\tilde{C} + \tilde{V})$: The "rate of profit" (more precisely – profitability).

All quantities in Table 1 are presented in the "labor values". All quantities in Table 2 are presented in the "prices of production". Let us introduce multipliers $x; y; z$ which transform the "labor values" into the "prices of production":

$\tilde{C} = C \cdot x$: The price of constant capital.
$\tilde{V} = V \cdot y$: The price of variable capital.
$\tilde{M} = z \cdot M$: The price of "luxury goods".

Marx's Transformation Rules

Marx postulated two "transformation rules:

1. **The first "transformation rule":** The surplus-value M embodied in the aggregate product produced during a year equals to the aggregate profit P:

$$\underbrace{M}_{\text{aggregate surplus-value}} = \underbrace{P}_{\text{aggregate profit}} \tag{1}$$

2. **The second "transformation rule":** The "labor value" and the "price of production" of aggregate output are equal:

$$\underbrace{C+V+M}_{\text{value of output}} = \underbrace{Cx+Vy+P}_{\text{price of output}} \tag{2}$$

Marx's "transformation rules" can be written also in another way:

3. The "labor value" and the "price of production" of the aggregate capital are equal:

$$\underbrace{C+V}_{\text{value of aggregate capital}} = \underbrace{Cx+Vy}_{\text{price of aggregate capital}} \tag{3}$$

4. The "rates of profit" in the value-form and in the price-form are equal:

$$r = \frac{M}{C+V} = \frac{P}{Cx+Vy} \tag{4}$$

Equality (3) follows from (1) and (2). Equality (4) follows from (1) and (3).

Any two equations in this system of equalities (1)-(4) can be chosen as the "transformation rules" because two other equalities follow from one.

The Balance-Conditions of Simple Production in the "Labor Values"

Figure 3 describes two value-forms of the economy with simple production.

1. **The value-form-1:** Describes "labor values" of products *produced* in the different sectors;
2. **The value-form-2:** Describes "labor value" of goods *consumed* in different sectors.

Since output of each sector is consumed in full in the economy with simple production we have the following equalities:

$$C = C_1 + V_1(1+m) = W_1 \tag{5}$$

$$V = C_2 + V_2(1+m) = W_2 \tag{6}$$

$$M = C_3 + V_3(1+m) = W_3 \tag{7}$$

Equalities (5)-(7) formalize (in the value-form) the balance conditions in the economy with simple production. The rate of surplus-value m determines the surplus-value produced in sectors. The rates $m_1; m_2; m_3$ connect labor value of luxury goods consumed by "capitalists" of the sector with the "labor value" of goods consumed by employees of this sector. The group "capitalists" in our model is the group of all the economic agents except employees. The "labor value" of "luxury goods" M consumed by "capitalists" is equal to the surplus-value $\widehat{M}$ produced in the economy:

$$M = m_1V_1 + m_2V_2 + m_3V_3 = m(V_1 + V_2 + V_3) = mV = \widehat{M} \tag{8}$$

The following equality follows from the balance conditions (5)-(7):

$$mV = m_1V_1 + m_2V_2 + m_3V_3 \tag{9}$$

Figure 3. Value-forms of the economy with simple production

	Value-form-2. Consumption of labor-value (labor commanded aspect).				
	C (means of production) (1)	V (goods for employees) (2)	M (luxury goods) (3)	m	W (value of goods consumed in each department) (5)
I	C_1	V_1	$M_1 = m_1V_1$	m_1	$C_1 + V_1 + M_1$
II	C_2	V_2	$M_2 = m_2V_2$	m_2	$C_2 + V_2 + M_2$
III	C_3	V_3	$M_3 = m_3V_3$	m_3	$C_3 + V_3 + M_3$
Σ	$C = C_1 + C_2 + C_3$	$V = V_1 + V_2 + V_3$	$M = M_1 + M_2 + M_3$		
	Value-form-1. Creation of labor-value (labor cost aspect)				
	C (transferring labor)	$\widehat{V}$ (necessary labor)	$\widehat{M}$ (surplus labor)	m	$\widehat{W}$ (labor cost of product)
I	C_1	V_1	mV_1	m	$C_1 + V_1(1+m)$
II	C_2	V_2	mV_2	m	$C_2 + V_2(1+m)$
III	C_3	V_3	mV_3	m	$C_3 + V_3(1+m)$
Σ	C	V	mV		

Strictly speaking, the rates $m_1; m_2; m_3$ are not the rates of "surplus-value" of sectors. The rates of surplus-value are identical in all three departments ($= m$) and characterize the rate of exploitation of labor-force.

The Balance-Conditions of Simple Production in the "Prices of Production"

Figure 4 describes the balance conditions of simple production in the "prices of production". We have the following equalities:

$$(C_1x + V_1y)(1+r) = Cx \tag{10}$$

$$(C_2x + V_2y)(1+r) = Vy \tag{11}$$

$$(C_3x + V_3y)(1+r) = Mz \tag{12}$$

Values Cx, Vy, Mz determine the "price of production" of goods ("means of production", "goods for employees" and "luxury goods") which are produced and consumed in the economy. Multipliers $x; y; z$ transform the "labor values" C, V, M into the "prices of production" of goods.

The following equality follows from the Equations (10)-(12):

$$r(Cx + Vy) = Mz \tag{13}$$

The Transformation Problem in the C-V-M Model of the Economy With Simple Production

We have the following: (1) the balance-conditions in "labor values" (5)-(7), (2) the balance-conditions in the "prices of production" (10)-(12), and two Marx's "transformation rules" (any two equalities from the list (1)-(4)).

Figure 4. Simple production in the prices of production. The $C-V-M$ matrix of simple production in the "prices of production".

	Price of constant capital	Price of variable capital	Profit	Sum
I.	C_1x	V_1y	$r(C_1x+V_1y)$	$(C_1x+V_1y)(1+r)$
II.	C_2x	V_2y	$r(C_2x+V_2y)$	$(C_2x+V_2y)(1+r)$
III.	C_3x	V_3y	$r(C_3x+V_3y)$	$(C_3x+V_3y)(1+r)$
Σ:	Cx	Vy	$P=r(Cx+Vy)=Mz$	

The balance conditions in "labor values":

$$\begin{cases} C_1 + V_1 + M_1 = C = C_1 + C_2 + C_3 \\ C_2 + V_2 + M_2 = V = V_1 + V_2 + V_3 \\ C_3 + V_3 + M_3 = M = M_1 + M_2 + M_3 \end{cases} \quad (14)$$

The balance conditions in "prices of production":

$$\begin{cases} (C_1x + V_1y)(1+r) = Cx \\ (C_2x + V_2y)(1+r) = Vy \\ (C_3x + V_3y)(1+r) = Mz \end{cases} \quad (15)$$

The transformation rules:

$$\begin{cases} P \equiv r(Cx + Vy) = M \\ Cx + Vy + Mz = C + V + M \end{cases} \quad (16)$$

We shall consider only the realistic solutions of the system (14)-(16) which satisfies the inequalities. The realistic limitations for the parameters of the $C - V - M$ model are as follows:

$$C_i > 0;\; V_i > 0;\; i = 1;2;3;\; m > 0;\; r > 0;\; x > 0;\; y > 0;\; z > 0 \quad (17)$$

The parameters $C_1; C_2; C_3; V_1; V_2; V_3; M$ are the coefficients in the system of the equations (15)-(16). We seek the solution of the system (15)-(16) i.e., an unknown coefficients of transformation $x; y; z$ and an unknown "rate of profit" r. We have five equations for four unknown values. Therefore, the system (15)-(16) can be solved if only the coefficients of this system $C_1; C_2; C_3; V_1; V_2; V_3; M$ satisfy to some additional condition. This additional condition (compatibility condition) guarantees that if any arbitrary equality in the system (16) is fulfilled, then the other equality in this system is fulfilled also. If this additional condition coincides with any equality of the system (14) (or with any consequence from this system), then the system (15)-(16) has a solution.

The following equality follows from the system (15):

$$r(Cx + Vy) = Mz \quad (18)$$

The first equality (the first transformation rule) in the system (16) is fulfilled if $z = 1$. The second transformation rule can be simplified as follows:

$$Cx + Vy = C + V \quad (3)$$

Thus, the system (14)-(16) can be rewritten as follows.

The balance conditions in "labor values":

$$\begin{cases} C_1 + V_1 + M_1 = C = C_1 + C_2 + C_3 \\ C_2 + V_2 + M_2 = V = V_1 + V_2 + V_3 \\ C_3 + V_3 + M_3 = M = M_1 + M_2 + M_3 \end{cases} \tag{14}$$

The balance conditions in "prices of production":

$$\begin{cases} (C_1 x + V_1 y)(1+r) = Cx \\ (C_2 x + V_2 y)(1+r) = Vy \\ (C_3 x + V_3 y)(1+r) = M \end{cases} \tag{15A}$$

The transformation rule:

$$(Cx + Vy)(1+r) = C + V + M \tag{16A}$$

The transformation rule $r(Cx + Vy) = M$ is fulfilled in the system of Equations (14)-(16A). We shall prove bellow in this Part of the chapter the following theorem.

Theorem about the existence of a realistic solution of the "transformation problem" in the three-sector model of the economy with simple production.

The system of the equations and the inequalities (14)-(17) has a solution in the only case when the matrix of simple production in the "prices of production" is symmetric. The symmetry of this matrix is the necessary and the sufficient condition for the existence of a realistic solution of the "transformation problem" in the three-sector model of the economy with simple production.

This Theorem consists of two Theorems.

Theorem E1: The sufficient condition for the existence of solution.

If the $C - V - M$ matrix of the economy with simple production is symmetric, the "transformation problem" has a realistic solution.

Theorem E2: The necessary condition for the existence of solution.

If the "transformation problem" has a realistic solution in the model of economy with simple production, the $C - V - M$ matrix is symmetric.

Let us consider the conditions of symmetry for the $C - V - M$ matrix of simple production. We have the following equalities.

The Conditions of Symmetry for the Matrix of Simple Production in the "Prices of Production"

$$C_2x = V_1y \tag{19}$$

$$C_3x = r(C_1x + V_1y) \tag{20}$$

$$V_3y = r(C_2x + V_2y) \tag{21}$$

If these equalities are fulfilled the balance conditions (15A) are also fulfilled. The converse is not true: the equalities (19)-(21) do not follow from the equalities (15A).

LEMMA-1: If the equalities (15A) and any (one!) equality of the system (19)-(21) are fulfilled, then *all three* equalities (19)-(21) are fulfilled, and the matrix of simple production in "prices of production" is symmetric.

Proof: We prove this statement for the case when the equalities (15A) and the equality (19) are fulfilled. We have the following chain of the mathematically equivalent transformations:

$$(C_1x + V_1y)(1+r) = (C_1x + V_1y) + (C_1x + V_1y)r = Cx = C_1x + C_2x + C_3x$$

We have the following result after simplification:

$$r(C_1x + V_1y) = C_3x \text{ - the formula} \tag{20}$$

$$(C_2x + V_2y)(1+r) = C_2x + V_2y + (C_2x + V_2y)r = Vy = V_1y + V_2y + V_3y$$

$$r(C_2x + V_2y) = V_3y \text{ - the equation} \tag{21}$$

The proof for other cases (the choice of the equality (20) or (21)) is analogous.

THE PROOF OF LEMMA-1 IS COMPLETED

We can conclude that the $C - V - M$ matrix of simple production in the price-form is symmetric if one of the equalities (19)-(21) is executed.

Let us rewrite the system (19)-(21) in the form of two equations for one variable:

$$C_2 t = V_1 \tag{22}$$

$$\frac{C_3 t}{V_3} = \frac{C_1 t + V_1}{C_2 t + V_2} \tag{23}$$

$$t = \frac{x}{y} \tag{24}$$

The system (22)-(24) has a solution if the coefficients satisfy to the following equality:

$$\frac{C_3}{V_3} = \frac{C_1 + C_2}{V_1 + V_2} = k \tag{25}$$

This equality follows from the Equations (22)-(23) if we substitute equality (22) into equation (23). Equality (25) determines the condition for the compositions of the capital (in the "labor values") k at the first and second sectors together and the composition of the capital in the third sector of the economy. The composition of the aggregate capital equals the composition of the third sector and the composition of the first and second sectors together:

$$\frac{C}{V} = \frac{C_1 + C_2 + C_3}{V_1 + V_2 + V_3} = \frac{k\left(V_1 + V_2\right) + kV_3}{V_1 + V_2 + V_3} = k = \frac{C_3}{V_3} = \frac{C_1 + C_2}{V_1 + V_2} \tag{26}$$

The conditions (26) are well-known as Sweezy's (1942) conditions when the solution of the "transformation problem" exists. As we proved above, these conditions follow from the conditions of symmetry of the $C-V-M$ matrix of simple production in the "prices of production". Thus, Sweezy's conditions are equivalent mathematically to the conditions of symmetry of $C-V-M$ matrix in the price-form. The conditions (26) are formulated via the "labor values" whereas the condition of symmetry is formulated for the $C-V-M$ matrix in the price-form. If the $C-V-M$ matrix of simple production in the "prices of production" is symmetric, a solution of the "transformation problem" exists because in this case the Sweezy's conditions are fulfilled. Thus, a symmetry of the $C-V-M$ matrix in the price-form is the sufficient condition for the existence of a solution of the "transformation problem".

The following lemma formulates Sweezy's result. We provide our own proof of this theorem.

LEMMA-2 (Sweezy, 1942): The solution of the "transformation problem" (the solution of the system of the equations (14), (15A) and (16A)) exists if the conditions (26) are fulfilled.

Proof: The first transformation rule $r\left(Cx + Vy\right) = M$ is fulfilled automatically in the system of equations (14), (15A) and (16A)). It is necessary prove the other transformation rule is also fulfilled.

We use Sweezy's equality $k = \frac{C}{V} = \frac{C_3}{V_3}$ for the proof.

The transformation rule (16A) can be rewritten as follows:

$$V(kx+y)(1+r) = V(1+k)+M \tag{27}$$

The following equality follows from the third equation in the system (14) and the conditions (26):

$$V_3(1+k) = M - M_3 \tag{28}$$

The following equality follows from the third equation of the system (15A) and the conditions (26):

$$V_3(kx+y)(1+r) = M \tag{29}$$

The next equality for the left part of the equation (27) follows from (29):

$$V(kx+y)(1+r) = \frac{VM}{V_3} \tag{30}$$

The next equality for the right part of the equation (27) follows from (28):

$$V(1+k)+M = \frac{(M-M_3)V}{V_3} + M = \frac{VM}{V_3} + \frac{MV_3 - VM_3}{V_3} \tag{31}$$

Let us substitute (30)-(31) into the equation for the transformational rule (27). The Equation (27) (and (16A)) is fulfilled if the rate of surplus value in the aggregate economy equals the rate of surplus value in the third sector:

$$\frac{M}{V} = \frac{M_3}{V_3} \tag{32}$$

The condition (32) is fulfilled since the rates of surplus-value are identical in all sectors of the economy. Thus the transformation rule (27) is fulfilled also.

THE PROOF OF LEMMA-2 IS COMPLETED

Sweezy's conditions follow from the symmetry of the $C-V-M$ matrix of simple production in the "prices of production". Therefore, if this matrix is symmetric the solution of the "transformation problem" exists. Subsequently, we proved the sufficient condition for the existence of a solution of the "transformation problem" in the $C-V-M$ model.

THE PROOF OF THEOREMA-E1 (SUFFITIENT CONDITION) IS COMPLETED

The necessary condition for the existence of a realistic solution of the "transformation problem" in the three-sector model of the economy with simple production.

Let us rewrite the system (14)-(16) in the following form:

$$\begin{cases} C_2 + C_3 = V_1(1+m) \\ V_1 + V_3 = C_2 + V_2 m \\ C_3 + V_3 = m(V_1 + V_2) \end{cases} \tag{E1}$$

The price-system (15A):

$$\begin{cases} (C_1 x + V_1 y)(1+r) = Cx \\ (C_2 x + V_2 y)(1+r) = Vy \\ (C_3 x + V_3 y)(1+r) = M \end{cases} \tag{E2}$$

Let us choose two transformation rules in mathematical form (1) and (4):

$$\begin{cases} r(Cx + Vy) = M \\ r = \dfrac{mV}{C+V} \end{cases} \tag{E3}$$

The first transformation rule in (E3) follows from the system (E2).

We consider so-called "consistency relations" i.e., relations between coefficients of the system of equations (E1)-(E3) under which this system has a realistic solution:

$$(m > 0; r > 0; x > 0; y > 0) \tag{E4}$$

The system of the equations and inequalities (E1)-(E4) formalizes the "transformation problem" in our model. The coefficients of this system are positive numbers.

The necessary condition for the existence of a solution of the "transformation problem" is formulated as follows.

If solution of the "transformation problem" exists, the $C-V-M$ matrix is symmetric.

Let us consider the system of equations (E1) as the system which determines the rate of surplus-value m in the economy with simple production. The third equation of this system is the consequence of the first and the second equations. We have two independent equations for one unknown value m in the system (E1). A solution exists only if the following relation between coefficients of this system is fulfilled.

The First Consistency Relation

$$V = C_2 + \left(\frac{V_2}{V_1}\right)(C_2 + C_3) \tag{33}$$

This relation follows from the first and the second equations of the system (E1). We rewrite this condition as follows:

$$VV_1 = C_2V_1 + V_2(C_2 + C_3) \tag{34}$$

Solution of the system (E1) is:

$$m = \frac{C_2 + C_3 - V_1}{V_1} \tag{35}$$

Let us introduce the new variable t:

$$t \equiv \frac{x}{y} > 0 \tag{24}$$

The following equalities follow from the third equation of the system (E2) and the equalities (E3):

$$r \cdot (Cx + Vy) = (1 + r) \cdot (C_3x + V_3y) \tag{36}$$

$$\left(\frac{mV}{C+V}\right) \cdot (Ct + V) = \left(1 + \frac{mV}{C+V}\right) \cdot (C_3t + V_3) \tag{37}$$

Let us substitute (35) into (37). We obtain the following equalities after some mathematical transformations:

$$t \cdot Q = P \tag{38}$$

$$Q = C_3 \cdot \left[V_1C + V(C_2 + C_3)\right] - VC(C_2 + C_3 - V_1) \tag{39}$$

$$P = V^2 (C_2 + C_3 - V_1) - V_3 \cdot [V_1 C + V(C_2 + C_3)] \tag{40}$$

$$V^2 (C_2 + C_3 - V_1) = V(V_1 + V_2)(C_2 + C_3 - V_1) + VV_3 (C_2 + C_3) - VV_3 V_1 \tag{41}$$

Let us substitute (41) into the formula (40). We find the following equalities after some transformations:

$$P = V(V_1 + V_2)(C_2 + C_3 - V_1) - V_1 V_3 (V + C) \tag{42}$$

$$\begin{aligned} Q &= V_1 C C_3 + V_1 V C + V C_3 (C_2 + C_3) - VC(C_2 + C_3) = \\ &= V_1 C C_3 + V_1 V C_3 + V_1 V (C_1 + C_2) - V(C_2 + C_3)(C_1 + C_2) = \\ &= V_1 C_3 (V + C) - V(C_1 + C_2)(C_2 + C_3 - V_1) \end{aligned} \tag{43}$$

Let us divide the first equation of the system (E2) to the second equation of this system. We obtain the following equation for unknown value t:

$$(CC_2) t^2 + (CV_2 - VC_1) t - VV_1 = 0 \tag{44}$$

Thus, we have two equations for one variable t:

$$\begin{cases} t \cdot Q = P \\ (CC_2) t^2 + (CV_2 - VC_1) t - VV_1 = 0 \end{cases} \tag{45}$$

The Second Consistency Relation

The system of the Equations (E1)-(E3) follows from the equations of the system (45):

$$(CC_2) \left(\frac{P}{Q} \right)^2 + (CV_2 - VC_1) \left(\frac{P}{Q} \right) - VV_1 = 0 \tag{46}$$

If consistency relations (33) and (46) are fulfilled, the system of equations (E1)-(E3) has a solution $(m; r; x; y)$.

The system (45) has a solution in two possible cases.

The First Case

Let variable t be the root of the second equation of the system (45). If a solution of the “transformation problem” exists, Sweezy’s condition is fulfilled (Lemma 2):

$$\frac{C_3}{V_3} = \frac{C_1 + C_2}{V_1 + V_2} \tag{47}$$

The chain of equalities takes place:

$$\frac{C_3}{V_3} = \frac{C_1 + C_2}{V_1 + V_2} = \frac{C}{V} = k \tag{48}$$

The following equality is fulfilled in this case:

$$P = \left(-\frac{V_3}{C_3} \right) \cdot Q \tag{49}$$

The root of the second equation in the system (45) is:

$$t = \frac{VC_1 - CV_2 + \sqrt{(VC_1 - CV_2)^2 + 4VCV_1C_2}}{2CC_2} > 0 \tag{50}$$

The second root is a negative number.

Let us substitute $t = \frac{V_1}{C_2}$ into the left part of the second equation of the system (45). It gives:

$$\begin{aligned}(CC_2)\left(\frac{V_1}{C_2}\right)^2 + (CV_2 - VC_1)\left(\frac{V_1}{C_2}\right) - VV_1 = \frac{CV_1^2 + CV_1V_2 - C_1V_1V - C_2V_1V}{C_2} = \\ = \frac{CV_1(V_1 + V_2) - VV_1(C_1 + C_2)}{C_2} = \frac{VV_1(V_1 + V_2) \cdot \left[\frac{C}{V} - \frac{C_1 + C_2}{V_1 + V_2} \right]}{C_2} = 0\end{aligned} \tag{51}$$

Thus, value $t = \frac{V_1}{C_2}$ is the positive root of the second equation in the system (45) if Sweezy’s condition is fulfilled. Let us compare the equality (49) and the first equality in the system (45). We see that the inequality $t = \left(-\frac{V_3}{C_3} \right) < 0$ takes place. But we obtained above the equality $t = \frac{V_1}{C_2} > 0$ which follows from the second equality of the system (45) and Sweezy's condition. Therefore, the equality (49) can be fulfilled if only values P and Q equals zero:

$$P = 0 \tag{52}$$

$$Q = 0 \tag{53}$$

Value $t \equiv \frac{x}{y} = \frac{V_1}{C_2}$ is the root of the second equation (45). It means the following equality is fulfilled:

$$x \cdot C_2 = y \cdot V_1 \tag{54}$$

Symmetry of the $C - V - M$ matrix follows from the equality (54) (Lemma 1).

The Second Case

$$P \neq 0 \tag{55}$$

$$Q \neq 0 \tag{56}$$

$$t = \frac{P}{Q} \tag{57}$$

$$(CC_2)\left(\frac{P}{Q}\right)^2 + (CV_2 - VC_1)\left(\frac{P}{Q}\right) - VV_1 = 0 \tag{58}$$

We have the following equality (59):

$$P(C_2 + C_3) - QV_1 = \frac{(C_2 + C_3)\left[V_1(C + C_2) + V_2(C_2 + C_3)\right]\left[C_2V_1 + V_2(C_2 + C_3) - V_1V\right]}{V_1}$$

This equation is easier to prove using the software "Mathematica". Let us find the difference between the left and the right parts of the formula (59) taking into the account the equalities (42) and (43). This difference equals zero after full simplification in the soft "Mathematica".

Multiplier $C_2V_1 + V_2(C_2 + C_3) - V_1V$ in the right part of the formula (59) equals to zero due to the first consistency relation (34). Therefore the next equalities follow from (59) and (38):

$$t \equiv \frac{x}{y} = \frac{P}{Q} = \frac{V_1}{C_2 + C_3} \tag{60}$$

$$x(C_2 + C_3) = V_1 y \tag{61}$$

We can substitute (61) into the first equation of the system (E2):

$$Cx(1+r) = Cx \tag{62}$$

This equality is fulfilled in three cases: 1) $x = 0$, 2) $C = 0$, 3) $r = 0$. All three cases violate the conditions (17). Consequently, we do not have realistic solutions in the second case.

Therefore, we proved the necessary condition for the existence of a solution of the "transformation problem": if the "transformation problem" has realistic solution, the $C - V - M$ matrix is symmetric.

THE PROOF THEOREMA-E2 (NECESSARY CONDITION) IS COMPLETED

The Matrix Formulation of "Transformation Problem"

We consider in this part the formulation and the solution of "transformation problem" in the many-industries economic system. Each sector of the economy consists of many industries. Aggregate output of each sector in the "labor values" or in the "prices of production" equals to the aggregate "labor value" or the "price of production" of all products produced by industries of this sector during the definite period (year).

The Designations

Let us introduce the following designations:

- $\vec{X}_I; \vec{X}_{II}; \vec{X}_{III}$ are the column-vectors of the physical outputs of the sectors I; II; III;
- $\vec{X}_{I;I}; \vec{X}_{I;II}; \vec{X}_{I;III}$ are the column-vectors of the "means of production" consumed (in natural form) as the intermediate input in the different sectors of the economy;
- $\vec{X}_{II;I}; \vec{X}_{II;II}; \vec{X}_{II;III}$ are the column-vectors of the "goods for employees" (in natural form) consumed by employees of the different sectors of the economy;
- $A_{I;I}; A_{I;II}; A_{I;III}$ are the matrices of direct requirements with the elements which equal the quantity of the "means of production" (in the physical units) expended per the physical unit of output

in the different sectors. These three matrices together form the Leontief's matrix of direct requirements;

- $A_{II;I}; A_{II;II}; A_{II;III}$ are the matrices describing the consumption of "goods for employees" (in natural form) per the physical unit of output. The elements of these matrices describe the consumption (in natural form) of the "goods" which the employees buy on the income earned for their labor in the production of the unit of goods;
- $N_I; N_{II}; N_{III}$ are the quantities of industries in the different sectors of the economy. We have the matrices of the following dimensions:

$$A_{I;I}\left(N_I \times N_I\right); A_{I;II}\left(N_I \times N_{II}\right); A_{I;III}\left(N_I \times N_{III}\right)$$

$$A_{II;I}\left(N_{II} \times N_I\right); A_{II;II}\left(N_{II} \times N_{II}\right); A_{II;III}\left(N_{II} \times N_{III}\right)$$

- The row-vector $\vec{v} = \left\{\vec{v}_I; \vec{v}_{II}; \vec{v}_{III}\right\}$ is the vector of the "labor-values";
- The row-vector $\vec{p} = \left\{\vec{p}_I; \vec{p}_{II}; \vec{p}_{III}\right\}$ is the vector of the "prices of production";
- The row-vector $\vec{l} = \left\{\vec{l}_I; \vec{l}_{II}; \vec{l}_{III}\right\}$ is the vector of the direct labor expenditures per the physical unit of goods.

Products of the first and of the second sectors are used in production. The product of the first sector is used as intermediate input consisting of the "means of production". These are equipment, raw materials, energy, and so forth. These goods are used directly in the process of production. Employees consume the "goods for employees". These goods are used indirectly in the process of production because the consumption of employees is the necessary condition for the maintenance of normal operation of the production.

Columns of the matrices $A_{II;I}; A_{II;II}; A_{II;III}$ describe the "real wage" of the employees i.e., the set of "necessity goods" which workers buy upon the compensation of the labor expended during the production of the unit of goods. The output of the third sector ("luxury goods") is not used in production.

The structure of the matrix of the direct requirements per the physical unit of goods is depicted in Figure 5. Abraham-Frois and Berrebi (1979) are used the name "socio-technological matrix" for the matrix consisting of the blocks $A_{I;I}; A_{I;II}; A_{I;III}$ and $A_{II;I}; A_{II;II}; A_{II;III}$.

The Mathematical Formulation of the "Transformation Problem"

The balance conditions for the physical outputs in the economy with simple production.

The condition of balance for the "means of production" is:

$$\vec{X}_I = \vec{X}_{I;I} + \vec{X}_{I;II} + \vec{X}_{I;III} \tag{63}$$

The condition of balance for the "necessity goods" is:

Figure 5. The socio-technological matrix of the direct requirements per the physical unit of goods

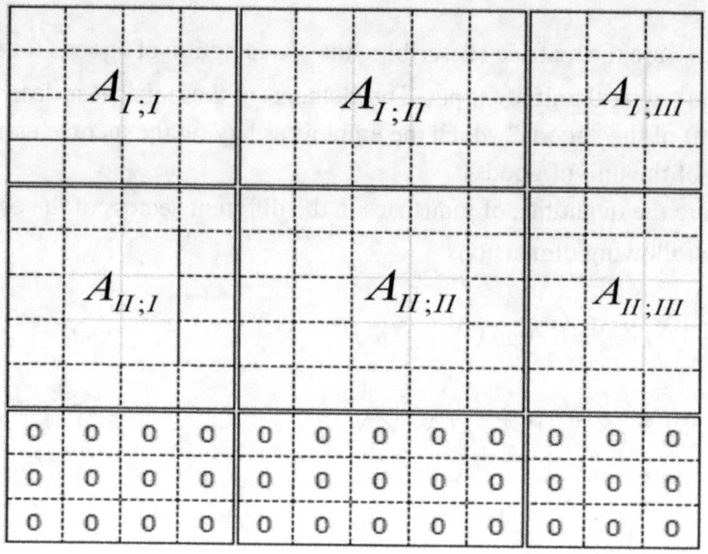

$$\vec{X}_{II} = \vec{X}_{II;I} + \vec{X}_{II;II} + \vec{X}_{II;III} \tag{64}$$

The flaws of goods produced in the sector $K = I;II$ and consumed in the sector $M = I;II;III$ are connected with outputs by means of the following relations:

$$\vec{X}_{K;M} = A_{K;M}\vec{X}_M \text{ (for example, } \vec{X}_{II;III} = A_{II;III}\vec{X}_{III}\text{)} \tag{65}$$

Therefore the following equalities for outputs are:

$$\vec{X}_I = A_{I;I}\vec{X}_I + A_{I;II}\vec{X}_{II} + A_{I;III}\vec{X}_{III} \tag{66}$$

$$\vec{X}_{II} = A_{II;I}\vec{X}_I + A_{II;II}\vec{X}_{II} + A_{II;III}\vec{X}_{III} \tag{67}$$

Outputs of the first and of the second sectors $\vec{X}_I$ and $\vec{X}_{II}$ can be calculated via the output of the third sector $\vec{X}_{III}$ as follows:

$$\vec{X}_I = \left(I - A_{I;I}\right)^{-1} \cdot \left(A_{I;II}B_{II} + A_{I;III}\right)\vec{X}_{III} = B_I\vec{X}_{III} \tag{68}$$

$$\vec{X}_{II} = B_{II}\vec{X}_{III} \tag{69}$$

$$B_{II} = \left[I - A_{II;II} - A_{II;I} \left(I - A_{I;I} \right)^{-1} A_{I;II} \right]^{-1} \cdot \left[A_{II;III} + A_{II;I} \left(I - A_{I;I} \right)^{-1} A_{I;III} \right] \tag{70}$$

$$B_I = \left(I - A_{I;I} \right)^{-1} \cdot \left(A_{I;II} B_{II} + A_{I;III} \right) \tag{71}$$

The vector $\vec{X}_{III}$ can be specified arbitrarily. Vectors $\vec{X}_I$; $\vec{X}_{II}$; are calculated on the basis of the equalities (68)-(71).

The Vector of "Labor Values" $\vec{v} = \{\vec{v}_I; \vec{v}_{II}; \vec{v}_{III}\}$

The following system of the equations determines "labor values" of goods:

$$\vec{v}_I A_{I;I} + \vec{l}_I = \vec{v}_I \tag{72}$$

$$\vec{v}_I A_{I;II} + \vec{l}_{II} = \vec{v}_{II} \tag{73}$$

$$\vec{v}_I A_{I;III} + \vec{l}_{III} = \vec{v}_{III} \tag{74}$$

The solution of this system:

$$\vec{v}_I = \vec{l}_I \left(I - A_{I;I} \right)^{-1} \tag{75}$$

$$\vec{v}_{II} = \vec{l}_I \left(I - A_{I;I} \right)^{-1} A_{I;II} + \vec{l}_{II} \tag{76}$$

$$\vec{v}_{III} = \vec{l}_I \left(I - A_{I;I} \right)^{-1} A_{I;III} + \vec{l}_{III} \tag{77}$$

The Balance Conditions in the "Labor Values"

The $C - V - M$ matrix of simple production in the "labor values" is depicted in Figure 6. This matrix describes the value-structure of the economy with simple production. The "labor value" of the "constant capitals" equals the "labor value" of the input-flows consisting of the "means of production". For example, the "labor value" of the constant capital C_{II} of the second sector equals the "labor value" of the input-flow $\vec{X}_{I;II} = A_{I;II}\vec{X}_{II}$ of the "means of production" consumed in the second sector during the definite interval of the time (the year). The "labor value" of the "variable capital" of a sector equals to the "labor value" of the "goods for employees" consumed by workers of this sector. For example, the "labor value" of the "variable capital" V_{II} of the second sector equals to the "labor value" of the input-flow $\vec{X}_{II;II} = A_{II;II}\vec{X}_{II}$ of goods consumed by employees of the second sector during the definite interval of time (the year).

We have the following system of equations for the balance conditions of simple production in the "labor values":

$$\left(\vec{v}_I A_{I;I} + (1+m)\vec{v}_{II} A_{II;I}\right)\cdot \vec{X}_I = \vec{v}_I \vec{X}_I \tag{78}$$

$$\left(\vec{v}_I A_{I;II} + (1+m)\vec{v}_{II} A_{II;II}\right)\cdot \vec{X}_{II} = \vec{v}_{II} \vec{X}_{II} \tag{79}$$

$$\left(\vec{v}_I A_{I;III} + (1+m)\vec{v}_{II} A_{II;III}\right)\cdot \vec{X}_{III} = \vec{v}_{III} \vec{X}_{III} \tag{80}$$

These equations must be fulfilled for an arbitrary vectors: $\vec{X}_I$; $\vec{X}_{II}$; $\vec{X}_{III}$. Therefore the following equalities follow from the Equations (78)-(80):

$$\vec{v}_I A_{I;I} + (1+m)\vec{v}_{II} A_{II;I} = \vec{v}_I \tag{81}$$

$$\vec{v}_I A_{I;II} + (1+m)\vec{v}_{II} A_{II;II} = \vec{v}_{II} \tag{82}$$

$$\vec{v}_I A_{I;III} + (1+m)\vec{v}_{II} A_{II;III} = \vec{v}_{III} \tag{83}$$

Figure 6. $C-V-M$ matrix of simple production in "labor values"

	C	V	M	W
I	$C_I = \vec{v}_I A_{I;I}\vec{X}_I$	$V_I = \vec{v}_{II} A_{II;I}\vec{X}_I$	$M_I = m\cdot\vec{v}_{II} A_{II;I}\vec{X}_I$	$W_I = C_I + V_I(1+m)$
II	$C_{II} = \vec{v}_I A_{I;II}\vec{X}_{II}$	$V_{II} = \vec{v}_{II} A_{II;II}\vec{X}_{II}$	$M_{II} = m\cdot\vec{v}_{II} A_{II;II}\vec{X}_{II}$	$W_{II} = C_{II} + V_{II}(1+m)$
III	$C_{III} = \vec{v}_I A_{I;III}\vec{X}_{III}$	$V_{III} = \vec{v}_{II} A_{II;III}\vec{X}_{III}$	$M_{III} = m\cdot\vec{v}_{II} A_{II;III}\vec{X}_{III}$	$W_{III} = C_{III} + V_{III}(1+m)$
Sum:	$C = C_I + C_{II} + C_{III}$	$V = V_I + V_{II} + V_{III}$	$M = M_I + M_{II} + M_{III}$	

The equalities (81)-(83) describe the decomposition of the "labor value" of the unit of goods into three parts: (1) the "labor value" of "means of production", $\vec{v}_I A_{I;K}$ ($K = I;II;III$), (2) the "labor value" of labor power, $\vec{v}_{II} A_{II;K}$, and (3) the "surplus-value", $m \cdot \vec{v}_{II} A_{II;K}$. The comparison of these equalities with the equalities (72)-(74) leads to the following equations:

$$\vec{v}_{II} A_{II;I} = \frac{1}{1+m} \vec{l}_I \tag{84}$$

$$\vec{v}_{II} A_{II;II} = \frac{1}{1+m} \vec{l}_{II} \tag{85}$$

$$\vec{v}_{II} A_{II;III} = \frac{1}{1+m} \vec{l}_{III} \tag{86}$$

These equations describe the relation between the "labor value" of the "labor-power" and the quantity of the direct labor expended per the unit of goods.

Let us substitute (75)-(77) into (84)-(86):

$$\vec{v}_{II} A_{II;I} = \vec{l}_I \left(I - A_{I;I}\right)^{-1} A_{I;II} A_{II;I} + \vec{l}_{II} A_{II;I} = \frac{1}{1+m} \vec{l}_I \tag{87}$$

$$\vec{v}_{II} A_{II;II} = \vec{l}_I \left(I - A_{I;I}\right)^{-1} A_{I;II} A_{II;II} + \vec{l}_{II} A_{II;II} = \frac{1}{1+m} \vec{l}_{II} \tag{88}$$

$$\vec{v}_{II} A_{II;III} = \vec{l}_I \left(I - A_{I;I}\right)^{-1} A_{I;II} A_{II;III} + \vec{l}_{II} A_{II;III} = \frac{1}{1+m} \vec{l}_{III} \tag{89}$$

Computation of the "Direct Labor" and the "Labor Values"

The Equation (87) gives the following expression for the vector $\vec{l}_I$ via the vector $\vec{l}_{II}$:

$$\vec{l}_I = \vec{l}_{II} \underbrace{A_{II;I} \cdot \left[\frac{1}{1+m} I - \left(I - A_{I;I}\right)^{-1} A_{I;II} A_{II;I} \right]^{-1}}_{S_I(m)} \tag{90}$$

Let us designate the matrix in the right part of this equation as $S_I(m)$. This matrix depends on the rate of surplus-value, m:

$$S_I(m) = A_{II;I}\left[\frac{1}{1+m}I - \left(I - A_{I;I}\right)^{-1} A_{I;II} A_{II;I}\right]^{-1} \tag{91}$$

We can rewrite (90) as:

$$\vec{l}_I = \vec{l}_{II} S_I(m) \tag{92}$$

Let's substitute the expression (92) into the Equation (88):

$$\vec{l}_{II} \underbrace{\left[S_I(m)\cdot\left(I - A_{I;I}\right)^{-1} A_{I;II} + I\right] A_{II;II}}_{S_{II}(m)} = \frac{1}{1+m}\vec{l}_{II} \tag{93}$$

Let us designate the matrix in the left part of the Equation (93) as $S_{II}(m)$:

$$\begin{aligned} S_{II}(m) &= \left[S_I(m)\cdot\left(I - A_{I;I}\right)^{-1} A_{I;II} + I\right] A_{II;II} = \\ &= \left[A_{II;I}\left[\frac{1}{1+m}I - \left(I - A_{I;I}\right)^{-1} A_{I;II} A_{II;I}\right]^{-1}\cdot\left(I - A_{I;I}\right)^{-1} A_{I;II} + I\right] A_{II;II} \end{aligned} \tag{94}$$

Let us rewrite (93) as the equation for the positive eigenvector of the matrix $S_{II}(m)$:

$$\vec{l}_{II} S_{II}(m) = \frac{1}{1+m}\vec{l}_{II} \tag{95}$$

Positive eigenvalue $\frac{1}{1+m}$ of the matrix $S_{II}(m)$ is the Frobenius's eigenvalue for this matrix. The Equation (95) has a solution if only the determinant of the matrix $S_{II}(m) - \frac{1}{1+m}I$ equals zero:

$$\det\left|S_{II}(m) - \frac{1}{1+m}I\right| = 0 \tag{96}$$

The norm of the "surplus-value", m, equals the real positive root of the equation (96). We can use the software "Mathematica" for the computation of the Frobenius's eigenvalue and of the eigenvector of the matrix $S_{II}(m)$. The components of eigenvector $\vec{l}_{II}$ can be multiplied onto the arbitrary positive number. Normalization of this vector depends on the choice of the unit of labor. For example, we can consider the quantity of the direct labor expended in the first industry of the second sector upon the production of the unit of goods as the definition of the unit of the labor. The normalization condition in this case can be described mathematically as follows:

$\left(\vec{l}_{II}\right)_1 = 1$ - i.e., the first component of the normalized vector $\vec{l}_{II}$ equals to unit

The vector $\vec{l}_I$ can be computed on the basis of formula (92). The vector $\vec{l}_{III}$ can be calculated from the Equation (89):

$$\vec{l}_{III} = (1+m)\cdot\left[\vec{l}_I\left(I - A_{I;I}\right)^{-1} A_{I;II} A_{II;III} + \vec{l}_{II} A_{II;III}\right] = \vec{l}_{II} S_{III}(m) \tag{97}$$

$$S_{III}(m) = (1+m)\cdot\left[S_I(m)\cdot\left(I - A_{I;I}\right)^{-1} A_{I;II} + I\right] A_{II;III} \tag{98}$$

The "labor values" of goods can be computed on the basis of the equalities (75)-(77). We see that the socio-technological matrix of direct requirements (Figure 5) contains the information about the "rate of surplus-value" (equalities (96)), about the vectors of the direct labor (formulas (95), (92), (97), (98)) and about the "labor values" of goods (equalities (75)-(77)). All these unknown quantities can be computed as only we choose the unit of labor.

The equalities (87)-(89) and (96) demonstrate that components of the vectors, $\vec{l}_I$, $\vec{l}_{II}$ and $\vec{l}_{III}$, are connected with the socio-technological matrix of direct expenditures. If the elements of this matrix are given then the vectors $\vec{l}_I$, $\vec{l}_{II}$ and $\vec{l}_{III}$ can be computed on the basis of the above-listed equations. The matrices $A_{I;I}; A_{I;II}; A_{I;III}$ describe the consumption of the "means of production" in the different sectors of the economy. The matrices $A_{II;I}; A_{II;II}; A_{II;III}$ describe the consumption of the "goods for employees" in the different sectors of the economy (via the consumption of employees). Therefore, the information about the consumption of the "means of production" and the "goods for employees" within sectors of the economy contains implicitly all information about the direct labor, the "rate of surplus-value" and the "labor values" of goods.

The "Prices of Production"

We have the following system of equations for the vector of the "prices of production":

$$\begin{cases} \left(\vec{p}_I A_{I;I} + \vec{p}_{II} A_{II;I}\right)(1+r) = \vec{p}_I \\ \left(\vec{p}_I A_{I;II} + \vec{p}_{II} A_{II;II}\right)(1+r) = \vec{p}_{II} \\ \left(\vec{p}_I A_{I;III} + \vec{p}_{II} A_{II;III}\right)(1+r) = \vec{p}_{III} \end{cases} \tag{99}$$

Strictly speaking, the Equations (99) determine the "prices of equal profitability".

The "prices of production" are slightly different from the "prices of equal profitability" because the "prices of production" are the prices which guarantee the equal profit for the equal advanced capitals. Nevertheless these two different kinds of prices often are identified in the researches devoted to the solution of the "transformation problem" (for example, in the papers Bortkiewicz (1907a; 1907b)). According to the first and the second equations of the system (99) the vector $\{\vec{p}_I;\vec{p}_{II}\}$ is the Frobenius's eigenvector of the matrix $\tilde{A}=\begin{pmatrix} A_{I;I} & A_{I;II} \\ A_{II;I} & A_{II;II} \end{pmatrix}$ with the Frobenius's eigenvalue $\lambda_F=\frac{1}{1+r}$. We can normalize the Frobenius's eigenvector $\{\vec{p}_I;\vec{p}_{II}\}$ in such a way that any one of Marx's transformation rules would be fulfilled. However, the other transformation rule is violated as a rule.

MARX'S TRANSFORMATION RULES

The First Marx's Transformation Rule

The surplus-value produced in the aggregate economy equals the aggregate profit of capitalists:

$$M=\left(\frac{m}{1+m}\right)\cdot\left(\vec{l}_I\vec{X}_I+\vec{l}_{II}\vec{X}_{II}+\vec{l}_{III}\vec{X}_{III}\right)=\vec{p}_{III}\vec{X}_{III} \tag{100}$$

The Second Marx's Transformation Rule

The "labor value" and the "price of production" of aggregate output are equal:

$$\vec{v}_I\vec{X}_I+\vec{v}_{II}\vec{X}_{II}+\vec{v}_{III}\vec{X}_{III}=\vec{p}_I\vec{X}_I+\vec{p}_{II}\vec{X}_{II}+\vec{p}_{III}\vec{X}_{III} \tag{101}$$

We can fulfill one of these equalities through the appropriate normalization of the vector $\{\vec{p}_I;\vec{p}_{II}\}$. However, according to the equalities (75)-(77) the normalization of the vector of direct labor $\vec{l}$ influences both onto the first (100) and on the second (101) transformation rule. Therefore in the general case we can't satisfy simultaneously equalities (100) and (101) through the choice of normalization of the vectors $\vec{l}$ and $\vec{p}$.

The balance-conditions of simple production (66)-(67) and Equations (99) give the following equality:

$$\vec{p}_I\vec{X}_I+\vec{p}_{II}\vec{X}_{II}+\vec{p}_{III}\vec{X}_{III}=\left(\frac{1+r}{r}\right)\cdot\vec{p}_{III}\vec{X}_{III} \tag{102}$$

The transformation rules can be rewritten as follows:

$$\left(\frac{m}{1+m}\right)\cdot\left(\vec{l}_I\vec{X}_I+\vec{l}_{II}\vec{X}_{II}+\vec{l}_{III}\vec{X}_{III}\right)=\vec{p}_{III}\vec{X}_{III} \quad (103)$$

$$\left(\frac{r}{1+r}\right)\cdot\left(\vec{v}_I\vec{X}_I+\vec{v}_{II}\vec{X}_{II}+\vec{v}_{III}\vec{X}_{III}\right)=\vec{p}_{III}\vec{X}_{III} \quad (104)$$

We have:

$$\left(\frac{m}{1+m}\right)\cdot\left(\vec{l}_I\vec{X}_I+\vec{l}_{II}\vec{X}_{II}+\vec{l}_{III}\vec{X}_{III}\right)=\left(\frac{r}{1+r}\right)\cdot\left(\vec{v}_I\vec{X}_I+\vec{v}_{II}\vec{X}_{II}+\vec{v}_{III}\vec{X}_{III}\right) \quad (105)$$

The vectors $\vec{l}_I;\vec{l}_{III};\vec{v}_I;\vec{v}_{II};\vec{v}_{III}$ can be expressed through the vector $\vec{l}_{II}$ according to the equations (92), (97), (75)-(77). The vectors $\vec{X}_I;\vec{X}_{II}$ can be expressed through the vector $\vec{X}_{III}$ according to the Equations (68)-(71):

$$\left(\frac{m}{1+m}\right)\cdot\vec{l}_{II}\left(S_IB_I+B_{II}+S_{III}\right)\vec{X}_{III}=\left(\frac{r}{1+r}\right)\cdot\vec{l}_{II}\left(U_IB_I+U_{II}B_{II}+U_{III}\right)\vec{X}_{III} \quad (106)$$

$$U_I=S_I\left(I-A_{I;I}\right)^{-1} \quad (107)$$

$$U_{II}=S_I\left(I-A_{I;I}\right)^{-1}A_{I;II}+I \quad (108)$$

$$U_{III}=S_I\left(I-A_{I;I}\right)^{-1}A_{I;III}+S_{III} \quad (109)$$

The condition (106) is not fulfilled automatically for an arbitrary socio-technological matrix and for an arbitrary vector $\vec{X}_{III}$. We can satisfy this equality by means of specific choice of vector $\vec{X}_{III}$ or by means of specific choice of socio-technological matrix of direct expenditures but this equality is violated in general case.

Therefore, the problem of transformation in general case (i.e. for the arbitrary matrix of direct expenditures and arbitrary vector $\vec{X}_{III}$) in the matrix formulation has not a solution.

Specification of the Matrices $A_{II;I};A_{II;II};A_{II;III}$

Let matrices $A_{II;I};A_{II;II};A_{II;III}$ satisfy the following equalities:

$$A_{II;I} = \vec{b} \cdot \vec{l}_I ;\ A_{II;II} = \vec{b} \cdot \vec{l}_{II} ;\ A_{II;III} = \vec{b} \cdot \vec{l}_{III} \tag{110}$$

The standard assumption is that the real wage of employees is proportional to their direct labor. A bundle of the "goods for employees" upon the unit of direct labor is designated as a vector $\vec{b}$. Since output of the second sector $\vec{X}_{II}$ is consumed by employees in full in the economy with simple production the vector $\vec{b}$ is proportional to the vector $\vec{X}_{II}$. The coefficient of proportionality equals the aggregate direct labor expended during the production of aggregate output:

$$\left(\vec{l}_1 \vec{X}_I + \vec{l}_2 \vec{X}_{II} + \vec{l}_3 \vec{X}_{III}\right) \cdot \vec{b} = \vec{X}_{II} \tag{111}$$

The columns of the matrices $A_{II;I}; A_{II;II}; A_{II;III}$ describe the real wage $\vec{w}$ of employees for their labor during the production of the unit of goods:

$$\vec{w}_i = l_i \cdot \vec{b} \text{ - is the real wage in the industry } i \tag{112}$$

Let's introduce the following designation:

$$\alpha = \frac{1}{\vec{l}_1 \vec{X}_I + \vec{l}_2 \vec{X}_{II} + \vec{l}_3 \vec{X}_{III}} \tag{113}$$

We can rewrite the Equations (110) as follows:

$$A_{II;I} = \alpha \vec{X}_{II} \vec{l}_I ;\ A_{II;II} = \alpha \vec{X}_{II} \vec{l}_{II} ;\ A_{II;III} = \alpha \vec{X}_{II} \vec{l}_{III} \tag{114}$$

Specification (114) of the matrices $A_{II;I}; A_{II;II}; A_{II;III}$ guarantees the balance condition (67) will be fulfilled for the arbitrary vectors $\vec{X}_I; \vec{X}_{II}; \vec{X}_{III}$. The balance condition (66) determines the vector $\vec{X}_I$:

$$\vec{X}_I = \left(I - A_{I;I}\right)^{-1} \left(A_{I;II} \vec{X}_{II} + A_{I;III} \vec{X}_{III}\right) \tag{115}$$

We see that elements of the matrices $A_{II;I}; A_{II;II}; A_{II;III}$ can be calculated via the vectors $\vec{X}_{II}; \vec{X}_{III}$, Therefore we can take an arbitrary positive vectors $\vec{X}_{II}; \vec{X}_{III}$. We can also choice the arbitrary vectors of direct labor $\vec{l} = \left\{\vec{l}_I; \vec{l}_{II}; \vec{l}_{III}\right\}$. The "labor values" can be calculated by means of the Equations (75)-(77). Let's substitute the equations (114) into the equalities (84)-(86). It gives the following equation for the rate of surplus-value:

$$\frac{1}{1+m} = \alpha \vec{v}_{II} \vec{X}_{II} \tag{116}$$

We can calculate the rate of profit and the "prices of production" using the equations (99). We can satisfy one of the two transformation rules (100)-(101) via the appropriate choice of normalization of the price vector but nevertheless the second transformation rule may not be satisfied in general case.

Therefore, the "transformation problem" in matrix formulation does not have the solution for the arbitrary socio-technological matrix of the economy. The mathematical formulation of this problem leads to a system of equations in which the number of equations is greater than the number of unknowns. The solution exists if the additional limitation is imposed on the structure of socio-technological matrix.

The Influence of the "Law of Large Numbers (LLN)" on the Structure of C-V-M Matrix

It is proved in the previous part of this paper that the symmetry of the $C-V-M$ matrix of simple production in the price-form is the necessary and the sufficient condition for the existence of a solution of the "transformation problem".

There are many variants for the calculation of the elements of $C-V-M$ matrix on the basis of above derived equations. These methods of calculation differ by the choice of input-data. We consider below only one of these possible methods of calculation.

Let us suppose that the elements of the matrices $A_{I;I}; A_{I;II}; A_{I;III}$; $A_{II;I}; A_{II;II}; A_{II;III}$ and the components of the vectors of direct labor $\vec{l} = \{\vec{l}_I; \vec{l}_{II}; \vec{l}_{III}\}$ are random numbers distributed on the basis of some statistic probability distribution laws.

The $C-V-M$ matrix (dimension 3×3) of simple production is depictured in Figure 7. We can model this matrix supposing that the elements of matrices $A_{I;I}; A_{I;II}; A_{I;III}; A_{II;I}; A_{II;II}; A_{II;III}$ and the components of vectors $\{\vec{l}_I; \vec{l}_{II}; \vec{l}_{III}\}$ are some random numbers with a definite statistic distribution (for example, "uniform distribution", "normal distribution", "inverse-power distribution law" etc). We can take arbitrary random sample of elements of the matrices $A_{I;I}; A_{I;II}; A_{I;III}; A_{II;I}; A_{II;II}; A_{II;III}$ and arbitrary random sample of components of the vectors $\{\vec{l}_I; \vec{l}_{II}; \vec{l}_{III}\}$ for the calculation of elements of $C-V-M$ matrix. If these random values satisfy definite probability distribution laws, the sums in Figure 7 (for example, the sum $\vec{p}_I A_{I;II} \vec{X}_{II} = \sum p_i a_{ik} X_k$) are equal approximately to the product of the quantity of items in the sum and the "mean value" of random items which are in this sum. For example, the sum

Figure 7. $C-V-M$ matrix in "prices of production" for the economy with simple production

	C	V	P	W
I	$\vec{p}_I A_{I;I} \vec{X}_I$	$\vec{p}_{II} A_{II;I} \vec{X}_I$	$(\vec{p}_I A_{I;I} \vec{X}_I + \vec{p}_{II} A_{II;I} \vec{X}_I) \cdot r$	$\vec{p}_I \vec{X}_I$
II	$\vec{p}_I A_{I;II} \vec{X}_{II}$	$\vec{p}_{II} A_{II;II} \vec{X}_{II}$	$(\vec{p}_I A_{I;II} \vec{X}_{II} + \vec{p}_{II} A_{II;II} \vec{X}_{II}) \cdot r$	$\vec{p}_{II} \vec{X}_{II}$
III	$\vec{p}_I A_{I;III} \vec{X}_{III}$	$\vec{p}_{II} A_{II;III} \vec{X}_{III}$	$(\vec{p}_I A_{I;III} \vec{X}_{III} + \vec{p}_{II} A_{II;III} \vec{X}_{III}) \cdot r$	$\vec{p}_{III} \vec{X}_{III}$

$\sum p_i a_{ik} X_k$ equals approximately the product of "mean value" of random quantities $p_i a_{ik} X_k$ and the quantity of items in this sum. The elements of $C-V-M$ (3×3)-matrix are almost equal the product of the quantity of items in the sums depictured in Figure 7 and the "mean value" of random items which constitute this sum. The difference between exact value of elements of the $C-V-M$ matrix and value computed as the product of the "mean value" and the quantities of terms in sum tends to zero when the quantity of industries tends to infinity. This is the consequence of the "law of large numbers (LLN)".

The elements of $C-V-M$ matrix contain the double summation: $\sum_{i;k} p_i^{(\alpha)} a_{ik}^{(\alpha\beta)} X_k^{(\beta)}$; $\alpha = I; II$; $\beta = I; II; III$. The "mean value", $M[...]$ of this sum of items equals the sum of the "mean values" for the random items which constitute this sum. We have the following equalities:

$$M\left[\sum_{i;k} p_i^{(\alpha)} a_{ik}^{(\alpha\beta)} X_k^{(\beta)}\right] = N_{\alpha\beta} \cdot M\left[p_i^{(\alpha)} a_{ik}^{(\alpha\beta)} X_k^{(\beta)}\right] \quad (117)$$

The quantity of components $N_{\alpha\beta}$ in double sum (117) equals multiplication of dimensions of the vectors $\vec{p}_\alpha$ and $\vec{X}_\beta$:

$$N_{\alpha\beta} = N_\alpha N_\beta \quad (118)$$

The "mean value" $M\left[p_i^{(\alpha)} a_{ik}^{(\alpha\beta)} X_k^{(\beta)}\right]$ of random items which constitute the sum equals the multiplication of the "mean value" of random values $p_i^{(\alpha)}$; $a_{ik}^{(\alpha\beta)}$ and $X_k^{(\beta)}$ plus correlation moment of these random values. Correlation moment of two random values can be computed as follows:

$$K_{uv} = M\left[(u - M[u]) \cdot (v - M[v])\right]$$

We obtain the following equality:

$$\begin{aligned} M\left[p^{(\alpha)} a_{ik}^{(\alpha\beta)} X_k^{(\beta)}\right] &= M[pa] \cdot M[X] + K_{(pa)X} = \\ &= M[p] \cdot M[a] \cdot M[X] + \underbrace{K_{pa} \cdot M[X] + K_{(pa)X}}_{\text{correlation moment}} \end{aligned} \quad (119)$$

If random quantities $p_i; a_{ik}; X_k$ are independent random quantities then the correlation moment in the equation (119) equals zero.

We performed the series of computer simulations of $C-V-M$ matrices varying the samples of the random elements in the matrices $A_{I;I}; A_{I;II}; A_{I;III}; A_{II;I}; A_{II;II}; A_{II;III}$ and the sample of random components of the vector $\vec{X}_{III}$. The uniform distribution of these random quantities was used. Simulations demonstrate that correlation moment is very small value which as a rule is diminishing when the number of industries increases. Therefore we can write the following approximate equality:

$$\sum_{i;k} p_i^{(\alpha)} a_{ik}^{(\alpha\beta)} X_k^{(\beta)} \approx N_\alpha N_\beta \cdot M\left[p_i^{(\alpha)}\right] \cdot M\left[a_{ik}^{(\alpha\beta)}\right] \cdot M\left[X_k^{(\beta)}\right] \quad (120)$$

If the number of industries in the economy is very large the sums depictured in Figure 7 can be replaced by the product of the "mean values" and quantity of terms as in Figure 8.

According to Figure 8, the compositions of capitals in the different sectors are equal:

$$k_I \equiv C_I : V_I = \frac{N_I M[p_I]}{N_{II} M[p_{II}]} \cdot \frac{M\left[A_{I;I}\right]}{M\left[A_{II;I}\right]} \quad (121)$$

$$k_{II} \equiv C_{II} : V_{II} = \frac{N_I M[p_I]}{N_{II} M[p_{II}]} \cdot \frac{M\left[A_{I;II}\right]}{M\left[A_{II;II}\right]} \quad (122)$$

$$k_{III} \equiv C_{III} : V_{III} = \frac{N_I M[p_I]}{N_{II} M[p_{II}]} \cdot \frac{M\left[A_{I;III}\right]}{M\left[A_{II;III}\right]} \quad (123)$$

If elements of each matrix $A_{I;I}; A_{I;II}; A_{I;III}$ (or each matrix $A_{II;I}; A_{II;II}; A_{II;III}$) are random numbers which are distributed on the base of the same probability distribution law, then the "mean values" for these matrices are equal:

$$M\left[A_{I;I}\right] = M\left[A_{I;II}\right] = M\left[A_{I;III}\right] \quad (124)$$

$$M\left[A_{II;I}\right] = M\left[A_{II;II}\right] = M\left[A_{II;III}\right] \quad (125)$$

Figure 8. $C-V-M$ matrix of simple production in price-form (the number of industries is very large)

$C-V-M$ **matrix of "mean values".**		
	C	V
I	$N_I^2 M[p_I] M\left[A_{I;I}\right] M[X_I]$	$N_I N_{II} M[p_{II}] M\left[A_{II;I}\right] M[X_I]$
II	$N_I N_{II} M[p_I] M\left[A_{I;II}\right] M[X_{II}]$	$N_{II}^2 M[p_{II}] M\left[A_{II;II}\right] M[X_{II}]$
III	$N_I N_{III} M[p_I] M\left[A_{I;III}\right] M[X_{III}]$	$N_{II} N_{III} M[p_{II}] M\left[A_{II;III}\right] M[X_{III}]$

If these equalities are fulfilled, then compositions of capitals in the different sectors are equal. In this case, the "labor value" and the "price of production" of output in each sector coincide subject to appropriate normalization of vector of prices. Thus, we can conclude:

If the equalities (124)-(125) are fulfilled the output of each sector calculated in the "labor values" equals to output calculated in the "prices of production" and the transformation of the "labor values" into the "prices of production" isn't required.

The equalities (124) describe mathematically sufficiently evident fact that the same "means of production" are used often in all three sectors of the economy. For example, petrol, metals, wood, motors, and so forth are used as "means of production" in all three sectors. Many goods can be used as both the "means of production" and the "goods for employees" (e.g., furniture and automobiles). Output of many industries can be used as raw material for manufacturing (the "means of production") and as the consumer goods. For example, flour, water, electrical energy, paper, and buildings can be used either in household or in manufacturing. Therefore, there are many industries influencing the elements of all three matrices $A_{I;I}; A_{I;II}; A_{I;III}$. Therefore, it is very likely that the statistical distributions of elements in each matrix must be almost identical.

Statistical distributions of elements in matrices $A_{II;I}; A_{II;II}; A_{II;III}$ depend on the expenditures of labor per the unit of goods and on the real wage. The real wage in natural form consists of the bundle of consumer goods which employees buy on the payment of a unit labor. The bundles of consumer goods bought per payment of a unit labor are approximately identical for all types of labor and consist of: the food, clothes, housing, and so forth. Many industries from the different sectors use the labor force of same kind. For example, the turners, drivers, sellers etc. work in all three sectors of the economy producing the "means of production", "goods for employees", and "luxury goods". Many kinds of labor are used often in the different sectors of the economy. For example, the labor used in manufacturing of flour must be accounted in the matrix $A_{II;I}$ if flour is used as the "mean of production" in bread making.

If flour is used in the households of employees ("goods for employees"), then this labor must be accounted in the matrix $A_{II;II}$. If flour is used for the production of delicacies ("luxury goods") we must account the labor expended upon the production of flour in the matrix $A_{II;III}$. Therefore, we can suppose the statistical distributions of elements in each matrix $A_{II;I}; A_{II;II}; A_{II;III}$ are almost identical. Equalities (125) describe this identity in the mathematical form.

The equalities (124) express the fact that the elements of all three matrices $A_{I;I}; A_{I;II}; A_{I;III}$ are distributed on the basis of the same probability law. The set of elements of each matrix is a sample having the same distribution law as elements of all three matrices.

Similarly, the elements of all three matrices $A_{II;I}; A_{II;II}; A_{II;III}$ are distributed according to a certain statistical law. Therefore, the probability distributions of the elements of each matrix are the same and the equalities (125) are fulfilled. Assumptions about the existence of the same probability distributions both for the elements of all three matrices together and for the elements of each individual matrix can be partially verified on the basis of stylized facts.

We shall consider the stylized facts for the economy of the United States in the next part of this chapter. These stylized facts definitely indicate that the equalities (124)-(125) are fulfilled likely in real economy.

COMPUTER SIMULATION OF C-V-M MATRIX. STYLIZED FACTS CONFIRMING THE EQUALITIES (124)-(125)

The calculations of the "labor values" and the "prices of production" are based on the equations of the previous part. The program in software "*Mathematica 8.1*" was written for the calculation of the elements of $C-V-M$ matrix in three forms:

Form 1: $C-V-M$ matrix in the form of the "labor values" – Figure 6.
Form 2: $C-V-M$ matrix in the form of the "prices of production" – Figure 7.
Form 3: $C-V-M$ matrix in the form of the "mean values" – Figure 8.

Description of the Program

The Program contains three blocks: A) the block of input-data, B) the block of calculations, and C) the block of output data.

Input-Data

The elements of matrices $A_{I;I}; A_{I;II}; A_{I;III}; A_{II;I}; A_{II;II}; A_{II;III}$ are given as an arbitrary uniformly distributed positive random numbers with the constants of distribution CR11; CR12; CR13; CR21; CR22; CR23 which determine the upper limits of uniform distributions. The components of the vector $\vec{X}_{III}$ are also positive random numbers uniformly distributed with the constant for the upper limit designated as $X_{\text{III max}}$.

Algorithm of Calculations

"*Mathematica 8.1*" generates the list of eigenvalues and the list of eigenvectors of the matrix. Frobenius's eigenvector and eigenvalue are on the first place in these lists. However eigenvectors are not normalized.

The vector $\vec{l}_{II}$ is the Frobenius's eigenvector of the matrix $S_{II}(m)$ (Equation (95).

The rate of surplus-value m is positive root of the equation (96) in which matrix $S_{II}(m)$ depends on m via the equation (94). The graph $f(m)$ of the function $f(m)=\left|S_{II}(m)-\frac{1}{1+m}I\right|$ visualizes approximate value m as the point where the function $f(m)$ intersect abscissa axis. This value is used as the first approximation. Newton's method is used for the computation of the root of the equation $f(m)=0$. Practically, we seek the root m of the equation $f(m)=0$ with accuracy $|f(m)|\le 10^{-20}$.

The vectors $\vec{X}_I; \vec{X}_{II}$ are calculated via the Equations (68)-(71).

The "labor-values" $v_1; v_2; v_3$ are calculated by means of the Equations (75)-(77).

According to the Equations (99) the vector $\{\vec{p}_I; \vec{p}_{II}\}$ is the Frobenius's eigenvector of the matrix

$$\tilde{A}=\begin{pmatrix} A_{I;I} & A_{I;II} \\ A_{II;I} & A_{II;II} \end{pmatrix}.$$

The rate of profit, r, is calculated via the Frobenius's eigenvalue $\lambda_{\tilde{A}} = \frac{1}{1+r}$ of this matrix.

The vector $\vec{p}_{III}$ can be calculated from the system (99) via the vectors $\{\vec{p}_I;\vec{p}_{II}\}$.

The constant of normalization for the price-vector $\{\vec{p}_I;\vec{p}_{II};\vec{p}_{III}\}$ is defined on the basis of the first transformation rule (100).

Since we use uniform distribution the conditions (124) are fulfilled if:

$$\text{CR1} \equiv \text{CR11} = \text{CR12} = \text{CR13};\ \text{CR2} \equiv \text{CR21} = \text{CR22} = \text{CR23} \tag{126}$$

Since elements of all six matrices $A_{\alpha;\beta}$ ($\alpha = I;II$; $\beta = I;II;III$) are random numbers, all quantities (for example the components of the vectors: $\vec{X}_I;\vec{X}_{II};\vec{p}_I;\vec{p}_{II};\vec{p}_{III}$) calculated by means of the equations of the $C-V-M$ model are also random numbers. The "mean values" for the random components of the vectors $\vec{X}_I;\vec{X}_{II};\vec{p}_I;\vec{p}_{II};\vec{p}_{III}$ were calculated via the function *Mean*[.] of the software "*Mathematica*" i.e. as the "mean value" for the sample of data. The elements $C_I;C_{II};C_{III};V_I;V_{II};V_{III}$ of the $C-V-M$ matrix in the form of the "mean values" are calculated via the formulas depictured in Figure 8. For example, the element V_I is calculated as the following multiplication: $V_I = N_I N_{II} M[\vec{p}_{II}] M[A_{I;II}] M[\vec{X}_I]$. The elements $M_I;M_{II}$ of $C-V-M$ matrix are calculated on the basis of the conditions of simple production:

$$M_I = C_{II} + C_{III} - V_I \tag{127}$$

$$M_{II} = V_I + V_{III} - C_{II} \quad (128$$

The element M_3 is calculated in the same way as the element in the price-form of $C-V-M$ matrix:

$$M_{III} = (C_{III} + V_{III}) \cdot r \tag{129}$$

Output-Data

The next facts were studied via series of the computer simulations of $C-V-M$ matrices for the different input data:

1. The approximate symmetry of $C-V-M$ matrix in all three forms;
2. The approximate coincidence of $C-V-M$ matrices in all three forms;
3. The approximate equality of the compositions of the capitals in three sectors;
4. The almost linear dependence of the rate of profit on the rate of surplus-value subject to the fixed structure of $C-V-M$ model.

The Results of Simulation

Figure 9 illustrates the results of simulation of $C-V-M$ matrix in three forms (the "value-form", the "price-form", and the "mean-value form"). We used in calculations the following constants:

$$X_{\text{III max}} = 1000\,;\ \text{CR11=CR12=CR13=CR21=CR22=CR23=0.025} \tag{130}$$

$$N_I = 40;\ N_{II} = 30;\ N_{III} = 10 \tag{131}$$

Simulation demonstrates that all three $C-V-M$ matrices are almost symmetric and almost identical. Symbol "Asym" in the table (Figure 9) designates the level of asymmetry of $C-V-M$ matrix in the value-form. This indicator is calculated on the basis of the following rule:

$$Asym = \frac{|C_2 - V_1|}{C_2} \tag{132}$$

We investigated the properties of the $C-V-M$ matrix by changing the values of the constants: CR1; CR2; N_I; N_{II}; N_{III}; $X_{\text{III max}}$

There are two nontrivial dependencies discovered on the basis of simulations:

1. The level of asymmetry $Asym$ diminishes when the quantity of industries $N = N_I + N_{II} + N_{III}$ increases. Figure 10 illustrates this dependence;
2. If the structure of $C-V-M$ model is fixed then the linear dependence exists between rate of profit r (profitability) and the "rate of surplus value", m. Figure 11 illustrates this dependence for two structures of the $C-V-M$ model.

The structure of $C-V-M$ model is fixed if the following quantities are fixed:

1. The quantity of industries in each sector: $N_I; N_{II}; N_{III}$;
2. The interrelation between the constants CR1:CR2.

The linear dependences depictured in Figure 11 correspond to the definite structures of $C-V-M$ model with varying constants CR1 and CR2 subject to the fixed ratio CR1:CR2 and fixed quantity of industries in the sectors N_I; N_{II}; N_{III}.

3. The computer simulations confirm the assumption (120). $C-V-M$ matrix in the form of the "mean values" calculated on the basis of equality (120) almost coincides with $C-V-M$ matrices in the "value-form" and the "price-form". Correlation moment in the Equation (119) is negligible quantity in comparison with the product of "mean values".

Figure 9. Numerical example of $C - V - M$ matrix in three forms (the "value-form", the "price-form", and the "mean-value form")

CR1	CR2	m	r	k1	k2	k3	Asym
0.025	0.025	0.401697	0.170139	1.364112	1.360222	1.445323	0.008665
			Value-form				
	C	V	M	W	k	m	r
I	2565.97	1881.16	755.657	5202.787	1.364036	0.401697	0.16992
II	1865.	1371.23	550.822	3787.052	1.360093	0.401699	0.170205
III	771.817	534.662	214.773	1521.252	1.443561	0.401699	0.164391
	5202.787	3787.052	1521.252	10511.09			
N1	40	X3 max	1000		N	80	
N2	30				Asym	0.008665	
N3	10						
			Price-form				
	C	V	M	W	k	m	r
I	2551.94	1870.77	752.475	5175.185	1.364112	0.402227	0.170139
II	1854.84	1363.63	547.586	3766.056	1.360222	0.401565	0.170139
III	768.409	531.652	221.191	1521.252	1.445323	0.416045	0.170139
	5175.189	3766.052	1521.252	10462.49			
			Mean-value form				
	C	V	M	W	k	m	r
I	2548.89	1871.55	768.19	5188.63	1.361914	0.410457	0.173781
II	1857.52	1362.25	563.135	3782.905	1.363568	0.413386	0.174899
III	782.214	549.111	226.51	1557.835	1.42451	0.412503	0.170139
	5188.624	3782.911	1557.835	10529.37			

Thus, if the equalities (124)-(125) are fulfilled, $C - V - M$ matrix (in prices of production) is almost symmetric. Therefore under these conditions the "labor value" and "price of production" of the output of each sector almost equal subject to the appropriate choice of the unit of price.

Thus, the "transformation problem" for the economy with simple production has solution if the equalities (124)-(125) are fulfilled. Exhaustive verification these equalities for the different real economic systems on the basis of stylized facts is a big and complex problem that goes beyond the scope of this chapter. We shall consider only main points of the procedure for verification of equalities (124)-(125) in this chapter.

Verification of the Equalities (124)-(125) on the Stylized Facts for the Economy of the United States, 2007

The following stylized facts were used for verification of the equalities (124)-(125):

Figure 10. The level of asymmetry, $Asym$ of the $C-V-M$ matrix in the "value-form" versus the quantity of industries

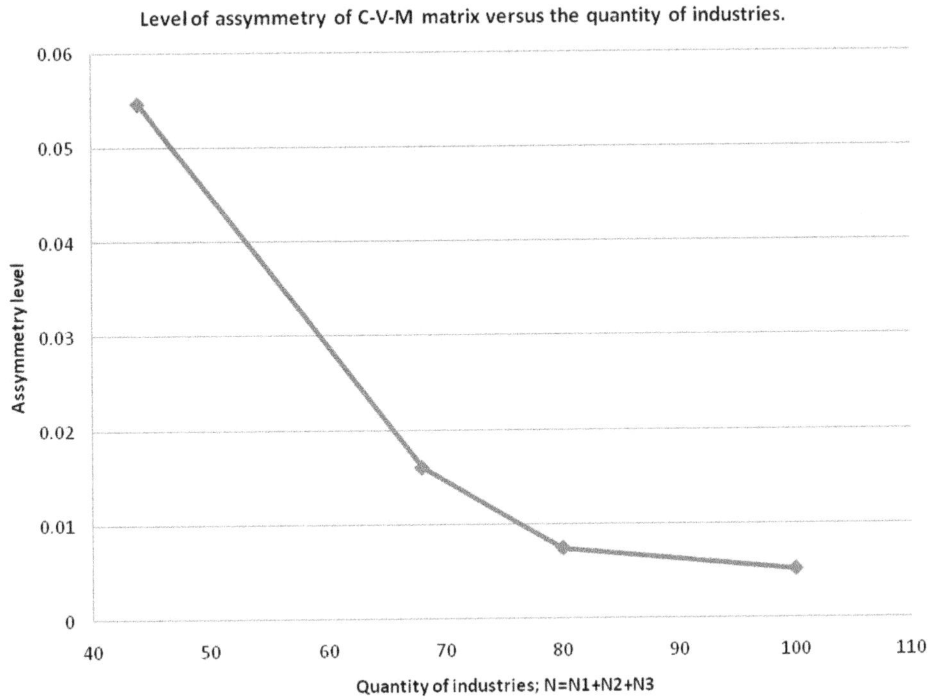

Figure 11. "Rate of profit" (profitability) versus "rate of surplus value"

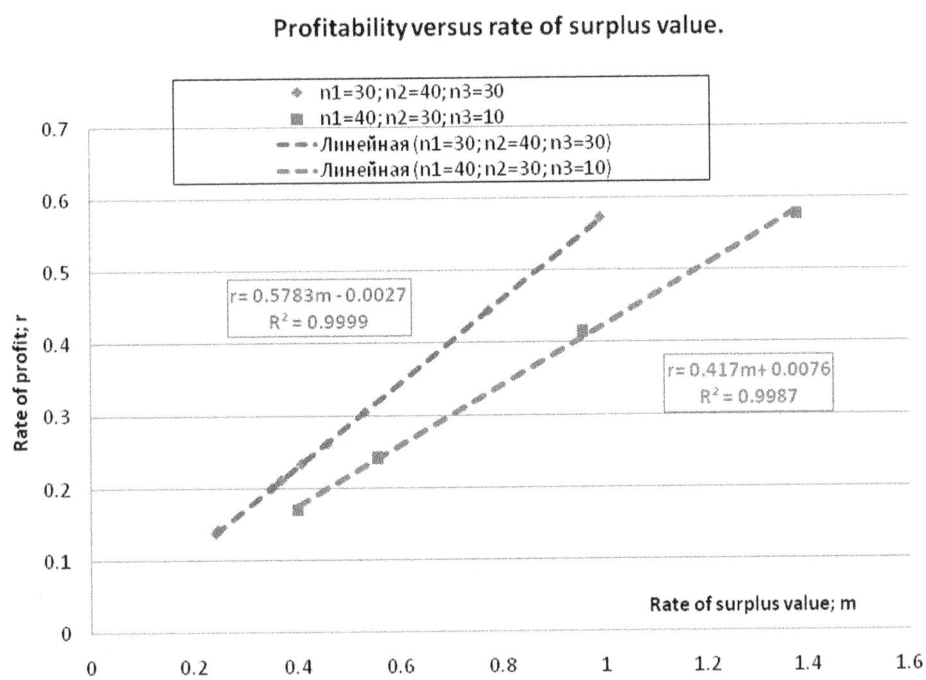

For a more accurate representation see the electronic version.

1. Use matrix before redefinition; 2007; 389 industries. Source: the U.S. Bureau of Economic Analysis: https://www.bea.gov/industry/xls/io-annual/IOUse_Before_Redefinitions_PRO_2007_Detail.xlsx;
2. Commodity-by-commodity total requirements table; 2007 year; 389 industries. Source: the U.S. Bureau of Economic Analysis: https://www.bea.gov/industry/xls/io-annual/CxC_TR_2007_Detail.xlsx.

The "commodity-by-commodity" matrix describes the total expenditures of all goods for the production of the definite commodity with the price in one dollar. Let us designate "commodity-by-commodity total requirements table" as the matrix B. The matrix A of "direct requirements" (i.e., the matrix of direct expenditures per one dollar of output) is connected with the matrix B by means of the following equality:

$$B = (I - A)^{-1} \tag{133}$$

The matrix A can be calculated as follows:

$$A = I - B^{-1} \tag{134}$$

Goods listed in "commodity-by-commodity total requirements table" can be divided into two large groups: 1) the "means of production" and 2) the "goods of final consumption". The second group of goods consists of the "necessity goods" (the goods bought by employees) and the "luxury goods" (all other goods of the second group). The rows and columns of the table of the first group of commodities form the matrix $A_{I;I}$. Summation of the elements disposed in the definite row of the matrix A shows that many sums almost equal to zero. Therefore, these goods are almost not used as "means of production". These goods can most likely be classified as a group of final consumption goods. Thus, these goods are the "goods of final consumption". Therefore, we seek the goods for which the sum of the elements disposed in the definite row almost equal zero. Practically, we used the following criterion: if the sum of elements disposed in the definite row lesser than 0.02 then the goods corresponding to this row is classified as the commodity of final consumption.

We have no information which could help us divide "goods of the final consumption" into two groups: the "goods for employees" and the "luxury goods". Therefore, we can only form the matrix consisting of all the "goods of the final consumption". This is the matrix $A_{I;II-III}$ which unifies the matrices $A_{I;II}$ and $A_{I;III}$ together. If probability distribution functions for elements of the matrix $A_{I;I}$ and the matrix $A_{I;II-III}$ coincide then the "mean values" calculated for elements of these matrices are equal. Thus, equalities (124) are fulfilled: (1) if probability distribution functions for the elements of matrices $A_{I;I}$ and $A_{I;II-III}$ coincide and (2) if probability distribution functions for the elements of matrices $A_{I;II}$ and $A_{I;III}$ also coincide. The second equality cannot be verified due to the absence of necessary information about the structure of spending of employees and all other economic agents. However, we can verify the first equality for the elements of matrices $A_{I;I}$ and $A_{I;II-III}$. Figure 12 confirms that probability distribution functions for the elements of these matrices indeed do coincide.

Figure 12. The probability distribution function for elements of the direct requirements matrix; the United States, 2007

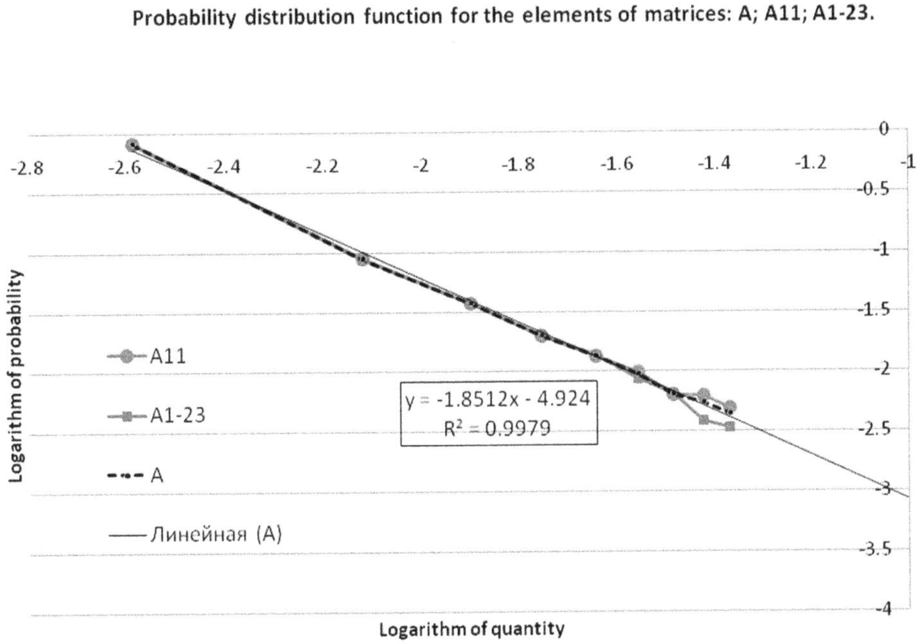

Figure 12 demonstrates that the probability distribution function (PDF) is approximated with high accuracy by the inverse power law: $p(a) \sim a^{-\beta}$ where a - the value of element of the matrix and $p(a)$ is probability of this value in the total massive of the elements of the matrix. The deviation of PDF from inverse power law is negligible when the quantity of the elements in matrix is large. Figure 12 shows a linear trend plotted for a full matrix consisting of matrices $A_{I;I}$ and $A_{I;II-III}$. Although we cannot construct the matrices $A_{I;II}$ and $A_{I;III}$ separately, it is possible to assert surely that the probability distribution functions for the elements of these matrices will also satisfy the same inverse power law.

The inverse power law for the distribution function is one of the “emergent properties” of complex adaptive systems (Pushnoi & Bonser, 2008; Pushnoi, 2014). The economic system is the concrete example of the complex adaptive system (Pushnoi, 2010, 2017). The general laws which act at a macroscopic level of the system are working also at all macroscopic parts of the system because all parts are interconnected. Therefore, it is most likely that probability distribution function found for elements of full matrix $A_{I;II-III} = A_{I;II} \cup A_{I;III}$ coincides with probability distribution functions for elements of each matrices $A_{I;II}$ and $A_{I;III}$. Therefore we can assert surely that “mean values” calculated for elements of matrices $A_{I;II}$ and $A_{I;III}$ are equal and the equalities (124) are fulfilled.

Let us consider elements of the matrices $A_{II;I}; A_{II;II}; A_{II;III}$. The columns of these matrices are the bundles of consumer goods bought by employees per wage paid for their labor expended during the production of the unit of goods. Each column can be represented as the product of a vector-column $\vec{b}$ of the real wage (bundle of consumer goods per the unit of labor) per the quantity of labor expended on the production of the unit of goods:

$$\vec{a}_k \equiv \begin{pmatrix} a_{1k} \\ a_{2k} \\ \dots \\ a_{Nk} \end{pmatrix} = \begin{pmatrix} b_{1k} \\ b_{2k} \\ \dots \\ b_{Nk} \end{pmatrix} \cdot l_k = \vec{b}_k \cdot l_k \tag{135}$$

The vectors $\vec{b}_k$ describe the structure of consumption of the employees in k-th industry. The structures of consumption of workers employed in the different industries are almost the same: food, clothing, and so forth. Therefore, the vectors $\vec{b}_k$ in different industries are almost identical. Thus, the probability distribution function for the elements of matrices $A_{II;I}; A_{II;II}; A_{II;III}$ depends mainly on probability distribution function of components of the vector of direct labor $\vec{l}$. Compensation of employees is almost proportional to their labor during the production process. Therefore, we can estimate the components of vector $\vec{l}$ using the information about compensation of employees per one dollar of gross output. This information is in the "Use Table". Probability distribution function for the components of the vector $\vec{l}$ is depictured in Figure 13.

The vector $\vec{l}$ consists of two parts: the vector $\vec{l}_I$ of direct labor in industries producing the "means of production" and the vector $\vec{l}_{II-III}$ of direct labor in industries producing the "goods of final consump-

Figure 13. Probability distribution function for the components of the vector $\vec{l}$

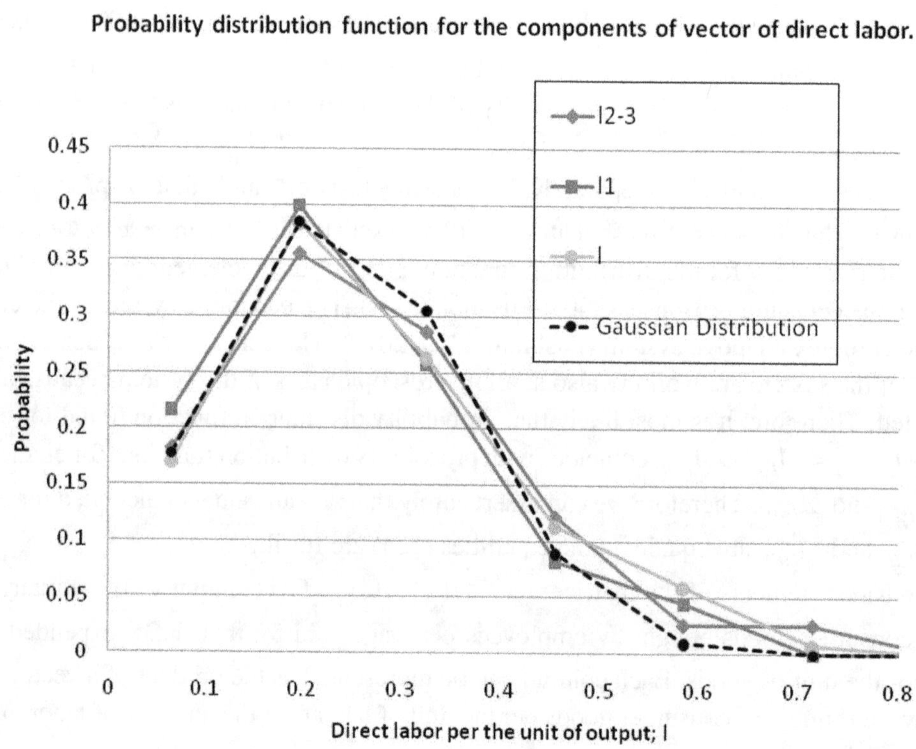

tion". Probability distribution functions for components of these vectors differ insignificantly. The vector $\vec{l}_I$ contains 269 components; and the vector $\vec{l}_{II-III}$ contains 119 components (388 in sum). These data are obviously not sufficient for constructing the probability distribution function with good accuracy. Therefore, curves of distribution for the vectors $\vec{l}_I$ and $\vec{l}_{II-III}$ are slightly different. However, it is very likely that we have here the same distribution for elements of both vectors, $\vec{l}_I$ and $\vec{l}_{II-III}$. This distribution is approximated with good accuracy by the normal Gaussian distribution with the "mean value" $\mu = 0.23$ and standard deviation $\sigma = 0.13$ (dotted curve).

Therefore, although we have obviously insufficient data for the final conclusion, the above calculations show that it is very likely that the laws of distribution of the elements of vectors $\vec{l}_I$ and $\vec{l}_{II-III}$ coincide. Therefore, it is very likely that the "mean values" for the elements of matrices $A_{II;I}$ and $A_{II;II-III}$ are equal. Figure 13 illustrates that probability distribution function for the components of the vector $\vec{l}$ is the most likely Gaussian normal law. If the components of the vectors $\vec{l}_I$ and $\vec{l}_{II-III}$ would be distributed according to the Gaussian law but with different parameters, the resultant distribution of the vector components $\vec{l}$ would not be a Gaussian distribution. Thus very likely that the "mean values" for elements of all three matrices $A_{II;I}; A_{II;II}; A_{II;III}$ are equal because the probability distribution functions for the components of all three vectors $\vec{l}_I; \vec{l}_{II}; \vec{l}_{III}$ are most likely same and the equalities (125) are fulfilled.

CONCLUSION

The "transformation problem" in Marxian economics has the long history. Ladislaus Bortkiewicz (1907a, b) proved in his articles that the Marxian rules for the transformation of the "labor values" into the "prices of production" cannot be performed for an arbitrary structure of $C-V-M$ matrix. In this chapter, we proved that solution of this problem exists only when the $C-V-M$ matrix (3×3) in the price-form is symmetric. The economy with large quantity of industries can be represented as the $C-V-M$ matrix with elements $C_I; C_{II}; C_{III}; V_I; V_{II}; V_{III}$ which can be calculated as a double sums: $\sum_{i;k} p_i^{(\alpha)} a_{ik}^{(\alpha\beta)} X_k^{(\beta)}$; where $\alpha; \beta = I; II; III$. These sums can be approximated as the products: $N_\alpha N_\beta \cdot M\left[p_i^{(\alpha)}\right] \cdot M\left[a_{ik}^{(\alpha\beta)}\right] \cdot M\left[X_k^{(\beta)}\right]$. The stylized facts about the economy of the United States indicate onto the existence of statistical distributions for elements of the matrix of direct requirements A and for the components of the vector of direct labor $\vec{l}$ per the unit of goods. Calculations demonstrate that probability distribution function for elements of the matrix of direct requirements is approximated with high accuracy by the inverse power law. Probability distribution function for the components of the vector $\vec{l}$ is approximated by the Gaussian law.

Since any sample of elements chosen from the set of random quantities satisfying the definite probability distribution law, satisfies also the same probability distribution law, the sums $\sum_{i;k} p_i^{(\alpha)} a_{ik}^{(\alpha\beta)} X_k^{(\beta)}$ located symmetrically within $C-V-M$ matrix (for example for elements V_I and C_{II}) are almost equal and the $C-V-M$ matrix is almost symmetrical.

Computer computation of the $C-V-M$ matrix was performed for a set of random uniformly distributed elements of the socio-technological matrix A and components of the vector $\vec{X}_3$ (physical output of the third sector). These calculations prove that the level of symmetry of the $C-V-M$ matrix increases when the quantity of industries grows.

Therefore, computer calculations and stylized facts definitely point that the "transformation problem" of the "labor values" into the "prices of production" in real economies consisting of tremendous quantity of industries is solved due to the action of the statistical "law of large numbers". Deviations of the "labor values" from the "prices of production" for the aggregate products of three sectors are negligible because the $C-V-M$ matrix becomes symmetric when the quantity of industries in the economy tends to infinity.

The algorithm for computation of the $C-V-M$ matrix and the results concerning the solution of the "transformation problem" open new possibilities for the exploration of economic systems. The economies of different countries can be represented in the form of $C-V-M$ matrices. Stylized facts about the economy can be used for calculation of the elements of the $C-V-M$ matrix. Therefore, the dynamic and structural properties of economies can be analyzed by using the $C-V-M$ modelling technique, so it is a new promising method for the study of economic systems.

ACKNOWLEDGMENT

I thank my friend Marina Bonser for her input into translation of this paper from Russian. I am grateful to Dr. Valeriy Kalyuzhnyi for the discussion of the basic ideas of this paper.

REFERENCES

Abraham-Frois, G. (1979). *Theory of value, prices and accumulation. A mathematical integration of Marx, von Neumann and Sraffa*. London: Cambridge University Press.

Bortkiewicz, L. von (1907a). On the Correction of Marx's Fundamental Theoretical Construction in the Third Volume of Capital (P. M. Sweezy, Trans.). *Jahrbucher fur Nationalokonomie und Statistik.*

Bortkiewicz, L. von (1907b). Wertechnung und Preisrechnung im Marxschen System. *Archiv fur Sozialwissenschaft und Sozialpolitik, 25*, 10–51.

Dumenil, G. (1980). *De la valeur aux prix de production*. Paris: Economica.

Dumenil, G. (1983-84). Beyond the transformation riddle: A labor theory of value. *Science and Society, 47*(4), 427–450.

Fine, B., Saad-Filho, A., & Lapavitsas, C. (2004). Transforming the Transformation Problem: Why the 'New Interpretation' is a Wrong Turning. *The Review of Radical Political Economics, 36*(1), 3–19. doi:10.1177/0486613403261091

Foley, D. (1982). The value of money, the value of labor power and the Marxian transformation problem. *The Review of Radical Political Economics, 14*(2), 37–47. doi:10.1177/048661348201400204

Freeman, A. (1996). The psychopathology of Walrasian Marxism. In Marx and Non-Equilibrium Economics. Cheltenham, UK: Edward Elgar.

Itoh, M. (1980). *Value and Crisis*. London: Pluto Press.

Kalyuzhnyi, V. V. (2014). *The Transformation Problem: Erroneous Arguments of Tugan-Baranovsky, Bortkiewicz and Steedman*. Retrieved from https://ssrn.com/abstract=2520362

Kliman, A.J. (2007). *Reclaiming Marx's "Capital". A Refutation of the Myth of Inconsistency*. Lexington Books.

Kliman, A. J., & McGlone, T. (1999). A Temporal Single-system Interpretation of Marx's Value Theory. *Review of Political Economy*, *11*(1), 33–59. doi:10.1080/095382599107165

Laibman, D. (2004). Rhetoric and Substance in Value Theory: An appraisal of the new orthodox Marxism. In A. Freeman, A. Kliman, & J. Wells (Eds.), *The New Value Controversy and the Foundations of Economics*. Cheltenham, UK: Edward Elgar.

Lipietz, A. (1982). The 'so-called transformation problem' revisited. *Journal of Economic Theory*, *26*(February).

Mariolis, T. (2006). A Critique of the 'New Approach' to the Transformation Problem and a Proposal. Published in *Indian Development Review: An International Journal of Development Economics*, *4*(1), 23–37.

Marx, K. (1885). Capital (vol. 2). Edited for publication by Engels in 1885.

Medio, A. (1972). Profits and surplus value: appearance and reality in capitalist production. In E. K. Huntand & J. Schwartz (Eds.), *A Critique of Economic Theory*. New York: Penguin.

Meek, R. L. (1956). *Studies in the Labour Theory of Value*. London: Lawrence & Wishart.

Morishima, M. (1973). *Marxian Economics*. Oxford, UK: Oxford University Press.

Morishima, M., & Caterhores, G. (1975). The transformation problem: a Markov process. In M. Morishima (Ed.), *Value Exploitation and Growth – Marx in the Light of Modern Economic Theory*. New York: McGraw – Hill.

Moseley, F. (1999). The 'new solution' to the transformation problem: A sympathetic critique. *The Review of Radical Political Economics*, *32*(2), 282–316.

O'Donnell, R. (1984). *Adam Smith's labour command measure of value*. UCD Centre for Economic Research, Working Paper Series; No. 21.

Park, C-S. (2009). The Temporal Single System: A retrospective critique. *Marxism, 21*.

Pushnoi, G. S. (2010). Crisis as Reconfiguration of the Economic Complex Adaptive System. *AAAI Symposium Series; AAAI Fall CAS Symposium*.

Pushnoi, G. S. (2014). Method of Systems Potential as Holistic Approach for CAS-Modelling. In M. Khosrow-Pour (Ed.), *Encyclopedia of Information Science and Technology* (3rd ed.). Hershey, PA: IGI Global.

Pushnoi, G. S. (2017). *Method of Systems Potential (MSP). Applications in Economics: Emerging Research and Opportunities*. Hershey, PA: IGI Global. doi:10.4018/978-1-5225-2170-9

Pushnoi, G. S., & Bonser, G. L. (2008). Method of Systems Potential as "Top-Bottom" Technique of the Complex Adaptive Systems Modelling. In A. Yang & Y. Shan (Eds.), *Intelligent Complex Adaptive Systems* (pp. 26–73). Hershey, PA: IGI Global. doi:10.4018/978-1-59904-717-1.ch002

Roberto, V. (2004). The Temporal Single-System Interpretation of Marx's Economics: A critical evaluation. *Metroeconomica*, *55*(1).

Roemer, J. E. (1980). A General Equilibrium Approach to Marxian Economics. *Econometrica*, *48*(2), 505–530. doi:10.2307/1911113

Samuelson, P. A. (1971, June). Understanding the Marxian notion of exploitation: A summary of the so-called transformation problem between Marxian values and competitive prices. *Journal of Economic Literature*, *9*(2), 399–431.

Shaikh, A. (1977). Marx's theory of value and the 'transformational problem. In J. Sohwartz (Ed.), *The Subtle Anatomy of Capitalism*. Santa Monica, CA: Goodyear.

Shaikh, A. (1984). The transformation from Marx to Sraffa. In E. Mandell (Ed.), *Ricardo, Marx, Sraffa*. London: Verse.

Smith, A. (1994). *The Wealth of Nations*. New York: The Modern Library. The. (Original work published 1776)

Steedman, I. (1977). *Marx after Sraffa*. London: New Left Books.

Sweezy, P. M. (1942). *The Theory of Capitalist Development*. New York: Monthly Review Press.

Sweezy, P. M. (Ed.). (1949). *Karl Marx and the Close of His System by Eugen Bohn-Bawerk and Bohn-Bawerk's Critism of Marx by Rudolf Hilferding*. New York: A.M. Kelly.

Tugan-Baranovsky, M. I. (1906). Theoretical foundations of Marxism (3rd ed.). J. "World of God".

Wright, I. (2007). Nonstandard labour values. *Open Discussion Papers in Economics, 69*.

Compilation of References

A Bad Climate for Development. (2009, September 17). *The Economist*. Retrieved on September 30, 2017, from: http://www.economist.com/node/14447171

Abraham-Frois, G. (1979). *Theory of value, prices and accumulation. A mathematical integration of Marx, von Neumann and Sraffa*. London: Cambridge University Press.

Acemoglu, D., & Autor, D. (2011). *Skills, Tasks and Technologies: Implications for Employment and Earnings*. NBER Working Paper No. 16082.

Acemoglu, D., Johnson, S., & Robinson, J. (2004). Institutions as the Fundamental Cause of Long-Run Growth. Cambridge, MA: Academic Press. doi:10.3386/w10481

Acemoglu, D., Johnson, S., & Robinson, J. A. (2001). The Colonial Origins of Comparative Development: An Empirical Investigation. *The American Economic Review*, *91*(5), 1369–1401. doi:10.1257/aer.91.5.1369

Acemoglu, D., & Pischke, J. (1999). Beyond Becker: Training In Imperfect Labour Markets. *Economic Journal (London)*, *109*(453), 112–142. doi:10.1111/1468-0297.00405

Adams, S. (2008). Globalization and income inequality: Implications for intellectual property rights. *Journal of Policy Modeling*, *30*(5), 725–735. doi:10.1016/j.jpolmod.2007.10.005

Adelmann, B. (2013). America's Reshoring of Jobs is Accelerating. *The New American*. Retrieved on August 3, 2014, from: http://www.thenewamerican.com/economy/markets/item/16616-thanks-to-america-s-fracking-boom-and-skilled-laborforce-the-re-shoring-of-jobs-is-accelerating

Aghion, P., & Howitt, P. (1992). *A Model of Growth Through Creative Destruction. Econometrica* (Vol. 60). The Econometric Society. doi:10.2307/2951599

Aguiló, E., & Rosselló, J. (2005). Host community perceptions: A cluster analysis. *Annals of Tourism Research*, *32*(4), 925–941. doi:10.1016/j.annals.2004.11.004

Ahvenniemi, H., Huovila, A., Pinto-Seppä, I., & Airaksinen, M. (2017). What are the differences between sustainable and smart cities? *Cities (London, England)*, *60*, 234–245. doi:10.1016/j.cities.2016.09.009

Aina, Y. A. (2017). Achieving smart sustainable cities with GeoICT support: The Saudi evolving smart cities. *Cities (London, England)*, *71*, 49–58. doi:10.1016/j.cities.2017.07.007

Aktan, Ç. C., & Vural, İ. Y. (2002). Gelir Dağılımında adalet(siz)lik ve gelir eşit(siz)liği: terminoloji, temel kavramlar ve ölçüm yöntemleri. In C. C. Aktan (Ed.), *Yoksullukla Mücadele Stratejileri*. Ankara: Hak-İş Konfederasyonu Yayınları.

Al-Amin, A. Q., Rasiah, R., & Chenayah, S. (2015). Prioritizing climate change mitigation: An assessment using Malaysia to reduce carbon emissions in future. *Environmental Science & Policy*, *50*, 24–33. doi:10.1016/j.envsci.2015.02.002

Albino, V., Berardi, U., & Dangelico, R. M. (2015). Smart Cities: Definitions, dimensions, performance, and initiatives. *Journal of Urban Technology*, *22*(1), 3–21. doi:10.1080/10630732.2014.942092

Alcacer, J., & Delgado, M. (2014). Spatial organization of firms and location choices through the value chain. *Management Science*, *62*(11), 3213–3234. doi:10.1287/mnsc.2015.2308

Alderman, L. (2014, January 3). Unemployed in Europe Stymied by Lack of Technology Skills. *New York Times*. Retrieved on September 22, 2017, from: http://www.nytimes.com/2014/01/04/business/international/unemployed-in-europe-hobbled-by-lack-oftechnology-skills.html?emc=eta1kills

Ali, F., Hussain, K., Nair, V., & Nair, P. K. (2017). Stakeholders' perceptions & attitudes towards tourism development in a mature destination. *Tourism (Zagreb)*, *65*(2), 173–186.

Allen, J., & Van Der Velden, R. (2005). *The Role Of Self-Assessment In Measuring Skills*. Paper For The Jacobs Foundation Conference Interdisciplinary And Cross-National Perspectives On Skill Formation And The Reform Of Vocational And Professional Training, Marbach, Switzerland.

Allen, F., Qian, J., & Qian, M. (2005). Law, finance, and economic growth in China. *Journal of Financial Economics*, *77*(1), 57–116. doi:10.1016/j.jfineco.2004.06.010

Allen, J., & Van Der Velden, R. (2001). Educational Mismatches Versus Skill Mismatches: Effects On Wages, Job Satisfaction, And On-The-Job Search'. *Oxford Economic Papers*, *3*(3), 434–452. doi:10.1093/oep/53.3.434

Almeida, F., Balbuena, A., & Cortés, R. (2015). Resident's attitudes towards the impacts of tourism. *Tourism Management Perspectives*, *13*, 33–40. doi:10.1016/j.tmp.2014.11.002

Alvarez, S. A. (2005). Theories of entrepreneurship: Alternative assumptions and the study of entrepreneurial action. *Foundations and Trends in Entrepreneurship*, *1*(3), 105–148. doi:10.1561/0300000003

American Institute for Economic Research. (2014). *2015-2016 Top college destinations ranked*. Retrieved on April 22, 2017, from: https://www.aier.org/american-institute-economic-research-unveils-2014-2015-ranking-best-us-cities-college-students

AMS. (2015). *Climate Services. A Policy Statement of the American Meteorological Society*. Retrieved on May 30, 2017 from: https://www.ametsoc.org/ams/index.cfm/about-ams/ams-statements/statements-of-the-ams-in-force/climate-services1/

Ana Carrasco. (2013). *A Model for Sustainable and Replicable ICT Incubators in Sub-Saharan Africa | infoDev*. Retrieved on May 3, 2015, from: http://www.infodev.org/articles/model-sustainable-and-replicable-ict-incubators-sub-saharan-africa

Andereck, K. L., & Nyaupane, G. (2011). Exploring the nature of tourism and quality of life perceptions among residents. *Journal of Travel Research*, *50*(3), 248–260. doi:10.1177/0047287510362918

Andriotis, K., & Vaughan, R. D. (2003). Urban residents' attitudes toward tourism development: The case of Crete. *Journal of Travel Research*, *42*(2), 172–185. doi:10.1177/0047287503257488

Antarctic Treaty. (1959). *Article I (2).*

Anthopoulos, L., Janssen, M., & Weerakkody, V. (2016). Smart service Portfolios: Do the cities follow standards? *Proceedings of the 25th International conference companion on world wideWeb: International world wide web conferences steering committee*, 357-362. 10.1145/2872518.2888618

Ap, J., & Crompton, J. L. (1998). Developing and testing a tourism impact scale. *Journal of Travel Research*, *37*(2), 120–130. doi:10.1177/004728759803700203

Arbache, J. S., Dickerson, A., & Green, F. (2004). Trade liberalisation and wages in developing countries. *Economic Journal (London), 114*(February), F73–F96. doi:10.1111/j.0013-0133.2004.00188.x

Ardalan, K. (2017). Driving force of globalization: A multi- paradigmatic look. *Research in International Business and Finance, 41*, 480–492. doi:10.1016/j.ribaf.2017.05.005

Arellano, M., & Bond, S. (1991). Some tests of specification for panel data: Monte Carlo evidence and an application to employment equations. *The Review of Economic Studies, 58*(2), 277–297. doi:10.2307/2297968

Arellano, M., & Bover, O. (1995). Another look at the instrumental variable estimation of error components models. *Journal of Econometrics, 68*(2), 9–51.

Arıcıoğlu, E. (2012). Kalkınma kavramına küreselleşme prespektifinden bir bakış. *Niğde Üniversitesi İİBF Dergisi, 5*(1), 36–53.

Aronsson, L. (2004). *The development of sustaniable tourism*. London: Thomson Learning.

Asteriou, D., Dimelis, S., & Moudatsou, A. (2014). Globalization and income inequality: A panel data econometric approach for the EU27 countries. *Economic Modelling, 36*, 592–599. doi:10.1016/j.econmod.2013.09.051

Atif, S.M., Srivastav, M., Sauytbekova M., & Arachchige U. K. (2012). Globalization and income inequality: A panel data analysis of 68 countries. *MPRA Paper No:42385.*

Audretsch, D., Sanders, M., & Zhang, L. (2017). International product life cycles, trade and development stages. *The Journal of Technology Transfer*, 1–44.

Australian Government. (2010). *Australian Government ICT Sustainability Plan 2010 - 2015 - Overview*. Retrieved on May 3, 2015, from: http://www.environment.gov.au/resource/australian-government-ict-sustainability-plan-2010-2015-2

Australian Sustinability Conference. (2012). *Australian Sustainability*. Retrieved on May 3, 2015, from: http://blog.australiansustainability.com.au/

Avcı, N. (2007). Turizmde taşıma kapasitesinin önemi. *Ege Akademik Bakış, 7*(2), 485–501.

Averill, J. R., & More, T. A. (2000). Happiness. In M. Lewis & J. M. Haviland (Eds.), *Handbook of emotions* (2nd ed.; pp. 663–676). New York: Guilford Publications.

Aykaç, A. (2009). *Yeni işler, yeni işçiler: Turizm sektöründe emek*. İstanbul: İletişim Yayınları.

Ayubu, J. C., Malongo, R. S. M., Siza, D. T., & Respickius, C. (2012). Understanding Farmers Information Communication Strategies for Managing Climate Risks in Rural Semi-Arid Areas, Tanzania. *International Journal of Information and Communication Technology Research, 12*(2), 45–58.

Bae, J. H., & Salomon, R. (2010). Institutional distance in international business research. *Advances in International Management, 23*, 327–349. doi:10.1108/S1571-5027(2010)00000230020

Bai, J., & Kao, C. (2006). Contributions to Economic Analysis: Vol. 274. On the Estimation and Inference of a Panel Cointegration Model with Cross-Sectional Dependence. Academic Press. doi:10.1016/S0573-8555(06)74001-9

Bai, J., Kao, C., & Ng, S. (2009). Panel cointegration with global stochastic trends. *Journal of Econometrics, 149*(1), 82–99. doi:10.1016/j.jeconom.2008.10.012

Bailey, D. A., de Ruyter, A., Michie, J., & Tyler, P. (2010). Globalisation and the Auto Industry. *Cambridge Journal of Regions, Economy and Society, 3*(3), 367–382. doi:10.1093/cjres/rsq021

Baker & McKenzie. (2015). *Chinese investment into Europe hits record high in 2014*. Retrieved from http://www.bakermckenzie.com/news/Chinese-investment-into-Europe-hits-record-high-in-2014-02-11-2015/

Bakıcı, T., Almirall, E., & Wareham, J. (2012). A smart city initiative: The case of Barcelona. *J. Knowl. Econ.*, *4*(2), 135–148. doi:10.100713132-012-0084-9

Bala, B. K., Arshad, F. M., & Noh, K. M. (2017). System Dynamics: Modelling and Simulation. Springer International Publishing AG.

Baltagi, B. H. (2014). Econometric Analysis of Panel Data (5ht ed.). Wiley.

Baltagi, B. H. (Ed.). (2015). *The Oxford Handbook of Panel Data*. Oxford University Press; doi:10.1093/oxfordhb/9780199940042.001.0001

Bandura, A. (1969). Social-learning theory of identificatory processes. In D. A. Goslin (Ed.), *Handbook of socialization theory and research*. Chicago: Rand McNally.

Bandura, A., & Wood, R. E. (1989). Effect of perceived controllability and performance standards on self-regulation of complex decision-making. *Journal of Personality and Social Psychology*, *56*(5), 804–814. doi:10.1037/0022-3514.56.5.805 PMID:2724068

Barro, R. J. (2000). Inequality and growth in a panel of countries. *Journal of Economic Growth*, *5*(1), 5–32. doi:10.1023/A:1009850119329

Barro, R. J., & Sala-I-Martin, X. (1992). Public Finance in Models of Economic Growth. *The Review of Economic Studies*, *59*(4), 645–661. doi:10.2307/2297991

Bartholomew, S. (1997). National systems of biotechnology innovation: Complex interdependence in the global system. *Journal of International Business Studies*, *28*(2), 241–266. doi:10.1057/palgrave.jibs.8490100

Bartlett, C. A., & Ghoshal, S. (1999). *Managing across borders: The transnational solution* (Vol. 2). Taylor & Francis.

Baş, K. (2009). Küreselleşme ve gelir dağılımı eşitsizliği. *Çanakkale Üniversitesi. Sosyal Bilimler Enstitüsü Dergisi*, *18*(1), 49–70.

Bayudan-Dacuycuy, C., & Lim, J. A. Y. (2017). Export Sophistication, Export-Led Growth and Product Space: Evidence from Selected Asian Economies. *Journal of Asian and African Studies*, *52*(1), 3–20. doi:10.1177/0021909614560241

Bechu, N. (1998). The impact of AIDS on the economy of the families in Cote d'Voire: Changes in consumption among AIDS affected households. In M. Ainsworth, L. Fransen, & M. Over (Eds.), *In confronting AIDS: Evidence from the Developing World*. Brussels: European Commission.

Becker, G. (1964). *Human Capital: A Theoretical And Empirical Analysis With Special Reference To Education*. New York: Columbia University Press.

Beck, T., Demirgüc-Kunt, A., & Levine, R. (2007). Finance, inequality, and the poor. *Journal of Economic Growth*, *12*(1), 27–49. doi:10.100710887-007-9010-6

Beck, U. (2000). *The brave new world of work*. Cambridge, UK: Polity Press.

Belisle, F. J., & Hoy, D. R. (1980). The perceived impact of tourism by residents: A case study in Santa María, Colombia. *Annals of Tourism Research*, *7*(1), 83–101. doi:10.1016/S0160-7383(80)80008-9

Bélissent, J., Mines, C., Radcliffe, E., & Darashkevich, Y. (2010). *Getting Clever About Smart Cities: New Opportunities Require New Business Models*. Cambridge, MA: Forrester Research.

Bénassy-Quéré, A., Coupet, M., & Mayer, T. (2007). Institutional determinants of foreign direct investment. *World Economy*, *30*(5), 764–782. doi:10.1111/j.1467-9701.2007.01022.x

Benjamin, M., Stoker, K., & Suri, T. (2013). The Economics of Slums in the Developing World. *Journal of Economics Perspectives*, *27*, 187-210.

Berdykulova, G. M. K., Sailov, A. I. U., Kaliazhdarova, S. Y. K., & Berdykulov, E. B. U. (2014). The Emerging Digital Economy: Case of Kazakhstan. *Procedia - Social and Behavioral Sciences, 109*, 1287 – 1291.

Bergh, A., & Karlsson, M. (2010). Government size and growth: Accounting for economic freedom and globalization. *Public Choice*, *142*(1–2), 195–213. doi:10.100711127-009-9484-1

Bergh, A., & Nilsson, T. (2010). Do liberalization and globalization increase income inequality? *European Journal of Political Economy*, *26*(4), 488–505. doi:10.1016/j.ejpoleco.2010.03.002

Berry, A. (2014). Global Integration And Innovation: Multicountry Knowledge Generation Within Mncs. *Strategic Management Journal*, *35*(6), 869–890. doi:10.1002mj.2140

Bevan, A., Estrin, S., & Meyer, K. (2004). Foreign investment location and institutional development in transition economies. *International Business Review*, *13*(1), 43–64. doi:10.1016/j.ibusrev.2003.05.005

Bhowmick, A., Francellino, E., Glehn, L., Loredo, R., Nesbitt, P., & Yu, S. (2012). *IBM intelligent operations center for smarter cities*. Armonk, NY: IBM International Technical Support Organization.

Bianchi, R. (2017). The political economy of tourism development: A critical review. *Annals of Tourism Research*. doi:10.1016/j.annals.2017.08.005

Bibri, S. E. (2013). *ICT for sustainable urban development in the European InformationSociety: A discursive investigation of energy efficiency technology* (Master Thesis). School of Culture and Society, Malmö University.

Bibri, S. E. (2015). *The shaping of Ambient Intelligence and the Internet of Things: Historico-epistemic, socio-cultural, politico-institutional and eco-environmental dimensions*. Berlin: Springer-Verlag. doi:10.2991/978-94-6239-142-0

Bibri, S. E., & Krogstie, J. (2017). Smart sustainable cities of the future: An extensive interdisciplinary literature review. *Sustainable Cities and Society*, *31*, 183–212. doi:10.1016/j.scs.2017.02.016

Bien, A. (2006). *A simple user's guide to certification for sustainable tourism and ecotourism* (3rd ed.). Washington, DC: Center for Ecotourism and Sustainable Development.

Bijlsma, L., Ehler, C. N., Klein, R. J. T., Kulshrestha, S. M., McLean, R. F., Mimura, N., ... Warrick, R. A. (1996). Coastal zones and small islands. In R. T. Watson, M. C. Zinyowera, & R. H. Moss (Eds.), *Climate Change 1995: Impacts, Adaptations, and Mitigation of Climate Change: Scientific-Technical Analyses. Contribution of Working Group II to the Second Assessment Report of the Intergovernmental Panel on Climate Change* (pp. 289–324). Cambridge, UK: Cambridge University Press.

Binoy, J., Joseph, I., & Raju, V. (2009). Labour Welfare in India. *Journal of Workplace Behavioral Health*, *24*(1&2), 221–242.

Birdsall, N. (2006). The world is not flat: Inequality and injustice in our global economy. *UNU World Institute for Development Economic Research (UNU -WIDER) WIDER Annual Lecture 9.*

Birnie, P., Boyle, A., & Redgwell, C. (Eds.). (2009). *International Law and the Environment* (3rd ed.). London: Oxford University Press.

Blamey, R. K. (2001). Principles of ecotourism. In D. B. Weaver (Ed.), *Encyclopedia of Ecotourism* (pp. 5–22). New York: CABI Publishing.

Blanchflower, D.G., & Andrew, J. O. (2004). Well-being over time in Britain and the USA. *Journal of Public Economics, 88.*

Block, P. (2011). Tailoring Seasonal Climate Forecasts for Hydropower Operations. *Hydrology and Earth System Sciences, 15*(4), 1355–1368. doi:10.5194/hess-15-1355-2011

Blomskog, S., & Schroder, L. (1997). Labour Market Entry, Vocational Training And Mobility In The Young Workforce In Sweden 1950-91. In S. Blomskog (Ed.), *Essays On The Functioning Of The Swedish Labour Market.* Stockholm: Swedish Institute For Social Research.

Blustein, D. (2005). *The psychology of working. A New Perspective for Career Development, Counselling, and Public Policy.* LEA.

Böckerman, P., & Ilmakunnas, P. (2005). *Elusive effects of unemployment on happiness.* Discussion Paper no. 47. Helsinki Center of Economic Research.

Bodvarsson, O. B., & Van den Berg, H. (2013). *The economics of Immigration: Theory and Policy.* New York: Springer Sciences and Business Media. doi:10.1007/978-1-4614-2116-0

Bookchin, M. (1996a). *Toplumsal Ekolojinin Felsefesi, Çev. Rahmi.* G. Öğdül, Kabalcı Yayınları, İstanbul, 197s.

Bookchin, M. (1996b). *Ekolojik Bir Toplumuna Doğru.* Çev. Abdullah Yılmaz, Ayrıntı Yayınları, İsyanbul, 300s.

Borghans, L., & De Grip, A. (2000). *The Overeducated Worker? The Economics Of Skill Utilization.* Cheltenham, UK: Edward Elgar.

Borjas, G. J., & Ramey, V. A. (1994). Time-series evidence on the sources of trends in wage inequality. *The American Economic Review, 84,* 10–16.

Bortkiewicz, L. von (1907a). On the Correction of Marx's Fundamental Theoretical Construction in the Third Volume of Capital (P. M. Sweezy, Trans.). *Jahrbucher fur Nationalokonomie und Statistik.*

Bortkiewicz, L. von (1907b). Wertechnung und Preisrechnung im Marxschen System. *Archiv fur Sozialwissenschaft und Sozialpolitik, 25,* 10–51.

Bosselmann, K. (2008). *The Principle of Sustainability: Transforming Law and Governance.* Farnham, UK: Ashgate.

Bourguignon, F., & Morrisson, C. (1990). Income distribution, development and foreign trade. *European Economic Review, 34*(6), 1113–1132. doi:10.1016/0014-2921(90)90071-6

Bozok, D., & Yılmaz, Ö. (2011). Turistik ürün çeşitlendirmesi. In N. Hacıoğlu & C. Avcıkurt (Eds.), Ekoturizm (2. Baskı) içinde (pp. 111-137). Ankara: Nobel Yayınları.

Brecher, R. A., Chen, Z., & Choudhri, R. A. (2002). Absolute and Comparative Advantage, Reconsidered: The pattern of international trade with optimal saving. *Review of International Economics, Vol, 10*(: 4), 645–656. doi:10.1111/1467-9396.t01-1-00355

Breitung, J. (2005). A Parametric approach to the Estimation of Cointegration Vectors in Panel Data. *Econometric Reviews, 24*(2), 151–173. doi:10.1081/ETC-200067895

Bretschger, L. (2017). Climate policy and economic growth. *Resource and Energy Economics, 49,* 1–15. doi:10.1016/j.reseneeco.2017.03.002

Breusch, T. S., & Pagan, A. R. (1980). The Lagrange Multiplier Test and its Applications to Model Specification in Econometrics. *The Review of Economic Studies*, *47*(1), 239. doi:10.2307/2297111

Briassoulis, H. (2002). Sustainable Tourism And The Question Of The Commons. *Annals of Tourism Research*, *29*(4), 1065–1085. doi:10.1016/S0160-7383(02)00021-X

Brida, J. G., Chiappa, G. D., Meleddu, M., & Pulina, M. (2014). A comparison of residents' perceptions in two cruise ports in the mediterranean sea. *International Journal of Tourism Research*, *16*(2), 180–190. doi:10.1002/jtr.1915

Brida, J. G., Osti, L., & Barquet, A. (2010). Segmenting Resident Perceptions towards Tourism - a Cluster Analysis with a Multinomial Logit Model of a Mountain Community. *International Journal of Tourism Research*, *12*(5), 591–602.

Brougham, J. E., & Butler, R. W. (1981). A segmentation analysis of resident attitudes to the social impact of tourism. *Annals of Tourism Research*, *8*(4), 569–590. doi:10.1016/0160-7383(81)90042-6

Brouthers, K. D. (2002). Institutional, cultural and transaction cost influences on entry mode choice and performance. *Journal of International Business Studies*, *33*(2), 203–222. doi:10.1057/palgrave.jibs.8491013

Brouwer, M. (1991). *Schumpeterian puzzles – technological competition and economic evolution*. Ann Arbor, MI: University of Michigan Press.

Brown, O., Crawford, A., & Campeau, C. (2008, June). *Environmental Change and the New Security Agenda: Implications for Canada's Security and Environment, International Institute for Sustainable Development*. Retrieved on September 29, 2017, from: http://www.iisd.org/PUBLICATIONS/pub.aspx?id=975

Brundtland Commission. (1987). *Our Common Future: Report of the World Commission on Environment and Development*. Oxford, UK: Oxford University Press.

Bruni, L. (2004). The "Happiness Transformation Problem" in the Cambridge Tradition. *European Journal of the History of Economic Thought*, *11*(3), 433–451. doi:10.1080/0967256042000246494

Bruton, G. D., Fried, V. H., & Manigart, S. (2005). Institutional influences on the worldwide expansion of venture capital. *Entrepreneurship Theory and Practice*, *29*(6), 737–760. doi:10.1111/j.1540-6520.2005.00106.x

Büchel, F. & Mertens, A. (2003). Overeducation In Europe. Cheltenham, UK: Edward Elgar.

Buckley, P., & Freeman, N. J. (Eds.). (1998). *Vietnam's Country Funds: An Emerging Investment Vehicle*. New York: St. Martin's Press.

Burkhauser, R. V., Crews, A. D., & Daly, M. C. (1997). Recounting winners and losers in the 1980s: A critique of income distribution measurement methodology. *Economics Letters*, *54*(1), 35–40. doi:10.1016/S0165-1765(96)00945-7

Busenitz, L. W., Gomez, C., & Spencer, J. W. (2000). Country institutional profiles: Unlocking entrepreneurial phenomena. *Academy of Management Journal*, *43*(5), 994–1003. doi:10.2307/1556423

Butler, R. W. (1980). The concept of a tourist area cycle of evolution: Implications for the management of resources. *The Canadian Geographer*, *24*(1), 5–12. doi:10.1111/j.1541-0064.1980.tb00970.x

Bygrave, W., & Zacharakis, A. (2008). *Entrepreneurship*. Hoboken, NJ: Wiley.

Byrd, E. T., Bosley, H. E., & Dronberger, M. G. (2009). Comparisons of stakeholder perceptions of tourism impacts in rural eastern North Carolina. *Tourism Management*, *30*(5), 693–703. doi:10.1016/j.tourman.2008.10.021

Cabral Vieira, J. A. (2005). Skill Mismatches And Job Satisfaction. *Economics Letters*, *89*(1), 39–47. doi:10.1016/j.econlet.2005.05.009

Cai, C., & Clacher, I. (2009). Chinese Investment Goes Global: The China Investment Corporation. Journal of Financial Regulation and Compliance, 17(1), 9-15.

Calderon, C., & Chong, A. (2001). External sector and income inequality in interdependent economies using a dynamic panel data approach. *Economics Letters, 71*(2), 225–231. doi:10.1016/S0165-1765(01)00374-3

Caleiras, J. M. A. (2011). *Para além dos números — as consequências pessoais do desemprego* (PhD Thesis). Faculty of Economics of Coimbra, University of Coimbra, Portugal.

Caleiro, A. (2011). *Desemprego e Felicidade em Portugal.* Working Papers no. 2011_05, Department of Economics & CEFAGE-UE, University of Évora, Portugal.

Campagnolo, D., & Gianecchini, M. (2015). *Oltre le ragioni: tempi e distanza nei processi di reshoring delle imprese italiane*. Padova: Padova University Press.

Can, M. & Doğan, B. (2016). Küreselleşme ve enerji tüketimi ilişkisi: Türkiye örnekleminde eşbütünleşme analizi. *Maliye Dergisi, 170.*

Canan, P., & Hennessy, M. (1989). The growth machine, tourism and the selling of culture. *Sociological Perspectives, 32*(2), 227–243. doi:10.2307/1389099

Cangizbay, K. (2003). *Sosyalizm ve Özyönetim: Reel Sosyalizmden Sosyalist Realiteye*. Ankara: Ütopya Yayınevi.

Can, M., & Dogan, B. (2017). The effects of economic structural transformation on employment: An evaluation in the context of economic complexity and product space theory. In F. Yenilmez & E. Kilic (Eds.), *Handbook of research on unemployment and labor market sustainability in the era of globalization* (pp. 275–306). Hershey, PA: IGI Global Publishing. doi:10.4018/978-1-5225-2008-5.ch016

Card, D. (1999). The Causal Effect Of Education On Earnings. In O. Ashenfelter & D. Card (Eds.), *Handbook Of Labour Economics, 3*. Amsterdam: Elsevier. doi:10.1016/S1573-4463(99)03011-4

Carlarne, C. (2014). Delinking International Environmental Law. *Michigan Journal of Environmental & Administrative Law, 4*(1), 1-62. Retrieved on September 25, 2017, from: http://repository.law.umich.edu/mjeal/vol4/iss1/1/

Carrion-I-Silvestre, J. L., & Sanso, A. (2006). Testing the null of cointegration with structural breaks. *Oxford Bulletin of Economics and Statistics, 68*(5), 623–646. doi:10.1111/j.1468-0084.2006.00180.x

Casella, A., & Rauch, J. (2002). 2002, Anonymous market and group ties in international trade. *Journal of International Economics, 58*(1), 19–47. doi:10.1016/S0022-1996(01)00160-X

Castel, R. (1995). *Les Métamorphoses de la Question Social: Une Chronique du Salariat*. Paris: Fayard.

Castilho, M., Menendez, M., & Sztulman, A. (2012). Trade liberalization, inequality, and poverty in Brazilian states. *World Development, 40*(4), 821–835. doi:10.1016/j.worlddev.2011.09.018

Castles, S. (2010, January). 2010, Understanding global migration: A social transformation perspective. *Journal of Ethnic and Migration Studies, 36*(10), 1565–1586. doi:10.1080/1369183X.2010.489381

Castles, S., & Miller, M. (2009). *The age of migration, International population movements in the modern world* (4th ed.). New York: Guildford Press.

Causey, J. E. (2014). *No shock, Milwaukee metro area has the worst segregation*. Retrieved on November 11, 2016, from: http://www.jsonline.com/news/opinion/no-shock-milwaukee-metro-area-has-the-worst-segregation-b99233242z1-252332071.html

CBRT. (2016). *Electronic Data Distribution System, General Statistics, Central Bank of the Turkish Republic*. Retrieved on November 24, 2017, from: http://evds.tcmb.gov.tr/

CCPIT. (2010). *Survey on Current Conditions and Intention of Outbound Investment by Chinese Enterprises*. China Council for the Promotion of International Trade.

Çevre & Komisyonu. (1991). *Ortak Geleceğimiz*. Türkiye Çevre Sorunları Vakfı Yayını, ss. 73-102.

Chadi, A. (2014). Regional unemployment and norm-induced effects on life satisfaction. *Empirical Economics*, *46*(3), 1111–1141. doi:10.100700181-013-0712-7

Chan, C. M., Isobe, T., & Makino, S. (2008). Which country matters? Institutional development and foreign affiliate performance. *Strategic Management Journal*, *29*(11), 1179–1205. doi:10.1002mj.705

Chang, C.-P., Berdiev, A. N., & Lee, C.-C. (2013). Energy exports, globalization and economic growth: The case of South Caucasus. *Economic Modelling*, *33*, 333–346. doi:10.1016/j.econmod.2013.04.027

Chang, C.-P., & Lee, C.-C. (2010). Globalization and Economic Growth: A Political Economy Analysis for OECD Countries. *Global Economic Review*, *39*(2), 151–173. doi:10.1080/1226508X.2010.483835

Chang, C.-P., Lee, C.-C., & Hsieh, M.-C. (2011). Globalization, Real Output and Multiple Structural Breaks. *Global Economic Review*, *40*(4), 421–444. doi:10.1080/1226508X.2011.626154

Chang, C.-P., Lee, C.-C., & Hsieh, M.-C. (2015). Does globalization promote real output? Evidence from quantile cointegration regression. *Economic Modelling*, *44*, 25–36. doi:10.1016/j.econmod.2014.09.018

Chang, J. (2013). *Empress Dowager Cixi: The Concubine Who Launched Modern China*. London: Jonathan Cape.

Chao, M. C.-H., & Kumar, V. (2010). The impact of institutional distance on the international diversity–performance relationship. *Journal of World Business*, *45*(1), 93–103. doi:10.1016/j.jwb.2009.04.005

Chen, D. H. C., & Suh, J. (2007). Introduction. In J. Suh & D. H. C. Chen (Eds.), *Korea as a knowledge economy: Evolutionary process and lessons learned. WBI Development Studies*. Washington, DC: World Bank.

Chirwa, E. W., & Muhome-matita, M. (2013). *Agricultural Growth and Poverty in Rural Malawi*. University of Malawi.

Choi, I. (2015). Panel Cointegration. In B. H. Baltagi (Ed.), *The Oxford Handbook of Panel Data* (pp. 46–75). Oxford, UK: Oxford University Press.

Choudhary, S. (2017). Employee welfare: A scheme of wise investment. *International Journal of Advanced Education and Research*, *2*(1), 1–6.

Christmann, P., Day, D., & Yip, G. S. (2000). The relative influence of country conditions, industry structure, and business strategy on multinational corporation subsidiary performance. *Journal of International Management*, *5*(4), 241–265. doi:10.1016/S1075-4253(99)00015-0

Chung, S. (2010). Innovation, competitiveness and growth: Korean experiences. In J. Y. Lin & B. Pleskovic (Eds.), *Lessons from east asia and the global financial crisis* (pp. 333-358). Annual Word Bank Conference on Development Economics.

Chung, M. (2008). *Shanghaied: Why Foster's Could Not Survive China*. Melbourne: Heidelberg Press.

Chung, M., & Mascitelli, B. (2013). Caught up in the Eurozone Crisis: The Case of Australia and China. *Journal of Modern Accounting and Auditing*, *9*(3), 416–426.

CIVITAS. (2018). Retrieved on January 30, 2018, from: http://www.civitas.eu

Clark, G. L., & Marshall, J. (2002). *Decision-making: models of the real-world and expertise*. Paper presented at National Association of Pension Funds, Edinburgh, UK.

Clark, A. E., & Oswald, A. J. (1994). Unhappiness and Unemployment. *Economic Journal (London), 104*(424), 648–659. doi:10.2307/2234639

Clawson, J. G. (2003). Level three leadership: getting below the surface (3rd ed.). Pearson Prentice Hall.

Clegg, J., & Voss, H. (2012). *Chinese Overseas Direct Investment in the European Union*. Europe China Research and Advice Network.

Coase, R. H. (1937). The Nature Of The Firm. *Economica, 4*(11), 386–405. doi:10.1111/j.1468-0335.1937.tb00002.x

Çoban, A. (2002). *Çevreciliğin İdeolojik Unsurlarının Eklemlenmesi*. Siyasal Bilgiler Fakültesi Dergisi Cilt 57, Sayı 3, ss. 3-30.

Çoban, A. (2013). Çevrecilik., iç. In Gökhan Atılgan & Atilla Aytekin (Eds.), Siyaset Bilimi Kavramlar İdeolojiler Disiplinlerarası İlişkiler. Yordam Yayınları, İstanbul, ss. 455-473.

Cohen-Charash, Y., & Spector, P. E. (2001). The role of justice in organizations: A meta-analysis. *Organizational Behavior and Human Decision Processes, 86*(2), 278–321. doi:10.1006/obhd.2001.2958

Collins, J. (2005). *Good to great and the social sector*. New York: Harper Business.

CONCERTO. (2017). Retrieved on November 11, 2017, from: http://concerto.eu/concerto/

Congress Library. (2014). *Recognising the People's Republic of China: The experience of Japan, Australia, France and West Germany*. Reprint from the collection of the University of Michigan Library, USA.

Cornia, G. (1999). *Liberalisation, globalization and income distribution, UNU world institute for development economics research*. Helsinki, Finland: UNU/WIDER.

Corporation, C. N. A. (2007). *National Security and the Threat of Climate Change*. Retrieved on September 22, 2017, from: http://www.npr.org/documents/2007/apr/security_climate.pdf

Covenant of Mayors. (2017). Retrieved on September 23, 2017, from: http://www.covenantofmayors.eu/index_en.html

Current Legal Challenges in Climate Change Justice. (2014). *Achieving Justice and Human Rights in an Era of Climate Disruption*. London: International Bar Association. Retrieved on September 28, 2017, from: https://www.ibanet.org/PresidentialTaskForceClimateChangeJustice2014Report.aspx

Da Fonseca, A. F. (2004). A ciência em busca da verdadeira felicidade! *FidelidadESPÍRITA Magazine*, 18.

Da Silva, R. B. C. (2011). *Valores e Felicidade no século XXI: um retrato sociológico dos Portugueses em comparação europeia* (PhD Thesis). Sociology Department, University Institute of Lisbon, Portugal.

Dabour, N. (2000). The role of foreign direct investment (FDI) in development and growth in OIC member countries. *Journal of Economic Cooperation, 21*(3), 27–55.

Dai, L. (2006). Chapter 1 From conventional technology to carbon nanotechnology: The fourth industrial revolution and the discoveries of C60, carbon nanotube and nanodiamond. In Carbon Nanotechnology. Elsevier B.V.

Dao, V., Langella, I., & Carbo, J. (2011). From green to sustainability: Information Technology and an integrated sustainability framework. *The Journal of Strategic Information Systems, 20*(1), 63–79. doi:10.1016/j.jsis.2011.01.002

Davies, B. (2015). *Internet of everything - Powering the smart campus & the smart city*. Armonk, NY: IBM Institute for Business Value.

Davis, D., Allen, J., & Cosenza, R. M. (1988). Segmenting local residents by their attitudes, interests and opinions toward tourism. *Journal of Travel Research, 27*(2), 2–8. doi:10.1177/004728758802700201

Davis, P. S., Desai, A. B., & Francis, J. D. (2000). Mode of international entry: An isomorphism perspective. *Journal of International Business Studies, 31*(2), 239–258. doi:10.1057/palgrave.jibs.8490904

de Groot, R. S., Wilson, M. A., & Boumans, R. M. (2002). A typology for the classification, description and valuation of ecosystem functions, goods and services. *Ecological Economics, 41*(3), 393–408. doi:10.1016/S0921-8009(02)00089-7

De Long, J. B. (1988). Productivity Growth, Convergence, and Welfare. *The American Economic Review, 78*(5), 1138–1154.

De Pinto, M. (2014, January). International Trade and Unemployment – the Worker-selection Effect. *Review of International Economics*. Retrieve on September 2, 2016, from: http://ideas.repec.org/p/mar/magkse/201127.html

De Rosario, A., Martín, A., Pérez, M., & Martínez, A. (2013). *Are the Smart Cities the most democratic?: The Spanish Case. EGPA Annu. Conf.*, Edinburgh, UK.

De Villiers-Scheepers, M. (2012). Antecedents of strategic corporate entrepreneurship. *European Business Review, 24*(5), 400–424. doi:10.1108/09555341211254508

Deakin, M. (2014). Smart cities: The state-of-the-art and governance challenge. *Triple Helix, 1*(7), 1–16.

Deininger, K., & Squire, L. (1998). New ways of looking at old ideas: Inequality and growth. *Journal of Development Economics, 57*(2), 259–287. doi:10.1016/S0304-3878(98)00099-6

Del Chiappa, G., Lorenzo-Romero, C., & Gallarza, M. (2016a). Host community perceptions of cruise tourism in a homeport: A cluster analysis. *Journal of Destination Marketing & Management*. doi:10.1016/j.jdmm.2016.08.011

Del Chiappa, G., Presenza, A., & Yücelen, M. (2016b). Profiling residents based on their perceptions and attitude toward sport event: Insights from the FIA world rally championship. *Tourismos, 11*(5), 26–51.

Demazière, D. (2006). *Uma abordagem sociológica sobre a categoria desemprego in: desemprego, trajectórias, identidade, mobilizações*. São Paulo: SENAC, Work and Society Series.

Demirkan, H., Goul, M., & Gros, M. (2010). A Reference Model for Sustainable E-Learning Service Systems:Experiences with the Joint University/Teradata Consortium. *Decision Sciences Journal of Innovative Education, 8*(1), 151–189. doi:10.1111/j.1540-4609.2009.00250.x

Denis, H. (2000). *História do Pensamento Económico*. Lisbon: Horizonte.

Denvir, D. (2011). *The ten most segregated urban area in America*. Retrieved on June 2, 2015, from: http://www.salon.com/2011/03/29/most_segregated_cities/slide_show/10

Desjardins, R., & Rubenson, K. (2011). *An Analysis of Skill. Mismatch Using Direct Measures of Skills*. OECD Education. Working Papers, No. 63. Paris: OECD Publishing.

Desroches, B., Francis, M., & Painchaud, F. (2006). Growth and Integration: The Emergence of China and India and the Implications for Canada. *ASSA Conference Paper*.

Deutsche Bank. (2017). *China 2018 outlook – Striving for a new growth model*. Retrieved from https://www.db.com/newsroom_news/2017/china-2018-outlook-striving-for-a-new-growth-model-en-11744.htm

Diakoulaki, D., Mavrotas, G., & Papayannakis, L. (1995). Determining objective weights in multiple criteria problems: The critic method. *Computers & Operations Research, 22*(7), 763–770. doi:10.1016/0305-0548(94)00059-H

Díaz-Díaz, R., Muñoz, L., & Pérez-González, D. (2017). Business model analysis of public services operating in the smart city ecosystem: The case of SmartSantander. *Future Generation Computer Systems, 76*, 198–214. doi:10.1016/j.future.2017.01.032

Dieguez, T., & Fonseca, J. (2016). Sustainable Entrepreneurship Lab, II. *Jornadas de Educação para o Empreendedorismo em Portugal*, 281-294.

Diener, E., & Suh, E. (1999). National differences in subjective well-being. In D. Kahneman, E. Diener, & N. Schwarz (Eds.), Well-being: The Foundations of Hedonic Psychology. New York: Russel Sage Foundation.

Diener, E., Diener, M., & Diner, C. (1995). Factors predicting the subjective well-being of nations. *Journal of Personality and Social Psychology, 69*.

Diener, E., Weiting, N., Harter, J., & Arora, R. (2010). Wealth and happiness across the world: Material prosperity predicts life evaluation, whereas psychosocial prosperity predicts positive feeling. American Psychological Association.

Diener, E. (2000). Subjective wellbeing: The science of happiness a proposal for a national index. *The American Psychologist, 55*(1), 34–43. doi:10.1037/0003-066X.55.1.34 PMID:11392863

Diener, E., & Lucas, R. (1999). *Personality and subjective well*-being. In D. Kahneman, E. Diener, & N. Schwarz (Eds.), *Well-being: The Foundations of Hedonic Psychology*. New York: Russel Sage Foundation.

Dirlik, A. (2012). *Küreselleşmenin Sonu mu? (çev. İ. Kovacı ve V. Batmaz)*. İstanbul: Ayrıntı Yayınları.

Dluhosch, B. (1998). Globalization and European labor markets. *CEPR Discussion Paper No. 1992.*

Doğan, B. & Can, M. (2016). Küreselleşmenin büyümeye etkisi: Güney Kore örnekleminde eşbütünleşme analizi. *Çankırı Karatekin Üniversitesi İktisadi ve İdari Bilimler Fakültesi Dergisi, 6*(2), 197-220.

Dollar, D., & Kraay, A. (2004). Trade, growth and poverty. *Economic Journal (London), 114*(493), F22–F49. doi:10.1111/j.0013-0133.2004.00186.x

Donnellan, B., Sheridan, C., & Curry, E. (2011). A Capability Maturity Framework for Sustainable Information and Communication Technology. *IT Professional, 13*(1), 33–40. doi:10.1109/MITP.2011.2

Donohoe, H. M. (2011). Defining culturally sensitive ecotourism: A Delphi consensus. *Current Issues in Tourism, 14*(1), 27–45. doi:10.1080/13683500903440689

Dornelas, A., Ministro, A., Ribeiro Lopes, F., Albuquerque, J. L., Paixão, M., & Santos, N. C. (2011). *Emprego, Contratação Colectiva de Trabalho e Protecção da Mobilidade Profissional em Portugal*. Portugal's Office of Strategy and Planning, Ministry of Labour and Social Solidarity.

Doxey, G. V. (1975). A causation theory of visitor-resident irritants: methodology and research inferences. *Conference Proceedings: Sixth Annual Conference of Travel and Tourism Research Association*, 195-198.

Doz, Y. L., & Prahalad, C. K. (1991). Managing DMNCs: A search for a new paradigm. *Strategic Management Journal, 12*(S1), 145–164. doi:10.1002mj.4250120911

Dreher, A. (2006). Does globalization affect growth? Evidence from a new index of globalization. *Applied Economics, 38*(10), 1091–1110. doi:10.1080/00036840500392078

Dreher, A., & Gaston, N. (2008). Has globalization increased inequality? *Review of International Economics*, *16*(3), 516–536. doi:10.1111/j.1467-9396.2008.00743.x

Dreher, A., Gaston, N., & Martens, P. (2008). *Measuring Globalization - Gauging its Consequences*. New York, NY: Springer.

Dreher, A., Gaston, N., & Martens, P. (2008). *Measuring globalization-gauging its consequences*. New York: Springer.

Dressen, E. (2009). *Sustainability and business: A narrative and annotated bibliography*. Retrieved on August 5, 2011, from: http: //www. web.ncf.ca/ct976

Drimie, S. (2003). HIV/AIDS and land. Case studies from Kenya, Lesotho and South Africa. *Development Southern Africa*, *20*(5), 647–658. doi:10.1080/0376835032000149289

Dryzek, J. (2013). *The Politics of the Earth: Environmental Discourses* (3rd ed.). London: Oxford University Press.

Dumenil, G. (1980). *De la valeur aux prix de production*. Paris: Economica.

Dumenil, G. (1983-84). Beyond the transformation riddle: A labor theory of value. *Science and Society*, *47*(4), 427–450.

Dunn, E. W., Gilbert, D. T., & Wilson, T. D. (2011). If money doesn't make you happy, then you probably aren't spending it right. *Journal of Consumer Psychology*. Retrieved on June, 2014, from http://www.wjh.harvard.edu/~dtg/DUNN%20 GILBERT%20&%20WILSON%20(2011).pdf

Dunning, J. H. (1980). Towards an eclectic theory of international production: Some empirical tests. *Journal of International Business Studies*, *11*(1), 9–31. doi:10.1057/palgrave.jibs.8490593

Dunning, J. H. (2000). The eclectic paradigm as an envelope for economic and business theories of MNE activity. *International Business Review*, *9*(2), 163–190. doi:10.1016/S0969-5931(99)00035-9

Duygu, A. E. (2004). AB'nin enerji bağimsizliği ve sürdürülebilir kalkinma politikalarinda biyokütle enerjisinin yeri: Üye, aday ülkelerdeki araştirmalar ve uygulamalar. *Türkiye IV: Enerji Sempozyumu*, 451-480.

Dyer, J., Gregersen, H., & Christensen, C. M. (2012). *The Innovator's DNA: Mastering the Five Skill of Disruptive Innovators*. Boston: Harvard Business Review Press.

Easterly, W., & Levine, R. (2001). *It's Not Factor Accumulation: Stylized Facts and Growth Models*. Central Bank of Chile, Working Papers, No:164.

Easterly, W., & Levine, R. (2001). *It's Not Factor Accumulation: Stylized Facts and Growth Models. The World Bank Economic Review*. Oxford University Press; doi:10.2307/3990260

Easterly, W., & Levine, R. (2003). Tropics, germs, and crops: How endowments influence economic development. *Journal of Monetary Economics*, *50*(1), 3–39. doi:10.1016/S0304-3932(02)00200-3

Ecevit, E., Yücel, A. G., & Yücel, Ö. (2016). Are Some Taxes Better than Others for Economic Growth? An ARDL Approach for Turkey. *The Empirical Economics Letters.*, *15*(11), 1129–1136.

Eden, L., & Miller, S. R. (2004). Distance matters: Liability of foreignness, institutional distance and ownership strategy. *Advances in International Management*, *16*, 187–221. doi:10.1016/S0747-7929(04)16010-1

Edwards, S. (1998). Openness, Productivity and Growth: What Do We Really Know? *Economic Journal (London)*, *108*(447), 383–398. doi:10.1111/1468-0297.00293

EESI. (2016). *Fossil Fuels*. Retrieved on January 10, 2017, from: http://www.eesi.org/topics/fossil-fuels/description

EİA. (2016). *What are greenhouse gases and how do they affect the climate*? Retrieved on January 10, 2017, from: https://www.eia.gov/tools/faqs/faq.cfm?id=81&t=11

Eichhorn, J. (2013). Unemployment needs context: How societal differences between countries moderate the loss in life-satisfaction for the unemployed. *Journal of Happiness Studies, 14*(6), 1657–1680. doi:10.100710902-012-9402-y

Elghali, L., Clift, R., Sinclair, P., Panoutsou, C., & Bauen, A. (2007). Developing a sustainability framework for the assessment of bioenergy systems. *Energy Policy, 35*(12), 6075–6083. doi:10.1016/j.enpol.2007.08.036

Ellerman, A. D., Jacoby, H. D., & Decaux, A. (1998). *The Effects on Developing Countries of the Kyoto Protocol and Carbon Dioxide Emissions Trading* (Policy Research Working Papers). The World Bank. 10.1596/1813-9450-2019

Emale, J. M. (2010). An examination of how conglomerates impact small-medium enterprises in their relationship. *Dissertation Abstracts International, 71*(5), 138A. (UMI No. 3407430)

EMRB. (2017). *Electricity Market Sector Report*. Energy Market Regulatory Board, Ankara, Turkey. Retrieved on June 2, 2017, from: http://www.epdk.org.tr/TR/Dokumanlar/Elektrik/YayinlarRaporlar/AylikSektor

Erdoğan, N. (2003). *Çevre ve (Eko)turizm*. Ankara: Erk Yayıncılık.

Erdoğdu, E. (2009). On the wind energy in Turkey. *Renewable & Sustainable Energy Reviews, 13*(6-7), 1361–1371. doi:10.1016/j.rser.2008.09.003

Erdoğdu, M., & Karaca, C. (2016). An Industrial Policy Recommendation for Raising Solar Energy Investments. In *Turkey and Its Possible Employment Effect", in Social and Economic Perspectives on Sustainability* (pp. 51–70). London: IJOPEC Publication.

Erik, P., Hoffmann, E., Laird, R. F., & Fleron, F. (1991). *Soviet Foreign Policy: Classic Issues in Soviet Foreign Policy: From Lenin to Brezhnev*. Transaction Publishers.

Ernst & Young. (2014). *Financial report 30 June 2014 (and interim financial report for the half-year ended 31 December 2014). Endeavour Managed Investment Scheme*. Retrieved on November 13, 2017, from: http://www.ey.com/Publication/vwLUAssets/EY-endeavour-managed-investment-scheme/$FILE/ey-endeavour-mis-2014.pdf

Eroğlu, Ö., & Albeni, M. (2002). *Küreselleşme, ekonomik krizler ve Türkiye*. Isparta: Bilim Kitabevi.

Esping-Andersen, G. (1996). After the Golden Age? Welfare State Dilemmas in a Global Economy. In G. Esping-Andersen (Ed.), *Welfare States in Transition. National Adaptations in Global Economies*. London: Sage. doi:10.4135/9781446216941.n1

Esteva, G. (2007). Kalkınma. Çev. Oktay Etiman, iç. Sachs, Wolsgangs (ed.), Kalkınma Sözlüğü Bir İktidar Olarak Bilgiye Giriş, Özgür Üniversite Yayınları, Ankara, ss. 17-50.

European Communities. (2003). *Using Natural and Cultural Heritage to Develop Sustainable Tourism*. Luxembourg: Office for Official Publications of The Europian Communities.

Eurostat. (2014). *Foreign Direct Investment*. Retrieved from http://ec.europa.eu/eurostat/web/-structural-business-statistics/global-value-chains/fdi

Evans, G. H. Jr. (1949). The entrepreneur and economic theory: A historical and analytical approach. *The American Economic Review, 39*, 336–348. Retrieved from http://www. AEAweb.org

Evans, T. R. (1993). *Resident's perceptions of tourism in selected New Zealand communities: a segmentation study (Master's dissertation)*. Dunedin: Dept. of Commerce, University of Otago.

EWEA. (2008a). Wind Energy Facts. *Environmental Issues*, 307-411. Retrieved on January 10, 2017, from: http://www.wind-energy-the-facts.org/images/chapter5.pdf

Feenstra, R., & Hanson, G. (1997). Foreign direct investment and relative wages: Evidence from Mexico's maquiladoras. *Journal of International Economics*, *42*(3-4), 371–393. doi:10.1016/S0022-1996(96)01475-4

Feld, C. S., & Stoddard, D. B. (2004). Getting IT Right. *Harvard Business Review*. Retrieved on December 12, 2013, from: http://www.scopus.com/inward/record.url?eid=2-s2.0-1542320698&partnerID=tZOtx3y1

Felstead, A. (2007). *How "smart" are Scottish jobs? Summary evidence from the Skills Surveys, 1997-2006*. Glasgow, UK: Futureskills Scotland Expert Briefing.

Fennell, D., & Dowling, R. K. (Eds.). (2003). *Ecotourism Policy and Planning*. Wallingford: CABI Publishing. doi:10.1079/9780851996097.0000

Fennell, D., & Weaver, D. (2005). The ecotourium concept and tourism-conservation symbiosis. *Journal of Sustainable Tourism*, *13*(4), 373–390. doi:10.1080/09669580508668563

Ferrari, F. (2015). *'Re-Shoring' and Skill Mismatch. Training Needs Analysis in School-to-Work Transition*. Paper to the 27th Annual Meeting of the Society for the Advancement of Socio-Economics, London School of Economics and Political Science, London, UK.

Ferrari, F. (2015a). *The back-shoring process and its impact on Human Resources Management practices. First empirical evidence and some issues for the future research agenda'*. Paper for the AIB Conference 'Breaking up the global value chain: Possibilities and consequences', Milano, Italy.

Ferrari, F. (2015b). *Knowledge Sharing in Family Business Transmission. Bad News From Italian SMEs*. Paper to the International Conference on Organizational Knowledge, Learning and Capabilities (OLKC), Milan, Italy.

Ferrari, F., & Emiliani, E. (2009). *Le Competenze E Il Mercato Del Lavoro. Un'analisi Dei Fabbisogni Formativi Tra Scuola E Impresa*. Roma: Carocci.

Ferreira, A., Demutti, C. M., & Gimenez, P. (2010). *A Teoria das Necessidades de Maslow: A Influência do Nível Educacional Sobre a sua Percepção no Ambiente de Trabalho*. In the XIII Seminar in Administration.

Fields, G. S. (1989). Changes in poverty and inequality in developing countries. *The World Bank Research Observer*, *4*(2), 167–185. doi:10.1093/wbro/4.2.167

Figini, P., & Gorg, H. (1999). Multinational companies and wage inequality in the hostcountry: The case of Ireland. *Weltwirtschaftliches Archive. Review of World Economics*, *135*(4), 135–145.

Fine, B., Saad-Filho, A., & Lapavitsas, C. (2004). Transforming the Transformation Problem: Why the 'New Interpretation' is a Wrong Turning. *The Review of Radical Political Economics*, *36*(1), 3–19. doi:10.1177/0486613403261091

Firebaugh, G., & Beck, F. (1994). Does economic growth benefit the masses? Growth, dependence, and welfare in the third world. *American Sociological Review*, *59*(5), 631–653. doi:10.2307/2096441

Fischer, M. M. (2011). A spatial Mankiw–Romer–Weil model: Theory and evidence. *The Annals of Regional Science*, *47*(2), 419–436. doi:10.100700168-010-0384-6

Fischhoff, B. (1994). What forecasts (seem to) mean. *International Journal of Forecasting*, *10*(3), 387–403. doi:10.1016/0169-2070(94)90069-8

Foley, T., & Zimmer, B. (2014, July 10). How to fix our cities. *CNN*. Retrieved on May 9, 2017, from: http://www.cnn.com/2014/07/10/opinion/foley-zimmer-fix-cities/

Foley, D. (1982). The value of money, the value of labor power and the Marxian transformation problem. *The Review of Radical Political Economics*, *14*(2), 37–47. doi:10.1177/048661348201400204

Foster, J. B. (2006). *Ekolojik Devrimi Örgütlemek*, iç. Ekolojik Felaket. *Özgür Üniversite Forumu Dergisi*, Ankara, ss. 99-108.

Foth, M., Hudson-Smith, A., & Gifford, D. (2016). *Smart cities, social capital, and citizens at play: A critique and a way forward.* Research Handbook on Digital Transformations.

Foxon, T. J. (2011). A co-evolutionary framework for analysing a transition to a sustainable low carbon economy. *Ecological Economics*, *70*(12), 2258–2267. doi:10.1016/j.ecolecon.2011.07.014

Frankauser, S. (2009). *The costs of adaptation.* Grantham Research Institute and Centre for Climate Change Economics and Policy. London: London School of Economics. Retrieved on September 17, 2017, from: http://www.lse.ac.uk/GranthamInstitute/wp-content/uploads/2014/02/WorkingPaper7.pdf

Frankel, J. A., & Romer, D. (1999). Does Trade Cause Growth? *The American Economic Review*, *89*(3), 379–399. doi:10.1257/aer.89.3.379

Fratocchi, L., Di Mauro, C., Barbieri, P., Nassimbeni, G., & Zanoni, A. (2014). When manufacturing moves back: Concepts and questions. *Journal of Purchasing and Supply Management*, *20*(1), 54–59. doi:10.1016/j.pursup.2014.01.004

Fredline, E., & Faulkner, B. (2000). Host community reactions: A cluster analysis. *Annals of Tourism Research*, *27*(3), 763–784. doi:10.1016/S0160-7383(99)00103-6

Fredline, L., Deery, M., & Jago, L. (2013). A longitudinal study of the impacts of an annual event on local residents. *Tourism Planning & Development*, *10*(4), 416–432. doi:10.1080/21568316.2013.779314

Freeman, A. (1996). The psychopathology of Walrasian Marxism. In Marx and Non-Equilibrium Economics. Cheltenham, UK: Edward Elgar.

Frei, T. (2009). Economic and Social Benefits of Meteorology and Climatology in Switzerland. *Meteorological Applications*, n/a. doi:10.1002/met.156

Frey, B. S., & Stutzer, A. (2002). What can economists learn from happiness research? *Journal of Economic Literature*, *40*(3).

Freyssinet, J. (1984). *Le Chômage*. Paris: La Découverte.

Frleta, D. S. (2014). Island destinations' tourism offer-tourists' vs. residents' attitudes. *Tourism and Hospitality Management*, *20*(1), 1–14.

Gaglio, C. (2017). Trade Liberalization and Export Performance: A Literature Review. *Revue d'Economie Politique*, *127*(1), 25–46. doi:10.3917/redp.271.0025

Gallo, C., Faccilongo, N., & Sala, P. (2017). Clustering analysis of environmental emissions: A study on Kyoto Protocol's impact on member countries. *Journal of Cleaner Production*. doi:10.1016/J.JCLEPRO.2017.07.194

Garau, J. B., Díaz, R. J., & Gutiérrez, D. (2014). Residents' perceptions of tourism impacts on island destinations: A comparative analysis. *International Journal of Tourism Research*, *16*(6), 578–585. doi:10.1002/jtr.1951

Gardner, N., & Hespanhol, L. (2017). *SMLXL: Scaling the smart city, from metropolis to individual.* City, Culture and Society.

Garifova, L. F. (2015). Infonomics and The Value of Information in The Digital Economy. *Procedia Economics and Finance 23*, 738–743. 10.1016/S2212-5671(15)00423-2

Gathmann & Schönberg. (2010). How General Is Human Capital? A Task-Based Approach. *IZA DP No. 3067.*

Gaur, A. S., & Lu, J. W. (2007). Ownership strategies and survival of foreign subsidiaries: Impacts of institutional distance and experience. *Journal of Management, 33*(1), 84–110. doi:10.1177/0149206306295203

Gautié, J. (1998). *Coût du Travail et Emploi*. Paris: La Découverte.

Gee, D. J. (2014, October 26). Millennials embrace our renaissance. *Buffalo News*. Retrieved on October 7, 2017, from: http://www.buffalonews.com/columns/denise-jewell-gee/millennials-embrace-our-renaissance-20141026Millennials embrace our renaissance

Gee, J., Loewenthal, D., & Cayne, J. (2013). Phenomenological research: The case of Empirical Phenomenological Analysis and the possibility of reverie. *Counselling Psychology Review, 28*(3), 52–62.

George, G., & Zahra, S. A. (2002). Culture and its consequences for entrepreneurship. *Entrepreneurship: Theory and Practice*. Retrieved on March 2, 2017, from: http://www. Entrepreneur.com/trade journals/article/91971828_1.html

Giddens, A. (2004). *Sociologia*. Lisbon: Calouste Gulbenkian Foundation.

Giese, K. (2003). New Chinese Migration to Germany: Historical Consistencies and New Patterns of Diversification within a Globalized Migration Regime. *International Migration (Geneva, Switzerland), 41*(3), 155–182. doi:10.1111/1468-2435.00245

Giffinger, R., & Pichler-Milanović, N. (2007). *Smart Cities: Ranking of European Medium-Sized Cities*. Academic Press.

Global Carbon Project. (n.d.). *Carbon Budget 2017*. Retrieved on November 20, 2017, from: http://www.globalcarbon-project.org/carbonbudget/index.htm

Global Entrepreneurship Monitor (GEM). (2015). *Executive Report*. Retrieved on February 7, 2017, from: http://www.gemconsortium.org/download/1300236130815/GEM_Global_15.pdf

Global Entrepreneurship Monitor (GEM). (2016). *2016 Global Report*. Retrieved on February 7, 2017, from: http://www.gemconsortium.org/report/49812

Goklany, I. M. (2007). Integrated strategies to reduce vulnerability and advance adaptation, mitigation and sustainable development. *Mitigation and Adaptation Strategies for Global Change*. Retrieved on September 20, 2017, from: http://citeseerx.ist.psu.edu/viewdoc/download?doi=10.1.1.167.857&rep=rep1&type=pdf

Goldberg-Koujianou, P., & Pavcnik, N. (2007). Distributional effects of globalization in developing countries. *Journal of Economic Literature, 45*(1), 39–82. doi:10.1257/jel.45.1.39

Gómez, A. M. M., González, F. A., & Bárcena, M. M. (2017). Smart eco-industrial parks: A circular economy implementation based on industrial metabolism. *Resources, Conservation and Recycling, xxx*, xxx–xxx.

Gon, M., Osti, L., & Pechlaner, H. (2016). Leisure boat tourism: Residents' attitudes towards nautical tourism development. *Tourism Review, 71*(3), 180–191. doi:10.1108/TR-07-2016-0025

Gordon, D. (2006). *The concept and measurement of poverty. In Poverty and Social Exclusion in Britain*. London: The Policy Press.

Görez, T., & Alkan, A. (2005). *Türkiye'nin Yenilenebilir Enerji Kaynakları ve Hidroelektrik Enerji Potansiyeli, III*. Mersin: Yenilenebilir Enerji Kaynakları Sempozyumu.

Gorz, A. (1988). *Métamorphoses du Travail: Quête du Sens. Critique de la Raison Économique*. Paris: Galilée.

Gourdon, J., Monjon, S., & Poncet, S. (2016). Trade policy and industrial policy in China: What motivates public authorities to apply restrictions on exports? *China Economic Review*, *40*, 105–120. doi:10.1016/j.chieco.2016.06.004

Government of Kenya (2014). *Homabay County Annual Report*. Author.

Government of Kenya. (2003). *Interim Poverty Reduction Strategy Paper 2002-2003*. Nairobi, Kenya: Author.

Government of Kenya. (2007). Kenya Vision 2030. Nairobi: Ministry of Planning, National Development and Vision 2030.

Government of Kenya. (2010). *Rachuonyo District Annual Report*. Nairobi: Government printers.

Gozgor, G., & Ranjan, P. (2017). Globalization, inequality, and redistribution: Theory and evidence. *World Economy*, *40*(12), 2704–2751. doi:10.1111/twec.12518

Graham, G. (2016). Smart cities and operations management. *Production Planning and Control*, *27*(6), 431–432. doi:10.1080/09537287.2016.1147100

Granger, C., & Newbold, P. (1974). Spurious regressions in econometrics. *Journal of Econometrics*, *2*(2), 111–120. doi:10.1016/0304-4076(74)90034-7

Green Digital Charter. (2015). Retrieved on February 20, 2016, from: http://www.greendigitalcharter.eu

Green, F., & Mcintosh, S. (2002). *Is There A Genuine Underutilization Of Skills Amongst The Over-Qualified?* Skope Research Paper, 30.

Greenaway, D., Morgan, W., & Wright, P. (2002). Trade liberalisation and growth in developing countries. *Journal of Development Economics*, *67*(1), 229–244. doi:10.1016/S0304-3878(01)00185-7

Green, F., & Mcintosh, S. (2007). Is There A Genuine Underutilization Of Skills Amongst The Over-Qualified? *Applied Economics*, *39*(4), 427–439. doi:10.1080/00036840500427700

Gregory, A. W., & Hansen, B. E. (1996). Residual-based tests for cointegration in models with regime shifts. *Journal of Econometrics*, *70*(1), 99–126. doi:10.1016/0304-4076(69)41685-7

Grier, K. B., & Tullock, G. (1989). An empirical analysis of cross-national economic growth, 1951–1980. *Journal of Monetary Economics*, *24*(2), 259–276. doi:10.1016/0304-3932(89)90006-8

Grimaldi, D., & Fernandez, V. (2017). The alignment of University curricula with the building of a Smart City: A case study from Barcelona. *Technological Forecasting and Social Change*, *123*, 298–306. doi:10.1016/j.techfore.2016.03.011

Grossman, G. M., & Helpman, E. (1991). *Innovation and Growth in the Global Economy*. Cambridge, MA: MIT Press.

Grubb, D. (1996). *Learnings To Work: The Case For Reintegrating Job Training And Education*. New York: Russel Sage Fundation.

Gurda, J. (1999). *The Making of Milwaukee*. Milwaukee, WI: Milwaukee County Historical Society.

Gurgul, H., & Lach, Ł. (2014). Globalization and economic growth: Evidence from two decades of transition in CEE. *Economic Modelling*, *36*, 99–107. doi:10.1016/j.econmod.2013.09.022

Gursoy, D., Chi, C. G., & Dyer, P. (2009). An examination of locals' attitudes. *Annals of Tourism Research*, *36*(4), 715–734. doi:10.1016/j.annals.2009.06.003

Gursoy, D., Chi, C. G., & Dyer, P. (2010). Locals' attitudes toward mass and alternative tourism: The case of Sunshine Coast, Australia. *Journal of Travel Research*, *49*(3), 381–394. doi:10.1177/0047287509346853

Haidine, A., Aqqal, A., & Ouahmane, H. (2016). Evaluation of communications technologies for smart grid as part of smart cities. In *Proceedings of the Mediterranean conference on information & communication technologies 2015* (pp. 277-285). Berlin: Springer. 10.1007/978-3-319-30298-0_29

Hakanson, L., & Ambos, B. (2010). The antecedents of psychic distance. *Journal of International Management*, *16*(3), 195–210. doi:10.1016/j.intman.2010.06.001

Hall, D. T., & Nougaim, K. E. (1968). An examination of Maslow´s need hierarchy in a organizational setting. *Organizational Behavior and Human Performance*, 3.

Hall, A. J., Yoganand, B., Sulaiman, R. V., Rajeswari, R. S., Shambu, P. C., Naik, G. C., & Clark, N. G. (2004). *Innovations in Innovation: Reflections on Partnership, Institutions and Learning*. Patancheru, Andhra Pradesh, India: International Crops Research Institute for the Semi-Arid Tropics.

Hallegatte, S. (2012). *A Cost-Effective Solution to Reduce Disaster Losses in Developing Countries: Hydrometeorological Services, Early Warning, and Evacuation*. Policy Research Working Paper Series 6058. Washington, DC: The World Bank.

Hallegatte, S., Bangalore, L., Bonzanigo, M., Fay, T., Kane, U., Narloch, J., … Vogt-Schilb, A. (2015). *Shock Waves: Managing the Impacts of Climate Change on Poverty*. Climate Change and Development Series. Washington, DC: World Bank. doi:.10.1596/978-1-4648-0673-5

Hall, R. E., & Jones, C. I. (1999). *Why Do Some Countries Produce So Much More Output Per Worker Than Others? The Quarterly Journal of Economics*. doi:10.3386/w6564

Hall, S., & Foxon, T. J. (2014). Values in the Smart Grid: The co-evolving political economy of smart distribution. *Energy Policy*, *74*, 600–609. doi:10.1016/j.enpol.2014.08.018

Hamlet, A. F., Huppert, D., & Lettenmaier, D. P. (2002). Economic Value of Long-lead Streamflow Forecasts for Columbia River hydropower. *Journal of Water Resources Planning and Management*, *128*(2), 91–101. doi:10.1061/(ASCE)0733-9496(2002)128:2(91)

Hamlyn, O. (2015). Sustainability and the Failure of Ambition in European Pesticides Regulation. *Journal of Environmental Law*, *0*, 1–25. Retrieved from http://discovery.ucl.ac.uk/1469006/7/Sustainability%20and%20the%20Failure%20of%20Ambition%20in%20European%20Pesticides%20Regulation.pdf

Hanson, G., & Harrinson, A. (1999). Trade and wage inequality in Mexico. *Industrial & Labor Relations Review*, *52*(2), 271–288. doi:10.1177/001979399905200207

Harding, R. (2006). Entrepreneurs: The world's lifeline? *Business Strategy Review*, *17*(4), 4–7. doi:10.1111/j.0955-6419.2006.00425.x

Harika, V. (2012) *Theories of Labour Welfare*. Retrieved on November 13, 2017, from: http://www.scribd.com/doc/52987735/2/THEORIES-OF-LABOURWELFARE

Harris, M. (2013, November 24). U.S. cities still struggling, but it doesn't seem so dire in Minneapolis. *Minneapolis Post*. Retrieved on May 3, 2016, from: http://www.minnpost.com/cityscape/2013/11/us-cities-still-struggling-it-doesn-t-seem-so-dire-minneapolis

Harris, M. J. (2000). *Sürdürülebilir Kalkınmanın Temel Prensipleri*, Çev. Emine Özmete. Retrieved on March 28, 2015, from: http://www.sdergi.hacettepe.edu.tr/makaleler/EmineOzmet2eviri.pdf

Hartog, J. (2000). Over-Education And Earnings: Where Are We, Where Should Se Go? *Economics of Education Review*, *19*(2), 131–147. doi:10.1016/S0272-7757(99)00050-3

Harvey, D. (2012). Yaratıcı yıkım olarak Neoliberalizm. *Atılım Sosyal Bilimler Dergisi*, *2*(2), 67-88.

Haughton, J., & Khandker, R. S. (2009). *The handbook on poverty and inequality*. Washington, DC: The International Bank for Reconstruction and Development, The World Bank.

Hausmann, R., & Hidalgo, C. A. (2011). The network structure of economic output. *Journal of Economic Growth*, *16*(4), 309–342. doi:10.100710887-011-9071-4

Hausmann, R., Hwang, J., & Rodrik, D. (2007). What you export matters. *Journal of Economic Growth*, *12*(1), 1–25. doi:10.100710887-006-9009-4

Hausmann, R., & Klinger, B. (2006). *The Evolution of Comparative Advantage: The Impact of the Structure of the Product Space. Center for International Development and Kennedy School of Government*. Harvard University.

Hausmann, R., & Rodrik, D. (2003). Economic development as self-discovery. *Journal of Development Economics*, *72*(: 72), 603–633. doi:10.1016/S0304-3878(03)00124-X

Hebert, R. F., & Link, A. N. (2006). Historical perspectives on the entrepreneur. *Foundations and Trends in Entrepreneurship*, *2*(4), 261–408. doi:10.1561/0300000008

Held, D., & Mc Grew, A. (2008). *Küresel dönüşümler büyük küreselleşme tartışması*. Ankara: Phoenix Yayınevi.

Helliwell, J., Layard, R., & Sachs, J. (2017). *World Happiness Report*. Retrieved on September, 2017, from: http://worldhappiness.report/ed/2017/.

Helliwell, J. F. (2006). Well-being, social capital and public policy: What's new? *Economic Journal (London)*, *116*(510), C34–C45. doi:10.1111/j.1468-0297.2006.01074.x

Helliwell, J. F., & Huang, H. (2014). New measures of the costs of unemployment: Evidence from the subjective well-being of 3.3 million Americans. *Economic Inquiry*, *52*(4), 1485–1502. doi:10.1111/ecin.12093

Hellmuth, M. E., Mason, S. J., Vaughan, C., van Aalst, M. K., & Choularton, R. (Eds.). (2011). A Better Climate for Disaster Risk Management. Columbia University.

Henisz, W. J. (2000). The institutional environment for multinational investment. *Journal of Law Economics and Organization*, *16*(2), 334–364. doi:10.1093/jleo/16.2.334

Henisz, W. J., & Zelner, B. A. (2003). The strategic organization of political Challenges and opportunities. *Strategic Organization*, *1*(4), 451–460. doi:10.1177/14761270030014005

Hernández, V., & Nieto, M. J. (2015). The effect of the magnitude and direction of institutional distance on the choice of international entry modes. *Journal of World Business*, *50*(1), 122–132. doi:10.1016/j.jwb.2014.02.002

Hersch, J. (1991). Education Match And Job Match. *The Review of Economics and Statistics*, *73*(1), 140–144. doi:10.2307/2109696

Heshmati, A. (2003). *The relationship between income inequality and globalization*. Retrieved from http://www.soc.iastate.edu/sapp/globalizationoutcomes4.pdf

Heshmati, A. (2004). *The relationship between income inequality, poverty and globalisation*. IZA Discussion Paper No. 1277.

Heshmati, A., & Lee, S. (2010). Human Dimension of Globalization The Relationship Between Globalization, Economic Growth And Income Inequality. *Journal of Globalization Studies*, *1*(2), 87–117. Retrieved from http://www.sociostudies.org/journal/files/jogs/2010_2/the_relationship.pdf

Hespanha, P. (2007). É o desemprego fonte de pobreza? O impacto do desemprego e do mau emprego na pobreza e exclusão social no Distrito de Coimbra. *EAPN Journals*.

Hidalgo, C. A., & Hausmann, R. (2009). The building blocks of economic complexity. *Proceedings of the National Academy of Sciences of the United States of America*, *106*(26), 10570–10575. doi:10.1073/pnas.0900943106 PMID:19549871

Hill, J., & Gale, T. (2009). *Ecotourism and Environmental Sustainability: Principles and Practice*. London: Ashgate Limited Company.

Hilmersson, M., & Jansson, H. (2012). Reducing Uncertainty in the Emerging Market Entry Process: On the Relationship Among International Experiential Knowledge, Institutional Distance, and Uncertainty. *Journal of International Marketing*, *20*(4), 96–110. doi:10.1509/jim.12.0052

Hilty & Lohmann. (2013). An Annotated Bibliography of Conceptual Frameworks in ICT for Sustainability. In *ICT4S 2013: Proceedings of the First International Conference on Information and Communication Technologies for Sustainability, ETH Zurich, February 14-16,2013* (pp. 288–300). Academic Press. 30010.3929/ethz-a-007337628

Hitt, M. A., Ahlstrom, D., Dacin, M. T., Levitas, E., & Svobodina, L. (2004). The institutional effects on strategic alliance partner selection in transition economies: China vs. Russia. *Organization Science*, *15*(2), 173–185. doi:10.1287/orsc.1030.0045

Høgevold, N. M., & Svensson, G. (2012). A business sustainability model: A European case study. *Journal of Business and Industrial Marketing*, *27*(2), 142–151. doi:10.1108/08858621211197001

Hom, E. J. (2014). *What is STEM Education?* Retrieved on May 9, 2015, from: https://www.livescience.com/43296-what-is-stem-education.html

Hoskisson, R. E., Eden, L., Lau, C. M., & Wright, M. (2000). Strategy in emerging economies. *Academy of Management Journal*, *43*(3), 249–267. doi:10.2307/1556394

Hummels, D., & Klenow, P. J. (2004). *The Variety and Quality of a Nation's Exports*. NBER Working Paper, No:8712.

Hunter, C. (1997). Sustainable Tourism as an Adaptive Paradigm. *Annals of Tourism Research*, *24*(4), 850–867. doi:10.1016/S0160-7383(97)00036-4

Hussung, T. (2017, February 10). *7 steps of the decision-making process*. Retrieved on July 22, 2017, from: https://online.csp.edu/blog/business/decision-making-process

Hwang, J. (2006). *Introduction of New Goods, Convergence and Growth*. Harvard University.

IATA. (2014). *Annual Review*. IATA.

İdem, Ş. (2009). *Toplumsal Ekoloji Nedir? Ne Değildir?* Retrieved on March 15, 2013, from: http://ecotopianetwork.wordpress.com/2009/11/17/toplumsal-ekoloji-nedir-ne-degildir-sadi-idem/

IFDC. (2015). *Promoting Agriculture Technology to Improve Productivity and Net Returns for Smallholder Farmers*. Retrieved on September 22, 2016, from: https://ifdc.org/promoting-agriculture-technology-to-improve-productivity-and-net-returns-for-smallholder-farmers/

Im, K. S., Pesaran, M. H., & Shin, Y. (2003). Testing for unit roots in heterogeneous panels. *Journal of Econometrics*, *115*(1), 53–74. doi:10.1016/S0304-4076(03)00092-7

Indiatsy, C. M. (2011). *Comparative analysis on the effects of social welfare facilities on employee motivation in Pan African Papermills and Mumias sugar company.* Doctoral dissertation.

Inmee, B., & Shi, Q. (2016). Impact of economic globalization on income inequality: Devoloped economies and emerging economies. *Global Economy Journal, 16*(1), 49–61.

International Monetary Fund (IMF). (2007a). World economic outlook: Globalization and inequality. Washington, DC: IMF.

International Monetary Fund (IMF). (2007b). *Reaping the benefits of financial globalization.* Retrieved from www.imf.org/extrenal/np/res/docs/2007/0607.htm

International Research Institute for Climate and Society. (2016). The enacts approach: Transforming climate services in Africa one country at a time. IRI Technical Note No. IRI-TR/05/1.

International Telecommunication Union. (2012). *Toolkit on environmental sustainability for the ICT sector.* Retrieved on May 9, 2015, from: http://www.itu.int/dms_pub/itu-t/oth/4B/01/T4B010000060001PDFE.pdf

Intriligator, M. (2004). Globalization of the world economy: Potential benefits and costs and a net assessment. *Journal of Policy Modeling, 26*(4), 485–498. doi:10.1016/j.jpolmod.2004.04.004

IPCC. (1996). Climate Change 1995: Impacts, Adaptations, and Mitigation of Climate Change: Scientific-Technical Analyses. Contribution of Working Group II to the Second Assessment Report of the Intergovernmental Panel on Climate Change. Cambridge, UK: Cambridge University Press.

IPCC. (2001). *Climate Change: Third Assessment Report.* London: Cambridge University Press.

IPCC. (2007). *Climate Change: Synthesis Report, Fourth Assessment Report of the Intergovernmental Panel on Climate Change.* London: Cambridge University Press.

IPCC. (2014). *Climate Change 2014: Impacts, Adaptation, and Vulnerability. Part A: Global and Sectoral Aspects. Contribution of Working Group II to the Fifth Assessment Report of IPCC.* Cambridge, UK: Cambridge University Press.

IPCC. (2014). *Climate Change 2014: Synthesis Report. Contribution of Working Groups I, II and III to the Fifth Assessment Report of the Intergovernmental Panel on Climate Change* (R. K. Pachauri & L. A. Meyer, Eds.). Geneva, Switzerland: IPCC.

IPCC. (2014). *IPCC Working Group III-Mitigation of Climate Change, Annex III: Technology-Specific Cost and Performance Parameters.* Retrieved on May 9, 2017, from: https://www.ipcc.ch/pdf/assessment-report/ar5/wg3/ipcc_wg3_ar5_annex-iii.pdf

Iredale, R. (2001). The Migration of Professionals: Theories and Typologies. *International Migration (Geneva, Switzerland), 39*(5), 7–24. doi:10.1111/1468-2435.00169 PMID:19186395

IRENA. (2016). *Renewable Energy and Jobs Annual Review 2016.* International Renewable Energy Agency. Retrieved on October 1, 2016 from: http://www.irena.org/DocumentDownloads/Publications/IRENA_RE_Jobs_Annual_Review_2016.pdf

IRENA. (2017). *Renewable Energy and Jobs Annual Review 2016.* International Renewable Energy Agency. Retrieved on November 21, 2017 from: http://www.irena.org/-/media/Files/IRENA/Agency/Publication/2017/May/IRENA_RE_Jobs_Annual_Review_2017.ashx

Isfol. (2006). *Organizzazione, Apprendimento, Competenze.* I Libri Del Fse.

Işığıçok, E. (1998). Türkiye'de gelir dağılımı ve 1987-1994 gelir dağılımı araştırmalarının karşılaştırmalı bir analizi. *Uludağ Üniversitesi İ.İ.B.F. Dergisi, 16*(1), 1.

Itoh, M. (1980). *Value and Crisis*. London: Pluto Press.

Ivancevich, J. M. (1969, August). Perceived need satisfactions of domestic versus overseas managers. *Journal of Applied Psychology, 54*.

J. W. O., & Bin Ismail, H. (2008, June 1). *Sustainable Competitive Advantage through Information Technology Competence: Resource-Based View on Small and Medium Enterprises*. Retrieved from http://shdl.mmu.edu.my/2912/

Jahoda, M. (1982). *Employment and unemployment: A social-psychological analysis*. Cambridge, UK: Cambridge University Press.

Jalil, A. (2012). Modeling income inequality and openness in the framework of Kuznets curve: New evidence from China. *Economic Modelling, 29*(2), 309–315. doi:10.1016/j.econmod.2011.10.012

Jameson, F. (2011). *Postmodernizm ya da Geç Kapitalizmin Kültürel Mantığı, Çev. Nuri Plümer, Abdülkadir Gölcü*. Ankara: Nirengi Kitap.

Johanson, J., & Vahlne, J. E. (1977). The internationalization process of the firm-a model of knowledge development and increasing foreign market commitments. *Journal of International Business Studies, 8*(1), 23–32. doi:10.1057/palgrave.jibs.8490676

Johnston, M., Gilmore, A., & Carson, D. (2008). Dealing with environmental uncertainty: The value of scenario planning for small to medium-sized entreprises (SMEs). *European Journal of Marketing, 42*(11/12), 1170–1178. doi:10.1108/03090560810903628

Jones, R. (2010). *Organizational Theory, Design, and Change* (6th ed.). New York: Prentice Hall Pearson Education, Inc.

Jonsson, J. O., Mood, C., & Bihagen, E. (2013). *Income Inequality and Poverty during Economic Recession and Growth*. GINI Discussion Paper 60.

Jorgenson, D., & Schreyer, P. (2015). *Measuring Individual Economic Well-Being and Social Welfare within the Framework of the System of National Accounts*. IARIW-OECD Special Conference. Harvard University and OECD.

Jurowski, C., Uysal, M., & Williams, R. D. (1997). A theoretical analysis of host community resident reactions to tourism. *Journal of Travel Research, 36*(2), 3–11. doi:10.1177/004728759703600202

Kadar, M., Moise, I. A., & Colomba, C. (2014). Innovation Management in the Globalized Digital Society. *Procedia: Social and Behavioral Sciences, 143*, 1083–1089. doi:10.1016/j.sbspro.2014.07.560

Kahneman, D., Diener, E., & Schwarz, N. (1999). *Well-Being: Foundations of Hedonic Psychology*. New York: Russel Sage Foundation.

Kalfagianni, A. (2014). Addressing the Global Sustainability Challenge: The Potential and Pitfalls of Private Governance from the Perspective of Human Capabilities. *Journal of Business Ethics, 122*(2), 307–320. doi:10.100710551-013-1747-6

Kalyuzhnyi, V. V. (2014). *The Transformation Problem: Erroneous Arguments of Tugan-Baranovsky, Bortkiewicz and Steedman*. Retrieved from https://ssrn.com/abstract=2520362

Karaca, C., & Erdoğdu, M. M. (2014). Sustainable Development and Turkey's Biomass Energy Potential. *Global Climate Change, Environment and Energy: Global Challenges and Opportunities to Global Stability*, 133.

Karluk, S. R. (1996). *Türkiye ekonomisi tarihsel gelişim yapısı ve sosyal değişim*. İstanbul: Beta Basım Yayım Dağıtım A.Ş.

Kassiola, J. (2002). Why Environmental Thought and Action Must Include Considerations of Social Justice. In M. Gillroy & J. Bowersox (Eds.), *The Moral Austerity of Environmental Decision Making Sustainability, Democracy, and Normative Argument in Policy and Law*. Duke University Press.

Katseli, L., Lucas, R., & Xenogiani, T. (2006). *Policies for Migration and Development: A European Perspective*. OECD. doi:10.1787/20771681

Kayakutlu, G., & Ercan, S. (2015). Regional Energy Portfolio Construction: Case Studies in Turkey. In *Sustainable Future Energy Technology and Supply Chains* (pp. 107-126). Springer International Publishing.

Kayemuddin, M. D. (2012). Leadership in small business in Bangladesh. *International Journal of Entrepreneurship*, 1625-1635.

Kayıkçı, M. (2012). *Çevre ve Kalkınma Söylemi, Birinci Baskı*. Ankara: Orion Kitabevi.

Kazar, A., & Kazar, G. (2016). International journal of economics and financial issues. *International Journal of Economics and Financial Issues*, *6*(2), 578–587. Retrieved from http://www.econjournals.com/index.php/ijefi/article/view/2125

Keegan, D., Lossenko, J., Mazar, I., Michels, P. F., Paulsen, M. F., & Rekkedal, T. (2007). *E-learning initiatives that did not reach targeted goals (MegaTrends)*. Bekkestua, Norway: NKI Publishing House.

Keleş, R. (1998). *Kent Bilim Terimleri Sözlüğü, İkinci Basım*. Ankara: İmge Yayınları.

Keleş, R., Hamamci, C., & Çoban, A. (2012). *Çevre Politikası*. Ankara: İmge Kitabevi.

Kenny, R., Law, C., & Pearce, J. M. (2010). Towards Real Energy Economics: Energy Policy Driven by Life-Cycle Carbon Emission. *Energy Policy*, *38*(4), 1969–1978. doi:10.1016/j.enpol.2009.11.078

Kenya National Bureau of Statistics. (2015). *Exploring Kenya's Inequality*. Nairobi: Government Printer.

Keohane, R. O., & Nye, J. S. (2000). Introduction. In J. S. Nye & J. D. Donahue (Eds.), Governance in a globalizing world (pp. 1-44). Brookings Institution Press.

Khanna, T., & Palepu, K. (1997). Why focused strategies may be wrong for emerging markets. *Harvard Business Review*, *75*(4), 41–48.

Khanna, T., & Palepu, K. (2000). Is group affiliation profitable in emerging markets? An analysis of diversified Indian business groups. *The Journal of Finance*, *55*(2), 867–891. doi:10.1111/0022-1082.00229

Kiefer, N. M., & Vogelsang, T. J. (2002). Heteroskedasticity-Autocorrelation Robust Standard Errors Using the Bartlett Kernel without Truncation. *Econometrica*, *70*(5), 2093–2095. doi:10.1111/1468-0262.00366

Kimberly, J. W., Thomas, H. T., & James, H. T. (2012). *Small business sustainability: What is the CPA's Role?* Retrieved on January 29, 2016, from: http://www.ijbssnet.com/journals/Vol_3_No_12_Special_ Issue June_2012/1.pdf

King, R. (2012). Toward a new map of migration to Europe. *International Journal of Population Geography, Wiley Interscience*, *8*(2), 89–106. doi:10.1002/ijpg.246

Kinkel, S. (2014). Future and impact of backshoring—Some conclusions from 15 years of research on German practices. *Journal of Purchasing and Supply Management*, *20*(1), 63–65. doi:10.1016/j.pursup.2014.01.005

Kiss, A. N., & Danis, W. M. (2008). Country institutional context, social networks, and new venture internationalization speed. *European Management Journal*, *26*(6), 388–399. doi:10.1016/j.emj.2008.09.001

Kliman, A.J. (2007). *Reclaiming Marx's "Capital". A Refutation of the Myth of Inconsistency.* Lexington Books.

Kliman, A. J., & McGlone, T. (1999). A Temporal Single-system Interpretation of Marx's Value Theory. *Review of Political Economy*, *11*(1), 33–59. doi:10.1080/095382599107165

Kolstad, I., & Wiig, A. (2012). What determines Chinese outward FDI? *Journal of World Business*, *47*(1), 26–34. doi:10.1016/j.jwb.2010.10.017

Koppenjan, J., & Enserink, B. (2009). Public–private partnerships in urban infrastructures: Reconciling private sector participation and sustainability. *Public Administration Review*, *69*(2), 284–296. doi:10.1111/j.1540-6210.2008.01974.x

Kormendi, R. C., & Meguire, P. G. (1985). Macroeconomic determinants of growth: Cross-country evidence. *Journal of Monetary Economics*, *16*(2), 141–163. doi:10.1016/0304-3932(85)90027-3

Kostecki, M. (2014). International Trade and Unemployment: On the Redistribution of Trade Gains When Firms Matter by Marco de Pinto Berlin, Heidelberg: Physica-Verlag (Springer), 2012. *World Trade Review*, *13*(03), 589–591. doi:10.1017/S1474745614000172

Kostova, T. (1999). Transnational transfer of strategic organizational practices: A contextual perspective. *Academy of Management Review*, 308–324.

Kostova, T., & Roth, K. (2002). Adoption of an organizational practice by subsidiaries of multinational corporations: Institutional and relational effects. *Academy of Management Journal*, *45*(1), 215–233. doi:10.2307/3069293

Kostova, T., & Zaheer, S. (1999). Organizational legitimacy under conditions of complexity: The case of the multinational enterprise. *Academy of Management Review*, 64–81.

Koten, M. M. L. (2013). *A Motivação do Trabalho dos Funcionários Públicos do Ministério da Justiça de Timor-Leste* (Master's Thesis). University of Minho, Braga, Portugal.

Kourtit, K., Nijkamp, P., & Steenbruggen, J. (2017). The significance of digital data systems for smart city policy. *Socio-Economic Planning Sciences*, *58*, 13–21. doi:10.1016/j.seps.2016.10.001

Kouzes, J. M., & Posner, B. Z. (2003). *Leadership the challenge* (3rd ed.). San Francisco, CA: Jossey-Bass.

KPMG International. (2012, February 15). Expect the Unexpected: Building Business Value in a Changing world. *KPMG*. Retrieved on December 22, 2017, from: http: //www.kpmg.com/global/en/issuesandinsights/ articlespublications/ages/ buildingbusiness-value.aspx

Krahn, H., & Lowe, G.S. (1998). *Literacy Utilization in Canadian Workplaces. Ottawa and Hull: Statistics.* Canada and Human Resource Development Canada.

Kroft, S. (2013). Are Robots Hurting Growth? "60 Minutes – CBS Television. *CBS News*. Retrieved on June 2, 2016, from: http://www.cbsnews.com/8301-18560_162-57601121/are-robots-hurtingjob-growth

Krüger, O. (2005). The role of ecotourism in conservation: Panacea or Pandora's box? *Biodiversity and Conservation*, *14*(3), 579–600. doi:10.100710531-004-3917-4

Krugman, P. (1990). *Increasing returns and economic geography (No. w3275)*. Washington, DC: National Bureau of Economic Research. doi:10.3386/w3275

Kulling, M. (2014). *Tackling Milwaukee's racial and economic disparity*. Retrieved on April 22, 2016, from: http:// www.milwaukeemag.com/article/7152014TacklingMilwaukeesRacialandEconomicDisparity

Kumar, S., & Yadav, S. S. (2002). Satisfaction level from labour welfare schemes in Sugar Factories of Gorakhpur Division. *Indian Journal of Economics*, *83*, 171–190.

Kuria, P. N. (2012). *The effects of employee welfare programmes on job satisfaction of employees within the flower industry in Kenya.* Doctoral dissertation.

Kuter, N., & Ünal, H. E. (2009). Sürdürülebilirlik kapsamında ekoturizmin çevresel, ekonomik ve sosyo-kültürel etkileri. Kastamonu Üni. *Orman Fakültesi Dergisi, 9*(2), 146–156.

Kuznets, S. (1955). Economic growth and income inequality. *The American Economic Review, 45*(1), 17–26.

Kwan, C. H. (2002). *The Rise of China and Asia's Flying-Geese Pattern of Economic Development: An Empirical Analysis Based on US Import Statistics.* Nomura Research Institute Working Paper, No:52.

La Vida Spain. (2013). *Spain Approves Immigration Residency Visa for 500,000 Euro Property Investment.* PR Newswire.

Labuschagne, C., Brent, A. C., & Van Erck, R. P. G. (2005). Assessing the sustainability performances of industries. *Journal of Cleaner Production, 13*(4), 373–385. doi:10.1016/j.jclepro.2003.10.007

LaFree, G. (2005). Evidence For Elite Convergence in Cross-National Homicide Victimization Trends, 1956 to 2000. *The Sociological Quarterly, 46*(1), 191–211. doi:10.1111/j.1533-8525.2005.00009.x

Lagat, A. C. (2012). *Contribution of Trade Unions in the Promotion of Employee Satisfaction: The Case of the UASU Egerton University Chapter, Kenya* (Unpublished Master of Human Resource Management Dissertation). Egerton University, Njoro, Kenya.

Laibman, D. (2004). Rhetoric and Substance in Value Theory: An appraisal of the new orthodox Marxism. In A. Freeman, A. Kliman, & J. Wells (Eds.), *The New Value Controversy and the Foundations of Economics.* Cheltenham, UK: Edward Elgar.

Lall, S. (2000a). *Skills, Competitiveness and Policy in Developing Countries.* QEH Working Paper Series, No: 46

Lall, S. (2000b). *Turkish Performance in Exporting Manufactures: A Comparative Structural Analysis.* QEH Working Paper Series, No:47.

Lall, S., Weiss, J., & Zhang, J. (2006). The "Sophistication" of Exports: A New Trade Measure. *World Development, 34*(2), 222–237. doi:10.1016/j.worlddev.2005.09.002

Lankford, S. V., & Howard, D. R. (1994). Developing a tourism impacts attitude scale. *Annals of Tourism Research, 21*(1), 121–139. doi:10.1016/0160-7383(94)90008-6

Latham, K., & Wu, B. (2013). *Chinese immigration to the EU, New Trends, dynamics and implications.* Europe China Research and Advice Network. Retrieved from http://eeas.europa.eu/china/docs/-division_ecran/ecran_chinese_immigration_into_the_eu_kevin_latham_and_bin_wu_en.pdf

Law, M., Stewart, D., & Pollock, N. (1998). *Critical review form – Quantitative studies.* McMaster University: Occupational Therapy Evidence-Based Practice Research Group.

Lee, C.-C., Lee, C.-C., & Chiou, Y.-Y. (2017). Insurance activities, globalization, and economic growth: New methods, new evidence. *Journal of International Financial Markets, Institutions and Money, 51*, 155–170. doi:10.1016/j.intfin.2017.05.006

Lee, C., & Chang, C. (2009). FDI, financial development, and economic growth: International evidence. *Journal of Applied Econometrics, 12*, 249–271.

Lee, J. (2006a). Inequality and globalization in Europe. *Journal of Policy Modeling, 28*(7), 791–796. doi:10.1016/j.jpolmod.2006.04.013

Lee, J. (2006b). Does globalization matter to income distribution in Asia? *Applied Economics Letters*, *13*(13), 851–855. doi:10.1080/13504850500425352

Lemos, M. C., & Morehouse, B. J. (2005). The co-production of science and policy in integrated climate assessments. *Global Environmental Change*, *15*(1), 57–68. doi:10.1016/j.gloenvcha.2004.09.004

Leung, Y. F., Marion, J. L., & Farrell, T. A. (2008). Recreation ecology in sustainable tourism and ecotourism. A streghtening role. In S. F. McCool & R. N. Moisey (Eds.), *Tourism, Recreation, and Sustainability: Linking Culture and the Environment* (2nd ed.; pp. 19–38). Oxon, UK: CABI Publishing. doi:10.1079/9781845934705.0019

Leuven, E., & Oosterbeek, H. (2011). Overeducation and Mismatch in the Labor Market. In Handbook of the Economics of Education. Elsevier Science. doi:10.1016/B978-0-444-53444-6.00003-1

Lewontin, R. (2013). *Üçlü Sarmal Gen, Organizma ve Çevre, Çev. Ergi Deniz Özsoy*. İstanbul: Say Yayınları.

Libosada, C. Jr. (2009). Business or leisure? Economic development and resource protectiond-Concepts and practices in sustainable ecotourism. *Ocean and Coastal Management*, *52*(7), 390–394. doi:10.1016/j.ocecoaman.2009.04.004

Lindert, P. H., & Williamson, J. G. (2001). *Does globalization make the world more unequal?* NBER Working Paper 2001:8228.

Lipietz, A. (1982). The 'so-called transformation problem' revisited. *Journal of Economic Theory*, *26*(February).

Li, Y. P., Huangb, G. H., Zhangc, N., & Nied, S. L. (2011). An inexact-stochastic with recourse model for developing regional economic-ecological sustainability under uncertainty. *Ecological Modelling*, *222*(2), 370–379. doi:10.1016/j.ecolmodel.2009.12.010

Lohan, D., & Johnston, S. (2005). *Bio-prospecting in Antarctica*. United Nations University and Institute of Advanced Studies Report. Retrieved on September 27, 2017, from: http://www.ias.unu.edu/binaries2/antarctic_bioprospecting.pdf

Lopez, R. (2002). Evaluating ecotourism in natural protected areas of La Paz Bay, Baja California Sur, Mexico: Ecotourism or nature-based tourism? *Biodiversity and Conservation*, *11*(9), 1539–1550. doi:10.1023/A:1016887417263

Lucas, R. E. Jr. (1988). On the mechanics of economic development. *Journal of Monetary Economics*, *22*(1), 3–42. doi:10.1016/0304-3932(88)90168-7

Luedi, T. (2008). China's Track Record in M&A. *The McKinsey Quarterly*, 3.

Lu, J., & Xu, B. (2006). The Impact of Foreign Firms on the Sophistication of Chinese Exports. *ASSA Conference Paper*.

Lundberg, E. (2015). The level of tourism development and resident attitudes: A comparative case study of coastal destinations. *Scandinavian Journal of Hospitality and Tourism*, *15*(3), 266–294. doi:10.1080/15022250.2015.1005335

Luthans, K. W., & Sommer, S. M. (2005). The impact of high performance work on industry-level outcomes. *Journal of Managerial Issues*, 327–345.

Lwoga, E.T., Ngulube, P., & Stilwell, C. (2010). Understanding indigenous knowledge: Bridging the knowledge gap through a knowledge creation model for agricultural development. *SA Journal of Information Management*, *12*(1). DOI: 10.4102ajim.v12i1.436

Maas, A., & Carius, A. (2010). *Territorial Integrity and Sovereignty: Climate Change and Security in the Pacific and Beyond.* Academic Press.

Mach, T. L., & Wolken, J. D. (2006). Financial Services Used by Small Businesses: Evidence from the 2003 Survey of Small Business Finance. *Federal Reserve Bulletin*. Retrieved on August 2, 2016, from: http://www.federalreserve.gov/pubs/bulletin/2006/smallbusiness/default.htm

Madić, M., & Radovanović, M. (2015). Ranking Of Some Most Commonly Used Non-Traditional Machining Processes Usıng Rov And Critic Methods. *Upb Sci. Bull., Series D, 77*(2), 193–204.

Madrigal, R. (1995). Residents' perceptions and the role of government. *Annals of Tourism Research, 22*(1), 86–102. doi:10.1016/0160-7383(94)00070-9

Maguire, S., Hardy, C., & Lawrence, T. B. (2004). Institutional entrepreneurship in emerging fields: HIV/AIDS treatment advocacy in Canada. *Academy of Management Journal, 47*(5), 657–679. doi:10.2307/20159610

Mahendra, S. (2016). *Economic Reforms, poverty and Inequality*. Mumbai: Indira Gandhi Institute of Development Research.

Mah, J. S. (2002). The impact of globalization on income distribution: The Korean experience. *Applied Economics Letters, 9*(15), 1007–1009. doi:10.1080/13504850210149124

Mah, J. S. (2003). A note on globalization and income distribution—the case of Korea, 1975-1995. *Journal of Asian Economics, 14*(1), 157–164. doi:10.1016/S1049-0078(02)00244-0

Mah, J. S. (2013). Globalization, decentralization and income inequality: The case of China. *Economic Modelling, 31*, 653–658. doi:10.1016/j.econmod.2012.09.054

Mahler, A., Jesuit, K., & Roscoe, D. (1999). Exploring the impact of trade and investment on income inequality. *Comparative Political Studies, 32*(3), 363–395. doi:10.1177/0010414099032003004

Majidi, A. F. (2017). Globalization and Economic Growth: The Case Study of Developing Countries. *Asian Economic and Financial Review, 7*(6), 589–599. Retrieved from https://ideas.repec.org/a/asi/aeafrj/2017p589-599.html

Maki, D. (2012). Tests for cointegration allowing for an unknown number of breaks. *Economic Modelling, 29*(5), 2011–2015. doi:10.1016/j.econmod.2012.04.022

Manacorda, M., & Petrongolo, B. (1999). Skill Mismatch And Unemployment In Oecd Countries. *Economica, 66*(262), 181–207. doi:10.1111/1468-0335.00164

Mankiw, N. G., Romer, D., & Weil, D. N. (1992). A Contribution to the Empirics of Economic Growth. *The Quarterly Journal of Economics, 107*(2), 407–437. doi:10.2307/2118477

Manolopoulos, D. (2006). What motivates R&D professionals? Evidences from decentralized laboratories in Greece. *International Journal of HRM, 11*(4).

Manzini, H. S., & Gwandure, C. (2011). The Provision of Employee Assistance Programmes in South African Football Clubs: A Case Study. *Journal of Social Sciences, 27*(2), 75–83. doi:10.1080/09718923.2011.11892908

Marber, P. (2004). Globalization and its contents. *World Policy Journal, 21*(4), 29–37. doi:10.1215/07402775-2005-1010

Marinova, D., & Raven, M. (2006). Indigenous knowledge and intellectual property: A sustainability agenda. *Journal of Economic Surveys, 20*(4), 587–606. doi:10.1111/j.1467-6419.2006.00260.x

Mariolis, T. (2006). A Critique of the 'New Approach' to the Transformation Problem and a Proposal. Published in *Indian Development Review: An International Journal of Development Economics, 4*(1), 23–37.

Marshall, A. (1920). *Principles of economics* (8th ed.). London: Macmillan and Co., Ltd. Retrieved on April 4, 2017, from: http://www.econlib.org/library/Marshall/marP.html

Martens, P., Caselli, M., De Lombaerde, P., Figge, L., & Scholte, J. A. (2015). New Directions in Globalization Indices. *Globalizations*, *12*(2), 217–228. doi:10.1080/14747731.2014.944336

Martin, X. S. (2002). *The world distribution of income (Estimated from individual country distributions)*. National Bureau of Economic Research. Retrieved from http://www.nber.org/papers/w8933

Marx, K. (1885). Capital (vol. 2). Edited for publication by Engels in 1885.

Maslach, C., Leiter, M. P., & Jackson, S. E. (2012). Making a significant difference with burnout interventions: Researcher and practitioner collaboration. *Journal of Organizational Behavior*, *33*(2), 296–300. doi:10.1002/job.784

Maslow, A. (1970). *Motivation and Personality*. New York: Harper and Row.

Matthews, S. (2014). *Older American Shun Retirement at 65 for risky startups*. Retrieved on December 2, 2016, from: http://www.bloomberg.com/news/2014-01-08/older-americans-shun-retirement-at-65-for-risky-startups.html

Mavromaras, K., McGuinness, S., & Fok, Y. (2009). *Overskilling dynamics and education pathways*. Institute for the Study of Labor (IZA), Discussion Paper 4321.

Mavromaras, K., McGuinness, S., O'Leary, N., Sloane, P., & Fok, Y. (2010). The problem of overskilling in Australia and Britain. *Manchester School*, *78*(3), 219–241. doi:10.1111/j.1467-9957.2009.02136.x

Mayborne, B. (2012). *Does Milwaukee have what it takes to fuel new growth?* Retrieved on May 9, 2017, from: http://www.mmac.org/wcnews/NewsArticle

Mayer, J. (2000). *Globalization, Technology Transfer And Skill Accumulation In Low-Income Countries* (UNCTAD/OSG/DP/150 No. 150). Retrieved from http://www.unctad.org/en/pub/pubframe.htm

McGuinness, S. (2006). Overeducation In The Labour Market. *Journal of Economic Surveys*, *20*(3), 387–418. doi:10.1111/j.0950-0804.2006.00284.x

McMichael, A. J., Campbell-Lendrum, D. H., Corvalan, C. F., Ebi, K. L., Githeko, A., Scheraga, J. D., & Wooward, A. (2003). *Climate Change and Human Health- Risks and Responses*. Geneva: World Health Organization.

McMillan, M., Rodrik, D., & Verduzco-Gallo, I. (2014). Globalization, structural change, and productivity growth, with an update on Africa. *World Development*, *63*, 11–32. doi:10.1016/j.worlddev.2013.10.012

Meadows, D. H., Randers, J., Meadows, D. L., & Behrens, W. W. (1972). *The Limits to Growth: Report for the Club of Rome's Project on the Predicament of Mankind*. New York: Universe Books.

Medio, A. (1972). Profits and surplus value: appearance and reality in capitalist production. In E. K. Huntand & J. Schwartz (Eds.), *A Critique of Economic Theory*. New York: Penguin.

Meek, R. L. (1956). *Studies in the Labour Theory of Value*. London: Lawrence & Wishart.

MENR. (2016). *Statistics, Balance Sheets, General Directorate of Energy Affairs*. Retrieved on November 24, 2017 from: http://www.eigm.gov.tr/tr-TR/Denge-Tablolari/Denge-Tablolari

Merico, C. (2015). *L'imprenditore va all'estero? La sua banca lo accompagna*. Milano: Selpress.

Meyer, J. W., & Rowan, B. (1977). Institutionalized organizations: Formal structure as myth and ceremony. *American Journal of Sociology*, *83*(2), 340–363. doi:10.1086/226550

Mikucka, M. (2014). Does individualistic culture lower the well-being of the unemployed? Evidence from Europe. *Journal of Happiness Studies, 15*(3), 673–691. doi:10.100710902-013-9445-8

Milanovic, B. (1999). World Income Distribution in 1988 and 1993. The World Bank.

Milanovic, B. (2002). True world income distribution 1988 and 1993: First calculations based on household surveys alone. *Economic Journal (London), 112*(476), 51–92. doi:10.1111/1468-0297.0j673

Milanovic, B. (2003a). *Can we discern the effect of globalization on income distribution? Evidence from household budget surveys. International Trade 0303004*. Econwpa.

Milanovic, B. (2003b). The two faces of globalization: Against globalization as we know it. *World Development, 31*(4), 667–683. doi:10.1016/S0305-750X(03)00002-0

Milanovic, B., & Yitzhaki, S. (2002). Decomposing world income distribution: Does the world have a middle class? *Review of Income and Wealth, 48*(2), 155–178. doi:10.1111/1475-4991.00046

Miller, D., Lee, J., Chang, S., & Le Breton-Miller, I. (2009). Filling the institutional void: The social behavior and performance of family vs non-family technology firms in emerging markets. *Journal of International Business Studies, 40*(5), 802–817. doi:10.1057/jibs.2009.11

Miller, K. D. (1992). A framework for integrated Challenge management in international business. *Journal of International Business Studies, 23*(2), 311–331. doi:10.1057/palgrave.jibs.8490270

Milwaukee History and Timeline. (2011). *Milwaukee county historical society*. Retrieved on October 11, 2016, from: www.https//milwaukee history. net

Minniti, M. (2008). The role of government policy on entrepreneurial activity: Productive, unproductive, or destructive? *Entrepreneurship Theory and Practice, 32*(5), 779–790. doi:10.1111/j.1540-6520.2008.00255.x

Mishkin, F. S. (2009). Globalization and financial development. *Journal of Development Economics, 89*(2), 164–169. doi:10.1016/j.jdeveco.2007.11.004

Mishra, S., & Bhagat, M. (2007). *Principles for successful implementation of labour welfare activities*. From police theory to functional theory. Retrieved on October 26, 2017, from: https://www.tesionline.com/intl/indepth.jsp?id=575

MMAC. (2012). *Demographic and Economic Profile - Metro Milwaukee*. Milwaukee, WI: Metropolitan Milwaukee Association of Commerce.

MOC. (2005). *Statistical Bulletin of China's Outward Foreign Direct Investment*. Beijing, China.

Molla, A., & Cooper, V. (2010, September 13). Green IT Readiness: A Framework and Preliminary Proof of Concept. *AJIS. Australasian Journal of Information Systems, 16*(2). doi:10.3127/ajis.v16i2.545

Monterrubio, J. C., & Andriotis, K. (2014). Social representations and community attitudes towards spring breakers. *Tourism Geographies, 16*(2), 288–302. doi:10.1080/14616688.2014.889208

Mora, C., Frazier, A. G., Longman, R. J., Dacks, R. S., Walton, M. M., Tong, E. J., ... Giambelluca, T. W. (2013). The projected timing of climate departure from recent variability. *Nature, 502*(7470), 183–187. doi:10.1038/nature12540 PMID:24108050

Morishima, M. (1973). *Marxian Economics*. Oxford, UK: Oxford University Press.

Morishima, M., & Caterhores, G. (1975). The transformation problem: a Markov process. In M. Morishima (Ed.), *Value Exploitation and Growth – Marx in the Light of Modern Economic Theory*. New York: McGraw – Hill.

Moseley, F. (1999). The 'new solution' to the transformation problem: A sympathetic critique. *The Review of Radical Political Economics*, *32*(2), 282–316.

Mota, G. A. L. (2009). *Three Essays on Happiness in economics. Exploring the usefulness of subjective well-being data for the economic analysis of welfare* (PhD Thesis). School of Economics and Management, University of Porto, Portugal.

Mulligan, C. E. A., & Olsson, M. (2013). Architectural implications of smart city business models: An evolutionary perspective. *IEEE Communications Magazine*, *51*, 80–85. doi:10.1109/MCOM.2013.6525599

Munasinghe, M. (n.d.). *Analysing the Nexus of Sustainable Development and Climate Change: An Overview.* Sri Lanka: Munasinghe Institute for Development (MIND).

Mundell, R. (1957). International trade and factor mobility. *The American Economic Review*, *47*(3), 321–335.

Murray, A., Skene, K., & Haynes, K. (2017). The Circular Economy: An Interdisciplinary Exploration of the Concept and Application in a Global Context. *Journal of Business Ethics*, *140*(3), 369–380. doi:10.100710551-015-2693-2

Muruu, R. W., Were, S., & Abok, M. A. (2016). Effects of Welfare Programmes on Employee Satisfaction in the Public Sector: A Case of the Public Service Commission. *Strategic Journal of Business & Change Management*, *3*(4), 1607–1633.

Mutlu, A. (2008). *Ekoloji ve Yönetim Toplumsal Ekoloji ve Sürdürülebilir Gelişme'nin Karşılaştırılması*. Ankara: Turhan Kitabevi.

Myers, N. (2005, May). *Environmental Refugees: An Emergent Security Issue.* Thirteenth Economic Forum, Prague, Czech Republic.

Namara, R. E., Makombe, G., Hagos, F., & Awulachew, S. B. (2007). *Rural poverty and inequality in Ethiopia: does access to small-scale irrigation make a difference?* International Water Management Institute.

Nanda, N., & Panda, J. K. (2013). Challenges and effectiveness of industrial relation environment in Indian Industries study on Rourkela Steel Plant. *International Journal of Financial Services and management Research,* *2*(6), 163-174.

Narayan, P. K., & Smyth, R. (2006). What determines migration flows from low-income to high-income countries? An empirical investigation of fiji-u.s migration 1972-2001. *Contemporary Economic Policy*, *24*(2), 332–342. doi:10.1093/cep/byj019

Naschold, F. (2015). *Why inequality matters for poverty*. Briefing Paper No 2 (2 of 3), 1–6.

Navaretti, G., de Simone, G., & Sembenelli, A. (2007). *Migration and Foreign Direct Investment: A review of the literature*. Centro Studi Luca d'Agliano.

Ndeto, J. (2009). Innovative financing mechanisms for municipal solid waste management in secondary cities of ethiopia: The case of Arba Minch city. *IUP J. Infrastruct.*, *7*, 79–102.

Nedelkoska, L., Neffke, F., & Wiederhold, S. (2015). Skill mismatch affects life-long earnings. *Policy Brief, proceedings of LLLight'in'Europe research project*. Retrieved on November 11, 2017, from: www.lllightineurope.com/publications

Nelson, D. L., & Quick, J. C. (2009). *Organizational behavior: Science, the real world, and you.* Mason, OH: South-western Cengage Learning.

Nelson, R. R., & Pack, H. (1999). The asian miracle and modern growth theory. *Economic Journal (London)*, *109*(457), 416–436. doi:10.1111/1468-0297.00455

Nepal, S. (2008). Residents' attitudes to tourism in central British Columbia, Canada. *Tourism Geographies*, *10*(1), 42–65. doi:10.1080/14616680701825123

NETL. (2013). *Power Generation Technology Comparison from a Life Cycle Perspective*. National Energy Technology Laboratory, US Department of Energy, Pittsburgh, PA. Retrieved on November 11, 2015, from: https://www.netl.doe.gov/File%20Library/Research/Energy%20Analysis/Life%20Cycle%20Analysis/Technology-Assessment-Compilation-Report.pdf

Nielsen, J. (2014). *When to Use Which User-Experience Research Methods*. Retrieved on August 18, 2017, from: https://www.nngroup.com/articles/which-ux-research-methods/

Nieto, G. (2003). The Chinese in Spain. *International Migration (Geneva, Switzerland), 41*(3), 215–237. doi:10.1111/1468-2435.00247

NIMET (2008). *Nigeria Climate Review Bulletin 2007*. Nigerian Meteorological Agency.

Nimpagaritse, F., & Culver, D. (2002). *A Broader Perspective of Measuring the well-being of Rural Farm and non-Farm Households*. Agriculture and Agri - Food Canada.

Nissanke, M., & Thorbecke, E. (2006). Channels and policy debate in the globalization–inequality–poverty nexus. *World Development, 34*(8), 1338–1360. doi:10.1016/j.worlddev.2005.10.008

Niza, C. F. (2007). *Economia da Felicidade e política social: contributos da ciência comportamental para orientação da acção pública com vista ao desenvolvimento humano* (Master's Thesis). School of Economics and Management, Technical University of Lisbon, Portugal.

Nogueira, S., & Ferreira, J. A. (2007). *A Realidade Psicossocial dos Sem-Abrigo: Breve Contributo para a sua Caracterização. Portuguese Pedagogy Magazine*.

Norris, P. (2000). Global governance and cosmopolitan citizens. In J. S. Nye & J. D. Donahue (Eds.), Governance in a globalizing world (pp. 1-44). Brookings Institution Press.

North, D. C. (1990). *Institutions, institutional change and economic performance*. Cambridge University Press. doi:10.1017/CBO9780511808678

NPC (National Planning Commission). (2004). *Meeting everyone's needs*. Abuja, Nigeria: National Economic Empowerment and Development Strategy.

NREL. (2016). *The Jobs and Economic Development Impact (JEDI) models*. National Renewable Energy Laboratory. Retrieved on 01 October 2016, from: http://www.nrel.gov/analysis/jedi/

Nunkoo, R., & Gursoy, D. (2012). Residents' support for tourism: An identity perspective. *Annals of Tourism Research, 39*(1), 243–268. doi:10.1016/j.annals.2011.05.006

Nunkoo, R., & Ramkissoon, H. (2012). Power, trust, social exchange and community support. *Annals of Tourism Research, 39*(2), 997–1023. doi:10.1016/j.annals.2011.11.017

Nyenzi, B., & Malone, L. (2005). *Challenges of Climate Prediction and its Application to the Agriculture Sector*. Retrieved on May 20, 2017, from: https://www.wmo.int/pages/.../mod5_climate_pred_apps_ag_sector.doc

O'Donnell, R. (1984). *Adam Smith's labour command measure of value.* UCD Centre for Economic Research, Working Paper Series; No. 21.

O'Rourke, K. H. (2001). *Globalization and inequality: Historical trends.* NBER Working Paper 8339. Cambridge, MA: NBER.

Obbard, J. (2017). APCEL Climate Change Adaptation Platform COP23 Bonn, Germany: The U.S. Stands Alone. Asia Pacific Centre for Environmental Law. National University of Singapore.

Obbard, J. (2017, December 12). *APCEL Climate Change Adaptation Platform COP23 Bonn, Germany: The U.S. Stands Alone.* Asia Pacific Centre for Environmental Law. National University of Singapore. Retrieved on January 15, 2018, from: https://law.nus.edu.sg/apcel/cca/COP23%20Bonn,%20Germany%20%20The%20U.S.%20Stands%20Alone.pdf

OECD. (1996). Transition From School To Work. In *Education At A Glance: Analysis*. Paris: OCED.

OECD. (1998). *Thematic Rewiew Of The Transition From Initial Education To Working Life: Interim Comparative Report*. Paris: OCED.

OECD. (2005). *OECD handbook on economic globalization indicators*. Retrieved from http://www.realinstitutoelcano.org/materiales/docs/OCDE_handbook.pdf

OECD. (2008). *OECD Benchmark Definition of Foreign Direct Investment* (4th ed.). Retrieved from http://www.oecd.org/daf/inv/investmentstatisticsandanalysis/40193734.pdf

OECD. (2013). *First International Report on PIAAC* (Vol. 1). Paris: OECD Publishing.

OECD. (2014). *Industry and technology policies in Korea*. OECD Publishing.

OECD-UNDESA. (2013). *World Migration in Figures*. OECD.

Oesterreich, T. D., & Teuteberg, F. (2016). Understanding the implications of digitisation and automation in the context of Industry 4.0: A triangulation approach and elements of a research agenda for the construction industry. *Computers in Industry*, *83*, 121–139. doi:10.1016/j.compind.2016.09.006

Official Records of the Diplomatic Conference on the Reaffirmation and Development of International Humanitarian Law Applicable in Armed Conflicts. (1975). Retrieved on September 15, 2017, from: Doc. CDDH/III/275 at 360.

Ogunyomi, O. O., Daisi, O. R., & Oluwashikemi, R. A. (2013). Economic globalization, income inequality and economic growth in Nigeria: A static data analysis (1986-2010). *ABC Journal of Advanced Research*, *2*(2), 55–68.

Ohtake, F. (2012). Unemployment and Happiness. Japan Labor Review, 9(2).

Oliver, C. (1991). Strategic responses to institutional processes. *Academy of Management Review*, *16*(1), 145–179. doi:10.5465/AMR.1991.4279002

Ollin, K., & Vej, J. (2012). Sustainability in business: Understanding meanings, triggers and enablers. *Journal of Strategic Marketing*, *20*(7), 625–641. doi:10.1080/0965254X.2012.711347

Oncel, S. S. (2017). Green energy engineering: Opening a green way for the future. *Journal of Cleaner Production*, *142*, 3095–3100. doi:10.1016/j.jclepro.2016.10.158

Önder, T. (2003). *Ekoloji, Toplum ve Siyaset*. Ankara: Odak Yayınları.

Onwuemele, A. (2013). *Understanding Information Communication Strategies among Farmers for Effective Utilization of Climate Research and Forecast in the Niger-Delta, Nigeria*. Paper Presented at the African Climate Conference, Arusha, Tanzania.

Onwuemele, A. (2014). Access And Utilization of Climate Services Among Vulnerable Communities in Nigeria: A Case Study of Isoko Communities in Delta State. *Journal of Environmental Issues & Agriculture in Developing Countries*, *6*(2-3), 15–24.

Onyekale, A. S. (2015). Access to Risk Mitigating Weather Forecasts and Changes in Farming Operations in East and West Africa: Evidence from a Baseline Survey. *Sustainability*, *7*(11), 14599–14617. doi:10.3390u71114599

Orams, M. B. (2001). Types of Ecotourism. In D. B. Weaver (Ed.), *The Encyclopaedia of Ecotourism* (pp. 23–36). Wallingford, CT: CABI Publishing.

Organisation for Economic Co-operation and Development (OECD). (2001). *Adoption of technologies for sustainable farming systems: Wageningen workshop proceedings*. Retrieved on June 2, 2016, from: http://www.oecd.org/greengrowth/sustainable-agriculture/2739771.pdf

Osterloh, S. (2012). Words speak louder than actions: The impact of politics on economic performance. *Journal of Comparative Economics*, *40*(3), 318–336. doi:10.1016/j.jce.2012.05.004

Öztürk, L. (2007). *Sürdürülebilir Kalkınma*. Ankara: İmaj Yayıncılık.

Pagani, M., & Pardo, C. (2017). *Industrial Marketing Management*. doi:10.1016/j.indmarman

Papageorgiou, C., & Spatafora, N. (2012). *Economic diversification in lic's: Stylized facts and macroeconomic implication.* IMF Staff Discussion Notes 12/13.

Papanek, G., & Kyn, O. (1995). The effect on income distribution of development. *Journal of Development Economics*, *23*(1), 55–65. doi:10.1016/0304-3878(86)90079-9

Park, C-S. (2009). The Temporal Single System: A retrospective critique. *Marxism, 21*.

Park, K. (2015). *A Study on the Effect of Company Welfare Forms on Workers Satisfaction* (Doctoral dissertation). Kounggi University, Korea. (in Korean)

Parul, P. B., & Ashokkumar, M. (2013). Provision of Welfare under Factories Act and Its Impact on Employee Satisfaction. *Journal of Business Management & Social Sciences Research*, *2*(2), 57–69.

Patro, C. S. (2012). Employee Welfare Activities in Private Sector and Their Impact on Quality of Work Life. *International Journal of Productivity Management and Assessment Technologies*, *1*(2), 18–29. doi:10.4018/ijpmat.2012040102

Patro, C. S. (2015). Employee Welfare Measures in Public and Private Sectors: A Comparative Analysis. *International Journal of Service Science, Management, Engineering, and Technology*, *6*(1), 22–37. doi:10.4018/ijssmet.2015010102

Patro, C. S. (2016). A Study on Adoption of Employee Welfare Schemes in Industrial and Service Organisations: In Contrast with Public and Private Sectors. *International Journal of Service Science, Management, Engineering, and Technology*, *7*(2), 16–33. doi:10.4018/IJSSMET.2016040102

Patro, C. S. (2017). Espousal of Welfare Schemes: A Means for Employees' Satisfied Work Life with Reference to Pharmaceutical Companies. *International Journal of Asian Business and Information Management*, *8*(3), 36–51. doi:10.4018/IJABIM.2017070103

Patro, C. S., & Kamakula, M. K. R. (2016). A Take on Employee Welfare Facilities and Employees' Efficiency. *International Journal of Asian Business and Information Management*, *7*(3), 54–70. doi:10.4018/IJABIM.2016070104

Patt, A. (2000). *Communicating probabilistic forecasts to decision makers: a case study of Zimbabwe. Belfer Center for Science and International Affairs (BCSIA) Environment and Natural Resources Program, Kennedy School of Government*. Cambridge, MA: Harvard University.

Patt, A., & Gwata, C. (2002). Effective seasonal climate forecast applications: Examining constraints for subsistence farmers in Zimbabwe Global Environmental Change. *Human and Policy Dimensions*, *12*(3), 185–195. doi:10.1016/S0959-3780(02)00013-4

Patz, J. A. (2002). A human disease indicator for the effects of recent global climate change. *Proceedings of the National Academy of Sciences of the United States of America*, *99*(20), 12506–12508. doi:10.1073/pnas.212467899 PMID:12271143

Paus, E., & Robinson, M. D. (1999). Real wage performance under greater trade openness: Lessons from Latin America and Asia. *Journal of Developing Areas*, *33*(2), 269–288.

Pekarskiene, I., & Susniene, R. (2014). The Assessment of the Manifestation of Economic Globalization: The International Trade Factor. *Procedia: Social and Behavioral Sciences*, *156*, 392–397. doi:10.1016/j.sbspro.2014.11.209

Pekarskiene, I., & Susniene, R. (2015). Features of Foreign Direct Investment in the Context of Globalization. *Procedia: Social and Behavioral Sciences*, *213*, 204–210. doi:10.1016/j.sbspro.2015.11.427

Pelling, M. (2003). Paradigms of risk. In M. Pelling (Ed.), *Natural Disaster and Development in a Globalizing World*. New York: Routledge.

Pellizzari, M., & Fichen, A. (2013). *A new measure of skills mismatch: Theory and evidence from the survey of adult skills (PIAAC)*. OECD Social, Employment and Migration Working Papers 153. Paris: OECD Publishing.

Peng, M. (2012). The Global Strategy of Emerging Multinationals from China. *Global Strategy Journal*, *2*(2), 97–107. doi:10.1002/gsj.1030

Peng, M. W. (2003). Institutional transitions and strategic choices. *Academy of Management Review*, 275–296.

Peng, M. W., & Luo, Y. (2000). Managerial ties and firm performance in a transition economy: The nature of a micro-macro link. *Academy of Management Journal*, *43*(3), 486–501. doi:10.2307/1556406

Peng, M. W., Wang, D. Y. L., & Jiang, Y. (2008). An institution-based view of international business strategy: A focus on emerging economies. *Journal of International Business Studies*, *39*(5), 920–936. doi:10.1057/palgrave.jibs.8400377

Perloff, H. S. (1957). Interrelations of state income and industrial structure. *The Review of Economics and Statistics*, *39*(2), 162–171. doi:10.2307/1928533

Perry, A., Wiederhold, S., & Ackermann-Pieket, D. (2014). How Can Skill Mismatch be Measured? New Approaches with PIAAC. *Methods, Data, Analyses, 8*(2), 137-174.

Person, T., & Guido, T. (1994). Is inequality harmful for growth? *The American Economic Review*, *84*(3), 600–621.

Pesaran, M. H. (2004). *General Diagnostic Tests For Cross Section Dependence in Panels* (CWPE 0435 No. 1233). Academic Press.

Pesaran, M. H., Ullah, A., & Yamagata, T. (2008). A bias-adjusted LM test of error cross-section independence. *The Econometrics Journal*, *11*(1), 105–127. doi:10.1111/j.1368-423X.2007.00227.x

Pete Foster. (2007). *The ICT Sustainability Index - The ICT Sustinability Framework*. Retrieved on May 3, 2015, from: http://www.ictsustain.com/the-ict-sustainability-index.html

Petralia, S., Balland, P. A., & Morrison, A. (2017). Climbing the ladder of technological development. *Research Policy*, *46*(5), 956–969. doi:10.1016/j.respol.2017.03.012

Pew Charitable Trust. (2013). *Pew Report: Cities Hit Late by Great Recession, Still Struggling to Rebound*. Retrieved on June 22, 2016, from: http://www.pewtrusts.org/en/about/news-room/press-releases/2013/11/11/pew-report-cities-hit-late-by-great-recession-still-struggling-to-rebound

Philipson. (2010). *A Green ICT Framework - Understanding and Measuring Green ICT. Connection Research Green Paper*. Retrieved from http://www.computersite.com.au/wp-content/uploads/2015/02/A_Green_ICT_Framework_CR.pdf

Phillips, N., Tracey, P., & Karra, N. (2009). Rethinking institutional distance: Strengthening the tie between new institutional theory and international management. *Strategic Organization*, *7*(3), 339–348. doi:10.1177/1476127009337439

Phillips, P. C. B., & Hansen, B. E. (1990). Statistical Inference in Instrumental Variables Regression with I(1) Processes. *The Review of Economic Studies*, *57*(1), 99. doi:10.2307/2297545

Phillips, P. C. B., & Moon, H. R. (1999). Linear Regression Limit Theory for Nonstationary Panel Data. *Econometrica*, *67*(5), 1057–1111. doi:10.1111/1468-0262.00070

Pieke, F. (2004). *Chinese Globalization and Migration to Europe*. The Center for Comparative Immigration Studies.

Pisano, G. P., & Shih, W. C. (2012). *Producing Prosperity: Why America Needs a Manufacturing Renaissance*. Boston: Harvard Business Review Press.

Poletaev, M., & Robinson, C. (2008). 2008). Human Capital Specificity: Evidence from the Dictionary of Occupational Titles and Displaced Worker Surveys, 1984-2000. *Journal of Labor Economics*, *26*(3), 387–420. doi:10.1086/588180

Pollin, R., Heintz, J., & Garrett-Peltier, H. (2009). *The Economic Benefits of Investing in Clean Energy: How the economic stimulus program and new legislation can boost US economic growth and employment*. Political Economy Research Institute, University of Massachusetts at Amherst.

Porter, L. W. (1963, April). Job Attitudes in Management: II. Perceived importance of needs as a function of job level. *Journal of Applied Psychology*, *47*.

Porter, M. E. (1980). *Competitive Strategy: Techniques for Analyzing Industries and Competitors*. New York: Free Press.

Porter, M. E. (1985). *Competitive Advantage: Creating and Sustaining Superior Performance*. Free Press.

Porter, M. E. (1990). *The competitive advantage of nations*. New York: Free Press. doi:10.1007/978-1-349-11336-1

Porter, M. E. (1990). The competitive advantage of notions. *Harvard Business Review*.

Potrafke, N. (2012). Political cycles and economic performance in OECD countries: Empirical evidence from 1951–2006. *Public Choice*, *150*(1–2), 155–179. doi:10.100711127-010-9695-5

Potrafke, N. (2015). The Evidence on Globalisation. *World Economy*, *38*(3), 509–552. doi:10.1111/twec.12174

Powell, W. W., & DiMaggio, P. J. (1991). *The new institutionalism in organizational analysis*. University of Chicago Press.

Presenza, A., Del Chiappa, G., & Sheehan, L. (2013). Residents' engagement and local tourism governance in maturing beach destinations. evidence from an Italian case study. *Journal of Destination Marketing & Management*, *2*(1), 22–30. doi:10.1016/j.jdmm.2013.01.001

Priti, S. (2009). *Employee Welfare*. Retrieved on October 20, 2017, from: http://www.citehr.com/176307employee-welfare.html#ixzz1zTZ8HheC

Prota, F., & Viesti, G. (2007). *La delocalizzazione internazionale del made in Italy*. Università di Bari, Cerpem.

Pushnoi, G. S. (2010). Crisis as Reconfiguration of the Economic Complex Adaptive System. *AAAI Symposium Series; AAAI Fall CAS Symposium*.

Pushnoi, G. S. (2014). Method of Systems Potential as Holistic Approach for CAS-Modelling. In M. Khosrow-Pour (Ed.), *Encyclopedia of Information Science and Technology* (3rd ed.). Hershey, PA: IGI Global.

Pushnoi, G. S. (2017). *Method of Systems Potential (MSP). Applications in Economics: Emerging Research and Opportunities*. Hershey, PA: IGI Global. doi:10.4018/978-1-5225-2170-9

Pushnoi, G. S., & Bonser, G. L. (2008). Method of Systems Potential as "Top-Bottom" Technique of the Complex Adaptive Systems Modelling. In A. Yang & Y. Shan (Eds.), *Intelligent Complex Adaptive Systems* (pp. 26–73). Hershey, PA: IGI Global. doi:10.4018/978-1-59904-717-1.ch002

PWC. (2013). *PwC's NextGen: A global generational study*. Retrieved on November 13, 2017, from: https://www.pwc.com/gx/en/hr-management-services/pdf/pwc-nextgen-study-2013.pdf

Quaglino, G. P., Casagrande, S., & Castellano, C. (1992). *Gruppo di lavoro, lavoro di gruppo*. Milano: Cortina Editore.

Quiggin, J. (2014). National accounting and the digital economy. *Economic Analysis and Policy*, *44*(2), 136–142. doi:10.1016/j.eap.2014.05.008

Qu, J., Zhang, Y., Luo, K., & Li, M. (2011). *Annual Report on Overseas Chinese Studies*. Beijing: Social Sciences Academic Press.

Radcliff, B. (2001). Politics, markets, and life satisfaction: The political economy of human happiness. *American Political Science Review*, *95*.

Rainer, G. (2018). Producing nature for tourism: A political ecology angle. *Annals of Tourism Research*. doi:10.1016/j.annals.2018.01.004

Rajamani, L., Brunnée, J., & Doelle, M. (2012). Introduction: The role of compliance in an evolving climate regime. In L. Rajamani, J. Brunnée, & M. Doelle (Eds.), *Promoting Compliance in an Evolving Climate Regime*. London, UK: Cambridge University Press. doi:10.1007/978-1-4614-1433-9_1

Raju, A., Lindmark, S., Delaere, S., & Ballon, P. (2013). A Holistic Impact-Assessment Framework for Green ICT. *IT Professional*, *15*(1), 50–56. doi:10.1109/MITP.2012.119

Ramón, J., & Serra, A. (2015). Segmentando residentes según sus actitudes: Revisión de la literatura. *PASOS: Revista de Turismo y Patrimonio Cultural*, *13*(4), 837–848.

Rao, B. B., Tamazian, A., & Vadlamannati, K. C. (2011). Growth effects of a comprehensive measure of globalization with country-specific time series data. *Applied Economics*, *43*(5), 551–568. doi:10.1080/00036840802534476

Rao, B. B., & Vadlamannati, K. C. (2011). Globalization and growth in the low income African countries with the extreme bounds analysis. *Economic Modelling*, *28*(3), 795–805. doi:10.1016/j.econmod.2010.10.009

Rao, J., Midega, C., Atieno, F., Auma, J. O., Cadilhon, J. J., Mango, N., ... Wesonga, M. (2015). *A situational Analysis of agricultural production and marketing, and natural resources management in West Kenya. ILRI/Icipe Project Report*. Nairobi, Kenya: International Livestock Research Institute for the Humidtropics CGIAR Research Program.

Ravallion, M. (2003). *The debate on globalization, poverty and inequality: Why measurement matters*. The World Bank, Policy Research Working Paper 3038.

Rees, D., Momanyi, M., Wekundah, J., Ndungu, F., Odondi, J., & Oyure, A. O. (2000). *Agricultural Knowledge and Implications in Kenya - Implications for Technology Dissemination and Development*. Agricultural Research & Extension Network Paper No.107, Overseas Development Institute. Retrieved on October 7, 2017, from: www.odi.org.uk/agren

REN21. (2016). *Renewables 2016 Global Status Report*. Renewable Energy Policy Networks for the 21st Century. Retrieved on August 4, 2017, from: http://www.ren21.net/status-of-renewables/global-status-report/

Rennen, W., & Martens, P. (2003). The Globalisation Timeline. *Integrated Assessment*, *4*(3), 137–144. doi:10.1076/iaij.4.3.137.23768

Reshma, S., & Basavaraj, M. J. (2013). Employee welfare measures in mining industry–A study with reference to statutory welfare measures in NMDC, Donimalai Iron Ore Mine, Bellary district. *EXCEL International Journal of Multidisciplinary Management Studies*, *3*(7), 157–164.

Ribeiro, M. A., Valle, P. O., & Silva, J. A. (2013). Residents' attitudes towards tourism development in Cape Verde islands. *Tourism Geographies*, *15*(4), 654–679. doi:10.1080/14616688.2013.769022

Richards, M. (2003). *Poverty Reduction, Equity and Climate Change: Global Governance Synergies or Contradictions?* London: Overseas Development Institute.

Ritchie, B., & Crouch, G. (2005). *The Competitive Destination A Sustainable Tourism Perspective*. Cambridge: CABI Publishing.

Ritchie, J. W., Zammit, C., & Beal, D. (2004). Can seasonal climate forecasting assist in catchment water management decision-making? A case study of the Border Rivers catchment in Australia. *Agriculture, Ecosystems & Environment*, *104*(3), 553–565. doi:10.1016/j.agee.2004.01.029

Roberto, V. (2004). The Temporal Single-System Interpretation of Marx's Economics: A critical evaluation. *Metroeconomica*, *55*(1).

Robinson, A., Sparrow, P., Clegg, C., & Birdi, K. (2006). Forecasting Future Competency Requirements: A Three Phase Methodology. *Personnel Review*, *36*(1), 65–90. doi:10.1108/00483480710716722

Rodrigues, S., & Child, J. (2008). The development of corporate identity: A political perspective. *Journal of Management Studies*, *45*(5), 885–911. doi:10.1111/j.1467-6486.2007.00750.x

Rodriguez, F., & Rodrik, D. (2000). Trade Policy and Economic Growth: A Skeptic's Guide to the Cross-National Evidence. In B. S. Bernanke & K. Rogoff (Eds.), *NBER Macroeconomics Annual 2000* (Vol. 15, pp. 262–338). MIT Press. Retrieved from http://www.nber.org/books/bern01-1

Rodriguez, P., Uhlenbruck, K., & Eden, L. (2005). Government corruption and the entry strategies of multinationals. *Academy of Management Review*, *30*(2), 383–396. doi:10.5465/AMR.2005.16387894

Rodrik, D. (2006). *What's So Special about China's Exports?* NBER Working Paper, No:11947.

Rodrik, D., Subramanian, A., & Trebbi, F. (2004). Institutions Rule: The Primacy of Institutions Over Geography and Integration in Economic Development. *Journal of Economic Growth*, *9*(2), 131–165. doi:10.1023/B:JOEG.0000031425.72248.85

Roemer, J. E. (1980). A General Equilibrium Approach to Marxian Economics. *Econometrica*, *48*(2), 505–530. doi:10.2307/1911113

Rogoff, E. G. (2007). Opportunities for entrepreneurship in later life. *Generations (San Francisco, Calif.)*, *31*, 90–95.

Romer, P. M. (1986). Increasing Returns and Long-Run Growth. *Journal of Political Economy*, *94*(5), 1002–1037. doi:10.1086/261420

Romer, P. M. (1990). Endogenous Technological Change. *Journal of Political Economy*, *98*(5), 71–102. doi:10.1086/261725

Roseiro, A. H. (2009). *Factores Psicossociais de Motivação nos Cientistas. Um estudo de caso no Instituto Gulbenkian de Ciência* (Master's Thesis). School of Economics and Management, University of Lisbon, Portugal.

Rosenfeld, R. B. (2014). Innovation and entrepreneurship: The invisible cycle. In *Sustainable entrepreneurship: Business success through sustainability* (pp. 39–50). New York: Springer Heidelberg.

Rutovitz, J. (2010). *South African Energy Sector Jobs to 2030", Greenpeace Africa by the Institute for Sustainable Futures. University of Technology*. Sydney: Greenpeace Africa, Johannesburg.

Rutovitz, J., & Harris, S. (2012). *Calculating Global Energy Sector Jobs: 2012 Methodology. Prepared for Greenpeace International by the Institute for Sustainable Futures*. Sydney: University of Technology.

Ryan, C., & Montgomery, D. (1994). The attitudes of Bakewell residents to tourism and numbers in comunity responsive tourism. *Tourism Management*, *15*(5), 358–369. doi:10.1016/0261-5177(94)90090-6

Ryan, C., Scotland, A., & Montgomery, D. (1998). Resident attitudes to tourism development-A comparative study between the Rangitikei, New Zealand and Bakewell, United Kingdom. *Progress in Tourism and Hospitality Research*, *4*(2), 115–130. doi:10.1002/(SICI)1099-1603(199806)4:2<115::AID-PTH105>3.0.CO;2-7

Saboor, A., Sidd, M., & Hussain, M. (2004). Life and Social Sciences Agricultural Growth, Rural Poverty and Income Inequality in Pakistan. *Pakistan Journal of Life and Social Sciences*, *2*(2), 168–173.

Sachs, J. D., & Warner, A. (1995). *Economic Reform and the Process of Global Integration* (Brookings Papers on Economic Activity No. 1). Retrieved from https://www.brookings.edu/wp-content/uploads/1995/01/1995a_bpea_sachs_warner_aslund_fischer.pdf

Şahin, Ü. (2003). *Ekolojizmi Çevrecilikten Ayırmak Yeniden Bir Düşünme Denemesi, Üç Ekoloji, Sayı 1*. Retrieved on March 27, 2015, from: http://www.ucekoloji.net/?p=89

Şahin, Ü. (2004). Bir Truva Atı Olarak Sürdürülebilir Kalkınma. *Üç Ekoloji*, Sayı 2, ss. 9-30.

Şahin, Ü. (2007). Antikapitalist Bir İklim Değişikliği Mücadelesine Doğru. *Birikim Dergisi*, Sayı 223. Retrieved on March 27, 2015, from: http://www.birikimdergisi.com/sayi/223/anti-kapitalist-bir-iklim-degisikligimucadelesine-dogru.

Sala-i-Martin & Schwab. K (2014). *Globabl Competitiveness Report 2014-2015*. Geneva: World Economic Forum.

Sala-i-Martin Xavier. (2002). *The disturbing rise of world income inequality*. NBER Working Paper No. 8904.

Salancik, G. R., & Pfeffer, J. (1978). *The external control of organizations: A resource dependence perspective*. New York: Harper and Row.

Samimi, P., Lim, G. C., & Buang, A. A. (2011). Globalization Measurement: Notes on Common Globalization Indexes. *Journal of Knowledge Management, Economics and Information Technology*, *1*(7), 1–20. Retrieved from https://ideas.repec.org/a/spp/jkmeit/1216.html

Samimi, P., & Jenatabadi, H. S. (2014). Globalization and Economic Growth: Empirical Evidence on the Role of Complementarities. *PLoS One*, *9*(4), e87824. doi:10.1371/journal.pone.0087824 PMID:24721896

Samimi, P., Lim, G. C., & Buang, A. A. (2012). A critical review on synthetic globalization indexes. *International Journal of Fundamental Psychology and Social Sciences*, *2*(1), 28–31.

Samuelson, P. A. (1971, June). Understanding the Marxian notion of exploitation: A summary of the so-called transformation problem between Marxian values and competitive prices. *Journal of Economic Literature*, *9*(2), 399–431.

Sands, P., & Peel, J. (2012). *Principles of International Environmental Law* (3rd ed.). London: Cambridge University Press. doi:10.1017/CBO9781139019842

Santos, E., Ferreira, J., Albuquerque, C., Almeida, H., Mendonça, M., Silva, C., & Almeida, J. (2010). Desemprego: experiências de transição. *Psychologica*, *52*(2).

Sarafidis, V., & Wansbeek, T. (2010). *Cross-sectional Dependence in Panel Data Analysis* (No. 20367). Retrieved from http://mpra.ub.uni-muenchen.de/20367/

Sarafidis, V., & Wansbeek, T. (2012). Cross-Sectional Dependence in Panel Data Analysis. *Econometric Reviews, 31*(5), 483–531. doi:10.1080/07474938.2011.611458

Sarma, S., & Sunny, S. A. (2017). Civic entrepreneurial ecosystems: Smart city emergence in Kansas City. *Business Horizons.*

Satayanarayan, M. R., & Reddi, R. J. (2012). Labour welfare measure in cement industries in India. *International Journal of Physical and Social Sciences, 2*(7), 257–254.

Sattinger, M. (1993). Assignment Models Of The Distribution Of Earnings. *Journal of Economic Literature, 31*, 851–880.

SBA. (2012). What is a small business? *United States Small Business Administration.* Retrieved on November 12, 2016, from: http://www.sba.gov/size/

SBA. (2014). Small Business, Big Impact: Celebrating Our Country and Small Businesses. *United States Small Business Administration.* Retrieved on April 8, 2017, from: http://www.sba.gov/

Schmidpeter, R., & Weidinger, C. (2014). Linking business and society: an overview. In *Sustainable entrepreneurship: Business success through sustainability* (pp. 1–10). New York: Springer Heidelberg.

Schooler, C. (1984). Psychological effects of complex environments during the life span: A review and theory. *Intelligence, 8*(4), 259–281. doi:10.1016/0160-2896(84)90011-4

Schott, P. K. (1999). *One size fits all? Specialization, trade and income inequality.* Retrieved from http://faculty.som.yale.edu/peterschott/files/research/papers/schott_cones_103199.pdf

Schott, P. K. (2006). *The Relative Sophistication of Chinese Exports.* NBER Working Paper, No: 12173.

Schott, P. K. (2003). Across-Product versus Within-Product Specialization. In *International Trade*. Yale School of Management and NBER.

Schroeder, T. (1992). Host community perceptions of tourism's impacts: A cluster analysis. *Visions in Leisure and Business, 10*(4), 43–48.

Schuller, M., & Schuler-Zhou, Y. (2013). Chinese investment strategies and migration – Does Diaspora matter? A case study on Germany. MPC Migration Policy Centre, 2013/08.

Schumpeter, J. A. (1942). *Capitalist, socialism, and Democracy*. New York: Harper and Brothers.

Schumpeter, J. A. (1982). *The theory of economic development: An inquiry into profits, capital, credit, interest, and the business cycle* (Rev. ed.). Edison, NJ: Transaction.

Schwarz, N., & Strack, F. (1999). Reports of subjective well-being: Judgmental processes and their methodological implications. In D. Kahneman, E. Diener, & N. Schwarz (Eds.), *Well-being: The foundations of Hedonic Psychology*. New York: Russell Sage Foundation.

Schwens, C., Eiche, J., & Kabst, R. (2011). The moderating impact of informal institutional distance and formal institutional Challenge on SME entry mode choice. *Journal of Management Studies, 48*(2), 330–351.

Scott, J. (1994). *Poverty and wealth: citizenship, deprivation and privilege*. New York: Longman Sociology Series.

Scott, W. R. (2001). *Institutions and organizations*. Thousand Oaks, CA: Sage Publications, Inc.

Sen, A. (2000). *Development as Freedom*. Oxford, UK: Oxford University Press.

Sertyesilisik, B. (2016). A preliminary study on the regenerative construction project management concept for enhancing sustainability performance of the construction industry. *International Journal of Construction Management*. DOI: 10.1080/15623599.2016.1222665

Sertyesilisik, B. (2016). Embedding Sustainability Dynamics in the Lean Construction Supply Chain Management. *YBL Journal of Built Environment*, *4*(1), 62–63. doi:10.1515/jbe-2016-0006

Sertyesilisik, B., & Sertyesilisik, E. (2016). Eco industrial Development: As a Way of Enhancing Sustainable Development. *Journal of Economic Development, Environment and People*, *5*(1), 6–27. doi:10.26458/jedep.v5i1.133

Sertyesilisik, B., & Sertyesilisik, E. (2017). Ways of Fostering Green Economy and Green Growth. In W. L. Filho, D. M. Pociovalisteanu, & A. Al-Amin (Eds.), *Sustainable Economic Development. World Sustainability Series*. Cham: Springer. doi:10.1007/978-3-319-45081-0_3

Seth, O. O. (2008). *Effects of HIV/AIDS Related Illnesses and Deaths on Agricultural Production: A Case of Nyando and Kericho Districts in Kenya* (Thesis). Egerton University.

Sezerel, H., & Cil, A. (2012). Connecting nature, culture, and art in the context of socially responsible ecological tourism. *MMV6 Conference Proceedings*, 266-267.

Shahbaz, M., Loganathan, N., Tiwari, A. K., & Sherafatian-Jahromi, R. (2015). Financial development and income inequality: Is there any financial Kuznets curve in Iran? *Social Indicators Research*, *124*(2), 357–382. doi:10.100711205-014-0801-9

Shaikh, A. (1977). Marx's theory of value and the 'transformational problem. In J. Sohwartz (Ed.), *The Subtle Anatomy of Capitalism*. Santa Monica, CA: Goodyear.

Shaikh, A. (1984). The transformation from Marx to Sraffa. In E. Mandell (Ed.), *Ricardo, Marx, Sraffa*. London: Verse.

Shane, S. (2008). *Technology Strategy for Managers and Entrepreneurs* (1st ed.). Upper Saddle River, NJ: Pearson.

Shaoming, C., Stough, R., & Jackson, R. (2009). Measuring and building high-quality entrepreneurship: A research prospectus. *Innovation: The European Journal of Social Sciences*, *22*, 329–340. doi:10.1080/13511610903399088

Sharma, B., & Dyer, P. (2009). An investigation of differences in residents' perceptions on the Sunshine Coast: Tourism impacts and demographic variables. *Tourism Geographies*, *11*(2), 187–213. doi:10.1080/14616680902827159

Sharpe, A., & Zyblock, M. (1997). Macroeconomic performance and income distribution in Canada. *The North American Journal of Economics and Finance*, *8*(2), 167–199. doi:10.1016/S1062-9408(97)90006-1

Sharpley, R. (2014). Host perceptions of tourism: A review of the research. *Tourism Management*, *42*, 37–49. doi:10.1016/j.tourman.2013.10.007

Shen, C. H., Lee, C., & Lee, C. (2010). What makes international capital flows promote economic growth? An international cross-country analysis. *Scottish Journal of Political Economy*, *57*(5), 515–546. doi:10.1111/j.1467-9485.2010.00529.x

Sheng, L., & Yang, D. T. (2016). Expanding export variety: The role of institutional reforms in developing countries. *Journal of Development Economics*, *118*, 45–58. doi:10.1016/j.jdeveco.2015.08.009

Silva, M. M. (2009). *O Mosaico de Desemprego* (PhD thesis). School of Philosophy and Human Sciences, State University of Campinas.

Silva, P. A. (1998). O RMG e a nova questão social. *Portugal, Society and Work*, *3*.

Silva, P. A. (2002). O modelo de welfare da Europa do Sul: reflexões sobre a utilidade do conceito. *Portugal, Sociology, Problems and Practices, 38.*

Silva, P.A., & Pereira, M.T. (2012). As políticas de proteção no desemprego em Portugal. *Portugal, Sociology, Problems and Practices, 70*, 133-150.

Sinclair-Maragh, G., Gursoy, D., & Vieregge, M. (2015). Residents' perceptions toward tourism development: A factor-cluster approach. *Journal of Destination Marketing & Management, 4*(1), 36–45. doi:10.1016/j.jdmm.2014.10.001

Sirakaya, E., Sasidharan, V., & Sönmez, S. (1999). Redefining ecotourism: The need for a supply side view. *Journal of Travel Research, 38*(2), 168–172. doi:10.1177/004728759903800210

Sklair, L. (1999). Competing conceptions of globalization. *Journal of World-systems Research, 5*(2), 143–163. doi:10.5195/JWSR.1999.140

Skousen, M. (2009). *The Making of Modern Economics: The Lives and Ideas of the Great Thinkers*. New York: M E Sharpe.

Slaughter, M. J., & Swagel, P. (1997). *The effect of globalization on wages in the advanced economies*. International Monetary Fund Staff Studies for the World Economic Outlook.

Smith, A. (1973). *Indagine Sulla Natura E Le Cause Della Ricchezza Delle Nazioni*. Milano: Isedi.

Smith, A. (1994). *The Wealth of Nations*. New York: The Modern Library. The. (Original work published 1776)

Smith, L. V., Leybourne, S., Kim, T.-H., & Newbold, P. (2004). More powerful panel data unit root tests with an application to mean reversion in real exchange rates. *Journal of Applied Econometrics, 19*(2), 147–170. doi:10.1002/jae.723

Solis, B. (2017). *The definition of digital transformation*. Retrieved on December 22, 2017, from: http://www.briansolis.com/2017/01/definition-of-digital-transformation/

Solo, V. (1984). The Order of Differencing in ARIMA Models. *Journal of the American Statistical Association, 79*(388), 916–921. doi:10.1080/01621459.1984.10477111

Solow, R. M. (1956). A contribution to the theory of economic growth. *Source: The Quarterly Journal of Economics, 70*(1), 65–94. Retrieved from http://www.jstor.org/stable/1884513

Song, M. (2003). Choosing Ethnic Identity. Blackwell Publishing Ltd.

Soskice, D. (1994). Reconciling Markets And Institutions: The German Apprenticeship System. In L. M. Linch (Ed.), *Training And The Private Sector*. Chicago: University Of Chicago Press/Nber.

Soubbotina, T. P., & Sheram, K. (2000). *Beyond economic growth: Meeting the challenges of global development*. World Bank. Retrieved from https://books.google.com.tr/books/about/Beyond_Economic_Growth.html?id=ZPQ1I8WuDcgC&redir_esc=y

Spaan, E., van Naerssen, T., & Hillmann, F. (2005). Shifts in the European Discourses on Migration and Development. *Asian and Pacific Migration Journal, 14*(1-2), 35–69. doi:10.1177/011719680501400104

Sraffa, P. (2010). *Malların Mallarla Üretimi İktisat Kuramını Eleştiriye Açış, Çev. Ümit Şenesen*. İstanbul: Yordam Yayınları.

Srinivas, K. T. (2013). A Study on Employee Welfare Facilities adopted at Bosch Limited, Bangalore. *Research Journal of Management Science, 2*(12), 7–11.

Standing, G. (2000). *Unemployment and Income Security*. Discussion Paper Prepared for Geneva 2000: Follow-up to the World Summit on Social Development, Programme on Socio-Economic Security Papers no 3. Geneva, ILO.

Steedman, I. (1977). *Marx after Sraffa*. London: New Left Books.

Steel, P., & Deniz, S. O. (2002). Personality and happiness: A national-level analysis. *Journal of Personality and Social Psychology, 83*.

Stein, E. W. (2013). A Comprehensive Multi-Criteria Model to Rank Electric Energy Production Technologies. *Renewable & Sustainable Energy Reviews, 22*, 640–654. doi:10.1016/j.rser.2013.02.001

Steinemann, A. C. (2006). Using Climate Forecasts for Drought Management. *Journal of Applied Meteorology and Climatology, 45*(10), 1353–1361. doi:10.1175/JAM2401.1

Stern, N. H. (2007). *The Economics of Climate Change: The Stern Review*. Cambridge, UK: Cambridge University Press. doi:10.1017/CBO9780511817434

Stewart, T. R., Pielke, R. Jr, & Nath, R. (2004). Understanding user Decision Making and the Value of Improved Precipitation Forecasts: Lessons from a case study. *Bulletin of the American Meteorological Society, 85*(2), 223–235. doi:10.1175/BAMS-85-2-223

Stiglitz, J. E. (1996). Some lessons from the East Asian miracle. *The World Bank Observer, 11*(2), 151–177. doi:10.1093/wbro/11.2.151

Stokey, N. L. (1989). Learning by Doing and the Introduction of New Goods. *Journal of Political Economy, Vol, 96*(:4), 701–717.

Stolper, W., & Samuelson, P. (1941). Protection and real wages. *The Review of Economic Studies, 9*(1), 58–73. doi:10.2307/2967638

Stone, S., Sourdin, P., & Legendre, C. (2013). *Trade and Labour Market Adjustment*. OECD Trade Policy Papers, No. 143. Paris: OECD Publishing. 10.1787/5k4c6spvddwj-en

Streeck, W. (1987). The Role Of The Social Partners. In *Vocational Education And Training In The Federal Republic Of Germany*. Berlin: Cedefop.

Stringer, J. (2006). *Unpublished results. Foreign direct investment and income inequality in developing countries: An exploration of the causal relationship using industry level FDI data.* Document prepared for the 2006 annual Midwest Political Science Association conference.

Stylidis, D., & Terzidou, M. (2014). Tourism and the economic crisis in Kavala, Greece. *Annals of Tourism Research, 44*, 210–226. doi:10.1016/j.annals.2013.10.004

Suarez, P. (2009). *Linking climate knowledge and Decisions: Humanitarian Challenges*. The Pardee Papers 7.

Sung, T. K. (2015). The creative economy in global competition. *Technological Forecasting and Social Change, 96*, 89–91. doi:10.1016/j.techfore.2015.04.003

Sweezy, P. M. (1942). *The Theory of Capitalist Development*. New York: Monthly Review Press.

Sweezy, P. M. (Ed.). (1949). *Karl Marx and the Close of His System by Eugen Bohn-Bawerk and Bohn-Bawerk's Critism of Marx by Rudolf Hilferding*. New York: A.M. Kelly.

Tachibanaki, T. (2006). Inequality and Poverty in Japan. *The Japanese Economic Review, 57*(1), 1–27. doi:10.1111/j.1468-5876.2006.00355.x

Tadelis, S., & Williamson, O. E. (2012). *Transaction Cost Economics*. Retrieved on May 9, 2014, from: Http://Ssrn.Com/Abstract=2020176

Tall, A. (2013). *What do we mean by Climate Services?* Intergovernmental Board on Climate Services. Retrieved on June 2, 2015, from: https://library.wmo.int/opac/doc_num.php?explnum_id=3224

Tall, A., Mason, S. J., van Aalst, M., Suarez, P., Ait-Chellouche, Y., Diallo, A. A., & Braman, L. (2012). Using Seasonal Climate Forecasts to Guide Disaster Management: The Red Cross Experience during the 2008 West Africa Floods. *International Journal of Geophysics*, *2012*, 12–25. doi:10.1155/2012/986016

Tasking, L., & van Bunnen, G. (2015). Knowledge Management Through the Development of Knowledge Repositories: Towards Work Degradation, New Technology. *Work and Employment*, *30*(2), 158–172. doi:10.1111/ntwe.12049

Taylor, A. M. (2002). *Globalization, trade and development: Some lessons from history.* NBE Working Paper No:9326, November.

TEİAŞ. (2016). *Türkiye 2015 Yılı Elektrik Üretim-İletim İstatistikleri. Türkiye Elektrik İletim A.Ş. Genel Müdürlüğü Planlama ve Stratejik Yönetim Dairesi Başkanliği Üretim Planlama ve İstatistik Müdürlüğü, Ankara.* Retrieved from http://www.teias.gov.tr/T%C3% BcrkiyeElektrik%C4%B0statistikleri/istatistik2015/istatistik2015.htm

The STEM Education Coalition. (2017). Retrieved on January 3, 2018, from: http://www.stemedcoalition.org/stem-ed-coalition-activities/legislation/

The White House Office of the Press Secretary. (2017). *Presidential Memorandum for the Secretary of Education.* Retrieved on November 7, 2017, from: https://www.whitehouse.gov/the-press-office/2017/09/25/memorandum-secretary-education

Theodossiou, I. (1998). The effects of low-pay and unemployment on psychological well-being: A logistic regression approach. *Journal of Health Economics*, *17*(1), 85–104. doi:10.1016/S0167-6296(97)00018-0 PMID:10176317

Thompson, M. (2018). Social capital, innovation and economic growth. *Journal of Behavioral and Experimental Economics*, *73*, 46–52. doi:10.1016/j.socec.2018.01.005

Thongmak, M. (2013). A Systematic Framework for Sustainable ICTs in Developing Countries. *International Journal of Information Technologies and Systems Approach*, *6*(1), 1–19. doi:10.4018/jitsa.2013010101

Thorbecke, E., & Charumilind, C. (2002). Economic inequality and its socioeconomic impact. *World Development*, *30*(9), 1477–1495. doi:10.1016/S0305-750X(02)00052-9

Thurow, L. C. (1975). Generating Inequality: Mechanisms Of Distribution. In *The U.S. Economy*. New York: Basic Books. doi:10.1007/978-1-349-15723-5

Thurow, L. C. (2000). *Building Wealth: The New Rules for Individuals, Companies and Nations in a Knowledge Base Economy*. New York: HarperCollins.

Thyne, M., & Lawson, R. (2001). Research Note: Addressing tourism public policy issues through attitude segmentation of host communities. *Current Issues in Tourism*, *4*(2-4), 392–400. doi:10.1080/13683500108667895

Tidd, J., & Bessant, J. (2009). *Managing innovation: Integrating technological, market and organizational change* (4th ed.). Hoboken, NJ: Wiley.

Tidmarsh, K. (2014). *Milwaukee: The most segregated and Polarized place in America.* Retrieved on September 9, 2016, from: http://www.governing.com/topics/politics/gov-milwaukee-most-segregated-polarized-place.html

TIES. (1990). *Global Ecotourism Fact Sheet.* The International Ecotourism Society. Retrieved on June 2, 2015, from: https://ibgeographylancaster.wikispaces.com/file/view/TIES+GLOBAL+ECOTOURISM+FACT+SHEET.PDF

Tiwari, P. (2011). Impact of selected HRM practices on perceived employee performance: An empirical study. *Global Management Journal*, *3*(1/2), 37–43.

Ton, G. (2013). *Finding the real impact of agricultural innovation support*. Retrieved on February 15, 2015, from: https://www.scidev.net/global/data/opinion/finding-the-real-impact-of-agricultural-innovation-support.html

Tovar, C., & Lockwood, M. (2008). Social impacts of tourism: An Australian regional case study. *International Journal of Tourism Research*, *10*(4), 365–378. doi:10.1002/jtr.667

Tretyakova, E. (2014). Assessing sustainability of development of ecological and economic systems: A dynamic method. *Studies on Russian Economic Development*, *25*(4), 423–430. doi:10.1134/S1075700714040133

Tsang, M. C., & Levin, H. (1985). The Economics Of Overeducation. *Economics of Education Review*, *4*(2), 93–104. doi:10.1016/0272-7757(85)90051-2

Tugan-Baranovsky, M. I. (1906). Theoretical foundations of Marxism (3rd ed.). J. "World of God".

TUIK. (2017). *Turkish Statistical Institute*. Retrieved on July 26, 2017, from: http://www.turkstat.gov.tr

Tweddle, A., Battle, K., & Torjman, S. (2013). *Welfare in Canada 2012*. Caledon Institute of Social Policy.

U.S. Census Bureau Data. (2014). *Population Reports U.S. Department of Commerce Economics and Statistics Administration*. U.S. Census Bureau. Retrieved on April 9, 2015, from: https://www.census.gov/content/dam/Census/library/publications/2015/demo/p60-252.pdf

U.S. Census Bureau Data. (2016). *Population Report, city of Milwaukee*. Retrieved on January 4, 2017, from: https://www.census.gov/quickfacts/fact/table/Milwaukeecitywisconsin/RHI125216

Uhlenbruck, K., Rodriguez, P., Doh, J., & Eden, L. (2006). The impact of corruption on entry strategy: Evidence from telecommunication projects in emerging economies. *Organization Science*, *17*(3), 402–414. doi:10.1287/orsc.1060.0186

UMCOR. (2013). *Disaster Risk Preparedness Saves Lives in India*. Retrieved on July 15, 2014, from: http://www.umcor.org/UMCOR/Resources/News-Stories/2013/October/1018-Disaster-

Um, S., & Crompton, J. L. (1987). Measuring resident's attachment levels in a host community. *Journal of Travel Research*, *26*(1), 27–29. doi:10.1177/004728758702600105

UNCHE. (1972). *Declaration of the UN Conference on the Human Environment, Stockholm, 5–16 June 1972*. Report of the UN Conference on the Human Environment, UN Doc.A/CONF.48/14.

UNCSD. (1996). Indicators of sustainable development—Framework and methodologies. New York: UNCSD.

UNFCCC. (2017). *GHG Inventories National Communications. United Nations on Climate Change*. Retrieved on January 10, 2017, from: http://unfccc.int/documentation/documents/advanced_search/items/6911.php?priref=600003580#beg

United Nations (UN). (1997). *Trade and development Report. United Nations Conference on Trade and Development.*

United Nations General Assembly. (1962). *Economic Development and the Conservation of Nature*. G.A. Resolution 1831 (XVII), UN GAOR, 17th Session, Supp. no. 17, UN Doc. A/RES/1831 (XVII).

United Nations. (1993). Results of the Earth Summit 1992. New York: UN.

United Nations. (2000). *We the Peoples: The Role of the United Nations in the 21st Century*. New York: UN. Retrieved on September 20, 2017, from: www.un.org/millennium/sg/report/key.htm

United Nations. (2015). *Inequality and the end of extreme poverty*. Oxfam Media.

United Nations. (2015). *World urbanization prospects*. New York: Department of Economic and Social Affairs. Retrieved on January 1, 2017, from: http://esa.un.org/unpd/wup/Publications/Files/WUP2014-Report.pdf

Urry, J. (1999). *Mekânları Tüketmek, Çev. Rahmi G. Öğdül*. İstanbul: Ayrıntı Yayınları.

USA Department of Education Office of Innovation and Improvement. (2016). *STEM 2026 A vision for innovation in STEM education*. Retrieved on February 22, 2017, from: https://innovation.ed.gov/files/2016/09/AIR-STEM2026_Report_2016.pdf

USAID. (2010). *Staple Foods Value Chain Analysis: Country Report-Kenya*. USAID.

USAID. (2013). *Climate Services: Better Information for Climate-Resilient Decision Making*. Retrieved on May 30, 2017, from: http://pdf.usaid.gov/pdf_docs/PA00KJWS.pdf

Van Cauwenbergh, N., Biala, K., Bielders, C., Brouckaert, V., Franchois, L., Garcia Cidad, V., ... Peeters, A. (2007). SAFE-A hierarchical framework for assessing the sustainability of agricultural systems. *Agriculture, Ecosystems & Environment, 120*(2–4), 229–242. doi:10.1016/j.agee.2006.09.006

Van der Meer, P. H. (2014). Gender, Unemployment and Subjective Well-Being: Why Being Unemployed Is Worse for Men than for Women. *Social Indicators Research, 115*(1), 23–44. doi:10.100711205-012-0207-5

Van Vuuren, D. P., Kok, M., Lucas, P. L., Prins, A. G., Alkemade, R., Van den Berg, M., ... Stehfest, E. (2015). Pathways to achieve a set of ambitious global sustainability objectives by 2050: Explorations using the IMAGE integrated assessment model. *Technological Forecasting and Social Change, 98*, 303–323. doi:10.1016/j.techfore.2015.03.005

Vareiro, L. M. C., Remoaldo, P. C., & Ribeiro, J. A. C. (2013). Residents' perceptions of tourism impacts in Guimarães (Portugal): A cluster analysis. *Current Issues in Tourism, 16*(6), 535–551. doi:10.1080/13683500.2012.707175

Vargas, A., Plaza, M. A., & Porras, N. (2009). Understanding residents' attitudes toward the development of industrial tourism in a former mining community. *Journal of Travel Research, 47*(3), 373–387. doi:10.1177/0047287508322783

Vargas, A., Porras, N., & Plaza, M. A. (2014). Residents' attitude to tourism and seasonality. *Journal of Travel Research, 53*(5), 581–596. doi:10.1177/0047287513506295

Veenhoven, R. (2006). Quality of life research. In C. D. Bryant & D. L. Peck (Eds.), *Handbook of 21st Century Sociology*. New York: Sage.

Ven, S. (2016). Residents' participation, perceived impacts, and support for community-based ecotourism in cambodia: A latent profile analysis. *Asia Pacific Journal of Tourism Research, 21*(8), 836–861. doi:10.1080/10941665.2015.1075565

Villaverde, J., & Maza, A. (2011). Globalisation, Growth and Convergence. *World Economy, 34*(6), 952–971. doi:10.1111/j.1467-9701.2011.01359.x

Viscusi, W. K. (1979). Job Hazards And Workers Quit Rates: An Analysis Of Adaptive Workers Behavior. *International Economic Review, 20*(1), 29–58. doi:10.2307/2526415

Vohs, K. D., & Baumeister, R. F. (2011). What's the use of happiness? It can't buy you money. *Journal of Consumer Psychology, 21*, 139-141.

Vujakovic, P. (2010). How to Measure Globalization? A New Globalization Index (NGI). *Atlantic Economic Journal, 38*(2), 237–237. doi:10.100711293-010-9217-3

Wade, R. H. (2001). The rising inequality of world income distribution. *Finance & Development, 38*, 37–36.

Wainaina, A. (2014). *Factors affecting perception on job performance in the Kenya financial sector A case study of an international bank with substantial operations in Kenya* (Doctoral dissertation). United States International University-Africa.

Wallerstein, I. (1997). *Tarihsel Kapitalizm, Çev. Necmiye Alpay*. İstanbul: Metis Yayınları.

Walsh, B. (2009). Q&A: The U.N.'s Ban Ki-Moon on Climate Change. *TIME*. Retrieved on September 25, 2017, from: http://content.time.com/time/specials/packages/article/0,28804,1929071_1929070_1947173,00.html

Wambugu, A., & Munga, B. (2009). *Growth, Poverty and Income Inequality in Kenya*. Nairobi: KIPPRA.

Wärmark, K. (2015). Assessment of water footprint for civil construction projects. The Department of Aquatic Sciences and Assessment, Swedish University of Agricultural Sciences (SLU) UPTEC W15 018, Digitally published at the Department of Earth Sciences, Uppsala University, Uppsala.

WCED. (1987). *Our CommonFuture: Report ofthe World Commission on Environment and Development*. WCED.

WDI. (n.d.). Retrieved from http://data.worldbank.org/data-catalog/world-development-indicators

Weaver, D. (2001). *Ecotourism*. Milton, Australia: John Wiley & Sons, Ltd.

Weaver, D. (2006). *Sustainable tourism: Theory and practice*. Oxford, UK: Elsevier Butterworth Heinemann.

Weaver, D. B., & Lawton, L. J. (2001). Resident perceptions in the urban-rural fringe. *Annals of Tourism Research, 28*(2), 439–458. doi:10.1016/S0160-7383(00)00052-9

Weaver, D. B., & Lawton, L. J. (2013). Resident perceptions of a contentious tourism event. *Tourism Management, 37*, 165–175. doi:10.1016/j.tourman.2013.01.017

Webb, K. J., Hodge, T. G., & Thompson, J. H. (2012). Small Business Sustainability: What is the CPA's Role? *International Journal of Business and Social Science, 3*(12), 1–7.

Weber, E., & Sonka, S. (1994). Production and pricing decisions in cash-crop farming effects of decision traits and climate change expectations. In B. Jacobsen, D. Pedersen, J. Christensen, & P. Rasmussen (Eds.), *Farmers' decision making – a descriptive approach* (pp. 203–218). Copenhagen: European Association of Agricultural Economists.

Weede, E. (1997). Income inequality, democracy and growth reconsidered. *European Journal of Political Economy, 13*(4), 751–764. doi:10.1016/S0176-2680(97)00028-1

Wei, S. J., & Wu, Y. (2001). *Globalization and inequality: Evidence from within China*. NBER Working Paper No. 8611. Retrieved from http://www.nber.org/papers/w8611.pdf

Weidinger, C., Fischler, F., & Schmidpeter, R. (2014). *Sustainable entrepreneurship: Business success through sustainability*. New York: Springer. Retrieved on April 22, 2016, from: https://www.researchgate.net/profile/Mara_Baldo/publication/300155089_Sustainable_Entrepreneurship_Next_Stage_of_Responsible_Business/links/57481dc608ae2301b0b9680b/Sustainable-Entrepreneurship-Next-Stage-of-Responsible-Business.pdf

Weiller, C., & Neely, A. (2013). *Business Model Design in an Ecosystem Context*. Cambridge, UK: University of Cambridge.

Wennick, B., & Ochola, W. (2011). Designing innovation platforms: Putting Heads Together, 396. Amsterdam: KIT Publishers.

Westerlund, J. (2008). Panel cointegration tests of the Fisher effect. *Journal of Applied Econometrics, 23*(2), 193–233. doi:10.1002/jae.967

Westerlund, J., & Edgerton, D. (2008). Simple tests for cointegration in dependent panels with structural breaks. *Oxford Bulletin of Economics and Statistics, 70*(5), 665–704. doi:10.1111/j.1468-0084.2008.00513.x

White, A. (2007). A Global Projection of Subjective Well-being: A Challenge to Positive Psychology? *Psychtalk, 56*, 17–20.

Wilber, K. (1997). An integral theory of consciousness. *Journal of Consciousness Studies*, *4*(1), 71–92.

Wilber, K. (2000). *Integral psychology: Consciousness, spirit, psychology, therapy*. Boston: Shambhala.

Williams, J., & Lawson, R. (2001). Community issues and resident opinions of tourism. *Annals of Tourism Research*, *28*(2), 269–290. doi:10.1016/S0160-7383(00)00030-X

Williamson, O. E. (1985). L'economia Dell'organizzazione: Il Modello Dei Costi Di Transazione. In R. C. D. Nacamulli & A. Rugiadini (Eds.), *Organizzazione & Mercato*. Bologna: Il Mulino.

Windmeijer, F. (2005). A finite sample correction for the variance of linear efficient two-step GMM estimators. *Journal of Econometrics*, *126*(1), 25–51. doi:10.1016/j.jeconom.2004.02.005

Winkelmann, L., & Winkelmann, R. (1998). *Why Are the Unemployed So Unhappy? Evidence from Panel Data. Economica*. The London School of Economics and Political Science.

WMO. (2006). Climate Information for Development Needs: An Action Plan for Africa, Report and Implementation Strategy. GCOS 108, WMO/TD No. 1358, Geneva

Wolfers, J. (2003). Is Business Cycle Volatily Costly? Evidence from Surveys of Subjective Well-Being. *International Finance*, *6*.

Wood, A. (1994). *North-South Trade, Employment, and Inequality: Changing Fortunes in a Skill-Driven World*. Oxford, UK: Clarendon Press.

Wood, M. E. (2002). *Ecotourism: Principles, practices & policies for sustainability*. Paris: UNEP.

Woods, N. (1998). Editorial introduction. Globalization: Definitions, debates and implications. *Oxford Development Studies*, *26*(1), 5–13. doi:10.1080/13600819808424142

World Bank. (1998). *Protecting Our Planet: Securing Our Future*. Washington, DC: Author.

World Bank. (2006). *World Development Indicators*. Washington, DC: Author.

World Bank. (2008). *Kenya Poverty and Inequality Assessment*. Economic Management Unit Africa Region.

World Bank. (2016a). The Cost of Air Pollution. *World Bank Group and IHME*. Retrieved on January 10, 2017, from: http://documents.worldbank.org/curated/en/781521473177013155/pdf/108141-REVISED-Cost-of-PollutionWebCORRECTEDfile.pdf

World Conservation Union. (1980). *World Conservation Strategy: Living Resource Conservation for Sustainable Development*. Gland, Switzerland: International Union for Conservation of Nature.

World Meteorological Organization (WMO). (2011). *Climate Knowledge for Action: a Global Framework for Climate Services–Empowering the Most Vulnerable: the Report of the High-level Taskforce for the Global Framework for Climate Services*. World Meteorological Organization.

World Meteorological Organization Greenhouse Gas Bulletin. The state of Greenhouse Gases in the Atmosphere Based on Global Observations through 2016. (2017). Retrieved on January 10, 2018, from: https://library.wmo.int/opac/doc_num.php?explnum_id=4022

World Wildlife Fund. (2009). *Arctic Still Unprepared for Major Oil Spill Twenty Years after Exxon Valdez*. Retrieved on August 30, 2017, from: http://arcticfocus.com/2009/03/23/wwf-arctic-still-unprepared-for-major-oil-spill-20-years-after-exxon-valdez/

Wright, I. (2007). Nonstandard labour values. *Open Discussion Papers in Economics, 69.*

Wuebbles, D. J., Fahey, D. W., Hibbard, K. A., Dokken, D. J., Stewart, B. C., & Maycock, T. K. (Eds.). (n.d.). USGCRP, 2017: Climate Science Special Report: Fourth National Climate Assessment (vol. 1). U.S. Global Change Research Program. doi:10.7930/J0J964J6

WUWM, Milwaukee Public Radio. (2013). *New ranking: Milwaukee still country's most segregated metro area.* Retrieved on May 3, 2017, from: http://www.wuwm.com/post/new-ranking-Milwaukee-still-countrys-most-segregated-metro-area

Xu, D., & Shenkar, O. (2002). Institutional distance and the multinational enterprise. *Academy of Management Review*, 608–618.

Xu, S. (1999). *Xibanya Huaqiao Huaren Xiehui Ji Lu Xi Huaren Shetuan Qingkuang [The State of Affairs between the Association of Chinese in Spain and the Sino-Spanish Community]. In Everybody Has a Chinese Heart.* Hangzhou: Zhejiang Renmin.

Ying, Y.-H., Chang, K., & Lee, C.-H. (2014). The Impact of Globalization on Economic Growth. *Journal for Economic Forecasting*, (2), 25–34. Retrieved from https://ideas.repec.org/a/rjr/romjef/vy2014i2p25-34.html

Yohe, G. W., Lasco, R. D., Ahmad, Q. K., Arnell, N. W., Cohen, S. J., Hope, C., . . . Perez, R. T. (2007). Perspectives on climate change and sustainability. In Climate Change 2007: Impacts, Adaptation and Vulnerability. Contribution of Working Group II to the Fourth Assessment Report of the Intergovernmental Panel on Climate Change. Cambridge, UK: Cambridge University Press.

Yü-Dembski, D. (2005). Huaqiao – Geschichte der Auslandschinesischen in Deutschland. von Groeling.

Yukl, G. (2010). *Leadership in organizations* (7th ed.). Upper Saddle River, NJ: Pearson Prentice Hall.

Zaheer, S., Schomaker, M., & Genc, M. (2003). Identity versus culture in mergers of equals. *European Management Journal*, *21*(2), 185–191. doi:10.1016/S0263-2373(03)00013-6

Zavadskas, E. K., & Kaklauskas, A. (1996). Determination of an efficient contractor by using the new method of multicriteria assessment. In *International Symposium for "The Organization and Management of Construction". Shaping Theory and Practice* (*Vol. 2*, pp. 94-104). Academic Press.

Zegarowski, G. (2007). Corporate sustainability after Sarbanes-Oxley linking social political initiatives and small and medium-sized enterprise resources. *International Journal of Disclosure and Governance*, *4*(1), 52–58. doi:10.1057/palgrave.jdg.2050043

Zhang, B. Q., & Fielden, K. (2011). Sustainable Economic ICT Strategy: A Proposed Framework. *All Sprouts Content.* Retrieved on May 9, 2015, from: http://aisel.aisnet.org/sprouts_all/443

Zhang, G. (2003). Migration of Highly Skilled Chinese to Europe: Trends and Perspective. *International Migration (Geneva, Switzerland)*, *41*(3), 73–97. doi:10.1111/1468-2435.00242

Zhao, S. (2017). *A time of test for the China model of economic growth.* Retrieved from http://www.eastasiaforum.org/2017/01/29/a-time-of-test-for-the-china-model-of-economic-growth/

Zhuhadar, L., Thrasher, E., Marklin, S., & de Pablos, P. O. (2017). The next wave of innovation-Review of smart cities intelligent operation systems. *Computers in Human Behavior*, *66*, 273–281. doi:10.1016/j.chb.2016.09.030

Ziemnowicz, J. (2010). *Joseph A. Schumpeter and Innovation.* Retrieved on April 11, 2017, from: https://link.springer.com/content/pdf/10.1007/978-1-4614-3858-8_476.pdf

Ziervogel, G. (2004). Targeting seasonal climate forecasts for integration into household level decisions: The case of smallholder farmers in Lesotho. *The Geographical Journal*, *170*(1), 6–21. doi:10.1111/j.0016-7398.2004.05002.x

Zizek, S. (2013). İdeoloji Hayaleti, Çev. Sibel Kibar, iç. Slavoj Zizek (Ed.), İdeolojiyi Haritalamak, Dipnot Yayınları, Ankara.

Zygiaris, S. (2013). Smart city reference model: Assisting planners to conceptualize the building of smart city innovation ecosystems. *J. Knowl. Econ.*, *4*(2), 217–231. doi:10.100713132-012-0089-4

About the Contributors

Bryan Christiansen is the Chief Executive Officer of Global Research Society, LLC in Michigan, USA. A former business lecturer at universities in Russia, Turkey, and the USA, he has traveled to 41 countries where he has conducted international business since 1985 in multiple languages and various industries with Global 500 firms and smaller. Christiansen received his Bachelor of Science degree in Marketing at the University of the State of New York in 1996 and his MBA degree at Capella University in 2003. The author of 22 Scopus-indexed Reference books on business, cultural studies, economics, and psychology, he is fluent in Chinese, Japanese, Spanish, and Turkish. Christiansen is currently working with a Russian theoretical mathematician on a new economic model for developing nations.

* * *

Daniel Álvarez Bassi, PhD in Economics and Business Management by the University of Deusto (Spain). He is Coordinator of the Centre for Research in Marketing and Tourism at the Faculty of Business Management, Catholic University of Uruguay (Uruguay).

Muhlis Can is an assistant professor at Hakkari University in Department of Economics and Finance. He holds a BA from Ataturk University in 2003. Thereafter, he started his career in the private sector. He has 6 years experience in various areas of the private sector, including marketing, export, and import. In 2011, he completed MA in Suleyman Demirel University. In 2015, he completed his Ph.D. at the same university. He writes on issues of international trade, energy, tourism, and globalization. He has collaborated actively with researchers in different universities around the world. In recent years, he has focused on econometric modeling. His researches were published in different peer-reviewed journals (indexing in SSCI, ESCI, Econlit) including Environmental Science and Pollution Research, Eurasian Business Review, International Journal of Alanya Faculty of Business, Akdeniz University Journal of The Faculty of Economics and Administrative Sciences.

Edward T. Chen is a professor of Management Information Systems of Operations and Information Systems Department in the Manning School of Business at University of Massachusetts Lowell. Dr. Chen has published numerous refereed research articles in scholarly journals and refereed chapters in academic books. His main research interests are in the areas of Project Management, Knowledge Management, Internet of Things, and Software Development.

Md Mahfuzar Rahman Chowdhury obtained LL.M from the department of Law & Justice, University of Rajshahi, Bangladesh. He has experience of working in NGOs and law-firms. Also, he is an advocate of the Bangladesh Supreme Court, Dhaka. Mr. Chowdhury is a published author of a book chapter titled, "Bridging the Public-Private Partnership in Disaster Management in Bangladesh" by Taylor and Francis. Recently, he participated on the 18th World Congress of Criminology held at O. P. Jindal Global University, NCR, New Delhi, India in December, 2016 where he presented a paper titled "Examining the Implication of Reducing Recidivism". Now, Mr. Chowdhury is working with a reputed law-firm, "The Legal Care". His areas of interest includes, disaster management, climate change, environmental law, criminology, amongst others.

Mona Chung is an expert in doing business in China. She addresses the major issues in doing business with China-overcomes the cultural gap. The vast cultural differences between China and the West have left many companies with large amount of written-downs. As a bi-cultural person she short-circuits processes and produce results that increase efficiency by between 70%-50%. Dr Chung specialises in strategic planning, cross-cultural negotiation, mediation and communication, management and marketing practice for international organizations with the understanding of the culture of the Chinese market first. Dr Chung is a frequent guest speaker at public forums.

James Dixon has a Doctor of Management in Organizational Leadership with a specialization in Information Systems and Technology (DM/IST) from University of Phoenix. He is an IT Specialist for US Army for over 20 years with broad experience in training, educating, evaluating, technical writing, and developing human capital resources in order to improve work processes, products, services, productivity, and performance. His research interests are the impact of technology on society, Management, Organizational Behavior, Curriculum Design, Educational Administration, and Instructional Technology.

Buhari Doğan was born in Isparta in 1985. He completed his primary and secondary education in Egirdir and Isparta. Then, he holds BA from Kocaeli University, Department of Economics of the Faculty of Economics and Administrative Sciences. He completed his MA in Department of Econometrics at Suleyman Demirel University, and then he completed his Ph.D. education in Department of Economics at the same university. Currently, he is working as Research Assistant in the Faculty of Economics and Administrative Sciences in Suleyman Demirel University. He writes on issues of energy, economic growth, and globalization. He was awarded in the category of the best academic paper in the International Conference of European Union Relations, Economics, Finance and Econometrics. His researches were published in different peer-reviewed journals.

Gwyneth Edwards is Associate Professor of international strategic management at HEC Montréal. Her research focuses on strategic practices in large, complex organizations. An engineer by training, Dr. Edwards focuses on high tech industries and has a particular affinity for all things technical. She teaches at the masters level and consults in executive development programs. She is the winner of the Governor General of Canada's Academic Gold Medal.

Filippo Ferrari holds a Bachelor degree in Work and Organizational Psychology and a Masters degree in Adult Training and Education. He currently serves as a Lecturer at Bologna University, School of Economics, Management and Statistics, where he teaches Organizational Behaviour and Design and Human Resources Management. His fields of interests are International Human Resources Management, Organizational Reliability, Adult Training.

Coskun Karaca is associate professor of economics at Cumhuriyet University in Sivas, Turkey. He has a PhD from Marmara University in relation to sustainable development and renewable energies. Since January 2012, he has been serving as the Chairman of Fiscal-Law Department at Cumhuriyet University, faculty of economics and administrative sciences. Until today, 11 books, 16 articles and many papers have been published on tax theory, fiscal policy, contemporary economic and financial problems, green buildings, energy and environmental politics. He is married and has two daughters.

Fatma Nur Karaman Kabadurmus, after completing her undergraduate studies at the Faculty of Business Administration (English), Istanbul University, completed her Master studies at Istanbul Technical University, Department of Economics and her Ph.D. at the Southern Illinois University Carbondale, Department of Economics. She started her academic career as an Assistant Professor at Kalamazoo College, Department of Economics and Business. She then was hired as an Assistant Professor at Yasar University. She is currently the International Office Department of Economics Coordinator and a member of Student Placement (Internship) Commission . Dr. Karaman is currently working as a full-time academician at Faculty of Business, Department of Economics at Yaşar University. Her research interests include international economics, development economics and economics of innovation.

Bruno Mascitelli is an Associate professor at Swinburne University of Technology in Melbourne, Australia. He specialises in European Union studies and is the President of the European Studies Association in Australia. He is the Jean Monnet Chair at Swinburne University and teaches European Studies at the undergraduate level. His research addresses many themes related to the European Union and China.

Andrew Onwuemele holds a PhD in Development Planning from the prestigious University of Benin, Benin City Nigeria. He is a well-trained and grounded social scientist, an Associate Research Professor with the Nigerian Institute of Social and Economic Research (NISER). He has Over 10 years of experience in international development management and assessment and Consulting with many of the most renowned donors (EU/EC, DFID, United Nations University, UNDP, UNICEF, Brookings Institution, UN Women, USAID, World Bank, etc.). Hands-on experience in M&E system development, strategic planning, capacity development and performance M&E. Excellent knowledge of PCM and Log Framework, experienced in the development, design of baseline studies, evaluation of projects with cross cutting issues including (i.e. water and sanitation, governance, education, human rights, environment, nutrition, youth, gender, HIV/AIDS, reproductive health, ICTs, poverty). Excellent analytical and interpersonal skills which enables to visualize, collect data, articulate, analyze and solve complex problems as well as communicate and interact with people from different background with ease and skilled and conversant with the 10 UNEG Norms, 4 institutional Norms for Evaluation as well as the 5 standards of evaluation.

Chandra Sekhar Patro is currently serving an Assistant Professor at Gayatri Vidya Parishad College of Engineering (Autonomous). He has a Ph.D in Faculty of Commerce and Management Studies from Andhra University, India. He has post-graduate degree in Master of Commerce (M.Com.) from Andhra University, Master in Financial Management (MFM) from Pondicherry University, and also MBA (HR & Finance) from JNT University. Mr. Patro has over 9 years of teaching experience in higher education. Mr. Patro has gained very good knowledge in Human Resource Management and Accountancy/Finance subjects. He has published number of research papers in reputed National and International Journals and also presented papers in National and International Conferences.

Garfield Plunkett has a Doctor of Management in Organizational Leadership from University of Phoenix. He is an entrepreneur who has created several businesses. He is the principal for GAP Investment and Management since 2006, and the principal for Plunkett Home Improvement and Construction since 2005. Recently, he has launched two new businesses: Upfront Protection LLC and Standard Property services LLC. Garfield considers himself as a social entrepreneur; he is a strong believer in giving back to the community. His research interests include management, leadership, organizational culture, community development, business and industrial development.

Grigorii S. Pushnoi graduated from St. Petersburg State University, physical faculty in 1992. It was time of tragic events in the history of new Russia. Many young scientists were compelled to leave science. Working as manager and economic analyst in several St. Petersburg' firms He investigated in practice the dynamics of many business-structures: why some organizations are successful, while others fail or disintegrate. Practical experience and self-education in CAS-field helped him to develop new understanding of some complex evolutionary processes – so-called "Method of System's Potential" (MSP). The method was offered in 2003 at 21st International Conference of the System Dynamics Society (New York). Several papers devoted to MSP were published in the Proceedings of the International A. Bogdanov Institute (2004-2005). Chapter devoted to MSP was included in book Yang & Shan (2008) "Intelligent Complex Adaptive Systems". MSP-Model of the Economic System was presented in 2010 at AAAI CAS Fall Symposium; USA.

Jose Ramon Cardona received a doctorate in business economics from the University of the Balearic Islands in 2012. He worked as lecturer in marketing at the University of Zaragoza, Pablo de Olavide University and the University of the Balearic Islands. He's a research associate of the research group Business Management and Tourist Destinations.

Arunasalam Sambhanthan is currently working as a PhD Research Scholar at the School of Information Systems, Curtin Business School at Curtin University, Perth, Western Australia supported by the Curtin Strategic International Research Scholarship. His current research focus is in the area of sustainability in IT organizations. He has a number of publications in peer reviewed journals and conferences. He has four years of industry experience in technical communication.

María Dolores Sánchez-Fernández, PhD in Competitiveness, Innovation and Development and a Lecturer at the University of A Coruña (Spain), Faculty of Economics and Business, Department of Business, Business Organization area. She is also part of the GREFIN (University of A Coruña) and GEIDETUR (University of Huelva) (Spain) research groups and associate researcher at the Centre of

CICS.NOVA.Uminho and Lab2PT research at the University of Minho (Portugal), GEEMAT (Brazil) and REDOR and RENUTEG (Mexico). She has been the author or co-author of several articles published in indexed journals. She has participated in over 150 communications in national and international conferences and is a member of the scientific committee. She reviews international scientific magazines in Spain, United States, México and Brazil. She is Editor in Chief International Journal of Professional Business Review (JPBReview). Her main research topics are: Corporate Social Responsibility, entrepreneur, quality, tourism, the hotel industry and human resources. Blog: http://mariadoloressanchezfernandez.blogspot.com.es/.

Begum Sertyesilisik is working as an Assoc. Prof. in the department of architecture in the Istanbul Technical University. She has been specialized in the construction project management, contracts, strategic management, sustainability, economics. She has written various international books, chapters, papers and proceedings in these fields.

Libi Shen has a Ph.D. in Instruction and Learning from University of Pittsburgh, PA. She started her college teaching career in 1989. She has been an online faculty for University of Phoenix since 2010. Libi is a contributing author for the following IGI Global books: (1) Educational, Behavioral, Psychological Considerations in Niche Online Communities; (2) Cases on Critical and Qualitative Perspectives in Online Higher Education; (3) Online Tutor 2.0: Methodologies and Case Studies for Successful Learning; (4) Emerging Priorities and Trends in Distance Education: Communication, Pedagogy, and Technology; (5) Identification, Evaluation, and Perceptions of Distance Education Experts; (6) Cybersecurity Breaches and Issues Surrounding Online Threat Protection; (7) Handbook of Research on Human Factors in Contemporary Workforce Development, and (8) Psychological, Social, and Cultural Aspects of Internet Addiction. She is also an author for Technology in the Classroom for Now and the Future. Her research interests include reading skills, curriculum design, distance education, online learning, communication, and instructional technology.

Gladys Wanjiku Thuita is currently a PhD student in Jomo Kenyatta University of Technology. In addition she holds an MBA in Finance, Bachelors in Business Administration (Accounting and Finance) and a Certified Public Accountant (K). She is coupled with over 10 years working experience in Accounting and Finance from a wide number of corporation which include the multinationals. Because of her passion in lecturing, Gladys left the corporate field to join the academia, where she first taught as an adjunct lecturer at Dedan Kimathi University of Technology and PAC University. She is a member of the Academy of International Business and have presented her paper titled" Investigation of the effect of tax incentives on the FDIs; a case of EPZs in Athi River Kenya" in the SSA academy of international business conference held at Riara University in August 2014. In addition have published in a peer-reviewed journal. With personal attributes such as being pro-active, self-driven, result-oriented, excellent technical, analytical and planning abilities, Gladys is set to add value in the academic field especially in the areas of research and lecturing. Currently she is at Riara University impacting knowledge in Accounting and Finance courses.

Recep Ulucak currently works at the department of economics, Erciyes University. Recep does research in Applied Economics, Econometrics. Ecological Economics, Environmental Economics, Energy Economics.

Index

A

adaptation 189, 192, 195, 197, 203-204, 206, 211, 215, 226, 228, 231-232, 240
attitude 152-153, 158, 245, 259, 275-277, 282, 290, 317

B

back-shoring 125-126, 130, 132-133, 136-138, 142

C

China 6, 11, 25, 76, 167-168, 170-171, 174, 176-177, 227, 229, 260-271
Chinese investment 260-261, 263-266, 269-271
Chinese migration 260-261, 263, 265-266, 269, 271
circular economy 188, 192, 202
climate change 10, 22, 89, 91, 96, 149, 187, 190-193, 197, 203-207, 211, 213-215, 220-221, 223-232, 314
cluster analysis 274, 278, 281-282, 290
COPRAS method 70, 73-74
County 84-85, 87-94, 96, 157, 161
CRITIC method 70-71, 74
culture 1, 48, 53, 61, 150, 158, 166, 191, 268, 278, 285-286, 316

D

Dematerialization 188, 192, 202

E

ecological approaches 46, 53, 57, 59-60
ecological sustainability 46, 56, 59
economic growth 1-6, 10-12, 23, 25, 29-30, 34, 51, 60, 84-85, 145, 148, 158, 161, 168-169, 172, 176-177, 189-190, 221, 232, 238-239, 242, 260, 263-264, 268, 291, 296, 304, 306
economics 3, 25, 106, 125-127, 130, 143, 147, 226, 237-242, 249, 251-253, 329-331, 369
Educational Mismatch 126, 129-131, 142
elasticity of demand 191, 195, 202
employability 127, 253
employee 128-129, 243, 291-297, 299, 301-303, 307-308, 310-311, 320-321, 326
employee productivity 291, 308, 310
entrepreneur 147, 156-157, 165, 188
environmental law 220, 224-227, 230
environmental treaties 227-228
European Union 2, 174, 222, 248, 260-263, 271

F

farmers 84-94, 96, 204, 206-207, 210
frustration 153, 157, 259

G

Gini index 29, 44
Global hyper competition 195-196
globalization 1-6, 10-12, 18, 20-30, 32, 34, 36-37, 44, 55, 188, 194
Gross domestic information and innovation impact 190, 202
Gross domestic information and innovation value 190, 202
growing global skills gap 196
growth 1-6, 10-12, 21, 23-25, 28-30, 32, 34, 47, 50-51, 60, 76, 84-86, 92, 103, 144-146, 148-150, 154, 158, 161, 165, 167-172, 176-178, 180-181, 189-190, 220-222, 225, 230, 232, 238-239, 242, 260, 263-270, 286, 291, 294, 296, 304, 306, 308, 331

H

happiness 237-242, 249-255, 259, 294-295, 308
Haters 276-277, 279, 290

heterogeneity 275, 282
HIV 85, 89, 96, 292
Homabay County 84-85, 87-89, 91-94
homogeneity 109, 168, 274
human resources 51, 90, 126, 137-138, 188-189, 195-197, 292, 295, 308

I

income 4-5, 20-30, 32, 34, 36-37, 44, 66-67, 84-91, 93-94, 96, 145-146, 168-170, 172, 203, 211, 215, 237-238, 242-245, 248, 252, 255, 259, 266-267, 276-277, 286, 294, 315
income distribution 20-30, 32, 44, 89
Individualist 259
industrial sector 310
industry 29, 49-51, 53, 67, 76-77, 146, 166, 187-195, 197, 204, 270, 276, 293-295, 310-311, 313-318, 353, 368
information intensive production 190, 202
inhabitants 27
innovation 3, 28-29, 88, 99, 105, 126, 130, 137-138, 149-151, 158, 160-161, 165, 168-169, 171, 177, 188, 190-193, 195-196, 198, 202
innovative agricultural practices 84-85, 87, 91-94
institutional development 100, 102-106, 109-110
institutional distance 99-101, 103-105, 107, 109-110
institutional uncertainty 100-104, 106-107, 109-110
Italy 130, 146, 261, 265, 268, 270, 277-278

J

Job Requirements Approach 142

K

KOF Index 4-6, 10, 18, 22-23, 28, 32
Kuznets Curve 20-21, 27, 30, 36, 44

L

Labor Welfare 310
Land Fragmentation 85, 89, 96
leadership 145, 152-154, 157-158, 160-161, 166, 296, 319

M

Maldonado 275, 282, 286
mitigation 205-206, 226, 228-229, 314
Mutual welfare 310

O

organisations 291-294, 297, 299, 301-308, 313
Organizational Culture 166

P

perceptions 107, 151-153, 158, 161, 275, 278-279, 282, 290
population 6, 21-22, 25, 29, 53, 85-87, 89-90, 96-97, 136, 145-146, 149, 190, 208-209, 211, 216, 220-223, 225, 231-232, 238, 241, 243-249, 263, 274-276, 279, 285, 318
Portugal 238, 244-245, 248-249, 253, 269, 278
private sector 193, 226, 232, 292-294, 301-306, 308, 311
product sophistication 167-168, 170-171, 177
productivity 4, 26, 85-90, 93-94, 105, 125, 130, 138, 147, 168, 170-174, 181, 223, 230, 237, 251, 267, 291-294, 296, 300, 302-304, 306-308, 310, 315
public sector 292-293, 301-306, 308, 311
Punta del Este 274-275, 281-282, 285-287

Q

quality of life 190, 237, 251, 259, 285, 294, 308

R

Relative Institutional Challenge 98, 100, 103-104, 109-110, 115
renewable energy 65-67, 69-70, 72, 74, 76-81, 196, 319
Re-Shoring 125, 142
resident 269, 274, 277, 279, 281, 285, 290
Resilient Supply Chain 202
resources 21, 28, 48-51, 53-54, 59, 66-67, 69-70, 74, 77, 79, 81, 86, 89-90, 102, 126-127, 129, 136-138, 147, 150, 170, 187-189, 191, 195-197, 204, 206, 208, 214, 220-223, 225, 227-228, 230-231, 243, 247-248, 261, 264-265, 270, 292, 295, 300, 308, 314, 317, 325

S

school-to-work transition 125-126, 128-129, 132, 136, 143
second generation panel data 1-2, 11
segmentation 274-276, 281-282, 286
service 25, 76, 90, 93, 152, 192, 203, 205-206, 208, 215, 245, 291-295, 301, 303-304, 306-308, 311, 314, 319
service sector 25, 76, 292-293, 301, 304, 306-307, 311
skill mismatch 125-126, 128-133, 136, 143
small business 144-146, 149-151, 154, 158-160, 166
SMEs 128, 137-138, 318
sorghum 84-85, 87-89, 91-94, 97
South Korea 20-21, 28-30, 36, 44
statutory welfare 295, 302-305, 311
Supporters 159, 274, 277-280, 282, 286, 290
sustainability 46-49, 51, 55-60, 145-147, 149-150, 156, 166, 187-189, 191-192, 194-197, 221-222, 224, 227, 229, 231, 241, 313-319
sustainable development 48, 52, 55-59, 65-66, 188-189, 206, 208, 213, 220-222, 225-226, 230-232, 315
sustainable economy 48, 197, 202
sustainable tourism 46-49, 51-53, 58-61, 274

T

tourists 47-53, 269, 285-286
training needs analysis 126, 132, 136
Transaction Cost Economics 125-127, 143

U

unemployment 25, 27, 50, 66-68, 80-81, 86, 128-129, 146, 188, 191, 196, 237-239, 242-249, 251-255, 300
Utilitarianism 259
Utility 242, 259

V

Voluntary welfare 311

W

Wage Scar 253, 259
welfare 1, 26, 28-29, 46, 48-50, 57, 90, 205, 238-240, 242-243, 259, 291-308, 310-311
welfare programmes 291-294, 296-297, 301-308
well-being 85, 190, 197, 221, 227, 230, 237-238, 259, 293-295, 307

Purchase Print, E-Book, or Print + E-Book

IGI Global books are available in three unique pricing formats:
Print Only, E-Book Only, or Print + E-Book. Shipping fees apply.

www.igi-global.com

Recommended Reference Books

ISBN: 978-1-5225-2016-0
© 2017; 375 pp.
List Price: $200

ISBN: 978-1-5225-0886-1
© 2017; 251 pp.
List Price: $160

ISBN: 978-1-5225-2075-7
© 2017; 2,266 pp.
List Price: $185

ISBN: 978-1-5225-1865-5
© 2017; 443 pp.
List Price: $200

ISBN: 978-1-5225-19614-4
© 2017; 365 pp.
List Price: $210

ISBN: 978-1-5225-1005-5
© 2015; 370 pp.
List Price: $205

Do you want to stay current on the latest research trends, product announcements, news and special offers?
Join IGI Global's mailing list today and start enjoying exclusive perks sent only to IGI Global members.
Add your name to the list at **www.igi-global.com/newsletters.**

Publisher of Peer-Reviewed, Timely, and Innovative Academic Research

IGI Global
DISSEMINATOR OF KNOWLEDGE

www.igi-global.com Sign up at www.igi-global.com/newsletters facebook.com/igiglobal twitter.com/igiglobal linkedin.com/igiglobal

www.ingramcontent.com/pod-product-compliance
Lightning Source LLC
LaVergne TN
LVHW060357300926
849162LV00006B/1291
* 9 7 8 1 5 2 2 5 5 7 8 7 6 *